The Struggle for the Soul of the Nation

The Harvard Cold War Studies Book Series
Series Editor
Mark Kramer, *Harvard University*

*Resistance with the People: Repression and Resistance
in Eastern Germany 1945–1955*
Gary Bruce

*Triggering Communism's Collapse:
Perceptions and Power in Poland's Transition*
Marjorie Castle

*Redrawing Nations: Ethnic Cleansing in
East-Central Europe, 1944–1948*
Edited by Philipp Ther and Ana Siljak

The Struggle for the Soul of the Nation

Czech Culture and the Rise of Communism

Bradley F. Abrams

ROWMAN & LITTLEFIELD PUBLISHERS, INC.
Lanham • *Boulder* • *New York* • *Toronto* • *Oxford*

ROWMAN & LITTLEFIELD PUBLISHERS, INC.

Published in the United States of America
by Rowman & Littlefield Publishers, Inc.
A wholly owned subsidiary of The Rowman & Littlefield Publishing Group, Inc.
4501 Forbes Boulevard, Suite 200, Lanham, Maryland 20706
www.rowmanlittlefield.com

P.O. Box 317, Oxford OX2 9RU, UK

British Library Cataloguing in Publication Information Available

The hardback edition of this book was catalogued by the
Library of Congress as follows:

Abrams, Bradley F., 1964–
    The struggle for the soul of the nation : Czech culture and the rise of
communism / Bradley F. Abrams.
        p.   cm. — (The Harvard Cold War studies book series)
Includes bibliographical references and index.
    1. Communism and intellectuals—Czechoslovakia—History. 2.
Intellectuals—Czechoslovakia—Political activity—History. 3.
Communism—Czechoslovakia. 4. Czechoslovakia—Politics and
government—1945–1992. I. Title. II. Series.
    HX528.A25 2004
    943.704—dc22
                                                                    2003026054

ISBN 0-7425-3023-X (cloth : alk.paper)
ISBN 0-7425-3024-8 (pbk. : alk.paper)

Printed in the United States of America

∞™ The paper used in this publication meets the minimum requirements of
American National Standard for Information Sciences—Permanence of Paper
for Printed Library Materials, ANSI/NISO Z39.48-1992.

Contents

Acknowledgments   vii

Introduction: The Cold War and Contemporary Understandings
        of the Communist Takeover of Czechoslovakia   1

Part I: Czech Intellectuals Enter the Postwar World

1   World War II and the East European Revolution   9

2   Intellectuals in the Czech Environment   39

3   Four Groups of Postwar Czech Intellectuals   53

**Part II: The Interpretation and Reinterpretation of Czech History
and the Reorientation of the Czech Nation**

4   The Communist Aim: The Creation of a New Czechoslovakia   89

5   The Battle over the Recent Past I: The Experiences of Munich
and World War II   104

6   The Battle over the Recent Past II: The First Republic and
Tomáš G. Masaryk   118

7   The Shift in Sensibilities and Generations: May 5, 1945, versus
October 28, 1918   139

8   The Reorientation of National Identity: Czechs between
East and West   156

Part III: The Meaning of Socialism

9 Socialism and Communist Intellectuals: The "Czechoslovak
   Road to Socialism"   178

10 Socialism and Democratic Socialist Intellectuals:
   The "New Socialist Ethos"   199

11 Socialism and Roman Catholic Intellectuals: The "Fateful
   Struggle between Spirit and Matter"   234

12 Socialism and Protestant Intellectuals: The "Kingdom of God
   on Earth"?   253

Conclusion: The End of Czechoslovak Democracy and the Rise
           of Communism in Eastern Europe   275

Appendix   289

Notes   296

Bibliography   347

Index   357

About the Author   363

Acknowledgments

In any large project, the number of people to whom the author owes a debt of gratitude far exceeds the space available to thank them, and that is certainly the case for this one. There are, however, several people and institutions without whom I could not have brought this work to its conclusion. First on this list are the members of the committee who oversaw the Stanford University dissertation from which this book grew: Norman Naimark and Paul Robinson of Stanford, and Tony Judt of New York University. Without their encouragement and support this study would not have borne fruit. After submission of the dissertation, I received insightful criticism from the twentieth century's dean of Czechoslovak historians, the late Gordon Skilling, in conjunction with a seminar on my work sponsored by the Woodrow Wilson International Center for Scholars. I also received valuable and generous criticism on the dissertation from Martin Myant and Igor Lukes, whose reports were commissioned by Columbia University's Harriman Institute.

In the course of revising the manuscript, I received advice from my colleagues in Columbia's history department, and valuable help in both revising the manuscript and navigating the world of publishing from the Harriman's Ron Meyer. Similarly, I received valuable criticism from many graduate students whom I forced to read the manuscript in varying stages of its completion. Special thanks in this regard go to Marci Shore, now a professor in her own right. In Prague, the staff of the National Library, and especially that of its Division of Formerly Prohibited Literature, provided great and occasionally heroic assistance. The Sociological Institute of the Czechoslovak (later Czech) Academy of Science lent extremely valuable technical resources, and its former head, Jiří Musil, contributed experiences and understandings that enriched this study.

The Fulbright Commission funded two years of research in Prague, and the Harriman Institute at Columbia University, through fellowships sponsored by PepsiCo, provided funds for two summers of additional work. The Harriman also generously provided funds to offset the costs of formatting and indexing, the latter of which was carried out by Kathy Stickel. The Joint Committee on Eastern Europe of the American Council of Learned Societies awarded my project generous financial support over the course of two years while I was writing up my findings, and the *Institut für die Wissenschaften vom Menschen* in Vienna provided a further six months in a working environment that can only be described as superb. The author also acknowledges the permission granted by the American Council of Learned Societies and the University of California Press to reprint sections of chapter 1 that were previously published in *East European Politics and Societies*. Finally, this project could not have been completed without the support provided by my parents in the United States, to whom this book is dedicated, the Janù family in Prague, and my wife wherever I am.

Introduction

The Cold War and Contemporary Understandings of the Communist Takeover of Czechoslovakia

[This is] a tense, thrilling struggle for the soul of the nation.

—Ferdinand Peroutka, "Co se stalo"

Today we are engaged with the bourgeoisie in a struggle for the faith of the nation.

—Klement Gottwald, *Spisy*

The Cold War is over, and it is a very good time to be a historian of Eastern Europe. The fall of the region's Communist[1] dictatorships led to the opening of formerly inaccessible archives and libraries, allowing historians both to gain a more complete understanding of events that have loomed large over the past half-century and to seek answers to questions we had previously not even dared pose for lack of reliable information. Beyond these material benefits, however, there are also those to be reaped from the removal of the region's history from the sphere of ideological contest. During the Cold War, at least for most American scholars, there was a clear demarcation line between "us" and "them." We stood on the side of those fighting against communism, and saw those dissenting from their regimes in Eastern Europe as our allies.

As in recent affairs, so in history: we saw those who had fought against the imposition of Communist dictatorships as our allies, and largely attributed their losses to the power of a group of local Stalinists supported by Moscow and directed unflinchingly toward the goal of gaining total power by any means necessary. It is largely this view that has been adopted since 1989 across Eastern Europe, and has been seen as telling the "true story" of Eastern Europe's slide into Communist dictatorship. The willingness of many

1

domestic accounts to mirror this Western interpretation has been succinctly noted by Norman Naimark:

> The historical model is transparent; a few Soviet puppets in each of the countries—encouraged by the NKVD and backed by the power and influence of the Red Army—successfully employed "salami tactics" (after the politics of Hungary's Matyas Rakosi) to capture free societies, halt the growth of democracy, and stunt the development of economic prosperity throughout eastern Europe. Western-style Cold War historiography, suppressed for so long in the countries of east central Europe, has come to dominate perceptions of the past.[2]

This is not to say that there is not considerable truth in this understanding of communism's rise to total power in the region. Certainly the combination of the presence of the Red Army, the activities of the Soviet secret police and their abuses of the domestic secret police organizations, and the desires, plans, and instructions of the Central Committee of the Communist Party of the Soviet Union and other Soviet organs played an important role in the imposition of the Communist monopoly of power. However, the reliance on the power of the Soviet Union and the construction of histories that make the installation of Communist regimes in Eastern Europe a prologue to the main drama of the Cold War render the societies of the region mere objects, deprived of power, influence, and even their own paths of historical development. Also, as I will argue in the first chapter of this study, World War II played an enormous role in creating conditions favorable to left-wing politics across the region, although the conflict by no means predetermined the victory of the region's Communist parties in its wake.

The predominance of the Cold War view can easily be seen in Czechoslovakia, where, since the fall of the Communist regime in the "Velvet Revolution" of 1989, there has been a flurry of interest in the short-lived Czechoslovak democracy of the immediate postwar period. This has been facilitated by the foundation of the Edvard Beneš Society (named after Czechoslovakia's president from 1935 to 1948), the domestic publication of many volumes by leading actors of that time, and public interest in finding out precisely how the Czech nation became subjugated to dictatorship.[3] While many members of the 1968 "Prague Spring" reform movement are still living, and are occasionally still carrying on the same debates they did more than three decades ago, this is not true for the leading actors of the 1945–1948 period. Instead, public debate has been muted by a wide but uncritical consensus that stresses the democracy of the postwar state and the heroism of its noncommunist leaders in their struggle against a Communist Party takeover.

The formation of this consensus is due partially to the widespread will to believe in the inherent democracy of the Czech people and their institutions, and partially to reasons stemming from the materials on which the popular understanding is based. First, the book market has been flooded by memoirs primarily written by the leading noncommunist politicians of the period. These often leave the impression that there existed a small group of valiant democrats fighting a losing, and even self-sacrificing, battle against a clique of uncompromising Communists who were heavily supported by Moscow and acting according to a preformulated plan that aimed at the subversion of the state and the installation of a Stalinist dictatorship.[4] On the one hand, most of these memoirs were published abroad before 1989 and served to strengthen a Western Cold War consensus on the danger of international communism. On the other hand, many of these works were published in the 1950s, while the major actors were all still alive, and were intended to pin the blame for the collapse of Czechoslovak democracy on a person or party either unrepresented or politically disadvantaged in the émigré debate.

The second problematic aspect of this literature concerns the fact that it concentrates on the events of the hectic days of February 1948, when the Communists took advantage of a government crisis to achieve a monopoly of power. For example, roughly a third of Hubert Ripka's and half of Jaromír Smutný's memoirs are devoted to the conversations and actions of that month. This has the effect of deemphasizing the years preceding the final struggle for power and the general atmosphere and changed political and social realities of the postwar era. It further contributes to the hothouse atmosphere created by the émigré debate by focusing on individuals' activities, based on occasionally faulty memories and buttressed by often self-serving interpretations. Because of the alignment of noncommunist versus communist forces at the time, this tendency to concentrate on the final month before the Communist takeover also increases the power of the popular interpretation. In February of 1948, the struggle for power culminated in a miscalculation on the part of the forces opposed to the Communists, when their representatives withdrew from the government, prompting a showdown that was largely played out at the highest levels of Czechoslovak politics. Given the small number of people directly involved, the idea of a few brave democrats attempting to stop a Communist Party "coup" in 1948 makes sense and corresponds to what today's Czech democrats want to believe.[5]

Further cementing the public consensus, these memoirs were almost exclusively written by leading members of the National Socialist Party, most of whom fled Czechoslovakia immediately after the Communist takeover. This party, not related to the similarly named German party, certainly represented the most vocal opposition to the Communists but was not the only force resisting Communist domination. In this respect, Roman Catholics, represented politically by the People's Party, have been largely ignored, although they consistently opposed the Communist Party throughout the period. The two leading People's Party politicians were captured while fleeing Czechoslovakia and died before the regeneration of the 1960s without being able to contribute their memories and interpretations to the debate. The firsthand interpretation to which the Czech public has had access is, therefore, a rather black-and-white one—National Socialists versus Communists—contributing to the Manichean view it has adopted.

Finally, much valuable historiography has not had a strong influence on the broader public. Karel Kaplan, by far the leading historian of the period, has published a number of works on the subject, but many of these have been released through the Institute of Contemporary History and aimed at a professional audience.[6] Even so, he self-consciously limits his examinations "to one, and the decisive side—power politics," and pays particular attention to the actions of the security forces.[7] Furthermore, his interest has shifted noticeably to the Stalinist period and particularly research on the crimes of that era.[8] In addition to Kaplan's work, the Czech public has been exposed to the relevant sections of Alexej Kusák's *Kultura a politika v Československu 1945–1956* and an essay in a volume entitled *The Sovietization of Eastern Europe*, among others.[9] All of these works are valuable and successfully present many of the problems that faced the state in the wake of the Second World War. In addition, they are supported by a number of interesting studies published in the reformist 1960s.[10] This historiographic fund has not been aided in presenting a more nuanced view of the period, however, by the explosion and popular consumption of memoir literature and Cold War–era popular history.

The material that has been presented to the Czech public has contributed to the development of an, on the whole, overly simplistic view of a crucial period in the nation's past. With the fiftieth anniversary of the Communist assumption of power now behind us, however, signs of a questioning of both the Cold War paradigm and the memoir-based party-political interpretations are apparent. This is particularly evident among younger Czechs, a group in Czech society that has a tradition of both castigating its elders and practicing national self-flagellation. Young Czechs, both historically minded and not, are asking the question of how their country became a communist state and demanding an answer that goes beyond the popular interpretation, and even beyond the solid party-political, social, and economic views offered by scholars such as Kaplan. In much the same way that German youth turned to their parents and asked them what they had done in the *Nazizeit*, Czechs in their twenties and thirties are asking their parents or grandparents what they did after the war and asking their nation disturbing questions about coresponsibility. This can be seen as a result of the fact that, despite the interpretive structures handed down to them, they have difficulty in finding satisfactory answers to a few fundamental questions. It is these questions that this study will be trying to answer: Why did the Communist Party gain 40 percent of the Czech vote in free elections in 1946? Why did its membership grow from 28,000 at liberation to almost 1.4 million by the end of 1947? Why did hundreds of thousands of people demonstrate in favor of Communist Party leader Klement Gottwald's solution to the government crisis in February of 1948, while only few thousand protested against it? What attracted this mass of people to communism? Why could the democratic forces not mobilize such support? And, most critically, what was the Czech nation thinking in its three-year hiatus from dictatorship? How did they understand their experience of the Second World War and the years leading up to it? What did they think of the Soviet Union, socialism, and communism?

In answering these questions, this study will predominantly concentrate on an important yet little known group of intellectual leaders who stood outside the communist movement and most often against it. In a sense, its aim is to resurrect these intellectuals from the historical death that accompanies political defeat by a totalitarian force. For almost fifty years their writings have lain undisturbed, in the East because of political taboos and in the West from a lack of access to the relevant materials. As a result, the following examination will be both descriptive and analytical. On the one hand, the politically crucial era in which they lived and their silencing after the Communist Party's claiming of total power demand that these men and women be allowed to tell their own stories. On the other hand, having the right to tell one's own story necessarily implies both bearing the responsibility for that story and an equal right for that story to be analyzed and criticized.

The enforced silence of these intellectuals for the past half-century has meant that they were largely forgotten in their homeland and very often remained unknown abroad. This fact has shaped this study in two ways. First, it has meant that the introduction of the main currents and characters must necessarily be more extensive than a similar study of, for example, French intellectuals. Several of the characters and institutions in this study will not be familiar even to scholars of Eastern Europe. A case in point is the Czechoslovak Church, which had over one million members in mid-1946, roughly one-eighth of the Czech population. This church, and its leadership, ideology, and activity, have escaped mention beyond an extremely rare footnote. Historical responsibility demands that these forgotten and excluded actors be placed in a historical, political and intellectual context that makes them graspable for an audience distant from them both geographically and chronologically. Second, the process of recalling these intellectuals to life also means allowing them to tell much of their stories in their own words. This has led to rather extensive, but I think justified, citation. This study aims to recreate and critically analyze the actions and ideas of noncommunist intellectuals in their active, living debates with their communist counterparts, an intent that demands quotation. Further, it should serve as a resource for other scholars attempting to come to grips not just with modern Czech history, but with such problems as the intellectual effects of World War II, the coming of the Cold War, the relationship of intellectuals to socialism, the impact of arguments over national heroes and histories on political development, and so on. Beyond the author's sense of historical duty, then, these intellectuals must have the opportunity to speak for themselves in order to make their thoughts accessible to, and usable by, the wider scholarly public.

Finally, in introducing this study, one methodological note is in order. The materials presented here are drawn entirely from published sources, and rely particularly on the most prominent six daily newspapers and roughly thirty journals that circulated in the Czech lands during the period in question. The decision not to include archival material that has in some cases become available over the past decade has not been taken lightly and springs from a notion central to the project as a whole. As we shall shortly see, Czech intellectuals historically, and particularly in the years immediately following World War II, played an almost unique and politically important *public* role. Their debates were carried out in extremely public venues, even mass-circulation newspapers, and often included responses from the broader public. Because of intellectuals' particular political and cultural influence on this wider public after the war, it is necessary to examine their public debates rather than those hidden from view. These lively and often acrimonious debates, because of the influence of the intellectuals involved, were primary in both creating and reflecting the *Zeitgeist* of postwar Czech society, and for shaping the larger political discourse of the era. Hence they are important for understanding the Communist Party's road to total power.

With this said, in this examination of the themes and arguments prominent in leading Czech cultural, intellectual, and political journals and focusing particularly on those intellectuals who stood in opposition to Communist Party dominance, two general arguments will be presented. First, communist intellectuals urged a "revision of the national character." In debates with their intellectual opponents they were largely successful in refashioning the Czech national self-understanding into a Slavic and socialist mold by gaining at least partial support from noncommunist intellectuals for both their interpretation of the recent Czech past and their vision of the nation's cultural orientation. Second, the postwar enthusiasm for socialism deeply affected even noncommunist intellectuals. This led to a weakening in the defenses of democracy whose perilous nature only became apparent in the critical days of February 1948. Though the study does not purport to fully explain the collapse of postwar Czech democracy, it does analyze the weaknesses in Czech political and intellectual thought that created a context in which the Communist Party could and did obtain widespread support, substantially easing its path to total power.

The first part of this study is composed of three chapters and discusses the broadly construed intellectual caste with which the study is concerned and the times in which they lived. In order to place the subjects of this book in their proper context, two introductory chapters are necessary. The first of these examines the effects of World War II in Eastern Europe as a whole, and advances the argument that the war created social, economic, and political preconditions favorable to left-wing radicalism. It concludes by assessing the experience of Czechoslovakia in the regional upheaval. The second chapter is largely devoted to an examination of the role intellectuals played in Czech national life before and during the Second World War, focusing on themes that recurred after that conflict. The chapter closes with a discussion of the intelligentsia's particularly prominent role in the postwar context. This is followed by the introduction of four groups of intellectuals active in the years 1945 to 1948: communist, democratic socialist, Roman Catholic and Protestant. The fundamental orientation and composition of the groups, the periodicals associated with each, and short biographical sketches of each group's leaders will be presented to acquaint the reader with the primary figures of the era.

Part II is composed of five chapters and is concerned with the debate over the politically sensitive interpretation of the recent Czech past and the communist attempt to reorient the Czech nation toward the Slavic and socialist East. Most importantly, the battles waged over this interpretation and reinterpretation set the stage for the debate over socialism discussed in Part III. Chapter 4 discusses the communist cultural strategy, which centered on the attempt to "revise the national character" by offering a reinvention of the meaning of the Czech nation and a persuasive interpretation of the traumas of the preceding decade. The following three chapters examine critical tests of the power of communist argumentation to control the discursive playing field of the recent past. The first analyzes the debate over the meaning of the Munich Accords and the Second World War. This is followed by an examination of the debate over the interpretation of the interwar Czechoslovak Republic and the struggle to claim the mantle of its leading personality and first president, the philosopher and sociologist Tomáš G. Masaryk. The third of these chapters directly contrasts interwar Czechoslovakia with its postwar reincarnation by investigating the celebration of two important holidays: October twenty-eighth (Czechoslovak Independence Day, declared in 1918) and May fifth (commemorating the Prague uprising at the end of the Second World War). It reveals an important fault line in postwar Czech society by highlighting the role of a prominent section of the youth, one that conceived of itself as a discrete and expressly socialist generation, one that had come of age with the Prague uprising and stood May fifth against their purportedly bourgeois elders' October twenty-eighth. The final chapter of Part II confronts the question implicit in all of the preceding, that of the nation's cultural orientation on an East-West axis.

Part III is composed of four chapters that discuss the political question around which all others revolved in immediate postwar Czechoslovakia: socialism. The first chapter explores the development of communist discussions of socialism, with particular attention devoted to the notion of a "Czechoslovak road to socialism" announced by the Communist Party in late 1946. Chapters 10 through 12 examine the remaining three groups' conceptions of the meaning of socialism in light of the communist offensive and center on notions of socialism, understandings of Marxism, and responses to the Communist Party and the key ingredients of its "Czechoslovak road to socialism." The conclusion assesses the crisis of February 1948 and discusses aspects of the postwar Czech mentality that aided the Communist Party in its seizure of power. Finally, the focus returns to Eastern Europe as a whole, offering hypotheses on similar developments outside of Czechoslovakia and suggesting avenues for further research on domestic aspects of the rise of communist dictatorships and the coming of the Cold War.

1

World War II and the East European Revolution

It is the contention of this chapter that the history of the rise of communism in Eastern Europe cannot be traced only to the period after the front lines had moved to the west of the individual Eastern European states. In fact, the war brought deep changes to the societies of the region, and its end left propitious circumstances for proponents of radical social and political change. Despite the urge to see 1945 as a *Stunde null* when the story of the Communist takeovers begins, that story's origins actually lie in the events of the war and have lines traveling as far back as 1918. The desire to commence with 1945 has long manifested itself in Western Cold War historiography of the region, since the real drama for these historians was the superpower duel taking place literally above the heads of Eastern Europeans. Since 1989, as Norman Naimark has observed and as I noted in the introduction, it has also become a facet of the region's own historiography.[1] The urge to begin with the war's end on the part of Eastern Europeans stems primarily from the wish to delimit a section of history that can be easily excised from the national narrative as aberrant. Also, and perhaps subconsciously, such a starting point allows regional authors to avoid the necessity of confronting questions of domestic complicity with Soviet actors, thus maintaining national pride. I, however, will argue that the war itself both constituted and spawned a social, economic, and cultural revolution and that the regimes that assumed power in its immediate aftermath served, on the one hand, to confirm a revolution that had already taken place on the ground and, on the other hand, to deepen and broaden it.[2]

One thing is clear: although local Communists seized power with varying levels of popular support across the region, their task was made considerably easier by the economic, political, social, and cultural changes brought by the

Second World War. As a result of the massive demographic, economic, and at-titudinal shifts resulting from the war, radical social change was on the agenda across the region and the Communist program was at least acceptable, and even preferable, to significant elements within these societies. Even if—as in Poland and Hungary—the Communists were dissatisfied with their electoral re-sults, the fact remains that regionally many people did vote Communist. Even more were amenable to, or accepting of, the Communists' aims and plans. Lo-cal Communist parties found support for wide-ranging changes in the struc-tures of their societies, and not only from opportunists or hangers-on. Sections of the working class, the bureaucracy, the youth and, most prominently, the in-tellectuals of Eastern Europe welcomed the chance to restructure their societies. This is not to say that they desired the oppressive and murderous Stalinism that came to the region, but only that they supported the more moderately stated aims offered by local Communists in the wake of the war, aims occasionally less radical than those of their social democratic counterparts.

The equation is simple: no Second World War, no Soviet-style communist Eastern Europe. However, it doesn't simplify further to imply that commu-nism came to the region on the backs of Soviet tanks. The presence of the Red Army was certainly important, but it was by no means the only or, in several cases, even the most significant factor encouraging radical experimentation in the wake of the war. In fact, I will argue that the more significant changes in Eastern European societies, economies, and cultures had already occurred before Stalinization appeared on the agenda in the late 1940s. The experi-ences of 1938 to 1945 ripped the fabric of the interwar societies, reconfigured social hierarchies, reorganized economies, reshuffled political allegiances, caused a reevaluation of both foreign and domestic political priorities, trig-gered a rethinking of the meaning of the nations involved, and catalyzed forces aiming at the fundamental restructuring of the states of the region. The experience of war, occupation, and liberation, of course, also had a serious, if less catastrophic, effect on Western Europe, and I hope, by focusing on the East, to illuminate truly pan-European developments.

In my argument, then, domestic actors and conditions will play the pri-mary role. In order not to be misunderstood, I would like to reiterate that, with the possible exceptions of Czechoslovakia, Yugoslavia, and Albania, the activities of the Soviet Union were a necessary if perhaps not sufficient condition for the consolidation of monolithic Communist power in Eastern Europe. At the very least, the presence of the Red Army in Poland, Romania, Bulgaria, Hungary, and Czechoslovakia at the conclusion of hostilities raised the immediate threat of a Communist seizure of power. This danger was heightened by the extensive jurisdictional powers that the Soviet armed forces held over a wide swath of land behind the front lines. They used this power, most prominently in Poland but also in Romania and Hungary, to liq-uidate individuals and groups opposed to, or suspected of being opposed to,

Communist politics.[3] These activities extended far beyond the generalized terrorizing of the region's population and included horrific and frequent incidents of pillaging and plundering, rape and robbery.

Furthermore, the Red Army organized military tribunals for suspected "collaborators," deported many thousands of potential opponents of the local Communist parties, and "assisted" in the creation of domestic courts intended to try those who had collaborated with the Axis. These latter courts were generally used to remove those deemed politically undesirable by the Communists from the public scene. Their activity reached a fever pitch in Bulgaria, where over eleven thousand people came under their purview, resulting in 2,730 death sentences and 6,424 sentences of twenty years or more.[4] Additionally, the Soviets aided in the wholesale purging of the Eastern European armies, integrating forces that had served alongside the Soviets and ensuring that the newly reorganized officers' corps were politically reliable. Finally, the continued stationing of Red Army troops in these five countries, although in Czechoslovakia only until December of 1945, raised the specter of "direct action" by domestic Communists supported by the Red Army. This was a danger that non-Communist political leaders had to take seriously in their consideration of steps that might attract unwelcome Soviet attention.

In addition to Soviet troops, the USSR aided local Communists in numerous other ways. Beyond Soviet diplomatic pressure on the international stage, the NKVD was an active presence in several of the countries of the region, intimidating non-Communist actors and, in the case of Poland, incarcerating suspected members of the anticommunist underground in, among other places, Auschwitz and Majdanek. Thousands of disappearances can also be laid at the NKVD's doorstep. The Soviets, both through the Red Army and through their control of the areas behind the front lines, also ensured a strong Communist presence in local governance, placing whatever local Communists were at hand on local administrative committees. At a higher level, the governments-in-exile either returned behind Soviet forces, as in the case of Czechoslovakia, or were prevented from returning by Soviet actions, as in the case of Poland. In all cases, the local Communists, often bolstered by leaderships returning from Moscow, were assured of disproportionately strong representation in the national front coalition governments. Further, the USSR saw to it that in most cases they controlled the "power ministries" of defense and the interior, as well as those of justice, information, and agriculture. These posts gave the Communists control over the armed and internal security forces, the intelligence bureaus, the media, and the distribution of land and other property seized from expelled ethnic minorities and collaborators.

Finally, the USSR was a dominating presence on the Allied Control Commissions (ACCs) that were set up in the defeated former allies of Nazi Germany: Hungary, Romania, and Bulgaria. The ACCs, composed of representatives of the United States, Soviet Union, and Great Britain, were responsible for

validating all measures taken by the reconstructed governments, from the local to the national level. Given a certain measure of Western indifference to developments in Eastern Europe, the Soviet commissioners were disproportionately able to influence the course of events in each of these three countries.
They had the power to decide on the acceptability or unacceptability of any
decision taken, any candidate for office, or any publication. As Jan Gross has
pointed out, the ACCs "provided local communists in all of these countries
with a wild card that they could always use against their opponents."[5] Soviet
ACC officials meddled extensively in local politics, and there were also serious
breaches at the national level. For example, the Soviet representatives to the
Romanian ACC consistently intervened to shuffle cabinets and demand governmental changes throughout the crucial autumn of 1944. Widespread abuses
also occurred throughout the ACC's tenure in Hungary, and significant interference, especially in the reorganization of local government, was also experienced in Bulgaria.

In these and many other ways the USSR strongly influenced postwar developments in Eastern Europe. The machinations of the Soviets can certainly
explain many facets of the process by which countries of the region became
Communist dictatorships. They cannot, however, explain many others, such
as the rapid growth of the regional Communist parties in the aftermath of the
war, and the concurrent support for the Communist and often quite radical
Social Democratic parties at the ballot box. While determining how many of
these newly minted Communists were true believers and how many hangers-on and opportunists is impossible, the rise of these parties is nonetheless
phenomenal. For example, the Bulgarian Workers' Party increased its membership from a meager 15,000 in October 1944 to 250,000 in March 1945 and
doubled that figure one year later. The Hungarian party grew from just over
3,000 in December 1944, to 300,000 by August 1945 and over 600,000 by January 1946. Even in traditionally anti-Russian and anti-communist Poland, the
Polish Workers' Party, which had between 20,000 and 30,000 members in
early 1944, could report 235,000 by the end of 1945 and over 550,000 a year
later. The Romanian Communist Party, numbering at most 1,000 people during the war, had swelled to almost 800,000 members by October 1945. The
Communist Party of Czechoslovakia, however, achieved the most spectacu-
lar growth of all. Barely 28,000 at liberation in May of 1945, by March 1946 it
could claim over one million members, making it the largest party in Czech
political history, a title it holds to this day.[6]

THE EFFECTS OF WORLD WAR II IN EASTERN EUROPE

What makes the Eastern European experience of the Second World War so
different from that of, say, France or Belgium or the Netherlands? Certainly, in

many ways it is not so different, and the difference is one of degree rather than of kind. Still, the answer depends on the meaning of the term Second World War. The conflict can be viewed in a number of ways, but essential differences can be delineated. These can be seen easily in the differences between the Pacific and European theaters, but equally strikingly between the forms and manners in which the war was conducted in the western and eastern halves of the European continent. In short, the Second World War was a multifaceted war, with battles between the belligerents overlaying guerilla wars of resistance, civil wars, and local wars over local political matters. These overlapping wars that constituted the Second World War were unequivocally more murderous, destructive, and brutal on the eastern half of the European continent than on its western half. The difference in scale was largely the result of the different policies Nazi Germany adopted toward the countries of Eastern and Western Europe, and hence of the Nazis' vision of the "New Order" they were intent on creating. The Holocaust and the leveling of Poland, for example, were tragedies brought about by Nazi desires to rid the continent of the "Jewish pestilence" and to prepare the East for resettlement by destroying the "subhuman" Poles, respectively. However, the decidedly more horrific Eastern European experience, and the more intensely felt desire and objective need for change, were also the result of differing local conditions, including the political constellations of the years prior to the commencement of hostilities, the actions of the countries' governments during the war, and the levels of political animosity reached as the conflict escalated.

The issue of the effect of total war has only infrequently been broached, and the focus has almost exclusively been on the experiences of the major belligerents.[7] Among these, Arthur Marwick's *War and Social Change* still stands as the groundbreaking work. Marwick delineates four major dimensions along which he charts the effects of the Second World War in Great Britain, France, the United States, Germany, and the Soviet Union: its "*destructive* aspects, its *test* aspects, its *participation* aspects, and its *psychological* aspects." By the first, he means "loss of life, loss of capital, the razing of houses and factories," by the second, "the supreme challenge to, and test of, a country's military, social, political and economic institutions," and by the third, the "greater participation on the part of larger, underprivileged groups in society, who tend correspondingly to benefit, or at least to develop a new self-consciousness"; by the last, he notes that war "involves many of the psychological responses more properly likened to those of the great revolutions in history" and argues that war brings changes in "social ideas . . . customs and behaviour . . . intellectual and artistic attitudes . . . [and] political . . . ideas."[8] Since a case study of these ideological, psychological, and attitudinal aspects of Czech society will constitute the remainder of this study, I will not discuss them here, but will return to the question for the broader Eastern European space in my conclusion.

What I intend to do in the following pages is to analyze briefly the effects of the Second World War on Eastern European society with Marwick's framework in mind, although I will not adhere strictly to it. In doing so, I hope to show both that the war in itself brought about revolutionary changes to these societies, and that these changes prepared the ground for their own institutionalization, broadening, and deepening by radicalized postwar political actors. Taken as a whole, the war and its effects created conditions propitious for radical reform, redounding to the benefit of the Communist parties of the region. In this sense, my analysis will have a hint of the teleological to it, as the search is directed toward understanding why people might be more willing to support, or at least be open to, radical left-wing politics in the wake of a terrible war. Nonetheless, radical and in some cases long overdue reform does not mean reform derived from the Soviet model exclusively, and my argument should not be taken to imply that these societies, if left to follow their own paths of development, would have ended up as Soviet-style communist ones. Western Europe underwent many of the same types of experiences as Eastern Europe, although to a less traumatizing degree, and did not foster Communist Party dominance despite a strong leftward surge after the war. Given that the Communist Party of France could become that state's largest and gain 28 percent of the vote in 1946, and the Italian Communist Party could become one of Italy's largest parties and gain 19 percent of the vote in the same year, why should one be surprised to find a similar state of affairs in the East? Communists had parliamentary representation in every European country after the first postwar elections, and won over 10 percent of the ballot in the first postwar elections in Belgium, Denmark, France, Italy, Luxembourg, the Netherlands, Norway, and Sweden. Even in the United Kingdom, where the Communists won only two seats in the House of Commons, the Labour Party won its first election ever, gaining 48 percent of the vote. Given the demonstrably more traumatic experience of the war in the east, one might legitimately ask why the Communists did not receive even greater support across the region, as they did in Czechoslovakia and Yugoslavia. Finally, although there will be a measure of overlap in what follows, this necessarily arises because each of the powerful effects of the war was felt in many different spheres of Eastern European society.

WORLD WAR II IN EASTERN EUROPE: THE DESTRUCTIVE ASPECTS

In keeping with Marwick, I will begin with the war's destructive forces, because they are both relatively straightforward and their effects reverberate through the succeeding aspects. At the most basic level of understanding, wars kill and destroy, and in this respect World War II was quite successful, particularly in Eastern Europe. While deaths came in large numbers in the

West, the loss of life was far greater in the East, and, moreover, a greater share of the burden fell on the civilian population. For example, Great Britain lost a total of 360,000 lives, representing slightly less than one percent of its population and France lost 590,000, less than 1.5 percent of her population. These numbers, terrible though they are, pale in comparison with those of Poland, which lost some 6 million souls, the vast majority of whom were civilians. This total represents roughly one-fifth of her prewar residents. Yugoslavia lost 10 percent of her population, over 1.5 million people, in war, resistance, and civil war. The losses of the other Eastern European nations, while not as catastrophic as these, are larger as a percentage of population than those of Western Europe in every case save Bulgaria: Romania 665,000 (3.4 percent), Hungary 436,000 (4.4 percent), Czechoslovakia (excluding ethnic Germans) 380,000 (3.7 percent), Albania 30,000 (2.7 percent), and Bulgaria 30,000 (0.5 percent).[9] The losses as a whole for the region totaled over 9 million dead, representing roughly 10 percent of Eastern Europe's prewar population. This average means that the region as a whole lost a greater proportion of its inhabitants than did even Germany, whose 5.6 million dead constituted just over 7 percent of her prewar population. Only the Soviet Union's losses, some 20 million of her 200 million inhabitants, approached those of Eastern Europe as a whole.

Beyond the deaths, there were millions of other casualties, in a more broadly defined sense. While exact figures are not available for the numbers of those wounded, either as participants, as what has become fashionable to call "collateral damage," as conscripts in forced labor battalions, or in other ways in the multilayered wars that constituted World War II in Eastern Europe, their number must run into the millions. Beyond those physically wounded, however, we must recall the larger brutality of the war, and its effects on the psyches of those who lived through it. Even those whose bodies were left relatively unscathed almost certainly had some experience of the physical brutality of the war in the East seared into their memories. In the most terrorized countries, Poland and Yugoslavia, one likely had relatives and friends among the dead, had seen the hanged bodies of resistance fighters, and had witnessed deportations to the concentration and death camps, if not the camps themselves. The mere experience of the brutality of the war years, I would argue, had severe effects on Eastern Europeans' perceptions of violence, coercion, and authority.

Added to this must be the experience of forced labor and displacement. Records indicate that in September 1944, there were just under 6 million foreign workers inside the Reich. Of these, over a third were from the Soviet Union, and a further quarter were from Eastern Europe. The vast majority of these, 1.7 million, were from the *Generalgouvernement* in Poland, but almost 325,000 were from Yugoslavia and Croatia, and a further 37,000 were from Slovakia.[10] In addition to the workers deported to Germany, millions of

Eastern Europeans fled, or were expelled, from their homes as a direct result of the war. This commenced with the flight of the mostly ethnic Czech inhabitants of the Sudeten regions handed to Nazi Germany as a result of the 1938 Munich Accords, and concluded with the immense "transfers" and exchanges of population after the end of the war. Indeed, the whole of Eastern Europe during the decade from 1938 to 1948 was in motion. To give just one example of wartime flight, a report from five months after the attack on Yugoslavia indicated that 160,000 ethnic Serbs had fled to Serbia: 104,000 from Croatia, 37,000 from Hungarian-occupied areas, and 20,000 from Bulgarian-occupied areas.[11] Certainly, however, the largest numbers of refugees fleeing battle had to be the millions of *Volksdeutsche* who fled the entire Eastern European region ahead of the Red Army in 1944 and 1945.

More important than flight before the front, however, were the expulsions and exchanges of population that occurred under the Nazi aegis during the war and with Allied consent after the cessation of hostilities. Between 1940 and 1943, for example, exchanges between Romania and Hungary involved 369,000 people and between Bulgaria and Romania a further 161,000. After the war, considerable attention has, correctly, been placed on the immense "transfer" of the German population of the region. For our purposes, however, it is not the virtual erasure of Germans from the ethnic maps of Poland and Czechoslovakia that is of primary importance (although the matter of their property is certainly of consequence), but rather the replacement of this population by Poles and Czechs. In the organized "transfers" of population, over 6.3 million Germans were expelled from Poland and Czechoslovakia. The concomitant depopulation of huge areas of those two states meant that in internal migrations, some 3.5 million Poles and almost 2 million Czechs and Slovaks were resettled in the formerly ethnically German areas of the "Newly Recovered Territories" and the Sudetenland. Over a million of the Poles involved in this resettlement came from the *kresy*, the eastern borderlands that had been assigned to the Soviet Union. A further 700,000 Poles returned to the territory of 1939 Poland from areas now lying in the Soviet Union. All told, in the years 1944–1950, an estimated 31,135,000 inhabitants of Eastern Europe—or roughly one-third of the prewar population—fled or were resettled.[12]

This massive loss of life and wounding of bodies, compounded by displacement, disorientation, and the desensitization of minds, was matched by material destruction unseen in the region since the Thirty Years' War.[13] While the damage was relatively slight in countries such as Bulgaria and Romania, it was greater in Czechoslovakia and Albania, and truly massive in Hungary, Yugoslavia, and Poland. In Yugoslavia, 822,000 buildings were destroyed, leaving some 3.5 million people, one-quarter of the population, homeless at war's end. Further, half of the railway lines, three-quarters of the locomotives and over four-fifths of the country's goods wagons were destroyed. Virtually all of its motorcars, two-fifths of its peasant carts, and almost half of its telephone and telegraph networks were ruined, and 60 percent of its horses and over half of its cattle, sheep, goats, and poultry lay dead. The loss has been estimated at 274 percent of Yugoslavia's entire 1938 national income. The condition of Poland was even more grave, as the Nazis' "scorched earth" policy took a brutal toll on the state's physical plant. The losses overall amounted to 38 percent of the national property, or three and one-half times the country's 1938 national income. Two-fifths of the country's prewar factories lay in ruins, and virtually all that remained had been stripped of their machinery. Eighty-five percent of the homes in Warsaw had been destroyed in the fighting, as had two-fifths of Polish railways. As in Yugoslavia, animals did not escape: 60 percent of Poland's cattle, 75 percent of its horses, and 80 percent of its swine died in the calamity, and one-quarter of Polish forests had been felled. Hungary was also hard hit, losing two-fifths of its railway lines and half its locomotives, in addition to all its primary river bridges. Half of the country's industrial plant was damaged and one-third of its engines and three-quarters of its machine tools lost, meaning that industrial production immediately after the war stood at less than one-third of its prewar level. Over half of the Hungarian stock of horses and four-fifths of its pigs and sheep were killed.

Even in the countries that were not as devastated by the wartime destruction, losses were substantial. Czechoslovakia managed to avoid much bomb damage, and the destruction in the state was localized, with the most significant area of devastation lying in central Slovakia, where the Slovak National Uprising of 1944 had taken place. Still, Czechoslovak losses totaled some 4.2 billion 1938 dollars, representing more than the state's national income of that year. Both Bulgaria and Romania escaped serious damage, with the exception of the Romanian oil fields, but their losses still constituted roughly one-third of their respective 1938 national incomes. Even tiny Albania did not escape unscathed, losing around one-third of its livestock and suffering the complete or partial destruction of more than half of its weak infrastructure of roads, bridges, mines, and factories. Two hundred villages had been destroyed and 18,000 houses burnt down, leaving 100,000 people homeless.

Finally, the war damage, German economic exploitation, the chaos of the passing of the front, and Red Army pillaging took their toll on the productive capacity of the economies of the region. In some ways this was even more serious a problem than the value of the lost capital assets. The sheer scale of the dislocation caused by six years of war resulted in a shortage of working capital, raw materials, components and facilities for repairs, and people with technical skills and in the sheer exhaustion of undernourished populations. The decline in national incomes in real terms from 1938 to 1946 (i.e., including one year or more of reconstruction) was staggering, especially in the East-Central European countries. Polish and Yugoslav national incomes are estimated to have dropped over 50 percent, the Hungarian by 40 percent, and that of Czechoslovakia by 25 percent. For comparison, those of France, the Netherlands, and Belgium experienced reductions of between 10 and 20 percent.[14] The most acute shortages that arose from this precipitous decline were in foodstuffs, as the populations of most of the states in the region were reduced to near-starvation levels of consumption.

What can one say about such widespread death, carnage, and misery, and how can it be related to support for radical politics in the wake of the war? Above all, the war in the East was much more of a *Vernichtungskrieg* (war of annihilation) than the war in the West, and the sheer loss of life created significant social mobility. This was even more the case because of the particular nature of the deaths, with Jews the primary targets of the Nazis' genocidal policies. For example, Jews constituted almost half of interwar Romania's commercial and banking class, and close to two-thirds of Poland's. They made up over half of Poland's doctors and one-third of its lawyers, while totaling almost half of Hungary's traders, and over half of that country's lawyers and doctors in 1920.[15] The Holocaust, then, meant not only the deaths of some 3.75 million Eastern European Jews, but also a significant depletion of the bourgeoisie as a class.

One other primary target of Nazi policy in the occupied lands was the intelligentsia, a group that included the writers, doctors, lawyers, journalists, army officers, academics, and middle bureaucrats and managers whom the Nazis saw as the bearers of a potentially dangerous national consciousness in the lands they occupied. These men and women were also members of the bourgeoisie, and found themselves selected for special treatment by the occupying forces. They were also hard-hit by their overrepresentation in the resistance movements, as the destruction of the Warsaw and Slovak uprisings attests.[16] Finally, the bourgeoisie was depleted in the immediate aftermath of the war by the expulsion of the German populations of, particularly, Czechoslovakia and Poland. In itself, the exhaustion of the middle classes need not be interpreted as strengthening the radical left in the region, but the physical weakening of the class with both the ability and inclination to oppose radical social change is certainly a factor that must constantly be borne in mind.

Because the scale of damage in the East was, on the whole, greater than that in the West, it therefore called for a more significant state presence in the relief and reconstruction efforts. The state literally had to provide food, clothing and shelter for millions of its homeless, repatriated or otherwise displaced citizens.[17] Furthermore, the state, as the region's traditional locus of modernization and industrialization, was the only entity strong enough to oversee the major reconstruction effort that was necessary. Only it could mobilize an undernourished and depleted population to clear the rubble, rebuild homes and factories, and reconstruct shattered road, rail, and communications networks. What was called for was unity in reconstruction, solidarity in suffering, and sacrifice for the common good. All of these watchwords of the left coincided well with the plans for the nationalization of major industries that were then being promulgated. Furthermore, they rang nationally true in states that had become, many of them for the first time, ethnically homogenous as a result of the murder of the Jews, the transfers of other ethnic groups, and the redrawing of borders.

Equally important for understanding the role of the state in Eastern Europe's postwar trajectory is that most of the states of the region had been fairly étatist before the war and had grown more state-centered under the pressures of the war and the dictates of the German *Grossraumwirtschaft*. This was equally true for occupied countries and those that maintained some degree of independence through alliance with Nazi Germany and Fascist Italy. Largely in an attempt to combat the Great Depression, the governments of Eastern Europe moved to adopt more autarkic economic policies, ones that fit well the increasingly autocratic nature of their governance. By the end of the 1930s, these states' promotion of industrial development had led to widespread state ownership and control of industry, especially in sectors of strategic importance. The Polish and Romanian states controlled the largest spheres of their economies, with Polish state ownership probably the highest of any European country save the Soviet Union. Beyond infrastructural holdings, the Polish state owned some 100 industrial companies employing about a million persons. Its share in certain sectors was quite large: 80 percent of the chemical industry, half of the metallurgical industry, 40 percent of the iron and steel industry, and 20 percent of the oil industry were in the government's hands. In Romania by 1939, the situation looked much the same, with the capital invested in state enterprises actually outdistancing that invested in the private sector. State ownership was less extensive in Yugoslavia and Bulgaria, and even smaller in Hungary and Czechoslovakia, but region-wide the state was an unusually prominent economic actor.[18]

The presence of the state looms larger when the regulatory cartels are taken into account. They fixed prices, allocated production quotas, and had broad powers in setting the conditions of trade. They contributed directly to the concentration of industrial production, often with the collusion of governments that saw them as useful policy tools. By the late 1930s, these cartels, often international in scope, accounted for a large share of the industrial product of the region. They accounted for two-thirds of the Polish, over two-fifths of the Hungarian, almost a quarter of the Romanian, and virtually all of the Czechoslovak industrial production. The dominance and structure of the cartels had political repercussions during the war, when German participation in them rose in the countries allied with the Axis. They also had deep effects in the first postwar years, making large sections of the economy natural targets for nationalization. In short, the mercantile bourgeoisie as a class was diluted by the strength of the state in the interwar decades and became subject to nationalization after the war.

Further, the changes in property relations between 1938 and the end of the war had been profound. In addition to those in the countryside caused by the German resettlement policy, "Aryanization" removed wealth and property from Jewish hands and gave it to the state, which either redistributed it or kept it. Moreover, by various financial devices, German banks were able to gain control over domestic banking and extended their control over domestic industry through the injection of large amounts of capital. This meant that, after the war ended, the new governments could easily conclude that a large proportion of the productive assets in the region were "enemy property," greatly facilitating the nationalization drive that the Communists and Social Democrats were advocating.[19] In fact, in the formerly Axis lands of Hungary, Bulgaria, and Romania, several joint ventures undertaken before or during the war with the Germans were simply converted, as part of reparations payments, into analogous enterprises with the Soviets as the new partners.

When the war ended, even more property fell under the state's control, as property "Aryanized" by the Nazis or their local collaborators that had been redistributed fell to the state when the Jewish former owners did not return from the camps (and occasionally even when they did). Similarly, at the time of liberation much of the region's industrial plant had been abandoned, and there were no legal representatives on hand to restart operations. In several of these cases, workers took it upon themselves to continue production, electing factory councils to oversee their work. When the governments regained control over their territory, the state quickly assumed the responsibility for administering these and, after this had occurred, it became virtually impossible to hand back these enterprises when the proper owners resurfaced, not least because of the objections of the workers themselves.

Finally, the industrial assets of the expelled ethnic minorities and others dropped into national property funds and fell under the state's economic discretion. These were most valuable in Czechoslovakia and Poland, since the largest expelled German populations came from these states. As Wladyslaw Brus has put it, "confiscation of ex-enemy property became by itself an act of nationalization," and these seizures can be considered the prelude to the great postwar nationalization projects.[20] In addition to the needs of reconstruction and the desires of the Communists and Social Democrats, there were other factors that encouraged nationalization, including the difficulties in sorting out property ownership and in deriving a method for property distribution. These conditions favorable to a policy of nationalization were backed by widespread support for the idea, as both it and land reform had been key components of wartime plans for national regeneration.[21]

Even before the Communists came to power, during the period of coalition government, wide-ranging nationalization proposals were put forward, often by social democratic parties. For example, in January 1946 all Polish factories having fifty or more workers were nationalized, and by November 1946 almost half of the employees in the Hungarian mining and industrial sectors were state employees. By 1947, half the industrial capacity of Bulgaria was in state hands, and decrees prompted and signed by President Beneš had placed 61 percent of the Czechoslovak workforce in the state sector by January 1946. All in all, the mixture of a high degree of state participation and the apparent failure of capitalism before the war, the increased étatization and the destruction of sections of the bourgeoisie during the war, and the needs of reconstruction after the war secured the radical social reformers sufficient preconditions for widespread nationalizations even before the Communists had achieved total power. Further, it created a framework not only for the more extensive nationalizations after the Communist takeovers, but also for the system of planning in the economy. Great strides toward the latter were also taken during the period of coalition government, again forced largely by the pressures of reconstruction.

The seizures of the assets of the expelled populations and collaborators also included huge tracts of land that laid the foundation for a land reform that severely weakened the rural bourgeoisie and destroyed the aristocracy, further enhancing the social power of the left. In Poland and Czechoslovakia, the area concerned was quite extensive, as can be expected from the size of the already-mentioned population transfers. In Czechoslovakia, 11,500 square miles was transferred to the state, while in Poland 38,200 square miles found their way into the state repository. Smaller totals fell to the disposition of the Romanian and Yugoslav governments, respectively, in the same way. These holdings paved the way for the land redistribution projects that had been in the platforms of all the major resistance organizations, and that were among the first orders of business transacted in the newly liberated states. In Poland, all estates over 100 hectares (247 acres) and those having 50 hectares (123 acres) of arable land were subject to redistribution, meaning that some 3.2 million hectares (over 12,000 square miles) were slotted to change hands. The reform was proportionally even more extensive in Hungary, where the aristocracy had maintained its political and economic dominance throughout the interwar years. In that country some 75,000 estates were expropriated, comprising over 11,000 square miles and constituting one-third of the state's territory. Even Bulgaria, where land had been fairly equally distributed before the war, all property over 20 hectares (roughly 50 acres) was confiscated and redistributed.

As in the case of the nationalizations, many factors contributed to the extent of the reforms. Above all, however, the perceived, and in many cases real, need for redistribution beyond that carried out in the years after World War I played a crucial role. In this way, the revolutionary changes on the land can be seen as part of a broader revolution that commenced in 1918. The disruptions of the Second World War brought two added elements, however. Most important, certainly, was the flight and later expulsion of the ethnically "enemy" populations, which provided an opportunity for thinking about more fundamental reforms and forced the creation of a framework for large-scale redistribution. Beyond this, however, the widespread rural poverty of the interwar years was linked with the collapse of world agricultural prices that came with the Great Depression. The vicious effects of the price scissors, rural overpopulation, and chronic peasant indebtedness raised serious questions about the effects of capitalism in the countryside. As with the other wide-ranging socialist reforms planned in the wartime underground movements, the chaos of war and occupation had provided the opportunity and created the will to tackle the most pressing problem faced by these heavily agricultural societies.

That the left generally and the Communist parties particularly (as holders of the appropriate ministries) were responsible for the implementation of these reforms certainly helped them in the eyes of the rural poor. Each recipient of land had been given, literally, a piece of the state by the left. While this did not automatically result in support for the individual national Communist parties, it certainly helped to bolster their credibility among a population notoriously suspicious of leftist politics. For example, the newly installed residents of the Sudetenland gave a majority of their votes to the Communist Party of Czechoslovakia in the 1946 elections, a substantially higher proportion than did those in the core areas of Bohemia and Moravia.[22] Many of these voters may have been Communists who received their grants because of their political allegiance, or may have been among the class of landless laborers who might have been inclined to give their votes to the left in any case. Nonetheless, one can have little doubt that overseeing the completion of a land reform stalled by the interwar right stood on the credit side of the Communists' balance sheet.

In summary, the human and material changes brought by the war created conditions encouraging for a radical reconstruction of the social and economic foundations of Eastern European society. The tremendous toll in lives and assets the war claimed pushed the state to the fore as the motor of the inherently social project of reconstruction. The state's power was further enhanced by the vast amounts of property that flowed into its hands. When linked to the popular desires for economic and land reform, these provided the springboard for the nationalization of industry and the seizure of rural estates for redistribution. The result was that the landed aristocracy and rural bourgeoisie were decimated by the land reform, and the urban bourgeoisie, already depleted by Nazi policies directed at Jews and the intelligentsia, was further weakened by the nationalizations and, in several cases, by the expulsion of the region's ethnic Germans. All of these destructive aspects of the war had effects that strengthened, at least relatively, the political left.

WORLD WAR II IN EASTERN EUROPE: THE TEST ASPECTS

By almost any standard one might choose, the Eastern European states' military, social, and political institutions failed the tests put before them in the years 1938–1945. Abandoned by her allies, Czechoslovakia capitulated to the Munich

Accords in 1938, split herself in two, and was forced to turn over Bohemia and Moravia to Nazi "protection" in March 1939. Albania dithered over an Italian ultimatum and was quickly occupied in April 1939. Poland chose the opposite course, fought courageously against impossible odds (especially after the Soviet invasion), and was again partitioned. Yugoslavia vacillated, decided to confront the Nazis, ripped herself apart and then spent four years not only fighting for liberation from the Germans and Italians, but also fighting bloody and brutal internecine wars along class and ethnic lines. Romania allied itself with Hitler, briefly came under fascist Iron Guard leadership, fought an increasingly unpopular war against the Soviet Union, and, finally, managed with relative adroitness to switch sides in August 1944. In the wake of this turnabout, Hungary, which had also allied itself with Hitler, attempted the same maneuver, failing dismally and allowing the fascist Arrow Cross to take the majority of the army with it in resisting the oncoming Soviet forces, resulting in the massively destructive siege of Budapest. Bulgaria, also allied with Hitler, was rather more successful, managing to satisfy her irredentist desires without committing troops to the eastern front. All of this came crashing down with the Romanian collapse and, in hastening to replicate that country's volte-face, Bulgaria found itself in the unique position of being at war temporarily with all of the major belligerents on both sides save Japan. No more successful were the two states the Nazis sponsored in the region. Slovakia, created at the same time as the Protectorate of Bohemia and Moravia, fought alongside Germany in the Soviet Union, then was herself torn asunder by a massive armed uprising within her own borders. Croatia, similarly, came into being with the destruction of Yugoslavia, and the Ustaša movement quickly set about alienating itself from its citizenry. Both of these lost considerable luster from their all too obvious reliance on Germany and Italy, and ultimately went down with their masters.

From this brief recapitulation of the wartime experiences of the governments and military forces of the region, a few general principles emerge. Above all, no government truly "won." It seems that one could either ally oneself with the Axis and win until Stalingrad, only to lose catastrophically thereafter (Hungary, Bulgaria, Romania, and the two puppet states), or one could capitulate to the Germans and Italians and then reach "victory" with the Allies in 1945 (Poland, Czechoslovakia, Albania, and Yugoslavia). Even their victory in defeat does not absolve these regimes of failing the test, for they were unable and also unwilling to recreate their states with the same political, economic, and social configuration as had existed before the conflict. This should come as no surprise, since it happened in the West as well. For example, in a referendum in 1946, 96 percent of the French voted against reviving the Third Republic. The war had made restoration untenable across the Continent for a number of reasons, not least because almost nobody wanted it, and the introduction of new groups with new powers and new aims onto the political landscape, covered in "participation" aspects below, meant that their voices counted.

The pan-European undesirability of restoration was raised to the level of impossibility for the sociopolitical regimes of Eastern Europe. With the exception of Czechoslovakia before the Munich Accords, all of the regimes of the region had been to one degree or another right-wing authoritarian dictatorships. Those that had allied themselves with Hitler were deeply discredited for having done so, as broad masses of their populations, particularly after Stalingrad, came to deeply resent having been dragged into a war they would soon lose in the service of the Nazis. As German economic exploitation increased during the war, so did the restiveness of the population. Starting with intellectuals and not a few politicians, and spreading throughout the population in the final years of the war, visions of reconfiguring the society came to the fore. These were largely drawn from the critiques leveled at the prewar regimes, and drew upon those regimes' perceived (and in most cases quite real) inadequacies, and even illegitimacy. The result was not just a reshuffling of the prewar political constellation, but the banning of those parties and movements deemed responsible for the inequities of the interwar years and the debacles of 1938–1945, whether in alliance with Hitler, defeat in battle, or capitulation and collaboration.

Above all, the interwar regimes had been self-consciously *right-wing*, either in the conservative-traditionalist sense (say, Hungary under Bethlen), modernization-dictatorial sense (Zog in Albania), national-unity sense (Pilsudski in Poland), right-radical sense (Gömbös in Hungary), or openly fascist sense (the Iron Guard interlude in Romania). What they all shared was an intense hatred and fear of "bolshevism," a term very broadly interpreted, and a clear dislike of other movements on the political left: independent trade unions, social democrats, etc. This stance was likely the result of the manner in which Eastern Europe was reorganized after the First World War. By and large, the same kind of revolutionary potential that existed at the end of the Second World War existed at the end of the First.[23] With the breakup of the German, Russian, and Habsburg empires and the subsequent drawing of state frontiers, the power of nationalism proved stronger than that of social discontent, on the one hand, and the newly established governments' promises of real reform (most importantly land reform) defused social radicalism, on the other. The country of the region that did experience socialist revolution, Hungary, was drawn into it more from an overwhelming national rejection of the perceived imminence of the state's dismemberment than from support for Béla Kun and his Republic of Councils. However, the specter of communism did, indeed, haunt Eastern Europe, or at least its leaders. Cognizant of the potentially explosive influence of the Bolshevik revolution, and having seen the eruption of communism in the region—in Hungary, but also in Bavaria and (briefly and farcically) in Slovakia—the new regimes encouraged national passions and promised social reforms as inoculation against the Red virus.

When the surge of post–World War I radicalism died down, the governments of Eastern Europe took three general steps that in many ways shaped the course of the ensuing thirty years. First, they commendably commenced on the course of political reform. Even if the attempts to implement these reforms were in cases half-hearted and soon collapsed under the weight of either their own contradictions, the ethnic, national, or class fragmentation of the polity, blatant corruption, or all of these, democratic parliamentary forms were created or enhanced. Their presence had two long-term effects. Decisively, the idea and ideal of participatory democracy and political representation were implanted in the consciousness of the broad public, even if only rhetorically. Equally importantly, democracy, such as it was, failed. Either the electoral system was so corrupt and abused that the whole charade hardly seemed to matter (as in Romania, Hungary, Bulgaria, and Albania) or representational government provided unwieldy, or ethnically unstable, coalitions unable to accomplish an acceptable minimum of effective action (Poland and Yugoslavia). This led to the general discrediting of democracy in its Western (or should one say bourgeois?) variant. Even in Czechoslovakia, largely seen as a paragon of Western democratic practices, parliament was run by the leaderships of the major parties (the "pětka") and no bill presented to that body failed throughout the interwar period. The failure of democracy to take root in the rocky soil of Eastern Europe led directly to the collapse of democratic politics and the rise of right-wing dictatorships under the strongmen of the region.

One final factor in the discrediting of democracy comes from the international arena. The Western democracies, and in particular France, enjoyed tremendous prestige and influence across Eastern Europe after World War I. Militarily and diplomatically, France was seen as the guarantor of the Versailles system and had alliances with Poland and the three countries of the Little Entente: Czechoslovakia, Romania, and Yugoslavia. After Germany's remilitarization of the Ruhr in 1936, it became apparent that France was in some ways disinterested in the fate of her eastern allies, and in other ways unable to gather the domestic unity to express a concerted interest. This progression culminated in the humiliating events of Munich—the abandonment of Czechoslovakia, the Eastern European democracy closest to Western standards—and the lack of forceful action on the part of the great Western democracies in September 1939. The democracies looked, at best, weak and fearful in the face of the Nazi threat or, at worst, like imperfectly self-interested collaborators with Hitler. In either case, their trustworthiness as allies and guarantors of Eastern European independence had been mortally wounded by the diplomacy of the 1930s. Just as democracy was failing domestically, the international order created by the Western democracies was also failing, and that failure could be seen as part and parcel of Western-style democracy.

Here we have several strands coinciding in Eastern Europe. States emerge, or are reincarnated, or change their borders in the wake of World War I, and the regimes of these states promise reforms on the Western model. These reforms fail, sometimes quite miserably, leaving the Western model of democracy damaged but having strengthened the idea of representation of the masses. The result is a group of right-wing dictatorships that either ally with the Nazis or become their handmaidens after occupation. There was, to be sure, little the right could do about this latter event. Right-wing political groupings were in charge when defeat came, and their bureaucracies, where allowed, merely remained in their posts, either to try to save what could be saved or out of a more deep-seated belief in authoritarian governance. In either case, they were discredited alongside the idea of democracy derived from the West. As François Furet has pointed out, the resistance movements during World War II were characterized by an antifascism that gave meaning to the terrible suffering of the war, but the war's end also "marked the victory of anti-Fascism rather than of democracy."[24]

The second step the regimes of Eastern Europe took in the wake of World War I was to promise social reforms to match those in the political sphere. Again, these were largely carried out only half-heartedly and left a legacy that was to have serious effects. Since most of these states were overwhelmingly agricultural, the example of land reform is the most instructive and critical. Every state in the region, save Bulgaria, promised large-scale land reform that was intended both as a matter of principle and as a palliative for socially radical passions in the countryside. In cases where the local large landholders were ethnically foreign, or perceived as such (as was the case in Czechoslovakia, where they were largely considered German), national passions mixed quite nicely with social ones. Many of the resulting land reforms, like their political counterparts, were delayed until the revolutionary potential generated by the experience and aftereffects of World War I had dissipated and failed to meet the desires or expectations raised by their initial announcement. Here we can witness, in Arno Mayer's famous phrase, "the persistence of the Old Regime," a particularly apt turn of phrase for Hungary. In that country, the strength and influence of the land-owning class inhibited any real reform after the abortive Kun regime's fall. By 1930, 0.1 percent of the population still controlled 23.7 percent of the land, while a further 0.8 percent controlled an additional 22.7 percent, meaning that less than 1 percent of the population was in possession of close to half the land of interwar Hungary. Land reform went only slightly better in Poland, where a little more than 10 percent of the state's arable land was affected, but only one-quarter of the land on large estates was expropriated, leaving 0.3 percent of the estates covering over one-quarter of Poland's land. The situation was similar in Czechoslovakia, where the promised land reform was to be quite radical, slating the expropriation of all holdings over 250 hectares, and those having arable land of over 150 hectares. By 1936, however, figures show that of all the land eligible for redistribution, 49 percent had been returned to the original owners and the fate of a further 18 percent had not yet been decided.[25] Even Romania's moderately successful reform left one million hectares (almost 2.5 million acres) subject to expropriation untouched and 0.8 percent of the farms controlling almost one-third of Romanian land.[26]

The result of these reforms was a persistent perceived need for land reform and a strong desire for such a reform on the part of the population. Much as in the case of political reform, the idea of land reform had been placed in the heads of the population to calm political passions in the aftermath of World War I and was (in the view of the peasantry) badly or even corruptly carried out. This gave the Communists a powerful tool during and immediately after the Second World War, for peasant land hunger was clearly an issue of the left. The Communists could plausibly claim that collectivization had been the correct response for Russia but was not on the cards for Eastern Europe, where intermediate forms would suffice. In making this argument, they could draw upon the strong cooperative movement that developed in some parts of the region between the wars. In Romania, for example, the number of cooperatives grew from 3,649 to 5,463 between 1940 and 1943, while in Czechoslovakia there were over 5,000 cooperatives already in 1930, excluding agricultural credit cooperatives, of which there were at least a further 10,000. The credit cooperative movement became strong across the region, largely as a result of the Great Depression. In these cooperative ventures lay the seeds of future collectivization, in much the same way as the centrally planned economy of communism could find roots in the autarky of the interwar years that was only nourished by the growing étatization demanded by the Nazi war economy and the subsequent requirements of reconstruction.

The third general step that the interwar authoritarian governments took that had long-term effects was the banning of the Communist parties of the region and the suppression of other left-leaning political groups. In response to the perceived threat of a replay of the Russian Revolution, the states of Eastern Europe quickly moved to ban local Communist parties. This happened even before the Second International in Hungary and Poland (both 1919), and within the ensuing few years in Yugoslavia (1921) and Bulgaria and Romania (both 1924). The only two places where Communists were not forced underground, hounded, imprisoned, tortured, and occasionally killed were Czechoslovakia, where the party consistently secured 10–13 percent of the vote before 1938, and Albania, which had no functioning Communist party to ban before 1939 (and no unified one before 1941). When the Communist parties were banned, they began to create front parties (with some measure of success) and to infiltrate the Social Democratic parties and trade-union organizations of their states. These latter institutions were kept on a very short leash, often faring only slightly better than the Communists themselves. With, again, the exception of Czechoslovakia, where the social democrats were a powerful party, moderate leftist parties were often persecuted by the governing parties. Their leaders were subject to harassment or worse, as in the Brześć affair in Poland in 1930, in which several thousand center-left antigovernment demonstrators, including 46 parliamentary deputies, were arrested and imprisoned. Further, social-democratic newspapers and other outlets to the public were subject to censorship or closure, trade unions' ability to organize was hampered, and left-wing activities were subject to surveillance and other hindrances. The governments of the region feared Bolshevism and anything that reminded them of it, and took steps to ensure that voices from the left remained muted at best.

In addition to doing damage to the idea of democracy, these measures had another longer-term effect, one that hinged on the relationship to Nazi Germany. During the war, the right-wing parties, and right-wing ideology more generally, became discredited. Whether these countries were allied with Hitler and had a strong native fascist movement, as was the case in Hungary and Romania, or had opposed Hitler, as in Poland and Czechoslovakia, the right lost its ideological resonance and its political base as the war drew on. Concomitantly, the left grew in stature, not least because of the socialist and communist involvement in the resistance, but also because everyone knew that the left was suppressed in the interwar years, although few had cared before the onset of the Great Depression. When that shattering event reached Eastern Europe in the years 1929–1932, however, the situation changed. The Western capitalist system professedly adopted by the states of the region was in disarray and, as was the case with Western-style democracy, lost much of its legitimacy. This encouraged the regimes to move to the right and begin to adapt their largely state-heavy economies to the corporatist model that seemed to be having such success in Germany. Even after the war came, Germany continued to look like a good model. When the war turned against the Axis, however, and the privations of the wartime economy began to be felt deeply, resentment against the corporatist path of escaping from discredited capitalism grew, as did sympathy for left-wing solutions.

This was bolstered by the effects of the regimes allied to or collaborating with the Nazis giving themselves over to anti-Soviet propaganda. After the attack on the Soviet Union in June 1941 this propaganda climbed to a fever pitch, and the sensibilities of sections of the Slavic populations must have been affected. It is impossible to measure this reaction, but there are two general cases that allow for speculation. Certainly, it affected the Slavic ethnic groups most deeply attached to pan-Slavic thought, the Czechs and the Bulgarians, the latter of whose governments avoided specifically anti-Russian propaganda and managed to keep from sending troops to the eastern front. However, it also disturbed some of the Croats and Slovaks, who were obligated to fight alongside the Nazis in their Soviet campaign. As the tide turned against the Axis, however, and the populations began to feel the strains and see the potential consequences, of their alliance with Hitler, to question the legitimacy of their right-wing governments, and even to undertake underground resistance actions (often alongside the Communists themselves), the propaganda began to have a hollow ring. In many of the states of the region—following the logic of "the enemy of my enemy is my friend"—when Nazi propaganda was revealed as nothing but lies, the ingrained understanding of the Slavic, socialist Soviets as subhuman incarnations of barbarism had also to be reconsidered. This was further affected by the attractions of socialism to the region's growing industrial working class, described below.[27]

In brief, in the quarter-century after the end of the First World War the regimes of Eastern Europe contributed mightily to their own demise. The early promises of real reform in the spheres of politics and socioeconomic organization had been successful in funneling the discontent of the final years of World War I away from social upheaval but were far less so in positively restructuring the region's societies. More critically, much of the population of Eastern Europe came to perceive their regimes as unjust under the weight of the pressures of the Great Depression and the political rise of Nazi Germany, neither of which was under the control of the states of Eastern Europe. At the same time, the worldwide economic crisis went far toward discrediting capitalism and the Western states that had been looked to as models for Eastern Europe's economic development. That the West was also given to appeasing a Germany that had come to dominate Eastern Europe only furthered its decline in Eastern European eyes. As pointed out above, the regional failure of Western-style democracy, for whatever specific combination of reasons, was matched by the international diplomatic failure of the guarantors of bourgeois democratic development. Still, the fires of the ideas of democratic governance and social reform, sparked in the first years after World War I, remained lit, a fact that benefited the left after the Second World War. The discrediting of the right bestowed an ambiguous credit on the left, which had suffered under the rightist regimes of the interwar and, after June 1941 at the latest, had given themselves over to resisting the Nazis. The left's credentials were further aided by the anti-Soviet propaganda of the Axis during the war and by the Soviet Union's subsequent victory. The tables turned internationally with Stalingrad, and they turned concomitantly domestically. This, of course, is not to say that the peoples of the region suddenly began worshiping Stalin and the USSR. Nevertheless, the delegitimization of the interwar Eastern European governments was matched by festering doubt about the reliability of the West and called all of the propaganda certainties of the previous twenty-five years into question, including those about the dangers of both left-wing politics and the Soviet Union.

WORLD WAR II IN EASTERN EUROPE:
THE PARTICIPATION ASPECTS

In a war that certainly deserves the adjective "total," there can be no doubt that almost every man, woman, and child in Eastern Europe participated in World War II to one degree or another. A catalogue of the entire range of experiences that differing segments of the population lived through in 1938–1945 would require a study of its own and clearly lies outside the purview of this introduction. However, Marwick's definition is somewhat more restrictive, and keeping with him in this regard is fruitful. He limits the notion of participation to the "greater participation on the part of larger, underprivileged groups in society, who tend correspondingly to benefit, or at least to develop a new self-consciousness."[28] With this in mind, the following will focus on three interrelated groups: the working class, the youth, and the communist movement.

Despite the fact that the economies of the region lay largely in ruin by 1945, the needs of the Nazi war machine created a boom in Eastern Europe during the first years of the war.[29] Because of the Axis need for war matériel, this boom was centered in the industrial and extractive sectors of the economy, while agriculture declined precipitously due to labor and capital shortages created by the calling up of conscripts and forced laborers and the priority given industry in war manufacturing. The one-sided prosperity and attendant industrial development were most notable in the Protectorate of Bohemia and Moravia, Slovakia, Hungary, Romania, and, to a lesser extent, Bulgaria. Dismembered Yugoslavia and Poland, alongside the resolutely nonindustrialized Albania, experienced none of the benefits of the boom of the early war years, while suffering greatly from the collapse and destruction that followed.

The Protectorate entered the occupation as the most industrialized territory in Eastern Europe, and the first years of the war witnessed an increase in Czech productive capacity, particularly in mining and heavy industry. Between 1939 and 1943, coal production rose by one-third, that of steel by one-ninth, and of electricity by almost half. This powerful advance in production was matched by an increase in the working-class population. Over the course of the war, industrial employment rose by one-quarter, with that of the mining, metallurgical, and chemical sectors leading the advance with an average growth of 64 percent. Alongside the growth in production came a rise in workers' wages. Although this existed simultaneously with wartime inflation, by 1941 real wages had increased by 3 percent. Less industrialized Slovakia experienced substantial expansion as well, as a result of significant German investment and technical assistance. In 1943, industrial production was over 60 percent higher than it had been in 1937, and employment in industry was over 50 percent higher. As in the Czech lands, these increases were centered in the spheres of capital goods and extraction. By the close of

1943, the production of producers' goods was almost twice as large as it had been in 1937, and employment in that sector was 60 percent higher. Despite the destruction caused by the war, upon liberation the reconstituted Czechoslovakia would have a larger share of its population in the industrial working class than ever before.

With some restrictions, the same can be said for Hungary, Romania, and Bulgaria. In these cases, German investment caused booms in the sectors the Nazis deemed most important for the war effort, although the generalized wartime demand for industrial and engineering goods created a significant rise in output, particularly in Hungary. Industrial production within Hungary's Trianon borders grew by 32 percent from 1938 to 1940, more than over the entire preceding twenty years. By 1942 the industrial labor force had grown by a similar amount, with the labor force in heavy industry growing by an estimated 60–70 percent by 1943. As in the Protectorate, the real wages of workers also rose, reaching a peak of 112 percent of the 1938 wage in 1942. Even when longer working hours are taken into account, real wages had risen by 8 percent over that period. Developments were much the same in Romania. Although the Germans were primarily concerned with assuring stable supplies of Romanian oil, steel production rose by some 30 percent by 1943 and there are indications that the output of Romanian industry as a whole expanded considerably in this period. Bulgarian industry likewise grew 19 percent in the years 1939–1941.

From these figures, it is apparent that in much of Eastern Europe German economic activity aided the industrialization of the region. To be sure, these gains were more than wiped out when German hegemony collapsed, and Yugoslavia and Poland (the areas incorporated into the Reich excluded) certainly sustained substantial losses throughout the period of German occupation. While there is no way to accurately assess the changes in workers' self-consciousness that the war brought, a few points can reasonably be made. Above all, the added industrial capacity across the region called for industrial workers, and hundreds of thousands of former peasants entered the industrial working class. The experience of factory labor was thus extended to a greater share of the population, which not only strengthened the working class at a propitious moment for the Communist parties of the region, but also contributed to a greater awareness of working-class problems and desires. To this growth of the working class must also be added the numbers of those whose first experience of factory life came with their arrival as forced laborers in the *Reich*. Furthermore, the booming early years of the war, coinciding with a generalized rise in the number of women in the workforce, led to a rise in workers' prosperity. Whether this resulted in stronger worker self-consciousness and a willingness on the part of workers across the region to make demands in the name of their class thereafter cannot be determined. However, the Czech working class certainly emerged from the war with a strong sense of its class power, and the necessity of appealing to the working class in the labors of reconstruction region-wide must have contributed to a sense of worker solidarity.[30] When the trade unions were consolidated over the course of the early postwar years, it not only gave the Communists an additional lever for controlling the working class, but also gave the working class an institutional home in which it could become more conscious of its social and political power.

The second group that emerged on the scene as a politically and socially important force at the end of the war was the youth, a feature that will require a bit of historical demography to understand. The spacing of the two major wars of twentieth-century Europe created a bifurcation in the age structures of the Eastern European populations. Largely as a result of World War I, the second decade of the twentieth century showed a decrease in the population of most of the countries of the region. Czechoslovakia, Hungary, and Bulgaria were the only ones to show a net increase between 1910 and 1920, and in the latter two cases this is largely attributable to an influx of co-nationals following the redrawing of international boundaries after the First World War. The territories of Poland and Yugoslavia were especially hard-hit, losing between 4 and 6 percent of their populations. The decade of the 1920s, however, more than made up for this, as a "vital revolution" swept over Eastern Europe.[31] Birthrates, which had been declining even before World War I, skyrocketed to over 32.5 per thousand in Yugoslavia and Poland, and over 37.5 per thousand in Romania and Bulgaria over the years 1921–1925. For the sake of comparison, rates in Germany, Great Britain, Scandinavia, and the Low Countries did not rise above 22.5 per thousand in those years. In combination with lower mortality rates, this meant that the populations of Eastern Europe grew remarkably rapidly in the 1920s. During that decade, the populations of Poland, Romania, Bulgaria, Albania, and Yugoslavia each grew by over 12 percent, and those of Czechoslovakia and Hungary by between 8 and 10 percent. This was roughly double the European average for the period. The extraordinarily rapid growth of the 1920s slowed after the onset of the Great Depression. Birthrates from 1936 to 1939, with the exception of the Romanian, did not eclipse 22.5 per thousand, and the rate of natural increase slowed in all countries. Still, the explosion of the first interwar decade had a lasting effect on the population of the region. Between 1920 and 1939, the population of Eastern Europe rose by over one-quarter, more than 50 percent faster than the rest of the Continent (excluding the USSR).

Taking all of these factors into account, a number of conclusions can be reached about the age structure of Eastern Europe in 1945. First of all, the military losses of the First World War meant a gash in the age pyramid at the level of 45–55 years of age. Correspondingly, the slowing birthrates in the years before and especially during that war weakened the cadre of those in their thirties and early forties. The boom in births in the first half of the interwar period meant that there was a spike in the population of those in ages ranging from 15 to 25, with much of the weight lying toward those born in the years of the highest birthrates in the early twenties. The net result is that one would expect a strong cadre of those who in the first years after World War II would have been between 18 and 28 years of age, having been born between the end of the First World War and the onset of the Great Depression, and this is in fact the case. A comparison of statistics derived from United Nations figures and national censuses reveals that a striking amount of the population was aged 15–25 in the immediate aftermath of the war.[32] In Czechoslovakia, the census of 1947 showed 17 percent of the population in that age group and, if we extend the parameters to age 30, we reach almost one-quarter of the population. The January 1949 census in Hungary reveals much the same: almost 17 percent in the 15–25 age group, and a little over a quarter was aged 15–30. Bulgaria, which suffered fewer casualties in World War II, was an even younger population, with over one-fifth of Bulgarians aged 15–25. Even in devastated Poland and Yugoslavia, the situation was no different. In Poland in 1950 17 percent of the population was aged 20–30, meaning that these Poles would have been between 15 and 25 in 1945. Finally, in war-torn Yugoslavia, the 1948 census shows that over 20 percent of the population was aged 15–25. For the sake of comparison, in 1970, near the height of baby-boomer radicalism and cultural influence, 17.4 percent of the population of the United States was aged 15–25.

What is the significance of having such a large portion of the population concentrated in their late teens and early twenties? Youths are traditionally held to be both more radical and more politically committed than their more pragmatic and conservative elders. While this is a truism that certainly does not hold in all cases, a strong argument for the existence of a cadre of radicalized, left-leaning youths across Eastern Europe can certainly be made. The generation of the post–World War I baby boom would have only scanty recollection of the measure of prosperity that emerged in the region in the 1920s. They would, however, have a living memory of the tribulations of the Great Depression. Similarly, they would have missed the relatively benign political climate of the first half of the 1920s, while having clear memories of the increasingly authoritarian dictatorships of the 1930s. Further, although generally too young to serve in the military in the late 1930s, they were disproportionately involved in the resistance movements of the region, ones which in many cases had a strong admixture of Communists. Finally, they were perhaps even more impressionable than their elders regarding the notions of Western appeasement, Nazi anticommunism, Soviet strength, and so on. It is difficult to believe that one could grow up in the greatest crisis modern capitalism has ever known, in countries under the leadership of right-wing dictators, beneath the shadow of fascist occupation (or in states allied with fascist dictatorships), and not have one's faith in capitalism and Western-style democracy deeply shaken. When the experience of taking up arms against the Germans, and perhaps even against one's own dictatorial government, alongside Communists, and then being liberated by the Red Army is taken into account, an urge for radical social change seems expectable, not just excusable. What made this politically important is not just that there were throngs of teenagers and young adults available to demonstrate their leftist sympathies with banners and placards on the streets, but that they had the vote. As one of the early postwar reforms, voting ages across the region were lowered, enfranchising many of these youths at a time when they were acutely vulnerable to left-wing political radicalism. The voting ages in Albania, Czechoslovakia, and Yugoslavia reached 18, that of Bulgaria 19, while those of Poland, Hungary, and Romania were lowered to 21.

Evidence for the radicalization of the youth can be drawn from the Communist and Communist-controlled youth organizations that dominated the scene where they could exist during the war, for instance in partisan-held territories of Yugoslavia, and that were quite strong across the region in its immediate aftermath. The Yugoslav Communist Youth League, for example, numbered 150,000 members at the end of hostilities, and provided the core of the United Anti-Fascist Youth League, which counted some 1.5 million among its ranks at war's end. Interestingly, of the 305,000 soldiers the Yugoslav National Liberation Army lost, about 50,000 were members of the party, while 70,000 were members of the Communist Youth League. The Bulgarian Workers' Youth Union was proportionally smaller, but nonetheless numbered 400,000 in 1945, and had provided the majority of the Bulgarian underground fighting force during the war.[33] Much as the unification of the trade unions contributed to both Communist domination of them and likely to worker self-consciousness and consciousness of group power, so the unification of the youth unions across the region, not least in Czechoslovakia, provided these radicalized youth with an institutional focus for their mutually infectious enthusiasm, as well as a mass platform for political expression.

The beneficiaries of the increased participation of the youth, in many cases, were the Communist parties of Eastern Europe, the third group that fits Marwick's criteria by achieving "greater participation" in the political lives of their nations, by having been "underprivileged" before the war and decidedly both "benefit[ing]" from and "develop[ing] a new self-consciousness" during the events of 1938–1945. As noted above, all the Communist parties of the region except the Czechoslovak were proclaimed illegal and operated underground during the interwar years, often under considerable police pressure. The coming of the war against the Soviet Union in 1941 and the beginning of resistance activities by local Communists only encouraged already anti-communist regimes to adopt harsher measures. Slovakia, for instance, imprisoned roughly 3,000 people for political reasons during the state's wartime existence, over half of whom were Communists. For their part, the Romanians decreed that if a Communist were to be found guilty of the decree-law of February 6, 1941, which criminalized broad categories of acts deemed threats to the existence and interests of the state, the punishment was to be doubled. Even ambivalent Bulgaria arrested 11,000 Communists during the war, imprisoning 6,000 in internment camps and shipping the remainder off to labor battalions. The conditions for Communists in the occupied countries were, of course, even worse than in these relatively benign cases. Given that most of these parties, working underground, were small before the war, it should come as no surprise that they were miniscule when it came to a close and that their domestic leaderships had been decimated. For example, the Communist Party of Czechoslovakia and the Communist Party of Slovakia each lost four underground central committees between 1939 and 1945.

Despite the increased levels of persecution, Communists participated in and often led the partisan and resistance movements aimed at liberating their lands from Nazi or Italian occupation, or overthrowing their domestic regimes that were in alliance with Hitler. These movements among Communists did not commence in any concerted fashion, of course, until after the invasion of the Soviet Union, but thereafter became considerably more active. Certainly the most pervasive Communist presence was in Yugoslavia, where by the end of the war Tito commanded some 800,000 partisans. Communists also constituted the primary force for active resistance in neighboring Albania, and provided the vast majority of Bulgaria's small resistance organization. Finally, Communists played disproportionately strong roles in the Czech, Slovak, Hungarian, and Romanian underground resistance movements. Only in the Polish resistance did the Communists play a marginal role, with the anticommunist Home Army and its political representatives running a virtual underground state and society. The Communists' presence in the anti-Axis struggle certainly redounded to their benefit after the war, but the experience of resistance itself can also be seen as a factor in fostering support for radical social change. As already noted, the plans for the future promulgated by the underground movements envisioned wide-ranging confiscations of German, Italian, Hungarian, and collaborator-owned property, nationalizations of key industries and the financial sector, and extensive land redistribution.

Taken as a whole, the changed structure of Eastern European society reveals several features that could be taken as beneficial for left-wing politics. The working class had grown during the course of the war, despite the destruction that came in its final years. Further, there was a bubble in the population that, in age and political memory and experience, was perhaps uniquely ripe for political radicalism. Moreover, the Communist parties of the region had gone from a hated and persecuted target of right-wing authoritarian regimes, to emerging as a powerful actor on the domestic political stage. Even without the aid afforded by the presence of the Red Army, the Communists had made a legitimate name for themselves in the wartime underground and would doubtless have played a significant, albeit minority, role in postwar developments. Finally, one must not lose sight of the flip side of "participation." The participation of a great many foes of the left had cost them their positions, or even their lives. This includes not only the discredited right-wing political groupings, which were subject to political justice after the war, but also a bourgeoisie that was either a target of Nazi oppression or tarnished by collaboration. Overall, the left emerged from its participation in the war in a very favorable position.

WORLD WAR II IN EASTERN EUROPE: THE CZECH CASE

That the left came out of World War II in a favorable position, however, should not be taken to mean that the experience of war preordained a communist Eastern Europe thereafter. Despite what I have said, I do not intend to replace the teleology of Cold War accounts—predicated on the power of the Red Army and the Soviet Union—with one based on the effects of the Second World War. Just as the role of the USSR and its military and political representatives was, in most cases, a necessary but not sufficient determinant of the direction in which the course of events moved, so the cataclysm of the war was a necessary spur to radical social change in the region, but it was not sufficient for determining the shape of Eastern Europe in 1950. Each country of the region followed its own, unique path to Communist dictatorship, influenced by its historical development before the war, the way in which the war played itself out, the domestic political and ideological constellation obtaining at war's end, and the behavior of the superpowers. The differences between them should not be overlooked, despite the commonalities of experience that they, to a greater or lesser degree, shared after 1918.

The case of Czechoslovakia, with which this study will be concerned, is unique and still reflects the general experience of the region. Founded in 1918 from parts of the Austro-Hungarian Empire, it shared many of its neighbors' struggles. Composed of the Czech lands (Bohemia and Moravia, taken from the Austrian half of the Dual Monarchy) and Slovakia and Sub-Carpathian Ruthenia (taken from the Hungarian half), the new state was confronted with problems of integration much like those of Poland, Yugoslavia, or Romania. In addition to the economic and administrative problems that accompanied state-building, there were nation-building ones arising from the differing histories of the Czechs and Slovaks. This problem was faced, with varying degrees of intensity, by all the lands of Eastern Europe, save Albania, Bulgaria, and Hungary, as these new or newly reconfigured states attempted to integrate co-nationals who had lived under different regimes before 1914. Additionally, each half of the new state had ethnic minorities, Germans in the Czech lands and Hungarians in Slovakia, that had formerly been dominant and were linked to powerful states anxious to revise the peace treaties of World War I. Such a condition was not unusual in the region, as the ethnic makeup of western Poland or Romanian Transylvania clearly shows. Czechoslovakia was unique, however, in that it had to confront threats from both Hungary and Germany.[34]

The interwar history of Czechoslovakia is often pointed to as being exceptional for the region, and there is a large measure of truth in this judgment. Unlike its neighbors, it did not succumb to right-wing authoritarianism until after it was truncated as a result of the Munich Accords. The reasons for this are too numerous to examine in great depth, but in some ways it can be seen as resulting from the "Westernness" of the political, economic, and cultural institutions and habits of the dominant Czech nation.[35] The Czech lands had been the most economically successful and highly industrialized region within the Austro-Hungarian Empire, making the Czechs at least as prosperous as many Western European peoples, and far more so than those elsewhere in Eastern Europe. Further, the expanding franchise and lively political activity of the last half-century of the Austrian half of the Dual Monarchy had created a vibrant civil society and a stable political culture, bequeathing the Czechs a fully articulated spectrum of political parties. In short, Czechs were accustomed to democratic politics and all of the interplay of interests that comes with it. These economic, political, and social legacies of imperial rule, not shared to the same extent by the other states of the region, or even by the Slovaks, contributed strongly to Czechoslovakia's development as a stable and prosperous democracy.

The state was not without its blemishes, however. The influence of the leaderships of the largest parties, the *"pětka,"* and the frequent invocation of caretaker governments worked to the detriment of interwar Czech democracy. However, they did provide continuity amid the numerous cabinet reshuffles that were as much a part of Czechoslovak political life as they were of that of the rest of Eastern Europe. Further, the Great Depression affected the Czechoslovak economy in much the same way as it did the others of the region. Three differences from the other countries of Eastern Europe should be pointed out here. Above all, the Depression exacerbated the ethnic tensions that existed between Czechs and Germans, paving the way for the growth of Konrad Henlein's Sudeten German Party, which came increasingly under the control of Hitler as the 1930s wore on. Further, as a far more industrialized society than the others of Eastern Europe, the effects of the price scissors and peasant indebtedness were far less severe. Finally, the arsenal of measures to treat the Depression in Czechoslovakia lacked one feature present in other states of the region: the expansion of trade with Germany. While Germany came to dominate the foreign trade of Hungary, Romania, Bulgaria, and even Yugoslavia, it only constituted roughly 15 percent of Czechoslovak imports and exports in 1937, a smaller share than in 1929. Similarly, by 1938 Germany contributed only 7.2 percent of the total foreign investment in the country, less than a quarter of Great Britain's share, and even less than that of the Netherlands.

The war came to Czechoslovakia in 1938, when an escalating series of Sudeten German demands, supported by the military might and diplomatic muscle of Nazi Germany, culminated in the Munich Accords. The sacrifice of Czechoslovakia by France and Great Britain was, as we shall see, a tremendous blow to the state. After the German annexation of the Sudetenland, a more authoritarian government was installed in Prague, with the intent of maintaining at least a vestige of Czechoslovak sovereignty. This step was to no avail, however, as German desires for the state's destruction coincided with Slovak secessionist tendencies some six months later. The Czech lands became the Protectorate of Bohemia and Moravia, while Slovakia gained a nominal independence under German tutelage. Taken together, the differing wartime histories of the two entities, covered *inter alia* above, make the Czechoslovak experience of the war roughly representative of the region as a whole, although neither part of Czechoslovakia fought initially. As in Yugoslavia, part of the country, Slovakia, was allied to the Axis, and part, the Czech lands, was occupied. Unlike Yugoslavia, though, resistance in both the Czech lands and Slovakia was generally low until the Slovak Uprising of August–October 1944. Like the other countries of the region, both experienced initial economic and industrializing gains that were wiped out in the final years of the war. Both suffered significant losses in life and property, more than those of Bulgaria but far less than those of Yugoslavia or Poland.

Despite these similarities in wartime experience, the differences between the trajectories of the Czech lands and Slovakia only reflect more deeply rooted differences between the two parts of the former Czechoslovakia. The weight given to the Czech lands, the current Czech Republic, over the preceding few pages has been deliberate, since the following chapters will analyze how Czechs argued about their experiences of the interwar republic, occupation, and war, and about their notions of socialism. While many of the sentiments they expressed found echoes among the Slovaks with whom they shared a state, the differing experience of each group in the thirty years before the Communists gained total power necessarily means that the views of Slovaks must be left to the side in what follows. Similarly, the differing experiences of Czechs and Slovaks over the centuries preceding and including Habsburg rule meant that the cultural, social, and political heritages of the two peoples were different. Most importantly for our purposes, this meant that the traditions, characteristics, and roles of the intellectuals with whom this study is concerned also differed, hence this study will be limited to the Czech case.

2

Intellectuals in the Czech Environment

Introducing a discussion of the intellectuals of any Eastern European land is both easy and difficult. On the one hand, for those familiar with the region it is simple and self-evident to refer to the "intelligentsia" when discussing its politics and culture. On the other hand, as Fiona Björling has put it, "to define the identity of this group of people, not to mention their function, is another matter." In laying the groundwork for a discussion of the group, we shall no doubt conclude with Björling that "the intelligentsia as such is real enough—but that most attempts at definition are at best intuitive."[1] In the following, I have elected to use the terms "intelligentsia" and "intellectuals" interchangeably to refer to a rather broad set of actors. They will designate people traditionally considered intellectuals in the United States: writers, academics, and so on. Further, however, it will be extended to lawyers, editorialists, religious leaders, and, perhaps most importantly, to political figures involved in the public debates of the times. This final category, perhaps counterintuitive from the American point of view, has been included for several reasons. Above all, politicians played a leading role in reflecting and defining the issues of the times, and their views cannot therefore be ignored in the debates analyzed here.[2] Further, many of them had been trained or professionally active in fields more traditionally considered the province of intellectuals. Finally, in the life of the Czech nation, as in the others of the region, the borders between political and cultural activity have often been so blurred as to make distinguishing them artificial and even arbitrary.[3]

Beyond their intrinsic interest, there is a solid historical foundation arguing for the importance of understanding the Czech intelligentsia and for the inclusion of political figures in the group. Like those of many other nations of Central and Eastern Europe, Czech intellectuals historically maintained a high degree of popular authority and political legitimacy. Their influence in their nation was powerful regardless of whether they engaged directly in political activity, and it reached a peak after World War II. In the following very brief sketch of Czech intellectuals' historical role, five aspects will be stressed: the national struggle in the Czech lands between Czechs and Germans; the substitution of intellectual and cultural activity for political activity in that struggle; the predilection for Slavism as a counterweight to German dominance; the importance of the intelligentsia's social origins for its continuing popular legitimacy; and the historical basis for both the direct and indirect participation of intellectuals in the nation's expressly political life.

From the time of the Hussite religious movement in the fifteenth century, the intelligentsia has been the driving force for the maintenance of Czech culture in its broadest sense. More than a century before Luther, Hussite preaching stressed the equality of individuals before God, and his credo that "truth will prevail" placed a premium on the individual search for truth, leading to an intellectual flowering. The movement also took on a nationalist aspect, with Czechs largely supporting it while the German population of Bohemia and Moravia largely identified with the Roman Catholic Church. When Hus was burned at the stake in 1415, this opposition flared into a series of wars that only ended close to two decades later. Hussitism festered for the next two centuries, and exploded again in the early seventeenth century, when a Czech conflict with the Vatican triggered the onset of the Thirty Years' War. With the defeat of Czech Protestantism at the Battle of White Mountain (1620) in the first decisive military confrontation of that war, came the imposition of a harsh counterreformation. The ruling Habsburg dynasty banned all forms of Protestantism and placed the educational system in the hands of the Jesuits. In addition, an estimated five-sixths of the Czech nobility fled into exile. The Habsburgs distributed these nobles' holdings and administrative positions to loyal local nobles and to mercenaries, who were predominantly ethnically German or adopted a German identity. Here we encounter one of the primary reasons the intelligentsia has loomed so large in Czech national life. Since the ruling strata in both the secular and religious life of the society came to be seen as both ethnically and religiously foreign, intellectuals became the bearers of statehood and national identity. The Habsburg nobility in the Czech lands was very small—totaling only some 2,300 people including family members—and became regarded as a group of intruders or invaders. In the Czech regions of the Habsburg Empire the lower levels of administration—village priests, small-town civil servants, etc.—often worked on behalf of the emerging nation but could have little effect on larger institutional wholes, which remained steadfastly *Kaisertreu*.[4] These conditions remained stable until the Enlightenment reached the Czech lands, spurring the commencement of the Czech "national rebirth."[5] As Antonín Liehm has pointed out:

The Czechs are the only people in Europe to have passed through most of the seventeenth century and all of the eighteenth without possessing a national aristocracy, and thus they were deprived of this traditional center of education, culture, and political power. As a result of the violent Germanization and counter-reformation which characterized these two centuries in our land, modern Czech political consciousness emerged as an attempt to revive the national language and culture. Those who took over this task—writers, linguists, scholars—assumed the role of the aristocracy; they became the spiritual elite of a subjugated nation, and eventually transformed themselves into a political elite. Thus, modern Czech politics was born at the end of the eighteenth century as a "cultural politics" and the connection between culture and politics had an organic basis from the very first. This situation persisted throughout the nineteenth century and into the twentieth. It was characteristic of the Masaryk era, as well as the Nazi occupation and the immediate postwar period. Only if we understand this historical background and the roots of the long-standing authority which writers enjoy among the people can we understand the tremendous power of Czechoslovak cultural publications.[6]

The intelligentsia both began and led the national revival of the nineteenth century. The historian and scholar of Slavic literature Josef Dobrovský commenced this age of cultural politics with his *Geschichte der böhmischen Sprache und Literatur* (1792). In his absence "the Czech language might well have been revived, but not in the classical form which he restored to it."[7] This "Age of Dobrovský," as Czechoslovakia's first president Tomáš G. Masaryk called it, was followed by wider activity in the second quarter of the nineteenth century, when the cultural movement around the *Matice česká* assumed the lead.[8] This largely literary society was controlled by two leading lights of the Czech national rebirth: the historian František Palacký (author of the multivolume *History of the Czech Nation*) and the linguist Josef Jungmann (the author of the first dictionary of the Czech language). In the 1830s, support for the *Matice* came largely from the clergy (40 percent) and students (20 percent), who sustained the organization's journal and limited publishing activities. In the period around the revolution of 1848 the *Matice* flourished, reaching a total of 3,773 individual and 95 institutional members.[9]

It is only at this time that we can begin to speak of a large group of intellectuals in the Czech lands, and the social origins and composition of the group are important for understanding its popular authority. With the exception of some members of the state bureaucracy and clerical establishment, the Czech intelligentsia was composed of members of the lower and lower-middle classes from small towns and villages. Miroslav Hroch found that over two-fifths of Czech "patriots" were born in places with a population of fewer than 1,500, and a further quarter in towns having between 1,500 and 4,000, people. He concludes that: "Most patriots came from the milieu of the towns and the largest group of them, in social descent, comes among the sons of tradesmen and shopkeepers. The share of the patriots from farm and intellectual families grew from the first patriot generation onwards."[10] Coming from smaller towns and the lower and middle classes, Czech nationalist intellectuals had considerably closer contacts with the common people, a fact which helped them to emerge "as a group of legitimate spokesmen, opinion leaders and organizers of the lower estates."[11]

As the industrial revolution spread throughout the Czech lands in the 1830s and 1840s, general education also spread, creating a wider audience for the growing intelligentsia. At the same time, the rising Czech urban bourgeoisie found itself in increasing competition with its German counterpart. Urbanization both created a milieu for intellectuals to meet one another and a larger, wealthier, and better-educated audience for their ideas. It also brought to the fore the latent national conflict in the Czech lands between a growing body of Czech nationalists, led by literary figures and historians, and the German population. As Gary Cohen observed, Czech nationalists "believed they had to establish an independent Czech social life in Prague and the other central Bohemian cities to stop the Germanization of upwardly mobile elements and to build a Czech society." This independent social life was founded on "clubs, balls, artistic and literary salons, and reading societies," and during the latter half of the century spread to all strata of Czech society.[12]

The events of 1848 played a central role in the development of the nationality conflict and illustrate many of the themes of this brief historical sketch, including the role of intellectuals as leaders of the Czech offensive and Slavism as a political force among Czechs. Stanley Pech noted that "the students and the young intellectuals" were the "one group that lent [1848–1849] its characteristic revolutionary flavor." Under the leadership of men such as Palacký, the fiery journalist Karel Havlíček and the Slavicist Pavel Josef Šafařík, the revolution was "Year One in the political life of the Czechs." It brought "the first Czech political program, the first constitutions, the first elections and political campaigns, the first political parties, the first popular assembly [and] the first great Czech daily newspaper."[13] Palacký served as chairman of the first Slavic Congress, which took place in Prague in June 1848. Some 385 participants from the Slavic world took part, representing "in the purest sense of the word the intellectual elite of non-Russian Slavdom." Although the practical effects of the Congress were slight, it strengthened contacts between the Slav nations and constituted a "special triumph" for the Czechs, who remained marked by pan-Slavic sentiment even beyond the Second World War.[14]

In the second half of the nineteenth century, a number of cultural endeavors became foci of the national conflict. The ultimate failure of the political strivings of 1848 and the return to absolutism in the Bach era led to added emphasis on the cultural aspects of the Czechs' national struggle. As one historian has noted: "Literature and its neighbors, aesthetics and history, became universally potent, became ersatz politics, ersatz philosophy, ersatz economics. They became an ersatz for those spheres for which the true basis was lacking."[15] As national consciousness took hold of the ever-growing Czech middle class, it spread to the working class as "great attention was devoted to the question of popular education in the widest sense." In this task Czech intellectuals solidified their ties to the swelling ranks of the urban proletariat, in a sense repeating the small-town and village activities of their predecessors in the age of the national rebirth.[16]

Perhaps the most important single symbol of the cementing of a widely held Czech national consciousness, however, was the building of the National Theater. From the early activity of the Committee to Build the National Theater in the bleak days of the 1850s, support swelled until the cornerstone was laid in 1867. The ceremony at the groundbreaking had tremendous symbolic importance because the funds for the theater's construction were raised from public contributions. Furthermore, the fact that 69 percent of the total came from individual donors reveals the importance of culture for the entire nation. Similarly, all classes of Czech society contributed to the fund, making the edifice worthy of its motto: "The nation to itself" (*Národ sobě*). Moreover, the visitors who attended the celebration made it "not only the most important Slavic 'open forum' since 1848, but also probably the most noteworthy Slavic 'congress' of the latter half of the nineteenth century." Among the more than 60,000 people who attended the ceremony were participants representing nine Slavic nations, and the closing words of the Committee's vice president's speech—"Success to the communality and solidarity of the Slavs!"—touched off a frenzy of mutual tribute-paying.[17]

It was also in the last quarter of the nineteenth century that certain Czech intellectuals began to play a direct role as political actors, some as leaders of a resurgent Pan-Slavism. Most famous among these politician-intellectuals was Tomáš Masaryk, who entered Czech political life in 1889 and was elected to the Austrian *Reichsrat* in 1891. Masaryk, a professor of sociology and later the first president of independent Czechoslovakia, was joined by the economist and sociologist Josef Kaizl and the economist and lawyer Karel Kramář in forming a group known as the "realists," which Jaroslav Opat has called the "brain trust" of Czech politics.[18] In these closing years of the century Czech-German relations were especially turbulent. The national struggle intensified to a fever pitch in 1897 when a set of ordinances making the Czech and German languages equal was announced and then withdrawn after widespread protests and rioting on the part of the empire's German subjects. With their withdrawal the likelihood of further internal reform faded and Czech intellectual and political leaders, particularly Kramář, began to look to a revival of Pan-Slavism for support.[19] This Neo-Slav movement gained strength after the Tsar introduced reform measures in the wake of the 1905 Russian Revolution. These reforms played a large role in Kramář's 1906 decision to propose an expansion of suffrage, an effort that appealed to the traditional concerns and social origins of the Czech intelligentsia. The Neo-Slavs' propagation of the "Slavic idea"—"an awareness of belonging to the Slav community of nations and a desire for increased contact and co-operation between the Slav peoples"—reached its peak during the Prague Neo-Slav Congress of 1908. The congress, held on the sixtieth anniversary of the 1848 All-Slav Congress, placed particular stress on cultural pursuits and was primarily attended by political, academic, and journalistic figures.[20]

The participation of intellectuals in the founding of an independent Czechoslovak state and their role in its public life are too extensive to address here, but a few points should be made. Above all, the state's first president, the philosopher and sociologist Masaryk, came from the ranks of the intelligentsia, revealing the popular authority and legitimacy given intellectual activity. His foreign minister and successor, Edvard Beneš, was also a trained academic and former professor of sociology. Further, in order to fashion and carry out his program for the new state, Masaryk created what was known as the "Castle Group." This was composed partly of leading politicians, but also of "democratic intellectuals. . . . Drawn from a variety of professions, they included economists, administrators, scientists, writers, and artists, and formed . . . a brains trust under Masaryk's leadership."[21] Even beyond this group, Czech intellectuals had further contact with the highest circles of power, as Masaryk and Beneš met with a group of leading cultural lights semi-regularly in the so-called "Friday Group." As Julius Firt, one of its members, later recalled:

> All were invited by [the writer] Karel Čapek. No longer was it only poets, now there were also painters and sculptors, journalists, university professors, actors and so on. . . . As a university professor before the war, he [Masaryk] was accustomed to visiting his cafe every afternoon, to read his newspapers and discuss matters with politicians, artists and academics. As president he no longer had this possibility, so [Ferdinand] Peroutka's invitation came as extremely welcome.[22]

Finally, there was a strong tendency toward left-wing politics among Czech intellectuals in the interwar republic, particularly among the literary elite. This, in conjunction with the already noted fact that the Communist Party was permitted to function above ground throughout the republic's twenty-year existence, lent left-wing radicalism a large measure of intellectual and cultural legitimacy.

Given these traditions from which to develop, the final reason for the markedly high status of Czech intellectuals in the 1945–1948 period was their service to the nation during the Second World War. The Protectorate of Bohemia and Moravia was undoubtedly harsh but, as is evident from the preceding chapter, constituted a far less brutal and indiscriminate experience than that of Poland or Yugoslavia. This was the case largely because it was in Germany's interest not to adopt overly harsh measures against the Czechs. The Protectorate was highly industrialized, and in order to maintain and even increase the levels of industrial production necessary for the German war effort, measures were taken to pacify

rather than to bully the population. As pointed out earlier, real wages for industrial workers rose at least through April 1941, rationing was introduced in the
Protectorate only after it had been in the Reich, and since "more women took
advantage of the new employment opportunities, the actual incomes of many
working-class families must have significantly increased."[23] As Václav Černý recalled in his memoirs, "the Germans did not want to provoke the workers, but
to win them over," a task at which he judged they were largely successful.[24] Further, the Protectorate as an institution was created early, and its eventual integration into the Reich was anticipated both for economic reasons and for reasons of historical desire on the part of the Sudeten Germans. Finally, Nazi racial
scientists and political leaders believed that "the majority of Czechs, being
racially close to the Germans, could be assimilated."[25] Since the Czech lands
were economically important to the Nazi war effort and the Czech population
largely assimilable, Nazi repression focused on Czech cultural life and its leaders
as the repository of Czech national consciousness.

Czech intellectual opposition to the Nazis, already stiff before Munich, became fully entrenched after the establishment of the Protectorate. While the
levels of resistance activity were never large in the Czech lands, and "at no
time did the Czechs challenge the Nazis with a significant resistance movement," they were particularly low in the first years of the war.[26] There were
several reasons for the small size and scope of the resistance movement: the
moral effects of Munich had been debilitating; the Czech army had surrendered in March 1939, meaning that their stockpiles of arms fell almost entirely into German hands; the Czech lands were, until the final phase of the
war, far from the front lines and possible supplies of foreign arms; the terrain
was unsuitable for partisan activity; and the Germans inherited an administrative network that had collected detailed personal data on every resident.[27]
The Czechs, having experienced centuries of Habsburg rule, cultivated a policy of coexistence and attempted to maintain their national language and culture, a tactic that placed the intelligentsia in the fore.

The first large-scale show of dissent occurred on the first wartime anniversary of Czechoslovak independence day, October 28, 1939, when
thousands of Czechs visited the tomb of the unknown soldier. There were
small-scale disturbances on the streets and during these demonstrations a
young student, Jan Opletal, was seriously wounded.[28] When Opletal died
two weeks later, 3,000 students and intellectual leaders took to the streets.
Although Czech police dispersed the demonstration, it brought a strong
German reaction. The Nazis placed placards on the streets, asserting that
"a group of Czech intellectuals has been attempting for some time . . . to
disturb peace and order in the Protectorate of Bohemia and Moravia
through greater or lesser acts of resistance. . . . Ringleaders of these acts
of resistance are to be found particularly in the Czech universities." As a
result, nine student leaders were executed and 1,200 sent to concentration

camps, and all Czech institutions of higher education were closed for three years.[29]

The repression of the students and their leaders corresponded with the Nazi goal of assimilating the majority of the Czech population. In order to prepare the nation for Germanization, the representatives and the institutions of the Czech language and culture had to be destroyed. The closing of the higher educational institutions was "part of a plan to eliminate Czech education and was followed by instructions for the gradual limitation of even Czech school education."[30] After the demonstrations of late 1939, the Nazis increasingly came to understand that the intelligentsia lay at the base of resistance activity, and took steps to destroy it. Already in 1940, they recognized that "the beneficiaries of the former regime and the majority of the puffed-up (*aufgeblähten*) intellectual caste hopes for our defeat and is irreconcilable," and that the intellectuals as a whole were "scarcely to be won over."[31] After Reinhard Heydrich became Reich Protector, in September 1941, Nazi rule became notably harsher. The eight months of his reign "meant a decisive turn towards the limitation of the Protectorate's autonomy and the Germanization of its administration."[32] This was particularly true of its treatment of intellectuals. Heydrich noted very early that their "hatred of everything German is unsurpassed," and his plan for the "solution of the Czech question" called for "un-Germanizable Czechs to be resettled in Siberia, and the especially dangerous intellectuals to be forced to emigrate overseas."[33]

Czech intellectuals came under particular pressure after Heydrich's assassination on May 27, 1942. Less than three hours after the attack, Hitler personally gave orders that 10,000 persons were to be taken hostage and 100 of the most important among them be shot that very night. Of the hostages "above all, the entirely oppositional Czech intelligentsia should be taken into custody," including "a strong contingent of civil servants, doctors, engineers, technicians, writers and artists . . . [and] a section of the teaching community." This was the most severe single blow to Czech intellectuals in 1942, a year that Václav Černý called "hellish for the Czech intelligentsia and Czech culture."[34] In the wake of Heydrich's assassination, the Germans destroyed a large part of the Czech resistance network, directing their repression "especially against the intelligentsia."[35] As the Communist underground was in disarray at that time, the vast majority of those taken were members of the non-Communist intellectual resistance.

The intelligentsia's role became even more significant after the tide began to turn against the Germans. At this time, much as the nationally conscious community flourished in the second half of the nineteenth century, the resistance movement began to grow. Small bands, primarily composed of intellectuals, were joined by increasing numbers of middle- and working-class Czechs. The intellectuals, who almost alone had comprised the non-Communist resistance, became the leaders of a wider movement. Their influence in the underground reached its peak during the Prague uprising of May

1945, when literary figures and academics composed the highest echelons of its leadership. Moreover, as the end of the Nazi regime and the restoration of Czechoslovakia increasingly became only a matter of time, thoughts turned to the nature and organization of the postwar state. Underground publications such as *In Struggle* (*V boji*) became centers for considering the form the Czechoslovak state would take after liberation. The most significant document of Czech political thinking during the war, *For Freedom. Into the New Czechoslovak Republic* (*Za svobodu. Do nové Československé republiky*), called for wide-ranging social, economic, and political changes to be realized in the immediate postwar years. According to Václav Černý, its composers were guided by the "ambition to broaden our democracy, hitherto only political, into a *social* democracy." For Černý, it was most important that "our own *national* resistance approved a program . . . for a *socialist* state, which concurrently would draw upon the wholly domestic tradition of progressive humanism that never intended to deny the ideals of civic, political and spiritual freedom for social justice, but rather strove for their synthesis."[36] We will meet with this democratic socialist desire for synthesis across a wide spectrum of issues in the postwar years, an impulse that became a political weakness.

In considering Czech intellectuals' experience of the war as a whole, several important facets become apparent. First and foremost, the intelligentsia was the primary target of a Nazi regime that wished to assimilate the largely passive Czech population. This population, while not driven to resist in large numbers, relied on the intelligentsia to maintain the nation's culture and language until better times arrived, much as it had during the centuries under Habsburg rule. Later, as the victory of the Allied forces became more apparent and the ranks of the resistance began to swell, intellectuals became the leaders of the underground. Consequently, increasing energies were directed toward rethinking the nature of the Czechoslovak state and envisaging its reconstruction as a socialist, although not communist, republic. Finally, the Nazi targeting of Czech intellectuals led to a magnification of the intelligentsia's prominence and authority. As Václav Černý noted, the bloodletting inflicted on the Czech intelligentsia's ranks brought increased responsibility in the postwar era:

Of all the groups in our society, the intelligentsia suffered the most. . . . Only a fraud can deny this. As a whole, our intelligentsia also showed the most character and faithfulness of all the groups in our society. I would say that in the years 1939–45 our intelligentsia acquired a moral legitimacy such as no other strata, or even the intelligentsia itself, had enjoyed since the time of the national revival. There was no doubt: if anyone had the right to speak about the future of our nation and state, it was [the intelligentsia.][37]

The service the Czech intelligentsia rendered their nation during the war was amply noted in pronouncements promulgated after its conclusion, and intellectuals were encouraged and occasionally even cajoled into assuming a leading role in public life. Political actors returning to their liberated state from exile in Moscow and London stressed the important role that intellectuals would play in regenerating the nation's moral health after the debilitating experiences of Munich and occupation. Many commentators noted the effort the Nazis had expended in their attempted decimation of the Czech intelligentsia, and argued that by its sufferings under German rule it had proven itself uniquely worthy of leading the nation.[38] It was considered intellectuals' duty to provide more than moral leadership, however. They were also called upon to take an active role in the political life of the new "People's Democracy."

Public figures were united in their desire that intellectuals hold a large share of direct and indirect political authority, and strove to commit them to the party-political structure of the National Front government. Only a very small number of decidedly noncommunist leaders attempted to defend a position "above the parties." They argued, as had Julien Benda before the war, that danger lurked in intellectuals "adopting political passions" and that the intelligentsia should stand outside the party-political arena. In their view, the intellectuals' responsibility to the nation was to remain independent and critical.[39] This position was rejected by the vast majority of public commentators, however, and was vehemently attacked by Communists and left-wing Social Democrats on Marxist grounds. In one of the two contemporary book-length studies of the intelligentsia, Bohuslav Kratochvíl presented the standard communist argument that although "part of the intelligentsia today stands for some kind of 'splendid isolation,'" this was merely an expression of the remnants of bourgeois ideology:

> The overvaluation of knowledge, founded on official bourgeois culture and faith in its fetishes, idealistically . . . leads the intelligentsia to the conviction that it is able to be the judge of political affairs and that its leading position is from above the parties.[40]

Other Marxists argued that the idea of standing above one's class was absurd, that the intelligentsia "cannot carry out a function 'above classes' in a class society." Furthermore, because "the intelligentsia did not see the social content" of their ideas, they "conjured up the idea of the 'eternal calling of the intelligentsia.'" This supposedly placed them above class and party interests, but actually helped "the ruling class deceive the masses of workers."[41]

The communist indictment of the attempt to remain outside of, or above, party interests found other, less theoretical grounds. One of the salient features of postwar communist discourse was the belief that the end of the war had brought the onset of a great new era. A side effect of this belief was an impatience with the pace of change that can be seen as a revolt against the largely passive waiting of the years of Nazi domination. Communist intellectuals saw the matter in a quite straightforward way: the intelligentsia must choose a political position, and if it is wise it will stand with the working people, under the leadership of the Communist Party. As *Tvorba*, the Central Committee's theoretical and cultural organ, put it: "In a situation created by the destruction of fascism and reaction and the introduction of the people's democratic government, the necessity of expressing itself unequivocally either for or against stands before our intelligentsia. . . . In this case no answer is also an answer."[42]

The pressure on intellectuals to choose a political affiliation did not come solely from the revolutionary left, however. Similar opinions, also arguing that in the postwar period "it is not possible for [the intelligentsia] to wait," came from the center of the political spectrum and from opponents of the Communist Party.[43] Their reasoning was substantially different, however. Perhaps disturbed by the rapid influx of members into the Communist Party, and particularly by the number of prominent intellectuals among them, intellectual supporters of the non-Communist parties saw the need to urge their like-minded colleagues to participate more directly in public life. Otherwise, communist activism would ensure the Communist Party control over developments in public life: "It is not possible to justify flight from political activity in any way. . . . The true intellectual must be brave. He must be an optimist. He is not allowed to be a deserter, not allowed to leave the field to lesser people."[44]

The Communists and their allies employed three arguments in coercing intellectuals to take part in the great experiment of what they called the Czech postwar "national and democratic revolution." Above all, they stressed the intelligentsia's traditional role in the leadership of the nation, emphasizing its service in the resistance and expressing confidence that it would not absent itself from the great new era of socialism. Much was made of the Czech intelligentsia's historical ties to "the people," referring to its origin and development in the small towns and among the lower classes. During this period of postwar revolutionary enthusiasm, the radical left argued, an intelligentsia that had "grown from the common people" would not allow itself to be isolated from the majority of the nation, despite "reaction's wish to drive cultural workers out of political life, to tear them away from the people."[45] Instead, it would "tie itself to the collective fate of the people and be the co-creators of this fate."[46]

The nobility of being seen as "of the people" during a wave of leftist populism was matched by communist praise for the intelligentsia's capacity and obligation to provide political and societal leadership. Intellectuals were seen as the only group with the "authority and ability to propagate the significance of the People's Democracy." The intelligentsia should therefore stand in "the first ranks, showing the way to our goal."[47] In order to accomplish this, left-wing intellectuals were welcomed into the ministerial machinery, particularly inside the Communist-dominated Ministry of Culture and Education and the Communist-controlled Ministry of Information. They had a duty to work in the civil service because, the radical left argued, the existing civil service still thought in the "old way," and the ascendant working class needed time to educate its own forces to take over these positions. Only at that time would intellectuals be freed from their public duty to return to nonpolitical pursuits.[48]

Moreover, the Communists and their allies also attempted to lure intellectuals into the political life of the "People's Democracy" by extolling visions of the benefits socialism would bring especially to them. These arguments were based on the "scientific certainty that socialism gives the intelligentsia so many and varied possibilities, such as no other system could give it." In their view, socialism would liberate the intelligentsia from the dependence on capital, which had served only to exploit those involved in cultural pursuits. Socialism would also exclude the dangers of superficiality and commercialization, as the nationalization of cultural institutions would ensure the "widest and most reliable possibilities for contact with the broader public." In the heady words of a leading communist writer, the People's Democracy would offer intellectuals "a chance to enact their ideas" such as they had never had before.[49]

Finally, a negative communist argument complemented both the praise heaped on the intelligentsia and the expectation that it would lead the nation to the bright tomorrow of socialism, namely the denigration of those intellectuals who argued for a position above politics, or who argued that devotion to intellectual labors had to take precedence over party-political activism. Those who argued against direct political participation were chastised for "dragging their heels," or being of "ill will."[50] They were proclaimed "people of little talent, with worm's eye views and Lilliputian ideas . . . whose 'spirit' is out of keeping with the spirit of the nation." In this view, their opposition to participation in political activism was, in the words of a leading journalist for the trade-union daily, "close to the Nazis and Nazi thinking."[51] At best, they were considered "expressly *negativistic.* This is not unpolitical, but a politics that is directed against the great deeds of the nation."[52] Communists threatened that there remained only one fate for recalcitrant noncommunist intellectuals: to be replaced by an intelligentsia educated under the People's Democracy. By not actively and publicly supporting the new "People's Democracy" through party-political activity, these intellectuals were proving themselves unreliable citizens. If they did not adapt to the new system, they were threatened that their actions "would mean the end of today's intelligentsia. The working people will *sweep them away* and create a new intelligentsia from their own midst."[53]

Noncommunist intellectuals were placed in a difficult position. They did not want to abandon the field to their opponents; conversely they were reluctant to condone too deep an involvement in party politics. Their criticisms were therefore not primarily directed at keeping noncommunist intellectuals out of politics but rather at minimizing the party-political character of any such involvement. Roman Catholic activists, representing the most conservative segment of Czech society, despaired that

> The collective betrayal of the intellectuals has not appeared in any other era of our history more visibly or worse. . . . Never has the intellectual so completely changed himself into a *party man*, never has the creative man more become a propagator who does not serve but does someone's bidding.[54]

They feared that the Czech intelligentsia, so united in the struggle against the Nazis, had "politically quartered itself" among the permitted parties, and that much of it had "exchanged its ideals for ideology."[55] Even Ferdinand Peroutka, one of the communists' most committed opponents, encouraged intellectuals to take part in politics, but under the conditions that they "not accept a lower level of morality, emotion and reason . . . [and] that they refuse to subordinate themselves to utilitarian political primitivism, merely carrying out the tasks given them by political secretariats."[56]

The Marxist left also had more programmatic ideas than their opponents on the tasks that intellectuals should accomplish in the new society. While the communists produced an avalanche of ideological rhetoric, they also set tangible goals.[57] Communist intellectual and political leaders stressed the importance of contact with the masses and thinking in terms of the collective in the attempt to foster social cohesion under the banner of socialism. Most importantly, they desired that intellectuals assume a larger share of responsibility in the civil service, which they argued was "as important as creative work and perhaps more so" because of the government's increased role in the functioning of society.[58] One may suppose that they did this because the Communist Party controlled the ministries most likely to attract creative intellectuals and wanted to create a staff that owed both loyalty and their positions to the party. The argument they presented, however, stressed the importance of their heritage of leading the nation for the task of building socialism and because there intellectuals could gain "experience that they can take advantage of in their own cultural creation."[59] Further, they called for intellectuals to take the lead in reaching out to other progressive nations, especially those in the Slavic world, and to strive for the creation of a Slavic and socialist Czech identity.[60]

The vague opposition to party strictures was echoed in the tasks that noncommunists wished intellectuals to carry out. With the exception of some Roman Catholic leaders, whose primary hope was for the "return of a Christian character to modern culture," most demands consisted of ambiguous calls to act as "the conscience of the nation."[61] In an obvious warning against an excess of revolutionary enthusiasm, intellectuals were called upon to "serve life and the world, not merely one interest." Most often, however, they were bidden to stand "on the side of truth" and other such goals that could not lead to the formulation of any programmatic vision that would unite the democratic intelligentsia.[62] Perhaps archetypal of the noncommunist view of intellectuals' activity was the both vague and tangled vision of the president, Edvard Beneš:

> Increasingly, the subject of all endeavors and strivings, both material and spiritual, will not be one party, one class, one nation and one state, but humanity, humanity as a whole. . . . [The intellectual's] role is non-political and at the same time highly political. He practices a so-called non-political politics and this is the best politics.[63]

Even in their strongest statements, leading democratic activists never pointed at communists by name, countering communist rhetoric only by calling on intellectuals to "fight against those who are harming the nation."[64]

In this short overview of the historical meaning of the Czech intelligentsia, several features have become apparent that are important for understanding its role and activity in the immediate postwar period. The Czech intelligentsia's authority was nourished by its deep roots in national-patriotic activity and its tradition of contact with broad segments of the population. Augmenting this, the intelligentsia had a tradition of acting either as part of the national leadership or as influential discussion partners of active politicians. In the immediate postwar period, intellectuals' authority on all levels was heightened by their sacrifices and heroism during the Second World War. They were called by the leaderships of all political currents to repair the damage to the nation caused by the devastating experiences of the "Munich betrayal" and six years of occupation. Czech intellectuals either willingly responded to these demands or were compelled to engage in political discussions when a position outside politics became untenable. In this period, their intellectual sensibilities were tinged by a historical inclination toward Slavism, which made them both more receptive to the revived Slavism of the era and to a socialism coming from the East. The history of the Czech intelligentsia also reveals that struggles over political matters were often fought out over issues only indirectly political, on the Czech intelligentsia's traditional battlegrounds of moral abstraction, history and culture. Finally, these struggles influenced not only public opinion, but also the directly political leadership as a whole, as the participation of President Beneš and Communist Party Chairman Gottwald in the discussion of the intellectuals' role shows. In reference to the immediate postwar period, Alfred French has noted that

> Writers in Western countries are accustomed to personal feuds or literary controversies involving politics: but almost never do such controversies have any decisive effect in the world of public affairs. However threatening, grandiloquent, or seductive are the voices of poets or novelists no one expects politicians to take much notice of them: and the polemics take on a reassuringly harmless image. This was certainly not so in Prague.[65]

3

Four Groups of Postwar Czech Intellectuals

The Czech intelligentsia of the immediate postwar years shouldered a heavy burden of responsibility for its nation's future. The question remains, however, of who these intellectuals were. In broad terms, the Czech intelligentsia was composed of four groups of cultural and political opinion-makers and -reflectors: communist, democratic socialist, Roman Catholic, and Protestant. Each group had different intellectual constituencies, political loyalties, and venues for presenting their ideas. The intellectuals who led these groups dominated the postwar Czech discourse, and the periodicals in which they publicized their views constituted the foci of intellectual, cultural, and political debate. As such, an understanding of the groups' political and intellectual orientations also provides an orientation to the complex world of postwar Czech politics.

COMMUNIST INTELLECTUALS

The circumstances in which the party found itself after liberation are of central importance for understanding the strategy and tactics of the Communist Party of Czechoslovakia's intellectual leadership. Together with the burst of revolutionary enthusiasm the Czech population exhibited in the war's wake came an extraordinary and overwhelming influx of members to the party, enabling it to win 40 percent of the Czech vote in the 1946 parliamentary elections. Although the Communist Party of Czechoslovakia had always enjoyed solid electoral support, its success after the war certainly cannot be deduced from its history. The party was formed in 1921 after splitting from the Social Democratic Party, following direct instructions from the Second Congress of the Third International. It seemed to have bright prospects, as the

Czechs had a tradition of support for socialist politics in the Austro-Hungarian Empire. Further, it remained a legal movement throughout the interwar republic, a condition unique among the Communist parties of Eastern Europe. Nonetheless, the party suffered from chronic internal feuding throughout the 1920s, making the party "a problem child for Moscow" and resulting in the loss of over 80 percent of its members between its birth and the final bolshevization of the party in 1929.[1] Despite this precipitous drop, the party managed to obtain 13.2 percent of the vote in the 1925 parliamentary elections, and 10.5 percent in those of 1929. The decade of the 1930s, while not seriously altering the party's fortunes at the ballot box, laid some foundation for its postwar growth. Under the leadership of Klement Gottwald, the party raised its electoral tally by 100,000 in the 1935 elections. While this was a healthy increase, it did not significantly alter the party's share of the ballot and showed that it was unable to benefit even from the Great Depression. The party did much for its postwar image in the Popular Front years, especially through its conduct during the Munich crisis. The party presented itself as a staunch supporter of the state and excelled in presenting its patriotism in such a way that its rallies during and immediately after the crisis attracted many non-Communists.

The Communists' service in the Second World War likewise stood them in good stead for the political battles thereafter. Despite the party's anti-war stance during the period of the Nazi-Soviet Pact, which could not have helped its image, there were cases even then of party members collaborating with groups of non-Communist resisters. The entry of the Soviet Union into the war rehabilitated the party, and the Nazis' virulent anti-Soviet propaganda only benefited the party in the public mind. Although the Communist resistance was no more effective than that of non-Communists, the party did suffer disproportionate losses. Twenty-five thousand party members were killed during the struggle, and an entire series of underground central committees were infiltrated and destroyed. In short, "the party paid a heavy price for relatively insignificant activity."[2] The most important result of Communist resistance activity was that the decimation of the party's leadership inside the country increased the power and influence of those leaders who had fled to Moscow. In the wake of the Soviet Union's first military successes, the Moscow exile group made further advances. This was cemented by the diplomatic gains achieved from the warm discussions on the future of Czechoslovakia that took place surrounding the signing of the Czechoslovak-USSR friendship treaty in December 1943.

The will to agree on the future shape of the republic, shown by representatives of all parties in both the exile government and the resistance movement at home, brought tremendous advantages to the communist movement in terms of political positioning. These bore fruit in the negotiations of March 1945, when their non-Communist partners, with only slight modifications, accepted the Communist Party's blueprint for immediate structural changes in the republic. These wide-ranging proposals determined the initial political, economic and social organization of the postwar state and made the Communist Party a leading actor. The outcome of these discussions created the basis for the National Front government's program, called the Košice Program because it was announced in the liberated Slovak city of Košice on April 4, 1945. The wholesale restructuring of the nation met with widespread popular approval. In May 1946 an opinion poll found that 62.9 percent of Czech respondents agreed "entirely" with the program, and 28.8 percent agreed "with reservations."[3]

The announcement of the Košice Program coincided with the naming of the first postwar government, composed of representatives from four Czech and two Slovak parties.[4] The banning of those parties deemed to have collaborated with the Nazis drastically altered the political landscape of the nation. Among those forbidden was the prewar republic's largest party, the Agrarians. Further, the truncation of the entire right wing of the prewar political spectrum left roughly half of the prewar electorate politically homeless.[5] In the division of portfolios, the Communists obtained the crucial ministries of interior, education, and culture. Furthermore, the Communists controlled the Ministry of National Defense, as the minister (and future president of the republic), Ludvík Svoboda, was a Communist Party supporter. He had asked Gottwald for membership and been denied on the grounds that the party needed "their man" in this position, which was slated to be occupied by a non-party expert. As a result of these moves the Communists had, from an administrative and institutional viewpoint, a strong position in determining future developments in the state.

The party could also rely on a number of international advantages in the liberated state. First among them was the great victory the Soviet Union had won in the war and the gratitude the Czech population felt toward their liberators. Although American troops had freed part of the republic, it was the Red Army that had accomplished the vast majority of the task.[6] Further, the friendship treaty of 1943 had made the USSR Czechoslovakia's primary ally and the guarantor of the state's future security. Additionally, the Soviet Union provided unwavering support for the expulsion of the ethnic German population from Czechoslovakia. This was critical in a country seized by an explicitly anti-German nationalism that was one of the central characteristics of the postwar environment. Moreover, the party bore no responsibility for the tragedy of Munich, since it had spent the entire interwar period in opposition. It could further claim that the USSR had stood behind Czechoslovakia and had been willing to fight for her freedom. Communist leaders saw the failure of the "bourgeois" republic to defend the state in 1938 as a primary reason for the necessity of a wholesale reinvention of Czechoslovakia. Also often reiterated was the point that, whatever its effectiveness, the Communist resistance had paid a high price in blood for the liberation of its homeland.

Finally, the Communists derived a crucial advantage from what can only be called the revolutionary élan of the times. The Czech populace had moved dramatically to the left during the years of Munich, occupation, resistance, and war. In the wake of these traumatic experiences, Czechs demanded changes in the entire organization of the state. Vilém Prečan has argued that

> [Czech society] immediately after the war, allowed itself to be carried away on a wave of utopian faith characteristic of a politically immature nation: that it would be able to solve all at once—and in the near future—the problems not only of its own external security, but also to ensure freedom, social justice and affluence. The measures enshrined in the Košice program corresponded well to the desires of the population, but many Czechs wanted to take them even further.[7]

The Communist Party was able to seize upon this generalized revolutionary enthusiasm and to exploit the consensus for the maintenance of the changes enacted by the Košice program by warning of plots to reverse them.

This revolutionary enthusiasm was particularly evident among the youth. This had political implications, since the age of enfranchisement was lowered in the liberated republic to 18 from the prewar level of 21. In one of history's ironies, this same generation that showed such enthusiasm for Stalin and communism later looked back in regret and attempted to reform the system in the 1960s. From the perspective of that later time, Zdeněk Mlynář rued that his generation had no mature experience of democracy and had become

> children of the war who, having not actually fought against anyone, brought our wartime mentality with us into those first postwar years, when the opportunity to fight for something presented itself at last. To the question whom to fight against and in what cause, the age offered a simple reply: on the side of those who were most consistently and radically against the past, who were not cautious, who made no compromises with the past but strove to sweep it aside, to overcome it in a revolutionary way.[8]

There was no doubt in the minds of many from that generation, no question of the final outcome:

> We launched into the new era with all the élan, enthusiasm, sincerity and sectarianism of our twenty years . . . [expecting that] with banners flying and bands playing [we] would march into the wide-open gates of the millennium. . . . We ran through those gates of paradise in 1945 and once again in 1948.[9]

It is possible to argue that the Communists took political advantage of the naiveté, enthusiasm and inexperience of the youth. Yet this fails to explain the hundreds of thousands of older men and women who rushed to join the party after liberation. At the conclusion of the Second World War the party had only 28,485 members, but the party rolls immediately began to swell, reaching 800,000 members by the end of 1945.[10] In December 1945, Chairman Gottwald set a target of 1 million members to be reached before the party's Eighth Congress in March 1946. The goal was easily met: the organizational secretary reported that the party had 1,081,544 members.[11] In 1947, in conjunction with the announcement of the "Czechoslovak road to socialism," Gottwald announced a target of 1,500,000 members to be reached before the parliamentary elections scheduled for 1948. As a result of a series of membership drives, the party ranks had swelled to 1,393,778 by the end of 1947, although only small gains were made among the targeted middle class.

The importance of these figures is twofold. Above all, the immensity of the party is indisputable: the Communist Party of the early postwar years was, and remains, the largest party in Czech history. At the end of 1947, there were 1,266,140 Communists in the Czech lands alone. Based on the returns from the 1946 parliamentary elections, this figure represents 23.1 percent of the voting public. The Communist Party dwarfed all the others, with the second-place National Socialist Party having less than half its number of members.[12] The party was also the most widespread, having offices in 96 percent of localities across the republic, while the other parties were organized in only between 60 and 70 percent.[13] It was strongly represented in Prague, where its 190,000 members composed over a quarter of the voting-age population. It was also relatively socially differentiated, drawing less than half of its membership from the ranks of industrial laborers.[14]

Significantly, the growth of the Communist Party also bears witness to the success of the party's moderate course, one similar to that followed by the Communist parties of the other young "People's Democracies." The party proclaimed the desire to follow a parliamentary road to socialism, while remaining silent about the characteristics their socialism would bear. They aimed to win the "hearts and minds" of the Czech population by satisfying its desires for a vaguely defined socialism and by offering a consistent alternative vision of the national character and the Czech past, particularly the crucial recent past. They portrayed their party as the legitimate heir to the greatest Czech traditions and therefore the logical actor to lead the nation into the future. This culminated in the twin announcements of the "specific Czechoslovak road to socialism" in the autumn of 1946 and the goal, announced in January 1947, of gaining 51 percent of the vote in the 1948 elections. Many of the party's members may well have been trying to cover for their collaborationist wartime past, and many may have been merely opportunists. Nonetheless, the sheer size of the party shows that many came to believe in its vision of the nation, its past and its future.

While it is important to note here that the promulgation of a "Czechoslovak road to socialism" found its impetus in Moscow, the landmark domestic event leading to its official announcement was the parliamentary elections of

May 1946. These were crucial because the Communist victory served as both justification for the party's moderate policies and the decisive element in assuring that this strategy would continue in the future. These elections were free and fair, occurring under what one leading noncommunist politician called "normal conditions." The non-Communist Minister of Justice, writing later in exile, drew the same conclusion:

> I consider it necessary to stress that in 1946 Czechoslovakia still had free elections. It is necessary to substantiate this because part of our public—and not an insignificant part—at that time denied it and did not want to recognize that these were free elections. . . . Czechoslovak society had, in 1946, a real possibility to decide how the liberated state would be administered. All statements to the contrary are incorrect.[15]

In these elections the Communist Party emerged as by far the strongest in the Czech lands, drawing over 40 percent of the vote (see table 3.1).

The outcome was clear. The Communists had achieved a substantial plurality in both of the Czech lands, as well as in the leading city of each region, Prague and Brno. The party won in 138 of the 154 counties in the Czech lands and gained the chairmanship of over half of the local committees. The party did particularly well in the border regions formerly settled by ethnically German citizens and among Protestants, as well as surprisingly well among rural voters.[16] For the non-Communist parties, the results came as "a shock."[17] In its self-congratulatory messages, the party accorded front-page importance to "the position manifested by our intelligentsia, which collectively stood on the side of the Communists."[18] One leading anticommunist, after his flight into exile, explained that one important cause for

> the movement to the left was the example set by Czech intellectuals, of whom a marked majority went over to the Communists, in so far as they were not [Communists] already. The Communists were skillful in taking advantage of this, and before the elections published long lists of intellectuals who had become members of their party.[19]

Table 3.1.   Returns of the General Election of May 1946 in the Czech Lands

	Bohemia	Moravia	Total
Communist Party	1,541,852 (43.26%)	663,845 (34.46%)	2,205,697 (40.17%)
National Socialists	898,425 (25.21%)	400,555 (20.79%)	1,289,980 (23.66%)
People's Party	580,004 (16.27%)	531,005 (27.57%)	1,111,009 (20.24%)
Social Democrats	533,029 (14.95%)	322,509 (16.74%)	855,538 (15.58%)
Blank	10,969 (0.31%)	8,484 (0.44%)	19,453 (0.35%)
Total	3,564,279	1,926,398	5,490,677
	(100.00%)	(100.00%)	(100.00%)

Before introducing the leading Communist Party intellectuals, a note on the Social Democratic Party is in order. This party, the oldest in the republic, emerged from the war in the worst shape of all the Czech political parties.[20] With much of its prewar leadership too old to continue, the party came under the leadership of politicians who had spent the war years in Moscow. Under the fellow-traveling chairman Zdeněk Fierlinger, this Marxist party entered into close alliance with the Communist Party, with whom a merger had been considered during the war (as had in fact occurred in Slovakia). Gravely damaged by the defection of most of its working-class support and much of its intellectual elite to the Communist Party, it managed to poll only 15 percent in the 1946 elections, making it the weakest of the Czech political parties.

Most importantly, the Social Democratic Party was internally riven between a left wing composed of fellow travelers and a right wing lying closer to the National Socialist Party. The left remained in control of the party, a condition reflected in the writings of intellectuals associated with it, until November 1947. At the party congress of that month, the centrist candidate supported by the right wing, Bohumil Laušman, replaced Fierlinger as chairman. Despite this, Laušman had little time, and no great inclination, before the crisis of February 1948 to restructure the party organization to reflect the victory of more moderate forces.[21] Because Social Democratic intellectuals will play a less prominent role in our story, and because those on the largely dominant left sounded like their colleagues in the Communist Party, they will be considered as part of the "communist" movement, but not of the party calling itself "Communist." Similarly, the fewer moderate intellectuals associated with the party will be considered as part of the forces of "democratic socialism."

The leading cadre of the Communist Party contained many actors with whom scholars of communism will be familiar. At the top of the pyramid stood Klement Gottwald, the party chairman and, after the 1946 elections, the prime minister. Also serving in the government were two prominent Communist intellectuals, Zdeněk Nejedlý and Václav Kopecký. Nejedlý, a historian by training, served as minister of education and culture and, subsequently, minister of labor and social affairs. His education and prolific publishing contrast with the demagogic character of Kopecký, who served in the critical post of minister of information. The three governmental Communist leaders were balanced by three leading theoretical and journalistic lights: Ladislav Štoll, Gustav Bareš, and Arnošt Kolman. The first two of these served as editors, respectively, of the party's major theoretical organ and its daily newspaper. Štoll later led the Stalinization of Czech literature, while Bareš's star faded. Kolman is noteworthy because he was the only trained philosopher who was also a Marxist in 1945 Czechoslovakia and was therefore regarded quite highly when matters of communist theory became problematic.

Finally, one particularly influential member of the younger generation is worthy of mention. Jiří Hájek was a prominent theater and literary critic who embodied the views of the communist youth, and his prominence in Communist intellectual circles lasted well into the 1970s.

These men—and there were very few prominent women in the party—were supported by scores of recognized writers, artists, and other figures, who had a number of publications in which to publish their views. Under Štoll's direction, the most important of these was the party's daily newspaper, *Rudé právo* (*Red Right*). It was both the physically largest newspaper in the republic and, at a half-million copies daily, had the largest circulation. As a telling signifier of the party's new image, the newspaper had made one major change to its prewar appearance: "Proletarians of All Nations, Unite!" no longer appeared above the title.[22] Second only to this was the Central Committee's theoretical organ, *Tvorba* (*Creation*), whose editor-in-chief was Bareš. Devoted to cultural, intellectual, and ideological affairs, the weekly had a large circulation (40,000), and excerpts from it often appeared in the daily press.[23] In 1947, *Tvorba* was joined by a second theoretical journal, *Nová mysl* (*New Thought*). Outside of direct party control lay the prominent radical weekly *Kulturní politika* (*Cultural Politics*), published by the talented avant-garde dramatist, musician, and poet Emil František Burian. His editorials supported communist cultural goals but became too idiosyncratic and independent for the post-February regime; the journal was shut down. The Social Democratic press was also open to communist intellectuals, although to different extents in different periods. Primary among these were the newspaper *Právo lidu* (*The People's Right*, 190,000 copies daily) and the cultural and political weeklies *Cíl* (*The Goal*) and *Směr* (*The Direction*).

In addition to Communist and Social Democratic Party organs, communist intellectuals had wide access to other periodicals sympathetic to their views. These included those of the 1,679,000-member Revolutionary Trades Union Movement, which was dominated by members of the Communist Party and left-wing Social Democrats.[24] This organization published the Czech lands' third-largest newspaper, *Práce* (*Labor*), whose 250,000 copies daily made it larger than the daily organs of either the Social Democratic Party or the People's Party, and the weekly cultural organ *Lidová kultura* (*The People's Culture*). Similarly, the enthusiasm of the youth for revolutionary change was reflected in the contents of the newspaper *Mladá fronta* (*The Youth Front*, 80,000 copies daily). The paper was occasionally more moderate, but frequently more radical, than even *Rudé právo*, and was accorded great importance by the Communist Party.

From this short introduction to the communists' intellectual and publicity resources, it should be evident that they had substantial opportunity to make their views known. Communist and left-wing Social Democratic intellectuals took advantage of the tribunes offered, and their editorials and transcripts of their speeches were a prominent feature of the daily and weekly press. In the first year after liberation these intellectuals used their visibility to drive the debate over the meaning of the Czech nation and its history, and by doing so they also drove in large measure the political vision and image of the communist movement. Their success was witnessed by both the Communist Party's rapid growth and its drawing power at the polls.

DEMOCRATIC SOCIALIST INTELLECTUALS

The primary intellectual opponents of the resurgent Communist Party of Czechoslovakia were the writers, social critics, and politically active journalists who will be grouped under the rubric of "democratic socialist."[25] The majority of these found their political home in the Czechoslovak National Socialist Party (*Československá strana národně socialistická*). The party was one of the older Czech political institutions, founded in 1897. Its program from that time onward was explicitly nationalist, and its moderate socialism was designed to attract non-Marxist adherents of the Social Democratic Party. After Czechoslovak independence in 1918, the party became one of the pillars of the interwar republic's coalition governments, failing to appear only between 1926 and 1929. Despite its prominent role between the world wars, it did not achieve widespread support, showing strength primarily among intellectuals (particularly university professors), civil servants, and skilled workers. It was most popular in Bohemia and drew its membership especially from the Czechoslovak Legions (World War I veterans who fought their way across revolutionary Russia to join allied forces) and the Sokol, a mass gymnastics organization. The party was perhaps most renowned for being the party of Edvard Beneš, who was a member from 1919 until his election to the presidency in 1935.

The Second World War brought both triumph and tragedy to the National Socialists. Its members occupied prominent positions in the London government-in-exile, gaining credibility and experience for their postwar political activity and reinforcing the tie to President Beneš. The party also acquitted itself well in the domestic resistance movement, its supporters playing a role second only to those of the Communist Party. Yet, these very facts also weakened the party. The underground activities of its members led to a decimation of its leadership, and only one member of its executive committee survived the war. The exile experience also brought significant detriments. It increased the party's dependence on President Beneš, a flaw whose depth was fully revealed in February 1948. Additionally, the decimation of the interwar leadership meant that the new leaders after the war were those who had found success in London and therefore had been nourished in the closeted world of diplomatic and exile politics rather than by leadership in domestic political organizing.

With these strengths and weaknesses the National Socialist Party entered the postwar world. It began as a formidably large party, reaching 500,000 members by the end of 1945. The future, however was not as fruitful. While the Communist Party continued its growth, the National Socialists expanded to only 593,000 members at the end of 1946 and added only 9,000 to this total by the end of January 1948. The party drew its support from much the same sources as in the prewar republic, with civil servants, the professoriate, and other middle-class groupings forming its core.[26] It also gained some members from the supporters of the parties banned for wartime collaboration. This proved problematic, however, as they tended to be wealthier and more influential and gave the party a profile of catering to the now-denigrated bourgeoisie. The economic weakness of the party, witnessed by the fact that at the end of 1946 only 63 percent of the membership was dues-paying, was reflected in persistent organizational weaknesses. In 1946, the party lacked local committees in 6,688 communities and had added only half of these to their lists one year later.[27] Despite these weaknesses, the National Socialists emerged as the second strongest party from the 1946 parliamentary elections, garnering 23.66 percent of the vote. This result came as a disappointing shock to the party, which had dreamt of occupying the first place in Czech politics.

The socialism of democratic socialist intellectuals close to the National Socialist Party will be examined in greater detail later in this study, but their beliefs will need to be seen against the backdrop of three major conceptual difficulties that the party faced. These were all related to the growing realization that the party had lost its share of control over the social revolution that had commenced in 1945. It had heartily approved of the early nationalizations and other preliminary measures of the National Front government, but as time passed it increasingly tried to curb the nation's revolutionary enthusiasm. As with all revolutions, the National Socialists discovered, once begun this one proved difficult to contain. This spawned the difficulty that, while the party wished to limit the revolution, it could not act in open opposition to the decisions of the National Front, whose program was based on the agreement of all its parties. It could argue against certain measures but, particularly after the Communist Party's electoral victory in the 1946 parliamentary elections, it did not have the power to win these arguments without support from all the noncommunist parties. In this sense, party leaders attempted to straddle two irreconcilable positions: "They seemed to be cautiously trying to canvass support from those who doubted aspects of the government's policies, but they were also trying to avoid being accused of playing the role of an opposition."[28] The party's limited room for maneuver in domestic affairs, partly of its own creation, was complemented in foreign

policy. Here the turn toward the Soviet Union, also partly the party's own doing, bound the party to definite policy positions. While the party could, and
did, add or remove socialist principles as necessary, the alliance with the
USSR could not be questioned. Finally, the recognition that the Czechoslovak postwar revolutionary fervor was not waning imparted a certain defen-
siveness to the party's statements. It is going too far to say that "the National
Socialists proved incapable of producing a new program" or that they had
"no serious program." Nonetheless, it is certainly true that they largely relied
upon doubts and uncertainties about the direction in which the state was
moving. The party's intellectual vanguard was outspoken but, like the party
itself, its members were often given to characterizing "their successes not in
terms of what they had achieved but what they had prevented."[29]

In addition to these difficulties, there is one defect for which the National
Socialist Party must bear the primary responsibility: the lack of unity within
the non-Communist political arena. All three parties, of course, can be
faulted for failing to create a coherent working agreement to contain the
Communist Party. In the historiography of the non-Communist parties, the
word "loggerheads" appears with stunning frequency in descriptions of mutual relations. Petty party politics, traditional in Czech politics, certainly
played a large role in this.[30] The National Socialists, as the largest and most
centrally positioned of the three non-Communist parties, were undoubtedly
the best placed to work toward agreement. In practice, as a United States
Embassy report made clear, the party's representatives "went their own way
and only occasionally put up a united front against the common foe."[31] The
National Socialists' problems with the People's Party stemmed from the realities of the postwar political environment. Of initial importance was the fact
that while the former was resolutely anticlericalist, the latter remained essentially a Roman Catholic party. Further, their convergence on some issues
made the two parties competitors for the same electoral constituencies.[32]
Finally, there were personality differences between members of the party
leaderships, noted as a major cause of the lack of unity by an American observer.[33] Much the same kind of difficulties afflicted the National Socialist–
Social Democratic relationship. The National Socialists and the right wing of
the Social Democratic Party also shared a constituency and competed for
electoral support. The situation became more tense after the 1946 elections,
which exacerbated the conflict between the two wings of the Social Democratic Party. At this point the two parties' traditional rivalry for the support of
moderate socialists intensified as the National Socialists "exerted great pressure to wean away the moderate wing of the Social Democratic Party."[34]

Despite these criticisms and those yet to come, there can be little doubt
that the National Socialist Party and those intellectuals who stood close to it
represented the most visible and vocal opponents of the Communist Party
and its goals. The battle that they waged, flawed though this study will argue

it was, represented the noble strivings of good men and women in a precarious situation only partially of their own making. Their task was made more difficult because they were faced with a Communist Party that was successfully recasting itself as moderate and patriotic. In an environment dominated by a yearning for social reform, and confronted with a Communist Party whose potential for malevolence they at least suspected, democratic socialist intellectuals attempted to fight for the ideals of social justice, freedom, and democracy as they understood them. They should not be berated for having done so and lost, but for their failure to formulate convincingly the differences between their ideas and those of the communists. Particularly, their acceptance of many facets of the communist reinterpretation of the meaning and calling of the nation made the Communist Party's road to power easier than it need have been.

As was the case with communist intellectuals and the Communist Party, the vast majority of the representatives of the democratic socialist current in postwar Czech thought were members of the National Socialist Party. On the one hand, this was a sign of the party's success in the campaign to draw noncommunist intellectuals into political life, and on the other a sign of the willing engagement of intellectuals in political affairs. Similarly, it was a mark of the era that political leaders publicized their views on intellectual and cultural issues. For this reason, National Socialist political figures familiar from political studies will also appear here. Among these, three figures in particular stand out: Hubert Ripka, Prokop Drtina, and Otakar Machotka. The first two served as ministers in the postwar government, while the last was a leading National Socialist ideologist. Minister of Foreign Trade Ripka and Minister of Justice Drtina are both well known from their memoirs of the immediate postwar era. Of similar stature in the cultural world was the art and literary critic František Kovárna, whose name is closely associated with the democratic socialist idea. He contributed widely to journals associated with the party, as well as its daily newspaper, and served on the party's committee on artistic affairs.

The roles of these four men, however, pale in comparison with the cultural influence of the three democratic socialist leaders: President Edvard Beneš, Ferdinand Peroutka, and Václav Černý. Earlier studies have concentrated particularly on the president as the defender of democracy in his political dealings.[35] In this study, his presence will be felt as the moral leader of the noncommunist forces. In this sense, he is rather more a symbolic presence than an actual political actor, and his statements on issues of moral and cultural significance will be read in the same manner as those of Ripka, Machotka, and Drtina. His views were of tremendous importance to the nation, as can be seen in the respect the "President-Liberator" enjoyed after his triumphant return in 1945. His immense popularity gave him a position from which he could have exercised vigorous leadership, but he took his status as being above the parties seriously, remaining largely aloof even from his own former party. Nonetheless, it is one of the intentions of this study to balance the weight of attention generally given to political actions and personalities in postwar Czech life, and especially the emphasis placed on Beneš. As the talented historian Jan Křen has pointed out:

> It is as clear as day that this is not about Beneš alone, but concerns the history of an entire, large grouping in society (with its core in the middle classes and with undervalued support in the military resistance) whose taste for a deep socio-political—in Beneš' terminology "socializing"—transformation created a real vision of a Czechoslovak socialism, a "socialism for 90 percent of the population."[36]

The intellectual strivings of this larger group found voice in the writings of Peroutka and Černý. They were the controversial giants of the noncommunist intellectual landscape, and in many ways divided the task of countering the Communist Party between them. They shared many things, and a comparative biography of the two would in many ways read like a cultural history of the Czech nation in the middle decades of the twentieth century. They were both critical minds, masters of cutting commentary who brought liveliness and invention to their use of the Czech language. Although politically somewhat divergent—Peroutka more moderate, Černý more radical—they shared a deep commitment to the freedom of the individual in artistic and critical expression, democratic government, and social justice. Finally, both suffered at the hands of the Nazis and resisted them, and immediately thereafter became the primary targets of vicious attacks by communist intellectuals.

Ferdinand Peroutka was perhaps the greatest Czech editorialist since Karel Havlíček. He won high praise from the acidly critical Černý, who called him "a culturally and politically sharp- and foresighted person, absolutely honorable, an ideologue and polemicist of clear thought and piercing formulations."[37] Peroutka first made a name for himself as an art critic and editor after World War I. He became an institution in 1924 with the publication of his *Who We Are* (*Jací jsme*), which examined the Czech national character and was fearless in pointing out its deficiencies. In that same year he launched the journal *Přítomnost* (*The Present*) with one million crowns granted him by no less than President Masaryk himself.[38] As a member of the famed "Friday Circle" of presidential intellectual companions, he was close to interwar political and literary leaders, particularly the author Karel Čapek. When Nazi tanks rolled into Prague in March 1939, Peroutka was among the first arrested. Although quickly released, his *Přítomnost* was banned after August of that year and Peroutka was again arrested, this time for the duration of the war. He spent almost six years in Dachau and Buchenwald, of which twenty-seven months were in solitary confinement.[39] Upon his return to his liberated homeland he became a fixture in the democratic press, controlling a weekly devoted to political news and opinion and editing a daily newspaper. There is some evidence that the Communist Party tried unsuccessfully to win him over, although he always remained close to the National Socialists, for whom he served as a member of parliament in the postwar Temporary National Assembly.[40] Within three days of the communist takeover he was expelled from the Union of Czech Journalists and the Syndicate of Czech Writers, and his new play *A Cloud and a Waltz* (*Oblak a valčík*) was shut down at the National Theater. He fled the country in April 1948, eventually settling in New York. There he became the head of the Czech section of Radio Free Europe in 1951 and continued to contribute reflections to the station long after he retired a decade later.[41] He devoted much of his time to writing both fiction and nonfiction and smoking his beloved pipes. The reburial of his ashes in 1991 at the Vyšehrad cemetery, the final resting place of so many Czech national heroes, attests to the continuing esteem in which he is held by Czechs today. Among others, President Václav Havel spoke at the event, and the reinterment was front-page news.[42]

Peroutka is difficult to label politically, as he was problematic for both the left and the right.[43] Recent discussions of his life, works, and views have only added to his contentious position. Philosophically he was a pragmatist and always felt close to the Anglo-Saxon tradition. Politically, he was a committed anticommunist (before World War II, he called communism "the root of all contemporary evil"), and he has been hailed as the most authentic Czech liberal of the twentieth century.[44] However, Peroutka's liberalism has also come under attack as differing "from socialism only 'spiritually': by stressing the personality and its creative power."[45] It is this critical sensibility that will pervade this work, in the hope of providing balance to the contemporary Czech mythologizing of Peroutka. As Eva Hartmannová has pointed out: "as long as Peroutka remains the subject of legend and myth, his rich works could contribute . . . to the intellectual stagnation of the recently liberated Czech society."[46]

Václav Černý, the foremost Czech literary critic after the death of F. X. Šalda, has been described as "a sharp and merciless critic, a sovereign lecturer, [and] a self-certain scholar of astonishing knowledge."[47] Younger than Peroutka, he first became prominent in the years just before World War II. His fame mounted after he founded *Kritický měsíčník* (*The Critical Monthly*) in 1938, which was immediately considered one of the leading literary journals of the time. Prominent in the wartime underground, he was captured by the Nazis and imprisoned in 1944, two years after his journal had been shut down, and only freed during the Prague uprising in May 1945. After the war he was named a professor of comparative literature at Charles University, renewed *Kritický měsíčník*, and contributed polemics to other noncommunist periodicals. Although which party he supported remains a subject of speculation, he was decidedly not enthusiastic about either the Communists or the National Socialists. He claims that both asked him to join, offers which he declined.[48] It seems reasonable, therefore, to conclude that he was a supporter of the Social Democratic Party, although this cannot be stated with certainty. His enthusiastically proclaimed socialism did not preclude him from sharply attacking communist intellectuals. Already before the war he had criticized historical materialism and socialist realism, and he repeated these postwar, with one difference: "the discussion had already ceased to be academic for Černý. At this time he was clearly aware that it was not about artistic criticism, approaches to artistic work or criteria, but political struggle. . . . [T]hese discussions were surrogates for far wider and more crucial problems."[49] After February 1948, Černý remained in communist Czechoslovakia. Although he voluntarily withdrew from its pages, *Kritický měsíčník* was shut down in October 1948, and Černý was removed from the university in 1951. He was imprisoned by the communist government in 1952, and released the following year. Academically rehabilitated during the Prague Spring of 1968, he was again removed from his post after the Warsaw Pact invasion. He was subsequently subjected to one of the most vicious of all the Communist smear campaigns in Czechoslovakia's history. Many of his works were smuggled abroad, where they were published and often smuggled back into Czechoslovakia. The most famous and controversial of these are his *Memoirs*, which run to several volumes and cover the years 1921–1972.[50] Like Peroutka, Černý is a character who has been the subject of much posthumous esteem in the years since the fall of the Communist regime in Czechoslovakia, as can be seen by the flood of works by him that have recently been published.[51] Personally self-assured to the point of intolerance and with some justification accused of anti-Semitism, he is nonetheless a mind deserving of respect.[52] His socialism remains unquestioned, as does his opposition to communist dominance.

Peroutka and Černý were particularly important for the journals they controlled, publications that gave direction to democratic socialist ideas. Peroutka was responsible for two periodicals, both sponsored by the Association of Cultural Organizations.[53] The first of these was the daily *Svobodné noviny* (*The Free News*, circulation 68,000).[54] Although smaller than the party dailies, it was widely discussed and was seen as a forum for the cultural reflections of the democratic socialist intelligentsia. It was described by a contemporary Western observer as "liberal and level-headed," and even the reform communist historian Jaroslav Kladiva had to admit that until 1947 it "succeeded in evoking a seeming objectivity and non-partisanship, thanks to the political dexterity and experience of F. Peroutka."[55] Nevertheless, it was constantly and justifiably criticized by the Communist Party as being under the control of the National Socialists.[56] Peroutka also stood as the guiding force behind the weekly *Dnešek* (*Today*), which has been aptly described by Eva Hartman-nová as "the most important platform of the noncommunist intelligentsia . . . the platform of an intellectual elite that was the primary source of rational in-spiration for orientation and the search for alternative methods for solving powerfully felt social, political and economic problems."[57] As with *Svobodné noviny*, *Dnešek* came under harsh communist fire throughout its existence, largely because it was clearly a renamed version of *Přítomnost* and lay very close to the National Socialist Party. Throughout the first postwar year, it was accused in bitter communist-led attacks of being under German influence, be-cause of its reportage on the violence and destruction that accompanied the expulsion of the Sudeten Germans.[58] Černý's *Kritický měsíčník* (circulation 22,000), for which Černý himself wrote the majority of the longer pieces, pro-vided the forum for the highest levels of artistic and literary debate in the country.[59] The intellectuals in the circle around Černý and Peroutka also cer-tainly had access to the pages of the National Socialist daily *Svobodné slovo* (*The Free Word*, circulation 300,000), and to its weekly journals *Svobodný zítřek* (*A Free Tomorrow*) and *Masarykův lid* (*Masaryk's People*), and the non-party weekly *Naše doba* (*Our Times*).[60] Furthermore, particularly after the right wing assumed tenuous control over the Social Democratic Party in November 1947, these intellectuals had some access to that party's daily, *Právo lidu*. Finally, they could contribute to the daily of the Community of Czech Legionnaires, *Národní osvobození* (*National Liberation*, circulation 40,000), although its smaller circulation and more diverse background render it less important for the debates under consideration here.

ROMAN CATHOLIC INTELLECTUALS

In this study, the group of Roman Catholic Church officials, People's Party ideologists, and intellectuals contributing to press organs addressing the con-cerns of these institutions will be considered exponents of the Catholic point of view. As the People's Party was the most visible public avenue for ex-pressing their ideas, with the Church playing only a subsidiary role, we can rightly call it a movement of "political Catholicism." This term has particular importance for delimiting the group, but may also be misconstrued and un-derstood as either too extensive or not extensive enough. The movement should not be regarded as one "created by, or [claiming] some sort of au-thorization from, the Papacy." In the postwar period, the People's Party claimed to be nonconfessional and was not subject to the direct influence of the Holy See. Equally, the party does not "include all Catholics who engaged in political action," as the vast majority of Czechs nominally belonged to the Roman Catholic Church while the forces of political Catholicism could claim only about one-fifth of the electorate. In short, the various strains of political

Catholicism are coalesced into this group "less from the fact that they were composed of individuals who could be categorized as Catholic believers, than from the Catholic goals and values" of the movement.[61]

The People's Party (*Československá strana lidová*) had its roots in the political conditions of the late nineteenth-century Habsburg Empire. It was created by the fusion of two rather different movements in Moravia, the more eastern and rural of the Czech lands: the Catholic-National Party (*Katolick-onárodní strana*) and the Christian Social Party of Moravia and Silesia (*Moravskoslezská strana křest'anskosociální*). The former of these, founded in 1896, was regarded as quite conservative and dependent on the Church. The latter, founded in 1899 by Jan Šrámek, grew out of the Christian social tradition. Despite the difference in their conceptions and supporters, they campaigned together in the 1911 *Reichsrat* elections and gained six seats.[62] These two strains of political Catholicism were forced together by the founding of the independent Czechoslovak Republic, when a flood of members left the Church, both to the Protestant sects and to the "nonconfessional" category. Between 1910 and 1921, the Catholic Church lost some 1,259,655 members in Bohemia alone and dropped from representing 95 percent of the Czech population to 78 percent. The Church was hardest-hit in Prague, where it lost 37 percent of its members.[63] In order to defend the Church's interests and to stanch the flow of souls, Catholic institutions closed ranks, one example of this being the forging of the People's Party in January 1919.

Throughout the interwar republic the People's Party maintained consistent although moderate support, gaining 7–9 percent of the Czechoslovak vote in parliamentary elections. The party was considered the consummate centrist party and as such placed ministers in almost every interwar government. Only a few facets of the party's development are necessary for understanding its political and social position after the war. The first concerns its electoral base. The party was largely Moravian, consistently drawing half or more of its statewide total of votes in parliamentary elections from the region and remaining its largest party throughout the interwar period. It drew above-average support in rural regions and those in which the Church was strongest.[64] Socially, the structure of the party in 1927 reveals that over half of its members were peasant farmers or cottagers (*domkáře* and *chalupníci*), while 20 percent were members of the working class. It also shows that women formed a fundamental component of the party, representing just under half of its membership.[65]

Its relations with the Vatican, although never ideal, evolved over the years of the interwar republic. In the early 1920s the Church, looking for a more radical defense of its interests, criticized the party. The turning point came in 1925, when Czechoslovakia became embroiled in a sharp conflict with the Vatican after the anniversary of the day Jan Hus was burned at the stake was made a national holiday.[66] The People's Party steered the parties toward compromise, and when a pact was finally ratified between the state and the Church in 1928, it was regarded domestically as a great victory for the party.[67] Despite the relatively good relationship that held between the party and the Vatican from that time onward, it is no doubt true that "the idea that the politics of the People's Party were always and completely identical to the politics of Church circles is unmaintainable. . . . [The] environment of the Czech nation had a far greater influence on Czech political Catholicism."[68]

The character of the People's Party was fully revealed in the struggle for the defense of the republic in the 1930s, a decade crucial for the party's reestablishment after the war. Even before the onset of the Depression, leading voices in the party had called for the recognition of the USSR, despite the party's criticism of the Soviet persecution of Christian believers and disagreement with its social system.[69] The party remained consistent in its position despite criticism from within the Catholic camp and from bourgeois parties. After Hitler's rise to power, the party maintained a consistently antifascist position, despite scattered elements sympathetic to fascist-style organization within the party. The uncompromising stance of support culminated after the government received the Munich ultimatum, when People's Party ministers were the only ones to vote unanimously against its acceptance. When this failed, they demanded the convening of parliament, arguing that only that body could constitutionally capitulate.

The party, and the cause of political Catholicism more generally, was credited in the postwar era for this stand and for its service during the war. In the wake of the Munich experience, the People's Party leadership fled the country, and chairman Šrámek served as chairman of the exile government in London. The dark days of the war seem to have brought many Czechs closer to the faith, as unusually large crowds attended pilgrimages in the early years of the occupation. Untainted by charges of collaboration, the Roman Catholic Church emerged in the liberated republic with considerable moral capital. With few exceptions its clergy had behaved courageously in the course of the Nazi occupation, and a great many had taken part in the national resistance. The Church paid for this in blood, as some five hundred priests were sent to concentration camps, where seventy-six of them perished, and perhaps some twenty-five more died in Gestapo custody.[70] The Vatican was apparently aware of the political importance of this, and immediately after the war named two well-known resistance figures and two former concentration-camp inmates bishops.

Despite their moral capital, Czech Catholics and their representatives in the People's Party suffered from two major types of defects, seen from the viewpoint of political activity. The first concerned questions in the Catholic community as a whole. Although after the war three-quarters of all Czechs declared themselves Roman Catholic, many were only nominally so, and took little part in Church affairs. A poll published in 1946 by a leading

Catholic journal, the aptly named *Katolík*, revealed that only 20 percent of the population declared themselves regular churchgoers, with 42.8 percent "occasional"; 13.6 percent attended only on major holidays and the remaining quarter less frequently or not at all.[71] Inside the Catholic community, the question of participation in political life was also salient. While the Church was the beneficiary of higher lay participation after the war, many of these believing Catholics faced the same dilemma we have seen confronting intellectuals in general. In the Catholic case, they questioned whether to take part in politics or to devote themselves to "silent" work, believing that "nothing today is more important than the apostolate, working for the spiritual renewal of the nation." Others argued that it was necessary to take part in order to "punch out *(proboxovat)* space in the political ring" for the Church.[72] In light of this, when the "Catholic" point of view is considered, it must be borne in mind that the views are those espoused by the politically active section of the believing Catholic population.

The second group of problems surrounding these Catholic political and cultural activists concerns the People's Party itself and can be broken down into defects in starting position, general political activity, and leadership. Despite chairman Šrámek's position in the exile government, the party was largely ignored during the crucial "Moscow discussions" of March 1945. From the party's viewpoint, these meetings had two important outcomes. It was at this time that the political character of the soon to be completely liberated state was discussed and, although the party was represented, it was accorded little weight in the negotiations. The relative unimportance of the party in Moscow continued in the months after liberation and was recognized even by one of the party leaders, Minister of Post František Hála. In the party's daily newspaper, he complained that it became apparent that "the socialist bloc will meet behind our backs and we will only have the opportunity to either agree or disagree."[73] This "socialist bloc" began to take shape in the discussions between the Communist and Social Democratic parties in Moscow and reached its final form just after liberation when the National Socialist Party joined. The development was very worrying for the People's Party, as it isolated the party on the right in Czech politics until the National Socialist Party withdrew from the bloc in late 1945. In many ways it seems that the party was reinstated in Czech political life as an admissible non-socialist force.

The second result of the discussions in Moscow was that the party would no longer be permitted to campaign as a specifically Roman Catholic party. Although it was not allowed to campaign confessionally, it could proceed under the banner of a nonconfessional Christianity. This measure represented only a small hindrance, because the party's historical ties to Catholicism could not be ignored and the Catholic character of the party remained evident both in its leadership and philosophy. It also had little effect on the composition of the party, as evidence from late 1945 reveals. At that time the party had 344,011 members (later growing to over 400,000), of whom the majority (183,379) lived in Moravia. Of this total, over 40 percent were small farmers and around 15 percent were working class. At that time the party had branches in only 55–60 percent of local communities, and its organization "was dense only in areas where the Catholic Church exerted strong influence, particularly among peasants."[74]

Just as the party's appeal had changed little from before the war, so its program remained relatively stable, with the difference that it was no longer in the center of the political spectrum, but relatively far out on the right wing.[75] In addition to defending Church property it took the lead in defending Church schools and religious instruction. This stance may have gained it some support, for in the same survey that revealed that only 20 percent of Czechs attended church regularly, 77 percent of the respondents thought children needed religious education (including 73 percent of working-class respondents), and 72 percent thought religious education should be a part of the school curriculum while only 16.5 percent disagreed.[76] Beyond these positions close to the Church, the party maintained its moderate stance. Like all parties in postwar Czechoslovakia, it applauded the Soviet Union and supported calls for at least limited social reform: symbolically, pictures of Edvard Beneš and Josef Stalin flanked the stage at the party's first postwar meeting.[77] On the other hand, its program was largely based on papal encyclicals and strenuously defended the rights of small businessmen and private farmers. The party also attempted to play on its rejection of the Munich capitulation, the Catholic wartime resistance, and its democratic credentials, which it contrasted with the Communists' history of obstructionism.

Given the revolutionary wave sweeping over the nation, the party made a virtue of necessity, by stressing that it was the only nonsocialist party, particularly as it had disputes with all of the other parties in the government. It was in a state of constant criticism of the Communist Party and warned that the Social Democrats were no better:

> Do not make a distinction between the Communists and the Social Democrats. . . . The two Marxist parties are merely two lures for different fish, while only one fisherman sits at both rods. . . . Only a strong People's Party . . . will decide whether our state will be characterized as a democracy or if we will again fall into dictatorship.[78]

Through this and their decidedly unenthusiastic stance toward the social revolution, they tacitly attempted to become a refuge for those Czechs left politically homeless by the banning of the interwar right-wing parties. It was this strategy that brought them into conflict with the remaining member of the National Front, the National Socialist Party. Both believed that they could gain the majority of the former supporters of the interwar period's largest party, the Agrarians. In the event, the People's Party appeared to be the choice of the plurality of its peasant support, while the National Socialists placed only third behind the Communists.[79]

The second major defect the party faced was one of leadership, a difficulty that partly stemmed from the party's position on the right wing of the Czech political spectrum. Partially as a result of an influx of new members from the recently banned parties, the People's Party suffered from a certain diffusion of viewpoints. Common to all were a commitment to Catholicism and moderation, but strategies for countering the postwar strength of the Communist Party varied. Three main trends can be distinguished within the party's political and intellectual leadership. The first and most left-leaning centered on Alois Petr and Father Josef Plojhar, both of whom served as ministers in the Communist government after February 1948. This wing had little power within the party, and was rarely heard in the Catholic press. At the center of events were Msgr. Jan Šrámek, the party's chairman and founder, and the government ministers Msgr. František Hála and Adolf Procházka, who stood slightly to Šrámek's left and right, respectively. Šrámek was the only non-Communist party leader to survive the war, a fact that lent the party a sense of continuity. Unfortunately, he was 75 years old and in poor health, which often prevented him from attending cabinet meetings. This led in practice to Hála managing the day-to-day affairs of the party, with Šrámek directing from above. A second problem with Šrámek was a certain dictatorial tendency directed primarily toward the right wing of his party, represented by a younger group of Catholic intellectuals, including the parliamentary representatives Helena Koželuhová (who was married to Procházka) and the historian Bohdan Chudoba, as well as the journalist Pavel Tigrid.

The dispute between the centrist leadership and the right boiled over after the 1946 elections, in which the party received 20 percent of the vote.[80] While *Katolík* saw "certainly no reason to lament" the outcome, it was still no time "to sit comfortably on one's hands."[81] The right wing, however, saw the result as reason for a serious reconsideration of the party's tactics. Koželuhová called for a change in leadership and a stiffer policy toward the Communists, and demanded an extraordinary congress for discussion of the party's future. Šrámek and the centrist leadership saw to it that she was promptly expelled from the party and, despite much dissatisfaction from lower party organs, she was not reinstated. The policy of surviving the revolutionary wave and waiting for more favorable times had maintained its position as the party's primary strategy.[82] Nonetheless, the episode caused the party leadership to lean slightly toward the right, becoming more critical of the Communists and attempting to work more closely with the National Socialists. The leadership's tougher stand against the Communists, and the increasing visibility of the intellectual representatives of the right wing who lay outside the party apparatus (such as Pavel Tigrid), seemed to firm up the party's basis. Among the non-Communist parties, the People's Party lost the least members to the Communist Party's membership drive in the winter of 1947–1948. The Communists' simultaneous attempt to infiltrate its National Front coalition partners also met with the least success in the People's Party, which was both the last and least infiltrated.[83]

In classifying the intellectual representatives of Czech political Catholicism, it is useful to focus on two main types of actors, which diverged according to the emphasis they placed on the component parts of the term "political Catholicism." The unitary definition casts the net sufficiently widely to ensure that all of the views with which we will be concerned contribute to its final form. Nonetheless, it is clear that one set of actors stressed political argumentation and maneuvering while relying on Catholic inspiration for their activity, whereas the second set placed more emphasis and discussed Catholic religious principles more intensively, drawing political conclusions from them. These two sets of actors are reflected in the two types of journals that were the tribunes of the People's Party and Czech political Catholicism.

The first, more politically oriented set was clustered around the weekly *Obzory* (*Horizons*), which had Pavel Tigrid and Ivo Ducháček heading an editorial board that also included Helena Koželuhová and Bohdan Chudoba. *Obzory* contained numerous articles criticizing Communist political practices and stood almost alone in its willingness to publicly contradict the rosy pictures of the USSR, publishing articles from the Western press on developments there. Beyond the criticism of communist politics, at the fore of which stood Tigrid, the journal provided a home to broader criticisms of dialectical materialism and to the explicitly Catholic political theorizing associated with Chudoba and S. S. [Simeon Simeonovič] Ghelfand. The accent on theoretical development may have been a result of Chudoba's influence. He was a historian and People's Party representative who authored one of the most programmatic Roman Catholic political texts, *What Christian Politics Is*. His views were amply reinforced and complemented by Ghelfand's numerous articles and his two book-length treatments, *Marxism and Christian Social Reformism* and *Dialectical Materialism*. *Obzory*'s criticisms of political developments both domestically and in the USSR made it a favorite target for radical socialists' ire. Its editorial positions and staff were derided, in letters to the editor and articles in the communist press for all manner of offenses. These ranged from indulging in "hateful slander" of the Soviet Union to being generally "harmful to our national interests."[84] The journal was calumnied as being "coordinated with the general plan of European reaction. . . . [which] is directed at the weakening and, in the longer term, the discontinuation of the alliance agreements of the Soviet Union with the Slavic states."[85] The revolutionary Marxist left tied itself in knots trying to explain how *Obzory* was able to gain its very problematic popularity among workers by its hostile position toward our working class, the United Trades-Union, the presidential decrees, etc.; among soldiers by its audacious attacks on the army; and among all honorable, consistent democrats and anti-fascists by its vile calumnies of the Soviet Union, its people and the Red Army, by its hypocritical "patronage" under the resettled Germans.[86]

The Communist minister of information even attempted to close the journal, but the measure was voted down in the council of ministers.[87] During that confrontation, *Obzory* received only a minimum of support from non-Communists outside the People's Party: the fellow-traveling Social Democratic chairman, Zdeněk Fierlinger, complained directly to František Hála about the journal's content and the National Socialist press echoed criticisms of Koželuhová.[88] Nonetheless, *Obzory* continued to publish, and Tigrid and Chudoba even managed to set up a second journal in the fall of 1946. Their *Vývoj (Evolution)* also came under communist fire and truly was, as *Tvorba* considered it, *Obzory*'s "younger brother." The weight placed on these two journals became clear in the tense days of February 1948, when one of the first acts taken against the People's Party was the immediate cessation of the printing of both journals.[89]

The second strain of Catholic activism had its roots much closer to the Church than to the People's Party, although this certainly did not keep its contributors from commenting on political developments or offering critiques of both Marxist theory and Communist Party practice. The most important representative of this strain was *Katolík*, which was surrounded by a group of like-minded journals, the most important of which were *Vyšehrad*, *Na hlubinu (To the Depths)* and the literary publications *Akord (Accord)* and *Archa (The Ark)*. The editor of *Katolík* was the Jesuit Adolf Kajpr, who concentrated around himself a group of leading Catholic intellectuals and young theologians. His credentials can perhaps best be established by noting that during the war he was imprisoned in Theresienstadt, Mauthausen, and Dachau. After the communist seizure of power he was sentenced to twelve years in the first anti-Catholic show trial and died while serving that sentence. *Katolík* published just under 13,000 copies and presented its last issue on 29 February 1948, ending without notice to its subscribers. One of the few historians of postwar Czech Catholicism noted that "its importance for the creation of postwar Czech Catholicism was extraordinary. It was not easy reading. *Katolík* was challenging and polemical (sometimes even too much so)."[90]

The other journals in this strain served rather in a secondary capacity, with *Katolík* largely setting the tone. In considering them as a whole, however, a few observations can be made. Above all, there was a great deal of overlap in authors among the four, with prominent Catholic writers from the prewar period, among them Jan Čep and Jan Zahradníček, often present. Further, the regional aspect of political Catholicism was maintained, as Moravia was very strongly represented: *Na hlubinu* was published by the Dominican Josef Silvestr Maria

Braito in Olomouc and *Akord* by the Association of Catholic Writers and Columnists in Brno.[91] Finally, the period is as equally dominated by the figure of the Moravian Dominik Pecka as it is by Prague's Kajpr and his *Katolík*. Pecka, a Benedictine, became a priest in 1918 after receiving special dispensation from the bishop since he had not yet reached the required age of twenty-four; he later became a professor of sociology at the Theological Institute in Brno. Before the war he had already served as an editor of both *Archa* and *Akord*, and continued to appear in their pages after the war, as well as publishing in *Na hlubinu* and more frequently in *Vyšehrad*. Omnipresent and interested in a wide range of topics, Pecka has been praised as "a teacher, literary figure, columnist, sarcastic polemicist and at the same time a serene man," who "had a great influence on the creation of the personality of more than one generation of Czech Catholic intellectuals."[92] In the figures of Kajpr and Pecka the more purely Catholic element of Czech political Catholicism found a fitting match for Tigrid's and Chudoba's more politically oriented leadership.

PROTESTANT INTELLECTUALS

Although Protestants comprise a far smaller portion of the Czech population than Roman Catholics do, they have traditionally maintained a profile and prominence far beyond their numbers. From intellectual roots in the Hussite tradition, their churches drew on that movement's powerful historical symbolism and the identification of the Roman Catholic Church with the Habsburg monarchy during their interwar growth period. Protestants' politically active stance, the worldliness of their doctrines, and the prominence of their leaders on the national level made them valuable political allies for proponents of radical change in the immediate postwar years. Although a variety of non-Catholic Christian sects existed in postwar Bohemia and Moravia, the two largest organizations were the Evangelical Church of the Czech Brethren and the Czechoslovak Church.

Despite its size and rapid growth after the war, the larger of the non-Catholic churches, the Czechoslovak Church, has been unjustly overlooked in all other studies of the era. Although it is not technically a Protestant church, this "free Christian" sect will be included under the rubric of Protestant for a number of reasons. Most decisively, its position was resolutely anti-Catholic, making it impossible to discuss its leaders in conjunction with Roman Catholic intellectuals. Further, it consistently strove to maintain good relations with non-Catholic Christians, sharing the Theological Faculty with the Evangelical Church and working for "friendly cooperation with the historic Protestant and Orthodox churches, and those assembled in the world ecumenical movement."[93] This was particularly true after the Second World War, when the church's second council adopted wide-ranging democratic reforms and the belief in a personal God. Here, in the words of the church's foremost historian, "a clear reference to the Protestant churches can be perceived, although the Czechoslovak Church neither then nor later counted among [them]."[94] Finally, the church's intellectual, cultural, and political views resembled those of the Evangelical Church, although they were far more openly radical.

The Czechoslovak Church had its roots in a group of reform-minded Catholic priests that began to meet under the umbrella of the Union of Catholic Clergy (Jednota katolického duchovenstva) in 1895. Its leader was Karel Farský, a professor of religion in Plzeň who was very active in the press, writing with special zeal for nationalist newspapers. Like the People's Party, the nascent Czechoslovak Church was called into being by the creation of an independent Czechoslovakia, organizing itself officially in January 1920, after voting 150–66 in favor of a split with Rome. Even before this, the organizers had lifted the celibacy requirement for priests and introduced the almost exclusive use of the Czech language in services. These steps, when seen in tandem with the church's theologically decisive repudiation of the Virgin Birth and the Resurrection, drew a sharp division between it and Roman Catholicism.[95] From its inception, the most visible characteristic of the church was the anti-Catholic tone of its rhetoric. Moreover, the church's anti-Catholicism was enflamed when its early strivings to become a national church met with failure precisely because of the Roman Catholic Church.[96]

A further crucial characteristic of the Czechoslovak Church was its modernity. In creating its message, the church borrowed freely from all Christian traditions, leading one critic to note that its "all inclusive pragmatism . . . is a peculiar mixture of everything, with something for everyone."[97] Elements in this mixture included a very strong inclination toward scientism and an emphasis on modern culture. At its first congress in 1921, a set of guidelines was approved that included the statement that "We are convinced of the universal validity and relevance of the law of evolution, to which religious thoughts are subject, and by which Christianity is regulated." Similarly, the opening paragraph of its first constitution, passed in 1937, held that the church was composed of "Christians who strive to fulfill the demands of contemporary morals and live in accordance with the advances of science."[98] This stress on science and contemporary thought was intended to create a context in which "from the Gospel of Christ and modern culture there would arise a unity, as there was in the Middle Ages."[99] The stance contributed much to the radical social beliefs of the church's leadership after the Second World War, when the church exhibited a tendency toward belief in "progress to the point of stupidity."[100]

Finally, the church exhibited a Slav-based nationalism and political progressivism that can be seen as part of its commitment to modernity and science. This facet fit particularly well with the Communist Party's postwar attempt to create a Slavic and socialist Czech identity. In its early years, for example, the church had entered into a long series of discussions with the Serbian Church.

These talks were aimed at uniting the two, but ultimately failed when the churches could not agree on a common program.[101] The church's Slavic feeling became even more prominent after the Second World War, when the church announced its aim of widening its cooperation with the other Slavic churches, with the goal of organizing "a defense against antipathy to the socialist world and the endangering of the essential interests of the Slavic world."[102] Although it claimed to be apolitical, in the interwar period certainly none of the church's members gave their votes to the Catholic People's Party, and the Social Democrats and Communists were rejected by the hierarchy for their openly antireligious stances. This left the church largely committed to the progressive but non-Marxist National Socialist Party.[103] With the softening of the Marxist parties' attitude toward religion during and most evidently after the war, the Czechoslovak Church's members could be both progressive and religious within the structure of these parties, and flocked to them. To a large degree, we can agree with Ludvik Nemec that the church was "truly a product of its times, and so much a product of all the components of modern secular Czech mentality": nationalism, patriotism, and dialectical thinking.[104]

An analysis of the church's membership reveals other important aspects of its character. In the census of 1921, the church could claim 525,346 adherents, representing 3.86 percent of the population of the new state.[105] Their number grew to 793,385 (5.39 percent) by 1930, some 864,000 by 1937, and an estimated 946,500 in 1945. Shortly thereafter, it became a million-member church, at approximately the same time as the Communist Party reached that plateau. This final figure represents roughly 8 percent of the population of Czechoslovakia as a whole. When the figures are scrutinized more carefully, however, a few interesting facts become apparent. Most significantly, while the church's name would indicate that it drew adherents from across the republic, the reality was quite different. The church was almost exclusively a Bohemian phenomenon, as over three-quarters of its members lived in this most westerly region, a condition that remained stable from the church's inception through the 1950s. Support outside of the Czech lands was almost nonexistent, as church members comprised less than 0.3 percent of the population of both Slovakia and Ruthenia in 1930. This means that the church membership represented just under 12 percent of the immediate post–World War II population of the Czech lands.[106]

Further, the church's membership was markedly urban and ethnically Czech. It was concentrated in the most thickly populated region of Czechoslovakia (Bohemia) and showed an especially high degree of support in the capital city of Prague, over 20 percent of whose inhabitants in 1945 were members. This made the church's influence greater than its share of the population because of its prominence in the center of political, economic, and cultural power. Beyond Prague, its highest levels of support were found in Kladno, a city known as "Red Kladno" for its support of the Communist Party, which was founded there in 1921.[107] The expulsion of the ethnic German population after the Second World War aided the church's relative power be-

cause, unlike other churches, it was also an overwhelmingly Czech phenomenon. The distribution of church adherents in 1930 reveals that in areas where
the ethnically German population was in the majority and there was also a
strong admixture of Czechs, the percentage strength of the Czech population
correlated positively with membership in the Czechoslovak Church.[108]

Perhaps most significant is the social distribution of the church's membership. While other denominations showed a distribution more or less consistent
with the social structure of the Czech population as a whole, the Czechoslovak Church showed marked support among the industrial working class. As
early as 1921, 46 percent of its members classified themselves as active in industry and 59 percent as "workers, apprentices and wage-earners," with 76
percent of the members from the industrial sector classifying themselves as
working class. In the 1930s, those who placed themselves at the cross of the
categories of "industrial sector" and "working class" represented 31 percent of
the church's total membership, constituting the largest single group.[109] Shortly
after World War II, the church proudly proclaimed that "of every 100 citizens
34.9 are employed in industry, of every 100 Czechoslovaks [i.e., Czechoslovak
Church members], however, there are fully 46.5 in industry. This shows that
the Czechoslovak Church is especially successful among the progressive
workers."[110] This made the church even more working class than the Communist Party, 43 percent of whose members came from the industrial sector.

The church's wartime experience brought several changes of emphasis,
with the church emerging radicalized from its dealings with the occupation
authorities. After the war the church claimed that 24 percent of its clergy in
Prague and 11 percent of its total clergy were imprisoned for resistance activities, although only twenty-eight were sent to concentration camps, where
a half-dozen died. Among the church members who lost their lives was Jan
Opletal, the student killed during the 28 October 1939 demonstrations.[111]
Despite these losses, the hardships placed on the church were relatively
slight. Obviously, after the creation of the Protectorate of Bohemia and
Moravia and an independent Slovakia, the church could not maintain the former state's name in its title. The Reich Protector's office demanded a change
after the protests in which Opletal was killed, and the church leadership responded by renaming itself the Czecho-Moravian Church (*Církev česko-
moravská*). Apart from this cosmetic alteration, the church was little hin-
dered in the early part of the war, as Rudolf Urban has described:

> In the first years of the German occupation the Czechoslovak Church could work
> comparatively undisturbed. . . . For a long time the Czechoslovak Church seemed
> to German authorities to be a suitable partner in their politics directed against the
> Catholic Church. Because the development of the Czechoslovak Church dis-
> played clear similarities to the Movement of German Christians promoted by the
> Reich government, it was believed on the German side that the two church
> movements must cooperate in some way.[112]

With an eye toward such cooperation, church patriarch Adolf Procházka met with Reichsbischof Ludwig Müller in 1940 and 1941, although the discussions proved fruitless because of the national and political gulf that separated the two. After the assassination of Reinhard Heydrich, the church suffered to the same degree as the general population and its primary organ, the weekly *Český zápas* (*The Czech Struggle*), was limited to biweekly distribution and later also limited in length.[113] Nevertheless, the church and some of its primary functionaries were accused of collaboration after the war's end, and the church was placed under the temporary administration of a communist-dominated Central Action Committee. It is certainly possible that this contributed to the church's procommunist stance in the postwar years, as the church perhaps attempted to unite with a surging Communist Party and overcome the charges of a less than pristine wartime past by subsuming itself in revolutionary politics.

The church had two other, internally compelling reasons to place itself close to the radical left. One arose from the church's stance in the matter of the expulsion of the ethnic Germans. The World Council of Churches raised significant opposition to this measure generally, and the methods with which it was being carried out particularly, while the Czechoslovak Church was one of its most vocal supporters. The church broke off contact with the Council, not reestablishing links until 1947 (after the vast majority of the expulsions had taken place), and not rejoining until 1962.[114] The motives for the church's radical stance were likely not purely nationalistic, however. The possibility of material gain surely contributed: the church wanted the National Front government to turn over to it the abandoned German evangelical churches and pastoral residences in the Sudetenland.[115] Since the distribution of the lands and property seized from the Germans was in the hands of a Communist-controlled government department, the church had much to gain by standing close to the Communists.[116]

The second internal reason for the Czechoslovak Church's close relations to communism arose directly from the war years. These brought several changes in the leadership of the church, changes that pushed it further to the political left. Patriarch Procházka died in February 1942, and although the vacancy was not officially filled until 1946, František Kovář took over the leadership of the church at that time. The bishop of Prague, the most important of the church's four dioceses, also died during the war and was replaced by Miroslav Novák, a representative of a younger, more progressive generation and a staunch ally of the Communist Party. These changes and the more widespread replacement of the founding generation of clergy by a younger one reflected a situation in which "the new church leadership was determined to engage itself more strongly in Soviet-style socialism."[117] Also important in this regard was the formation of a Communist group inside the leadership of the church's institutions and administration. As Karel Kaplan has pointed out, Communist Party members "occupied leading positions and in 1946 they pushed through support for the socialist changes in the land at the church's general assembly."[118]

The result of these circumstances was a Czechoslovak Church that was committed to radicalism and quite popular, indicating the strength of both the church and its idea of social revolution. Without delving too deeply at this stage into the church's view of socialism, a few examples of the tone of its rhetoric should serve to establish its revolutionary pedigree. The first two tasks that the church set itself in national life after the war were "to support the transformation of the republic into a People's Democratic state" and "to strengthen the moral conviction of the Czechoslovak people in favor of socialism." In the liberated homeland, the church promised to place itself "consistently and with the whole weight of its spiritual authority behind the striving towards constructing the republic as a national, People's Democratic state heading towards socialism." The gallop towards socialism in the church's rhetoric often affected even its theological formulations. For example, a letter from the leadership to the first postwar prime minister, Zdeněk Fierlinger, stressed that in its works the church would "give expression to its conviction that the ethos of Jesus' Gospel is the ethos of the classless society."[119]

Although the leadership, particularly after the communist assumption of power, revealed itself to be more radical than its followers, the voice of the Czechoslovak Church was one of the most unequivocal to be heard in the immediate postwar era. Because of the "democratizing" principles adopted in 1946, the church had no single dominant figure. Nonetheless, there was a group of central leaders who largely represented the public face of the church. Primary among these was Patriarch Kovář, who served as the church's leader from 1946 until 1961. In 1928, he had founded one of the church's most influential journals, *Náboženská revue* (*The Religious Review*) and published widely in it after the war. Kovář's second-in-command, Miroslav Novák, also played a large role in formulating church policy from his position as Bishop of Prague. Outside the church hierarchy, František Hník and Alois Spisar (a cofounder of the church) forcefully furthered the church's views on cultural, social, and political issues. Both were professors of theology in Prague and frequently appeared in the pages of the church's two primary organs, *Náboženská revue* and *Český zápas*. In addition to these four men, one further religious theorist will be considered as a primary representative of the Czechoslovak Church's views, František Linhart. A professor of church history and philosophy, Linhart published the landmark *Dialectical Materialism and Religion*, which strongly influenced the church leadership's position on Marxism. Although ordained by the Evangelical Church, in the postwar period he published almost exclusively in Czechoslovak Church organs, attended its theological conference, and published his book with the imprint of the latter's publishing house. For these reasons, he will be considered among the Czechoslovak Church's intellectual leadership.

The unabashedly positive stance of these leaders, and the very warm attitude of the church as whole, toward the Communist Party and its aims was reciprocated. The Communists furthered the candidacy of numerous church representatives for positions in the Office for Religious Affairs in the National Front government, as well as in the State Office for Church Affairs. More significantly, there was considerable support within the higher echelons of the party for the idea of using the church as the basis of a national church under Communist leadership. Although these plans later fell through—not least because of the church's miniscule support in Slovakia and relatively weak position in Moravia—the church declared its strong approval of the new regime after the events of February 1948. The church proved particularly useful when its anti-Catholicism coincided with the new regime's attacks on the Vatican in the early 1950s.

There is, however, evidence that the radical tendencies of the church leadership eventually outraced the enthusiasm of its lower clergy and many of its believers. In 1950, in a move to reassure the regime of its support, the leadership removed from its central administration what it termed "a certain number of clergy, who have contact with reactionary elements and express themselves conservatively," replacing them with "entirely reliable" members. Similarly, the hierarchy instituted political schooling for the clergy. Yet these measures had the opposite effect from the one the church's leaders intended. The Communist administration "began to fear that the leadership had begun to lose touch with the pastorate and believers and had fully lost influence over them." Although in the church's 1951 synod its leaders publicly acknowledged the existence of differences, the Communists had lost interest by that time in the plan to make from it a national church.[120]

Some historical perspective is necessary to understand the position of the other prominent non-Catholic denomination, the Evangelical Church. After the seventeenth-century defeat of the Protestant forces in the Czech lands, all Protestant churches were banned. This situation obtained until Josef II announced his *Toleranzpatent* in 1781, which granted Evangelicals of the Augsburg and Helvetian confessions the right to practice their religions in private, while maintaining the Roman Catholic Church's exclusive dominance of the public domain. Despite the number of difficulties posed by the lack of trained clergy and the relative obscurity of the sanctioned creeds in the Czech lands (the Helvetian confession had not even been printed in the Czech language at the time), some 70,000 Czechs were affiliated with evangelical churches by 1787.[121] Although difficulties remained, the faiths were allowed to hold services publicly as a result of gains stemming from the revolutions of 1848. The first attempts to unite the two confessions also took place at this time, rising and falling with the revolutionary wave.

Progress toward legal equality with the Roman Catholic Church continued throughout the second half of the nineteenth century. After the Habsburgs lost the 1866 war with Prussia, and especially in the period surrounding the 1870 Vatican Council, organizational matters progressed and sharper anti-Catholic tones revealed themselves. Still, the dream of unifying the two confessions remained unfulfilled. Discussions in 1868 and 1869, spawned by the upcoming celebration of the 500th anniversary of the birth of Jan Hus, fell apart over the question of which confession represented the true descendant of the Czech Brethren.[122] This infighting did not stop the churches from growing, however, and by 1880 there were 32,000 Czechs subscribing to the Augsburg confession and 109,000 to the Helvetian confession.[123] The two confessions again drew closer as the century came to an end, when the tensions between Czechs and Germans reached fever pitch and the anti-Catholic *Los-von-Rom* movement gained strength.[124] Internally, the rapprochement was made possible by the appearance of new sets of leaders and increasing contacts between their respective intellectual elites and journalistic establishments. Further contacts were encouraged by the confessions' joint participation in the laying of the foundation stone for Prague's famed Hus monument (1903) and the 500th anniversary of Hus's death (1915). At this time, the first institutions for evangelicals without regard to confessional differences were created: the Association of Czech Clergy (Spolek českých duchovních, 1904) and The Union of Constance (Kostnická jednota, 1905). The latter of these began to publish the journal *Kostnické jiskry* (*The Sparks of Constance*), which became one of the two most influential Protestant organs and remained so after the Second World War.[125]

The collapse of the Habsburg Empire and the creation of an independent Czechoslovakia gave the final impetus to unification. The national cleavages revealed by the First World War supported the ongoing efforts toward uniting the two sects under the banner of an anti-Austrian and anti-Catholic (or, in the positive sense, Czech-national and Hussite/Czech Brethren–traditional) conceptual matrix. With the founding of the Czechoslovak Republic, all the elements were in place for the merging of the two confessions, which took place in December 1918. The new church, christened the Evangelical Church of the Czech Brethren (Českobratrská církev evangelická), benefited from a number of initial assets. Primarily, it could draw upon its Hussite heritage as well as the traditions of the Czech Brethren, important symbols in a time of nation building. Institutionally, the new church was granted permission to create the Hus Theological Faculty, which trained pastors and carried on theological research and discussion from 1919. Finally, the new republic's adulated president, Tomáš G. Masaryk, was a member, having converted from Catholicism to the Reformed Church in 1880. His widely shared belief that the meaning of Czech history lay in the Hussite traditions of democracy and humanism gave the church important intellectual and political visibility.

Under these conditions the church prospered, as Czechs moved away from a Roman Catholic Church tainted by its association with the perceived national oppression of the Habsburg Empire. Already in 1921, the time of the first postwar census, 231,213 residents of the Czech lands claimed affiliation to the church, representing 2.16 percent of the population and just under 60 percent of the evangelical population. By 1930, the Evangelical Church had grown to 290,994 members, or 2.54 percent of the population and still just under 60 percent of the evangelical population.[126] This represented a growth of almost 100 percent (140,000) in the twelve years since the church had been founded, with most of the increase coming from the ranks of disaffected Roman Catholics. Similarly, the number of parishes grew from 123 in 1921 to 161 in 1932.[127] By 1949, there were 330,000 members of the Evangelical Church of Czech Brethren, representing three-quarters of the Protestant and 3.7 percent of the total population of the Czech lands, both populations having declined considerably with the expulsion of the ethnic Germans.[128]

The church played an active role in Czech cultural and intellectual life from its birth. Theologically inclusive and committed to seeing itself as part of the wider European Reformation, the church was composed of two generational parts, a condition reflected in the development of church positions. The older generation achieved prominence before the founding of Czechoslovakia and was politically rather conservative, most often choosing to remain outside political debate. This generation was eventually forced to share power with a younger cadre that began to emerge from the Theological Faculty in 1924. With the onset of the Great Depression, these more progressive clergymen, under the leadership of J. L. Hromádka, began to involve the church more deeply in political and social issues. They emerged from the Second World War radicalized and in firm control of the church. Their sympathies lay on the political left, and one Roman Catholic commentator has argued that "in not a few places the local or district secretariats of the Communist Party took up headquarters in the residences of these Protestant pastors."[129] While this overstates the tightness of the bonds, it is certainly true that there was a strong correlation between regions with a high proportion of Protestant voters and those with high percentages of communist electoral support.[130]

Already before the war the church's influence had centered on two important journals and three outspoken leaders that all survived the war and stood at the very core of the church's conceptual foundation. Two of the leaders of the church, František Bednář and Josef Souček, were professors of theology who were central to the formation of the church's view of the People's Democratic regime. Bednář was widely known as the author of numerous works on theology and history and contributed many articles on contemporary issues to periodicals both within and outside the church press. Souček, whose father had been instrumental in uniting the two confessions in 1918, served as the secretary of the church's synodal council for fifteen years. During the war, he directed the church's underground theological seminary, thereafter serving as a professor at the Evangelical Theological Faculty. In the immediate postwar period he also co-edited the influential church journal *Křest'anská revue* (*The Christian Review*).

The figure who dominated the currents of Evangelical thought in both prewar and postwar Czech cultural and political life, however, was Josef Lukl Hromádka. Despite the major contributions made by Bednář and Souček, Hromádka was the primary representative of his church both at home and abroad for four decades, until his death in 1969. His views both reflected the positions of his church and guided its ideas and ideals. As such, he will play an important role in our story, and deserves careful attention. After eight years as a pastor, and studies in Prague, Aberdeen, Heidelberg, and Vienna, Hromádka became a professor of theology in 1920 and was named dean two years before the war. Cofounder (with the eminent Emanuel Rádl) of *Křest'anská revue* in 1926, he played an active role, particularly among the youth of interwar Czechoslovakia. Shortly after the Nazi occupation of March 1939, Hromádka fled to the United States, convinced by his older colleagues that as the youngest leader he bore the responsibility for maintaining the church's profile during the war. While in the United States, he taught at the Union Theological Seminary (alongside Reinhold Niebuhr) and at Princeton. He returned to Czechoslovakia for three months in 1945, another three months in 1946, and permanently in 1947, when he resumed his career at the Theological Faculty. In placing Hromádka in the context of this study, the critical features of his character are his relationship to the Czech religious community (particularly to the younger members of his church), the development of his theology and its relationship to socialism in light of the events of the Second World War, and his response to the communist seizure of power in February 1948.[131]

Hromádka was generally representative of the younger generation of his church. He was the youngest professor at the Theological Faculty when he joined, and quickly solidified a leading position among the youth (for example, Souček was his student). His influence over younger clergymen was to become important when that politically more progressive generation came to lead the church in the postwar era. He was instrumental in the 1927 creation of the YMCA movement in Czechoslovakia, becoming its chairman and delivering a series of lectures on Marxism and Christianity to its members in the early 1930s.[132] He was also very active in the ecumenical movement, having good relations with the entire spectrum of smaller Protestant churches, as well as with the Czechoslovak Church. In this respect, too, he was representative of his church's position. He distanced himself only from his church's critical view of Catholicism, a religion whose "solid conceptual system" he praised.[133] Interestingly, in the interwar period Hromádka also devoted much attention to the Russian Orthodox Church, finding that for it "the revolution and all that has followed is perhaps a necessary purifying fire. . . . The Soviet Russian revolution is possibly the greatest good in religious history."[134]

The sympathy with which Hromádka viewed socialism was reinforced by his theological formulations in the wake of the watershed event of Hromádka's pre-1948 life: Munich. The abandonment of Czechoslovakia by her Western allies and the state's failure to fight had, in Hromádka's eyes, caused permanent damage to his nation's soul: "We will carry it to our graves, our children and grandchildren will feel it inside them and will find no surgeon who can operate and remove it from their inner being."[135] For him, the collapse of liberal democracy before fascism was especially painful, leading him to rethink the entire foundation of his social and political beliefs. His rethinking developed into what has been called a "theology of crisis" during the war. Hromádka formulated the precept that the Western liberal democracies' betrayal at Munich was only one symptom of a much larger crisis of Western civilization. Liberal democracy had failed to show "a far-sighted understanding" of social problems, and Hromádka doubted that it was capable of organizing a new order on the basis of "real social justice and equal opportunity." In place of the defensive character of a sickly Western democracy, he argued that "what the peoples of Europe . . . badly need is the spiritual, intellectual and moral power to cope with their national, political and cultural issues."[136] Hromádka would find this power in socialism, and would conversely find in all other politics, both at home and abroad, the stamp of a "reaction" that was in his mind synonymous with the evil of Munich. Hromádka's philosophy of history also played an important part in forming his political stance, coming to the fore in his postwar enthusiasm for socialism. For Hromádka, Czechs "cannot go back. We cannot impose our abstract formulas and blueprints on the events of current history. Behind history, the Risen Lord is doing his work." In the apt words of Charles C. West, Hromádka's philosophy of history "emphasizes the fullest kind of Christian involvement in the world, in the complete confidence that Christ is sovereign over it and asks of his Church a joyful affirmation of the creative possibilities inherent in the new society which the Communists are building." Behind his crisis theology, with its twin beliefs that liberal democracy would be unable to overcome its crisis and that Jesus stood behind the screen of human events, there lurked "a longing for a *kulturchristliche* unity of religion with social power."[137] He found the opportunity to join the two in postwar Czechoslovakia.

Although Hromádka was in Hungary during the February events, he signaled his approval of the communist assumption of power upon his return. He was a member of the Action Committee of the Theological Faculty and wrote editorials that cemented his stand behind the new regime. In keeping with his historical consciousness, he argued that "history cannot be stopped! He who wants to stop it will be pushed into insignificance . . . I accept the February events as a step towards the irrevocable and just process of social change."[138] Hromádka's support for the communist takeover once again put him in a position of a shepherd leading his flock, many of whom met the changes less than enthusiastically. As Hromádka himself noted in his autobiography:

> Pastorally, it was difficult work: not to reinforce people in their incorrect political judgments and in their old social (class) interests and to still have understanding for their personal or family hardships, and especially for their moral and political disagreement with . . . the new society.[139]

Hromádka deeply believed in the cause of socialism, despite claims to the contrary in works that have tried to exculpate him from the charge of co-responsibility for his nation's fate. Certainly, in making his choice he was concerned that if his church did not stand behind the regime it would be pushed to the margins,[140] and his "'yes' to the state [was] more for the human goals of Marxism than for the political reality in his land."[141] Nonetheless, he was undoubtedly naive in his socialist convictions, and his continued support of the regime did nothing to help create the *kulturchristliche* unity of Evangelism and socialism he desired. In the years after 1948 he became so concerned with finding reasons for hope that he ignored the question of power. He maintained an eschatological hope for members of his church, granting

> to the Communist movement the ideology and the right to interpret and control the immediate movements of history. . . . The question of power realities [was] overridden in his mind by his basic sense of the historical rightness of the Communist revolution.[142]

Hromádka's loyalty to the regime was shown in the following years through many different channels. Domestically, he continued to teach at the Theological Faculty, serving as dean from 1950 until 1966 and occupying a variety of positions both inside and outside the State Office for Church Affairs. He condemned the United Nations' action in Korea and spoke out against the Hungarian revolt of 1956, arguing that "the Hungarian tragedy shows the consequences of anti-Soviet hysteria."[143] His books, especially *The Gospel for Atheists*, made him popular among "thoughtful Marxists" in Czechoslovakia, and he won two Orders of the Republic (in 1954 and 1959).[144] In addition, he became an important international representative of communist Czechoslovakia, serving as a leader of the Christian Peace Conference.

These four groups of intellectuals—communists, democratic socialists, Catholics and Protestants—represent a wide range of political ideas and fundamental cultural orientations, testifying to the breadth and liveliness of the postwar Czech intellectual environment. The prominence of both the individuals and the periodicals in which they published ensured that their ideas were read by political representatives, civil servants, and others to whom the political future of Czechoslovakia had been entrusted. Furthermore, the visions and reflections of the postwar intelligentsia reached the wider Czech public and contributed to a great extent in the formation of the public mood of the times. The debates carried on among the groups, and occasionally within them, reveal much about the way Czechs conceived of their nation and its history, meaning, and calling. The strengths and weaknesses of these men and women reflected those of their nation as a whole and contribute much to understanding not only what happened in Czechoslovakia in the fateful February of 1948, but also why it happened in the manner it did.

4

The Communist Aim: The Creation of a New Czechoslovakia

The period immediately following liberation was universally regarded as a unique moment in the history of the Czech nation. Czechs viewed the infamous betrayal at Munich, an event that had profound effects on the national psyche, as the prologue to the war. This tragedy was followed by the disturbing declaration of Slovak independence, occupation by German forces, modest resistance, a major uprising in the city of Prague, and liberation. Czechs emerged from these experiences remarkably changed and in a Europe very different from the one that had existed before the war. In the immediate postwar years, Czechs sought to regain a sense of certainty lost in the maelstrom of war. Responding to this, and capitalizing on the revolutionary wave that washed over the nation after liberation, Communist and left-wing Social Democratic intellectuals demanded what they called the "revision of the national character" and offered a new conception of the nation, one that drew on the intrinsic historicism of Czech consciousness and the postwar resurgence of nationalism. The Czech radical left performed a simultaneous two-sided transformation: the Communist Party became super-patriotic, and Czech history was reinterpreted to make the communist movement the logical inheritor of the best values of the nation, by portraying the Communist Party as walking in the footsteps of the greatest figures of Czech history.

In the wake of the war, many non-Marxist intellectuals and especially those from the religious communities also believed the nation was in the midst of a deep crisis. Although they disagreed on the exact date of its commencement, they saw the crisis as having been heightened immensely by the war, as having primarily a spiritual as opposed to an economic or political character, and as demanding immediate attention. Because of this perception, noncommunist intellectuals were acutely aware throughout the period from May 1945 until the communist seizure of total power in February 1948 that the decisions they made would have decisive implications for the future of their nation. As the Roman Catholic novelist and essayist Jan Čep noted: "Each of us is certainly aware that we are living at a very serious time; that we are probably living through one of the most fateful moments in human history."[1] Correspondingly, articles with titles such as "At the Crossroads," "On the Threshold of a New Era," or "A Watershed in the Nation's Cultural Development" appeared constantly in noncommunist periodicals throughout the period.[2] Appearing just as frequently were articles with titles such as "Why Today's Moral Chaos?" "The Roots of the Cultural Crisis," and "A Crisis in Cultural Life?"[3] Noncommunist intellectuals clearly understood the gravity of the times and their responsibility to carry the nation over the "threshold" and through the "crisis."

Different groups of intellectual activists ascribed different causes to the perceived crisis. Among democratic socialists adhering to the right wing of the Social Democratic Party and to the National Socialist Party, the crisis had two material sources. The first was external to the nation, lying in the German population that had in their view destroyed the prewar Czechoslovak state. The German danger had been eliminated by the mass expulsion of this perceived ethnic "fifth column." The second source was, as communists also argued, the unresolved social question. Democratic socialists intended to solve this problem less radically than the communists, although their plans for socialization were also extensive. In addition to these material sources, however, many noncommunists also perceived a crisis in the consciousness of the nation, a crisis that needed to be resolved in order to ensure the success of the nation's ethnic and social reconfiguration. For example, the fiery Ferdinand Peroutka argued that "the spiritual question is not only idealistic, but also practical: if there is no spiritual order, neither will there be order in material affairs."[4] Even President Beneš, the figure perceived as the stabilizing force of the nation and its tie to the state's prewar democracy, stressed throughout his *Democracy Today and Tomorrow* that democracy itself was in a prolonged crisis. In his 1946 radio address to the nation, he called the postwar era a time of a "great *moral shift.*"[5]

Roman Catholic intellectuals heavily stressed this moral aspect, seeing the crisis as arising from mankind's distance from God and the increasing secularization of modern society. One leading Catholic journal argued that humankind had come to the abyss of World War II because "in the main, humanity today lives only from the ruins of Christianity." Christianity, by which Roman Catholic commentators meant their denomination, had been pushed out of everyday public life, a displacement that had abetted the rise of Nazism and brought about the war.[6] The Catholic cure for the crisis was summed up by Pavel Tigrid: a rejection of Marxism and a return to the "ideals from which our Helleno-Christian civilization originated," values that had led civilization for two thousand years.[7] In a society demanding change, however, a back-ward-looking solution such as this could find little support outside the politically more conservative community of active Catholic believers.

Many noncommunists believed that part of the confusion and tension of the era arose from its transitional character, as Czechoslovak society moved from capitalism to socialism and from a "bourgeois" or "liberal" democracy to a "people's" democracy. Čep himself recognized the impact of the ongoing social transformation with the Communist-style formulation that "the forms of human life and human societies recreate themselves before our eyes. Old societies die out and new ones are born." He held that the transition was bound to sow seeds of confusion among the population.[8] Rather than seeing the "bright tomorrows" and ultimate victories the Communists predicted, however, these thinkers saw the transitional ferment as a warning sign demanding increased vigilance. For them, the "old order has been disrupted, but the new has not yet taken form. There has never been a time when leaders have borne heavier responsibility."[9]

Consciously aware of both the critical nature of the coming years and their own heightened responsibility in them, noncommunist intellectuals engaged their communist opponents in what both conceived as a "struggle for the soul of the nation." They hoped that in the as yet amorphously reconstituted republic they could protect the values they cherished while carrying out an extensive transformation of the social and economic spheres. For this reason, some democratic socialist intellectuals deliberately attempted to separate the moral and cultural crisis they perceived from the social question for which the vast majority of the nation desired a generally socialist solution. Jan Patočka, the eminent philosopher and student of Husserl and Heidegger, argued this position:

> We must ask ourselves again what the bases of modern man's crisis are . . . and what can provide the means for solving it . . . [It is] a crisis that it is naturally not possible to cure solely by social reforms, but only with simultaneous internal renewal. The social solution and the metaphysical-moral solution are *two* items that we must necessarily conceive separately.[10]

However prestigious the democratic advocates of such a separation, their voices were certainly overwhelmed by the voices of those for whom "unity" was a rallying cry. The necessity of national unity was one of the main themes running through the entire period, and calls for unity reflected the differing concerns and stances of the various actors. Many noncommunists believed that Czechoslovakia's socialist but noncommunist position—and indeed its independence—could be saved only by the continuation of some form of unity between the wartime allies. Similarly, unity was a theme inside the borders of the country, as there was a need to reintegrate Czechs and Slovaks after their vastly different wartime experiences. Also domestically,

Communist and left-wing Social Democrats stressed in particular the need for unity within the working class for the task of rebuilding the country, and used the desire for the unification of the trade unions and other associations and organizations to further their influence in them.

More important for the resolution of the state of crisis in Czech consciousness were the calls for *conceptual* unity, for the rebuilding of a sense of intellectual and spiritual certainty that had been shaken by the war. These ranged across the political spectrum. The Roman Catholic Pavel Tigrid cited the need for a "pan-European ethical codex," obviously referring to the Catholic perception of the abandonment of religious principles and a need to return to Church guidance.[11] The apolitical poet and translator Kamil Bednář similarly bemoaned that "our era has no world view, no interpretation acceptable to all."[12] Representatives of the Protestant denominations took this demand for conceptual unity the farthest, however. The prominent Evangelical theologian J. L. Hromádka argued that modern mankind had lost the moral and cultural anchors that, in the distant past, had been provided by the Roman Catholic leadership and more recently by other actors.[13] More directly, the Czechoslovak Church's Alois Spisar argued that the "moral chaos" of the times had arisen, because

> Our era does not have a unified world view or conception of life and therefore does not have a unified morality or unified ethics. The modern world view does not have a solid center, a strong unifying point of support. . . . [P]eople feel that the cause of the moral disintegration lies in their heads and in their hearts, that is, in *conceptual disintegration, in the conflict of faith* and science and *in the lack of unity in philosophical thought.*[14]

For Czechoslovak Church intellectuals, the only way to reestablish a sense of moral authority in the postwar era was to educate people in "one theory of life, and a unified view of life is possible only, *only* with a unified theory, with a unified world view."[15]

Communist intellectuals rushed to fill this *Weltanschauung* vacuum. As will be discussed subsequently, the economic and social aspects of their position became enshrined in the "Czechoslovak road to socialism" only *after* the popularity of the Communist Party of Czechoslovakia had been tested and proven in the elections of 1946. Communist intellectuals, however, began to lay the crucial cultural foundation immediately after liberation. The primary elements of communist cultural argumentation—patriotism, national traditions, the progressive quality of the national character—were already in place when the directly political argumentation of the "Czechoslovak road" was formulated. It is significant that the debates over the creation of a new content for the nation's self-understanding commenced *before* the Communist Party's discussion of a "Czechoslovak road." The acceptance that the communist interpretations received played a role in the Communist Party's election victory and certainly made natural and plausible the party's adoption of a political strategy calling for a calm and parliamentary road to socialism. Communist intellectuals' public calls for a rethinking of the essence of the Czech character began at the moment of liberation. Less than three weeks after his return to Czechoslovakia from his Moscow exile, the new Communist Minister of Education and Culture Zdeněk Nejedlý declared: "The years just past . . . force a revision of the conceptions of our national character."[16] He was immediately followed in the party's leading theoretical organ, *Tvorba*, by the radical young theater critic Jiří Hájek, who argued that the experience of the war demanded that Czechs "carry out a wide and incorruptibly honest revision of all the positive and negative qualities of the Czech national character."[17] Although both of these men used the same terminology, different formulations appeared in the public pronouncements of other leading communists. For example, Minister of Information Václav Kopecký eagerly anticipated the "new era of our new Czechoslovak culture," and *Tvorba* editor Ladislav Štoll inaugurated the new *Nová mysl* with a call for "a critical revision of everything that seemed stable for ages. . . . a great revaluation of all values."[18] This proliferation of terms indicates that there was no pre-formulated Communist strategy dictated by the political leadership. Rather, many Communist and left-wing Social Democratic intellectuals desired to recreate the Czech self-conception, believed it was necessary, and were searching for a manner in which to portray their aim.

This reinterpretation developed through the years of the "struggle for the soul of the nation," and became more strident after the Communist Party's election victory in 1946 and the subsequent announcement of the "Czechoslovak road to socialism." In this respect, the Two-Year Plan of late 1946, seen as one of the linchpins of the political strategy, was interpreted by Gustav Bareš as changing "not only the economy, but also social relations, morality and people themselves." Further, by the labor expended toward its fulfillment "the thought and spiritual life of the nation are being reshaped. Here *a new national character is being fashioned.*"[19] In order for radical social transformation to be politically possible, winning the hearts and minds of the Czech people was crucial. Here the importance of the broadly construed intellectual caste cannot be understated, and the Communist Party maintained its commitment to intellectuals and ideas throughout the period. Even as late as January 1948, Václav Kopecký assigned communist intellectuals the following task:

> To create, to formulate, and to validate among the widest masses the ideology of the new Czechoslovakia. . . . The ideology of the new Czechoslovakia will be the ideology of the new People's Democratic republic and the ideology of transition on the road from capitalism to socialism.[20]

These ideological commitments directly corresponded to the "Czechoslovak road" political strategy, emphasizing the importance of the People's Democracy and the evolutionary, rather than revolutionary, character of Czechoslovak developments.

A few words here are necessary concerning what communist cultural leaders claimed *not* to intend by their new conceptualization of the Czech character. Even the demagogic Václav Kopecký was careful to avoid laying himself open to the charge that the communists wanted nothing more than the wholesale transplantation of Soviet culture onto Czech and Slovak consciousness:

> *We do not want merely to imitate someone else's culture. Our task is to create our own, Czech* and *Czechoslovak* culture, and create it as the culture of a *new Czechoslovakia*. What will this culture be? Not socialist in its content, but corresponding to the new creation we are now building in the republic. . . . Our new culture, the culture of the new Czechoslovakia, should be national in form, and in content democratic, from the people, and progressive.[21]

Communist intellectuals repeatedly emphasized that they aimed at the creation of a truly national culture, one "that on the one hand reflects the nation, its character, history and aspirations, and on the other hand acts on the nation, forms it and teaches it how to understand itself."[22] In keeping with the Communist Party's softer postwar face, this task would not be accomplished by mimicking methods applied in the Soviet Union. Rather, communist intellectuals proclaimed themselves in favor of "the tactics of explaining and convincing, not for police methods. . . . the tactics of schooling and thorough work in ideas and education."[23]

The concept common to all of these formulations was the nation. The "truly national culture," the "renaissance of national culture," and so forth implied taking cultural life out of the hands of elitist capitalists and transferring it to a wider society led by the working class. More importantly, alongside their reinvention of the nation, Communist intellectuals were also reinventing their party, refashioning it as a patriotic, at times even nationalist party. This reinvention was absolutely essential if the party intended to achieve electoral success, because of the wave of nationalism that swept over Czechoslovakia after the war. This nationalism was primarily negative, directed against Germans, both those in the destroyed Third Reich and those ethnically German citizens of the Czechoslovak Republic. The virulence of Czech anti-Germanism may have arisen from their less than illustrious resistance record, coupled with the needs of compensating for the humiliations of Munich and occupation. In this respect, the cause of communism derived great advantage from the Soviet Union's absence at Munich and its early assent to the expulsion of the German population, and from the constant reiteration from all political quarters that the alliance with the USSR constituted the bulwark against any German revanchism.

Communist intellectuals' drive to attune the party's image to Czechs' nationalist sentiment had first to overcome the roadblock of the movement's ideological internationalism. They achieved this through differing styles of argumentation. Often they used pure demagogy, as when Václav Kopecký claimed that communists "never understood internationalism" in a way that would allow Germans to overrun Slavs.[24] They also often employed a fair bit of obfuscation, such as the usually clear Zdeněk Nejedlý's statement that "every true communist is an internationalist, but internationalism is not anationalism [*beznárodnost*], with which people still confuse it. If I want to be international, I must on the contrary also be national, even if not nationalistic."[25] Finally, in late 1947 came a clear argument, when *Tvorba* argued that "patriotism and internationalism are merely two sides of the same coin." The author held that there was no way to help people around the world in the service of the great idea of socialism if one did not help those close to oneself. Conversely, one could not love one's nation if one did not love all people and work for the progress of all humanity. The conclusion of such reasoning was obvious:

> That is why a person who loves and cares about his nation and about the people is—in the interests of the nation and of the people—an uncompromising warrior against capitalism, is a builder of socialism, is an internationalist, is a patriot.[26]

With this contradiction at least rhetorically resolved, communist intellectuals were free to proclaim themselves the vanguard of "*the new Czechoslovak patriotism*, in the front for freedom, democracy, peace and progress!"[27] In addition to the main task of building socialism, the content of this new patriotism included correctly learning the lessons of Munich and World War II, reinterpreting the interwar republic while maintaining the stature of its still-revered head Tomáš G. Masaryk, and reorienting the nation's culture eastwards. As proof of their patriotism, the Communists constantly stressed their party's wartime service, formulating it partly in terms of the struggle against a fascism understood as the final stage of imperialist capitalism. However, they also continually reminded the public that "25,000 Members of the Party Sacrificed Their Lives for the Freedom of the Nation," and that Communists had shown their "deep love for the nation in the most critical times, at Munich and in the Second World War."[28] Further, they used the gifts of hundreds of thousands of hours of labor by party members in the physical reconstruction of the republic as a sign of their devotion to the homeland.[29] Finally, they stressed their hatred of collaborators, demanding the harshest sentences against those brought before the courts.[30]

Politically engaged noncommunist intellectuals were unsure how to respond to this communist self-representation. While some tried to paint communism as inherently "un-Czech," others, particularly in light of the massive influx of members to the party, were more sanguine about the party's reinvention. Even Ferdinand Peroutka expressed his openness to the party by attempting to allay the fears of those who saw the Communist Party as an enemy, rather than as a political opponent: "If the qualities of the Czech people are good, do not fear. They will have an effect inside the Communist Party. . . . We are who we are, and things will turn out in accordance with who we are. Still, we must always remember that by this 'we' it is necessary to understand also the Communists."[31]

Many leading democratic socialist politicians both publicly and privately expressed their—in hindsight perhaps shocking—convictions that the Communist Party leadership was composed of patriotic Czechs. Some of these expressions may have been prompted by a desire to keep the communists in the National Front fold by reassuring them that they were integral to the political life of the nation, or alternatively by a desire to reassure the Western Allies that Czechoslovakia was still a reliable partner.[32] Nonetheless, these statements could only reinforce the communist propaganda offensive. More worrying are similar sentiments expressed in *private* by leading anticommunist political actors. For example, Robert Bruce Lockhart, a British diplomat with long experience in Czechoslovak affairs who was a good friend of Foreign Minister Jan Masaryk, describes President Beneš as saying to him in May of 1947 that Klement Gottwald was a "man who believed in parliamentary democracy." Lockhart was similarly perturbed that Beneš and Masaryk were convinced that "Czech Communists were not [like] other Communists," a common feeling according to many sources.[33] Hugh Seton-Watson reported, after a visit to the country in 1947, that "it was widely believed among non-Communist Czechs at this time that Gottwald, a man of personal amiability, was 'more Czech than Communist.'" Josef Korbel, the non-Communist ambassador to Yugoslavia, later pointed out that "the idea that Czechoslovak communists were first of all Czechoslovaks, and only secondarily communists, gained credence. Some people began to say that these people were not really communists at all."[34] The electoral victory of the Communist Party in 1946 was in large measure attributed to its success in recreating itself as the most patriotic party.[35] That even experienced political leaders believed the communist reinvention stands as proof of its plausibility. It also reveals a disconcerting willingness to overlook the party's problematic factual past in favor of its cooperative, but as yet hypothetical, future.

Although the communist reinvention of the nation took on many aspects, one of its primary foci was the reinterpretation of the meaning of Czech history. History and its interpretation have always played a remarkable role in Czech culture. This was recognized with particular acuity by communist intellectuals like Gustav Bareš, who noted that even "foreigners who come to our country stress *historicism* as the marked feature of the Czech character."[36] Zdeněk Nejedlý, in an influential article entitled "History and Its Meaning for Us," noted that "among the Czechs there has never been a *more national* discipline than history."[37] This view was not limited to communists commencing a wholesale reinterpretation of the nation's history, nor was history important only to historians. This was argued most directly and eloquently by the Roman Catholic commentator František Marek, in a view worthy of lengthy citation:

A strong historicism flows in us partly from a wealthy and glorious history and partly from anxiety about our existence. . . . That is why the position of historians was always somewhat exceptional in our land, that is why the struggles over the interpretation of historical periods were so intense and were not settled only among experts, but with the participation of the whole nation. As the recent congress [of historians] showed, history has not ceased to be politics. . . . The struggle for the present and for the future, the struggle for the soul of the Czechs does not take place in sociology, or philosophy, or in any field of scholarship other than history: *the struggle for the future manifests itself among us above all as a struggle over the past*. . . . A nation with a strongly acting history and with such a strong weight of historicism constantly looks over its history for instruction for the future and tries to continue following the most authentic elements of its history. In such a nation, the politician will always take pains to refer to the hallowed names of the national history and attribute his ideas to them in some form. He will say to the nation that the ideas that serve him have ancient indigenous roots, that they were part of the striving of the nation in its most glorious eras, for example in Hussitism, and that therefore it is necessary to adopt them.[38]

This passage reveals precisely why the communist reinterpretation was so crucial, and describes one of the primary methods communist intellectuals employed in achieving their large measure of success in reframing the meaning of the nation.

The communist reinterpretation of the Czech past was wide-ranging and complete, beginning with the introduction of Christianity in the ninth century and concentrating on the interpretation of the crucial years of the interwar republic and the Second World War. In this history, communist intellectuals traced one thread running through the centuries: socialism. Thus, the editor-in-chief of the trade union daily, *Práce*, argued that "revolutionary socialism grew from the needs of the nation. . . . it is an essential part of the nation's currents of thought, it is its acme and fulfillment." Foreshadowing the as yet unformulated "Czechoslovak road," he maintained that despite the existence of the USSR, "Czech scientific socialism, provably pure Czech socialism, not only grows from our soil . . . [and] does not flirt with foreign models, but applies the universal foundations of scientific socialism to the specifically Czech conditions."[39]

The classic text of this reinterpretation was Zdeněk Nejedlý's *Communists: The Inheritors of the Great Traditions of the Czech Nation*. Nejedlý made the argument not only that the lower classes were the bearers of the national traditions of "democratism, progressivism and revolution," but also and more importantly that the postwar Communist Party was the final product of a glorious tradition stretching back through the centuries. As such, Communists were the logical choice to carry the national traditions into the future:

> [There is] a common line that runs through and links these historical elements and phenomena in one chain, from the lesser nobility in the Middle Ages, through the Hussite peasant and artisan and the national awakeners, up to today's proletariat.[40] . . . We, Czech communists . . . are *the most recent phase* in this development of the nation. . . . All this is therefore no chance occurrence, nor is it or can it be only some kind of mask. It is . . . deeply historically logical that precisely the communists feel so nationally close to our people. . . . We truly are the continuers and inheritors of the best and most national strivings and yearnings of the popular layers—and therefore the best elements—of our nation.[41]

Communists invoked variations on this argument frequently throughout the immediate postwar period, an era in which the use of national traditions as political argument reached a crescendo. For example, the postwar expulsion of the Germans and the redistribution of their lands was conceived as the overturning of the 1620 Battle of White Mountain, which had resulted in the destruction of the Czech nobility and its widespread replacement by nobles loyal to the Austrian Habsburgs. Similarly, school reform was carried out under the banner of the seventeenth-century bishop and educator Komenský (Comenius). As 1948 approached, the question of national traditions came increasingly to the fore, since that year was to see the celebration of many anniversaries laden with meaning: the 600th anniversary of the founding of Prague's Charles University, the 100th anniversaries of both the first All-Slav Congress (held in Prague) and the revolution of 1848, the thirtieth anniversary of the founding of an independent Czechoslovakia, and the tenth anniversary of the Munich Accords. Moreover, with these anniversaries looming, there was an election campaign in progress. By January 1948, Zdeněk Nejedlý felt confident enough in the power of the communist historical argument to imply that it would form the foundation of for the Communist Party's campaign.[42]

While communist intellectuals comprehensively reconsidered the national heritage, their debates with their noncommunist opponents focused on the recent past. Nonetheless, even the distant past was employed in the drive to secure political victory. Paradigmatic in this regard is the age of Jan Hus, the fifteenth-century religious reformer whose preaching and martyrdom led to a series of religious wars. He was, and still is, considered the greatest of the Czechs (with his only possible competition coming from Tomáš G. Masaryk) and his era has always been considered by his nation as among the high points, if not *the* high point, of its history. In 1946, the Hussite era ranked first in a survey of the "most glorious" periods of Czech history, followed closely by the reign of the fourteenth-century King Charles IV and, perhaps surprisingly to many today, "the present time." In the same survey, Hus himself ranked third on the table of figures the Czechs esteemed most, behind only Masaryk and President Beneš.[43]

Hus nurtured the reformist ideas of John Wycliffe, preaching against indulgences and other Church abuses, and served as dean of the philosophical faculty of Charles University. His spirited reformism gained much support from Prague's Czech population and especially among Czech university students, who coupled protest against the Church with national demands springing from their minority position on the university's decision-making bodies. The contemporary king, Václav IV, granted the Czechs' university demands in a 1409 speech in Kutná hora, resulting in the exodus of 1,200 ethnically German students, a move that contributed to the ethnic isolation of the reform movement. The movement was further boosted when the pope interdicted all religious services in Prague until Hus stepped down. Hus went to the countryside, where his demands found support from the Czech peasantry. His actual doctrine, however, was not exceedingly radical, and he never advocated a complete break with the Roman Catholic Church. Hus became a martyr for the cause of reform after the Council of Constance declared him a heretic and ordered him burned at the stake in 1415. Discontent across the land increased until Hus's followers stormed Prague in 1419, and King Václav called for military aid against the Hussite forces. The Hussites' demands, which were primarily religious, were condensed into the Four Articles of Prague, which demanded the free preaching of the Gospels (against priestly privilege), the right of all to take communion in both kinds (bread and wine, later conceded by the Vatican), the condemnation of the inquisition and the sale of indulgences, and the Church's relinquishing of its worldly holdings. A series of wars were fought from this time until papal forces and their moderate Hussite allies decisively defeated the radical Hussite "soldiers of God" in the 1434 Battle of Lipany. One center of the movement was the Bohemian town of Tábor, which was the seat of the Hussite military leader Jan Žižka and became a sort of commune, with residents required to surrender all their money and valuables upon entrance.[44]

If the communists were to be successful in reinventing the Czech nation and placing themselves at the end of a glorious tradition, the Hussite movement had to be incorporated in their reconfiguration. Even they considered Hussitism "the fount of not only our national history, but also of our national character and traditions."[45] Toward this end there was no shortage of historical material, and communist intellectuals focused their reinterpretation on a few core issues. Most crucially, and in keeping with their rebirth as convinced Czech patriots, they stressed the nationalist aspects of the Hussite struggle. This had two components: an anti-German one and a Slavic one that dovetailed with their desire to reorient the nation toward the east. King Václav's Kutná hora decrees received special attention, and the Hussites' largely Czech ethnicity was made salient. Because Hus had supposedly confronted "German imperialism," *Tvorba* editor Ladislav Štoll cast him as "the head of a powerful Czech national revolutionary movement."[46] A comparison of the Hussite times with the war just concluded became similarly prominent, as the Hussite struggle was seen as finding "its recapitulation in the struggle of the Czech Communists with Nazism."[47] This use of the war opened space for unsubstantiated claims that "in its spirit, Hussitism was Slavic."[48] Zdeněk Nejedlý cleverly derived from this that the Czechs greeted the Red Army as "not only liberators, but as some kind of new 'soldiers of God.'"[49] This link to the Slavic east was greatly reinforced by a chronological coincidence that placed the national holiday for Jan Hus on the same day as the 1946 and 1947 celebrations of Slavic brotherhood. Further, communist intellectuals characterized Hus as "the first modern *revolutionary*" and understood his movement as primarily social rather than religious, even as "the first people's democratic revolution."[50] For them, although Hussitism was "in its form a religious reformation . . . in its content it was a social revolution. . . . A struggle for the social equality of all people, for a new social order against oppression."[51] The communists stressed the worldly demands of the movement and the social makeup of its supporters, who came largely from "the people": peasants and small-town dwellers.

Finally, in conjunction with the reinterpretation of the Hussite movement as social-revolutionary, the communists highlighted the socially radical Tábor faction and the Hussites' military leader, Jan Žižka. In Zdeněk Nejedlý's formulation, Tábor was "democratic politically, . . . socially, . . . and economically (private property was abolished in it, and property communism—admittedly utopian, but still communism—was introduced)."[52] The Táborites were to be considered the most consistent in the Hussite camp because of their social radicalism, a view that also had a wartime analogue. Hus's slogan that "truth will prevail" traditionally had been seen as testifying to the moral and spiritual, rather than physical and military, character of Czech strength. Communist intellectuals urged the nation to maintain its commitment to the truth (their truth, as revealed in scientific socialism), but in the wake of a war in which the strength of Czechoslovakia's great ally the USSR was seen as the decisive force, this element of the Czech character needed revision. Nejedlý attempted to persuade the nation that "truth is not enough, if there is not the strength to protect and defend it. That Hus alone does not suffice, Žižka is also necessary, for only the two together yield a victorious truth."[53]

The communist brain trust was certainly capable of explaining the consequences of this interpretation of Hus, Žižka, and their era to the nation. In its view, the movement was primarily social, even socialist, and therefore the communists were the logical and consistent inheritors of its tradition. The

Hussite conflict with Rome and its allies was "a struggle for the oppressed against the oppressors and a struggle against the old, wicked order for a better new order—a struggle that in new forms we [communists] are leading today."[54] For Nejedlý, Hus had instilled the spirit of revolution in the Czech nation. He went the furthest in trying to remove Hus from the religious tradition and place him at the service of the party, claiming that

> It is therefore absolutely ahistorical to think that Hus would today . . . be in any way a theologian. Today Hus would be the head of a political party. . . . And his party would be very close—about this we can be certain—to us Communists.[55]

Czech communist intellectuals gained valuable support for this reinterpretation from the rapidly growing Czechoslovak Church, whose million-member faith had particular stake in the political use of the Hussite movement. Growing out of the "Los von Rom" movement, its anti-Catholic stance had been sharpened by the wartime Protectorate's symbolic use of the Catholic Saint Václav. Furthermore, the Czechoslovak Church's socially radical position made the communist view of Hus more than acceptable to its intellectual leadership. Václav Lorenc agreed that the stress traditionally laid on spiritual and conceptual aspects of Hus's teachings had led to a distortion of the epoch's true meaning:

> The overwhelming majority of historians, and scholars in general who have been engaged in the evaluation of the Hussite revolution, have seen only one side of it, that is the ideas. They have interpreted the Hussite revolution as a purely religious movement, in some cases as ethnic. This manner of valuation . . . has clouded the view of the real social forces that in their totality made up the Hussite revolution. . . . [It concerned] much more than only the rectification of the *church* administration, for them it was about the reform of the *entire* society. We strive to present the Hussite revolution in its full, that is, its social, extent.[56]

The Czechoslovak Church was quick to learn the lessons of this reinterpretation. In a book in which he viewed the whole of Czech history through the prism of the Hussite movement, František Roháč concluded that Nejedlý's assessment of what Hus's political sympathies would have been were he to have been alive presently was correct. The movement's "*revolutionary character*" made it clear "where Hus would stand and what he would do if he were with us today."[57] This view was shared by Lorenc, who commented on the similarity between the Hussite era and contemporary times:

> Just as we are witnessing today the deep crisis of the capitalist order, in that time the era was characterized by the deep crisis of the feudal order. . . . It is our moral duty to stress clearly the social content and the social consequences of the Hussite revolution. . . . [We must] defend ourselves against the representatives of the exploitative capitalist order, which is no less cruel and despotic than was the Roman Catholic Church.[58]

Although for understandable reasons Roman Catholics stayed out of the discussion of Hus and his times, other representatives of the democratic forces attempted to keep the communists from politically monopolizing the Hussite movement. In this they had the opportunity to rely on the quintessential authority of Tomáš G. Masaryk. In his study of Hussitism, he argued that the Czech Reformation was "above all and in the first order religious," and argued directly against the view postwar communist intellectuals were attempting to inculcate:

> Never and nowhere is a *religious* movement born . . . from *national* and *economic* oppositions. *If religion is religion*, i.e., a singular and independent spiritual and cultural power, then it is not possible to derive it from another power, neither from *nationality*, nor from *economics*, nor *from anything at all other than religion.*[59]

However, democratic socialist intellectuals—either from noble conviction in the ideal of blending socialism and democracy, naiveté, or blindness—chose to adopt in large part the positions of their communist opponents. The celebrated Evangelical philosopher Jan Kozák wholly accepted the interpretive method communist intellectuals applied to the question of Hus. He argued that "we will interpret the Hussite brotherhood in a more worldly, less religious, and more economical way than this or that historian would accept," thereby tacitly rejecting scholarly discussion in favor of political expediency.[60] Similarly, another journal controlled by the National Socialist Party incorporated the anti-Germanism and unproven Slavism of the movement, writing that in the fifteenth century "the military as well as the political power of the German neighbor was greater than the Czech priests' ideal consciousness of Slavic belonging."[61] Finally, although these democratic socialists certainly filled the term with different content than their communist counterparts, they also saw the postwar People's Democracy as growing from Hus.[62]

The only defense democratic socialist intellectuals mustered was to counter the most overt and outrageous political uses of the Hussite heritage. One National Socialist commentator devoted a long article to an examination of Nejedlý's *Communists: The Inheritors of the Great Traditions of the Czech Nation*, attacking both his placement of Hus's sentiments in contemporary politics and the book's overall conception. "Nejedlý has posthumously rendered Hus an agitator for the Communist Party," he wrote, and correctly concluded that Nejedlý had "simplified history: only communists, in the past and in the present, fight against the oppressors."[63] Similarly, the National Socialist mayor of Prague condemned the communists' placing of the Tábor faction close to their own positions as both incorrect and ahistorical. He argued that while the Táborites were undoubtedly the most revolutionary element of the Hussite tradition, they were "above all 'soldiers of God,' therefore in some manner 'idealists,' in contradistinction to materialist communism," and noted that there existed "a great historical abyss between the Táborites and the communists who claim them."[64]

As is clear from this one crucial example from the distant past, non-communist intellectuals gave much ground to the Communists' aim of establishing themselves as patriotic, nationally oriented, and the dominant force in the interpretation of the Czech past. The democratic socialist intelligentsia certainly drew a line beyond which it would not support the communists' sculpting of the Czech self-understanding. Nonetheless, it also accepted many of the fundamental positions of the communist reinvention of the nation and its character, a factor that weakened its ability to resist further communist cultural encroachment and lent credence in the public mind to other communist interpretations. More significantly, by accepting aspects of communist argumentation while attempting to defend a core of values, they appeared unsure, unclear, and often in internal disagreement. The triple shock of Munich, occupation and war left the Czech public yearning for unity and certainty, and the democratic forces were able to offer only reasoned argument, compromise, and synthetic judgments. Meanwhile, Communist and left-wing Social Democratic intellectuals presented a consistent, unified view that offered the Czech public much-desired certainty. The following chapters will consider the most crucial topics in their attempted "revision of the national character." This "struggle over the soul of the nation" reached its height in the interpretation of the most recent past, including the interwar republic, Munich, and the war. The entire nation understood the political import of the way in which these events were interpreted. The success of the communist intelligentsia in forming a coherent, plausible interpretation of these years revealed a shift in how Czechs viewed themselves and their cultural orientation, as the nation was increasingly encouraged to look eastwards for cultural and political inspiration. This shift in the Czech self-understanding rendered the Communists' "Czechoslovak road to socialism" more plausible and facilitated the Communist Party's assumption of power in the critical days of February 1948. In these battles, as in the battle over Hus, communist intellectuals were aided by the backing of Protestant leaders and gained at least partial support of their democratic socialist opponents, finding consistent opposition only from the Roman Catholic intelligentsia.

5

The Battle over the Recent Past I: The Experiences of Munich and World War II

The experiences of the Munich Accords of September 1938 and the Second World War shook the pillars of the Czechs' self-conception and fostered a crisis of identity in Czech consciousness, providing fertile ground for communist intellectuals' postwar call for a wholesale "revision of the national character." The idea of "Czechoslovakism"—that Czechs and Slovaks were the component parts of one nation—had been dealt a crushing blow by the March 1939 proclamation of an independent Slovak Republic under the aegis of Nazi Germany. Further, Czechs' faith in the heritage of the interwar Czechoslovak Republic was shaken by its failure to defend the state and increasingly for its perceived social injustice. The final psychological pillar of prewar Czechoslovakia, its reliance on the Western Powers and the nation's self-identification as belonging historically and culturally to the West, was gravely damaged by the events of Munich. Finally, the liberation of the vast majority of the country by units of the Soviet armed forces played a pivotal role in raising the question of national orientation.

This examination will concentrate on several symbolic interpretations of the traumatic years of 1938–1945 that were introduced into Czech consciousness immediately after the war. The Munich Accords will be seen from the vantage point of the postwar Czech perception that they represented the culminating act in the moral and spiritual decline of the West. This view had a dual composition: the West had become so morally weak that it no longer had the strength to resist fascist aggression, and the West was determined to use Hitler's Germany to destroy the Soviet Union and the socialist promise it carried. These had as their corollary that the moral and physical strength of the Soviet Union had made it both resistant to Munich and ultimately victorious in the war. Finally, the Munich experience aggravated a sore spot in

Czechs' self-understanding: the perception of their own "smallness" (*malost*). The fact that the decisions taken in Munich were made without the participation of Czechoslovak representatives dealt a severe blow to Czech self-conceptions and aspirations.

The war and Nazi domination, in addition to the physical damage they brought, fostered certain other elements in postwar Czech political thought and behavior. Above all, the war was seen as the height of a moral and spiritual crisis, proving itself "the graveyard of the values on which Europe stood." Moreover, the relatively small scale of underground resistance activities in the wartime Protectorate of Bohemia and Moravia gave rise to the postwar fear that the nation was having difficulty in ridding itself of the stigma of collaboration. After the Communist victory in the May 1946 parliamentary elections, the impression that a servile and malleable "Protectorate mentality" had survived the war gained new importance in noncommunist rhetoric. Finally, observers across the political spectrum noted the belief that the remnants of fascist methods survived in the nation's political consciousness. This was perceived intensely by communist intellectuals, who saw fascism as the final stage of a capitalism whose eradication was part and parcel of their reinterpretation. On the other side of the political fence, democratic socialist and Roman Catholic intellectuals saw the remnants of fascism in the methods of political struggle employed by their Communist opponents. Taken as a whole, Munich and the war served as both a catalyst of, and a lever for, the communist "revision of the national character," creating the intellectual and cultural preconditions for the Communist Party's rise to total power.

The Czechoslovak Republic had not yet reached its twentieth birthday when it became the focus of an international confrontation with Nazi Germany, centering on the problem of Czechoslovakia's German minority. British envoy Lord Runciman's reprehensible visit as an ostensible mediator and President Beneš's acceptance of the Sudeten Germans' ultimatum as encapsulated in the "Carlsbad Demands" only served to spur German calls for further concessions, which were supported by the diplomatic and military might of Nazi Germany. In an atmosphere of fear over the growing possibility of war, Neville Chamberlain and Edouard Daladier met with Adolf Hitler and Benito Mussolini in Munich on 29 September 1938 in a final attempt to solve the dispute. The agreement they reached was presented as a *fait accompli* to Czechoslovak representatives, whose state was forced either to accept its conditions or be left to fight Nazi Germany alone. The latter option had become militarily hopeless after the *Anschluss* of Austria in March 1938, which had substantially lengthened the Reich's frontier with Czechoslovakia. In the event, the government in Prague accepted the Munich Accords, and the Third Reich rapidly occupied border areas inhabited by the majority of Czechoslovakia's German minority. President Beneš abdicated his post and a government responsive to the wishes of the Reich assumed power.[1]

The effects of the Munich Accords on both Czech political and cultural consciousness were searing, and Czechs have long argued for its crucial importance for the historical development of the postwar state. As Vilém Hejl has noted:

> The Munich capitulation did not mark our life only for a few years until the recognition of the Czechoslovak government in exile, until the revocation of the Munich Agreement by the Western Powers, or until the return of the president to the reestablished Czechoslovakia. . . . In the time that has passed since Munich—and it has already been five decades—we have seen that its content influenced our entire lives.[2]

Western scholars have been more cautious in their assessments of Munich's effects. This can be partially explained by the psychological nature of the long-term consequences wrought by Munich. Western scholars have concentrated primarily on political and economic developments in the postwar period and have found it difficult to plot the precise relation between Munich and the postwar Czech mood along those axes. Furthermore, many Western analyses have focused on the period 1945–1948 as if it existed in isolation from the events that preceded it. This study will argue, alongside Bohuslav Lohniský, that "the modern history of the Czech nation began to be written at Munich."[3] Further, this chapter aims to reveal the cultural and intellectual effects of Munich as expressed in the interpretive patterns of those who had experienced that trauma. Munich was the gateway to both the wartime oppression of the Protectorate and to the understandable questioning of the value of Czechs' Western friendships.[4]

The explanation most commonly given by postwar Czech intellectuals for the Western Powers' appeasement of Hitler at Munich took both moral and politicoeconomic forms. The moral explanation was undergirded by its relation to the sense of crisis perceived by many Czech intellectuals. The wider European crisis was seen as affecting only the western half of the European continent. Part of the reason for this was a certain circularity of hindsight allowing for two arguments to offer mutual support. Seen from the vantage point of 1945, because there was a moral crisis in the West in the interwar period, the West was willing to conclude an agreement with Hitler at the expense of Czechoslovakia. Simultaneously, the West's appeasement of Hitler was taken as proof of the crisis of Western European culture. Therefore, Czech intellectuals argued the matter both ways: because there was a crisis, Munich was bound to happen, and because Munich happened, there was necessarily a crisis.

This argument was made particularly frequently by the intellectual representatives of the Roman Catholic community, not surprising given their stress on the moral aspects of the crisis. The majority of Europeans, in their view, had "through weakness, negligence, dilatoriness and baseness arrived at the crime" of Munich.[5] According to *Katolík*'s Adolf Kajpr, the Western Powers revealed their "weakness toward fascism and their betrayal of the ideals of democracy" by appeasing Hitler at Munich.[6] This weakness was not understood as a short-term divergence, but rather as "a symbol of the deep crisis of the great Western democracies, a spiritual and moral crisis. . . . The visible defeats and catastrophes of these nations were already long ago decided by the invisible corrosion of faith in spiritual values and the weakening of clear understanding and judgment."[7] The abandonment of these values had made appeasement possible, and the subsequent struggle against Nazi Germany had not repaired the West's damaged moral fiber. As Pavel Tigrid pointed out, France in particular was still in the throes of a "moral-political crisis" after the war's end.[8]

The more common argument concerning the Munich events, however, condemned the Western Powers' sociopolitical motives in their dealings with Hitler. As could be expected, communist observers most frequently made this argument, but, surprisingly, commentators outside and even staunchly opposed to the Communist Party delivered it just as stridently. Even the National Front government as a whole ascribed blame for the tragedy to "world and domestic reaction."[9] Václav Lorenc, an editorialist for the Czechoslovak Church's *Český zápas*, presented one of the most shrill examples of this argumentation. His sect repeatedly proved itself the politically most radical in the Christian community and revealed its closeness to communist views in its assessment of responsibility for Munich. Lorenc argued that Munich was not the result of blindness on the part of Western leaders, but grew "organically from the fear of a Slavic, socialist Russia" and was part of an attempt to "make an anti-Russian wall out of Germany." The lesson for Czechoslovakia was simple: "The unprecedented betrayal . . . [showed] that our people have their most reliable ally in the people of Slavic Russia."[10] The fundamental components of the interpretation are revealed in these statements. The stress on Slavism was a vital element of the radical socialist attempt to reorient Czech identity toward the East and away from the Czechs' traditional self-conception as a nation nurtured on, and contributing to, Western European values and culture. Moreover, Lorenc made a powerful link between socialism and opposition to Munich. The estimation of the Soviet Union among Czechs was raised by that state's absence from the Munich proceedings and by its plausible claim that it would have fought for the integrity of Czechoslovakia had the opportunity presented itself.[11] Lorenc made the link between the Soviet Union, socialism, and the rejection of Munich explicit, writing that "world reaction (fascism was only its most perverse form) . . . reached agreement, and the war against the progressive forces of the world commenced."[12] The Czechs must continue to fight against the "men of Munich," Lorenc argued: "To spot them is easy, for they all have in common the mark of Cain that unites them: hatred of socialism."[13]

The argument that a Western European plot directed against the Soviet Union was responsible for Munich was not the exclusive preserve of communist sympathizers, however. Such argumentation had resonance even among leading noncommunists in the government. President Beneš was careful to argue neutrally that the blame for Munich and the war could not be ascribed to any one side but rather arose from "the failure to maintain solidarity" among the European nations.[14] Conversely, the National Socialist Minister of Schools and Education, Jaroslav Stránský, maintained that the Munich experience was as elementary as the "ABCs and 123s" for determining the state's future orientation towards the USSR, a state to whom, Stránský argued, the Czechs were tied not just by ethnography and geography but also by spiritual affinity.[15]

More alarmingly, the National Socialist Minister of Justice, Prokop Drtina, found himself making an argument that could have come from the pen of any leading Communist. He became embroiled in a conflict with *Rudé právo* over the policy Czechoslovakia had followed in the critical September of 1938. Maintaining that capitulation before the Accords was the only realistic course of action open to the state, he attempted to refute the claim that he was anti-Soviet by arguing that the USSR would have aided Czechoslovakia even beyond its treaty obligations. In his view, Munich was the fault of the international forces of reaction, which had hoped to divert Hitler toward the USSR by sacrificing the Czechoslovak Republic.[16] Under pressure from the communist press, he went even further, arguing that "*the military opposition of Czechoslovakia with Soviet aid would have called into being a coalition of the reactionary governments of Great Britain and especially France with Hitler and Mussolini against us.*"[17] Although this claim sounds extreme today, the fact that it was penned by a leading political opponent of the Communist Party reveals both the profound effect Munich had on Czech political consciousness and the extent of the shift away from the West toward the Soviet Union and socialism.

Views like these are representative of the vast majority of comments on Munich. There were, however, isolated attempts—primarily in the Roman Catholic press—to argue that while Munich had been a grave miscalculation on the part of the Western Powers, it was one that had been atoned for in blood. For example, Pavel Tigrid pointed out that in 1946 everyone recognized Munich was wrong, but he argued that it was a typical example of power politics and that the appeasing nations had paid the harshest price for their actions. Further, he condemned labeling Great Britain and France as reactionary, maintaining that "evil and immoral acts should be called such, not reactionary. And those, as we know, recognize neither borders nor ideologies."[18] Similarly, Adolf Kajpr noted that "the nations that agreed with [Munich] or remained silent about it" received "a horrible punishment."[19] In accord with the more widespread interpretation, *Vývoj* agreed that the USSR had been willing to fight for Czechoslovakia, although "unfortunately many contemporary politicians were more afraid of Josef Stalin than Adolf Hitler." On the other hand, it also found that "the most central moral and political meaning of Munich" was that

> It was a desperate attempt of two Western states—France and Great Britain—to turn away from war and defend peace at least for some period of time. . . . The freedom of a small nation was sacrificed and the representatives of this small nation had no say in it. It was simply a *Diktat* of the great and powerful to the small and weak. The word of a small nation meant nothing.[20]

This citation points to one of the underlying psychological effects of the Czech experience of Munich. The pain of the abandonment by their Western allies was matched by the Czechs' feeling of powerlessness and humiliation as the dismemberment of their state was decided without their participation. One of the two Czech observers at Munich related that "Mr. Chamberlain yawned without ceasing and with no show of embarrassment" as the Czechs were informed of their state's fate, adding insult to injury.[21] In fact, Adolf Kajpr argued, "perhaps the most disturbing and humiliating part of the Munich tragedy was that they met there completely without us. . . . How it hurt, how we felt our smallness as we felt the injustice of it."[22] The Czechs' understandable distress at having decisions made "about us without us" (*o nás bez nás*) was multiplied by the accent it placed on the size of their nation. As early as 1905, the future first president of Czechoslovakia, Tomáš G. Masaryk, had written a long essay entitled *The Problem of the Small Nation*, in which he argued that Czechs' obsession with their nation's smallness was detrimental to them and instructed them to rely on their spiritual strength and the humanism of their national traditions.[23] The manner by which the result of Munich was reached only intensified the "anxiety from smallness" (*strach z malosti*) that was, despite Masaryk, a facet of the national character.[24] As Václav Lorenc plaintively asked: "Does [Munich] mean . . . that we are condemned only to hopeless, passive waiting?"[25]

This sensitivity to the nation's smallness was one of the traits communist intellectuals most wanted to erase from Czech consciousness. In their call for a "revision of the national character," they found the elements of the desired Czech character in the Slavic virtues embodied by the nation's great ally, the Soviet Union. The dynamic young literary and theater critic Jiří Hájek castigated Czechs for their "constantly calculating adaptability," in which he saw "the core of the problem of our smallness." Further, he argued that:

> This hidden inferiority complex of our small nation was the source of the Protectorate psychosis that manifested itself in the idea that in this enormous worldwide struggle nothing depended on our powers, that we can—even that we must—wait and see "how it turns out," that we are merely the plaything of the powerful, that others will decide for us and about our fate.[26]

Gustav Bareš concurred with Hájek, writing that "the custom has taken root . . . to speak of the nation only as a suffering and passive object of history, and to cry over its cruel fate." Such a self-conception had grave implications for the nation, Bareš maintained:

> This weepy, passive sentimentality is not worthy of a nation that has decided to rebuild itself into a state both internally and externally more solid and stronger, relying on the Slavic nations and above all on the Russian nation, to rebuild itself into a state able to defy the surging military aggression of German imperialism and all new Munichs. . . . The nation must feel . . . that when all is said and done its fate and future lie *in its own hands*. At the same time, we must learn to distinguish between forces in the world friendly to us and those that are unfriendly.[27]

This passage reveals very important elements of the communist call for the "revision of the national character," as it both hints at the attempt to reorient the nation's cultural self-identification towards the East and employs the tragedy of Munich to further this aim. When Hájek argued for strengthening the positive aspects of the national character, he defined them as "those aspects of our character that bring us closer to the national character of the Eastern and Southern Slavs," who had shown their power and virtue during the war.[28] A further signifying characteristic is the stress placed on strength. Unlike Masaryk, who conceived of the Czech nation's power as spiritual, communists emphasized the virtues of physical strength. This view redounded to the benefit of the Soviet Union, which not only was widely perceived in the Czech lands as the true victor of the war but also was the sole remaining continental great power. The change in the relative weights placed on physical and spiritual strength can be seen plainly in a statement by Zdeněk Nejedlý. Writing in *Tvorba*, he argued that "it will be necessary to lead our nation away from the beautiful, but today unmaintainable, Enlightenment dream of the power of truth . . . to show our nation that truth is not enough if there is not also strength."[29] This mirrored his argument that the Czech nation needed not just Hus, but also the military leader Žižka.

The strength Nejedlý encouraged was found in the alliance with the Soviet Union. Its prestige had been raised not only by not taking part in the Munich conference but also and to an even greater extent by its share in the Allied victory, including its liberation of most of Czechoslovakia. After his flight into exile, the noncommunist leader Jan Stránský noted in his study of the immediate postwar period, "yesterday, calling for all proletarians to join in the last battle, [communism] lifted their hearts by the idea of the moral force which was on their side. To-day it encourages them much more by the idea of material force: the strength of the invincible Soviet Union."[30] All political currents in the nation expressed their gratitude to the Red Army and Stalin, and proclaimed their devotion to the Czechoslovak–Soviet alliance. More visibly, at public speeches and in schools pictures of President Beneš and Marshal Stalin, accompanied by the flags of their respective states, flanked the podia. This outpouring of gratitude was untempered by criticism of the occasionally reprehensible behavior of Red Army troops on Czechoslovak soil.[31]

Communist intellectuals certainly agreed that the Soviet Union's victory grew from the physical strength of that state. In contradistinction to Stránský and other democratic socialists, however, they also saw it as springing from the state's socialism and the culture that system fostered. Gustav Bareš stressed this cultural strength in arguing that it was

> the strength of progressive ideas and spiritual currents that protected human civilization and culture against the Nazi barbarians . . . and this strength defeated the Nazi enemies of culture. There is no doubt that the most powerful, most lively culture . . . is internally carried by those ideas and progressive spiritual currents that emerged victorious from the horrible burdens and tests of the last six years.[32]

Taking this argumentation a step further, Zdeněk Nejedlý argued that the war had represented not only the defeat of fascism and its ideology, "but also every other ideology and their philosophical systems. Only the materialism on which Soviet science is built survived the war victoriously."[33] Nejedlý's understanding of the war's consequences was mirrored by the renowned communist poet Vítězslav Nezval. He raised the Soviet Union's victory to the plane of philosophy, writing that it was "the great land of socialism whose truth was victorious."[34] The tacit contrast to the crisis many noncommunist intellectuals saw gripping Western nations and their democratic and liberal truths is clear.

The noncommunist opposition found it difficult to argue with such logic, given both the press restrictions stringently limiting criticism of the USSR and the gratitude felt by a large number of Czechs to their Soviet liberators. Nevertheless, it is significant to note that questioning of the particularly *socialist* preconditions for the USSR's military victory were very rare. The point most often made was that the war had not been won by the USSR alone, and that Czechs were indebted to all the Allies for their ultimate liberation. The Roman Catholic Adolf Kajpr was the most prominent speaker to raise his voice against the communist interpretation, writing, "it wasn't just followers of Marxism-Leninism who won the war. They would not have won it without the aid of others, non-Marxists. And even if we were to accept that they won it alone, that would still not be an argument for Marxism." He closed by questioning directly whether the USSR was victorious *because* of its Marxism.[35] Despite this argument, a fellow Catholic editorialist could not avoid noting that the experience of the war had "split the concepts of democracy and economic liberalism. Today it is no longer possible to place an equal sign between them. . . . Liberalism has lost its guiding idea, its ideological authority."[36] Other noncommunist voices were even less willing to contradict their political opponents. Drtina was again found among those who followed the communist line. In a striking article entitled "The Victorious Revolution and Our Victory," he argued that the war had been "the victory of the Red Army and the USSR, but also the victory of the November Revolution [i.e., the Russian Bolshevik Revolution]. . . . Whether one is a Communist or not, November seventh created the preconditions for the strength, perseverance, self-consciousness, self-sacrifice and patriotism of today's Soviet citizen."[37]

The point of these arguments is clear: the Soviet Union had proven itself the Czechs' ally in the their darkest hour at Munich, and its victory in the war was due to both its strength and its virtue. Communist, Protestant, and democratic socialist intellectuals alike perceived the West as spiritually degraded, weak before the threat of fascism, and both anti-Soviet and anti-socialist. Conversely, the Soviet Union—and this despite the Nazi-Soviet Pact[38]—was seen as resistant to fascism, willing to fight for Czechoslovak independence, and both physically and morally strong. Only Roman Catholics attempted to view Munich politically and to accord the Western Allies full credit for their share in the Axis defeat. The alliance with the USSR was the logical outgrowth of this reading of the international situation, and was praised by all, including Roman Catholic leaders. The inference had further ramifications: if the Soviet Union was the guarantor of Czechoslovak sovereignty and international solidarity, who other than its local representative, the Communist Party of Czechoslovakia, could be seen as the reliable domestic guarantor of the same national interests?

Intellectuals sympathetic to communism could reap a bountiful harvest for their attempt to revise the national character from the events of Munich and the victory of the Soviet Union. Moreover, the moral and cultural damage the war had caused to the Czech consciousness created space for their interpretations. As the Roman Catholic editorialist Marie Voříšková pointed out in a particularly elegant evocation of the harm done to the Czech mentality, the years of fighting and occupation had "scorched everything, cities, cathedrals, houses, and people and even the values by which we lived . . . What remains of the foundation of our being, the foundation of our culture?" In her view, World War II was worse than even the Thirty Years' War—which had killed between one-third and one-half of the population of Bohemia and lay ruin to much of the land—because it was "truly the graveyard of the ideas and values on which [Europe] stood."[39] The prominent Protestant theologian J. L. Hromádka, who had spent the war years in the United States, perceived the effects of the war on his countrymen in much the same way, writing during his first visit to his newly liberated homeland that the war had "shaken this society to its very *foundations*."[40]

In contrast to the First World War, which had brought Czechoslovakia into existence and was remembered in a rather heroic light, the focal point of the Second World War was the suffering of the Czech people. Only a few commentators took pains to point out that Czech losses, both material and human, had been proportionally less than those in most of the rest of Eastern and Central Europe.[41] As a whole, however, Czechs were acutely aware that Nazi racial policies had made this a war for "the defense of our bare existence."[42] The Nazis had suppressed the Czech language, considered the life blood of the nation, and then closed Czech institutions of higher learning, leading many to fear for the future of the nation. Nazi policy foresaw the extinction of the Czechs as a people, with those having "Slav" racial determinants shipped East, and those with "Aryan" characteristics assimilated.[43] In this respect, Czech intellectuals were correct to consider that in this war their nation had "stood at the abyss between being and non-being."[44]

Czech intellectuals, and particularly those opposed to the Communist Party, noted many deficiencies in the national character that they attributed to the nation's wartime experience. From the perspective of the political battle being waged between communist and noncommunist forces in the country, the discussion centered on two related conceptions: the existence of a "Protectorate mentality" engendered by six years of Nazi rule, and the notion that the virus of fascist behavior had not yet been extracted from the Czech character. The two concepts differ in having evoked two different sets of behavior patterns—the former marked by servility and adaptability, the latter by dominance and intolerance. However, they are related not only in the sense that they both arose from dealings with the Nazi occupiers, but also because they constituted flaws that made it easier for the Communist Party and its sympathizers to dominate the field of discourse.

Communist intellectuals found little in the "Protectorate mentality" to criticize, holding that only collaborators, not true patriots (i.e., Communists), could suffer from such a defect. They followed the dual strategy of casting the bourgeoisie as the bearers of collaboration (and hence also those who would suffer from the "Protectorate mentality") and praising the Czech people—Communist-led, of course—for waiting to resist until the war had virtually reached its end. The Marxist philosopher Arnošt Kolman admitted that "six years of slavery could not pass without certain effects on the character of some Czechs," but praised the "deliberation" of the Czech character. This had kept the nation from "giving itself over to open struggle . . . [leading it to] calmly wait for the end and thereby preserving much of the national strength." Despite the years of passive waiting, "the overwhelming majority of the Czech nation did not lose its earlier character. . . . Therefore it will not be so difficult to rid ourselves of individual blemishes."[45] These imperfections were to be laid at the feet of the capitalist ruling class, which, in the words of Jiří Hájek, "found thousands of reasons to excuse cowardice and collaborate in good will with the enemy."[46]

In contrast, noncommunist intellectuals expressed grave concern about the effects of the Protectorate of Bohemia and Moravia on the national character, despite the political necessity of praising the nation's bravery in resistance. Their concern regarding the negative effects of the Protectorate took an expressly political nature as they attempted to come to terms with the results of the May 1946 parliamentary elections. As the noncommunist forces sought to explain—or perhaps explain away—their poorer-than-expected showing, the destructive power of the "Protectorate mentality" and its persistence in the Czech postwar political consciousness came to figure more centrally in their discourse. The fears expressed by a panel of noncommunist philosophers in early 1946 that "the purity of [Czech] democracy had been adulterated by the long years of a lack of freedom of thought and action" seemed to have been realized in the Communist electoral victory.[47] In the immediate aftermath of these elections, noncommunist observers ascribed negative qualities in Czech patterns of thinking to the experience of the war. They saw these not only as insufficiencies in the overall culture of political life, but also as specifically aiding the Communist Party. In the week after the elections, both Pavel Tigrid and Ferdinand Peroutka cited "indifference" as one of the primary traits inherited from the years of occupation. Peroutka expressed his shock that "in six years of Nazi rule people had become so indifferent" to their national traditions and to freedom itself. However, he did not see the solution in attacking the supporters of the Communist Party, rather in arguing for democratic values: "More important than fighting against the communists . . . is to convince them of the rightness of certain ideas."[48] Tigrid thought along the same lines, writing in reference to reported abuses in the Communist Party's electoral campaign that the lingering effects of the Protectorate could be witnessed in the "indifference of people to injustice and abuses, so far as they themselves are not concerned." He concluded that "the elections only showed what was apparent already: that Nazi domination did not have only economic and political consequences, but also moral ones."[49] Noncommunist critics also noted, as did the writer Bohuslav Brouk, that "it has taken us long enough after Nazi enslavement to be able to criticize anything at all. However, we have only found the courage to say that constructive criticism is criticism. . . . Real criticism is still called destructive criticism and sabotage."[50]

It was also Brouk who most strongly made the claim that the flaws that had entered the Czech character during the occupation aided the Communist Party. In Peroutka's *Dnešek*, he made one of the period's most vociferous attacks on the party, writing that

A great many people join the Communist Party and remain in it because of their defeatist, Protectorate mentality. To be sure, they came to know in the occupation how badly it goes for politically unorganized people in a state with only one party, and our Communists dream of a similar state. It is perhaps not possible to hold it against all people whose political affiliation is motivated by such reasons, for not everyone is courageous enough or values spiritual freedom more than a cushy job, a better existence. . . . It is very disturbing that German tyranny cultivated chicken-heartedness (ustrašenost) in the souls of many of our people, instead of pugnacity and opposition to dictatorship.[51]

Other writers less stridently attacked those whose "Protectorate mentality" led them to ally themselves with the communists, who, in the words of Jan Stránský, "turned the way the wind was blowing."[52] Tigrid claimed to be surprised that a "great percentage of those who voted for the communists did so for reasons of personal gain."[53] Father František Hála of the People's Party also noted the selfish "party-political interests of some individuals and groups," which he "wanted to especially stress [are] results of the Protectorate mentality, by which the Nazis corroded and weakened the national spirit, and especially that of weaker individuals, who perhaps are willing to sell their convictions for selfish reasons."[54]

The tendency to conform to the powerful, highly organized political force the Communist Party represented was only one aspect of the wartime legacy, however. As Ferdinand Peroutka noted, while Czechs had learned under the Protectorate to bend in the direction of power and "to reinvent themselves in front of the Germans," such behavior simultaneously led to the unwitting assumption of some of the qualities of fascism.[55] This had occurred despite the fact that the prewar Czech fascist movement had been miniscule, constituting no more than a sixteenth of one percent of the population.[56] All political currents held that elements of fascism remained in the Czech character after liberation. President Beneš maintained that "it will take entire generations before we are rid of it," an assessment with which other critics agreed.[57] On the political right, Pavel Tigrid urged that "we must fight . . . against the very roots of this, the greatest evil of our times—and these roots are in *us*, in our thoughts." The hard-line Communist ideologue Nejedlý similarly admonished Czechs: "We must not think that we were as immune to fascism as we told ourselves. We have more of this fascism in ourselves than we think. . . . We must destroy it also in us."[58]

Communists could easily link the task of eradicating the absorbed elements of fascism to their attempt to "revise the national character." They viewed fascism as the last, most virulent and imperialist stage of capitalism, and only by creating a Slavic and socialist Czech character and a socialist Czechoslovakia could the remnants of fascism be stamped out. The communists held that to strengthen antifascist elements in the Czech character it was necessary to learn from the socialist Soviet peoples, the strength of whose antifascist ideals had resulted in their great wartime victory. Representatives of the Czechoslovak Church, virtually always allies of communist interpretations, also adhered to this view of fascism. Lorenc, who had scathingly condemned the Western Allies for their capitulation at Munich, amply illustrated his vehemence on this topic in *Český zápas*:

> The capitalist order, which has fulfilled its historical task and is becoming a brake on further development, carried on its last struggle against the unstoppable advent of the socialist order. Fascism was consciously and intentionally summoned in order to delay the fall of capitalism. . . . We must understand the president's words about the danger the remnants of fascism still present as a call for the mobilization of all moral forces against the desires of those who are trying to turn back the wheel of history because they know that they will be removed from their privileged, exploitative, and sinful positions.[59]

Lorenc's colleagues as a body concurred in this assessment, with the Church Assembly's Resolution proclaiming that fascism "has its origin in the historical development of class society, in its necessary internal contradictions," and that "there can be no real peace" from fascism until socialism is established.[60]

In contrast, intellectuals opposed to the Communist Party took a much more nuanced view of the origins of fascism.[61] More importantly, however, they attempted to argue that it was the communists themselves who had absorbed fascist qualities most deeply by drawing parallels between their methods and aims and those of the Nazi occupiers. They usually did this tacitly, for overt expressions of similarity ran the risk of harsh recriminations from the communist press and might have been interpreted as being in contravention of the strict press laws enforced by the Communist-controlled Ministry of Information.[62] Nonetheless, in the face of the flood of virtually identical Marxist statements proclaiming fascism the most barbarous (and truest) face of capitalism, even President Beneš felt compelled to introduce an element of evenhandedness into the debate, arguing that

> It is only a small step from good, old-time conservatism to fascism. And in view of the fact that Nazism and fascism took over many socialist features, just a few steps from some varieties of socialism or communism are sufficient to lead to the Nazi totalitarianism that was realized in Germany.[63]

Instances such as this will be discussed in more detail when democratic socialist and Roman Catholic responses to socialism and communism are examined. Postponing the discussion of this subject is most appropriate because it concerns criticisms of Communist political activity, not fascism, its origin, its development or its methods. Roman Catholics in particular were neither hesitant to link Nazi and Communist Party methods nor reluctant to elaborate a theory of totalitarianism that criticized the potential shape of socialist society. In the democratic socialist camp, however, such criticisms were rare before the 1946 elections and remained infrequent thereafter, although references to totalitarianism became more common.

This may have been the case because democratic socialists were, relative to Roman Catholics, more willing to believe that the Communist Party had undergone a radical change during the war. Further, as the National Front declaration shows, the three socialist parties were united in the belief that fascism had sprung from a capitalism they all rejected. Therefore, not only was it a logical contradiction to see fascist qualities among Marxists but, furthermore, the argument on fascism's origins provided democratic socialists with ammunition against oppressive capitalism. Finally, and most importantly, the arguments that democratic socialists adopted regarding other elements of the interpretation of the war had made it clear that they accepted the oppositions USSR/Germany and communism/fascism. The recognition of the sacrifices of the communist resistance, the moral value placed on the USSR's absence from Munich, and the Soviet Union's ultimate victory all made the equating of fascism and communism close to an intellectual impossibility.

In the eyes of many Czech intellectuals, the experiences of Munich and the war had truly been "the graveyard of European values." In their view, these events had placed the Czech nation at what the Protestant theologian František Hník called "a crossroads of ages. . . . we have been forced by our recent experiences into the retesting of all certainties."[64] For communist intellectuals, the Western betrayal at Munich and the glorious victory of the socialist Soviet Union made not only the retesting but also the revaluation of prewar certainties a necessity. Their call for "the revision of the national character" aimed at replacing the Czech prewar conception of their nation as one nurtured by, sharing in, and contributing to Western European cultural, political, and social development with a new Slavic and socialist identity, based on the model of the victorious Soviet Union. They held, with the poet and chairman of the Association of Czech Writers František Halas, that the experiences of 1938–1945 were "waiting for the purification of socialism, for its love and moral force."[65] In order to shift the locus of Czech self-conception and value orientation to the east, however, communist intellectuals and those sympathetic to them first had either to rebut or to assimilate the values with which Czechs had entered the war. This meant confronting the prewar Czechoslovak Republic and the towering figure of Tomáš G. Masaryk, the state's first president and an enduring national symbol.

6

The Battle over the Recent Past II: The First Republic and Tomáš G. Masaryk

By almost any standard of judgment, the interwar Czechoslovak Republic was an at least moderately successful state. From its inception at the close of the First World War until its demise as a result of the Munich Accords, the "First Republic" was, in the words of Joseph Rothschild, "the most prosperous, progressive and democratic state of East Central Europe."[1] While certainly not perfect, it became an island of relative democracy and stability in the region until the Great Depression and the rise of Nazism sowed the seeds of its destruction by inflaming ethnic and national discord. The Czech lands had been the most industrialized region in the Austro-Hungarian Empire, and provided the foundation for an economy that became the world's tenth largest. The republic's excellent educational system was reflected in the high level of literacy (almost 96 percent of those over ten years of age were literate in 1930) and the state's large pool of skilled labor. Its progressive social policy was anchored by legislation mandating, among others, the eight-hour day, unemployment insurance, protection of women and children, family allowances, holidays with pay, and housing and agrarian reform. On the international stage Czechoslovakia was a loyal member of the League of Nations and a military ally of France and, later, the Soviet Union. Its fall at Munich, wrote Hugh Seton-Watson, "was not only a strategical but a moral loss to all of Europe."[2]

The following examination of views of the First Republic and its founding father and leading personality, Tomáš G. Masaryk, will show one aspect of the way in which Czech attitudes changed during the war. It will also reveal how successful communist intellectuals were in effecting their claim to be the logical inheritors of the nation's glorious history. Communist Party intellectuals and those sympathetic to them viewed the First Republic as at best a necessary failure that provided the foundation for a national state but failed to achieve socialism. At the same time, however, they strove to claim Masaryk's legacy by portraying him as a heroic ally of the working class and a forerunner of their socialist ideas, despite his sometimes biting criticisms of Marx. By doing this, they attempted to deny the era, while at the same time assuming the mantle of the man universally regarded as its personification. The Communists were not alone in claiming to be the heirs of Masaryk's heritage, however. All political factions sought to claim Masaryk as their own, whether—as an editorialist for the Roman Catholic *Obzory* pointed out— their world views corresponded with his (as was perhaps closest to the truth for the National Socialist Party) or not (as was the case with the Communists).[3]

Throughout most of the interwar period the Communist Party considered Czechoslovak democracy a sham, a mere mask for the exploitation of the working class by the bourgeoisie. Despite the party's support at the ballot box, which regularly placed it among the four strongest parties in the country, the Communists remained in firm opposition. In the republic's final years, however, with the Nazi threat looming and the Comintern's announcement of the "Popular Front," the party came to the defense of the republic. The road for this was made considerably clearer by the conclusion of Czechoslovakia's pact of mutual assistance with the USSR, signed in 1935. From that time onward, the state and its democratic system of government became worth defending for the Communists, and they remained its supporters until its end at Munich. In the aftermath of the war, however, the desire to build a socialist state required the Communists to resume their critical views of the First Republic. Although many of their criticisms are typical of Stalinist attacks on "bourgeois democratic" systems, a few representative examples culled primarily from the Central Committee's *Tvorba* clarify the particulars of the Czech case. The First Republic's reforms, which had ranged from land reform to social welfare and insurance reforms, had been characterized by some interwar political leaders as part of the republic's "growing into socialism." However, from the postwar Communist point of view, as expressed by Karel Kreibich, the question after World War I had been "simply this: either a socialist takeover, if necessary even with violence, or a fascist takeover, aggressive imperialism and a new war." According to Kreibich, the interwar republic's attempts to grow through reform had been insufficient to meet the tasks international events would place on its agenda. Further, its capitalist leadership would necessarily capitulate before fascism. The state's celebrated "humanist democracy" therefore prepared the way for fascism, and by defending capitalism the First Republic was led by its bourgeoisie inexorably to Munich.[4] This mechanical communist argument allowed for no other possibility, since the logic of history could lead the bourgeois state nowhere else: "[The Czechoslovak bourgeoisie's] class selfishness made it too short-sighted to evoke heroic acts. The only thing it could accomplish was capitulation, by which it surrendered its state and its nation's fate to German fascism over the protests of the people. With this, however, it lost its role in the nation."[5]

That the First Republic under the leadership of the bourgeoisie had been too weak to maintain the independence of the state was a common line of argument among Communists and left-wing Social Democrats. In addition, however, they pointed out that although 28 October 1918 had brought political independence, much economic power had remained in the hands of foreign capitalists. They compared this condition with that holding in the new post–World War II republic, in which the expropriation of Sudeten German property and the nationalizations proclaimed by President Beneš ensured that by 1946 the "nation controls its destiny more than ever before." Gustav Bareš argued that in the First Republic "foreign capital, and especially German or that tied to Germany, had a dominant position and decided many important matters." For him the influence of the "bankocracy and the industrial and landowner oligarchy" had two destructive manifestations: domestically the Czech great bourgeoisie was responsible for "the millions of unemployed," while in the international arena its betrayals "reached their height in Munich and the occupation."[6]

Bareš found trenchant support from Jiří Hájek, who borrowed Masaryk's term to argue that the nation had been abandoned by the failure to "de-Austrianize." True democracy—"the appeal to broad segments of the people to participate in the administration, the economy and the creation of national history"—was therefore not realized. He also made the similar although more sophisticated argument that the Great Powers after World War I had wanted no changes in European social arrangements, such that economic sources remained in the same hands as in the late Austro-Hungarian Empire. Since these were driven by profit and not by ties to the nation, they were ultimately bound to end in defeat. As he pointedly, and not without merit, argued: "For the securing of our geographic foundation against German and Hungarian revisionist pressure our democracy had to pay by participation in securing the society against revolutionary pressures."[7] The poet and professor of Russian literature Bohumil Mathesius enlarged on this, with a caustic and dramatic formulation: "Our culture in the golden age of the Czech bourgeoisie was built on poverty and suffering."

The charge that the interwar republic was distant from "the people," so often a part of communist rhetoric, was not aimed solely at the system of government, however. Even the Czech literary avant-garde, which had been prominent in its support for radical socialist causes, came in for criticism. For example, the leftist intelligentsia of the interwar period was subjected to harsh criticism in an unusually long letter to the editor in *Tvorba*, which argued that "by its mentality, customs and economic condition it was a bourgeois intelligentsia, a liberal one that through considerable spiritual schooling taught itself to be conceptually vigorous and progressive." In this view, the bourgeois intelligentsia had learned to respect progressivism, but not to think fundamentally differently from the liberal society in which it was rooted. While the interwar left-wing intelligentsia by no means rejected socialism, it was concerned with it only theoretically, leaving it "rather an individualistic than a socialist [intelligentsia] that flirted coquettishly with socialism with its ballots."[8] Nonetheless, most communist intellectuals saw the interwar avant-garde as the brightest hope of those years. Bareš condemned all nonsocialist intellectuals from the period, maintaining that "everything in the First Republic that had artistic value was on the left, was in opposition, held a position critical of the ruling regime." Similarly, bourgeois culture was seen as co-responsible for Munich, since it was "those so-called intellectuals, those sycophants, who gave their support to each of the successive governments . . . [that] under the pressure of reaction evolved to the right and finally betrayed the republic."[9]

A final example of the types of criticisms Communists and their allies leveled against the First Republic can be seen in the comparison Jiří Hendrych makes between the moralities of pre- and postwar Czechoslovakia. In an article entitled "The Morality of Our Era," the leading Communist politician, theoretician, and member of the party's Central Committee (a post he retained until 1971), argued: "From the viewpoint of the new morality, what is moral is that which aids in the definitive defeat of the old world, the world of oppression and poverty, and helps build the new world that is rushing toward socialism." The morality of the "old world" of the First Republic had been dominated by capitalist oppression, resulting in a social culture defined by fear of unemployment and strike-breakers. The republic spawned a morality in which "anything could be bought," a weakness that eventually led to "bankers, large-scale capitalists and agrarian magnates selling our entire country" at Munich. For Hendrych, the morality of the "new world" was visibly different. He argued that since so many Communists had spent time in concentration camps, the necessity of solidarity and optimism had been more deeply impressed upon them. As evidence of the results of these experiences, he pointed to the "work brigades, gifts of working hours [to the state] and higher productivity."[10]

In response to the avalanche of communist criticism leveled against the First Republic, democratic socialist intellectuals attempted to show that the prewar republic had not been such a terrible place. This is not to say, however, that they publicly expressed a desire for its return. Even if some among them may have harbored a private yearning for a resumption of the path of development ended by Munich, the socializing spirit of the times and the logic of party-political competition made such statements impossible. In fact, even among the intellectuals most ardently opposed to the communists none openly maintained that such a revival could, or should, take place. Therefore, they often joined in the criticism of the interwar republic, although for reasons different from those of their Marxist competitors. That noncommunists proclaimed the final death of the First Republic and joined in the anti-eulogies being given at its grave caused František Weyr to wonder in the pages of *Svobodné noviny* why the admirers of the First Republic were not "only *excluded* and *shamed*, but even consistently silenced." He argued that the criticism was "so universal and consistent that it cannot be by chance." All four parties and the press paid so little attention to commemorating the deeds of the First Republic and its leading personalities (with the exception of Masaryk), Weyr noted, "that the non-party observer sometimes has the impression that he is watching some kind of plan in action."[11] Jaroslav Blažek also plaintively asked why only negative comments were heard about the First Republic; and although his view is certainly less conspiratorial, it is far more resonant. He found it to be a result of a generational divide. While the older and middle-aged generation needed no lessons on the positive aspects of the First Republic, those under twenty-five years of age could only personally recall their frightful experience of the state's final years. Their negative impressions, drawn from the Great Depression and an era of rising ethnic and international tensions, were reinforced by school policy during the occupation, when neither history nor geography had been taught in Czech schools. The closing of all Czech institutions of higher education after the demonstrations of October 1939 compounded this information deficit. The circumstances in the Protectorate led Blažek to conclude, "gaps originating this way cannot be filled and will severely hinder the political education of this generation."[12]

In general, however, democratic socialists in postwar Czechoslovakia expended little intellectual energy in attempting to salvage the political and social reputation of the First Republic. They preferred to work toward maintaining links to Masaryk's philosophical heritage, hoping thereby to defend the fundamental pillars of the interwar republic: democracy, social welfare, and the Western humanist tradition. This may seem surprising, given the exemplary record of interwar Czechoslovakia in comparison with that of her neighbors. However, democratic socialists' choice of strategy both rested upon their particularly cultural understanding of socialism and represented a tactical step necessitated by the wave of revolutionary excitement that accompanied liberation. These intellectuals, particularly in the immediate postwar months and after the Communist Party's 1946 electoral victory, were fighting a rearguard action. In order to save the spiritual essence of the First Republic, it seemed to many of them that its less socialist material features would have to be disowned.

As a result, a cult of "no return" emerged even among confirmed opponents of the Communist Party. Ferdinand Peroutka wrote an editorial in November 1945 bearing the title "There is No Return," which can be seen as archetypical of this point of view. In this essay, Peroutka writes: "After six difficult years we yearn for the return of that which was, for a return to a lost paradise. Yet here we must say that there is no return to that time, that the Third Republic in fundamental ways will differ from the First Republic. . . . Perhaps it is necessary to repeat it more sternly: It will not return." While there were definite features of Czech public life that would certainly not return, Peroutka claimed, there were others that could not be abandoned:

> In essence, these are moral and national questions. . . . No one can diverge from the Czech traditions . . . [that] contain moral principles for how people should treat one another. We sum them up under the name of humanist principles. May God grant that there will be no struggle over them!

It was these principles that the democratic socialist intelligentsia was fighting to maintain. Yet their struggle was taking place in a domestic political context flooded by radical left-wing voices. It seemed obvious that Masaryk's 1924 dictum "developments are moving to the left" had proven true; and Peroutka argued that in the epochal change "he who does not understand this will be lost and will err, in politics he will err intolerably." In such a political context, he argued, the worst position to take was one of yearning for the past. Rather than wistfully dreaming for a return to the conditions of the First Republic, Peroutka counseled Czechs to "work on the foundation as it is given."[13]

The "no return" chorus represented a widespread phenomenon, whether brought by honest sentiment or a rather colder calculation of political realities.[14] Even the pages of publications with close ties to the First Republic proved no exception. For example, the historian and editor of the Masaryk-founded journal *Naše doba*, Josef Macek, reminded readers in the first pages of the renewed journal that "we have in our memory the mistakes from which the pre-Munich democracy suffered," and argued that Czechs should continually "warn [them]selves of them" in renewing the nation's democracy.[15] He argued that the First Republic's system of proportional representation had led to governments composed of too many coalition partners, resulting in compromises satisfying no one.[16] Similarly, Karel Hrbas, writing in the daily of the Czech Legionnaires, an organization that was composed of soldiers who had fought against both the Austro-Hungarian Empire and then the Red Army (eventually controlling large portions of Siberia), saw Masarykian democracy as "the faith of our life," but also argued that "what we saw in the First Republic could never satisfy us."[17]

The understanding of the notion of democracy had so changed during the war that a return to prewar norms was unacceptable, as is evident even in the writings of President Beneš. In his *Democracy Today and Tomorrow*, Beneš argued that democracy must experience a transformation and presented an extensive argument explaining the fall of the European

democracies in the interwar period.[18] "Liberal bourgeois democracy . . .
after today's world war cannot return to its previous position," he wrote.
This was the case because interwar democracy had not proven itself capable of solving either its economic or political problems. In the economy, it
revealed that it "did not have the courage or ability to forcefully and systematically solve the main social problems and intervene more sharply in
the economic structure of modern society," while the political system was
plagued with numerous egoistic political parties, whose leaders had become oligarchic.[19]

Certainly, the criticisms leading democratic socialists directed at the First
Republic were balanced by an attempt to recognize its positive aspects.
While conscious of "everything that it lacked and what should be perfected
in it," Beneš pointed out that the First Republic was "one of the best and
most successful" European democracies of its era.[20] Peroutka, who had been
close to leading interwar politicians, was the most visible of this group. In an
attempt to stem the tide of criticism against the First Republic, he argued for
a more balanced view of both the prewar and postwar states, and tried to
link them. By presenting the postwar Third Republic as a continuation and
expansion of the interwar First Republic, Peroutka also likely aimed to temper the revolutionary surge by stressing the sense of renewal rather than of
novelty. Writing on the first anniversary of Czechoslovak independence celebrated after the liberation, he pointed out that the First Republic lived on in
the Czech nation and argued that the storm of retrospective criticism betrayed a typically Slavic character flaw: "the quality of self-laceration is not
foreign to us. How brilliantly Slavs sometimes accuse themselves and what
joy it sometimes brings them!" All of the insufficiencies of the First Republic
had been privately discussed at the time, and Czechs should "not [be] allowed to forget that we can say much good about it." In fact, Peroutka argued with a telling qualification, "in a certain sense it was the golden age of
the Czech nation." Finally, he cautioned Czechs against glorifying their present too much at the expense of ignoring their past: "we didn't arrive in the
world for the first time last May." The nation had been developing for ages,
Peroutka concluded, and it would be dangerous to consider that "everything
good had suddenly arrived among us this year for the first time."[21] Elsewhere
Peroutka related that, when asked whether he considered the First or the
Third Republic better, he had to answer that while "things are much better
now," he also had to note that "things were also much better then" than people tended to recall.

This sentiment was echoed by Roman Catholic intellectuals. Writing in the
pages of the People's Party daily, *Lidová demokracie,* Jaroslav Pavela commented that "if someone who hadn't lived in the First Republic stepped out
of the grave and heard the incessant lamenting about how bad we had it
then, he would get the idea that he could suffer only a few years of such

freedom." All states have shortcomings, Pavela argued, and he prophetically speculated that "possibly we will have complaints about the present one in a few years."[22] Other Roman Catholic commentators were less approving, however. In keeping with the Catholic view that the crisis the nation was experiencing was a result of people's distance from God, Bohdan Chudoba condemned the indifference to religion expressed by some groups in the First Republic.[23] Elsewhere he depicted the fragmentation of the sense of solidaric community (pospolitost), a result of the waning influence of the Church, as responsible for the fall of the republic, an argument echoing many noncommunists' criticisms of the fragmented party-political structure of interwar Czechoslovakia.[24]

In short, the communists' arguments on the weakness of the interwar republic largely became the interpretation of postwar Czechoslovakia. They portrayed the First Republic as a state dominated by an alliance of a foreign (i.e., German) and domestic bourgeoisie that exploited "the people" before betraying it into the hands of imperialist fascism. In the face of this onslaught, democratic socialist intellectuals—many of whom had been active in the interwar years—responded weakly. On the one hand, they urged the public to relinquish any hope of a return to the "bourgeois republic," a position whose implications we will consider in more detail in the examination of their visions of socialism. On the other hand, their primary defense of the First Republic lay in presenting the postwar Third Republic as the fulfillment of its less glorious predecessor's promise. By arguing the latter, they may have been acting to preserve the moral core of the interwar republic, but they thereby praised and legitimized a state in which their political opponents in the Communist Party played the leading role. Furthermore, here the Communists' argument that they were the logical inheritors of the best traditions of the nation found both its perfect analog and increased plausibility: the First Republic had developed into the far superior Third Republic and flawed bourgeois leadership had developed into far superior Communist leadership.

The views of Tomáš G. Masaryk, who had loomed so large in the life of the First Republic, provide a different lens on the interpretation of the prewar period. Although J. L. Hromádka recognized that the time could rightly be called "The Era of Masaryk," since he was "not only officially, but also essentially our sovereign representative personality," he also noted that there were some problems with the label. For him, its deficiency lay in the way the period "empowered so many elements of our life that consciously or unconsciously denied all for which Masaryk stood," a view foreshadowing the communist interpretation's maintenance of Masaryk as a hero, while denying much from the era traditionally given his name.[25] As his statement shows, the identification of the period with the man was sometimes seen as problematic in the postwar era. Nonetheless, all political currents scrambled to claim Masaryk as their predecessor. Masaryk's political charge and the manner in which his relationship to the state he ruled was viewed thus provided a lively field for abuse. As another Protestant, the philosopher and former Evangelical cleric J. B. Kozák, noted:

> The incorrect identification of President Masaryk with the First Republic can be committed similarly tendentiously by those who want to swim across the moat between the two republics [i.e., the First and Third] and those who yearn for some aspects of that era that are not returning. Of course, President Masaryk represented the First Republic until 1935, but it was his reflection only sometimes and partially.[26]

Czech intellectuals viewed Masaryk primarily with respect to the political benefits that could be gained from appropriating his heritage. He and other noted figures from Czech history represented for postwar activists "opportunities to caricature their programs and their statements, to dress them up for momentary interests and needs."[27]

There was some postwar concern over whether Masaryk, who died in 1937, still occupied a primary place in the pantheon of Czech heroes. This apprehension was expressed by *Svobodný zítřek* particularly with a view to the younger generation, which "lived its most important six years in war and knows nothing about Masaryk." More worryingly, there was also concern that Masaryk was alive for the older generation "only in dim memories as the liberator of the nation" and that even this generation was being "confused by both hidden and explicit attacks on Masaryk's tradition."[28] Hájek, alone among communist intellectuals, shared the double concern that Masaryk was losing real importance and being abused for purely political ends. He argued in *Tvorba* that one negative aspect of the Czech national character was its propensity for turning its heroes from the past into "cold statues" and that there was a danger that Masaryk was becoming "a bronze statue to visit once or twice a year." These visits, he wrote, were becoming little more than an opportunity for political maneuvering:

> As a rule, political preachers undertake adventurous excursions to the sacred groves with solemn orators. Around the symbols a somewhat comical whirl of political bidding occurs, the whirl of those who, in their practicality, get it into their heads that the bronze of the sacred statues could be a very appropriate object for breaking the noses of political opponents or a fitting decoration for their grimy trafficking.[29]

While the charge of political opportunism was certainly true, the concern for Masaryk's importance was just as certainly misplaced, as the intensity of the battle for claiming rights to his legacy clearly demonstrates. In a letter for the inaugural meeting of a society devoted to the study of Masaryk, in itself a sign of Masaryk's enduring importance, President Beneš maintained that

"what he meant for us during World War II is clear to all," and that the meaning of Masaryk for postwar Czechoslovakia was "*what is at stake!*"[30] Similarly, Kozák noted that Masaryk was studied diligently underground during
the occupation, and that postwar developments would show whether he had
been well understood.[31]

Clearly, the figure of Masaryk was not one whose importance to the Czech
nation communist intellectuals could simply deny, nor could they ignore him
if they intended to claim that they were "the inheritors of the best traditions
of the Czech nation." As the noncommunist editorialist Jiří Zhor noted, communist ideologists had "to incorporate the Masaryk cult into their agitation,
whether they want to or not. . . . Communists, if they do not want to come
into conflict with the soul of the Czech people, must take this fact into consideration."[32] Communists clearly recognized this, as even such an important
Communist Party ideologue as Václav Kopecký argued that while the Communists were "led by the ideas of Marx, Lenin and Stalin," they "could not
ideologically build the new Czechoslovakia without the foundation of
Masaryk."[33] The main thrust of their strategy was to include Masaryk as one
of the figures in their revision of the national history, a revision that followed
two complementary paths. On the one hand, they reinterpreted the pantheon of Czech heroes—figures such as Jan Hus, Jan Amos Komenský, Karel
Havlíček-Borovský, and F. X. Šalda—to stress the Slavism and socialism of
their achievements. On the other hand, they strove to introduce lesser-
known socialists from the nineteenth century into the main currents of Czech
history. While the more intellectually responsible Hájek could maintain that
the communists did not "want to make a socialist of [Masaryk] if we
know that he was not one," the prominent Communist poet and essayist
Lumír Čivrný was more typical. He ranted against the "ideological war" noncommunist forces were waging by "abusing" Masaryk's name:

> We cannot sit back . . . [and permit] the best figures of our history to be falsified
> and the best parts of their labors to be pushed into the background. [We will not]
> allow everything from their actions that today serves the people's democratic re-
> public to be extracted or artificially construed and then directed against the
> working people, against scientific socialism.[34]

At times, communist attempts to integrate Masaryk were unconvincing to
the point of absurdity. Such was the case with an early 1948 attempt in *Rudé
právo* to link Masaryk to the USSR because his birthday, March 7, fell on the
same day as the 1918 battle of Bachmač, the first time Czechs and Slovaks
fought on the same side as the Soviet army.[35] Most examples, however, were
plausible efforts at reconciling a thinker who had criticized Marx with a politics predicated on Marxism. Perhaps unsurprisingly, the less convincing
strategy of simply directly expropriating the right to Masaryk's heritage was
adopted by Václav Kopecký. He claimed that since Masaryk stood "opposed

to the agrarian-nationalist coalition" as had the Communist Party, "the bourgeoisie has not even the least right" to claim the former president. In fact, he maintained, "if anyone is to talk of Masaryk, it should be us."[36] He went on to criticize anticommunist "provocateurs" for attempting to use Masaryk to poison the youth against the People's Democracy. This was a repetition of a strategy he had employed earlier, when he had claimed that "all real and politically honorable students of Masaryk stand today in one rank with the people's revolutionary forces and sincerely support our new people's democratic regime" against "provocateurs," many of whom, Kopecký claimed, had "supported the Nazis."[37]

A primary strategy communist intellectuals employed in their struggle to assume Masaryk's mantle was placing emphasis on his conflict with the bourgeois establishment of the late Habsburg Empire. The foundation for this lay in the response Masaryk evoked by his leading role in two causes célèbres: the "Hilsner Affair," in which Masaryk defended a Jew accused of ritual murder, and the "Manuscript Controversy," in which Masaryk correctly maintained that supposedly ancient manuscripts invoked by Czechs in nationalist disputes with the Czech lands' Germans were forgeries. The two affairs were undoubtedly central to the creation of the vision of Masaryk as a ceaseless destroyer of illusions in the quest for truth. Communist intellectuals saw the outraged reaction in the late nineteenth century to Masaryk's stance in these two affairs as proof that "all reactionaries stand against Masaryk."[38] Notably avoiding the politically more problematic question of Masaryk's relationship to the First Republic, they portrayed him as "miles from the bourgeoisie," a man who was "above all an opponent of bourgeois humanist mythology," the latter claim baldly contradicting Masaryk's emphatic humanism.[39] They also pointed out that Masaryk's conception of Czech history, the source of much intellectual conflict around the turn of the century, opposed that of the Catholic bourgeois historian Josef Pekař (although they ignored its equally sharp opposition to the ideas of Zdeněk Nejedlý). Finally, they argued that Masaryk's *The Social Question* was a treatise whose primary purpose was the condemnation of liberal capitalism.[40]

This last point was particularly problematic and called for more delicate handling. In *The Social Question* Masaryk certainly criticized the excesses of laissez-faire capitalism, but devoted the overwhelming majority of the work to presenting an extensive critique of Marxism, a problem that communist intellectuals were forced to confront. While implicitly recognizing Masaryk's criticism, they argued that much had changed both in the interpretations of Masaryk himself and especially in the practice of Marxism since the time of *The Social Question*'s publication. Zdeněk Nejedlý admitted that Masaryk had considered Marx "overcome," but argued that the situation was far different in the mid-1940s than it had been in the late 1800s.[41] The leading Communist ideologist Ladislav Štoll similarly argued that Masaryk's criticism of

Marx had been the root of a "misunderstanding" between Masaryk and the working class. This had been inflamed when "the teachings of Marx and Engels were continued by Lenin and Stalin," leading the working class to break with Masaryk. Far from a negative event, this break showed the working class's "sincere relationship to him" and was now dialectically overcome in the harmony of the people's democratic system.[42] Vladimír Procházka more explicitly accepted Masaryk's criticisms of Marxism, but argued that the time Masaryk devoted to the study showed how seriously he took the subject. He pointed out that while it was true that Masaryk himself had no faith in the Bolshevik revolution he also wanted no interference in developments in the Soviet Union.[43] Procházka also insisted that Masaryk approved of Marx's critique of capitalism and differed only "in the manner of realizing the new, more just social order."[44]

In the desire to counter Masaryk's rejection of Marx's teachings while not disavowing Masaryk himself, Procházka's final remark hints at the most nuanced of the communist strategies. In this reading, Masaryk was exonerated of his criticisms of Marx for reasons of historical development. Having lived the majority of his life in the nineteenth century, he experienced all of society's great problems as a man of that era, "with all the typical contradictions" that accompanied it.[45] As the leading communist dramaturge E. F. Burian argued, "the life of our first president was in essence a collection of societal contradictions in one person" and his writings, not least *The Social Question*, must be seen in the context of the times in which they were written.[46] Ludmila Koutníková agreed with this assessment, noting that Masaryk could not "cross the borders of his bourgeois progressivism in the direction of social revolution, to scientific socialism, to Marxism." She excused Masaryk on the historical grounds that his "thoughts and struggle were revolutionary for that discrete developmental stage."[47] This argument was also made by the theater critic and dramaturge Jaroslav Pokorný, who recognized that Masaryk was "a personality conditioned in his ideas and activities by his times." He was a figure who was "limited to a definite role in the development of our nation" by the era in which he lived. The liberal democracy he founded, while representing "progress vis-à-vis monarchy," was nonetheless "a reactionary form in comparison with the soviets being realized in Russia at the time."[48]

Seeing Masaryk as a revolutionary, albeit one who could not fully escape his bourgeois era, allowed communist intellectuals to place him firmly on the side of progress as a heroic warrior for the working class. With more than a bit of rhetorical contortion, Masaryk could be seen as "a socialist even if he was never a socialist . . . as a result of the social function he fulfilled in Czech life."[49] Procházka argued that, despite the differences Marxists had with Masaryk over *The Social Question*, there was no doubt that he "heroically struggled for a better tomorrow, [that] he had a beautiful relationship with the workers, with whom he behaved as an equal among equals."[50] This was manifested especially in his striving for the passage of universal male suffrage in the early years of the twentieth century. Although originally he had been opposed to the idea, communist intellectuals viewed Masaryk's eventual support, in tandem with that he offered the striking miners of Kladno in 1900, as establishing Masaryk's leftist pedigree.[51]

Masaryk was not only claimed for his activities in support of the working class during his lifetime, however. He was also appropriated to support the post–World War II socialization measures. Communist commentators repeatedly maintained that were Masaryk still to be alive, he would applaud the accomplishments of the postwar People's Democracy under the leadership of the Communist Party. "If he had lived," Kopecký claimed, he would stand "with the people" and approve of the nationalization of industry and the banking system. This was the era, he crowed, in which "all [Masaryk's] ideals are being realized."[52] Procházka chimed in, asking "who could believe that he would be against our people's democratic state?"[53] The most resolute, however, was Burian, who argued that while Masaryk had laid the foundation for the Czechoslovak state in 1918, the Czech and Slovak people had fought for its true realization in May of 1945: "*Yes, T. G. Masaryk would have already at that time, in 1918, agreed with the popular measures pushed through in the national revolution of 1945.*"[54]

The success of the communist assumption of Masaryk's mantle and the depth which pro-socialist sentiment reached can be judged by their opponents' responses. Though Masaryk was undoubtedly a progressive politician, he was by no means a Marxist. Yet even while his ideas were more in harmony with those of National Socialist or right-wing Social Democratic intellectuals, these figures found it difficult to assume Masaryk's inheritance without also supporting many of the communists' arguments. This was particularly the case regarding the social foundations of the postwar People's Democracy, to whose creation and administration they had contributed. Their position was made doubly difficult by popular sympathy for the Communist Party. With an eye toward political advantage, they considered it unwise to harp too extensively on Masaryk's anti-Marxism for fear of being labeled "reactionaries," a charge that carried significant weight in the postwar era. Some, according to the essayist Robert Konečný, were even "afraid to pronounce his [Masaryk's] name from the fear that it is not a name that would have the revolutionary charge of the era."[55]

It was this kind of cowardice that concerned Ferdinand Peroutka. Politically shrewd, he recognized that "only one who is free of the suspicion of social reaction can fight in Masaryk's way for spiritual ideals." Two implications here are disturbing. The claim that only socialists could legitimately invoke the name of Masaryk excluded Roman Catholics, a step that both weakened broad-based noncommunist cooperation and buttressed communist claims to Masaryk. More troubling, however, is that the implication that one must prove oneself free from "social reaction" *before* staking a claim to Masaryk's spiritual heritage could lead to a similar strategy in the political arena. Such a strategy could mean that political concessions on the practical issues of socialism would be made in good faith in return for less tangible gains anticipated thereafter. Still, Peroutka at least asked:

> Are there those among us who will succeed similarly [to Masaryk]? Standing face to face with evil, if it should arise, will we be more cowardly than Masaryk was against the evils of his time? . . . Masaryk was an activist in every situation. One who waits until everything somehow turns out on its own, or lets others guide events, is not Masarykian. . . . As he said: "About myself I can say that I never twiddled my thumbs."[56]

Despite this call to arms, many noncommunists adopted in large part the views of their opponents, and this was true even at the highest levels of the political and intellectual establishment. Masaryk's successor Beneš was one of the leaders in this respect. In harmony with the communists' placement of Masaryk at the service of the new People's Democracy, he argued that "no one here should think that what we are doing today means any kind of departure from Masaryk. It is rather a continuation and completion of his program and his ideas . . . to their logical conclusion."[57] This argument resembles the attempt to tie the postwar republic to its prewar antecedent. Perhaps as a means of self-justification, Beneš pointed particularly to the expulsion of the Sudeten Germans (a result of his intense diplomatic lobbying of Allied governments), the first wave of nationalizations (carried out at best semi-democratically under his presidential decree), and the Communist-dominated system of national committees as measures of which Masaryk would approve.[58]

Masaryk's successor was in good company in interpreting him in a light comparable to that of the communists. This was the case with Czechoslovakia's foremost Russian historian, student of the famed Josef Pekař (to whose name the communists almost universally attached the epithet "reactionary") and former director of the Russian Archive of the Ministry of Foreign Affairs, Jan Slávik. He found fault with the argument that Masaryk denied Marxism and agreed with the Marxists' claim that developments since the time of the publication of *The Social Question* had rendered much of Masaryk's criticism invalid. "How could the bourgeoisie be happy," he wrote, when near its end *The Social Question* concludes that "even if Marxism were completely mistaken, and even if Marxists were to fully recognize this, socialism would not fall."[59] Jan Patočka similarly noted that the name of Masaryk "has a different sound than in the First Republic. It has freed itself from the officiality and veneer of liberal banalities," making the necessary "corrections" of Masaryk possible. At the same time, however, he also expressed the fear that "we are clearly somehow factually distant from Masaryk, no matter whether we judge this interval positively or negatively." He argued that the present reinterpretation of Masaryk's thought was a positive development, for it showed that the nation's "future life could not be imagined without an organic tie to him."[60] The Protestant philosopher Kozák also noted that Masaryk's ideas were open to further development. He observed in a public debate that Masaryk had experienced only early Bolshevism (a form deemed unsuitable for Czechoslovakia), and argued that the revolution begun by the 1945 Prague uprising "was not so far from Masaryk's foundations as it seemed at first," although he also hoped that the communists' newfound interest in Masaryk would help to temper their more radical views.[61]

In the view that the First Republic's "bourgeois democracy" was inherently un-Masarykian, Beneš was joined by the eminent professor of philosophy and sociology Josef Král. For Beneš, Masaryk's desire was for "a truly humanist democracy, i.e., a democracy superior to bourgeois democracy."[62] The ultimate conclusion of Masaryk's democracy lay, in Beneš's view, in a "socializing democracy," in "democracy as a political, economic and social system, a new postwar democracy—in contrast to prewar democracy—*in its present reconstruction in a socialist sense.*"[63] Král similarly saw Masaryk as "not satisfied with the common political definition of democracy," but striving for it to be understood "economically and socially, as a desire for economic and social justice, as socialization."[64]

Masaryk was undoubtedly a political progressive much in the mold of those cited here, and these statements should be understood with caution. Above all, the vision of the final shape the "socializing" state would take was unclear for these avowedly socialist, but undoubtedly noncommunist, leaders. It was, however, certainly different from that of their Marxist opponents, who looked to the USSR as at least a general model. Furthermore, the enthusiasm for socialism and the attempt to place everything good, including Masaryk, on its side was an expression of both democratic socialists' beliefs and political reality. The support for socialist measures was large, as the 80 percent of the Czech vote for the three explicitly socialist parties in the 1946 parliamentary elections witnesses.[65] Democratic socialist receptivity to more radical interpretations may have represented as much an attempt to dilute Communist Party support as an endeavor to construct a viable socialist but noncommunist ideology.

Nonetheless, two claims need to be kept in mind with respect to democratic socialists' socialism. The first holds that while the leftward tendency in their thinking was in some ways the result of the national mood in the wake of the war, it also represented in some sense its spur. The democratic socialist intelligentsia's profound faith in the moral correctness of socialism contributed greatly to propagating political support for a socialist society they defined vaguely and analyzed inadequately. All rejected bourgeois society, and the battle lines were drawn between positions all claiming to be socialist, rather than between clear-cut ideas representing a broad political spectrum. The disputes were a matter of degree but not kind, and they relied on consistency, clarity, and plausibility for gaining and maintaining political and cultural support. The second claim is related to the first in holding that the socialist rhetoric of all non-Catholic intellectual leaders had the effect of rendering Communist Party rhetoric seemingly less radical, thereby aiding that party's rise to total power. The party, as we shall see, took advantage of this by playing up its more moderate stances, which culminated in its late-1946 announcement of the "Czechoslovak road to socialism."

Much democratic socialist comment therefore sounds today as if it could have come from the pens of moderate Communist Party members. Even such a staunch opponent of the communists as Lev Sychrava was not immune. As editor-in-chief of *Národní osvobození*, Sychrava argued that Masaryk belonged equally to the East and the West, to "Western democracy" and "the history of Marxism," and that he contributed to "the Western development from liberalism to socialism and at the same time belong[ed] to the Russian Revolution." While the revolution that Masaryk led was not socialist, Sychrava admitted, "his criticisms of democracy and liberalism were socialist and today's socialism is unthinkable without him."[66] In an even more startling comment, J. B. Kozák argued that "only a blind man cannot see that a great part of the world is going with the current of new life. . . . One must be on the correct side of world change, and live and face the future, as Masaryk always did."[67] In its tacit teleology, this claim is suspiciously close to that made by the Marxist-oriented philosopher Ladislav Rieger, that Masaryk's famed humanism meant "socialism. . . . Masaryk moved forward and did not turn back. In this we will follow him."[68]

The elements of Masaryk's philosophy that all noncommunist intellectuals stressed were perfectly compatible with their brand of socialism and opposed to Marxism in their implications. Above all, they accented the former president's evolutionary, rather than revolutionary, philosophy. Even here there was occasionally deep rhetorical confusion, implying a lack of conceptual clarity. On the one hand, President Beneš pointed out that Masaryk was "a revolutionary of the spirit, who would push for a real revolution of hearts and minds." On the other hand, he stressed that Masaryk would oppose any new oppression replacing the old and any "violence or terror either spiritual or physical," because "his evolutionism played a fundamental role."[69] Josef Král similarly argued that in certain circumstances Masaryk would approve of revolution but noted pointedly that "Masaryk did not recognize continuous, or 'permanent' revolution."[70]

The fundamental difference in the manner in which communists and noncommunists interpreted Masaryk's legacy lay in the importance placed on the spiritual aspect of the question of socialism. Communist ideological maneuvering attempted to link Masaryk to the tangible political, economic, and social facets of the "building of socialism." Their emphasis on the actual socializing measures of the first postwar months, and the claim that Masaryk would have approved of both them and the people's democratic system, bore witness to this. Conversely, democratic socialists in part stressed the moral and spiritual aspects of his thought, aspects that corresponded to their cultural and moral understanding of socialism, thereby positively establishing their socialist credentials in the public mind and providing justification for their more moderate socialist aims. Negatively, they strove to defend the spiritual values they held dear (democracy, freedom of expression, and the rights of the individual) against the threat they perceived from their communist opponents. In attempting to contain the revolutionary potential of the era, noncommunists accepted the economic and social changes that had occurred in the immediate wake of the war but stressed the need for the nation to consider its preparedness for further change. In this task, Masaryk's heritage proved useful, as Vladimír Úlehla surely recognized when writing that "Masaryk often stressed, even directly warned, that such changes are only possible and successful as far as we are also prepared for them morally."[71]

Ferdinand Peroutka cautioned the Czech nation more strongly, writing that while Masaryk would see the changes that had already been made as "necessary, even desirable, and would sympathize with them in principle. . . . [He] would not cease to call attention to the fact that alongside the economic question there exists also a moral question." Peroutka recognized the irreversibility of the decision for large-scale economic and social change but warned that "in other matters the nation stands at a crossroads and must decide: humanity or something else . . . freedom or bondage? Our own national face or a borrowed mask?" He argued:

> It is consequently necessary to consider social reform a fundamental and irreversible fact. We repeat, it is possible to fight against whatever bad that happens alongside it, against it, only from Masaryk's premises, such that the one fighting will not come under the suspicion of social reaction. . . . One who wants to contribute something to public life today must implore morally. . . . Here it is most necessary to look for inspiration in Masaryk.

For Peroutka, there were only two forces that stood opposed to Masaryk's heritage: fascism and communism. Fascism had been defeated, but he argued that "much of our fate depends on how much this lively and powerful movement [i.e., communism] is willing to accept from Masaryk's heritage and how much the rest succeed in defending it."[72]

In staking this moral claim, many prominent noncommunist intellectuals cited Masaryk's strong religious grounding. His argument for democracy was based on each individual's possession of an eternal soul, which allowed noncommunist intellectuals to repeatedly stress the importance of individual freedom. Similarly, one of the primary bases of Masaryk's socialism was the tenet "Love thy neighbor," which democratic socialists used to bolster their argument for a socialism based on brotherhood across class boundaries as opposed to Marxist class antagonism.[73] Not surprisingly, the religious view of Masaryk and his socialist beliefs was particularly evident among Roman Catholic intellectuals, as the example of the *Lidová demokracie* editorialist Jan Strakoš demonstrates. In three long, front-page articles, Strakoš laid out the Catholic view of Masaryk and placed his heritage firmly in opposition to Marxist materialism. While agreeing with the generally held position that one of Masaryk's foremost achievements had been to turn Czechs intellectually away from Germany—a point often mentioned by communists in order to increase the relative importance of Russia in Czech cultural development— he saw Masaryk's value in this respect lying primarily in bringing Anglo-Saxon thought to the fore. Notably, in listing the Germans whose influence Anglo-Saxon thinkers had replaced, Strakoš places Marx near the top of the list.[74] While recognizing that Masaryk also looked toward Russia, Strakoš stressed the critical nature of his reflections. He cited Masaryk's criticism of the lack of social development in late nineteenth-century Tsarist Russia, the backwardness of the Orthodox Church, and especially Czech Russophiles' idealization of the East and the emotion and mysticism of their arguments.[75]

The Roman Catholic view, as represented by Strakoš, was closest to the democratic socialists' in its highlighting of the religious aspects of Masaryk's thinking (on which it naturally placed more emphasis) and the spiritual nature of social reform. The first of these was encapsulated in Masaryk's credo "Jesus not Caesar," which was often repeated in the writings of Catholic intellectuals.[76] Masaryk's humanist program was understood as based on the eternity of God's creation. Similarly, the foundation of his democracy was seen as a religious argument based on the individual's immortal soul, such that democracy was the political form of the principle "Love thy neighbor."[77] The rejection of radical socialism was couched in the same terms. Strakoš argued that Masaryk was always conscious of the danger posed by an orthodox Marxist doctrine that would have as its final phase the denial of individual freedom, and placed emphasis on the implications of this for spiritual life. According to Strakoš, the choice was simple: go with Masaryk or against him, "with democratic freedoms or with a totalitarian dictatorship, with Christian humanism or with materialistic egoism, with social reform or with the complete socialization of the state and the individual."[78] Not only was Marxism a totalitarian movement, but as the last clause of the citation indicates, it was the wrong way to solve the social question. "Dialectical materialism does not serve the true goals of socialism," Strakoš concluded in each of his three articles, arguing that the impulse must base its strength on "an appeal to individual conscience." Therefore, the People's Party could make the claim that with their brand of "social reformism" they *consciously acknowledge the heritage of Tomáš Masaryk.* Consequently, our program is a profession of faith in the ideals of *truth and freedom*, realized in a democracy filled by Christian spiritualism in the sphere of scholarship and art, and by solidarity in the social questions of daily life."[79]

Given that they held divergent positions on the question of socialism, it should come as no surprise that Protestant interpretations of Masaryk differed from those of their Roman Catholic counterparts. The more balanced Protestant interpretation was that of the Evangelical Church. In *Křesťanská revue*, Miloslav Trapl and presidential aide František Škarvan attempted to discern Masaryk's relationship to Marxism in order to help Evangelical Christians solve this dilemma:

> Should I, and can I, actively participate in the socialist struggle, a struggle being carried out today by the Marxist philosophy of dialectical materialism, an antireligious and consciously amoral philosophy? This is a fundamental question, on which essentially everything depends.

Škarvan praised Masaryk's *The Social Question* as "creative criticism" of Marxism from the viewpoint of "a great spirit, imbued with Christian experience," which provided "a correction to the schematism" of Marx and Engels, but at the same time he mirrored the communist view that already much had been corrected by Lenin and Stalin.[80] Trapl similarly recognized the book as "one of the sharpest expressions of [Masaryk's] criticism," but also noted that Masaryk only criticized views "that he liked, that he respected, that he considered to be important." It was impossible, according to Trapl, to deny the "essential and deep differences" between Marxist views and those of Masaryk, since the former president had denied Hegelian dialectics (which he had termed "hocus pocus") and both philosophical and historical materialism. Trapl also argued, however, that "in the criticism of historical materialism Masaryk went too far." In Trapl's judgment, "historical materialism is a sociological question, *quaestio facti*, which can be valid even without the foundation of philosophical materialism. Dialectical oppositions are a social reality." Reflecting the communist interpretation, Trapl found Stalin to have corrected Marx's teachings and pointed out that Masaryk criticized most bitingly the bolshevism he found in the first years of the Russian Revolution. The mature USSR could therefore not be held responsible for the errors of those early years. This was balanced by his concluding critique, which bears much resemblance to democratic socialist interpretations in its emphasis on the importance to Masaryk of the spiritual and moral preconditions and prerequisites for "true socialism," summed up in the slogan "Men, not Measures."[81]

Finally, Czechoslovak Church commentators interpreted Masaryk in a style commensurate with their more radical social agenda. Among the least strident was František Hník, who argued that because Masaryk was no "tool of foreign interests" (meaning the despised Germans) he was "a convinced socialist." He followed this by emphasizing Masaryk's denial of all "class, nationalist, and church imperiousness," through which he took aim both at communist exaltation of the working class and at the Roman Catholicism's wavering claim to national representation.[82] The Church's *Český zápas* took a more revolutionary view of Masaryk than even the communists. In its pages Masaryk was lauded for his prophetic vision that "the future of Europe (and Czechoslovakia in it) is possible *only* as a *socialist* future." Masaryk's objections to Marxism were viewed in a fashion that cleaved to the communist interpretation: they were "conditioned partly by the fact that Masaryk was himself a politician of the bourgeois class . . . and partly because he was president of a republic in which the bourgeois class was the leading political stratum." As a result, Masaryk's "faults" in criticizing Marxism were excused, and the communist division between the man (who was good) and the republic he presided over (dominated by the evil bourgeoisie) was maintained.[83]

The view of Masaryk as a prophet was also stressed by the founder of the Association of Religious Socialists, František Linhart, who had close ties to the Czechoslovak Church. Rather than emphasizing his core of religious beliefs, as Roman Catholic commentators had done, Linhart employed Masaryk in the service of both a religious and socialist revolution. Masaryk's conception of religion represented "a return to the prophetic type of religion, to the religion of the prophets of Israel and to the religion of Jesus, in which this religion reached its height." Further, Masaryk's prophecy represented "a new conception of religion, a revolutionary conception opposed to the traditional." The traditional conception of religion was "dualist, basing itself on the assumption of a natural, terrestrial world and a supernatural, holy world."[84] Masaryk, interpreted as a revolutionary bringing religion into closer contact with the world, thereby served the central goals of the Czechoslovak Church. He pointed the way toward the redemption of Christianity from its perceived crisis through the revitalization of faith, and provided a path leading through worldly social change that would redeem the nation from its crisis.

Several important conclusions can be drawn from the discussion of the heritage of the interwar Czechoslovak Republic and its president. Above all, communist intellectuals were largely successful in throwing the First Republic into disrepute, both for its bourgeois nature and for the weakness it revealed in connection with Munich. The latter of these had implications ranging beyond domestic political relations. Democratic socialists did little to defend the interwar republic against communist criticism. Their agreement on at least the inadequacy of the interwar republic both represented the socialist consensus of the times and helped to encourage and spread that consensus. This was also the case with the battle over Masaryk's heritage, although here Marxist intellectuals were less successful than they had been with the First Republic. Democratic socialist and Roman Catholic intellectuals mounted relatively stiff resistance to communist attempts to appropriate Masaryk. This proved the case despite the fact that the Evangelicals and especially Czechoslovak Church leaders lent much support to the Marxist view. Roman Catholics, as always, placed spiritual matters to the fore and by doing so rejected the communist assumption of Masaryk's mantle. The position of the democratic socialist intelligentsia was far more problematic. By enlisting Masaryk in the battle against "reaction" and in the cause of the "socializing" republic, and partly dissociating him from the interwar republic, they encouraged communist appropriation of him in the name of world socialism. The People's Democracy was manifestly Communist-led, and casting its institution and aims as a fulfillment of Masaryk's promise could not but aid the Communist Party in its battle to portray itself as the inheritor of his heritage. Their urge to use Masaryk—with "corrections"—to validate their hope for a synthesis of Masarykian humanist democracy and radical social reform revealed a programmatic ambiguity that did not well serve their cause.

7

The Shift in Sensibilities and Generations: May 5, 1945, versus October 28, 1918

Communist intellectuals furthered their dominant position in the understanding of the interwar First Republic and complemented the inroads they had made toward an appropriation of the heritage of its president, Tomáš G. Masaryk, by means of a two-pronged move that revealed the depth of the changes in Czech consciousness. This was aimed toward both the appropriation of Czechoslovak Independence Day, October 28th, and its replacement by May 5th. The movement will be examined here by contrasting the role October 28th played in national life and political consciousness with that played by May 5th, the new holiday commemorating the commencement of the Prague Uprising in 1945. For many Communist Party members and their intellectual allies May 5th represented the state's true independence, as the uprising rapidly transformed from an anti-German military action intending to secure the physical liberation of the nation into the first act of the "national and democratic revolution." This revolution had as its "national" component the expulsion of close to 3 million ethnic German citizens of the prewar Czechoslovak Republic and as its "democratic" component wide-ranging economic and social reforms. Young Czechs played perhaps the most important role in the attempt to replace October 28 with May 5. They conceived of themselves as a clearly determined generation whose defining moment had been the days of the uprising. As a result, radicalized young intellectuals—who had come of age during the Second World War, had little personal recollection of the pre-Depression republic, and identified themselves with the postwar "People's Democracy"—viewed May 5th as "their" holiday, in opposition to the October 28th of their elders. Conversely, noncommunist intellectuals of the older generation attempted simultaneously to confirm the social changes of the immediate postwar period and to limit the revolutionary élan expressed particularly by this generation of radicalized youths.

Communist intellectuals were greatly aided in both claiming May 5th and appropriating the established October 28th by certain chronological features peculiar to the postwar period. May 5th falls only four days after the internationally recognized Day of Labor, which was traditionally the high point of the Social Democratic and Communist calendar. Furthermore, May 9th was celebrated from 1946 as "Liberation Day," since it was on this day in 1945 that the first Soviet Army troops entered Prague.[1] This combination of holidays created a seamless web of relationships built on the solidarity of the international labor movement, the drive for national and economic self-liberation, and the final liberation by the forces of the world's only socialist state. The power this association wielded was enormous, and from the end of April through the second week of May newspapers such as the Communist Party's *Rudé právo* and the Union of Czech Youth's *Mladá fronta* presented readers with an uninterrupted stream of self-congratulatory editorializing and praise for the glorious Soviet Union.[2]

Communist intellectuals' appropriation of October 28th benefited from similar circumstances. Several important events that established the gains of the "national and democratic revolution" took place on that date in 1945 and 1946. For example, the Temporary National Assembly, the revolutionary parliament that sat until the first postwar elections in May 1946, convened for the first time on October 28, 1945, and the first nationalization decrees signed by President Edvard Beneš came into effect on the same day. The following year, on October 28, 1946, the bill enacting the postwar Czechoslovak two-year plan was signed by Beneš, and the President and Prime Minister Gottwald declared the main phase of the expulsion of the Sudeten Germans to be at an end.[3] The more radical journals of the period commemorated these events with enthusiasm, celebrating October 28th as "Nationalization Day"—its official designation throughout the period of Communist rule—as much as for its connection to the state's 1918 declaration of independence.

Lauding the recent achievements that had taken place on the anniversary of the republic's independence was by far the most common strategy communists employed in their efforts to appropriate the holiday. Klement Gottwald highlighted the significance of the recent events associated with the day in a front-page article in *Rudé právo*:

The holidays of October 28th have become important landmarks in our new state's development. The proclamation of the nationalization decrees on October 28, 1945, and the signing of the two-year plan by the President of the Republic on October 28, 1946, clearly mark advances in the construction work that we have begun in our new, free national life.[4]

Similarly, the philosopher Ladislav Rieger, in an article entitled "October 28th—The Holiday of National Construction" in the cultural weekly of the communist-dominated trade unions, *Lidová kultura*, decried the lack of "conscious meaning" the holiday had borne in the interwar First Republic and proclaimed that the two-year plan had "opened a new era in the life of our state."[5]

The stress on the two-year plan is noteworthy, for it reveals a important difference: Communist Party intellectuals and their supporters celebrated the holiday as a signpost toward future glories, while their opponents commemorated it as a recognition of the past. As Josef Smrkovský, at that time chairman of the National Land Fund but later a leader of 1968's Prague Spring reformers, pointed out, the two-year plan brought a new feeling to October 28th. It was no longer a commemoration, in the sense of occupying itself primarily with the past, but rather turned Czechs' attention to the future. "The era of merely speaking about goals and ideas is ending," Smrkovský wrote, and it was now time to realize hitherto only rhetorical ideals within the framework of the economic plan.[6] His perception was certainly correct, for the writings of noncommunist commentators showed a marked tendency toward commemoration and remembrance, while those in communist-dominated periodicals concentrated on the postwar changes and the active responsibilities these brought for the future.[7] This difference in styles was mirrored in the interpretations of several other political and economic issues. The effect was to create the impression that the radical left represented a young and vibrant force, in contrast to the traditional and occasionally formulaic statements of its democratic socialist and Roman Catholic opponents.

The communist endeavor to appropriate October 28th was complemented by moves aimed at undermining the traditional meaning of the holiday. Communists often attempted to establish a connection between the Russian Revolution and the establishment of the Czechoslovak Republic. Indeed, the National Front government as a whole had made this link already in 1945, and the slogan it used, "Without November 7th in Russia, There Would Have Been No October 28th, 1918, Here," was printed on posters and distributed widely by the Communist Party to support the argument.[8] *Rudé právo*'s editor-in-chief, Gustav Bareš, was one of the primary propagators of this line, arguing that "an independent Czechoslovakia could only originate as a concession on the part of the Western Powers to the powerful revolutionary wave accompanying the Russian Revolution."[9]

A further strategy mirrored communist intellectuals' criticisms of the First Republic by attacking the socialist credentials of October 28th. Communist intellectuals saw the day as a symbol of the quashing of the nation's true revolutionary desires by a small circle of reactionary politicians and economically powerful individuals. In this respect *Rudé právo* viewed the general strike of October 14, 1918, and the subsequent declaration of a socialist republic by the Socialist Council (which ended in failure the day it was proclaimed) as the true heritage of the birth of the republic. However, many left-socialist critics conceded that in 1918 the national question had achieved predominance over social objectives. As the Social Democratic daily *Právo lidu* noted, the insufficiencies of October 28, 1918, came about because "the revolutionary wave did not have sufficient strength, in addition to breaking the shackles of political and national bondage, also to overthrow the yoke of class oppression."[10] However, Ladislav Štoll argued that it was not merely that "the people were dazzled by freedom" that acted as a brake on the revolution. Returning to the influence of the Russian Revolution, he argued that powerful reactionary elements in Czechoslovakia "keenly felt the earthquake, the shifting of the social ground that another, *living revolution* caused one year before October 28, 1918." In order to ensure that the Czechoslovak revolution would not reach full flower, Štoll confidently concluded, reactionaries took steps to "isolate this great day from a wider historical connection to the developments of twentieth-century European society, namely from the Great Russian Revolution, whose influence on our national liberation is obvious."[11]

To be sure, a number of moderate commentators argued for the maintenance of October 28th's leading position among Czech national holidays. The noted writer Eduard Bass, editor of *Svobodné noviny* until his death in October 1946, wrote a long paean to the freedom Czechoslovakia gained after the "300 years of bondage" in the Austro-Hungarian Empire.[12] One year later Peroutka, his successor as the newspaper's editor, argued that "no other day can be allowed to be in competition with October 28th in the life of the nation."[13] In this view he was supported by the Roman Catholic commentator Vladislav Sís, who reformulated the communist slogan by noting that without October 28th "there would not have been the later, today more celebrated, May 5th," and warned against those "who today are attempting to push the meaning of October 28th into the shadow of May 5th."[14] That forces were working to subordinate October 28th to May 5th was similarly recognized by the mayor of Prague and chairman of the National Socialist Party, Petr Zenkl. He lashed out at those who denigrated October 28th because of their enmity toward the First Republic:

> It is admittedly true that after last year's May revolution it has become fashionable in certain circles to describe the first October 28th as something very imperfect—as an opportunity whose fruits we did not turn to our advantage—and to look upon the First Republic as some kind of mistake, almost as a new Dark Ages. We are told how we did everything, or almost everything, poorly, and how it is now necessary to draw a thick line through all this and begin everything anew from the foundations.[15]

The Social Democrats were deeply split after their 1946 election defeat between a left wing that pushed for even closer alliance with the Communist Party and a more moderate wing that urged the party to define itself against both the center and left wings of the political spectrum. Accordingly, the party maintained an ambiguous middle ground on the issues of October 28th and the interwar republic generally. For example, Jan Vaněk argued in the party daily *Právo lidu* that while Czechs should

> remain conscious that the First Republic did not fulfill all the hopes 1918 gave us. . . . [it] would be gross ingratitude if we were uncritically and indiscriminately to condemn all that the First Republic gave us and what October 28th meant for us during the era of the First Republic, which had many positive qualities.[16]

In this way the party could proclaim its dissatisfaction with the whole of the interwar republic, while remaining free to reprove criticisms of it.

Nonetheless, the National Socialists' Petr Zenkl also saw the "*social* content" of May 5th as "the harmonious complement to our first, *national* revolution." This formulation was echoed in the comments of many other leading democratic socialists, and represented almost an "official line" for them.[17] A National Front statement in 1945 proclaimed August 29th (the holiday commemorating the Slovak National Uprising of 1944) and May 5th the "successors" to October 28th. Eduard Bass similarly saw springtime's May 5th as the natural complement to autumn's October 28th.[18] The leading National Socialist ideologist Otakar Machotka also saw the two holidays as "organically linked in *logical unity* . . . [as] two sides of the same coin."[19] This argument also found resonance among both Evangelicals, who were broadly sympathetic to communist viewpoints, and Roman Catholics, who were opposed to the communists. The Evangelical Church's *Kostnické jiskry* proclaimed that the "original national revolution [of 1918] reached its heights here in the social revolution," and the People's Party daily *Lidová demokracie* asked whether the nation could want anything more than "what October 28, 1918 brought, what August 29th hallowed, and what May 9th confirmed."[20] This strategy clearly recalls the attempt by noncommunists to maintain some degree of respect for the interwar republic by stressing its postwar successor's ties to it.

However, the National Front proclamation also stressed that Czechoslovak "independence has a secure foundation only in the social and economic liberation of the people."[21] This statement represented the left-wing side of the compromise proclamation and is a formulation that left open the path for the future. Zenkl, the victim of one of the harshest Communist Party slander campaigns of the period, called attention to the social side of postwar developments in a fashion similar to that of communist intellectuals. Writing in the National Socialists' *Svobodné slovo*, he argued that "The political freedom instituted on October 28, 1918, and renewed by the revolution of May 5, 1945, has already been completed on October 28, 1945, by the idea of economic and social freedom."[22] Taken as a whole, these views represent an attempt to integrate the experience of the "national and democratic revolution" into the historical traditions of the Czech nation enshrined in the semantic coding of October 28th. In reading these statements, it becomes clear that noncommunists emphasized the regaining of lost freedom rather than the revolutionary changes accompanying the uprising. Democratic leaders saw the revolutionary phase of the postwar period as completed, and they viewed May 5th and October 28, 1945, in the past tense as having "confirmed" or "completed" the work of October 28, 1918. The noncommunist historian Jaroslav Werstadt tried to bring the two dates even closer, noting the similarities between them. He pointed out that they were both born from resistance movements abroad, relied primarily on domestic forces, "occurred spontaneously from below, from the people . . . earlier than the political leadership planned," and both represented "the closing act and general symbol of our liberation struggle rather than its deciding moment."[23]

Communist critics viewed May 5th less as a completion or fulfillment of the tasks given the nation by October 28, 1918, than as a "corrective" to the "mistakes" made at the inception of the First Republic. Albert Pražák, the literary historian who had served as chairman of the Czech National Council that had directed the uprising, pointed out that the fundamental meaning of the two holidays was the same: "the freedom of the state and nation." Nonetheless, he termed May 5th "the uncompromising and radical correction," the "magnificent corrective" of October 28th. He contrasted the "celebratory demonstrations" and "German capitulation" of Independence Day with the "revolutionary" character and the "German defeat [in] a day of fighting" of May 5th and condemned the First Republic for failing to follow through on the socialist and nationalizing plans of its first days.[24] These sentiments were echoed by the Communist Party Central Committee member Vilém Nový, who, like other Communists, faulted October 28, 1918, for failing "to satisfy the social and socialist desires of the working class" and allowing the ruling class to "curtail the democratic rights of the people." For this reason, May 5th had "corrected the mistakes, insufficiencies, and halfheartedness of October 28, 1918, and given it a deeper, more popular [lidovější], and more democratic character."[25]

The politically astute Peroutka attempted to rebuff these criticisms by defending October 28th as "the greatest symbol of our independence." He was forced to concede that in 1918 "the greatest of our social traditions did not show themselves," but maintained that the moderate pace of social reform was not the fault of October 28th but rather of later developments and the European context as a whole. He condemned all attempts to place the social question in opposition to the heritage of October 28th, arguing that for him the holiday was "in no way tied to a definite economic system. We place no capitalist mark upon it." He expressed confidence that the patriotism and socialism represented by October 28th and May 5th need not be mutually antagonistic but could be reconciled in the new republic as "two colors on the same banner."[26]

In considering communist and noncommunist intellectuals' views of Czechoslovak Independence Day, it seems that neither side's interpretation was strong enough in itself to be politically valuable, although the communists were able to diminish significantly the holiday's traditional meaning through dilution. The communist link to the Russian Revolution, and their stress on the social-revolutionary potential of Czech society in 1918, failed to find the resonance their interpretations of other events had achieved. Nonetheless, they were able to draw on the enthusiasm among intellectuals and the broader public alike for the nationalizations, the Two-Year Plan, and the expulsion of the Sudeten Germans to raise competing understandings of precisely what was being celebrated. Noncommunists, particularly democratic socialists, expressed limited interest in preserving the symbolic content of the holiday. By proclaiming May 5th its complement, democratic socialists reiterated their strategy in countering the communist criticism of the First Republic. This aimed at calming the tenor of the times by emphasizing continuities. However, this line of reasoning also accepted the social nature and importance of May 5th, rendering the communist appropriation of that holiday both easier and symbolically more important, for noncommunists themselves had contributed to crowning it the successor to October 28th.

In analyzing the notions of May 5th, both similarities and contrasts are evident between the views of communist intellectuals and more moderate forces. One point on which both sides agreed was the crucial significance of the Prague Uprising in the history of the Czech nation. In keeping with his view of the complementary nature of the two holidays, Otakar Machotka noted that October 28th had perhaps "passed too calmly and happily for such a tremendous and historic event." He argued that the Czech nation had been given the unexpected opportunity on May 5th to "seal its freedom in blood. . . . and to repay by fierce struggle the debt incurred in 1918."[27] The heroism of the Czech people and the historic nature of their struggle were stressed in all reflections. "For the first time ever in the history of the Czech nation," Machotka observed, "an army of a hundred thousand men turned its weapons over to Czech hands."[28]

The psychological meaning of the Prague Uprising for the Czech nation of the immediate postwar period cannot be underestimated. During the war, collaboration had been the dominant strategy of the Czech nation, and the uprising can be seen as an attempt both to punish an oppressive occupier and to regain a measure of self-respect. In this sense, the celebrated Communist poet Vitězslav Nezval, in an article entitled "May 5th—The Life Blood of Our History," could characterize the uprising as "the brilliant rehabilitation of the Czech nation . . . [that] returned self-consciousness to the Czech people."[29] On the other side of the political spectrum, Otakar Machotka could view the uprising as "simultaneously an act of liberation and a moral purification." More tellingly, Machotka concluded his comments with a revealing observation: "The greatest war in history condemned the majority of Czech men to the role of powerless observers, incomplete men. On May 5th they became, through their will, complete men again."[30] This statement points to one element in the complex of psychological effects tied to the experience of Munich, the problem of "smallness" so keenly felt when Czechs were forced into the role of onlookers as the fate of their nation was being decided. One of the communist recipes for relieving the psychological burden of this "smallness" was to define the nation in terms of its ties to a resurgent and powerful Slavism that had the victorious Soviet Union at its head.

Over the past half-century, several scholars have posited a link between Czechs' wartime collaboration, the Prague Uprising, and the Communist Party's rise to total power. More surprisingly, two commentators in the immediate postwar period perceived the same link. A political analyst writing in Peroutka's *Dnešek*, noted that the events of

> May led many of those who had remained outside of political life into the Communists' ranks. . . . People who, not incorrectly, supposed that their insufficiently patriotic behavior during the war could be expiated by a sudden spasm of postwar radicalism also arrived there. . . . Those who arrived in the Party at five past twelve want by their present defector's zeal to incinerate their wartime pasts.[31]

Even more harshly, the poet and essayist František Halas castigated the same behavior already in late June 1945:

> People who yesterday remained in cowardly silence and kowtowed to Nazism are trying to creep into Military Tribunals and Courts of Purification. As far as possible, they wear the most conspicuous five-pointed stars on their jackets, suspiciously red, and denounce and slander one another, supposing that by the radicalism of their phrases their wretched pasts will be hidden in the fog.[32]

Whether from psychological motives engendered by the humiliations of Munich and occupation, cynical motives of political self-defense, or political conviction, we have seen that Czechs rushed to join the Communist Party. Democratic socialists' attempt to view this as evidence of a defensive opportunism, while psychologically plausible, also reveals how poorly they had estimated the true support the communist cause could muster in the country. Not all of the hundreds of thousands of new Communist Party members were susceptible to punishment as collaborators. The democratic socialist preference to see the growth in the Communist ranks as less a criticism of their own message and more a result of the impeachable morality of the nation is telling.

While radical socialist and more moderate forces in Czech culture agreed on the fundamental meaning of the May 5th uprising for the nation, they differed in their assessments of its aims. More conservative Roman Catholic commentators viewed the uprising as primarily a military operation aimed at freeing the nation from Nazi domination. As Helena Koželuhová, the fiery People's Party journalist and parliamentarian, argued, "our so-called revolution of May 5th was not a revolution, but a military action and uprising against the German enemy. . . . It was not a revolution directed toward fellow citizens, but a heroic battle versus the enemy."[33] Most other Catholic observers did not go so far as to deny the revolutionary character the struggle had assumed, but they did refuse to commemorate the event as a specifically *socialist* revolution. Karel Severa, writing in the political weekly *Vývoj*, recognized that a "spontaneous, unorganized revolution" had commenced on May 5th but viewed it as a "revolution of the entire nation against the foreign invader . . . a revolution of legality against illegality . . . that in essence had as its intention nothing more than a return to the legal conditions of Masaryk's republic."[34] Severa's observation that the entire nation took part was echoed by many of his fellow Roman Catholics. This stood in opposition to communist attempts to appropriate May 5th by claiming that the working class had stood in the vanguard of the uprising, while the bourgeoisie had remained in the background. While clearly expressing gratitude to the Soviet Union, Catholic writers at the same time decidedly emphasized that the success of the uprising was a result of the unity of all classes in the nation, and because "all the conditions" necessary for its victory had been "prepared from the reservoir of national forces."[35] In keeping with their view that the uprising was almost exclusively an anti-German action, the Catholic press emphasized its commemorative aspect, detailing the events of those crucial days and providing extensive reportage on the memorial services surrounding May 5th.[36]

In contrast to the Catholic view, communist editorialists looked forward, seeing the uprising as the beginning of a work still very much in progress, a position comparable to their treatment of October 28th. In direct opposition to Severa, Karel Štainer-Veselý presented an argument in the trade-union daily *Práce* that contained the primary points of the communist view. The uprising had not only a negative purpose—the destruction of fascism—but also represented "the crystallization process of progressive ideas." The working class, in his view, had provided the foundation for the resistance to Nazi rule; because of its leading role in the uprising "the new republic shall not be like the First Republic."[37] Similarly, Albert Pražák argued that May 5th aimed not only "to free the nation," but also to "fully liberate the people. . . . This is our new national truth, for which every other, earlier truth must make way."[38] The communist press accused the Roman Catholic intellectual leadership of both shirking its duty to the nation on May 5th and failing to understand the fundamental change the nation had undergone. It asked where Roman Catholic "intellectuals were on the day of the uprising, that they let these [i.e., revolutionary] realities slip."[39] Smrkovský also

warned against the reactionary motives of "some circles of the Czech bourgeoisie . . . among whom functionaries of the National Socialist Party created an essential element, [who] wanted a return of October 28, 1918," during the uprising. He meant this both in the sense of a peaceful transfer of
power through negotiation with German military representatives and in the
sense of a more generalized return to prewar norms. For Smrkovský, an
armed uprising had been necessary both to liquidate "all the intrigues of the
Czech reaction" and because "the Czech nation had to consecrate the birth
of the new republic with its blood."[40]

The youth were among the most strident in taking up the socialist calling
of the new republic, seeing October 28th as a holiday whose time had
passed with the generation of their parents. The young poet who served as
editor in chief of the Union of Czech Youth daily *Mladá fronta* and director
of the publishing house of the same name, Jaromír Hořec, was typical of his
generation.[41] While he conceded that October 28, 1918, had laid the democratic foundation of the republic, he decidedly subordinated it to May 5th,
writing that "the main task for valuing and understanding October 28th is to
show the continuity between it and May 5th." The "great progress and
strength" of the latter had made Independence Day merely the "symbolic expression of our first democratic republic."[42] This opinion was by no means
unusual, as it was also often heard in the democratic socialist camp, but it
was decidedly among the more restrained coming from leading representatives of the younger intellectual generation. Albert Pražák observed that the
older generation had a warmer relationship to the symbolism of October
28th; E. F. Burian similarly noted that "my generation and the generation of
older people think of it [Independence Day] differently than the generation
raised in the First Republic."[43]

It was the dynamic Hájek who most programmatically defined his generation of intellectuals, linking it explicitly to both the uprising and Marxism.
In an article with the significant title "The Generation of October 28th and
the Generation of May 5th," he accepted the symbolic meaning October 28th
had during the interwar First Republic but argued that its significance had
been overshadowed by the historic events of 1945–1946:

> In the First Republic, October 28th was the axis of our national and political cal-
> endar. . . . In the new republic October 28th has received a new meaning: last
> year the Temporary National Assembly was convened and this year the two-
> year plan was approved. . . . What has value for our time from the content of
> October 28th will live on in the new forms of democracy . . . but the axis of our
> national and political calendar, the foundation of the new historical era, is May
> 5th. It is not a denigration of the real meaning of October 28th and the whole
> era of the First Republic if we say that the May revolution of 1945 gave a much
> more solid and broad foundation to our national life than did October 28,
> 1918.[44]

The generation he represented, which had come of age during the final years of the First Republic and under the Nazi-directed Protectorate of Bohemia and Moravia, leveled serious criticisms at the Czechoslovakia its parents had built. The First Republic had offered the youth "few constructive opportunities," and the Depression had reared the generation to "a feeling of its own expendability and lesser value."[45] In the decade between the onset of the Depression and the outbreak of the Second World War, Hájek argued, his generation experienced "more than the generation of our fathers did throughout their entire lives. We ripened under the pressure of rapidly developing historical events, such a stampede of events as had never been experienced before us." It was during this onslaught that what Hájek called "the most active core of the generation" came into contact with socialism and there found the answer to its yearnings and dreams, the key to its future. He explained that the youth was pushed toward dialectical materialism by the collapse of capitalism under the weight of its contradictions and the necessary rise of reactionary fascism. This lent credence to the noncommunist view that the youth had experience only with the worst years of the First Republic. In giving itself over to Marxism, Hájek maintained, his generation knew it was not choosing an easy road but that "for us it was for keeps: we knew clearly what was at stake here."[46]

In Hájek's view, the two events discussed in chapter 5 were the crucible in which the generation was forged. First came the experience of Munich, in which the "Agrarian Party and reaction showed their true face and sold out the republic without a shot being fired." Although he did not explicitly condemn Great Britain and France for their participation in the Munich Accords, a condemnation is implicitly contained in his assertion that dialectical materialism provided "the correct interpretation" of the event. The First Republic's government bore the brunt of his criticism in this respect. In capitulating to an agreement that the young generation was "prepared to fight under any circumstances" the First Republic's leaders had committed a "moral sin" against the entire nation, "the youth in particular."[47] Hájek also saw the burdens of the occupation as falling overwhelmingly on younger Czechs, "with the exception of the Protectorate children of the greater bourgeoisie." His generation had "lived through its most personal human experience in the years of German occupation." It had been "definitively thrown from the so-called normal course of life. . . . Its development was halted for six years." One result of the youth being sent in disproportionate numbers to Germany as forced labor was that young intellectuals and workers came to know one another, further cementing ties to socialism. Hájek argued that for young intellectuals dialectical materialism had, in the experience of forced labor and concentration camps, became something more than a mere doctrine: "How could the people from the salons know what dialectical materialism came to mean in these years and these situations? It was not just a fixed point in the center of the war . . . but a strong anchor in our most inner personal life. . . . A faith, if you like."[48]

Given this view of the formative fifteen years of a generation of young Czech intellectuals, it is perfectly natural that they "took up the revolution and uprising as theirs" on May 5, 1945.[49] Nor is it surprising that after the war they strove to claim the holiday for themselves and to place it in opposition to their elders' October 28th, or that they became champions of the socialist yearnings first publicly expressed in conjunction with the uprising. It should be reiterated here, however, that there had been virtually complete consensus within the resistance movement during the war on the necessity of social change in the postwar republic, although the conceptions of the pace and extent of the changes differed among the political factions represented. As Hájek observed in an article entitled "We Are the Bearers of a New Era," the youth had become "the bearers of the trump of May 1945" by virtue of their large-scale participation in the uprising. Moreover, because they understood "the spirit and tempo of the times," they must therefore also "be the bearers of the new era of their history." The youth had proven themselves victorious in the uprising and must continue their work, for there were new victories yet to be won: "Young people rose to important positions not only with weapons . . . [but] also as managers and administrators of their liberated land."[50] Here we can see a reflection of both the cult of youth and the intergenerational social mobility brought about by the war.

Hájek was the cultural critic who concerned himself most completely with characterizing and championing the conception of a clearly delineated and consciously socialist generation of youth. He served as editor of the aptly named *Generace*, around which many young intellectuals of a similar political orientation gathered. Although politically tempered by the journal's semi-monthly format, *Generace* explored many of the cultural and artistic themes that united the radical socialist youth.[51] However, the Union of Czech Youth's daily *Mláda fronta* presented this generation of young intellectuals with a more immediate forum for its views. The examination of the issues of this fairly radical publication in the days surrounding the May 5th holiday shows the depth of its commitment to the heritage of the uprising and the youth's role in it. Articles with titles such as "May 1945—Our May" and "The May Uprising—The Revolution of the Youth" appear frequently, and reports on the activities of the younger generation in the uprising were extensive.[52] Claims on the heritage of May 5th ranged from the metaphorical, as in Stanislav Maleček's comment that "it is symbolic that it was a young month, a month of new life that brought new freedom to our homeland," to the more dogmatic statement of Václav Kutný, who argued that "it was not a matter of indifference to us how our new liberated republic would look. . . . We not only demanded national purification, but also that there would be a government of working people in the republic."[53]

The coalescence of this generation was not only recognized by its members, however. The Communist press lavished much attention on socialist youth leaders and the activities of the Union of Czech Youth, and the slogan "Youth to the Fore!" (Mládež kupředu!) was often repeated at party congresses and in party publications. Noncommunist forces also perceived that a shift in the relationship between the younger and older generations was taking place, and the younger generation's commitment to democracy was a source of concern for them. One democratic socialist intellectual cited the youth's radical orientation as the "most oppositional dividing line between the prewar and postwar generations."[54] The Roman Catholic editorialist Antonín Pimper pointed out that over the ensuing few years a transfer of power would take place between the generations and worried that the young generation considered their elders "superannuated and less valuable for today's developments. Some members of the younger generation are afraid of [their elders'] excessive conservatism." However, he saw the cause of this lying in fascism's emphasis on youth rather than in the allure of Marxist ideology, and maintained the hope that young Czechs could be won over by more moderate political forces.[55]

In an article written shortly after the Communist Party's victory in the May 1946 elections, Pavel Tigrid was less optimistic about the younger generation's ability to resist being carried away by the revolutionary élan of the times. He cited "the fanaticization of the younger working-class and student generation" as one of the alarming signals the election result had brought.[55] He ascribed the decline primarily to the effects of the Nazi occupation on the value system of the Czech youth. In this he was joined by Peroutka, who argued that it was necessary to understand that the war and occupation rendered more complicated and lasting harm to the realm of the spirit than to the physical infrastructure of the nation. He believed this was particularly true for the youth: "Can we say that today's youth, educated in German-dominated schools, obtained a strong moral character from good education?"[57]

Democratic socialists' concern regarding the damage the war had caused to the spiritual underpinnings of Czech culture and its effects in increasing young Czechs' susceptibility to revolutionary enthusiasm constituted part of a larger theme: revolution and the need for its limitation. Democratic socialists were not opposed to seeing May 5th in a social-revolutionary light, but they wanted to see the revolutionary phase of postwar development as a completed phenomenon. Therefore, they found themselves attempting to contain the socialist enthusiasm they themselves had helped to foment in the first postwar months. This placed them in a difficult position. On the one hand, they had to sanction the concept of revolution generally, with a view toward winning over the more conservative elements in the population for the postwar changes. On the other hand, they struggled to stifle the continuation of revolutionary activity by more radical elements in the Czech polity.

In assessing the first of these tasks, Josef Grňa, one of the leaders of the wartime resistance movement, recognized that many Czechs were uncomfortable with the idea of revolution because of their basic conservatism. However, Grňa argued that Czechs needed to understand that their revolution was "fighting for the realization of moral and universal ideals."[58] Similarly noting that European traditions were essentially conservative, meaning that revolutions were therefore occasionally necessary, the lawyer and Charles University professor Vratislav Bušek balanced this view by stating already in late 1945 that the National Socialist Party "want[s] to consider this stage as overcome. We believe in reasonable development without violence."[59] This attempt simultaneously to celebrate the revolution and to place it in the past was echoed in the same journal a few months later: "only the superficial viewer sees nothing good in revolution." Yet at the same time "the newly received values need calm for their continued development."[60]

The apparent fear of democratic socialist critics was that the revolution had escaped their control and that the extension of the wave of revolutionary enthusiasm would play into the hands of their left-wing competitors. The National Socialist Minister of Schools and Education, Jaroslav Stránský, argued that continuing revolution or "permanent revolution [means] insane revolution or disguised counterrevolution."[61] Peroutka can be seen as representative of the stance of many democratic socialist political observers in this respect. Similar to the manner in which noncommunists attempted to salvage at least part of Masaryk's heritage, Peroutka argued that there were material and spiritual aspects to every revolution and hoped "that the material and cultural sides will not set themselves against one another as enemies in our revolution."[62] Moreover, in his *Dnešek* he attempted to curb the revolutionary spirit of the times, issuing a warning to those who would take the revolution too far:

> But what is a healthy relationship for the nation to have to revolution? This: accept its results and then part with its fever. One who denies the results of revolution causes the same harm as one who extends revolutionary chaos. . . . The goal of our revolution, which has lasted since 1939, was freedom. Only by cheating, by smuggling, would it be possible to carry this pugnacious and victorious nation to some other stage. And only by violence would it be possible to maintain it.[63]

This citation clearly demonstrates the ambivalence in the democratic socialist position. He simultaneously condoned and discouraged revolutionary sympathies and decidedly placed the revolution in the past by setting it in the context of a resistance struggle against Nazi occupation that had liberation as its endpoint.

Roman Catholic observers were less ambiguous in their relationship to revolution. Helena Koželuhová's denial that the events of May 5, 1945, constituted a revolution did not preclude her from recognizing that a revolution was in fact taking place. In March 1946 she asked rhetorically why revolution was valued so positively and concluded that it was due to there having not yet been elections. The elections would restore democratic government after the ten-month intermezzo of "revolutionary government" that the defeat of Nazi Germany had brought.[64] Other Roman Catholic commentators were less certain that the revolutionary wave would ebb, and Karel Severa was particularly vehement in contending that "revolution is not a program" and warning against the "fetish of revolution." He argued that the publicly visible "revolutionary fever, revolutionary psychosis, revolutionary craze" corresponded to "an internal confusion, an unrest in people who have lost the sense of connection, continuity, tradition . . . in people who are no longer tied to anything—to the country, to the family, to society, to God, even to themselves." He maintained that the constant intoning of "revolutionary" slogans should not be understood as constituting a program, for the word could be filled with any content the speaker desired, and the rhetorical battle risked becoming "a childish game with the words 'revolution' and 'counterrevolution.'" Most ominously he warned "hotheads" that playing with revolution can have dire consequences, noting that Hitler too "had carried out his own national and social revolution." He concluded that the safest and truest course for the republic was a return to normal life, for "nothing is more dangerous to any kind of totalitarian regime than a calm and continuing condition of civic prosperity, of a standard of living, of orderly, satisfied, everyday civic life."[65]

The more pious Catholic journals *Katolík* and *Vyšehrad* maintained a similar line. In contrast to Peroutka, the Jesuit-controlled *Katolík* warned against accepting the revolutionary changes of the post-liberation months and concluding that the revolution was completed, for "revolutions are not satisfied with partial solutions." Catholic readers should therefore be wary of all the socialist elements of Czech society. The journal also tacitly drew the comparison to Nazi totalitarianism by noting that "just as the German danger is not eliminated, neither is revolution eliminated."[66] The influential Catholic professor Dominic Pecka, responding to the use of May 5th's revolution to justify both democratic socialist and communist conceptions of socialism, argued that "in an era when everything is 'revolutionary' . . . freeing ourselves from such empty 'revolutionary' terminology would possibly be the most revolutionary act of our 'revolutionary' era."[67] The view of revolution expressed by both wings of Czech political Catholicism was primarily aimed at countering sympathies for the Marxist parties. However, a critique of democratic socialist ambiguity is also visible. By warning that "revolution is not satisfied with partial solutions," Catholic intellectuals implicitly criticized their democratic socialist compatriots' encouragement of revolutionary social change in the first postwar months. Although they were now striving to curb the enthusiasm they had helped to further, they were battling with the communists over who was the exponent of the true Czech socialism, a "childish game with the words 'revolution' and 'counterrevolution.'"

The sharp divide between Roman Catholics and Protestant leaders sympathetic to the aims of radical socialism also revealed itself in the debate over revolution. The Czechoslovak Church again was the more radical of the two major Protestant groupings, with professor of theology František Bednář unambiguously proclaiming that "not a single European is threatened by the present explosion of revolutionary forces."[68] In its programmatic statement, "Tábor Is Our Program," the leadership urged the church faithful to embrace fully the revolutionary spirit of May 5th and observed that it should not be "seen with wonder that a religion could have a positive view of revolution." The tradition claimed by the young church was self-consciously "heretical" and held that "rebellion against the arresting of development is . . . the embodiment of religious purity. This purity is the glory of all revolutions." Consistently the most radical of the religious groups in postwar Czechoslovakia, the Czechoslovak Church was committed to both social and religious revolution and enthusiastically pronounced: "We see our new religion also as a source of revolutionary events in human history."[69]

The views concerning the relationship between the two holidays reveal important factors in postwar Czech developments. By their willingness to attach comparable weight to May 5th, democratic socialist intellectuals showed the extent to which they were active participants in the construction of a new socialist semantic structure. This was true even of many figures strongly opposed to the Communist Party, although the ultimate duration and destination of the "national and democratic revolution" begun on May 5th was undoubtedly different for them than it was for their more radical counterparts. Further, particularly in the comments of democratic socialist leaders, the accent on the "complementary" or "completing" character of May 5th may have represented an attempt to gain political support, as the social and economic changes the immediate postwar regime instituted were proving quite popular. At the same time, by invoking October 28th in conjunction with May 5th, democratic socialist intellectuals also strove to fashion a rhetorical brake on the revolutionary troika of May first, fifth, and ninth by stressing continuities with calmer times. By reminding the public of its heritage, it is very likely that more moderate commentators were attempting both to strengthen the weakened reputation of the First Republic and to dampen left-wing enthusiasm for future changes that would take the state even further from its prewar configuration.

This strategy revealed two major flaws, which had the effect of confusing the wider Czech public over what was at stake in the confrontation between the Communist Party and its allies in other groupings and noncommunist forces. By consciously or subconsciously echoing the statements of communist politicians, their statements made radical rhetoric sound less extreme, thereby narrowing the perceived differences between the two positions. Moreover, the tendency toward rhetorical compromise had the effect of requiring democratic social reformers to fight their ideological battles on the home ground of revolutionary Marxism. The national identity crisis many perceived in postwar Czech culture demanded the search for an axis of moral and intellectual certainty. Perhaps because of its moderate political position, the Roman Catholic Church found itself in a weakened position to assert authority across the population. Further, the nation's traditional Western orientation had been disrupted by the experience of Munich. The result of this was that the ideological allure of the certainty Marxism embodied was extremely powerful. By proclaiming faithfulness to the ambiguous socialist aims of May 5th, noncommunist intellectuals forced themselves into the difficult position of defining and defending their compromise positions against the complete interpretation and unified strategy of the Communist Party and its allies. A final crucial factor in postwar Czech culture revealed here is the revolutionary enthusiasm of young intellectuals. Radicalized by the war and recalling little good before it, this generation was ripe for revolution. The disorienting era of Depression, disintegration, occupation, and war had pushed many of them into the arms of a Marxism that seemed to hold the certainty of preventing such events from recurring. The political import of this was magnified by the extension of the franchise to all those over eighteen years of age.

8

The Reorientation of National Identity: Czechs between East and West

Mezi Západem, Východem, Moskvou a Paříží
leží svobodná, nesvobodná země.
Ó, rci mi, kam moudrý hlas touhy tvé zahlízí?
Východ či Západ? Co zvítězí ve mně?
Rci mi, co vyvolíš?
Jsi stáří světa? Jsi mládí?
Jsi myšlenka? Skepse? Jsi čin?
Západu šum a let, lesk tě svádí?
Rozkoš moci mezi bohatstvím a hladem?
Závrat' mezi vítězstvím a pádem?
Či snad přísná, chladná, spravedlivá,
mladá revoluce, jež zpívá
čin, čin, čin?

Vol, vyvol! Ted', nebo nikdy.

Between East and West, Moscow and Paris
lies a free, unfree land.
Oh, tell me where the wise voice of your yearning looks?
East or West? Which will be victorious in me?
Tell me, which will you choose?
Are you the old of the world? Are you the young?
Are you thought? Skepticism? Are you action?
Does the noise and flight of the West tempt you?
The lust for power amid the wealth and hunger?
The giddiness amid victory and defeat?

Or perhaps the disciplined, cool, just,
young revolution, which sings
act, act, act?

Choose! Choose! Now, or never.

—Josef Hora, "Západ a Východ"

The question of the nation's cultural orientation between East and West has preoccupied Czech intellectuals throughout the nation's modern history. It has constituted, in the words of Pavel Tigrid, "The Eternal Question of Our History."[1] Czech intellectuals developed politically significant answers to this question in the aftermath of the experiences of Munich and the Second World War. They reveal a transformation of the Czech self-conception along one of its most fundamental axes. Propelled by communist intellectuals' drive to "revise the national character," many Czechs shifted their allegiances away from the capitalist and liberal West and toward the Slavic and socialist East. The question of cultural orientation became the nexus at which opposing cultural, political, social, and intellectual views met. All of the debates over history and patriotism, Hus, the meaning of Munich and the war, the interpretation of the interwar republic and Masaryk reflected a fundamental divergence between the adherents of Western cultural, political, and social positions and those who looked to those of the East. As the talented historian and art critic Jindřich Chalupecký noted, "The sense that we find ourselves in a decisive historical moment leads to the most varied contemplations. These concentrate themselves around the formulation *East or West*."[2] The way in which various groups of intellectuals answered this question was accorded tremendous importance, with one observer holding that the choice was as "fateful" as when the nation "chose between the Catholic South and the Protestant North."[3] As such, the debate over the nation's future orientation became one of the primary dividing lines between left and right and constituted one of the most acrimonious and longest-running debates of the period, commencing publicly with the war's end and continuing until the Communist Party's assumption of total power in February 1948.

The precondition for the questioning of Czech self-identification was clearly the Second World War, which one observer called "the midwife of a new society."[4] With its bookends of the Western betrayal at Munich and liberation by the Red Army, many Czechs could agree with Klement Gottwald that "Munich [and] the war years definitively made the sign of the cross over theories of balancing between East and West."[5] The experience of Munich gravely damaged Czech willingness to rely on the West for the state's security, which manifested itself in Czechoslovakia's close military alliance with the Soviet Union. Seen pragmatically, "the Munich disappointment drives the national instinct for self-preservation to the East."[6] It was not just Western foreign and defense policy that was called into question, however, but also its moral standing. Even noncommunists judged that "Munich showed the terrible moral weaknesses of the liberal democracies."[7] In such a climate, "almost everything that makes us uncomfortable in a survey of the politics of the Western superpowers awakens painful memories of Munich."[8]

As the converse of the moral failure attributed to the West for those policies leading to Munich, the moral prestige of the Soviet Union had been raised by its wartime successes. As we have seen, the Soviet victory was seen by many as springing from the strength of its socialist system and the heroism this inspired in its citizens. In contrast to the condemnation of the West's appeasement of Hitler, the USSR was celebrated by communists and their political opponents alike as the main opponent of Nazi expansion and the principal liberator of Czechoslovakia. This certainly contributed to the Communist Party's victory in the 1946 parliamentary elections, as Czech voters were "grateful to the USSR and equated being an ally of the USSR with communist ideology."[9] The victory the Soviet Union had won over Nazi Germany and its liberation of the majority of Czechoslovakia clearly made it "the most reliable ally" for the renewed state.[10] Yet, rather than seeing the alliance as merely an expression of geopolitical reality, many intellectuals ascribed to it a more fundamental meaning. They referred to the USSR as "the guarantor of the national state of Czechoslovakia" and argued alongside the most respected Czech historian of Eastern Europe, Josef Macůrek, that without a turn to the East "our nationality will not continue to exist."[11] The strength of these feelings derived directly from the Czech perception that the war against the Nazi regime had represented a struggle for their nation's very survival.

The geopolitical attraction of alliance with the Soviet Union was heightened because, although Germany was occupied and lay in ruins, the threat of a resurgent Germany weighed extremely heavily on the minds of leading Czechs. As one noncommunist commentator put it, "the Czech question is an anti-German question."[12] The fear of a revived Germany was especially apparent in the speeches and writings of President Beneš, who warned his countrymen that "today the situation is different, but in five or ten years there will be a German problem again. . . . Don't take your eyes off Germany!" This sentiment was echoed by Macůrek, who argued, "the German danger will certainly return in one form or another." In preparing for this, it was "necessary to recognize that it is not possible to rely on other forces [i.e., other than the USSR] with trust."[13] The relationship to Germany directly impinged on the question of national orientation, as one noted painter and writer revealed when he plaintively asked, "how will the 'West' look to us when the German nation again finds itself in a normal situation?"[14]

Related to this, and perhaps even more important, was the effect of the expulsion of almost 3 million ethnically German citizens of the prewar republic. The nineteenth-century Czech historian and politician František Palacký had found the meaning of Czech history in the interaction and rivalry of Germans and Czechs in Bohemia and Moravia, and the expulsion of the Germans left a discernible gap in the nation's self-understanding. As the Evangelical minister and historian František Bednář incisively commented:

> Today the Germans have gone and in the souls of many Czechs there is some kind of vacuum. . . . [H]ow to fill the empty Czech soul . . . which after the departure of the Germans has somehow lost its existential program? . . . We reject their ideology and condemn it, but mere *negation* is not a program and calls for complete clarity on what our nation stands for and what *its* ideal is.[15]

In the attempt to define the nation's postwar character, steadfast and assured communist views rushed to fill this vacuum with the ideals of Slavism and socialism. As we shall see, the noncommunist response, offered during a period in which calm reason was less persuasive than powerful rhetoric, again showed a tendency toward compromise and introduced synthetic views that left them in a conceptually and politically weak position.

In the debate over the nation's cultural orientation, the victory of the Soviet Union was generalized such that it was widely perceived as a victory for the Slavs as a whole. Since we have seen that one of the sharpest blows Munich delivered to the Czech psyche was the "smallness" Czechs felt, many Czech intellectuals seem to have taken the USSR's victory as also a victory for their nation. The notion of a greater Slavdom acted as compensation for the nation's perceived "smallness." Communist public figures exploited this, arguing that "the victory over fascism is also the victory of the Slavs," casting the Russians as the defenders of the smaller Slavic nations.[16] This phenomenon represented more than a psychopolitical ploy on the part of communist sympathizers, however. Even President Beneš recognized the ascription of such a role to the USSR, praising "the great role of the Soviet Union in this struggle, [and] the heroism of the Red Army, which fought not only for the Soviet Union but also for the rest of the Slavic nations."[17] Claiming the victory over Nazi Germany for all the Slavic nations through the role of the USSR was the first link in the forging of a conceptual chain binding Czechs to the East. Communist intellectuals and those allied with them trumpeted supposed "Slavic virtues" endlessly, placing the power of the Soviet Union and the justice of its social system at the center of attention. The present discussion will center on two arguments communist intellectuals presented to allay noncommunists' fears and control the field of discourse: that the East represented the true inheritor of the Western tradition, and that socialism, as embodied by the USSR, was the direction in which the world—both East and West—was turning.

The article "East and West" by Ladislav Štoll was seminal for the communist position, presenting the model for subsequent communist argumentation.[18] Writing only three months after liberation, Štoll took issue with the idea that

Our orientation to the East . . . is a requirement of our gratitude, an obligation of public cultural equity, a necessary result of the power-political constellation. Some also stress that the Czechs in their spiritual essence are apparently Western. They see a Hamletesque meditation of a divided soul and language.

Štoll argued that the question of orientation should not be reduced to one of sides of the world, but should be a search for "spiritual and cultural influences" bearing worldwide importance. The influences that had earlier been decisive—the Renaissance and Reformation, and the British and French revolutions—had become less important after the Czech national movement gained wide support in the nineteenth century, not least because they had been received through the mediation of the now completely discredited Germans. In the aftermath of the Second World War, it was apparent to Štoll that there was only one possible direction for Czech culture to turn. After the West had discredited itself by appeasing Hitler at Munich, he asked, who would want "to return to the Westernism that reacted with such indifference to the calls of our threatened culture in 1938?" In any case, the West itself, and especially France, had been forced by the war "to carry out a fundamental revision of its traditions" and to "turn to the East and learn from the Russians to honor [their] own national revolutionary democratic traditions."

Russia, according to Štoll, had not only contributed its own ideas to the world, but had proven the most fertile ground for Western ideas, for it was the Russians who "elaborated, enhanced and developed them." In this respect, the USSR stood in much the same relation to the West as did the Communist Party in relation to Czech traditions:

> It was the Russians who became not only the true inheritors of the great cultural traditions of the West, but who also took the initiative and ran ahead of the West economically, socially, culturally, and morally. They became the defenders of European culture and civilization [against the Nazis] because their culture was stronger, more vigorous, and more powerful.

Communists, to be sure, still looked to the great traditions of the West—to Greece, Rome, and France—but these belonged to the past while "the present and future" belonged to the East. The Russian language, according to Štoll, was poised to act as the language of the twentieth century, as Latin had served in the Middle Ages and French in the eighteenth and nineteenth centuries. Those who maintained the East/West geographic division, rather than deciding cultural orientation on the basis of the locus from which progressive ideas flowed into the country, were "not true Westerners (*západníci*)" but "new Czech parochialists (*zapecníci*)." For Štoll, these intellectuals were "afraid of this great breath of the European historical spirit, which is creating on the soil of Europe a new epoch of civilization and culture." They should, he argued, be proud that it was "the Russian nation and the culturally and spiritually related

Slavic nations" bringing this to the world. By virtue of this mission, the Slavic nations were guaranteed "a respected place in European civilization, where the culture of the Slavic nations had often been looked down upon."

This article encapsulates all the major points communist intellectuals invoked in the debate over the national cultural orientation. Above all, Štoll rejected the notion that a purportedly Western Czech soul was being forced by external affairs into the Eastern orbit—what Ferdinand Peroutka called in his diary "loving a beautiful woman and having to marry an ugly one."[19] However, this notion decidedly undergirded some noncommunist views. Furthermore, the view that Western ideas had come to Czechs through the mediation of a Germany that was now "completely bankrupt," implying that the ideas were suspicious by association, was commonly asserted by communist observers.[20] Some democratic socialists also supported this position. Similar to Štoll, they warned that, while the war had finally brought a definitive end to "German power and cultural hegemony," influences from the West preceding it also had been "deformed by Germany."[21]

The characteristic of communist argumentation that best served to deflect the "Westerners'" concerns was Štoll's characterization of the Soviet Union as the inheritor of Western-created values. This was evidently an attempt to counter noncommunists' doubts about whether the USSR was sufficiently steeped in Western culture to appreciate the differences between its country (and its socialism) and the Czech cultural, geographic, political, social, and economic heritage and position. The noted communist writer Lumír Čivrný argued: "The East, led by the Soviet Union, is the inheritor of [the progressive culture of the West] and the realizer of the world's best spiritual values."[22] These sentiments were echoed by a fellow communist writer, Václav Řezáč:

> The ingenious conception of social transformation in the West was no less ingeniously realized in the East. The burning flame of human progress lay in France during the French revolution but has since moved to the East. . . . The great heritage of European culture . . . cannot be lost . . . and will not be lost. New, stronger arms are taking it, leading it forward and augmenting its content.[23]

That the East, embodied in the guiding ideas and social organization of the Soviet Union, constituted the logical inheritor of the Western tradition was a conception that found much support among democratic socialists as well. For example, the view of Lev Sychrava was analogous to that expressed by leading communists:

> The Russian Revolution . . . was built on the ideas of the British and French revolutions. . . . Masaryk in his book *Russia and Europe* showed how Russian socialism came out of Western thought. . . . The Slavs are building on the great fundamental values of the Western revolutions and in many respects are ahead of the West.[24]

For many democratic socialists, the idea extended even beyond the revolutionary heritage. Surprisingly, these views found expression in the primary intellectual forum for opponents of the Communist Party, *Dnešek*, in a pair of articles by Antonín Klatovský. He held that beyond the implementation of Western social thought, the Soviet Union "had taken over all the values of liberal civilization: the cult of technology and the organization of production, the monetary system and the ideal of material wealth. Therefore, it is not entirely untrue that communism is truly the last phase of liberalism."[25] In fact, he found that "the West and the East are not only close to one another in the cult of technology, but also in what is called national character." To demonstrate this he used the statements of American aviators fighting on the Eastern front during the war, who claimed in reference to the Russians that they "had never met with a nation that was fundamentally so close to the American people: in its realism, frankness, good-heartedness, and sense of humor."[26]

In fact, noncommunist intellectuals most often held that Marxism had made the East *more* Western, rather than less so, because they viewed the philosophical foundation on which the Soviet Union was built as a direct product of the West. Even Václav Černý, the most vociferous and visible of the "Westerners," called attention to this in his defense of the West:

> Marx is, I think, the fruit and expression of *Western* thought and, if I'm not wrong, even a convinced *Westernist*. And I think that perhaps there is no doubt about the line to which Lenin belongs. It is so obvious that the Russians themselves proudly call attention to the fact that the strivings of Soviet civilization are attached firmly to Europe and act as an indivisible part of Western culture.[27]

The comments of Otakar Machotka, one of the National Socialists' chief ideologists, were the most specific in analyzing how Marxism drew the Soviet Union closer to the West. In a long article in *Svobodný zítřek*, Machotka argued that the Russians had acquired "many facets of Western culture by the adoption of Marxism, with its rationality, systematism, strength and its sense of organization . . . that in many ways blurred the Slavic soul." While he noted that there were still many negative qualities in the Russian national character, he implied that at least some of these could be disregarded since they came from "a pronounced German influence."[28]

Štoll's fourth argument, that while the past certainly belonged to the West the future belonged to the East, constitutes a familiar part of communist rhetoric.[29] More interesting is the resonance that it had among noncommunists across all political divisions. The Evangelical leader J. L. Hromádka believed that "all Europe, not only Czechoslovakia, is on the road to socialization. It is a historical fact."[30] Only the leaders of the Czechoslovak Church trumped the determinism of this statement. In their coverage of the session of Congress of Czech Historians devoted to the Slavic East, they stressed their "*certainty of faith in the historical progress*" coming from the East.[31]

Intellectuals from the democratic socialist camp also voiced their belief that humanity's future lay in the East. Like Štoll, the social and literary critic Karel Polák encouraged Czechs to look for new and creative ideas in deciding their state's future, and in the postwar world he saw these ideas coming "principally from the East."[32] Similarly, the National Socialist government minister Jaroslav Stránský argued that not only was "the East closer to the *sources* of beauty and the good" than the West but was "itself the source of the future moral, artistic, social, and scientific values."[33] Only Václav Černý dared raise his voice against this kind of thinking, arguing that Czechs must not "do away with the West by exceedingly lazily and simplistically [claiming] that the West is for us admittedly a monument to the great cultural traditions of the past but that the present and future lies exclusively in the East."[34]

The fervor expressed in these lines regarding the rosy future of socialist progress was expressed equally for its presumed bearers, the Slavs under the leadership of the USSR. This renewed interest in the Slavic world clearly aided the communists in capturing center stage in the public discourse over the country's cultural orientation. Many Czechs saw the radiant socialist future of the East as an opportunity to extol the great virtues Slavs could now bring to the world. In juxtaposition to the "smallness" they had felt at Munich, Czechs could join their Slavic brethren and command the international respect they had lacked in 1938. Praise for "the great Slavic world," anticipations of the "wealth Slavs [will] contribute to the world" and expressions of certainty that "the future belongs to the Slavs" were rife across the political spectrum.[35] Josef Macůrek noted that, in contradiction to the helplessness felt over Munich, "history does not make itself, we cannot and are not allowed to look at events as merely passive observers. . . . People create history and people change it. Today we have more means for this than at any other time." He saw Slavism, which he defined as "a faith in the Slavs and their great future," as the most powerful tool for creating this glorious history, since it tautologically bestowed upon the Slavs "a special historical mission."[36]

These sentiments, even among noncommunist intellectuals, occasionally took on an explicitly anti-capitalist veneer in addition to expressing an at best ambivalent view of the West. Sychrava, in a statement that encapsulates a whole range of attitudes from anti-Germanism to a Slavic pride yoked to socialism, maintained that Czechs cannot "close [their] eyes to the anti-Slav prejudices that have existed since time immemorial across the whole world, prejudices that have been fed by German propaganda and now by the Western bourgeoisie's fear of social upheaval."[37] The psychological pain and the feeling of "smallness" suffered acutely in the experience of Munich could be overcome through the tie to the great socialist movement and the larger Slavic world. In the words of one prominent art historian,

The present revolution is not limited spatially or in content. It is taking possession of the whole world. When the society of the Middle Ages originated, the
Slavs did not appear on the main stage of world history, they were on its pe-
riphery. Now they are among the main actors of the new order. . . . They will no
longer be passive objects of world history.[38]

Zdeněk Nejedlý neatly summed up the tie between the socialist future and
the heightened self-confidence of Czechs through their ties to the Slavic
world, portraying Czechs as living in

an era begun by the October Revolution. This means the end of Slavs' often ar-
tificially maintained second-class status. Hitherto, for example, in the majority of
world histories a supplemental Slavic chapter has been added to the histories of
all the other nations. In the future that simply will not be. The Slavic world . . .
is conscious of its historic path and importance.[39]

Distinctly messianic interpretations of Slavism represented a significant
part of the discourse over the nation's orientation and were exploited by
communist ideologues such as Nejedlý. Interest in forging links between the
Slavic nations, however, was not restricted to such views. Less overtly ideological interest in "renewing" and "deepening" contacts with Slavic nations
was widespread and was reinforced by President Beneš's aim of building a
"new Slavic politics." The ideas he expressed in his *Reflections on Slavism*
serve well as an introduction to the democratic socialist view of the Czech
relationship to the Slavic East and reveal Slavism's political and cultural
power in the early postwar era.[40] Much of his book is devoted to an examination of the historical roots of Slavic reciprocity and the development of
Slavic thought. For Beneš,

the struggle for the freedom of the Slavic nations was always and above all the
struggle of the Slavic *people* in the widest sense of the word . . . some of whom
suffered under domestic tyranny and reaction (Russia), others under foreign
tyranny and reaction (Poles, Yugoslavs, Bulgarians) and some from both (Poles,
Czechoslovaks). Slavic society in the past could only be a society of revolutionary struggle against all tyranny and reaction. All Slavic nations are by their nature exceedingly democratic and naturally exhibit stronger egalitarian tendencies than the other European nations.[41]

This struggle against "reaction" had culminated in the war against fascism,
"the largest, spiritually most vulgar and nauseating reaction," and resulted in
"all the Slavic states emerging after this war with truly popular (*lidové*) democratic regimes."[42]

The use of the politically loaded term "reaction" and the emphasis placed
on revolution are hallmarks of Beneš's discussion and certainly aided in
forming a postwar discourse conducive to communist discursive domina-

tion. The ambiguity of his attitude can be seen even in his declaration of opposition to the messianic position described above. He explicitly rejected all messianism, including communist messianism, and expressed the fear that

> The enormous victory of the USSR in World War II gave it such great political and power prestige among the Slavic nations that the mystical idea of new Russian messianism with a communist varnish forced itself, almost automatically, not only on Soviet actors, but also the simple masses in the other Slavic nations.[43]

At the same time, however, he argued, "for the future, Slavic solidarity (souručenství) is tied only to the idea of modern, popular, and radical democracy," and claimed that the lead in creating a new Slavic politics should be taken by the young, who are "unburdened by the old politics and understand the meaning of the First and Second World Wars and the Russian Revolution."[44] Similarly, Beneš underestimated the potential threat of Soviet domination. While he warned against an imperialist and expansionist Soviet Union attempting to integrate the Slavic states into the USSR, he argued this because he believed that such an attempt would fail.[45] He gave the USSR the task of showing that the "People's Democracy" was a goal rather than a means for "communizing" states, and admitted that it was legitimate to question whether "the [Communist Party of the Soviet Union] and under its influence the USSR will return to pure doctrine after the war and whether its Slavism will not remain only a tactical move as a result of this."[46] At the same time, he argued that "Soviet socialism and Russian communists have learned from the terrible world crisis after 1938." Revealing a mixture of wounded pride from Munich and renewed self-confidence gained from reinvigorated Slavism, he proclaimed that the main goal of practical Slavic politics should be "*the gaining of a new place for all Slavic nations and cultures in Europe and in the world.* Slavs as a whole and as individual nations have not been valued as they should have been valued."[47]

While the effect of the president's positions on the discourse of Slavism is impossible to measure precisely, at the bare minimum his words did much to encourage wider discussion of the question, with inevitable effects on the larger dialogue over the nation's cultural orientation. With the imprimatur of the nation's most influential noncommunist personality, efforts to raise the profile of the Czechs' Slavic ties had widespread support, and more radical arguments were thereby made difficult to rebut. Representatives of the Czechoslovak Church were the most vocal of the supporters of the "new Slavism," joyfully celebrating that the USSR's example of "unwavering will, resolute labor, and self-denying suffering for the realization of a truly humane society" had brought Czechs "closer than ever to the family of Slavic nations."[48] The church's representative at a conference entitled "Which of the Christian Churches Has the Greatest Importance for the Unification of the Slavs?" placed his church firmly behind strivings for a unified Slavic world:

> The Czechoslovak Church will strive to unify the Slavs by supporting all of the desires which have hitherto unified the Slavs and placing them on the foundation of pure Christianity, freed from superstitions and outdated ideas, so that a synthesis between religion and scientific endeavors can be brought about.[49]

Occasionally, the enthusiasm of the church's spokespeople for Slavic solidarity led them to make deeply irresponsible statements, in which their political radicalism led to the abuse of their theological responsibility. For example, Jaroslav Pravda argued overzealously in a set of articles that both "Europe and Asia have served Satan over the centuries in his war of extermination against a Slavic world whose calling is to establish the Kingdom of God and social justice on Earth." Further, he called for all Slavs to be taken "out of the hands of non-Slavs," for Slavs must "not trust anyone in the wide world: we have not one friend there."[50]

It was precisely this variety of Slavism that provided Roman Catholics, the religious group on the opposite end of the political spectrum, with an opportunity to criticize the lurch to the Slavic East. The People's Party leader Adolf Procházka maintained that the country should be a "true Slavic brother" and continue good relations with the USSR, but virtually no other intellectuals from the Roman Catholic camp were willing to go further than this lukewarm expression.[51] While they recognized the international and domestic necessity of maintaining a positive relationship with the Slavic world, they criticized what Jan Strakoš called the "idealization of the East" and the hijacking of the Slavic issue by "revolutionaries," who were taking advantage of "the revolutionary mania following our liberation."[52] The control these revolutionaries exerted over the 1946 All-Slav Congress in Belgrade led to its dismissal in the Roman Catholic press as "four days of . . . ideologically colored manifestos and speeches."[53] Following President Beneš, Pavel Tigrid went perhaps the furthest, when he condemned the implicit racism in many of the expressions of Slavism, denouncing what he called the "validating [of] the thought of Slavic brotherhood by racist hatred of all others."[54]

Despite the pronounced lack of enthusiasm on the part of Roman Catholic intellectuals, it is apparent that their communist opponents had succeeded in capitalizing on the USSR's share of victory in the Second World War and setting the terms of the debate over the nation's orientation. The resonance that so many of their ideas found among members of the democratic socialist and Protestant intelligentsia placed them in a dominant position in the postwar conceptual field and carried them far in their "revision of the national character." Their popular linking of Slavism and socialism placed their democratic socialist opponents, in particular, in a politically difficult position, for they, too, supported socialist reforms and increased contacts with their Slavic neighbors. The problem democratic socialist intellectuals confronted was one of measure: how to support a limited turn to the East, without appearing to be merely weak copies of their communist counterparts? The case made by democratic socialist intellectuals in this great debate reflected their tolerance, open-mindedness, and socialist convictions, as well as their recognition that in the aftermath of the war the balance of cultural, political, and economic power on the European continent had shifted markedly to the East. In their attempts to come to terms with the latter half of this statement, however, they placed themselves in a political position that left them appearing far less confident and assured than their communist opponents. In a period marked by the rethinking of the meaning of the Czech nation, they adopted synthetic and idealistic positions on a question as fundamental as the nation's cultural orientation. While honorable and reasonable in themselves, these left them appearing at best unsure and disunited and at worst poor mimics of communist positions. In either case they ultimately appeared incapable of fulfilling the desires of a public yearning for concrete solutions and the security that black-and-white interpretations offered.

Much as Ladislav Štoll set the parameters of the communist strategy in the attempt to redefine the Czech cultural orientation, the eminent Václav Černý encapsulated the varying responses of noncommunist intellectuals to the national reorientation. In three articles appearing in his *Kritický měsíčník*, Černý defined what he meant by "East" and "West," placed Czech culture historically in the Western camp, called for Czech intellectuals to synthesize the thought of both East and West while remaining critical of both, and mirrored the messianic rhetoric of his communist opponents in proclaiming this synthesis the highest task of "Češství," a term embodying all of the qualities of the Czech character.

In contrast to his communist counterparts, Černý defined in his first article precisely what he meant by the terms *East* and *West*. Narrowly construed, the East was Russia, while more broadly interpreted it included all of the Slavic lands. He noted that since the time of the Enlightenment Czechs had looked to Russia for cultural impulses, so that the current interest in the USSR was in no respect out of the ordinary or a matter of concern: "That the old Russophilism of our culture is gaining quasi-official certification alarms me in no special way. It is only an official seal on what has been long dictated by a natural and unforced love."[55] Nevertheless, Černý had no doubt that Czech culture was essentially Western. A professor of comparative literature who had attended the Lyceum in Dijon as a young man and concerned himself professionally with French literature, he not surprisingly saw the core of the West residing in France. In the broader West, he included the remainder of the Latin world and Great Britain. In Černý's view, Czech culture had made its decision for the West during the battles between Eastern and Roman Christianity in the ninth through eleventh centuries. The choice was "above all about spiritual life itself, about the conception of civilization, the way of thinking and social and personal behavior [dějstvování]." In opting for the West, Czechs had internalized two fundamental Western ideas—Greco-Roman "humanitas" and Christian "caritas"—that had "defined our later development." In later centuries, the Western character of Czech culture became even more pronounced, as "the Reformation, Enlightenment, ideas from the French Revolution, and the entire nineteenth century show the Western character of our modern culture." The political thought of the nation was an essential outgrowth of this cultural orientation, with Havlíček and Masaryk growing "directly from the conceptual substance of the West."[56] Černý argued that these figures were more than just expressions of Western ideas in the Czech character, but were symbols of the nation itself and, by extension, of its exclusively Western character. He asked whether it was any wonder that:

> The names of these most convinced of our modern "Westerners" are simultaneously the symbols of the most honored Czechness [*češkost*]? The stress on the absolute unity of Western culture and Czechness [*češství*], that in our national life the West has played a thoroughly constructive role, that it formed us, reinforced us, and led us to the recognition of our own spiritual essence and our historical tasks, all this . . . is not even subject to debate. It is absolutely self-evident. After more than ten centuries, "homo bohemicus" understands his striving for a more perfect and more complete humanity, his self-perfection, and the full realization of his calling on Earth as part of the larger role that Western Man is fulfilling in the world.[57]

This did not mean, however, that Černý meant for Czechs to look exclusively to the West for cultural regeneration after the cataclysm of war. Although the Czechs were "a Western nation by our ancient culture" they were not allowed "to evade even one of [the East's] fruitful impulses, not even one little part of its wealth." By urging a cultural orientation directed toward both East and West, Černý hoped to give "a clear answer to an unclear question, East or West? Neither the West in place of the East or the East in place of the West, but the East *and* the West."[58] This clear answer, however, could be criticized as an example of the kind of reply Štoll criticized as "Hamletesque." Perhaps better than any other commentator, Černý recognized that "everything is a political matter." Yet he rejected solving matters of culture by bare political categories, by "narrow party propaganda," claiming that his analysis had avoided this danger. He insisted that his binary cultural perspective had been motivated by the correct reading of the cultural situation, "absolutely not by any Hamletism."[59]

One of the most important characteristics of Černý's instruction to look both East and West was that the reception must be critical. Czechs were obliged by Černý to follow Havlíček and Masaryk in adopting critical attitudes toward Russia, although similarly they should not accept Western cultural trends without question.[60] Consequently, he directed his attention primarily toward communist intellectuals and their sympathizers, in whose enthusiastic panegyrics he perceived a danger to the free development of Czech culture. While he did not believe that the USSR would "prescribe" developments in postwar Czechoslovakia, he defensively warned his "Eastern-oriented countrymen" that West-leaning intellectuals were "at least as qualified as they to speak about our nation's spiritual affairs." In Černý's view, Czechs must choose for themselves: "We simply will not ask Russia what of the spiritual essence of the West is good for us or will nourish us, just as we will not ask the West what we will assume from Russian models."[61]

The endpoint of Černý's analysis was a rejuvenated and world-significant Češství, one that necessarily entailed learning from both the USSR and the Western democracies. He directed Czechs in their position between East and West to ensure that their culture "remain Czech, to be in the future as it was in our greatest eras: not only Western, not only Eastern, but truly human!"[62] Although Czechs could draw upon "the model and support of the moral example" of the USSR, this was not to be taken as "a model for blind imitation." He supported his argument with quotations from Marxist classics, including one from Stalin's *Questions of Leninism* that maintained that socialism "will be realized in forms corresponding to the languages and mores of [the individual societies'] nationalities." Černý concluded, "we want to build a culture of Czech socialist humanism. In that we are all agreed. But we will not build anything either Czech or cultural if we are not able to create entirely freely. . . . Our socialist humanism will be different from the Russian, simply because it will be Czech."[63] Emphasis on the freedom of cultural expression alongside the citation of classics of communist theory was a hallmark of Černý's arguments, as we shall see later in this study.

Finally, Černý's call contained a messianic view that mirrored the way in which the new Slavism was seen by communist intellectuals and acknowledged by many democratic socialists. Instead of investing the larger Slavic world with a redemptive function, however, he ascribed it to the Czechs alone, on whose ability to synthesize East and West the world's future depended. Černý recognized that the task would not be easy to accomplish, for it required Czechs "to harmonize two types of human life. . . . in no way to establish a temporary compromise of both, but to digest, fuse, and unite them in a new, internally consistent higher organism." On the resolution of this dialectic within the Czech character the fate of the world depended: "future peace is possible only at the price of its [a "*Czech* synthesis of cultural forces'"] success."[64] Czechs should regard this task not as a burdensome responsibility but as an honor, since through it they could serve not only themselves, but also Europe and ultimately humanity as a whole:

> Western European intellectuals literally *hope* [for our success] and this consequently places a higher duty upon us. At this time we are in the position of a *privileged* nation in the world, being—apart from the horribly exhausted Poles—the *only* nation expressly *Western* in culture entering into a sphere

decidedly under the politico-cultural influence of *Russia.* The question of a much longed-for synthesis is given to us, we are charged to solve it first, possibly *as an example* for all Europe.[65]

[This is] a task of great honor! A task of honor in that the duty to the nation here expands into a duty to humanity. A task of honor in that such a task could not be entrusted to just anyone and Czechs are not today, nor have they ever been, a nation given just any task, whatever is at hand. Czechness [*Češkost*] should again also be worldliness [*světovost*], our solution should be a supranational example and have supranational validity.[66]

The messianism this widely held view reveals bears evident political risks, risks that will become more apparent when we see its recurrence in democratic socialist intellectuals' understandings of socialism.

Černý found both support and dissent among his democratic socialist compatriots. Their multiplicity of views stood in contrast to the united front presented by Communist Party intellectuals and augmented by the intellectual representatives of the Protestant churches and even some democratic socialists themselves. While his conception of the East as the USSR and the Slavic lands of Eastern Europe found no disagreement, several observers questioned his attribution of France as the locus of the Western world. They agreed that France had served as the focus of Czech cultural life before the war, but argued that its wartime defeat, attributed to moral and cultural defects, had caused it to lose pride of place among the Western nations. In the words of Černý's colleague, professor of literature J. B. Čapek, the Second World War had ended "not only the forced power hegemony of Germany, but also the long voluntarily accepted cultural hegemony of France that reached its height after the First World War." As a result of the French collapse, Čapek argued, the meanings of East and West had correspondingly changed: "before the war the East-West problem appeared to Czechs as the opposition Soviet Union/France . . . today it appears to the thoughtful observer above all as the antithesis Soviet Union/the Anglo-Saxon world."[67] This way of viewing the East/West dichotomy in light of the postwar geopolitical situation was the most common, being shared by both Roman Catholics, such as Minister Procházka, and several communist commentators.[68] In the only significant deviation from this pattern, Communist Party leaders, such as Gottwald, occasionally attempted to imply that the dichotomy was in fact the USSR versus Germany, although these found little resonance.[69]

That other noncommunists did not share Černý's sentiments on the importance of France did not mean that they objected to his characterization of the Czech nation as overwhelmingly Western. For Roman Catholic intellectual leaders like Pavel Tigrid, Czechs belonged "morally, politically, culturally, and religiously to Western European civilization. We had the Western interpretation of the Bible in the Middle Ages, Greek and Roman philosophy, and social-revolutionary impulses from the West. The sources of our national rebirth [and] of our liberalism lie in the West." In Tigrid's view, the communist attempt to change the nation's orientation was doomed to failure: Czechs "could be turned into Easterners only through programmatic action. [E]ven if the Communist Party were victorious. . . . even if the Communist Party had unlimited power [it could not be achieved] because of the unshakable and centuries-old obstacle" of Czech Westernness.[70] Other comments were in unison with this historically based conception, holding that Czechs were "obviously and indisputably" Western and that their culture "was, is, and will be predominantly Western."[71]

Černý's slogan "the East *and* the West" found much support throughout the noncommunist camp. From the Roman Catholic government minister František Hála through Protestant leader J. L. Hromádka to Václav Běhounek writing in *Práce*, voices across the spectrum agreed that Czechoslovakia had "the best preconditions for striving for a unified European civilization."[72] For the professor of literature history Albert Pražák, one of the leaders of the 1945 Prague Uprising, "Generations long past already decided in favor of both 'East and West.' We have always been for incorporating everything in the world that furthers the role of the spirit." Others similarly called for a synthesis that would not be "a mere arrangement, a halfway measure. True synthesis is a creative creation [*tvůrčí tvar*]," or stressed that "the synthesis, before whose realization we have been placed, is that of a *real* synthesis."[73]

What did the noncommunist intellectuals mean when they called for a real synthesis? Leaving aside the ambiguities in the conceptions of socialism yet to be discussed, the disappointing answer is that they did not attempt to delineate the synthesized culture of the Czech future. The most identifiable tendency was to call for the simultaneous realization of the aims of both the French and the Russian revolutions. They hoped that in "the synthesis of the Western understanding of freedom and the Eastern requirement of equality it is possible to arrive at a system in which all will receive both bread and freedom."[74] Rather than describing how the East and the West would be synthesized, many avoided the problem by positing the future convergence of the two systems. Many in the intellectual caste held with the historian Zdeněk Kalista that the modern world with all its technological advances "is leading more and more distinctly not only to osmosis, a mixing of one culture with another, but directly to some kind of cultural syncretism. . . . In the future we will be deciding between the two cultural regions less and less."[75] In this view, the West would be learning socialism from the East and the East democracy from the West. It appears that these Czech intellectuals hoped to leap ahead to the point of ultimate convergence by creating a living synthesis of the two.[76]

Most interesting is the outright rejection of the idea that Czechoslovakia could serve as a "bridge" between the two, despite the sympathy with which it was viewed in the months immediately following the war, and the wide resonance the term has found in later commentary on the period. The initial importance of the conception was ascribed by Jindřich Chalupecký as constituting "part of the Czech character to search for some kind of 'something in-between.'" For Chalupecký the adoption of such a position was doomed to failure, since Czechs "are and will remain a part of Europe and we will not wrench ourselves from its fate, from the struggle between the 'Eastern' and the 'Western' conceptions, between socialism and capitalism. Nor will we be a 'bridge,' where these two conceptions would meet."[77] Chalupecký's view was reiterated across the political spectrum. Communists condemned the idea, holding that "the conception of a 'Czechoslovak bridge'" maintained "the compromised link to Western capitalism."[78] Moreover, voices from the highest levels of the noncommunist camp agreed with President Beneš's statement, "for us the function of a so-called bridge between East and West does not exist."[79] These ranged from assessments that found, like Černý, that Czechoslovak culture was so rooted in the West that it could not serve as a bridge, to those that considered the geopolitical situation and superpower relations too discouraging for the Czechs to fulfill such a function.[80]

While Czech democratic socialist intellectuals rejected the notion of the "bridge," they overwhelmingly supported synthesizing elements of both cultures and generally followed Černý's final two arguments. Almost universally, they urged the adoption of a critical stance toward both East and West, warning particularly against the vulgar assumption of Soviet culture. Moreover, in a related rhetorical strategy, they called for their countrymen to remain true to themselves, stressing the value and strength of domestic traditions and urging self-reliance. This acted as a brake on the stress communists placed on developing the purportedly "Slavic" qualities of the Czechs' Soviet allies. From the moderate National Socialist press to the Social Democratic leader Bohumil Laušman there were demands that Czechs "must look at all sides of the world and choose from everywhere . . . the more critically, the better."[81]

A few observers were more persistent on the point, however, and hinted at the looming danger of Soviet cultural domination. They took aim at the uncritical, glowing praise for all facets of Soviet life produced by communist intellectuals and their allies. Part of this condition may be attributed to the press restrictions that strictly limited criticism of the Soviet Union. As one anonymous author pointed out, since communists controlled the Ministry of Information, Czechs were better informed about the insufficiencies of the West: "those who have their mouths filled with communism, who are full of reverence for the Soviet Union, do not care for us to be thoroughly informed about the USSR."[82] In light of this, the calls for Czechs to be as critical of the East as they were of the West were largely directed against "those who wanted to gain sympathy for Russia by uncritical puppeting or servile kowtowing [*nekritickým papouškováním nebo podlezavým poklonkováním*]."[83] It is important to note that these comments did not attack the Soviet system even as an abstraction, but rather argued that "we cannot bow down to [the USSR] as devotedly as did our predecessors toward France, we will not fawn over it and sing to the glory of Stalin, but rather strive to learn."[84] Democratic socialists like Sychrava argued that "foreign models and examples can be a stimulus for us, but in no way a pattern." However, they also expressed their concern over the popularity of the simple and certain rhetoric of the communists among the population, noting that maintaining a difficult balance "assumes critical thinking. . . . And thinking as we know hurts, and so we have among us . . . superficial fanatics of Eastern methods."[85]

There were certainly political costs associated with criticizing either the deepening of contacts with the Slavic nations or a cultural and political orientation directed toward the Soviet Union. It was noted in the National Socialist *Svobodný zítřek* that the "basic orientation toward the USSR" was "undoubtedly popular among the population, who would overwhelmingly support any vote on it."[86] In light of this, it comes as no surprise that much noncommunist rhetoric stressed the more limited goal of maintaining a specifically Czechoslovak orientation. Several noncommunist intellectuals characterized the debate over the national orientation as "a question of spiritual independence."[87] This allowed them to avoid appearing in the uncomfortable position of opposing the wave of popular support for both socialism and its Soviet embodiment. Noncommunist intellectuals believed they could not win "the struggle for the soul of the nation" with rhetoric directed in any way against the Soviet Union, nor were they inclined to such a position.

Noncommunist and particularly democratic socialist intellectuals could also use this strategy in their attempt to formulate a Czech self-identity that was socialist but not bound to the cultural and political forms of the USSR. While they maintained that Czechs should be open to all that was "new and creative," shorthand for socialist culture and mores, what was accepted into their state's culture must be "elaborated [*zpracováno*] in a Czech way."[88] It was only through adapting ideas from other lands, and primarily those from the USSR, to Czech traditions and conditions that Czech intellectuals could "truly serve the nation."[89] This line of argument was summed up in an article in the National Socialist weekly *Masarykův lid*:

> Only if we do not deviate from our Czech or, if you like, Czechoslovak path, directed by our traditions and our culture will it mean a boundless enriching and deepening of our national being. This is what the reflections about East and West are truly about. That in all earnest and open cooperation with the West and the East we not lose ourselves, that we remain faithful to ourselves.[90]

In addition to attempting to stem the tide of the communist "revision of the national character," the emphasis placed on remaining faithful to themselves revealed concern for the battering Czech self-conception had taken since the debacle of Munich. As one noted writer observed about the entire question of national orientation, "sadness emanates from this question, from the fact that it was necessary to ask it. Has faith in ourselves and our traditions . . . vanished?" Another hoped that, despite the "hot-blooded dispute" over the national cultural orientation, the nation was so critically and culturally developed that "any trend can influence it only in passing, incidentally, opportunistically, most often in times when we are searching for more solid ground under our feet."[91] In the wake of the experiences of Munich and the Second World War, however, Czechs *were* making such a search. After the traumatic events of 1938–1945, the confident, assured, and resoundingly optimistic communist rhetoric—backed up by the material and moral example of the USSR and the powerful notion of a new Slavism—stood in stark contrast to the calm and rational, but also more diffuse and hesitant, public pose of the democratic intellectuals. Again, Roman Catholics were alone in maintaining a firmly Western stance. Diametrically opposed to the Catholics, here as in every other issue, stood Czechoslovak Church intellectuals who had grasped the notion of Slavism and sought the unification of all the Slavic peoples.

As should be evident from each individual topic analyzed in the preceding chapters, as well as their overall tenor, the communists dominated the conceptual limits of discourse with their "revision of the national character." On issues so vital for the national self-understanding—from the interpretation of national heroes such as Hus and Masaryk to the issue of the fundamental cultural orientation of the nation—communist intellectuals largely determined the field of debate and the issues over which debates would take place. They successfully won widespread support for their reinterpretation of Jan Hus, for their criticism of the interwar republic, and for their interpretations of the fundamental meanings of Munich and the Second World War. Despite their failure to appropriate completely the heritage of President Masaryk, they were remarkably successful in parlaying the USSR's wartime victory into a consensus on the value of the East and could rely on the widespread sympathy for Slavism in reorienting the national cultural self-understanding toward a Slavic East with the USSR at its head. These debates revealed a deep shift in the Czech national self-conception. In place of the prewar pride in the First Republic and in belonging to the Western family of nations, a new Slavic and also socialist Czech identity was being forged, which found its institutional embodiment in the "People's Democracy" and in that system's domestic social configuration and international political orientation.

Communist intellectuals could not have achieved this without the considerable assistance of groups of intellectuals who saw themselves as supporters of the communists' efforts. Here the support of Protestant intellectuals should be highlighted. Little noted and rarely discussed in examinations of postwar Czech political, cultural, and intellectual history, their influence has been unjustly overlooked. The intellectual and spiritual leadership of the

Czechoslovak Church, which represented roughly one-eighth of the Czech public and was markedly strong in Prague, not only stood behind the communist reinterpretation but actively drove it forward, occasionally outdistancing even communist intellectuals themselves. The alliance of that church, with its desire for a radical reformulation of Christianity, and forces aiming to radically reform the nation's self-understanding made sense. Dangerously, however, Czechoslovak Church leaders occasionally allowed their social radicalism to trump their theological responsibility. This trait, as we shall see, was especially pronounced in their understandings of socialism. Evangelical leaders similarly supported communist views but remained more restrained. In many ways, as a group they behaved more like intellectuals from the democratic socialist group, while intellectuals from the Czechoslovak Church behaved like communists.

The communists also gained much support from their opponents in the democratic socialist camp. These men and women undoubtedly believed that there were defects with the Czech national self-understanding and saw the traumas of Munich and World War II as having their postwar consequences. In their efforts to rebuild the Czech nation, however, a number of disturbing characteristics recurred. Above all, democratic socialist intellectuals were often quick to place themselves close to communist interpretations, whether in criticizing the First Republic or trumpeting the heroic values and rosy future of Slavism. The adoption of these positions had the effect of lending credence to at least parts of the communists' much larger attempt to radically reorient the nation's self-conception—a goal with which they could not agree. For this reorientation, the communists had a coherent and complete interpretive structure, composed of Marxism and a nationalist Slavism, that could provide forceful and believable explanations for the ordeals the nation had experienced. The elements were all linked in an easily recognizable whole, whereby democratic socialist support for individual elements redounded to the plausibility and conceptual power of that whole. Democratic socialists appeared largely incognizant of this, and of the political and cultural implications their support bore.

Further, even when democratic socialist intellectuals disagreed with their communist opponents, they were careful not to do so too sharply, and phrased their responses as a set of careful and reasoned compromises. These may have genuinely reflected their considered opinions of the matters at hand but bore the weaknesses pointed out so often in the preceding pages. Their statements lent at least partial credence to communist argumentation, contributing to the notion that perhaps the communists had the correct interpretation after all. Simultaneously, democratic socialists' reasoned compromises left them looking divided, since they often stressed different elements in arriving at somewhat different conclusions. This often happens when truth is the goal sought, but it indirectly contributed to the appealing cogency, clarity, and explanatory power of the communist reinvention of the nation. In combination with the communist ideas that democratic socialists supported, democratic socialist argumentation contributed to a decided fuzziness of exactly what the essential differences were between the intellectual positions of the Communist Party (and left-wing Social Democrats) on the one hand and National Socialists (and right-wing Social Democrats) on the other. This confusion had immeasurable yet distinct political ramifications. Democratic socialists' compromises too often left them appearing as diluted communists, unable to travel the full path to communist belief. Their attempt to break with the revolutionary tide they had helped to create found expression in argumentation that said to the communists "this far and no farther" in matters of interpretation, but it also gave away much rhetorical ground before raising opposition.

Perhaps most disturbing was the messianic zeal with which many democratic socialists viewed the nation's calling. This aspect pervaded, tacitly or not, much of their argumentation here as well as in their notions of socialism yet to be discussed. Whether in the striving toward perfection from the imperfect interwar republic, in the sense that May 5th was a "correction" or "completion" of strivings begun on October 28, 1918, in the inflated notions of Slavdom, or in the Czechs' calling to synthesize East and West synergically into a higher unity that would serve humankind, these intellectuals believed they were playing a historic role. The nation they led would internally perfect itself and thereby heal the contradictions of a larger world. The notion of this special mission represents a flight from the realm of the politically wise, and perhaps even from the politically possible. It encouraged the wider public to believe that all things were possible and that the Communist Party's dominance in Czechoslovakia would necessarily have different effects than in neighboring countries, about which it was notably ill-informed. It contributed to the notion that all circles could be squared simply because of the fact that it was the Czech nation performing the action. This had grave consequences when the form and nature of the Czech socialism then being constructed were on the intellectual agenda.

Finally, the Roman Catholic intelligentsia played a role remarkable for both its continuous opposition to one-sided communist interpretation and its internal consistency. These generally calm men and women fought, often alone, against every point in the communist interpretive program without appearing obstinate, obstructive, or uninformed. They defended the role of the West in the Munich tragedy as evenhandedly as possible, repeatedly stressed that the West was also responsible for the liberation of Czechoslovakia, defended the First Republic and Masaryk, expressed grave concerns about the political savvy and revolutionary enthusiasm of the youth, and tied themselves to a Western cultural orientation. Their worldview was predicated on a solid Catholic foundation that naturally opposed them to communism from the outset but also gave them an underlying fount of ideas and understandings that together formed a complete whole. This distinguishes them from their Protestant counterparts in the Czechoslovak Church, who often appeared to let their Christian ideas be overwhelmed by their desire for radical social change. It also distinguishes them from democratic socialists, who lacked an internally consistent and solid conceptual matrix that could have provided them with a forceful bastion from which they could securely defend their positions and coherently counterattack communist arguments in a concerted fashion. The strategies and attitudes adopted by all these groups on the issue of the "revision of the national character" were repeated, clarified, and intensified when discussion turned to the central question of postwar Czech society—socialism.

9

Socialism and Communist Intellectuals: The "Czechoslovak Road to Socialism"

Communist intellectuals' broad cultural offensive and their widely successful attempt to reformulate the national identity prepared the public for the debate over socialism, a debate that gained intensity only after the 1946 elections. The Communist Party's refraining from discussing its vision of socialism during the first year after liberation benefited the party and its allies. Above all, the silence allowed time for communists' reinvention of the nation to develop and for their own reinvention as Czech patriots to gain plausibility. Furthermore, the advances made in that sphere were not threatened by fears raised by disturbingly radical statements on exclusively political and social matters. The silence thus reinforced the party's popular image and made it possible for it to gain a mass of new members and emerge victorious from the 1946 elections. Moreover, as their party was considered the repository of true socialist thought, communist intellectuals' silence on the matter of socialism placed pressure on their opponents to define their positions on this central issue. In the atmosphere of revolutionary enthusiasm that dominated the first post-liberation months, noncommunist leaders were forced by Communist Party silence, public pressure, and their own sensibilities to proclaim their allegiance to the task of socialist change.

Even after their victory at the ballot box, the Communist Party's intellectual and political leaders stated their goals moderately. Knowingly or unwittingly, they played on the perception that Czech Communists were not like other Communists by formulating their aims as a "specific Czechoslovak road to socialism." While the impetus for this formulation came from Moscow, the national road strategy fit Czechoslovak circumstances extremely well. Without specifying the final form Czechoslovak socialism would take, the Communist Party fashioned a program that stressed already existing elements of which the public overwhelmingly approved: the People's Democracy, the National Front government, and the Two-Year Plan for the economy. All of these reassured the public that the party did not intend a radical shift toward a Soviet-style regime. The plausibility of this calm, parliamentary road was bolstered by communist intellectuals' reinvention of the nation, the Communist Party's reinvention of itself, and by the party's announcement of the goal to win a majority of the vote in the 1948 elections.

The battle over the meaning of socialism was a crucial one for the Communist Party and its fellow-traveling allies on the left wing of the Social Democratic Party. It constituted the political and social twin of the cultural battle over the revision of the nation's self-understanding and orientation. In presenting their side of the debate, Communist intellectuals showed considerable flexibility in their relationship to their party's ideological foundation in Marxism-Leninism, and in particular to the central notions of dialectical materialism and the dictatorship of the proletariat. This flexibility, partly a cause and partly a consequence of the "Czechoslovak road" policy, placed their opponents on the defensive. Thus, as was the case in the debate over the "revision of the national character," communist intellectuals were able to set many of the terms and boundaries of the field of debate.

With these topics we encounter a set of thorny historiographical disputes. The Czechoslovak communist regime, particularly in the 1950s, maintained that the developments of the 1945–1948 period were cut from one piece of cloth. In this view, the "national and democratic revolution" grew naturally and spontaneously under disciplined Communist Party leadership into a truly socialist revolution that placed the Communist Party in power.[1] On the other side of the Iron Curtain, émigré political leaders repeatedly stressed an argument that appealed to Western cold warriors, that the Communist Party leadership had returned to its liberated homeland with a clear plan for seizing total power. In the words of one National Socialist Party leader, from March 1945 the Communists "knew exactly by what means and in what circumstances they would come to power."[2] Both the Stalinist and émigré arguments share the conception of a Communist Party that had a program that had been worked out beforehand and was implemented in order to gain total power for the party.[3] The Communist Party and its intellectual supporters certainly wished to create a socialist Czechoslovakia oriented toward the East. However, they came with neither a preconceived, preformulated strategy designed to carry them to power nor a complete conception of how the state would look at various stages along the way. Instead, like all of the other parties in immediate postwar Czechoslovakia (and, in fact, political parties generally), the Communist Party responded to events as they occurred and designed its strategy accordingly, including that of the "Czechoslovak road." In this we can agree with the 1960s reformist historian Václav Pavlíček that "this specific road was not a precisely elaborated and comprehensive model, but was developed in response to concrete conditions."[4] These conditions certainly included Soviet needs and desires, as well as reflecting international developments. That Soviet behavior, particularly between 1945 and 1947, corresponded well to the domestic needs of the Communist Party of Czechoslovakia was a happy coincidence for the party.

In order to understand the meaning and importance of the "specific Czechoslovak road to socialism" one must again look back to the war and the changes that it catalyzed in Czech Communists' conception of their socioeconomic system. Already in the Moscow exile, it has been argued, the idea of a Czechoslovak road to socialism emerged, even if its name and contours were not yet fixed. Moreover, the ideas of the exile leadership were paramount because of the decimation of the prewar communists in the course of the resistance. Party casualties during the war reached 25,000, and fewer than 29,000 of its prewar members remained after liberation. Finally, the unity witnessed among all parties during the war, both at home and abroad, in their general demands for the reconstitution of the republic led to the adoption of many of the Communist Party's immediate goals. This final point takes us far in understanding why Communists were reticent to discuss their vision of socialism in the early post-liberation months. The reorientation of foreign policy toward Moscow, the limitation on the number of political parties, and the position the party came to occupy in the political system as a result of the Moscow discussions of March 1945 certainly worked to their advantage.

With the parties' points of fundamental agreement enshrined in the Košice program, there was little need for the party's intellectual or political leadership to make concrete statements concerning its view of socialism. They were quite obviously the supreme party of socialism: as Toman Brod has aptly put it, "All the rest [of the parties] mouthed the name of socialism in vain. Only the communists were the Chosen Party."[5] The revolutionary élan of the Czech populace in the first months after the war's end, reflected by the massive influx into the Communist Party, meant that the party was not compelled to place detailed plans for the future before the public and risk losing its growing support. Instead, communist intellectuals came to the fore, attacking on the cultural front while the political battle over socialism remained nascent. The victory in the battle for the refashioning of the Czech national self-conception thus was the crucial precondition for the battle over the political future of Czechoslovakia. This was tacitly recognized by the historian Josef Belda in 1967, when his attempt to unravel the problem of the "Czechoslovak road" led him to conclude about the Communist Party's activities before the 1946 elections that:

> It is certain that political power, the political leadership of society, is a precondition for acting and leading in the other spheres. However, in certain circumstances (and by this I mean at a time when the relationship of forces between the bourgeoisie and the proletariat is essentially balanced) influence and action in the other, non-political spheres can predominate or precede.[6]

Simultaneously, the identification of the Communist Party with socialism and that party's rapid growth put pressure on the noncommunist parties to formulate their own, distinctive answers to the question of social organization. If the public believed the Communists were exemplary patriots as well as the most consistent socialists, the noncommunists were in serious need of a strategy of their own.

Finally, the adoption of almost all of the Communists' immediate aims in the Moscow discussions had bequeathed the party a position for which it had anticipated it would have to fight. The party's ideological elite could therefore adopt a "wait and see" attitude while judging the mood of the nation. The upshot of these circumstances is that the first article in *Tvorba* with a form of the word *socialism* in its title does not appear until over seven months after liberation and is, moreover, a historical article.[7] Likewise, Brod reports that Chairman Gottwald first mentioned socialism as the direction in which events in Czechoslovakia were moving only on March 10, 1946, some ten months after liberation. In light of these circumstances, we can certainly agree with his assessment: "The theme of the socialist development of Czechoslovakia . . . was for many months after May 1945 *taboo* for the communists."[8]

Communist Party political and intellectual leaders instead stressed that the nation was carrying out what they called a "national and democratic revolution." This movement had two principal aims. The "national" component consisted of the expulsion of prewar Czechoslovakia's 3 million ethnically German citizens and the exchange of its Magyar minority for ethnic Slovaks living in Hungary. This was to be followed by the nationalization of the holdings of the expelled population and the transferal of much of this property to poorer Czechs and Slovaks. In this way, Klement Gottwald stressed, power would pass "from the hands of the oppressor nation, the nation of occupiers, the German nation, into the hands of the formerly oppressed nation, the Czech and Slovak nation—in this sense our revolution is a national revolution."

The nationalization measures and the redistribution of the property of the expelled ethnic minorities and collaborators, as well as the banning of those political parties deemed to have collaborated, constituted the democratic component. Thus Gottwald similarly stressed: "As far as our struggle, our revolution, is directed against Czech and Slovak treason and reaction and its political and economic bearers, our revolution is simultaneously a democratic revolution." In order to erase all doubt in the minds of his party's most active members, Gottwald emphasized, "it is necessary to again and again be aware that at this stage we are moving along the path of a national and democratic revolution, and in no way along the path of a socialist revolution."[9] The program of this national and democratic revolution was taken by Gustav Bareš to be the Košice program, which supports the contention that the communists had gained more than they had anticipated in the discussions over its formulation.[10]

Nonetheless, already in the first months after liberation, the Communist Party came under criticism from its own ranks for its moderation. Radical elements within the party, notably among those who had fought in the domestic resistance, condemned the line as "opportunist."[11] They had expected the institution of a dictatorship of the proletariat immediately after liberation. Extremists within the party's ally, the Social Democratic Party, similarly accused it of having "betrayed the working class, practicing coalition politics and making a pact [*paktuje*] with the bourgeoisie."[12] The party remained cautious even in the face of insistent demands from its bulwark of support within the trade union movement for more rapid and extensive progress on the issue of the nationalizations.[13] In sum, the Communist Party's conception of its politics of moderation did not change from the end of the war until at least the spring of 1946.[14] This despite the fact that it was apparent to communist and noncommunist activists alike that the party could have seized total power already in 1945.[15]

In fact, the Communist Party's line remained unchanged through its Eighth Party Congress of March 1946. At that meeting, the party faithful were given the news that the Communists had reached the million-member mark, becoming the largest party in Czech history.[16] This in itself was ample testimony to the success of the party's moderate course, a course that the leading political lights of the party emphasized, flanked by portraits of Gottwald and Beneš. The party general secretary, the later-executed Rudolf Slánský, coolly stressed that the communists were devoted to "calmly and peacefully . . . building the republic."[17] The themes of Slavism, patriotism, and national traditions explored in part 2 of this study were emphasized throughout, and the usually rabid Václav Kopecký even took time to reassure the Roman Catholic Church of the party's commitment to religious freedom and tolerance. He proclaimed that the party had "nothing against socialism and communism being proclaimed as the realization of Christian equality and Christian community," and singled out both the Czechoslovak Church and the Evangelical Church as "loyal and convinced helpers" of the new regime.[18]

It is true that there was no talk of a "Czechoslovak road" at the Eighth Party Congress, but there is evidence that already at that time elements that became the foundation of the policy began to appear. This is particularly the case for the words of party chairman Klement Gottwald. In the Congress's telegram to Stalin—signed by no less than Gottwald, Slánský, and Minister of the Interior Nosek—the great leader was thanked for giving Czechs "the possibility to build our new, free state according to our own democratic decisions."[19] In hindsight, this can be seen as foreshadowing the permission for the "national roads" that Stalin was to grant several months later. In his speech to the delegates, Gottwald stressed the importance of the Košice program and the National Front system of government. He placed particular emphasis on the factors that he would shortly thereafter claim had made the adoption of the "Czechoslovak road to socialism" possible: the defeat of Nazi Germany, the USSR's role in that defeat, "the complete ideological, political, and moral bankruptcy" of the bourgeoisie and the unity of the Czechoslovak people. In keeping with the party's reticence, he refrained from even mentioning socialism. Only at the end of his speech did he add, "The final meaning of our entire endeavor . . . is the realization of the great and sacred ideals of socialism. We are on the right road."[20] The moderation of the entire Congress and its foreshadowing of the oncoming "Czechoslovak road" are important for refuting the later Communist argument that a direct ideological line can be drawn from the Congress to the party's assumption of power in February 1948. In fact, the opposite is closer to the truth, as Jaroslav Opat has pointed out:

> The connection between the line of the Eighth Congress and February 1948 is *not* programmatic. It is only indirect. The line of the Eighth Congress was—in its undeformed [by Stalinist historiography] shape—a line of the struggle for socialism in the broadest sense of the word. A line that grew from the conditions of 1946. In its way, it was a program for a specific road to socialism.[21]

Clearly, the Communist Party's impressive victory in the May 1946 parliamentary elections opened the way for the more full development of the party's earlier themes and emboldened it to enter into a more specific discussion of socialism. The Communists, as the leading party in the government, needed to come forward with their interpretation of the term "socialism." This was perceived by the new prime minister, Klement Gottwald, who recognized in October 1946 that "[we] have not talked much about socialism in the past 16 months."[22] The party's possibilities for doing so were exponentially expanded by the words of one man: Josef Stalin. In the summer of 1946 he held a conversation with British Labour Party leaders in which he proclaimed the possibility of various roads leading to socialism.[23] This Soviet ideological offensive, aimed primarily at the West, nonetheless also showed vibrancy in Eastern Europe. Soon thereafter, "national roads" began appearing across the region, proclaimed in Bulgaria, Romania (by Patrascanu), and Poland (by Gomulka), among others. Undoubtedly, however, the Eastern European communist party that benefited the most from Stalin's words was the Communist Party of Czechoslovakia, in whose country the conditions were the most favorable for its application. The party had gained over 40 percent of the Czech vote, and the fact must be faced that only the Yugoslav Communists could surpass the Communist Party of Czechoslovakia's authority among its populace.[24] The party's careful reinvention of itself and its constant stress on Slavism, patriotism, the national history, and the nation's traditions of democracy and social justice had laid the perfect foundation for a specific "Czechoslovak road" to socialism. To some extent, it seemed that Stalin himself had blessed the Czech Communists' politics.

Gottwald, whose speech to the party congress seemed to foreshadow the Marshal's words, wasted little time in taking advantage of the changed Soviet line. Upon his return from a visit with Stalin in Moscow, he told the Central Committee of the results of his journey:

> You have certainly read in the press news about the conversation of Comrade Stalin with the delegation of British Labourites, in which Comrade Stalin referred to the various roads to socialism. . . . I had a similar conversation with Stalin during my latest visit to Moscow. Comrade Stalin said that, as experience has shown and the classics of Marxism-Leninism teach, there does not exist only one road to socialism. . . . He expressly mentioned our land, saying that here a special road to socialism is possible, one which does not necessarily have to lead through the soviets and the dictatorship of the proletariat. . . . We will follow our own road to socialism. We have a model in the Soviet Union, but neither Stalin, nor we ourselves, will disguise that this road is our own, special, longer, slower, more complicated and more winding.[25]

> We have already gone part of the way on our specific road to socialism. We have learned how to travel on it and we will continue down this road resolutely and firmly.[26]

The policy of a calm, peaceful and parliamentary road to socialism was announced to the public shortly thereafter, and it was left largely to party intellectuals to elaborate the initially vague concept.

The primary task confronting communist intellectuals was that of explaining why the "Czechoslovak road" had arisen only recently, and why the parliamentarianism criticized before the war had now become a cornerstone of communist politics. As a result, the history of communism was reinterpreted to argue that even Russia could have followed a parliamentary road, had its exponents not made a pact with the bourgeoisie, making the Bolshevik revolution that country's only truly socialist option. The Czech party's stress on the dictatorship of the proletariat in the interwar republic was likewise seen as stemming from the power of the bourgeoisie, leaving Czech communists no other choice.[27] The Second World War had changed all this. Gottwald's speech at the Eighth Congress was invoked as communist intellectuals explained the four components that had made a "Czechoslovak road" possible. Most important was the defeat of fascist Germany and its domestic reactionary helpers, who had revealed their "moral, political, and ideological bankruptcy."[28] The communists had been largely successful in painting the Munich Accords as the result of "reactionary" capitalist and Western actions, and that argument could logically be brought to bear here. The leading role the USSR had played in the defeat of Germany was likewise stressed, drawing on the already elaborated argument concerning Slavism, the Soviet Union, and the nation's orientation. The third component was the leading role of the Communist Party in the resistance movement and the losses the party had suffered. The Communists' reinvention of themselves as Czech patriots and their uncompromising position on the expulsion of the Germans reinforced this stance. Finally, the unity of the nation under the leadership of the working class, as embodied by the Communist Party, and its position as by far the largest party made such a peaceful road possible.[29] In these formulations, the intellectual debates surrounding the "revision of the national character" were translated from cultural arguments with political significance and overtones into the background for a directly political strategy.

Similarly, the components of the "Czechoslovak road" were almost exclusively drawn from the existing organization of the state. Throughout the first postwar years all parties lauded the government's nationalization program, the national committees instituted from the level of small localities, land reform, and reform of the state administration and army. All these institutions were to a greater or lesser degree both integrated into the conception of a "Czechoslovak road to socialism" and subsumed under the conception of the "People's Democracy." Most importantly, communist political and cultural leaders proclaimed their commitment to maintaining this people's democratic system. Although all parties pledged their allegiance to the "People's Democracy"—the pleonasm was recognized even by communists[30]—the Communists carved out a claim on it by virtue of their party's electoral dominance under the system. Furthermore, party ideologists such as Kopecký and Bareš devoted special attention to the conception. Above all, it was integrated into the theory of the "Czechoslovak road"—and was occasionally seen as having made the policy possible[31]—as the foundation for the transition from capitalism to socialism: "We are heading toward socialism. The People's Democracy is the road to it."[32] Moreover, they used it to distance the party from Soviet practices, including the dictatorship of the proletariat, and to stress that it corresponded to *Czechoslovak* needs. In this view, the People's Democratic system was "no longer a bourgeois democracy and also not the dictatorship of the proletariat. It is not a soviet arrangement. It is a specific type of state, which grew from the concrete historical situation and under our own conditions."[33] The special place given the "People's Democracy" by the party and the increasing identification of the party with it proved significant in limiting the field of debate for noncommunists.

Two other concepts, however, are also worthy of deeper investigation: the Two-Year Plan and the stated goal of gaining a majority of the vote in the elections scheduled for 1948. These facets need to be singled out because they were the only completely new items on the list of those associated with the "Czechoslovak road." The party could count on support for its other ideas, as they had all been both contained within the Košice program and worked out with the other National Front parties. Moreover, together with the "People's Democracy," they elicited more extensive comment from non-communist intellectuals. Finally, they became, in effect, shorthand for the "Czechoslovak road" and the dominance of the Communist Party in Czech political life. As Bareš noted, "The ensuring of our road to socialism is equivalent to the fulfilling of the Two-Year Plan plus the gaining of a majority of the nation for the politics of the Communist Party."[34]

Not addressed in the Košice program, the idea of planning was new. The aftereffects of the war, including the nationalization decrees and the concomitant extension of government control over the economy, however, made it a natural development. The Communist Party was the first to discuss the matter and put the idea in their election program some two weeks before the balloting in the 1946 elections.[35] Although the other parties ignored its initiative before the election, loyalty to the Two-Year Plan became part of the programs of all of the Czech parties thereafter. Noncommunist enthusiasm for planning was spurred by the realization that the idea was proving very popular. In a survey taken in 1946, 73 percent of the respondents claimed to have at least some knowledge of the plan's contents, and 77 percent believed it would be at least partly successful.[36] Moreover, the Western European lands to which Czech noncommunists looked were adopting similar measures. The seriousness with which the government took the plan can be seen in the penalties for disrupting it: "intentional behavior" that would "make difficult the successful course" of the plan could be punished by up to two years' imprisonment, and serious damage by up to ten years' imprisonment and a fine of one million crowns.[37] One young communist sympathizer even felt that noncommunist talk of freedom and democracy should be considered punishable under the same rubric: "We know that we will not allow anyone to sabotage the Two-Year Plan with their hands. Should we not also try to limit the sabotage of minds? We are not afraid to be ruthless to these saboteurs, no matter how they gesticulate with their conception of democracy."[38]

The Two-Year Plan was of particular importance to the party, making the laudatory responses of noncommunist intellectuals important in solidifying the Communists' leading role in the state. Primarily, Communists saw it as central to the "Czechoslovak road to socialism," as Gottwald made clear:

> The main arena, around which everything will turn this year, will be the struggle to fulfill this year's plan for the Two-Year Plan. What I have said, that the Two-Year Plan and its fulfillment are links in a chain that we must grasp in order to pull the entire chain, stands today in full force.[39]

> Fulfilling the Two-Year Plan will be an important stage on our road to socialism.[40]

Consequently, the plan was seen by communist intellectuals, like Arnošt Kolman, as part of overcoming the capitalist past by following "the road we began with the Two-Year Plan, Gottwald's road to socialism."[41] The citation from Kolman indicates a further reason the Two-Year Plan was so crucial to the party: prestige. In the minds of the Communist leadership, much hinged on the success or failure of the plan. It was closely associated with the name of the party chairman and was often referred to in the communist press as "Gottwald's Two-Year Plan."[42] Moreover, the prestige of the party itself was seen as being at stake. As one American journalist pointed out, "The opponents of the Communists will tell you that, although all parties agree with the Two-Year Plan, the communists have the main share of the planning and are the soul of its implementation."[43] The plan was the centerpiece of the first Communist-led Czechoslovak government, and as such was a test of the party's governing ability. Gottwald was aware of this, arguing that a successful result

> will be even more important in that we will decisively prove to all critics and prophets of doom that our regime of people's democracy, national committees, and nationalized factories has proven itself in the economic field, in a sector that is always a measuring stick for the ability of every regime. We will prove that we know how to produce more, better, and more cheaply than the old system.[44]

The party's emphasis at the Eighth Congress on its work in rebuilding the republic now naturally shifted to the plan, as the party faithful were reminded that "our road leads through labor" and were exhorted to "*be the best workers on the Two-Year Plan by being the most model builders of the republic and sacrificing the most in working for its happiness, strength, and blossoming.*"[45] As indicated by the personification of the plan and the effusive language used to describe it, the communist propaganda machine went into overdrive in its support for the Two-Year Plan. The communist weeklies were saturated with praise for it, and cartoons and poems in honor of the plan became an admittedly silly commonplace. This was probably taken the farthest by *Lidová kultura*, which for weeks ran a "Fairy Tale about the Two-Year Plan," in which the plan came alive and dispensed pearls of wisdom to the journal's trade unionist readership.[46] More seriously, the intellectual big guns of communist activism also deified the Two-Year Plan, albeit in a more sophisticated manner. Bareš rejected the notion that the plan was a mere question of economics and manufacturing. It symbolized, he argued, "*the great spiritual transformation of the nation,*" and had as its goal "the person—the free builder [*budovatel*] of socialism, his heroism, his sacrifice, his new moral and ethical questions."[47] The communist poet Lumír Čivrný perhaps took this the furthest when he tied the plan directly to the revision of the Czech national character by claiming that, seen from "the moral point of view," the plan was in fact "the road to the new type of the Czech character."[48]

The other new component of the "Czechoslovak road" structure was the party's stated goal of acquiring a majority of the vote in the elections scheduled for 1948. Inside the Central Committee, Gottwald had ruminated on the possibility of gaining a majority through parliamentary means as early as the end of May 1946, when the favorable result of the parliamentary elections became known.[49] His first public mention of the idea came in late September of that year in conjunction with the announcement of the "Czechoslovak road." At this juncture, however, he remained vague: "Most important for every revolution, and for all progress whatsoever, is to gain for the matter concerned the majority of the nation, the majority of the people."[50] The policy was made public in January 1947, under the banner of the slogan "For a Majority of the Nation!" In this campaign, the party stressed its new, patriotic image, and Bareš noted that the party would "rely on the best patriotic feelings" of the nation for the strategy's successful completion.[51]

Did the Communist Party really mean to achieve socialism by means of the ballot box? While the question of intent regarding the whole of the "Czechoslovak road" will be taken up shortly, a few comments on this particular issue are in order. The leadership was split between those who desired continued cooperation with the other parties of the National Front and those who called for sharper attacks on noncommunist political positions.[52] The announcement of the intention to gain a majority was intended for the latter, while to satisfy the former the party's intention to remain in the National Front partnership was constantly intoned.[53] More significantly, the party administration clearly took Gottwald seriously and initiated a membership drive in order to gain the members considered necessary for the task.[54] Furthermore, the goal of 51 percent was maintained both publicly and privately through the eve of February 1948. The Central Committee's November 1947 internal "strategic plan" for the upcoming elections, formulated by Gottwald, repeatedly stressed the task and closed with the words that the party "*will gain this majority!*"[55]

Did the party really stand a chance of gaining 51 percent of the ballot? This has been the source of much speculation, since free and fair elections were not held in 1948. The standard view has been propagated by defeated democratic politicians living in exile, and holds that one reason the February crisis occurred was that the Communists feared the results of the upcoming elections. In the vote, it is argued, the Communist Party would have gained only between a quarter and a third of the Czech ballots. This was apparently also the result of National Socialist Party surveys of voter opinion.[56] However, the National Socialist prognosis should be treated with caution. The party had estimated that the Communist Party would only win 30 percent of the vote in 1946 and that the communists would do better in Slovakia than in the Czech lands, both of which were seriously errant predictions.[57] The Communists, however, had proven themselves better readers of the public mood in 1946, estimating that they would gain 41 percent of the Czech vote.[58] On the basis of surveys similar to those of 1946, the party estimated in January 1948 that it would gain 55 percent of the vote.[59]

Nonetheless, for obvious reasons the National Socialist prognosis was the one that became part and parcel of the Western, Cold War view of the communist takeover when exiled National Socialist politicians began to tell their stories. More objectively, Dana A. Schmidt estimated in 1953 that the Communist Party would gain only 28 percent of the vote.[60] Schmidt relied on a survey of public opinion carried out in January 1948, a survey that has been often cited as showing a decline in the Communists' popularity. However, the analysis of this survey was not completed at that time, since after the party had seized power such surveys became largely superfluous. During the Prague Spring of 1968 two researchers went back to the data and completed the analysis, finding that:

> The results . . . do not confirm that the Communist Party could have obtained more than 50 percent. Because, however, among some respondents a rise and among others a loss of votes [for the Communist Party] was registered, it is likely . . . that if the elections had been held immediately the Communist Party would have maintained its leading position with on the whole an insignificant loss of votes.[61]

Therefore, the party would likely not have reached its goal of a majority, but would have maintained its support at roughly the 40 percent level.[62] In such a case, it is difficult to imagine how the delicately balanced National Front could have emerged from deadlock without either a communist coup or the exclusion of the Communist Party from the government, the latter of which would likely have resulted in direct action by the party.

The twin announcements of the gradual, parliamentary "Czechoslovak road to socialism" and the party's intention of gaining a majority at the ballot box brought important responses both within the party and from its competitors. Although the People's Party, as the only expressly nonsocialist party, remained undamaged, the other two Czech parties stood to suffer from the Communists' announcement. The Communist Party had been having difficulties with its Social Democratic ally since the early months of 1946, and the new policies struck at the latter's very existence. Having received only 15.5 percent of the Czech vote in the 1946 elections, it was the smallest party in the National Front government, and moreover was internally riven by a deep left-right split. After the elections, the party had begun to distance itself from the Communists, having come to the conclusion that voters viewed it as dependent on its far larger ally.[63] The announcement of the "Czechoslovak road" caused grave problems for this strategy, for now the party had no niche to fill. As one internal National Socialist memorandum from April 1947 noted:

> Since officially departing from Marxism, the Social Democrats can claim neither V. I. Lenin and J. V. Stalin (for the Communist Party claims them) nor the German theoreticians Bebel, Lasalle, Bernstein, and Adler (for national reasons). Formerly they could claim a difference in tactics between themselves and the

Communist Party, as they placed evolution against revolution and the dictatorship of the proletariat. However, after the Communists announced that communism is not tied to the dictatorship of the proletariat and that the concrete situation of the Czechoslovak Republic demands that they push socialism through by a democratic road, Czechoslovak Social Democracy lost its *raison d'être*.[64]

The Communist call for a majority represented a two-sided blow: it betrayed the party's sharp lack of faith in its ally, and it was clearly directed at gaining the Social Democratic Party's members for itself. In the wake of these blows, and with the internal conflict reaching fever pitch, the party quite correctly felt itself "especially endangered" and was reduced to proclaiming a "foggy democratic socialism."[65]

The party's announcements also caused difficulties for its main competitor, the National Socialist Party. Some in the party attempted to portray the declaration of the "Czechoslovak road" as an admission of the bankruptcy of Marxism, and as a justification for the National Socialists' moderate, traditional, and democratic socialism.[66] Others, such as Minister of Justice Drtina, "could not escape the impression that [the "Czechoslovak road"] was taken from his campaign speeches," and recognized the implicit threat.[67] As the statements of leading Communists lessened the rhetorical distance between their party and the National Socialists, intellectuals in the latter party "endeavored to show a differentiation of philosophical and sociological views . . . departing from abstractly formulated Masarykian humanism . . . [and advocating] a so-called progressive socialism based on spiritualism."[68] This strategy had fundamental weaknesses. Above all, the vagueness of democratic socialist views within the party, particularly among its intellectual leadership, left them looking less sure about the future they envisaged than the Communists. The latter were anchored by the party's identification with the concrete institution of the "People's Democracy" and had the tangible measure of the Two-Year Plan as a goal. Moreover, democratic socialists' signals to the public—encouraging the development of a socialist culture and morality and then attempting to limit the enthusiasm thus produced—sent a confusing message to potential voters, who could easily compare its proclamations for socialism with the moderate Communist "Czechoslovak road" and that party's consistent ideology.[69] Nonetheless, we can safely conclude that the threat to the party's electoral base was slight, and certainly far less than that posed to the Social Democratic Party.

The announcement of the "Czechoslovak road" also gave rise to dissatisfaction within the Communist Party itself. Most vocal were those elements who had been disappointed that it had not followed a revolutionary course immediately after liberation. Their voices returned in late 1946, when several openly disturbed local party organizations called for clarification of the policy. Occasionally, as in the case of one group from Prague, they urged the party to take a "short road" to power.[70] The party leadership could justify its moderation by pointing to the great election victory just won, and was quick to condemn these expressions of radicalism. At a meeting of the Central Committee, Gottwald made the point that this would not be tolerated: "It is necessary to be wary that our so-called leftist, rogue, petit bourgeois, often Trotskyite element does not force us from the correct path of a broad National Front, the path of a large and responsible governing party."[71] To this end, *Tvorba* condemned such positions publicly:

> We also heard the voices of people . . . who asked whether the Communist Party of Czechoslovakia is following the correct road and has not lost sight of its socialist ideals [. . . whether it has] abandoned the road of communism, tossed the teachings of Marx, Lenin, and Stalin overboard, and borrowed demands and goals from other "socialisms." [. . . .For them] the words of Klement Gottwald are appropriate: "The political art of every party consists in how it comes to discriminate between what must be done today and what tomorrow."[72]

The party's election victory had made the achievement of socialism by parliamentary means a possibility, and therefore we can agree with Jaroslav Opat that the "Czechoslovak road" was "an *attempt* to ground *theoretically* the politics of the party at the time."[73] The task of this theoretical grounding was taken up by party intellectuals, who were disproportionately enthusiastic about the new line and showered its personification, Gottwald, with high praise. They drew on the works of Lenin and Stalin to show that the "Czechoslovak road" was only the practice of "what was foreseen theoretically by Marxist classics."[74] Furthermore, they appealed to the Slavic feeling they were inculcating among the Czechs by noting that it was predominantly the Slavic societies that were forging ahead along the new roads to socialism. The "Czechoslovak road" even found support in Russian history, when communist intellectuals argued that the Russian Bolsheviks themselves had not followed a pre-scripted plan. Lenin himself, they claimed, had always chosen the calm road when possible, so that "Lenin's work is with us, in our free land, in . . . our specific, calm road to socialism, which would not exist if there had not been Lenin."[75] Gottwald, the father of the "Czechoslovak road," was portrayed as "the archetype of the creative Marxist," the man who had "fulfilled Lenin's teaching that it is necessary to seek out new forms for the entrance into socialism."[76]

The enthusiasm communist intellectuals expressed for the "Czechoslovak road" was mirrored in the way in which they discussed socialism and dialectical materialism. The measures already taken, including the massive nationalizations that had made 61 percent of the workforce employees of the state, were considered a healthy beginning, but only the preliminary steps toward a socialist paradise. They rejected the view of many in the National Socialist and People's parties that the enacted changes had gone far enough (or even too far) and that "socialism" had already been achieved. Václav Kopecký summed up the view in January 1948: "We still do not have socialism in the new republic. If we were to have it, we would be happy." Nonetheless, even at this late date he enthusiastically supported the democratic road in a chapter entitled "Victoriously Continue the Present Course!":

> Everything has gone calmly, peacefully, legally, democratically. Yes, with the guarantee of the support of the popular masses, *with the guarantee of the strength and power of the people*, it appears possible in Czechoslovakia to travel to socialism on the road of the new democracy, a calm and peaceful road and *in no way the road of the dictatorship of the proletariat. In this sense, we want to continue victoriously down the present road, the road of the People's Democracy. . . . Our developmental road came out of the May revolution, is tied to the revolution, and carried onward in the spirit of the revolutionary yearning of the Czechoslovak people.* It is a democratic road, we democratically administer the power the people democratically gave us. We see no reason to doubt that the present road will take us to our great socialist goal.

For him, as for many other communists, socialism was *"the most beautiful and most noble human idea."*[77] Although waxing poetic about the as yet undefined future state of Czech socialism that lay at the end of the "Czechoslovak road" was a commonplace, it is interesting to note that even the hardnosed theoretician, Arnošt Kolman, could not avoid it. In his *What Is the Meaning of Life?*, he posited that the title question would be irrelevant in the coming socialist era:

> The people of a socialist society will not ask what the meaning of life is, doubting its meaning, its value. They will pose a different question. They will ask what the meaning of death is, denying this meaning. Because for a person living a full socialist life, death will be a thing much more undesirable than it is for us today.[78]

The communist "radiant future" offensive was complemented by their attitude toward Marxism and dialectical materialism. Communist intellectuals were under constant pressure on these issues from Roman Catholic intellectuals and People's Party leaders, who portrayed them as proof of a materialistic conception of life incompatible with the spiritual and philosophical heritage of the Czech nation. Nonetheless, the wide-ranging discussion of Marxism in the press organs of the Communist, Social Democratic, and National Socialist parties forced Roman Catholic activists to recognize that already "in the first months of the newly established state, revolutionary Marxism became in [Czechoslovakia] admittedly something less than an official teaching, but something more than the affair of one ruling group."[79] This was the case even though the Communists encountered practical difficulties in inculcating Marxist theory among the Czechs. The party emphasized the task but had only one trained Marxist philosopher at its disposal (Kolman). Despite the fact that the party ran lecture series with such titles as "What Is Communism?" "What Does the Soviet Union Mean for Us?" and "Our Road to Socialism," the dissemination of Marxism ran into difficulties. Even the party schools had practical problems, as Jaroslav Kladiva has noted: "The main problem of internal party education was the lack of educated Marxist teachers." The two great victories of the party in this respect were the institution of over 5,000 "Gottwald libraries" of communist literature in communities across the land and the publishing and distribution of large numbers of copies of communist classics. This testifies to both the public's lack of and thirst for knowledge of Marxism-Leninism.[80]

The Communist Party unequivocally proclaimed its allegiance to the fundamentals of dialectical materialism and followed a two-sided strategy to support its philosophical foundation: one defensive and the other offensive. Communist intellectuals contended that not only did non-Marxists caricature the materialism of the theory, but also that it in fact rested on an ethical and humanist foundation (an argument resuscitated in the thaw of the 1960s by philosophers looking at the young Marx). In the communist view, the objections raised with particular frequency by Roman Catholic intellectuals (for example, "Marxism is crudely materialistic; it does not have an ethical system; it does not perceive human actors; it is a German teaching; Marx in his time wrote unflatteringly about the Slavs and God knows what else") were completely unfounded. Communist leaders continually emphasized that Marx had stressed the creativity of the human will and that, even if he had not concerned himself directly with morals, "his work was deeply ethical in its conclusions."[81] Marxist intellectuals in both the Communist and Social Democratic parties strove to establish a monopoly on a socialism both morally fulfilling and yet scientifically rigorous enough to answer all questions:

> The socialist teaching itself is based on the deep foundations of universal morality, even if its scalpel, historical [materialism], was long depicted with relish as a horrible, terrible "materialism [*hmotářství*]" to denote socialism as an immoral teaching. Even today there are some pseudosocialists attempting to divide socialism into a materialist [*materialistický*] one—worthy of condemnation—and their humanitarian, or spiritual and moral, or Christian, etc. one: the true one, the only one suited to the average Czech [*malý český človĕk*].[82]

In conjunction with this, communists went on the offensive, attacking the credentials of those criticizing communist theory. They ridiculed the idea that Marxism had somehow been "overcome" and pointed out that such statements had been made so often in the past that they had become essentially meaningless.[83] Those who dared criticize the hallowed pantheon of communist theoreticians were denounced as having obviously not read the complete works of Marx, Lenin, and Stalin, a reproach that, under the circumstances, could not be refuted. Furthermore, they were portrayed as being "linked by one thing . . . recoiling in the face of socialism." The strivings of democratic socialist thinkers for less radical social reform were denounced as "unscientific," serving "only as a *political weapon against socialism.*[84] This reached a peak in Štoll's use of a charge that many noncommunists, Roman Catholics in particular, were using against the communists themselves: the accusation of harboring Nazi sympathies. Although he admitted that the charge was not true for a large proportion of the party's members, he maintained that the "anti-Marxism" of the National Socialist Party bore a resemblance to that of its German namesake.[85]

Throughout the 1945–1948 period, and especially after the announcement of the "Czechoslovak road to socialism," the party relied on a yearning for certainty that it perceived the Czech population desired. While such a yearning cannot be demonstrated, it is not only plausible, given the traumatic experiences of Munich and occupation, but has been noted in many memoirs from the period and is witnessed by the wide-ranging discussions of the Czech nation's history and meaning.[86] Just as the communists' reinterpretation of national traditions, interpretation of the recent past, and presentation of a new cultural orientation offered a complete and internally consistent cultural view, so their version of Marxist theory presented the same for the political and social reorganization of the land. Kopecký clearly contrasted the diffuse, vague, and, on occasion, internally inconsistent views of the communists' political opponents with the rigorous nature of Marxism:

> Yes, we ask *who alive* in the camp of the Czech bourgeoisie proclaims some kind of philosophy, some kind of conception, some kind of idea that is able—in another way than the one we Communists use—to show the nation and the Czech people a road forward? . . . This is how it appears in the camp of our opponents: *reaction, decadence, pessimism, nihilism, existentialism, marasmus, putrefaction, finality, death!* That is how it looks among those anticommunists![87]

The twin announcements of the "Czechoslovak road" and the goal of gaining a majority of the nation brought one significant theoretical advantage to communist intellectuals. It provided them with the ammunition for a legitimate defense against the charges that communist theory prescribed the introduction of the dictatorship of the proletariat and that the party was aiming toward installing such a totalitarian dictatorship even if it required a putsch. Nazi Germany had discredited the word "dictatorship," and there was little way to give a positive connotation to the dictatorship of the proletariat. In February 1946, before the announcement of the "Czechoslovak road," a group of party theoreticians met to discuss the question, "Can we reach socialism without the dictatorship of the proletariat?" Even at that time, while the consensus was that the "transformation to socialism cannot be achieved without [it]," some theoreticians were searching for ways around this. Kolman looked optimistically toward the upcoming elections: "The dictatorship of the proletariat is the unlimited power of the working class. . . . At this time there is hope for the elections. We cannot know if the unlimited power of the working class will be necessary."[88] The proclamation of the "Czechoslovak road" rendered such theoretical discussions obsolete, as Communist intellectuals could crow that noncommunists could no longer use the dictatorship of the proletariat against the party. The concept was relegated to the status of a measure necessary only if occasioned by the actions of reactionaries. Kolman summed up the communist argument:

> You ask if we, Czechoslovak Communists, have dictatorship in our program? No, we do not, as the leadership of our party pronounces over and over, and as our politics of the road of calm development, the specific Czechoslovak road on which our party is treading, bears witness. No, we do not, because we are convinced that, thanks to historical developments, our land has every possibility to achieve a socialist order without any kind of shattering attempts at disruption by reaction.[89]

The threat of Communist Party totalitarianism, either stated or implied by its opponents, was handled similarly. The party's announcement of its intention to gain an electoral majority gave rise to claims that should the party achieve its aim, a tyranny of the Communist 51 percent over the non-Communist 49 percent would result. Communist ideologues refuted this by relying on the moderation the party had hitherto displayed, and invoked the calm tones of the "Czechoslovak road." They also observed that the "totalitarianism, terror and violence" prophesied in some quarters if the Communist Party emerged victorious from the 1946 elections had not come to pass.[90] Finally, communist intellectuals like Bareš pointed out that in lands such as Great Britain and the United States parties strove for and gained 51 percent of the vote, but that they were not accused of totalitarianism. He concluded his argument with the comment: "We have not forgotten that for entire decades—in times when it was a practical impossibility—adherents of socialism were told: Gain a majority and there will be socialism. Why should this be 'totalitarianism?'"[91]

Communist intellectuals could also use the "Czechoslovak road" and the call for a majority as the ultimate proof that the party had no plans to gain power by force, that it "counted on power-political shifts *inside* the given political system and in the framework of the given . . . socio-economic structure."[92] They characterized such concerns, whether expressed in public or private, as "dirty, evil, reactionary gossip."[93] Party intellectuals repeatedly emphasized both that they had no such plans and that they, in fact, did not need to take over the state violently. As late as January 1948, Kopecký could claim:

> We have no reason to doubt that the present road will take us to our great socialist goal. *We have no reason to reach for power in another way than the People's Democracy.* We have a great share of power, which the people gave us, and we are convinced that the people will give us even more power and *that a majority of the nation will give us power.*[94]

The view that the party would not bid for power through illegal methods or even employ such methods to gain an absolute majority was held by many, including the American ambassador.[95] Furthermore, the Communist Party's policy of pursuing a calm, evolutionary road allowed it to cast itself as the defender of freedom and democracy. To be sure, these terms held different content for the communists than for their opponents, but communist intellectuals were able to maintain the rhetorical position that their socialism equaled true freedom and democracy. For communist intellectuals, "democracy and socialism are indivisible in this epoch, and the road of consistent, true democracy leads to socialism."[96] As for democracy, so for freedom: the People's Democratic state offered far more freedom than that enjoyed by citizens of West European lands, and the party was committed to "the freedom of political, conceptual, and theoretical conviction," barring only fascism.[97]

Paralleling the party's proclamations of allegiance to the ideals of freedom and democracy, the party adopted a soft line when attacking its enemies. Gone were the vicious prewar assaults on the entire bourgeoisie; now only "big capitalists" came in for party scorn. Already in March 1946, the slogan of the party's Eighth Congress reflected this. No longer did the party trumpet, "The Struggle against the Bourgeoisie!" but rather "The Struggle against Reaction!" This changed formulation implied that the party was prepared to form a common front with elements of the bourgeoisie who were amenable to socialist development against those who were opposed to socialism. Party ideologues were vague about defining a reactionary, at various times condemning those opposed to state ownership, those who expressed concern over the expulsion of the Germans, or those disconcerted by the closeness of the state's relationship to the USSR. More generally, all who were opposed to the People's Democratic system, and later those who opposed the Communist Party, were labeled "reactionary." They were accused of preparing a "new Munich," in order to return the country to the hands of greedy capitalists. The fury against reactionaries intensified as February 1948 drew closer, and Kopecký placed all "Westerners" and anticommunists in the reactionary camp:

> At the time of the birth of the new republic [in 1945] . . . the love of these people for their nation and motherland ceased. They no longer liked anything about the republic. . . . On the contrary, they *like everything foreign*, Western and, above all, everything American. . . . *in their spirit they are already gone, they are in spirit already in emigration.* . . . *Their Westernism* is imbued with a hatred of their own land, of their own nation. Their way of thinking borders on high treason. . . . [Their] anticommunism is really high treason.[98]

Looming over all of the preceding is the question of whether the "Czechoslovak road" was meant to be a specific Czechoslovak *road* to a socialism whose model was the USSR, or whether it implied a specific *form* of socialism. The latter understanding became salient in the reformist 1960s, as historians sought to ground the "Prague Spring" in the history of Czechoslovak communism. Reform-minded historians argued that Stalinist "deformities" dictated the eventual shape of Czechoslovakia, and that the "Czechoslovak road" in reality "accents the development of Czechoslovakia not only from the Soviet *road*, but also expressly suggests also the possibility of a *system* different from the Soviets."[99] Other authors have perceived an indeterminacy in the proclamation of a "Czechoslovak road," without being willing to subscribe to the view that a system of non-Soviet socialism was intended.[100] On the other side of the debate, the samizdat and émigré historian Vilém Prečan holds that "there was talk about various roads to socialism, but the concept of socialism was understood to be *only* socialism of the Soviet type."[101] The truth, as is so often the case, lies between these two perspectives. As neither the party's political nor intellectual leaders ever discussed the contours of the socialism that lay at the end of the "Czechoslovak road," we cannot be absolutely sure what they intended. While the creation of a different kind of socialism was not expressly intended by the "Czechoslovak road," this does not imply that such ideas lay outside the thinking of the mass membership of the Communist Party, or even outside its leadership circles. More likely, given the increasing regional convergence in socialist developments before February 1948, the Czechoslovak leadership decidedly had at least the model of the Soviet Union firmly in mind. Therefore, while party leaders may not have intended a complete copy of the conditions of the USSR, Karel Kaplan has aptly summed up this leadership's view by commenting that it was one of the "Czechoslovak road to the Soviet model of socialism."[102] This was particularly the case after the September 1947 Cominform meeting, in which the French and Italian Communist parties were harshly criticized for their moderation. Although the Czechoslovak delegation narrowly avoided becoming the subject of a similar attack, the implications were clear, and must have become common knowledge in top party circles.[103] From reading the statements of the intellectuals affiliated with the party or sympathetic to it, it is evident that they counted on both wider and deeper variance between the Soviet Union and Czechoslovakia than perhaps did sections of the political leadership.

A further overarching question is whether the "Czechoslovak road" was a mere tactical bagatelle or a serious attempt at the creative Marxism so highly praised at the time. That it was *ex post* considered a tactical move on the part of the Communist Party by internal dissidents, such as Prečan, and by exiles groomed during the Cold War, is to be expected. They saw the announcement of the "Czechoslovak road" as "a carefully prepared program for winning the minds of the Czechoslovak people," that was neither innovative nor seriously meant.[104] Communist intellectuals at the time, however, argued, "It is obvious that those who suspect us of temporary tactical maneuvering are falsifying reality. This is not about politicking, but is a fundamental, scientific solution for the new problems that the new situation has presented."[105] Václav Pavlíček has argued that, similar to the resistance offered by party radicals to its announcement, "even among the advocates of the 'specific road' were those who considered it a purely tactical move on the part of the party to achieve a monopoly of power." Nevertheless, he still maintains that those who consider "the

slogan of the Communist Party about the specific road as only a trick necessary for gaining victory in the state . . . are incorrect."[106]

In a larger sense, however, the entire dispute over the possible underlying
tactical nature of the declaration of the "Czechoslovak road" is, as Toman
Brod put it, "irrelevant. The bare fact that the Communist Party did not exclude the possibility that they could achieve a monopoly of power through
electoral procedures . . . bears witness to the distinctness of their conception."[107] Whether the Communist leadership or the intellectuals who gave
themselves over to the concept believed in the long-term viability of the
"Czechoslovak road" or whether they subscribed to it because it was the party
line has little effect on its actual importance. Even Josef Korbel, who believed
it was merely tactical, admitted that it "succeeded to a considerable extent."[108]
As the erudite wife of a leading communist killed in the show trials of the
early 1950s pointed out, "no one except maybe the Soviet agents doubted that
we would be able to run our own show in a way that was quite different from
the Russian totalitarian model. A national road to socialism was basic to our
thinking."[109] Finally, it should be noted that those who proclaimed the virtues
of the "Czechoslovak road" in the late 1940s in many cases paid for their "adventurism," to use Brod's word, with their lives in those show trials.[110]

In a broader sense it is truly irrelevant whether leading Communists believed in the future of the "Czechoslovak road" or whether they saw it as a
temporary tactical position.[111] Its announcement and propagation had a deep
impact on how Czech communists and noncommunists alike viewed political
developments in their land, and created the framework within which debates
over the form and content of Czech socialism took place. Created after the
communists had largely won the debates over the "revision of the national
character," the "Czechoslovak road" had a plausibility and a consistency that
caused clear concern among noncommunist political and intellectual leaders.
In the following three chapters, the noncommunists' views of socialism will
be examined and should be seen against the backdrop of the Communist
Party's presentation of its socialism. Both the party's silence and the eventual
announcement of the "Czechoslovak road" forced noncommunist intellectuals to define their positions on socialism. While this exposed the depth of
unity between the moderate, stated goals of the Communist Party and those
of their democratic socialist opponents, it also revealed the considerable ambiguity and idealism present in the latter camp. Likewise, the Communist policy forced the hand of Roman Catholic intellectuals, who manifested strong
opposition to communism while walking the tightrope of "Christian social reformism." Finally, it created space for the revolutionary enthusiasm of Czech
Protestants, allowing the communists to reap the benefits of their support
while appearing both moderate and disciplined in comparison.

10

Socialism and Democratic Socialist Intellectuals: The "New Socialist Ethos"

> Marx expressed the view that the spirit has often made itself ridiculous
> when it proceeded independently, unconnected to material interests. He
> was undoubtedly right. Still, again and again the spirit must give itself over
> to such adventures.
>
> —Ferdinand Peroutka, "Článek nikoliv lhostejný"

Like their communist counterparts, democratic socialists developed their
ideas on the single most important question of the period over time, both in-
fluencing and being influenced by the social, cultural, and political realities
of their environment. Nonetheless, there were constants in the democratic
socialist discourse: a complete rejection of capitalism, an ambivalence toward Marxism, and a sincere belief in a socialism interpreted as a moral and
cultural rather than a socioeconomic phenomenon. These comprised the
core of the democratic socialist conceptual matrix throughout the period.
Their expectations from, and reactions to, the 1946 parliamentary elections,
and their responses to the Communist Party's subsequent announcement of
the "Czechoslovak road to socialism," however, marked a major turning
point in the development of their thought. At this time, and markedly after
the Communist Party's announcement of the aim of securing a majority of
the vote, democratic socialists moved off the socialist offensive and adopted
a defensive position centered on the twin issues of democracy and freedom.
They attempted to avoid the label of "reactionary" and paint their communist
opponents as potentially totalitarian, while arguing for a higher synthesis of
Eastern socialism and Western notions of democracy and freedom. One important flash-point of their struggle with communist intellectuals—the battle
between the communist *Kulturní obec* (The Cultural Community) and the

democratic socialist *Kulturní svaz* (The Cultural Union)—reveals the weaknesses of their position and supports a critical assessment of the democratic socialist endeavor.

Throughout the 1945–1948 period, democratic socialist intellectuals were driven by a firm belief in the moral rectitude of socialism. Their socialism, however, was not derived from an elaborated political, philosophical, and economic theory and thus had none of the support that Marxism could offer Communists and left-wing Social Democrats. Instead, it was based on a set of related conceptual premises. Above all, it was founded on the certainty that the era of capitalism had ended. Capitalism had been discredited by the Great Depression and the war that followed, and was worthy only of intellectual scorn. Further, their socialism regarded Marxism as a valuable tool in the struggle for social justice, yet also saw it as problematic as a result of its association with the communist movement. While democratic socialist intellectuals attempted to secure the theoretical legitimacy of their socialism by associating themselves with portions of the Marxist canon and its terminology, they rejected Marxist theory as a complete whole and castigated communist intellectuals' dogmatism in employing it. Finally, it is clear that their socialism sprang from an essentially cultural and ethical understanding, which expressed itself in terms such as "socialist culture," "socialist humanism," and the struggle for the "new man."

Democratic socialist intellectuals rarely discussed capitalism and never analyzed it with significant critical depth. At first glance, this may seem surprising, as they opposed the workings of the capitalist system not only in economics but also politics ("bourgeois democracy," "liberal freedom") and culture ("bourgeois thinking" [*měšťáctví*], the conceptual opposite of "people's culture" [*lidová kultura*]). On a deeper level, it seems that it was not an important issue for them because the Great Depression and the war had proven the defeat of capitalism: there were simply no proponents of capitalism to argue against. Moreover, the political steps enshrined in the Košice program had established the foundations of what President Beneš had declared a "socializing democracy."[1] Much like their communist counterparts, these intellectuals were engaged in a struggle to define the meaning of socialism and found little need to devote their attention to a capitalism that all political and cultural actors agreed was dead. This is not to say that they were not aware and critical of what they saw as its most virulent forms—fascism and reaction—but that they did not fill their reflections with such diatribes against capitalism as appeared in the communist press.

Their concern with capitalism, therefore, primarily lay in writing the system's epitaph. Ferdinand Peroutka, a man whose realism in public affairs was unquestioned by democrats of all political orientations, took the lead in this task. Shortly after he returned from Buchenwald it became apparent to him that, as the title of his already discussed editorial put it, "There Is No Return" to the past of the First Republic's capitalism.[2] Particularly in the months preceding the 1946 elections, he endeavored to explain to "those who yearn for the renewal of capitalism as for redemption" that the "decisive fact" was that capitalism had "politically and irrevocably lost."[3] As a result of the Great Depression, "capitalism stood before the world as a sinner" whose fall had been a "necessity" that gave rise to the new regime.[4] The teleological nature of this statement bears more than a passing resemblance to Marxist doctrine. Democratic socialist intellectuals' only further concern with capitalism grew directly from the proclamation of its death. Capitalism was both a defeated political enemy and a self-destructive economic system unworthy of intellectual support. Therefore, the re-education of the public was the proper mission for Czech intellectuals. Capitalism had greatly damaged public morality, and for Peroutka the task of the intellectual was clear: "There are no doubts about the capitalist hierarchy: barbaric priority to hankering after profits; reason, humanity, and culture only in the second tier. The natural goal of the intelligentsia must be to overturn this hierarchy."[5] Although capitalism was gone, its aftereffects lingered in "a certain mentality" that could only be described by the word "capitalist."[6] For democratic socialist intellectuals, such a mentality was not present only in the capitalist class but pervaded their entire society. "Capitalism, capitalist thoughts and feelings" still existed in Czech society, and democratic socialists believed that "a long education will be necessary before these feelings and thoughts give way to others."[7] The conviction that they must change the hearts and minds of the Czech nation lay at the core of the democratic socialists' conception of socialism and their emphasis on the creation of a socialist culture.

It proved more difficult for democratic socialists to come to terms with the Marxist vision resident on their political left, however. The interest in Marxist theory, as we shall see, ranged across all political boundaries in postwar Czechoslovakia. As Nikolaus Lobkowicz has pointed out, in the aftermath of the war "Marxism-Leninism had become academically '*salonfähig*'. . . . [I]t had become almost a national duty to take the Soviet Union and with it Marxism-Leninism at least seriously."[8] Additionally, because of the popular interest witnessed in the sales figures for Marxist-Leninist classics and because of the rise of the Communist Party, democratic socialists recognized that "whatever the final result, it is necessary to confront and come to terms with this world view."[9] Fundamentally ambivalent, they desired the freedom both to praise and rely on Marxist classics for critical support, yet also to escape commitment to the limiting theories of dialectical and historical materialism. Marx himself, however, was almost untouchable from a critical viewpoint. Democratic socialists praised him as "a cultivated and philosophically schooled man" who had "truly wonderfully" analyzed the weaknesses of capitalism.[10]

These intellectuals, and particularly those more inclined to literary pursuits, often cited Marxist classics to buttress their arguments. A case in point is the writing of Václav Černý, who used Marx to defend the West in the argument over national orientation, and at other times relied on Engels, Lenin, and Stalin. However, this did not prevent him from maintaining that

> I am not a historical materialist. . . . I fully accept . . . the goals of the communist transformation of human society. I do not accept the explanation for these goals or the interpretation of development as given by historical materialism. I do not explain my socialism and I do not explain human beings and human life only with Marx.[11]

Therefore, Černý used Marxist classics for support, denied the theory that undergirded them, and proclaimed his support for the goals set by those who accepted that theoretical foundation. As we shall see, such volatile mixtures of ideological commitment were more the rule than the exception among democratic socialists.

For their part, Communist intellectuals saw such uses of Marxist thinkers as an attempt to appropriate them for ends aimed against the Communist Party. In response, they moved to protect their intellectual heritage, condemning the democratic socialist use of Marxist thinkers as "illegitimate" and denouncing the borrowing of Marxist conceptions by those who were "standoffish" to the theory as a whole.[12] Even some intellectuals outside the Communist Party rejected what they saw as the politically motivated use of Marxist terminology by those opposed to the party. One young writer took specific aim at both Peroutka and Černý, believing that the latter thought that "without the socialist catechism in his titles his opinions will not make headway" and calling on his colleagues to "expose [Černý's and Peroutka's] *ex tempore* improvisation" with Marxist terminology. He concluded that it was "necessary to keep an eye on their half-truths and to polemicize with them."[13] Politically viewed, democratic socialists' use of Marxist-Leninist terminology and writings indirectly augmented the authority and prestige of the communist movement, which had a self-evident claim to the Marxist heritage, and brought damage to their own cause by augmenting the power and validity of Marxist theory.

Democratic socialists' internal theoretical disagreements over the nature of historical and dialectical materialism only magnified this weakness. Roman Catholic intellectuals, as we will see, founded their united opposition to Marxism on its materialism, which they placed in opposition to the spiritual values embodied by Christian teaching. While democratic socialist intellectuals were undoubtedly, and even primarily, concerned with protecting much the same spiritual values, the allure of Marxist theory rendered the attainment of such a firm position impossible. Most democratic socialists attempted to occupy a middle ground in the dispute between communist "materialists" and Catholic "spiritualists." In a strategy symbolic of their attempts to come to grips with Marxism, some attempted to separate its theoretical materialism from what they saw as the essentially ethical political movement to which it gave rise. Otakar Machotka maintained that "the theoretical foundation of [communism] excludes the moral viewpoint," while simultaneously arguing that there was a moral aspect to the communist movement that even the Communist Party did not recognize.[14] Similarly, the prominent sociologist Arnošt Bláha did not deny Marxism's materialism but argued, "In practice, however, this theoretical materialism was linked with ethical idealism . . . [and] was directed by an eminently ethical idea."[15] Even Černý, while rejecting the materialist foundation of Marxian socialism, held that any

> revolutionary socialism is for me today above all *an enormous moral capital*. . . . [It would not] bother me, a non-Marxist, to recognize loyally and deservedly that this ethical force was to a large extent radiated by a materialist type of socialism. . . . Socialism, whatever its explicit philosophy of development . . . *is* cultural and ethical in its deepest inspiration.[16]

It was this ethical inspiration that guided democratic socialist cultural understanding of socialism.

Democratic socialists' main difficulty lay, therefore, not in the materialism of Marxist theory. They were more than willing to discuss Marx and Marxism, but were thwarted in this because the matter had "ceased to be material for discussion, the subject of reflection or experiment, and has changed into a law, reaching the state of sacrosanctity."[17] They repeatedly criticized the dogmatism that characterized the communist employment of Marxist teachings, and condemned the implication that if one were not an exponent of dialectical materialism, one could not be a good socialist, relying on President Beneš for support. In his speech at the Congress of Czech Writers, often singled out as of fundamental importance in the struggle between democratic and communist forces, he pronounced that "the acceptance or non-acceptance of dialectical materialism must no longer influence the question of whether or not a modern person is a socialist."[18]

It was the communists' dogmatic defense of the exclusive right to the use and interpretation of the Marxist canon that led democratic socialists to conclude that dialectical materialism acted as a faith for the communist movement. While this argument was adopted more elegantly and consistently by Roman Catholics aiming to counter the Marxist emphasis on the "scientific" certainty their teaching could offer, democratic socialists used it to return Marxism to the stage of public debate. They wanted "to engage [Marxism] as a temporal matter, not an unchanging, immortal one."[19] The widespread public interest in Marxism accorded political benefits to those seen as the guardians of its pure meaning, and democratic socialists wished to claim a portion of this by sharing in its interpretation. They wanted to be free to criticize Marxist theory, but simultaneously to use it to win support for their view of the nation's future in socialism. The tension between these can be seen in Peroutka's words: "No theory by itself has ever redeemed the world, and many good ideas have become torments when poorly practiced."[20]

This statement also reveals one primary strategy employed by democratic socialists in their debate with their communist opponents. They argued in favor of socialism throughout the 1945–1948 period, sometimes imprudently enthusiastically, but maintained that they had the truest vision of its final shape and possessed the means for its most successful implementation. The postwar environment had placed these noncommunist intellectuals in a difficult position, one that in many ways demanded such a strategy. On the one hand, they both truly desired and supported the socialist reorganization of their state. Because of the wave of revolutionary enthusiasm sweeping over the land, and because the Communist Party was quickly recognized as the socialist party *par excellence*, democratic socialists were forced to repeatedly protest that they, too, were committed to socialism. On the other hand, their natural inclinations, as well as their cultural and political constituencies, lay on the more moderate end of the socialist-dominated political spectrum. This demanded that they mark out a dividing line both to the right, in regard to the People's Party, and to the left, primarily against the Communist Party. They succeeded in establishing the demarcation on their right and legitimating their ardor for socialism, perhaps too well. Because of this, and perhaps also because of their belief in the essential democratic integrity of the Communist Party, they failed to establish a firm bulwark on their left.

All political currents in the nation, with the exception of the People's Party, strove to portray themselves as both nationalist and socialist. As communist intellectuals were well established on the latter of these issues, they devoted their energies to reinventing the Communist Party as patriotic and resting on national traditions. Democratic socialists had the opposite task. The national and patriotic pedigree of the National Socialist Party was in no doubt, so its intellectual vanguard strove to reinforce its socialist credentials. While it was impossible to question communist intellectuals' commitment to socialism, even the undoubtedly socialist Černý was called upon again and again "to prove to those who simply do not want to believe (for *it is convenient for them not to believe*) that I am a socialist."[21]

In the following discussion of democratic socialist intellectuals' conceptions of socialism, the material state of Czechoslovak society must be borne in mind. The Košice Program of April 1945 proclaimed extensive confiscations and nationalizations. In addition to the state's seizure and partial redistribution of the property of ethnic Germans, Hungarians, and collaborators, it called for the nationalization of the entire financial and credit system, all insurance companies, and the whole of the state's natural and energy resources. Then, by his decrees of October 1945, President Beneš nationalized industries employing over 60 percent of the economically active population. At the same time, a decree on factory councils gave broad powers to employees in these industries. These actions meant that by the end of 1945, workers had a large share of workplace control and that the share of combined government and nationalized sectors in national output was almost twice as large as in France, Austria, or Britain.[22] These moves in industry were matched by a wide-ranging land reform, involving some 11,374 square miles or roughly 8.8 percent of the area of Czechoslovakia, which accompanied the property confiscation. This was furthered by a law promulgated in 1947 that limited private land holdings to no more than 50 hectares, with holdings in excess of this figure allocated to smallholders or retained by the state. This sweeping socialist transformation, which Czechoslovak society experienced almost overnight, has major implications for any analysis of democratic socialists' relationship to socialism. First and foremost, one can only wonder where in precise terms these intellectuals wished to guide their society, when they urged it toward socialism. For communist intellectuals, the USSR was clearly a model for ideas and institutions, even if not necessarily one to be perfectly imitated. Additionally, with property, industrial, labor, and institutional relations already in such a state, democratic socialist intellectuals' lack of either an elaborated theoretical framework or an extant model may have led them to their adoption of an abstract cultural, moral, and ethical view of socialism.

In this environment democratic socialists constantly asserted that there was no other way forward than socialism. The purpose of this was to convince those on their right that there could be no return to the Czechoslovakia that had existed before the war. With capitalism discredited, the task for democratic socialists was, as Peroutka put it, to persuade the nation that "the road to the future leads only through the gates of socialism."[23] In light of the reforms just mentioned, it was deemed impossible to alter the direction in which the country was heading even before the nation had been consulted in the 1946 elections:

> Even if some of our parties were to speak out after the elections for the removal of socialization . . . and even if this standpoint were to gain a majority among the people and in the parliament, it would be determined that it is impossible. The social process has intervened so deeply in our economy that the sudden removal of its consequences would mean economic catastrophe . . . not to mention that other nations commonly pay a bitter price in the moral field for similar steps backward.[24]

Cautious statements such as these were backed up by enthusiastic proclamations of socialist feeling and depictions of the new world of socialism. The road to socialism stood clear, and Czech intellectuals were eager to travel it: "We are riding the wave of the future," one pronounced.[25] Not only was socialism exalted as an idea that "professes human freedom in contrast to economic oppression and exploitation," but as the system that "guaranteed the greatest degree of personal happiness and wealth."[26] Socialism was, in short, "the moral duty of all people. . . . the *ideal of humanity realized in a new societal organization.*"[27] These are just a few examples of the promising statements that were splashed across the pages of democratic socialist journals and newspapers.

The infectious enthusiasm also gripped the two intellectual leaders of their camp, men who were widely looked upon as defenders of moderation and viciously attacked as backward-looking by the communist press. Černý found in socialism "expressly and primarily *the exultation of individual moral qualities.*" For him, it was "not possible to imagine a future world, one better than before, other than as socialist."[28] Even the moderate and realistic Peroutka envisaged socialism's bright future: "Socialism is greatly and intimately in agreement with the psychological and material forces of the present and future. . . . Socialism agrees with the moral condition of the majority of humanity." In his usually sober view, socialism was the rosy future "to which sooner or later the whole world will turn." Czechs must therefore contribute to the creation of this future, so that they would "be able to say with pride: I was there for it, I helped."[29] Nonetheless, he balanced his optimism with concern over the form of socialism to which the nation was rushing:

> Our situation is this: only socialism is possible, but what kind of socialism is possible? Socialism can bring humanity undreamed-of enrichment, but also undreamed-of impoverishment, according to which elements in it gain predominance. It can be a joyous invitation to work, but it can also suddenly reverse into the most detestable, dry system of barriers, restrictions, regulations, supervision, and suspicion, into a disaffection with humanity that hacks off everything higher. Behind it there can be eyes inflamed by creative enthusiasm, but also eyes green with envy. . . . Socialism can order public affairs according to the most refined or the most backward of its members. It can support good or bad qualities.[30]

The characterizations of socialism in terms of morals, qualities, and liberation reveal the salient point of the democratic socialist understanding of socialism. It was less a question of nationalization, institutional reorganization, and industrial policy than one of creating what Černý called "*a new socialist ethos*" that was most often characterized as a socialist humanism.[31] In promoting this conception, democratic socialists hoped to achieve two aims. They hoped to create, in the words of František Kovárna, a "socialism that looks for its origin and grounding in an ethical decision" by establishing a foundation for their socialist convictions which did not rely on Marxist theory.[32] They also sought to place the debate over the future of Czechoslovak socialism on their home ground of ethical and moral abstractions. Without the creation of an explicitly new humanism, they argued, socialism would be "nothing but a dry new arrangement of ownership and economic conditions."[33]

Democratic socialists rested their social-humanist offensive on the long tradition of Czech humanism that had reached a pinnacle with Masaryk. By doing so, their socialism could be seen as part of "a great inheritance from the past." The socialist component could then be extrapolated from the failure of capitalism, which was the underlying meaning of the suffering of the war. Finally, the concept bore the imprimatur of President Beneš, the rallying point for noncommunist forces. In his often quoted speech to the Congress of Czech Writers in mid-1946, he argued that "the subject of all our endeavors and strivings . . . will be the struggle—and is already today the struggle—*for a new humanism.*" In this struggle, he called upon intellectuals to serve as "the pioneers, the warriors for this new world, this new humanism."[34] He made the source of the new humanism clear in a speech one month later, saying that "through the use and explication of the principle of economic democracy we must and will arrive at a new socialist morality."[35]

Democratic socialist intellectuals followed their president's lead, declaring that humanism was "undoubtedly the goal of socialism."[36] Even Machotka argued, "Socialist society must also have a *new, socialist morality.*" More ominously, he assigned the intelligentsia the role of enforcers in this new moral regime: "In the socialist state, every individual must be formed to be a suitable and effective element of the whole social organism. . . . [As the USSR shows,] the building of a new socialist society makes a rigorous upbringing in the socialist morality necessary."[37] Beneš' military rhetoric was thereby raised to nothing less than a blueprint for a national re-education program aimed at "forming" the individual into a new socialist citizen. Given this urge, it comes as no surprise that in tandem with the struggle for socialist humanism came "the struggle for the new man," proclaimed by no less than Beneš and taken up by others.[38]

What, then, would be the components of this new, socialist morality? The answer to this question reveals a lack of positive content that was mirrored in so much democratic socialist writing. It would be "heroic, active, [and] against evil," read one definition. More precisely, it would be characterized by "a positive position on socialist organization, the understanding of one's own vocation as a service to the whole, the understanding of labor as *a joyous duty for the whole* . . . and the striving for a socialist society."[39] This final characteristic, a concept absolutely devoid of content that hinged on the definition of socialist culture itself, was explained by Černý as being "a magnificent search. . . . And there must be a search because it [socialist culture] must be found!"[40] Even the president admitted that he had no precise idea of where he was leading his nation: "A new world and a new life are being created. We do not have a precise and entirely clear conception of these new things, but we are searching for them, we are struggling with them."[41]

These vague goals were supplemented by a much clearer view of what socialist culture would *not* be, one that corresponds to the middle course democratic socialist intellectuals were attempting to steer. As the proclamation of the Congress of Czech Writers proudly stated, "we resolutely stand for the new, socialist humanism that is fighting for the liberation of the human being, and are against a callous and merely abstract liberal humanism."[42] While the bourgeois era was perceived as "incapable of style," the new socialist Czechoslovakia would, in the words of Kovárna, "free the strata already liberated from material oppression from the spiritual oppression . . . of bourgeois influences. We must aid in the creation of the new socialist lifestyle [*životní styl*]."[43] As in all other spheres of public discussion, the adjective "bourgeois" was pejorative and, no matter how vaguely defined, the adjective "socialist" commendatory. Moreover, while "socialist culture cannot—thankfully—be considered or elaborated in a spirit directed *against the communists*," it would be no mere copy of conditions in the Soviet Union.[44] Citing the Soviet slogan, "a culture socialist in content, national in form," Černý summed up this requirement:

> We want to build a culture of Czech socialist humanism. In this we are all as one. But we will not build anything either Czech or cultural if we are not allowed to create entirely freely, i.e., without foreign prescriptions or even only recipes. Regarding this construction work we have before our eyes a wonderful example: Russia. It is a model that simultaneously [provides] a moral example and support. An exemplary model, in no way however a model for blind imitation . . . . Our socialist humanism will be different from the Russian one simply because it will be Czech.[45]

The final sentence of Černý's view of socialist humanism perceptively describes a primary unifying feature of democratic socialists' conception of socialist society: it would somehow be "Czech." This description of moderate socialists' aims was, like the majority of the preceding statements, particularly prominent in the run up to the 1946 parliamentary elections. Machotka's *The Socialism of the Czechs*, Ripka's calls for "democracy and Czechoslovak socialism," and even the demand that Czechs should "in the realization of our socialist ideals [follow] our own road," were all part of an attempt to create the impression that the Communist Party was somehow foreign, that it would introduce a foreign, i.e., Soviet, socialism into the nation, or that it would bring a slide into totalitarianism.[46] To make this point clear, Ripka argued:

> To vote for the Communists (and their help-mates or servants in the Social Democratic Party) means to vote for the communization of Czechoslovakia, . . . [which] would lead inexorably to a dictatorial regime of economic, political, and cultural totalitarianism. The bearer and means of this totalitarianism will be the dictatorship of the proletariat.[47]

The specifically Czech socialism that would prevent this apocalyptic scenario and still lead to the joys of socialism was never clearly defined, and was often presented as a socialism that was in harmony with Czech traditions. This foundation was certainly less than a stable one, as the Communist Party was enjoying success in casting itself as patriotic, and communist intellectuals were in the process of reinventing precisely these traditions, with not inconsiderable support from their democratic socialist opponents. Democratic socialists seem to have believed that Czech national traditions stood unquestionably behind them, and devoted themselves to propagating good will toward socialism, as we have just seen. In the words of Eva Hartmannová, they called for "character [and] ideals" to bring about a "vaguely defined and, in its concrete form, unanalyzed 'socialism,'" revealing a dichotomy between "a seemingly inexorable material reality and a psychic dimension on which hopes were placed."[48]

Despite these weaknesses, democratic socialists believed that the National Socialist Party would claim victory in the 1946 parliamentary elections. At least one thought the party would gain roughly 45 percent of the vote, and others held that the Communist Party would be reduced to only a "minor" party.[49] Peroutka was the only commentator to correctly understand that his colleagues had overestimated their position. Two months before the election, he warned those who believed that the Communists would meet their Waterloo:

> This is an illusion the more dangerous the more one is inclined to deduce from it. This dream conceals the real political conditions in the state and is estranged from an understanding of the facts of the times. . . . Far from a real defeat awaiting it, the Communist Party will emerge from the elections as the first or second party, more likely the first, and will again present itself as an influential, likely the most influential, governing party.[50]

Democratic socialist intellectuals blamed the National Socialist Party's subsequent electoral defeat on several factors. The most superficial explanations laid the blame on external circumstances, such as gratitude toward the USSR.[51] Others held that the Communist Party had gained the votes only of people "without character," who had either been somehow bought by the Communist Party or lured by its voting tricks. Peroutka noted that this was the desperate reasoning of those who had believed most deeply in a National Socialist victory and retorted, "One illusion is dead, long live another illusion!"[52] Finally, the most exhaustive analysis of the defeat stressed the success of the Communist Party's reinvention. Since the time of the prewar republic, it had moved from minority self-determination to vociferous support for the expulsion of the Germans; from oppositional to governing; from rejection of all cooperation with the bourgeoisie to solid support for the National Front; from class warfare to social solidarity and national unity; from a base in the proletariat to support from intellectuals, technicians, farmers, and small traders; and, finally, the party had moved "from the Red flag to the national flag." In hoping to pinpoint the social strata in which the National Socialists should try to shore up their vote, this commentator observed, "*Consequently, the whole nation voted for the Communists*—not only one class and fragments of others."[53] The only people who escaped public blame were the creators of the ideas that had led the party to defeat in the pre-election debates and at the ballot box. Averell Harriman was not so kind, however, ripping into the political and ideological leaders of Czech democracy for their "lack of backbone" and their failure to offer "effective democratic counterpropaganda."[54]

Peroutka offered a lesson in realism to those who believed that the Communist Party victory was a fluke caused by the new international constellation and gratitude to the USSR. Whereas before the elections he argued that the public needed to be taught that capitalism was dead, now he maintained,

> A strong and influential Communist Party is one of the primary facts of our contemporary politics. It is necessary to teach all people concerned with politics to count on this. Essentially, people still tell us, "We want a situation in which the Communist Party is not strong!" Fine. But we do not have such a situation, we cannot offer it. We are not a model showroom [*výběrna vzorků*]. There is what there is.[55]

In recognizing that the Communist Party was and would remain a political force, he warned against the adoption of a stringently anti-communist course. There were, in his view, Czechs who "cannot see in the Communists anything else than enemies—not political opponents, but simply enemies." The election returns had shown this to be wrong, for "if the Communists really were enemies of the Czech and Slovak nation, of the Czechoslovak state, of the Czechoslovak people . . . a great portion of the nation would be enemies of the nation." In these and other statements, he poured cold water on those who had complacently believed in a Communist Party defeat, and after the elections sought to explain away the National Socialist loss. Nonetheless, his urging to treat the Communist Party as a political foe, rather than as a potentially anti-democratic force, contributed to a weakening of democratic defenses. It also reveals the profound difference between democratic and communist conceptions of politics. His conclusion bears more than a trace of fatalism: "The one real hope the nation always has is faith in its people. . . . If the qualities of the Czech people are good they will have an effect even within the Communist Party."[56] Such reliance on the innate qualities of the Czech people hardly substitutes for a coherent and convincing ideological platform for democratic politics.

The question of conjuring up Harriman's "effective democratic counterpropaganda" still remained for these intellectual and political elites and was a question that remained unanswered for some time. It was apparent that relying on Czech traditions and a claim to Masaryk and Beneš as the intellectual foundation for a noncommunist "Czech" socialism had failed to convince the electorate. Democratic socialists' ability to claim these could not match the communist exploitation of the same and had proven, in the words of one *Dnešek* contributor, "too lazy a means to scare their rival."[57] Similarly, their enthusiasm for socialism had narrowed the rhetorical distance between themselves and their Communist Party opponents, thereby confusing the electorate both about the differences between the National Socialist and Communist parties and about the precise nature of National Socialist socialism. For example, *Dnešek* received a letter from one National Socialist that demanded clarification of the party's understanding of socialism. The writer closed by asking, "whether we would not breathe much more easily and live much more easily if we universally learned to say clearly and understandably: Marx's socialism = Masaryk's humanism!" The reply was that while there were different kinds of socialism, all agreed that "institutional exploitation" must be abolished, that nationalization was one means of accomplishing this but "in itself is not socialism," and that "socialism is not a personal matter, nor one of the proletariat's class interest, but is the moral duty of the people." The only distinction made vis-à-vis the Communist Party was that while Marxists overvalued institutional change, non-Marxists overvalued changing the way people think. Even this moderately self-critical statement was further tempered by noting that both methods were necessary.[58] This reply is symptomatic of both the democratic socialists' commitment to a moral, ethical, and cultural conception of socialism and their inability to clearly formulate what precisely differentiated them in a positive sense from their Marxist opponents.

Democratic socialists' attempt to found a political ideology based on a particularly "Czech" brand of socialism was dealt a serious blow by the Communist Party's announcement of the "Czechoslovak road to socialism" in late 1946. After that announcement, National Socialists continued to maintain that "'the Eastern system,' i.e., state capitalism in conjunction with the dictatorship of the proletariat and the Marxist world view," was not *the only and best road to socialism*" and that the Communists' new strategy was only what the National Socialists had long maintained.[59] Nonetheless, there is no doubt that the announcement of the "Czechoslovak road" lessened even further the rhetorical distance between these two camps, to the benefit of the Communist Party. It gravely damaged a democratic socialist line based on the "foreign" nature of the Communist Party or the suspicion that the Communists would impose a Soviet system on Czechoslovakia. Although National Socialists could still claim to be a home-grown socialist phenomenon, the nationalism of the Communist Party detracted considerably from the political power of this argument.

Perhaps surprisingly, the "Czechoslovak road" was generally welcomed by democratic socialist intellectual and political leaders. Immediately after its announcement, Hubert Ripka published an article entitled "Stalin Revives Hope," and Kovárna proclaimed his gratitude that it was "possible for us to embark on our own road to socialism, as Prime Minister Gottwald assured us."[60] This response seems to have been drawn from the supposition that it indicated that the Communist Party recognized the unsuitability of rigid Marxism for Czechoslovakia and implicitly grasped the validity of the democratic socialist course. As one contributor to *Dnešek* observed, the Communist announcement

> was not an unwise act. The leaders of the Communist Party were certainly aware of two facts: that it is far more valuable to achieve power by the road this nation has always traveled, the road of democratic elections, and that it is a specific quality of the Czech character that it above all demands persuasion and not orders.[61]

Thereby showing their respect for the political wisdom and cultural sensitivity of the Communist leadership, it was only a small step to believing that the strategy represented the culmination of a shift in the Communist Party and the Soviet Union itself, one that had begun even before the war. This was what democratic socialists wanted to believe, as Lev Sychrava showed in 1947 when he mirrored the words of Klement Gottwald:

> Our communist movement, already from the time Hitler rose to power, began to change its opinion of the Czechoslovak national and state idea. . . . This rapprochement and cooperation, sanctified by blood, is not temporary or a matter of chance, because it corresponds to the profound contemporary change in the Soviet Union's revolutionary theory, which only erroneously can be considered a mere tactical shift.[62]

The belief that the Communist Party's transformation was part of a broader change in the thinking of the Soviet Union's leadership was widespread. President Beneš relied on this for his conception of the state's foreign policy, and the Communists' abandonment of the dictatorship of the proletariat must have come as confirmation of both his belief in the Communist Party's reformation and of his international policy convictions:

> You will certainly find exponents of communism who maintain the necessity of the dictatorship of the proletariat. I myself hold that it is not necessary in the great majority of lands, that it is against the principle of developmental democracy. . . . The Soviet Union and Russian communists today recognize that the transition from liberal democracy to its higher level—to socializing democracy—can and should today happen gradually, step by step, through reasonable development according to the natural economic, social, geographic, moral, and legal conditions of the respective national societies.[63]

Endorsements like these of the essential rhetorical message of the "Czechoslovak road" from the head of Czech noncommunist politics certainly played a role in the plausibility accorded the policy, but also something more. If democratic socialists truly believed in the reformed nature of Czechoslovak Communism, then it was even more crucial that they develop a coherent idea of their own socialism. Peroutka's stricture that democratic socialists should "convince" their communist counterparts implied that they must create arguments capable of doing so.

The democratic socialist response to the component parts of the Communist "Czechoslovak road" were similarly favorable, particularly for the emphasis placed on the Two-Year Plan and the conception of the People's Democracy. For example, democratic socialists saw the People's Democracy—despite its recognized terminological redundancy—as "indisputably a step forward on the road of democracy."[64] For democratic socialist intellectuals like Arnošt Bláha, as for President Beneš and also the communists, the "bourgeois democracy" of the prewar period was "only formal democracy, because it was only political. It was not an economic democracy . . . nor was it a cultural democracy."[65] For democratic socialist intellectuals, the mission of the People's Democracy was to overcome the failures of bourgeois democracy in the political, economic, and especially cultural fields. Pavel Tigrid later ruefully noted the proliferation of the use of what he called "fraudulent labels and slogans," citing the People's Democracy as a particular example:

> Not only communists thought these up, all of us patented democrats used them and operated with them without shame. Obviously, it did not bother us that the term "People's Democracy" was an awkward pleonasm. . . . The National Front was neither national, since it excluded from the nation the politically most powerful component of the First Republic, nor was it a front, but a closed club of the spokespeople of the mutually permitted parties, in which it was calculatingly agreed what had to be approved by the government and parliament.[66]

Although introduced openly by the Communist Party, democratic socialists responded as warmly to the idea of planning as they had to the "people's democratic" system. Given Peroutka's criticism of the "anarchy" of capitalism, it should come as no surprise that he argued, "The main mistake of the old democracy, despite all the appealing features that mark it, lies in its incapacity for great activity, for an extensive plan."[67] More surprisingly, he called the Two-Year Plan "the axis and skeleton of the government plan," a statement that bears remarkable similarity to Gottwald's argument that "the Two-Year Plan and its fulfillment are links in a chain that we must grasp to pull the entire chain."[68] In Peroutka's view, the plan was integral for the maintenance of the National Front, an institution of questionable democratic legitimacy but one guaranteeing noncommunist participation. In contrast, for Gottwald it was integral to the Communists' "Czechoslovak road" and the party's control of the state. Peroutka, however, seems distinctly moderate in comparison with some of his colleagues, particularly in terms of implications. Robert

Konečný was unsatisfied with the extent of the plan's provisions, and demanded, perhaps incredulously to our ears today, "a general plan . . . like the Soviet Gosplan, for all aspects of state life."[69] The taste for planning among democratic socialists extended beyond according the state extensive control over the economy, however. K. J. Beneš also faulted the plan for not going far enough: "We lack something else much more useful in the overall plan, and that is—we are not frightened by the words—a *Central Union of Cultural Interest Organizations*, which would correspond to the important and well-functioning analogous unions in the economy."[70] This brush with cultural planning was not understood as potentially inhibiting the freedom of artists, the protection of which was a bulwark of the intellectual resistance to communist power. However, Beneš (and he was not alone) revealed a blindness to the potential for abuse inherent in such planning that is striking. Perhaps most crucially, democratic socialists believed that economic planning would require much the same ideological retraining for which Machotka had called and for which communist intellectuals—with their "revision of the national character"—were striving: "The planned economy obviously demands certain changes in the thinking of the citizens."[71]

In the wake of the Communist Party announcement of the "Czechoslovak road," and particularly after that party proclaimed its aim of securing a majority of the vote, democratic socialists settled on a few fundamental strategies. The comments that follow will analyze these critically, but any account must recognize that these men and women were limited by a number of factors. Above all, the Communist Party had seized much of the nationalist and socialist high ground, leaving little space for the ideological exploitation of either social or patriotic issues. Furthermore, that party's announcement of the "Czechoslovak road," as the twin of the communist cultural offensive, gravely weakened any advocacy of a socialism based on Czech traditions or a vaguely defined Czech "national character." Moreover, democratic socialists' belief in the moral rectitude of socialism prevented them from launching any general critique of the developments in the state. Finally, their past encouragement of socialism and cooperation with the communists, as well as their approval of the linchpins of the "Czechoslovak road" made it difficult for them to find grounds on which to criticize the communist position.

As Ferdinand Peroutka's warning made clear, the mass support for the Communist Party made it politically unrealistic, if not impossible, to attack that party as an outright enemy. The Communists' reinvention as patriotic and committed to national goals also rendered such a strategy rhetorically implausible. How then did democratic socialists see their communist opponents? With an eye perhaps toward electoral gains from the communist ranks, democratic socialists were careful to distinguish between various types of communists and different motivations for joining the party. For all of the potential targets for democratic socialist ideas who currently supported the Communist Party, Peroutka believed, "communism as a movement, an ideal, probably attracts them more than the Communist Party in all of its concrete manifestations."[72] This insight prompted democratic socialists to strive to both grasp the ideals of communism and separate them from their incarnation in the Communist Party. This was the spring for Ripka's argument that "the majority" of communist sympathizers were subject to a "naive faith that the communists want only what they proclaim today."[73] It also stood behind *Dnešek*'s argument, produced during the government crisis of February 1948, that communism did not strive for the same things that individual Communist parties did.[74] J. B. Kozák had reached a similar conclusion already before the 1946 elections, stressing that democratic socialists and communists differed in methods, but not in aims:

> The methods of our Communists are not, in our judgment, the best path. If someone were to ask us whether the Communist program is too much for us, we would answer: By no means. In some areas it is too little for us. A Communist government in our country would, by its methods, separate us from its own goal of socialism rather than bring us closer.[75]

Kozák's final comment reveals a recurring theme of democratic socialist criticism brought by their commitment to socialism. They were forced to admit, as did Peroutka, that while democratic socialists may wish that the communists would base their "constructing" work on a non-Marxist basis, there was no doubt that their labors were "in the interests of socialism."[76] In essence, their pre-election argument that communism was somehow foreign and that a socialism based on Czech traditions was necessary was refitted for further duty. Now that they could no longer plausibly claim to hold a patent on Czech socialism or even Czech traditions, democratic socialists maintained that they could introduce socialism into Czech society in a better way. They did not argue that the concrete final form of their socialism would necessarily be different from that of the communists, but rather that they had better methods for instituting socialism and that their socialism was more inclusive. This allowed them both to escape precisely analyzing their socialism's content and to characterize it as one predicated on the defense of freedom and democracy. This defensive definitional posture, coupled with the affirmation of socialism, characterized the democratic socialists' intellectual position until their ultimate exclusion from the public stage in 1948.

The defensive posture was understandable for reasons beyond democratic socialists' political position and sensibilities. First, they were certainly aware of not only the mass support, political power, and potential danger of the Communist Party of Czechoslovakia, but also of the developments in neighboring lands. Nonetheless, they refrained from critically commenting on regional developments, perhaps for the same reasons that criticisms of the Soviet Union remained outside of public discussion. The state of democratic socialist political actors' knowledge of events in Poland and Hungary can be seen from their memoirs. The broader public, however, remained poorly informed on events in these countries, as they were discussed in a condemnably superficial manner. With the exception of the Roman Catholic *Obzory*, which reprinted Western journalists' reports on Eastern European affairs without comment, Czech reporting and commentary focused on the strides toward socialism taken in the "fraternal people's democracies" and the solidifying of cultural, economic, and political ties among them. In this respect, democratic socialists must bear the responsibility for their failure to adequately inform the public of abuses taking place just across Czechoslovakia's borders. This may have contributed to the inability to organize effective resistance to the communists in February 1948.[77]

Furthermore, communist intellectuals succeeded in placing their democratic socialist counterparts on the defensive by questioning their socialist credentials, and accusing them of being the bearers of "reaction," thereby inducing a defensive response. The charge of representing reactionary forces was increasingly leveled at democratic socialists in the National Socialist Party. Roman Catholics were far less concerned about, and politically less vulnerable to, such labeling and, as supporters of the openly non-socialist People's Party, were not the targets of Communists' "Czechoslovak road" ideology. Democratic socialists, however, were more sensitive to the charge, both because of their belief in socialism and because of their position in Czech politics. Communist intellectuals saw an opportunity to capitalize on their identification with true socialism and to wean away democratic socialists' popular support through such charges.

Democratic socialists pursued several distinct courses in coming to terms with the charge of reaction. Before the 1946 elections, and in their immediate aftermath, democratic socialists dismissed as unwarranted the worries about reactionaries. Already at that time they realized the potential damage the label could have in all spheres of public life: "To be declared a literary reactionary is almost as ignominious as to be called a political reactionary."[78] Nonetheless, for them reaction constituted no threat; it was as powerless as the capitalism it represented: it was "defeated" (Kozák), "without influence . . . [and] without character" (Peroutka).[79] For this reason, it was not worth more democratic socialist attention than was capitalism. As time passed, however, these same intellectuals perceived that they, and their brand of socialism, had become the primary subjects of the communist search for "reactionaries." As a group, they repeatedly protested that they were progressive socialists and not reactionaries bent on thwarting socialism. After the Communist victory in the 1946 elections, however, the term had obviously changed content in the communist discourse: it no longer applied only to the political right, but to all opponents of communist power.

Černý and Peroutka both fell victim to the charge of "reaction" and their responses to the attacks are telling. Černý condemned his attackers and noted that communist strategy toward him had developed from arguing with him, to placing him in the reactionary camp, and finally to mere "name-calling." This did not keep Černý from indulging in much the same behavior, however. In a departure from his normally reasoned, if hyperbolic, style, he took to calling his opponents "pole-cats and worms clinging to our culture and our socialism."[80] Peroutka's response was more interesting, for he reversed field and conceded that reaction did in fact exist and did constitute a threat. As he directly attacked his own former position, his rhetoric mirrored that normally seen in the communist press:

> Some people who themselves are undoubtedly close to reaction make it look as if reaction did not exist at all and try to expose the term itself to ridicule. . . . There is no doubt that reaction exists and that it is waiting, prepared to one day take advantage of an opportunity and its strength, or to exploit the weakness or mistakes of others. The number of people who personally lost in these transitional events [i.e., the socialist changes after liberation]—what a reservoir of reactionary forces.

He clearly characterized what constituted reaction in the economic sphere: "open or secret opposition to the great work of nationalization cannot be considered as anything but reaction." In the fields of politics and culture, however, he maintained that the content of the term was far less clear. Here he displayed his capability for innovation by asking a series of questions. These constituted precisely the list of concerns about, and criticisms of, the Communist Party he had often expressed. He asked, "Which principle is progressive and which reactionary—one party or more parties? Democracy or dictatorship? . . . Is communism the only progressive movement and are all other kinds of socialism reactionary? Is there no progressivism apart from materialism?"[81] By phrasing his response in this way, he avoided criticizing the Communist Party (or the Soviet Union) directly, while clearly implying that the party itself was a reactionary force biding its time, waiting for a mistake by its opponents.

Peroutka's article constitutes one of the relatively few democratic socialist attempts to paint the communists with their own "reactionary" brush. Isolated other endeavors observed that there could also be reactionaries inside the communist ranks and that Marxist theory and ideology did not meet the rigorous standards of empirical sociology and therefore could not be progressive.[82] In this vein, Jan Slavík, who labeled the Communist Party's goal of obtaining 51 percent of the vote reactionary, made the sharpest attack:

> Reaction is raising its head. Who is not convinced that in a democratic state it is necessary even for those who achieve 51 percent of the vote to respect the political minority? . . . Reaction is raising its head, writes the communist press. Here, however, it is necessary to ask: "About whom are you speaking?" *You are speaking of yourselves.*[83]

The identification of the Communist Party aim of achieving an electoral majority with reaction hints at one of the few offensive strategies employed by democratic socialist intellectuals. They realized, as did Peroutka, that the open declaration of such a goal by any party could not "be a common aim of the National Front," and that it could lead to a breakdown in the delicate system of the People's Democracy.[84]

The charge that the Communist Party pursued totalitarian aims and the similar strategy of equating communism with fascism were relatively common but not forcefully made. President Beneš noted, "Just as Nazism and fascism adopted many socialist features, from some varieties of socialism or communism it is only a small step to Nazi totalitarianism." His close associate Ripka, while maintaining that his "anticommunist standpoint" had never meant that he "could not see the essential differences between communism and fascism," also noted that "unfortunately some communists sometimes use methods that it is possible only with difficulty to distinguish from fascist methods." Finally, Slavík, in the article just cited, asked communists to "explain the surprising similarity of some ideas and methods of fascism and communism."[85] Other commentators were more explicit, comparing young communists to the Hitler Youth or condemning communist materialism, but such attacks were rare.[86] On the whole, democratic socialists trod very lightly on the issue, appending qualifiers to their statements. As in the cited examples, they most often only tacitly drew the comparison, allowing the reader to draw his or her own conclusions. Most significantly, Peroutka triumphantly claimed in January 1947, "The year 1946 decided whether Czechoslovakia will become a totalitarian or a democratic state."[87] Although he undoubtedly revised his opinion as 1947 progressed, the fact that he was willing to proclaim the period of danger ended is some indication of democratic socialists' estimation of the threat. This stands in stark contrast to Roman Catholic intellectuals who, perhaps because they were not bound by the same socialist sensibilities and electoral calculations as democratic socialists, explored and exploited the similarities between communism, fascism, and totalitarianism.

Democratic socialists' commitment to social change made it intellectually difficult for them to view the Communist Party as a potential threat rather than as an ally in the process that was the "socializing democracy." As Černý admitted in his *Memoirs*:

> It occasionally seemed to me, and I was not an exception among democratic intellectuals, that it was possible to expect a guarantee of true national regeneration and of the just social transformation of our national society only from the pressure and unyielding character of the communist element in the National Front.[88]

This sentiment led democratic socialists to reject any possibility of intellectually throwing out the communist baby because of the potentially totalitarian bath water. Instead, as Peroutka's recommendation to "convince" the communists indicates, democratic socialists attempted to sway their communist counterparts by appealing to the undefined goal of socialism they both shared. Therefore, they advised their communist counterparts to shed any tendencies toward totalitarianism not because they would be met with stiff resistance, but because they would damage the cause of socialism: "*All attempts to turn back democracy . . . and introduce the dictatorship of one party will not benefit, but damage socialism. . . .* Above all, they have the disastrous consequence that out of socialism, whose complete success in Europe has already been decided with finality, they make a dangerous specter."[89] This yoking of democracy to socialism was also a hallmark of communist argumentation, which made the democratic socialists' claim to represent the true defenders of freedom and democracy more difficult to uphold.

Democracy and freedom were the conceptual cornerstones of democratic socialists' hopes to create a successful, if undefined, socialism in Czechoslovakia. For them, democracy was a "character trait" of the Czech nation.[90] The democracy and freedom they now advocated were new and qualitatively different from those inherited from the Czech past, however. Whether trumpeted as "socializing democracy" (Beneš), "humanist democracy" (Konečný), or a "political democracy . . . completed by economic democracy" (Peroutka), they all drew upon the ideas expressed by President Edvard Beneš in his *Democracy Today and Tomorrow*, lacked a precise content and defined themselves by their opposition to liberal democracy.[91] Finally, the same messianic sense of a special Czech calling that characterized democratic socialist intellectuals' attempts to unite East and West in a higher synthesis also played a role in their struggle to maintain democracy and freedom.

Liberal democracy and the freedoms it guaranteed were favorite targets of the proponents of the "new democracy." As democratic socialists showed only slight reservations about taking part in the criticism of their own interwar republic, it should come as no surprise that theoretical liberal democracy came under harsher fire. Liberal democracy "truly created a feudal order of wealth," and created the conditions for "anarchy and cultural, political, and economic licentiousness."[92] As for democracy in liberal society, so for the liberal notion of freedom. "The same freedom for all," wrote Antonín Klatovský, "is in reality freedom for the most powerful, often not in terms of abilities and character, but of rapacity and ruthlessness."[93] For democratic socialists as a whole, as Černý put it, "[We must remember] Lenin's statement about freedom that it can also mean 'the freedom to shout, to lie and to write whatever one likes.' In no way shall we invoke such freedoms! We know that there cannot be true freedom in a society based on the power of money and social inequality."[94]

What then did they intend to put in place of liberal democracy and freedom, if not their wholesale replacement by precisely the kinds of democracy and freedoms on offer from the communist movement? The answer to this question is extremely unclear, and the proliferation of terms denoting the new democracy that democratic socialists wished to create did little to improve conceptual clarity. The system for which they strove would be a "correction" of earlier conceptions of democracy that would result in "a state realizing spiritual democracy and economic and social democracy."[95] The two elements of democracy and freedom were certain to be components, but its formal character was predicated on the moral concerns for the new, socialist culture and socialist humanism already discussed. It appeared to democratic socialists that "for the clear majority of Czechs and Slovaks, democracy without socialism seems formal, incomplete, without living content."[96] To paraphrase a Czech proverb, it seems the wish became the father of the thought, and democratic socialists' profound faith in the power of their abstract conceptions of socialist culture and morality led them away from a careful consideration of the legal, institutional, and conceptual foundations of freedom and democracy. For example, the future of freedom was discussed in terms that both glorified the new democracy and ignored democratic socialists' own lack of content for it:

> This freedom is not in conflict with, but will be made easier by the new order. The former system led to the isolation of the individual and to all the consequences that brought chaos into the inner person and sometimes even made a beast of him. The new order will lead the individual from pernicious isolation and thereby save him. It will liberate us from an entire set of slaveries (above all, the slavery to money), liberate the personality [*osobnost*] and make it possible for individuals to develop their personas [*osobnost*]. . . . It is about clearing the path so that the individual can be truly good.[97]

Here is an example of democratic socialist messianism, although in this case it is ascribed to the system rather than the nation. Other democratic socialists were more circumspect, but the notion was widespread that the new socialist order would free both the society as a whole and the individuals within it for higher creation. In many ways, even freedom was understood as a subordinate factor to this socialism. This is not meant in the sense that democratic socialists would sacrifice freedom for socialism. Rather, freedom's value was often described in terms of the contribution it could make to the efficient achievement of the goal of socialism. As Antonín Klatovský put it, with more than a hint of messianism:

> *Our calling is not to provide proof that it is possible to socialize with the preservation of spiritual freedom, but to prove that with the preservation of spiritual freedom it is possible to arrive more rapidly and successfully at socialism.*[98]

The sense that the achievement of a syncretic synthesis was somehow a specific Czech "calling" recalls the debate over the Czech cultural orientation on the East-West axis, and the two are tightly related. Czech democratic socialist intellectuals had set themselves the task of synthesizing the cultural and intellectual fruits of the Slavic Eastern Europe and liberal Western Europe into a new and higher culture. Similarly, their vaguely defined socialism was often interpreted as being the synthesis of Western political traditions and freedoms with Eastern socialism. For example, in an article with the telling title, "Our National Individuality," Oldřich Procházka argued that the West represented political freedom and the East economic freedom.[99] Similarly, Peroutka's *Dnešek* maintained in 1947 that the task was to "combine the fruits of the French and Russian revolutions."[100] Peroutka himself argued that the unification of "socialism and freedom" must be achieved, and he characterized the task for the nation as "to evaluate everything that has happened since the revolution from the higher viewpoint of synthesis . . . : the harmonious integration of victorious socialism with the ancient spiritual assets of European culture."[101] Even Ripka, the National Socialist minister of foreign trade—neither a man nor a post commonly identified with flights of intellectual fancy—was not immune. In a statement of this desire that comes close to being programmatic, he argued that

> Our social order should express the fundamental ideas of democracy and socialism, and it should realize them in organic, harmonious unity. We are fundamentally convinced that socialism is in no way the overcoming of democracy but, on the contrary, its consummation, its organic continuation and fulfillment, that it is its developmental form and more perfect content.[102]

These intellectuals seemed to have found the meaning of history, and desired to see it realized.

Democratic socialist intellectuals were aware of the immensity of the goal they had set and, as in the case of the debate over the Czech national orientation, relied on a strong sense of messianism to carry their argument. They believed that the future of their nation, and perhaps even the world, hung on their ability to carry out this synthesis. As Vratislav Bušek argued, 1948 would decide the fate of "a specific Czech synthesis, guaranteeing full and real democracy in the political, social, and economic spheres . . . , a synthesis whose success is the fate of our nation, for better or worse."[103] This view was shared by Klatovský, who, after arguing for both the West's view of freedom and the East's measure of socialism, expanded upon it by observing, "The ideological opposition between East and West seems insurmountable. If it were to be so . . . the situation of humanity would be despair and hopelessness."[104] Czech democratic socialists set themselves the task of overcoming this opposition and, through the creation of a new and higher order of democracy, saving both their country and humanity from rising Cold War tensions and the apparently unbridgeable ideological gap between the West and the East.

A CASE STUDY OF COMMUNIST–DEMOCRATIC SOCIALIST CONFLICT: *KULTURNÍ OBEC* VERSUS *KULTURNÍ SVAZ*

The weaknesses we have just seen in the defense of freedom and democracy were even apparent in the case of artistic and scholarly freedom, a subject implicit in the intellectual idea and one over which democratic socialist intellectuals made their strongest stand. For several weeks in late 1946, democratic socialist and communist intellectuals engaged in an open conflict that contrasts markedly with the series of sniping actions that characterized the 1945–1948 period. At the outset, communist intellectuals committed a tactical error that handed their democratic socialist opponents an opportunity to seize the positive issue of artistic and scholarly freedom and exploit it to initiate a broader critique of communist intentions. Nonetheless, by the conclusion of the dispute, democratic socialists' willingness for intra-socialist compromise and their occasionally messianic belief in synthesis had led them to join their communist opponents and sacrifice the potential cultural and political gains on offer. In this regard, the battle can be seen as paradigmatic of democratic socialists' aspirations and, more importantly, of the internal weaknesses of their position.

The conflict began on October 6, 1946, when the Communist Party's *Rudé právo* published an appeal to Czech intellectuals. This announced the founding of *Kulturní obec* (The Cultural Community) and appealed for cultural figures to join the organization "in the spirit of active and fighting humanism and scientific socialism."[105] With this act the proclamation's 40 signatories touched off a furious cultural and political battle that, although short, encapsulated many of the themes of the democratic socialist–communist debate and centered on an issue that lay near to democratic socialists' hearts: intellectual freedom in a socialist society. The announcement came at a critical juncture in the battle between communist and democratic socialist intellectuals. The preceding weeks had seen the condemnation of the journals *Zvezda* and *Leningrad* and the writers Zoshchenko and Akhmatova by the Central Committee of the Communist Party of the Soviet Union. While this example of the stiffening of the cultural line in the USSR drew little direct protest from Czech democratic socialists, it did elicit many calls directed at securing a Communist promise that such an action would not be repeated in Czechoslovakia. The hesitation on the part of the Communist political and intellectual leadership—apparently caught off guard both by the news from Moscow and by the response in Prague—to give such assurances raised concerns about the Communist commitment to artistic and scholarly freedom and, by extension, to the notion of freedom more generally.[106] Moreover, the announcement of the formation of *Kulturní obec* coincided with that of the "Czechoslovak road." Thus it appeared that the two were related offensives, aimed at securing the Communist Party's domination of not only the issue of socialism, but also of the socialist culture that lay at the core of democratic socialists' view of Czech society's future. Finally, the debate between the adherents and opponents of *Kulturní obec* took place as other events contributed to the rising tensions. These included the parliamentary debate over the formulation of the Two-Year plan (passed October 26), the upcoming anniversary of the founding of the Czechoslovak Republic (October 28), strong communist showings in the French and Bulgarian elections, and the official end of the expulsion of the Sudeten Germans.

According to Jaroslav Kladiva, the decision to form *Kulturní obec* came at the end of a long set of discussions within the framework of the Communist Party's Cultural Propagation Committee. That body's "May Call"—which gathered signatures from figures in various fields of cultural activity pledging support for the party in the run up to the 1946 elections—had obtained nearly one thousand signatures, and the party's strong showing in that election certainly contributed to the decision to launch *Kulturní obec*. Kladiva points out that the replacement of the Communist Nejedlý by the National Socialist Jaroslav Stránský as Minister of Education and Culture provided the impetus to the committee's decision. By forming the organization, the party aimed to create a unified cultural organization that would aid in carrying out the tasks given to culture within the framework of the two-year plan then being debated in the legislature.[107]

The appeal founding *Kulturní obec* was based on the call not only to "heal the moral consequences of the Second World War and overcome the Czech 'anxiety from smallness' [*strach z malosti*] and indifference to public affairs, but also awaken the self-consciousness of a democratic nation living from its own labor." The experience of the war was a defining one for the younger generation of intellectuals and one which caused all Czech thinkers to probe the interwar years to find its causes. In this respect, *Kulturní obec* laid the blame at the feet of Czechoslovakia's "pernicious pre-Munich relationships, both international and domestic." Other elements of the communist call for the "revision of the national character" appeared in the document and were summed up in the declaration's demand that the nation "justify its existence through the progressive development of the national character."

Because of its similarity to other statements of communist cultural goals, the proclamation seems to contain little that would ignite an intellectual firestorm. The only exception to this might be the closing call to work in the spirit of "scientific socialism," but even this was balanced by the opening promise to work on "a broad and solid conceptual foundation." The problem lay in the list of organizers, which contained very well-known intellectuals from all fields of creative endeavor, but was composed entirely of Communists. This fact prompted the response published in the National Socialist daily *Svobodné slovo* one week later, which announced the formation of *Kulturní svaz* (The Cultural Union).[108] Its proclamation, while similarly recognizing the "moral breakdown" brought by the war and standing behind the democratic socialist mantra of building "a new social and economic order . . . an economic and social democracy," emphasized the need to ensure artistic and creative freedom. The clear rebuff to the perceived communist attempt to dominate even competing socialist elements in the national culture can be seen in the *Kulturní svaz* pledge to defend "the freedom of the individuality of spiritual labor . . . against any kind of interference or attempts to subordinate it to power and party or political influences." The proclamation, signed by 66 leading democratic socialist intellectuals, was buttressed by citations from the president's speech at the Congress of Czech Writers that had taken place the previous June. The skirmishes that took place at that meeting broke into open confrontation with this debate, which clearly demarcated the battle lines by compiling and publishing lists of the two organizations' adherents.

The two proclamations evoked an immediate response from the across the political spectrum. A small minority greeted the formation of rival institutions positively,[109] but the vast majority of observers viewed the unfolding events with angry concern. The schism in the cultural front was held to have grave consequences for the sense of unity created in the state in the months after the May 1945 revolution. This was particularly evident in the view of the *Mladá fronta*. The paper, usually supportive of the Communist Party, may have seen the weakness of the communist intellectuals' position, and urged the forging of a unified cultural organization similar to that obtaining in the trade unions, i.e., under communist domination. The dangers of returning to the cultural divisions of the interwar republic, in which leftist intellectuals were pitted against their right-wing counterparts, were often alluded to, while the pressing need for a unified cultural organization to argue for the needs of culture in a planned economy were similarly stressed.[110] The cause of the split was almost universally seen to lie in the "politicking" (*politikáření*) of the hyper-politicized postwar environment, rather than in legitimate political or intellectual differences. This gave rise to the general belief that a unified organization would be created.[111]

Democratic socialist supporters of *Kulturní svaz* certainly saw the formation of *Kulturní obec* as a Communist Party attempt to hijack the nation's culture. They seized the issue of creative freedom primarily from the conviction that the communists represented a danger to freedom of expression. It is also clear, however, that the vehemence of their response partly stemmed from a sense that this was a political trump card, one which would assure them of support from wide sections of the public. Ferdinand Peroutka justified the foundation of *Kulturní svaz* as a "forced move . . . the reflexive movement of one who has been attacked." He argued correctly that the communists had erred by having the committee that announced the formation of *Kulturní obec* composed entirely of Communist Party members, and berated their implicit claim to represent Czech culture: "What is the difference between this method and dictatorship? If anything is totalitarian then it is this: *we* represent Czech culture, nothing else and no one else is any longer necessary." He also argued that, in the wake of the Zoshchenko-Akhmatova affair, creative freedom had become a major theme and that this made the formation of *Kulturní svaz* imperative.[112] While the need for a unified cultural organization was not denied by the supporters of *Kulturní svaz*, they argued that *Kulturní obec*'s program made it too narrow to fulfill that function.[113]

The first communist responses to these attacks refused to admit that any mistake had been made, and angrily rejected the contention that communist intellectuals wished to limit artistic freedom in any way. The vehemence of their responses and the subsequent retreat from many of the positions taken at the outset indicates both that the communists were surprised by the strength and size of the support given to *Kulturní svaz* and that democratic socialists had found a winning issue. Communist intellectuals portrayed the cooperation of such a wide array of forces in *Kulturní svaz* as an attempt to create an anticommunist cultural front, one which necessarily included dangerously reactionary elements.[114] This claim was bolstered by the perhaps inopportune expressions of support by National Socialist Minister of Education and Culture Stránský.[115] The argument that the *Kulturní svaz* was an attempt to form an anticommunist front would appear to have some merit. Noncommunist intellectuals certainly saw the tactical mistake on the part of the founders of *Kulturní obec* as an opportunity both to express their fears of communist domination and to articulate their positions from a protected political position. In a larger sense, the use of the danger of an anti-communist front can perhaps best be seen as an attempt to discredit *Kulturní svaz*'s breadth of membership while *Kulturní obec* struggled to obtain the signatures of as many noncommunists as possible in order to give its membership some semblance of balance.

That democratic socialists saw a threat from the creation of *Kulturní obec* is beyond doubt. Equally apparent from the reading of the documents is that communist intellectuals realized that they were in danger of isolating themselves. Although both sides had published lists of further signatories—with *Kulturní obec* gaining over 250 additional members and *Kulturní svaz* claiming slightly fewer before deciding not to publish further lists of adherents—*Kulturní obec*'s second proclamation had a distinctly defensive air about it.[116] Published one week after the formation of *Kulturní svaz*, on October 20, the document opened by stating that *Kulturní obec* had been formed "with a sense of conviction that our public life vitally needs such an organization." The appeal continues with a rather abruptly toned explanation, which notes that Czech culture needs to be conscious of the problems it faces and repeats the list of problems contained in the first manifesto. It argues that all who are truly working to solve the problems of Czech culture know "that it is possible today to fulfill such tasks only with the forces of *scientific truth, socialism, and fighting active humanism*," which represented a softening from the "scientific socialism" construction of its opening document.[117]

On that very same day the first important external response, under the banner headline "Culture Should Unify the Nation," reached the public. It was the brainchild of an extensive group of younger intellectuals centered around *Mladá fronta*. Although the authors castigated the hyperpoliticization of the cultural and intellectual debate, the need for unity was the central issue of the "Proclamation of the Young Cultural Workers." The "unifying function of culture," albeit in a "multifaceted unity," was considered "part of the historical calling of the new Czechoslovakia." They stressed the need for synthesis and urged their older counterparts to "be aware of the urgency of the tasks" awaiting all cultural workers.[118] This proclamation was seconded five days later, on October 25, by a group of Moravian intellectuals composed mainly of university professors. In addition to scolding their colleagues for splitting cultural life, they pointed out that the country's political life was based on the cooperation of the four permitted parties in a National Front government, and the fracturing of cultural life along party-political lines could have "ominous" consequences for the state as a whole.[119] The immediate result of these two proclamations, and of a slew of other newspaper and journal articles, was to spur the hastily called series of meetings between representatives of the two opposing organizations that had been taking place without public knowledge since October 22.[120]

On November 4, these meetings bore fruit and the first unified proclamation was released to the public.[121] In many ways the document represented a compromise between the standpoints of the two groups, although the content with which the warring parties filled the conceptual formulations agreed upon here and in other, similar documents diverged widely. This led to fundamental misunderstandings of the goals toward which the various parties were striving and the means to be employed in achieving them. *Kulturní obec*'s formulation of "active humanism" remained, although the modifier "fighting" was dropped.[122] The emphasis on perfecting democracy, a Masarykian phrase employed to represent the shift from the "bourgeois" democracy of the First Republic to the still developing People's Democracy of the postwar republic, was neutral. Finally, the stress placed on the value of the individual—although tempered by the ambiguity of the necessity of a freedom that was "disciplined [and] responsible to the whole"—and the freedom of research, creation, and (again "responsible") criticism certainly represented a victory for *Kulturní svaz*.

In its general tone and in the formulation of many of its phrases, the document strikes at the heart of the democratic socialists' lack of clarity. As in so many documents that bear the marks of the democratic socialist hand, socialism is seen as the "primary tool" of humanism. The role of the intellectual in this socialism lay in "the creation of its spiritual and moral content." While this may have been intended by democratic socialist intellectuals as a rejection of materialism, it points to their abstract understanding of the socialist venture.

Similarly, a hint of democratic socialist messianism comes through in concern for the mission of Czech history and in calling upon intellectuals to serve their nation and thereby "serve the world." The open character of the "spiritual and moral content" of socialism and of the imprecisely modified conceptions of freedom leave these central notions open to the kinds of political manipulation and strategic abuse that communist intellectuals had proven themselves amply able to perform. In this sense, the compromise the parties reached was precisely *not* a "real" one, and the uniting of the *obec* and *svaz* was exactly the mechanical "*ob-vaz*" (bandage) that some had feared.[123]

The response to the joint announcement was positive, as representatives from all factions rushed to claim that their side had been the first to call for unity. It is significant, however, that many of the more vocal antagonists were less than enthusiastic, even though they themselves had been among the participants in the joint consultations. Hence E. F. Burian, who had devoted three consecutive editorials in his weekly *Kulturní politika* to the affair, gave no public comment on the meetings and left it to the moderate linguist Pavel Eisner to welcome the proclamation and call for the organization to adopt a vigorous action program.[124] Ferdinand Peroutka, while refusing to assess winners and losers in the dispute, also expressed his reservations, writing that the announcement was "in no way more than a beginning, since it is always easier to agree on common words than on their interpretation."[125]

On April 27, 1947, more than 600 intellectuals assembled in the Rudolfinum to witness the proceedings officially establishing the unified *Kulturní jednota* (Cultural Unity) organization.[126] The resolution of the new institution, despite its perhaps necessarily vague quality, reads suspiciously like a communist document.[127] The members of *Kulturní jednota* merely do not "renounce" their "individuality of ideas and creativity" and agree to "subordinate" themselves to "the interests of the whole." Thus, the freedom for which democratic socialists had struggled for five months disappears almost entirely. Not only did democratic intellectuals fail to secure at least a verbal guarantee of artistic and scholarly freedom, but the word freedom appears only once, in relation to the communist-driven idea of Slavism, in the phrase "under the Slavic sun of freedom." In contrast to this, the communist "revision of the national character" appears as a common desire of communist and democratic socialist intellectuals: "We want our culture to be . . . the co-creator of a new, robust national character." Similarly, the organization committed itself to "burn off the remaining centers of fascism and injustice and to support . . . new, higher forms of democracy" with the aid of "all the democratic forces of world culture." This implied that the People's Democracy was perhaps not democratic enough, and that further reforms (obviously drawing on experiences from the East) were necessary. Finally, the most prominent democratic socialist element in the resolution is the emphasis on "cultural synthesis," which is seen as an "urgent" task because "humanity is at a historical turning point."

The three inaugural speeches given there by the head of the organizing committee, J. B. Kozák, the democratic socialist František Kovárna, and the Communist Ladislav Štoll, lent added significance to the event. These explore some of the main themes of the democratic socialist–communist debate and, taken with President Beneš's address to the Congress of Czech Writers, were considered by Václav Běhounek the most important speeches of the period concerning culture.[128] Kozák, a well-known democratic socialist professor of philosophy and a former Protestant cleric who had served in the London exile, began by offering his thoughts on how the schism developed and how *Kulturní jednota* had acted to heal the rift.[129] He argued that the mistake did not lie in the creation of two organizations, but rather in the way the dividing line had been drawn. Even though some noncommunists had joined *Kulturní obec* relatively rapidly, the public perception was that it was an exclusively communist affair with *Kulturní svaz* lying on the opposite side of the divide, a "powerful political reality" that could not be overcome easily. The manner chosen to elude the problem was to stress the point on which both parties agreed, an undefined socialism, rather than the thorny dispute over freedom in which the democratic socialists had the political upper hand. The joint document was not merely an attempt to be as inclusive as possible, but excluded some points of view as well. As Kozák proclaimed: "No uncritical or biased *laudator temporis acti*, praiser of times past, will be satisfied with it because it is progressive. No one can sign it who really is not a socialist."[130] Beyond the implicit rejection of the interwar republic, this reinforces one central point: the vague, mediative quality of the noncommunists' formulations and the willingness to compromise (often at almost any cost) made them weak rallying points for a public reeling from the combined effects of Munich, war, and occupation. This left communist intellectuals, who stood on the firm ideological ground of "scientific socialism," appearing the most self-assured and disciplined force in the nation.

In this time of great change, Kozák continued, it was necessary to realize fully the depths of the change, and that was the task of the intellectuals and their new organization. He argued, "There is not one among us who would be committed to the hope that changes in the social structure, changes in the property and productive orders will automatically create complementary and suitable types of people." Czech intellectuals had the responsibility of ensuring that the tendency of rising classes to assume the traits and cultural markings of the classes they displace (i.e., that the Czech proletariat might assume the tastes of the bourgeoisie) was avoided.[131] For this reason Kozák held that it would be nonsensical to mouth slogans proclaiming *Kulturní jednota* "above the parties" or claim to be engaging in "non-political politics." Clearly, the role he envisioned for the Czech intelligentsia involved extending the enthusiasm for socialism and Machotka's "forming" of the socialist individual. Echoing *Mladá fronta*'s editorial commentary to the Young Cultural Workers' proclamation, he argued that Czech intellectuals' main concern was to be "on guard against reaction . . . Among us Czechs there is certainly less [reaction] than anywhere to the west or southwest of us, but we must pay attention to the trends that strengthening reaction could call out elsewhere in the world."[132]

Kozák then took the democratic socialist yearning for synthesis one step further. He maintained that "the development of the various types of socialism is not divergent, but convergent. . . . All socialists are heading toward a classless society." Kozák was no longer striving for a synthesis between East and West or, respectively, their notions of socialism and democracy. Instead, he was manufacturing a bizarre form of convergence theory between different types of socialism, predicated on the endpoint of a classless society. In a recapitulation of democratic socialist messianism, he held that Czechs occupied an advantageous position, because of their prolonged Germanization after the Battle of White Mountain. The "negative democratization" the Czech social structure had then undergone made the Czechs "closer to classlessness than the majority of nations." Because of the head start on the road to a classless society that Habsburg oppression had given Czechs, Kozák concluded, "It is necessary immediately to begin educating [the people] to a classless spirit," a formulation that again echoed Machotka, but took him dangerously further.[133] Such expressions, and his reflections on classlessness and reaction in general, place Kozák on the more radical wing of the democratic socialist movement. They in no way exclude him from it, however. He had signed the *Kulturní svaz* proclamation and had been accepted by that organization's leaders as the head of the organizing committee of *Kulturní jednota*, as well as being personally responsible for reporting to President Beneš on developments in the inter-organizational discussions. Had the democratic socialist leadership believed that his views were unrepresentative, he would not have attained such prominence or addressed the general assembly.

Štoll, representing the communist *Kulturní obec*, then delivered a short lecture on "Freedom and Truth." He also noted that the times were changing, and reassuringly stressed that "we want to follow our own Czech road" to socialism. The use of the term freedom, according to Štoll, becomes subject to conscious or unconscious abuse when individual and creative freedoms are discussed. While *Kulturní jednota* must guard the freedom of individual and cultural creation as well as the freedom of the collective, it must be made impossible to equate the terms "freedom and arbitrariness, freedom and anarchy, freedom and privilege, freedom and license."[134] The meaning of freedom is different in different spheres and the objectively correct measure of freedom in each must be found, Štoll maintained. In economics, liberal freedom had dug its own grave through the oppressive creation of monopolies and trusts, and socialism was in the process of returning freedom through national collective ownership "to the millions of people dispossessed and stripped of their freedom." Štoll linked the idea of freedom to that of objective truth, arguing that there are axioms in human life as in science. For example,

The individual does not have the right to live at the expense of the work of other people. . . . Our nation can hold on as a nation only on the side of world progress. . . . [and with] the necessity of planned labor across the whole of national life. . . . The freedom to shatter these truths means the freedom to shatter not only the foundations of the freedom of the nation but also the freedoms of the individual.[135]

That Štoll was attempting here to calm the cultural waters can be seen when these words are compared with his earlier statements, made during the weeks when the struggle between the two organizations was at its height. At that time, he recognized a fundamental difference between *Kulturní obec*'s conception of freedom and that of *Kulturní svaz*, claiming that the latter concentrated only on the subjective, unrestrained side of freedom, which Štoll characterized as the privilege of people "who *personify the right not to care about questions that are in the interest of the national fate.*" By doing so, he argued that *Kulturní svaz* had revealed that its demands for freedom were a cloak for "insane anti-communism . . . in essence, a logical outgrowth of *anti-democratism.*"[136] Given the favorable statement the incipient *Kulturní jednota* had approved, it seems evident that the usually fiery Štoll moderated his stance in order not to rekindle a debate on freedom that had initially placed communist intellectuals on the defensive.

The final speech was delivered by *Kulturní svaz*'s Kovárna. He attempted to delineate explicitly the two organizations' differing conceptions of socialism. While both shared the goal of a classless society, acknowledged the role of ideas in society, and recognized cultural autonomy (whether as a fact of development within the ideological superstructure or as a moral requirement), Kovárna saw crucial differences in their views. The first of these concerned the relationship between the individual and the state. What he termed "collective socialism" placed the state above the individual, with it attempting to build on the "public man," on people defined by their relationships in the society. Contrary to this, "individualist socialism" saw the concomitant personalizing of institutions as a brake on true socialism and a potential barrier to the achievement of a classless society. Here the argument that democratic socialists knew better *how* to implement the ideal of socialism is recapitulated, in essence criticizing communists from the communist standpoint of an intellectual heading toward a classless society.

Kovárna also saw a divergence in the amount of faith communists and democratic socialists placed in the ability of economic change to create a culture-wide shift to socialism. While collectivist socialists aimed to change the social structure and the ideological superstructure by changing the economic foundation, individualists called for the subordination of economics to morality not just through appeals to the citizenry's moral nature but by "positive laws." Even though their methods differed, Kovárna saw their basic agreement in goals as a force compelling cooperation:

Perhaps I speak for all when I talk about the feeling we have at a time when it is not possible for us to go into tomorrow on any other than a socialist path. It seems to us all, I think, that history and our situation have directly endowed us with a definite disposition toward socialism. . . . An example of such a situation is found certainly in the era of the occupation, when for all of us, not only socialists, the existence of the nation was at stake. And in mentioning the occupation, I would like to call attention to the experiences that washed over, changed, and branded each of us, and even more so the socialist individualist. We had the opportunity not only to think through but also live through the recognition that our individuality itself has its social side.[137]

The only irreconcilable difference that Kovárna could see lay in the conception of morality. While collectivists saw morality as a product of its era, individualists tended to see it as above human activity, more than mere mores or customs, and hence the two sides would act differently from their differing conceptions of morality. Nonetheless, Kovárna messianically concluded, as long as the Czechs maintained the rule of law on the road to socialism, "precisely us, a Slavic nation raised in Western civilization, can do something meaningful for socialism."[138]

The speeches given by the two democratic socialist intellectuals at the founding of the *Kulturní jednota* reveal the noble yearnings and political weaknesses of the group's larger intellectual endeavor. Their commitment to socialism affected their understandings of freedom and democracy such that the three terms became tightly intertwined. The symbolic expression of this intertwining was the socialist culture for which they strove, an abstraction that served as shorthand for a socialism both vaguely defined and dissociated from practical aims and policies. The expression resulted in the instrumental view that freedom and democracy had worth beyond their intrinsic values, because they could aid both the pace and quality of the socialist transformation of Czechoslovak society. The apparent intention was to create a society that was even more fully socialist than the "socializing" one of 1946–1947, but one that was not a communist society.

By constantly trumpeting the abstract moral and ethical qualities of their socialism, democratic socialists committed several errors. Above all, such rhetoric obscured the lack of clarity surrounding their venture, rendering them, if not unable to see the dangers they faced, at least unable to directly confront them. As Toman Brod has put it: "They served the nation poorly; instead of words conveying hard truths and self-recognition, they covered it with the laurels of victory. They did not perceive that [the nation] lacked the weapons for a battle that was already raging."[139] Moreover, their belief in the moral rectitude of socialism and their cherished socialist culture made them willing to condone actively measures that they might, at another time, have rejected. Democratic socialist intellectuals not only applauded the "Czechoslovak road" and largely accepted the patriotism and democratic instincts of the

Communist Party, but glorified the People's Democracy and urged further steps in social engineering. The most dangerous element in this was their willingness to undertake the task of a massive re-education of the Czech nation, so that it would be more in line with economic planning, their notions of a socialist morality, or, in Kozák's case, a classless society. The implicit anti-democratism of this notion bothered them far less than the possibility that an undefined bourgeois mentality or outdated bourgeois notions might survive among the Czech people.

Perhaps most importantly, their commitment to socialism brought with it the adoption of what can only be termed communist rhetorical standards. Democratic socialist intellectuals talked of the struggle for "the new man," and the battles for and glories of an unanalyzed "new democracy," "socializing democracy," "socialist lifestyle," "socialist humanism," and "socialist culture." Conversely, they condemned "liberal freedom," "liberal democracy," and any term containing the adjective "bourgeois." In a state with an active and well-organized Communist Party and a common border with the Soviet Union, such language was politically and electorally dangerous, if not intellectually irresponsible. Democratic socialists like Peroutka—who, again, was among the most circumspect and vociferously opposed to communism in this camp—argued for treating the Communists as "political opponents" and not enemies, implying that they could and should be beaten at the ballot box. Given a strategy of public political competition, the mimicking of communist sloganeering could only spread one of two notions among the wider public. On the one hand, one might assume that the Communists had the correct positions, and that democratic socialists were trying rapidly to amend their interpretations. On the other hand, one might opportunistically calculate that since all socialist parties sounded largely the same and proclaimed themselves for largely the same goals, why should one not vote with the Communists, who after all had the most resources with which to reward loyal supporters? In either case, such language contributes to a weakening of the political and cultural defenses against a communist takeover. Vilém Hejl neatly summed up this weakness in reference to President Beneš, but it is equally valid for the other democratic socialist intellectuals: "To what percent of the vote did Beneš politics help the Communists, when both he and the Communists spoke the *newspeak* of the 'People's Democracy?'"[140]

Finally, democratic socialist intellectuals often allowed their sense of a shared socialist mission with their communist opponents to overwhelm their concerns over possible communist totalitarianism. This was aided both by the value they placed on synthesis—East and West, or democracy and socialism—and by their notion of a special Czech calling. This messianism is especially disturbing because, beyond enhancing their special position inside the purportedly special Czech society, it allowed Czech intellectuals to escape from political and practical reality. Rather than leading to a careful consideration of the developments in their state and its neighbors, the perceived "national individuality" of the Czech nation allowed democratic socialist intellectuals to continue their bold experiment in squaring the circle blinkered from the disturbing light of either critical self-analysis or an honest assessment of regional developments. Traces of this sense of Czech specificity may also have fed democratic socialists' belief that Czech Communists were also somehow different from those elsewhere. As Otto Friedman hinted,

> But, of course, the Czechoslovak democrats thought and asserted that the Czech and Slovak Communists were more democratic than other Communists. Why? Because they were, above all, Czech patriots. But were they? . . . [The conception] is based on a national prejudice, the idealization of all members of one's own nation in whom their "national instinct" is expected to prevail over all other inclinations.[111]

Democratic socialist intellectuals' messianism was guided by the notion that the Czech nation was specially qualified, both culturally and morally, to reconcile what has proven to be irreconcilable. Their failure does not detract from the nobility of their intentions, but neither does the nobility of their intentions exculpate them from the charge that they ill served their nation. As the Communist Lumír Černý later noted, "Great evils may have their origins in periods of apparent prosperity and enthusiasm, and people of goodwill may unwittingly help to turn the course of historic events to unfortunate channels."[142] In an hour in which the Czech nation needed clarity and conviction, it received ambiguity and compromise; in an hour in which it needed democracy, communist and democratic socialist intellectuals alike were there with the "People's Democracy."

11

Socialism and Roman Catholic Intellectuals: The "Fateful Struggle between Spirit and Matter"

Of all the major cultural groupings in postwar Czechoslovakia, Roman Catholics showed the most consistently oppositional stance toward communism. Their group antipathy can be witnessed most visibly in the results of the 1946 parliamentary elections, when the weakness of Communist Party support correlated directly to the intensity of Catholic feeling in the three regions of the country. As one moved toward the more pious east, the vote for political forces allied with Catholicism rose as the Communist vote fell.[1] Throughout the period, Catholic cultural and political leaders attacked communism, Marxism, and socialism more generally. Their parties provided a home for many of the former members of the banned right-wing parties and those disaffected by the pace and extent of the postwar social changes.

In opposing communism Roman Catholic intellectuals grouped around the People's Party closely resembled their coreligionists in Western Europe and characterized their dialogue with communist intellectuals as a struggle to maintain the position of spiritual values against those of materialism. They attacked both the theory of dialectical materialism and the practice of communism as embodied in the Communist Party, occasionally resorting to smear tactics more commonly associated with communist rhetoric, such as stressing the German (read "fascist") roots of Marxism. Much like democratic socialists, they also attempted to turn the label of "reactionary" back on the communists themselves, although from a resolutely nonsocialist stance. Partially in deference to the enthusiasm for the reordering of Czechoslovak social relations, they condemned capitalism as well, but argued that socialism was the spiritual descendant of capitalism and contained precisely the same evils. Socialism was more pernicious, however, as its achievement was held by Catholic intellectuals to be impossible without the institution of dictatorship. In conjunction with their critiques of capitalism and socialism, they enunciated a coherent theory of "Christian solidarity" or "Christian social reformism" that closely approximated Catholic political ideas then current in Western Europe.

John Whyte has delimited two varieties of Catholicism in modern Western European politics, one "open" and one "closed."[2] The open variant has existed in periods during which Catholic political parties deemphasize their links with the Church or declare themselves nonconfessional, Catholic trade unions and social organizations work closely or even unite with their nonsectarian counterparts, and Catholic religious leaders prove less willing (or less able) to give strong political guidance to their flocks. Conversely, in periods of closed Catholicism, Catholic parties emphasize the Church's role in the formation of their policies, Catholic trade unions and social organizations assert their distinctiveness, and the pulpit is used to sway the laity. Whyte argues that in the immediate aftermath of World War II strong forces encouraged the growth of an open Catholicism in Western Europe. Catholics' experience of working with socialists and communists in the resistance across the region nourished postwar cooperation. Further, institutional pressure for the open variant was created by the general unwillingness to restore prewar Catholic parties. These were replaced by interconfessional groupings in France, Belgium, Germany, and Austria.[3] Finally, the unification of various trade union movements (Italy, Germany, and Austria) or the greater cooperation of Catholic and socialist trade unions (Belgium, the Netherlands, and France) encouraged open Catholicism.

However, Whyte argues, these developments in part diminished of their own accord and in part were countered by moves in the opposite direction, leading to the solidification of a closed Catholicism by 1960. Centripetal forces in the trade unions caused ruptures in Italy in 1948 and Germany in 1955, while in France, Belgium, and the Netherlands Catholic unions increased their proportional strength. The extension of the franchise to women in France, Italy, and Belgium also spurred the growth of closed Catholicism, as "public opinion polls showed that, in the nineteen-fifties, women were markedly more likely to support parties of Catholic or Christian orientation."[4] The re-emergence of the issue of Church schools contributed to the growing intervention of clerics in political life, such that "over much of continental Europe, the bishops imposed a more continuous direction on the voters in the period 1945–1960 than they had done before."[5] Most important, however, were the rising tensions of the Cold War (especially after the papal condemnation of all collaboration with communism in 1949) and the growing distinctiveness of Catholic social doctrine (as elaborated particularly from the encyclicals *Rerum novarum* and *Quadragesimo anno*). Taken as a whole, these forged a situation in which, by 1960, "closed Catholicism [had] reached its peak of development in continental Europe" and "parties of Catholic inspiration had, everywhere except in France, roughly reached the limits of their natural development."[6]

Given this set of factors, how can we assess the development of the Czech variant of political Catholicism, the Czech People's Party? How closely does it correspond to developments on the western part of the continent? Above all, several conditions encouraging the development of an open variant of Catholicism lay outside the People's Party's control. For example, the trade unions were forcibly united into one mass organization, the Revolutionary Trades Union Movement (*Revoluční odborové hnutí*), a move that rendered impossible the resuscitation of the interwar Catholic unions. Moreover, the party was forbidden to campaign on a confessional platform, although as with similar parties in Western Europe this did not preclude public recognition of its Catholic orientation. Finally, the institution of the National Front government forced politically active Catholics across the state into cooperation with leftist politicians and cultural leaders ambivalent or antipathetic to the aims of political Catholicism.

However, as in Western Europe, other factors were eating away at the openness of Czech political Catholicism. Women had always constituted a significant proportion of party membership and played much the same role as in the development of Western European Catholic politics. Further, although there could be no rebirth of the Catholic trade unions, other organizations were reestablished on a confessional basis and met with some success. While Church-sponsored youth organizations had difficulties in attracting a large following, the Congress of Young People's Party Supporters drew 110,000 followers to Prague in May 1947. Although participation levels for organizations, celebrations, and meetings cannot be established with certainty, the sheer number of events testifies to the richness of Catholic associational life.[7] Finally, as in Western Europe, the clergy and especially academic theologians played an increasing role in political debate. This held true for all facets of the nation's political reconstruction, but "above all concerned Church schools and property."[8] All these factors bear considerable resemblance to those operating on Catholic political actors in the West. The crucial final two—the Cold War and the consolidation of Catholic social doctrine—were played out in the development of the party's political position. Heightened East-West tensions were reflected in the increasing sharpness of the stance Catholic activists and People's Party leaders adopted. Similarly, over the course of its three years of relatively free operation, the party elaborated a reformist but resolutely nonsocialist doctrine that relied heavily on papal encyclicals, as was the case in the West.

The shift from the open to the closed variant of Catholic politics appears more pronounced in the People's Party than in its analogues in the West, however. Czech Catholicism emerged from the war with both the rejection of Munich and a solid record of resistance service standing to its credit, but the People's Party emerged rather disorganized and politically marginalized. Catholic rhetoric was neither strong nor united enough to be considered that of a closed Catholicism, and the enthusiasm throughout the land for social change demanded from the party a stance that did not lie too far to the right, since its moderation already isolated it on the right of the Czech political spectrum. After the 1946 parliamentary elections and the partial reorganization of the People's Party, the political, intellectual, and clerical leaderships of Czech political Catholicism drew closer, presenting a more united front. This can be seen as the Czech variant of closed Catholicism, and relied on the intertwining of Whyte's final two criteria. The Communist Party's victory in those elections, and the extent of the public sympathy for socialism generally, forced politically moderate Catholic believers to close ranks. This pressure only heightened after the initial Cominform meeting labeled the Church a reactionary force in the fall of 1947. Further, the party, which in 1946 could campaign only on a platform of being the sole non-socialist party in the Czech lands, thereafter developed a coherent anti-Marxist message that presented a distinctly Catholic social-reformism. In terms of the two wings of the movement, this message was spread both by the more "political" wing and lay leaders like Pavel Tigrid and Bohdan Chudoba, as well as by the more "Catholic" wing led by theologians like Adolf Kajpr, Dominik Pecka, and S. S. Ghelfand. While it impossible to predict how Czech Catholicism would have developed had the communists not risen to total power, elements heralding the rise of closed Catholicism are evident. These would likely have continued to gain strength, particularly following the Pope's anticommunist pronouncement of 1949, resulting in the coalescence of a Christian Democratic movement similar to that familiar to Western observers.

Roman Catholic political and intellectual leaders took seriously the threat of socialism, by which they almost exclusively meant the Marxist variant. Activists like S. S. Ghelfand saw the Marxists' endeavor to transform Czech society as part of a "fateful struggle" between the theistic forces of the spirit and the materialist soldiers of atheism. Therefore, the nation must choose: "Either Christianity or Marxism. In this lies the meaning of today's struggle over the spiritual and material content of human life."[9] For Catholics, no synthesis of Marxist theory and Christian principles, such as the one for which we shall see the Czechoslovak Church yearned, was possible. They conceived of their struggle as one to the death: as one commentator noted, only the future would tell whether communism would be written about in the history books of the Church or vice versa.[10] As the general secretary of the People's Party observed, the struggle against materialism had been carried on for nearly 2000 years, but the threat of communism made it "necessary today to adopt a militant position in this truly dramatic struggle for the victory of the spirit."[11] In this battle, his party considered itself the "spokesperson" of those who characterized themselves as defenders of the primacy of the spirit.[12]

In contrast, communist intellectuals adopted a decidedly soft rhetorical position toward religion through the first year after liberation, and only showed a harsher face after the Communist Party's victory in the 1946 elections. As this was directed at Roman Catholics, it contributed to the sharpness of the shift between open and closed Catholicism in Czechoslovakia, while other Christian sects could still bask in the glow of communist tolerance and even praise.[13] In 1946, the Communist Party's Eighth Congress proclaimed its respect for the freedom of conscience and religious affiliation. As Karel Kaplan has noted:

> The Communists tried to maintain good relations with the Church and not come into conflict with it. In their own ranks, they silenced and condemned the voices of their prewar members—activists of the Union of Agnostics in the majority—who wanted to launch atheistic propaganda with attacks against the Church. Many of these . . . proclaimed the incompatibility of membership in the Communist Party with religious affiliation.[14]

For example, the Communist minister of education and culture, Zdeněk Nejedlý, spoke before 380 priests at a meeting in November 1945. He praised the clergy for its conduct during the war and declared his opposition to the complete separation of church and state. This statement from one of the founders of the Union of Progressive Freethinkers was received "unexpectedly enthusiastically."[15] Although it seems apparent that the binding of the Church to the state made the control of the former by the latter easier, at that time Catholics did not consider a Communist Party's electoral victory and its domination of the government likely.

On the theoretical plane, however, this "soft" line was maintained longer than it was in the sphere of practical politics. In a book published in 1948, Nejedlý argued for socialism and against religion, but none of the ranting that later became the stock in trade of communist anti-religious rhetoric is apparent. Instead, Nejedlý interpreted "original" Christianity in much the same way he had interpreted Jan Hus, viewing it as a religion of the weak and oppressed that played a "socially revolutionary role" in ancient society. This original Christianity survived, although the Roman Catholic Church in later eras served the wealthy and powerful, and reappeared in the Czech lands with the Hussite movement. After the Hussite defeat, "original" Christianity remained dormant until the modern era, when it "found new expression not in religious progress, but in scientific progress—in socialism." In his interpretation, communists need not condemn religion, because Marxism "offers a better and more convincing understanding . . . [and] makes religion unnecessary." For Nejedlý, "the retreat of religion is an entirely natural and necessary result of the development of socialism as a new, stronger, and more effective force, both socially and ideologically." He reached absolute agreement with his Catholic counterparts on only one point. For him, as for

Catholic intellectuals, there could be no thought of uniting Christianity and Marxism: "[It is] a vain attempt . . . because Marxism is at a far higher level in solving their common questions."[16]

This is not to say that he did not see the Marxist movement as standing in opposition to the Church as an institution. At the same time as he welcomed believers to the Communist Party, he painted the Church as an entity dangerous to the development of the People's Democracy. Religious feeling exists in all people and can be overcome, but "there are powers that markedly abuse it: In the first place, churches, and first among them, the Catholic Church." The party did not reject religion as a whole, no surprise given its support in Protestant quarters, "only [its] abuse . . . for other, reactionary goals." Priests were particularly castigated for "taking advantage of religious tendencies . . . A priest today does not have time for religion, for him the church is only the formal setting for his own political agitation."[17] The point that the institutional hierarchy of the dominant church stood in opposition to the transformation of society was also taken up by *Tvorba*, which usually restricted itself to attacking People's Party policy positions. According to *Tvorba*, the struggle was much the same as it had been in Hus's time:

> It is not entirely by chance that the Vatican heirs of the Popes and Councils, who executed Hus, do not like the people's democratic politics of the new Czechoslovakia. Today, just as in Hus's time, they are the moral defenders and supporters of the old world of prerogatives and privileges. Today, not being able to agitate wars of the cross against us, through their henchmen they subvert the building of a democratic republic in our country.[18]

While the Communists stressed the worldly interests of the Church, Catholic intellectuals devoted attention to the necessary atheism of communism. Naturally, this was more pronounced on the religious wing of Czech political Catholicism. Thus the Jesuit editor of *Katolík*, Adolf Kajpr, could stress that the "communists are obviously atheists, consistent opponents of religious conceptions and representations of the world" and label this "the fundamental insufficiency of socialism."[19] As far as religious persecution under communist rule was concerned, Czechs should be grateful to the USSR for the liberation of their homeland, but Catholics "will not forget those Christians who lost their lives in the struggle against communism during the time of the atheist offensive."[20] Such attacks in *Katolík* no doubt represented "preaching to the converted," as loyal readers would undoubtedly be antipathetic to communism from the outset. It is important to note them, however, so that we do not lose sight of the deeply held religious convictions of the Catholic opponents of communism.

Beyond the objection to communist atheism, intellectuals from both wings of Czech political Catholicism rejected both the theory and practice of Marxism and devoted much effort to countering it. The communists clearly recognized that "in the new republic, the greatest number of books and brochures directed not only against Marxism, but against any kind of socialism, come from the Catholic ranks."[21] The general popularity of Marxism as a complete worldview posed a dangerous threat to Catholic ideological and moral power because of the combination of its all-encompassing nature and the less than fervent religious beliefs of the majority of Czechs. The nation's freethinking and progressive traditions made it susceptible to the "scientific" claims of Marxism, and Catholic intellectuals from the religious establishment took pains to point out that Marxism in general and dialectical materialism in particular were "faith, in no way science."[22] In one of his series of articles on the intellectual and spiritual condition of the postwar era, Dominik Pecka gave the most eloquent and incisive presentation of this view, also linking Marxism to fascism:

> This collectivism has assumed all the markings of Christ's Church. It is self-redemptive, single, holy, and infallible. It does not arrive as a social force, but as a worldview. It has its Bible, whether it is *Mein Kampf* or *Das Kapital*. It has its visible head, its leader, Führer or Duce, a head absolutely infallible in all things economic, social, political, and military. Everything called for by the interest of the collective is morally permitted. Violence, murder, thievery, the violation of one's word, assault, and war are sanctified by the final goal, which is the good of the collective. The collective has its hierarchy, leading elite and a strata devoted to the head, its values and honors, but also its heretics and schismatics, its banishments and excommunications, sanctions and punishments. It has its censors, preachers, prophets, philosophers, and ideologues. It has its orthodoxy and its general line of correct thinking. It has its liturgy, holidays and celebrations, it has its cults, reliquaries, saints, heroes, and martyrs, its ceremonies, symbols, and hymns.[23]

Despite its pseudo-religious aspects, however, Marxism was a mere pretender to the throne in the eyes of Catholics. Its commitment to atheism left it, in Pavel Tigrid's words, with no "*great ideals* that would nourish the insatiable yearning for the absolute."[24] Without belief in God, Marxism was left with no fixed moral compass, no immutable moral laws. As both Catholic political and religious journals pointed out, it was a philosophy of constant change, with truth being only "agreement with present class interests, as they are understood in the thought of the leaders."[25] Instead of eternal truths, Catholics often argued that all dialectical materialism could offer was a narrow view of humankind, one that saw the individual as no more than "a purely economic creation." That this should be so struck Ghelfand as odd, given that so many communists had given their lives in the service of Marxist ideas, rather than out of any economic necessity.[26]

A critique of the increasing mechanization of life provided a link between rejection of the economic view of the individual and the wider spirit/matter debate. In a society in which, as Pecka argued, "A person seemingly liberated by technology is becoming the slave of the machine, seemingly liber-

ated by social and economic organization is becoming only a cog in the social machine," it was a fundamental failure of Marxist materialism to believe
that "the bettering of economic and productive relations will also better the
person." He argued that in the "step from 'I' to 'us,' a step from the depths of
isolation onto the solid ground of society, . . . [i]t does not suffice to create
'us' only externally and mechanistically: it is necessary to find 'us' internally
and spiritually."[27] This point was also made by Catholic political editorialists
like Pavel Tigrid, who condemned Marxists for believing that social health
necessarily leads to moral health.[28]

A further objection concerned the revolutionary character of Marxist philosophy. Here Catholic intellectuals placed themselves in a difficult position,
for there was also an urge to bridge the rhetorical gap and take advantage of
the nation's postwar revolutionary élan by claiming that Christian ethics
were also revolutionary. Nonetheless, the tenor of the movement was over-
ridingly anti-revolutionary, as Catholics like Ghelfand called for social reforms rather than social revolution, placing them in opposition in his *Marxism and Christian Social Reformism.*[29] Recalling the groundstone of the
entire debate, Catholics argued that there could be no revolution without "a
revolution of the spirit" and that although the broader European tradition
certainly did not exclude revolution, there were "correct and incorrect traditions," with Marxist revolution clearly belonging to the latter.[30] Finally, the
People's Party leader and Minister of Health Adolf Procházka stood even
firmer in his conviction, declaring that "revolution has no place in a democratic system."[31]

The Catholic position on Marxism found the doctrine of class warfare particularly objectionable, emphasizing it while communists showed reluctance
to discuss the problematic notion. Terming it mere "class selfishness,"
Catholic intellectuals stressed that through their Christian universalism they
alone consistently pursued the good of the community, the *pospolitost.*[32] This
stance was also part and parcel of the People's Party position, one that emphasized that it was a national, not a class-based, party. This position dovetailed with their observation that capitalism and Marxian socialism were very
much alike, making Christian social reformism the best hope for the nation.
For Catholics, class warfare and the eventual dictatorship of the proletariat
amounted to nothing more than the same Darwinism that guided capitalism,
as one commentator made clear: "Marxist theory [is] derived from *Darwin's
well-known evolutionary theory . . . in which only the stronger is victorious
. . .* [Christian reformism] is against the rule of one class over another in the
form of the dictatorship of the proletariat."[33] Furthermore, the dictatorship of
the proletariat, some Catholics argued, would in practice not mean that the
proletariat actually ruled over the other classes, but something far more sin-
ister: "the proletarianization of all layers and then the limitless, cruel, and
long-term government of a narrow layer of privileged officials over a huge

proletariat."[34] That class warfare was one of the fundamental, if unstressed, doctrines of Marxist theory only proved to Catholics that the communists were not truly thinking of the whole, for they could not see "another way to social justice than the striving for the equality of all in the slavish worship of the state."[35]

The final aspect of the Catholic representation of communist theory concerns the two book-length Catholic studies published during the period in question, both by the Jesuit S. S. Ghelfand. His *Dialectical Materialism* and *Marxism and Christian Social Reformism* were apparently written for use by Catholic students in preparing for exams in history and dialectical materialism.[36] The former was published in a not inconsiderable print run of some 3,000 copies, and was described as "the most popular book of its kind" by one of Ghelfand's leading critics.[37] As mentioned earlier, Ghelfand spread his views in the People's Party press as well as through these books, and he also delivered public lectures on the topic. As many of the arguments in his books have appeared above or will appear below, no complete explication of their contents is necessary. Ghelfand maintains roughly the same positions in the two books, and his years of concern with Marxism ensured that the books neither radically distort Marx's teaching nor subject it to mockery or ridicule. In fact, Ghelfand stresses in both that Marx himself was "very moral, empathetic and full of love for humanity."[38]

The most significant facet of these two works is an argument that particularly aroused the wrath of his communist opponents. Ghelfand argued that industrial and technological progress will ultimately disprove Marx's theory of surplus value. As machines perform more and more of the labor now performed by people, productivity will rise and the profit the manufacturer makes can no longer be correctly understood as the unpaid portion of exploited laborers' wages.[39] He uses examples of factories performing huge amounts of work with no more than a handful of wage laborers to show that Marxist teaching has no explanation for how "machines create capitalist profit without the participation of wage labor in modern mechanized production."[40] The two communist critiques directed specifically against him devote much space to this argument, seeing it as "the core of Ghelfand's book."[41] Both argue that machines are no more than the congealed labor of exploited workers (to which Ghelfand responds that the factory owner could buy the machines in the USSR!), and that someone must supervise the machines (although Ghelfand clearly states that they could be family members of the owner, or even co-owners).

Most significant is that both communist responses conclude with rhetorical attacks external to the argument over theory. One held that the main point was "*who* will profit from this technological progress, the owner of the means of production or the whole of society?" The other concluded by noting that the producer could sell his machine-made goods at a lower price, and would therefore "take part to an even greater extent in the *exploitation of the entire working class by the entire capitalist class.*"[42] These responses reveal important conditions about the debate over Marxism in postwar Czechoslovakia. Above all, as already discussed, there were many *politically* trained communists, but a grave shortage of *philosophically* trained Marxists to counter arguments criticizing theory. Moreover, the communists' retreat on the conceptual level and the simultaneous strengthening of the rhetorical attack lend credence to the position taken in *Obzory*, that Marxism

> is a tendentious philosophy, construed for political goals, extended and argued by political means, and, consequently, it is not easy to refute it by the mere calm reasoning to which philosophers are accustomed. . . . [Today] all of these teachings of Marxist philosophy seem unquestionable, and that is why it is the worst heresy to doubt their truth, to reveal at all their weaknesses.[43]

Despite the threat they perceived in Marxism and the power of socialism in the liberated Czechoslovakia, the idea of a People's Democracy was not unacceptable to Roman Catholic intellectuals. Even as stalwart a proponent of Catholic politics as Bohdan Chudoba recognized in early 1946 that, although the term was redundant, it was not only an economic necessity but also "a moral command."[44] Rather than contrasting it to capitalism, however, Catholics termed "the People's Democracy, in which socialist and private capitalist sectors work together, a better and higher form of human coexistence than a socialist order."[45] Catholics, like the staunch anti-communist Helena Koželuhová, were confident that such a socialist order could never come into being in Czechoslovakia because in no place where there had been a choice had communists been voted into power.[46] The results of the 1946 parliamentary elections came as a shock, and the consolidation of the party's ranks after Koželuhová's expulsion was undoubtedly a step in the right direction. Still, there was certainly no call for the kind of optimism expressed in the pages of *Obzory* only a few weeks before the communist assumption of power. The contributor argued that the danger for the nation had passed, because in the first months after liberation the communists could have relied on support stemming from the presence of the Red Army, the need for strong authority, and respect for communist war losses to take total control of the state. In January 1948, the situation had been changed by the detrimental effects of communist power politics and the party's occasionally "SS-like actions": "So it is decidedly certain that Czechs—and absolutely certain that Slovaks—will never give the Communist Party uncontrollable, monarchistic power voluntarily."[47] Within six weeks the communists had acquired just such power. Although power was not handed over voluntarily, the communist acquisition of it more closely approximated legality—and particularly the legal norms of postwar Czechoslovakia—than did their rise to total power almost anywhere else in Eastern Europe.

More often than making bluff claims that a communist rise to power was an impossibility, Roman Catholics attempted to inspire distrust in the Communist Party's claims to democracy and defense of freedom. They warned the public that the communists would stop at nothing and would abandon all of the Czech political, ethical, and cultural traditions embodied by Masaryk.[48] Communist claims, made in conjunction with the announcement of the "Czechoslovak road," that their definition of democracy included political and economic freedom were ridiculed as a "paradox," for they had until recently remained "the avowedly express antipodes of democracy." Readers were warned to closely compare Communist theory to practice, for "this leopard may not have changed its spots."[49] Catholics argued that the Communists' victorious election campaign had been an exercise in deception, in which they had kept their final goals hidden, preferring to play to the tastes of the voting public.[50] Some, like Pavel Tigrid, stressed that the Communist Party was concerned with "political tactics more than political programs" in pursuit of the goal of power.[51]

Catholics' conviction that the Communists were deceiving the public in a bald attempt to seize power naturally extended to the Communist goal of securing 51 percent of the vote and their theory of a "Czechoslovak road" to socialism. The existence of the latter was denied outright, since Catholics argued that if Marxism was the philosophy of the Communist Party it must necessarily be taken as a whole, a worldview that could not be reconciled with Czech Communists' claims of specificity:

> Do not believe that there can be some kind of "other," perhaps "Czechoslovak" practice of Marxism. That is an attempt to deceive not only our voters, but also all naive voters in Europe today. Do not believe that the character of any nation can influence Marxist practice in the least.[52]

Catholic attacks were particularly aimed at the Communist Party's calls for 51 percent of the vote in the 1948 elections. Even though Catholics were convinced that the Communists' aim could not become reality, they questioned why it was necessary to set this goal.[53] If the Communists were truly democrats and not striving for a one-party state, Tigrid asked, why were they striving for 51 percent, rather than seeking to work with the other parties?[54] The implication that a majority vote for the Communist Party was inconsistent with democracy was often made and occasionally linked to expressions of optimism that the nation would see through their plans and would deny it the necessary support. As *Obzory*'s "younger brother," *Vývoj*, put it, the majority of the nation had "an instinctive mistrust of the politics of 51 percent," for it "knows and not just supposes that its victory would mean a catastrophic limitation of democratic freedoms and would develop beyond this into totalitarianism."[55]

Communists, with increasing frequency and venom, strove to paint Catholics with the colors of "reaction." Communist calls to expel "reactionaries" from the People's Party incited both a vigorous defense from Catholic commentators and claims that it was the communists themselves who were the "reactionaries." Such an argument was also made by democratic socialists, but where they attacked communists from the standpoint of socialist purity, Catholics went further. This strategy was adopted by both Tigrid and Ghelfand, and thus represented a common tactic of both wings of Czech political Catholicism. Ghelfand's argumentation was quite simple: if one defined progress as "the realization of Christian principles in society," then "the striving to realize socialist goals is anti-progressive, hence, reactionary."[56] Tigrid used a variety of different definitions to paint the Communist Party as harboring reactionaries who were "trying to abuse and take advantage of the revolution" for ends that were "anti-democratic." For him, the "Czechoslovak road" was a sham, the device "of a reaction that says democracy but thinks totalitarianism." Many of those who voted for the Communist Party were also condemned as "truly reactionary," since they had chosen to side with power and not ideals, a variant on the larger spirit/matter argument.[57] In short, Tigrid called for debate with the communists, arguing that if both sides were "to precisely define what is and what is not democratic, what agrees and what does not agree with the demand for freedom and a legal order in a democratic state . . . then we would know instantly who is progressive and who is reactionary, who is a democrat and who imitates fascism."[58]

The similar tactic of playing the "fascist card" by either implying or arguing openly that fascism and Marxism were essentially the same was employed with particular frequency by the political wing of Czech political Catholicism, as the above characterization of the communists' actions as "SS-like" indicates. This was done over communist objection that such comparisons had only "become the fashion among those who know Marxism only superficially."[59] Occasionally the inference was left to the reader, as when *Obzory*'s editors called attention to the fact that the journal was "was not against Marx and Engels because they were Germans," or when the People's Party leader Ivo Ducháček warned that "in the hasty march toward the socialization of everything, the freedoms of thought, criticism, and religion [should] not be collectivized—or as the workers party of Adolf Hitler used to put it '*Gleichgeschaltet*' (neglajšaltovala).'"[60] More direct commentators, like S. S. Ghelfand, stated outright, "If the fascist state and Nazi *Reich* is totalitarianism based on mystic idealism, the socialist state is materialist totalitarianism."[61] *Obzory* went the furthest, when in late 1947 the journal compared the two in a number of aspects and found both mass, uniform movements characterized by the regimentation of culture, demagogy, and state-socialist capitalism.[62] Jaroslav Richter, whose *Socialism and Christianity* was one of the primary texts of the newly consolidated Catholic position, noted that the Nazi program "contained truly socialist points." Further, both were directed against liberalism: fascism in the sphere of politics and socialism in economics.[63] Finally, both Nazism and communism were viewed as the philosophical descendents of Hegel, and Catholics placed particular stress on Hegel's notions of the state and its powers, which they considered "the primary component of the fascist-communist striving for political totalitarianism."[64]

This emphasis on Hegel's theory of the state was most powerfully seen in the Catholic conception of how a socialist society would appear, one that diverged greatly from both Protestant views and the visions of democratic socialist intellectuals. In contrast to the position of Czechoslovak Church leaders, for Catholics it was self-evident that "atheist communism cannot build the Kingdom of God on Earth." In a slap at the rapidly growing church, Kajpr argued that the claim that such a paradise could be built was an illusion that could "only exist in the notions or promises of those who wish to gain for their teaching the widest possible support."[65] In this inter-confessional debate, Chudoba argued that true "Christians never maintain that some revolution will change the world into paradise and human society into a perfect society." The Czechoslovak Church's enthusiasm and liturgical support for a classless society was, therefore, completely misplaced, because it relied on the assumption that Czechs could choose between a class-based and classless society: "In reality it is possible only to choose between two kinds of class society: one in which membership in the higher economic class is determined by economic abilities, and one in which membership in the higher economic class is determined by abilities other than economic ones."[66]

This last point provided ammunition for a critique of communism relying on the untrammeled power of the state. Catholics like Jaroslav Richter believed, in an opinion that later became sociological fact, that in a communist state there would be two classes, "a surely enormous class of workers and employees (like today's proletariat and even larger) and a narrow directorial class." Class struggle would still exist, but under socialism it "would not be allowed to discuss it at all."[67] For Catholics, the introduction of socialism would necessarily lead to precisely what in fact later arose in Czechoslovakia: all would be employees of an all-powerful state, which owned virtually everything (making it far worse than even the worst cartelization of capitalism), and whose idea of equality was at best the reduction of all to the level of workers, mere cogs in its machine.[68] It would be, in the words of Dominik Pecka, nothing short of "a police state . . . whose true name is slavery."[69]

There is no doubt that Catholic intellectual leaders believed committed communists were striving to be masters over this enslaved society. How, then, did they view the 40 percent of the Czech electorate that gave its vote to the Communist Party? It seemed that the public had failed to see that "the socialist state cannot exist without absolute power over everything." The control over the workforce necessary in a socialist economy—"including [over its] thoughts"—was something communists obviously would not mention in their polemics. In fact, Richter argued that there were supporters of communism who would reject the movement if they saw what it would mean if taken to its logical conclusions.[70] While many supporters of socialism were motivated by personal advancement or ambition to rule others, the most dangerous group, according to *Obzory*, was made up of those resembling the democratic socialists of this study:

> The socialism of so-called humanitarian collectivists springs from the confused yearning of every normal person, from the otherwise noble struggle for equality, justice, and humanity. In this lies the greatest danger of humanist socialism, that it will take advantage of noble motives to support a human society on a road leading to collectivist dictatorship and to an enslaving state. . . . It is precisely these people who conceal the true content of socialist demands and the true socialist reality with slews of words and phrases, and create from them an inviolable myth similar to the Nazi myth of race and blood that should hide organized injustice and the disintegration of society. In this way these humanists, not knowing humankind, fulfill the prophetic words of Grillparzer: "From humanity through collectivism to bestiality." . . . Socialism is not a drug against capitalism but its logically consistent culmination.[71]

The last sentence of this polemic points to one way Catholic intellectuals and political commentators attempted to bring Czech voters back to the fold, and signals a shift away from the examination of Catholic criticism of socialism to that of the coalescing Catholic program of social reform. Nonetheless, Catholic social critics needed to establish an anti-capitalist pedigree to win electoral support and to carve out political and rhetorical space for their positive ideas. They clearly stated that they did not want a return to laissez-faire capitalism and that capitalism was "not more acceptable because it [stands] as we do against communism." In fact, they argued that after "the internal renewal of the sixteenth century, Christianity began a struggle with capitalism that it could not, until our times, end victoriously."[72] With their anti-capitalist credentials thus established, they could link them to their anti-communist stance by portraying Marxian socialism as the inheritor and magnifier of the evils of capitalism. Catholics contrasted this with their own program, which they maintained offered the true alternative to capitalism. In doing so, they painted Christian principles as the long-resisting opponents of capitalism and atheist Marxism, both of which represented forms of oppression. The danger for Czechoslovakia, as Catholics saw it, was that the socialist cure for the disease of liberal and individualistic capitalism would be a tightly regimented, collectivist, and dictatorial communism, for "it has been human fate to treat one evil with another: in wanting to overcome and abolish one extreme we fall into another."[73]

Intellectual leaders on the religious wing of Czech political Catholicism stressed the atheism of both capitalism and communism. For them, capitalism was "worshipping the golden calf," whose promise of material benefit was copied by communism. Both endangered the Christian worldview, for in its

most fundamental aspect "the extra-Christian world is as one: replace the worship of God with idolatry."[74] The obsession with enrichment in modern capitalism and the materialist denial of God in communism inculcate a view in
which the individual is "reduced to a mere thing. . . . Modern capitalism, just
like modern collectivism . . . regards the individual as something that it is possible to use and take advantage of, as a thing." By denying the individual soul,
Marxism was "the direct descendant and continuer of capitalism."[75] Finally,
both communism and capitalism strove to bar religion from public life. Capitalism had made religion a private matter excluded from the public sphere of
politics. In short, communism, despite the relative openness expressed by the
contemporary Communist leadership, was viewed as absolutely antithetical to
not just Catholic political activity, but religion as a whole.

On the political wing, Bohdan Chudoba championed the view that Marxist socialism was nothing more than state capitalism, a view seconded by
both Ghelfand and Pecka. For Chudoba, "Capitalists—and it makes no difference whether they are the private capitalists of liberalism, or the state capitalists of communism—recognize only the citizen and the state." While the
value placed on the role of each varied widely, neither saw the range of local and regional networks emphasized by Catholic social doctrine.[76] Chudoba argued that the guiding idea of socialism was the same as that of nineteenth-century capitalism, with the difference that capital accumulated to the
state instead of trusts. The same enormous factories, deplorable working
conditions, and demeaning labor that nineteenth-century Marxism had condemned were now exalted by the communist system: "huge factories are
considered by communists to be the most modern, even the only, manner of
production, and the concentration of workers in a small number of locations
continues."[77] Ghelfand concurred that the distinction between communism
and capitalism lay only in the ownership of capital: "in everything else they
agree: common to both are the ideas of the importance of economics in societal life, the primacy of production and philosophical materialism."[78]

The primacy of matter over spirit united Catholics' belief that Marxism was
merely the fulfillment of capitalism with their criticisms of Marxist theory. For
a broad spectrum of Catholic commentators, "the fundamental idea of [com-
munism and capitalism] is one and the same: the world is a collection of objects ruled by material laws."[79] The promises of the radiant future awaiting
socialist societies came in for similar criticism. While socialist intellectuals of
all stripes believed that economic planning would bring both social justice
and generalized wealth, Catholics held that the stress placed on material
benefit made socialism no more than the idea of capitalist progress in a new
guise.[80] Marxism was portrayed by many leading Catholic intellectuals as
"the final stage of liberalism, for it is apparently the acme and universaliza-
tion of the bourgeois ideal of material welfare. . . . In the teachings of Marx
we barely find anything that would not be the fruit of the bourgeois spirit:

the variations are only in the application."[81] From the Catholic point of view, therefore, capitalism and communism did not represent real philosophical alternatives. For them, the choice was not between what they termed private capitalism and state capitalism, but rather "the true dilemma reads: communism or Christian social reformism."[82]

Catholic intellectuals recognized that the Church had not traditionally stood in the forefront of social progressivism, and stressed that Catholicism "must recognize its sins, namely its sins of omission."[83] In postwar Czechoslovakia, Catholic political thinkers could not "delude themselves into supposing that all this talk about the social question is completely out of place."[84] Faced with a wave of revolutionary enthusiasm, they tried to present Catholic doctrine in such a way as to amass popular working-class support—as one article attempted with the title "Comrade Jesus Christ"—without sacrificing their moderate, centrist membership.[85] Drawing on ideas from the papal encyclicals *Rerum novarum* and the more recent *Quadragesimo anno*, they attempted to adapt to the mentality of social change in the postwar Czech lands. In much the same way as Michael Fogarty has seen Christian democracy in Western Europe developing, Czech Catholic intellectuals stressed that their ideas were "Personalist, not Individualist," and "Pluralist, not Collectivist," with an emphasis on "'Horizontal' Pluralism—From the Neighborhood to the International Community."[86]

In place of both capitalist and socialist materialism, they offered a world-view in which the spiritual would be the "decisive component" but would be "in step with the material."[87] Catholic intellectuals saw themselves as "reasonable realists, reasonable spiritualists." Their stress on the realism of Christian politics drew on Masaryk's heritage and mirrored their condemnation of communist theory as no more than faith. With dialectical materialism dismissed, they could argue that Catholic social doctrine was no "less realistic than socialism or communism."[88] Catholic intellectuals close to the People's Party presented this "realistic" and moderate line to a target audience composed of those who looked at the problems of liberal society and asked "How not to be a socialist?" and at the problems of socialism and asked "How to be a socialist?" They argued that their Christian social politics was the only way to break out of "the bleak and primitive dichotomy of capitalism–communism."[89] Czech political Catholicism aimed to constitute a third force, one which could satisfy the true desires of the Czech public. According to Ghelfand, the Czechs yearned for a "beautiful, majestic ideal of the future . . . a synonym for progress, loving thy neighbor and social justice." However, he held that this is "'social feeling' [sociálnost]: a yearning and striving for justice in society, social reformism. In no way, however, is this socialism." By maintaining a moderate role in the National Front Government, the People's Party could claim that they fulfilled these desires, and "could equally well call itself a Christian Social Democratic party."[90]

Throughout their writings, politically activist Catholics from both wings of the movement stressed their reliance on the Christian principles that underlay their politics of solidarity. They reiterated that they were not concerned with benefiting merely one class, but the whole of society, and saw their politics as the natural outgrowth of the biblical teaching to "love thy neighbor." Dominik Pecka argued that all of the ideas that made the nation great—humanity, democracy, equality, and brotherhood—"are only an elaboration of the Gospels' fundamental teaching concerning loving thy neighbor."[91] This conception was criticized at the First Congress of Writers by Jaromír John, who argued that such a foundation represented only naive idealism and that in practical terms socialism had "*given humanity more in the hundred years of its organized activity than the moral sermonizing and all the Christian proclamations of love thy neighbor over the course of two thousand years.*" To counter this, Catholics replied: "It is equally naive to expect that people's natural selfishness will disappear by the mere socialization of all production, and that then a perfect commune will be created."[92]

On the question of the nature of Catholic politics, an interesting divergence is evident between the periodical press and books laying out the theory of Catholic social policy. In the heat of the rhetorical battle to seize the hearts and minds of a Czech populace enthusiastic for change, *Obzory* in particular stressed that Catholic ideas were revolutionary. Pavel Tigrid argued that Christian parties were strong, with "a revolutionary, modern conception for the economic and social organization of society." This conception was based on Christian principles, but these had been given new meaning in the turbulent recent decades, becoming, in *Obzory*'s view, "newly revolutionary . . . a *revolutionary* Christian ethics."[93] The Catholic intellectuals responsible for the more exhaustive explication of their positions stressed that Czech political Catholicism would follow only the "*evolutionary path,*" because it was "*in its essence a social reform movement and in no way a revolutionary movement.*"[94] This is not to imply a contradiction within the Catholic camp, but to show that it did differentiate between the message it presented to the wider public through journals and the one it presented to its secure and more conservative electoral hinterland.

Catholic leaders' views of the future economic development of the state conceived of a diversified ownership pattern. Consequently, they maintained a far more restrained attitude toward two central issues: the role of planning and the course of nationalization. In contrast to the enthusiastic stance adopted by Protestant leaders, Catholics saw some degree of planning as a necessity, and realized that to "oppose the need for planning is absolutely in vain." They argued instead that it should be limited to the state and cooperative sectors and that a healthy and robust private sector should remain outside its purview.[95] Their view of the recurring waves of nationalization was identical with this. The nationalization of banks, mines, and the largest industrial concerns by presidential decree (which placed almost 60 percent of industrial output under state control) was praised, as was a less extensive further nationalization. Catholic intellectuals saw large property holdings by individuals as "immoral," but consistently stressed the importance of small and medium-sized producers to the economy. They reiterated that they and their People's Party had approved of the early nationalizations but would go no further. "Nationalization is a drug, a costly enough drug and one full of danger," and therefore they needed significant proof that more was necessary before their support would be forthcoming.[96]

The one economic issue on which the Catholic view differed significantly from that of the other groups was the uncompromising stance it took in defense of private property. In keeping with their view of the necessity of having three different types of ownership—nationalized, cooperative, and private—Catholic intellectuals strongly supported private property rights in both the abstract and in economic reality. In a statement whose perceived necessity reveals the radical mood of the early postwar years, Tigrid declared, "*The defense of private property is not a crime.*" This does not mean that Catholics held that the right to private property was unlimited, since Catholic doctrine had "always stressed the social function of ownership."[97] Nonetheless, as Jon Bloomfield has noted about the People's Party, Catholics "wished to retain a considerable private sector, which could be more easily achieved once the existing popular radicalism had waned."[98] This defense of private property was tied to calls for several ameliorative measures, including worker joint-ownership in factories, appeals for a vague "deproletarianization" of the proletariat, and Ghelfand's demand for a "just wage."[99]

Finally, Catholic intellectuals differed from their Czechoslovak Church and Evangelical counterparts in their stringent defense of freedom. While Protestant intellectuals showed little concern for issues of individual freedom, Catholics viewed them as a fundamental element in the struggle between spirit and matter: "on one side stand the potentially weaker defenders of the individual . . . on the other the powerful adherents of the freedom of the nation-state, the class and anti-individual freedom."[100] This simplified view of the matter nonetheless took into account communist intellectuals' argument that they were in fact the true defenders of freedom and that the Communist Party was having some success with this strategy. Catholics recognized all too well that in the experience of war and revolution "some terms have lost their original meaning" and resolved to "let democracy and freedom mean something entirely different for us than for the communists."[101] They pledged themselves to struggle to maintain freedom in their country no matter what the costs may be. Their passion on the issue of freedom makes more clear the dangerous unconcern shown by the intellectual leaderships of the other Christian denominations: "Better poverty and struggle and, if necessary, slavery and again liberation, new struggle and, if necessary, death, just so we do not give up our free spirit!"[102]

Postwar Czech political Catholicism represented a clear alternative to the political visions of the other groupings. Most significantly, both wings of the movement consistently criticized the theory, practice, and developmental potential of socialism. In hindsight, this commendable position unwittingly contributed to weaknesses in postwar Czech politics, however. By equating socialism with communism (and with Marxist theory), Roman Catholic intellectuals made cooperation with their potential democratic socialist allies more difficult. Although the primary responsibility for this must lie with democratic socialists who feared the accusation of consorting with reaction, Roman Catholics also deserve a share of the blame.[103] They certainly did not clear the path to alliance by seeing "humanitarian collectivists" as the most dangerous adherents of socialist ideas. Catholicism's conceptual foundation provided Roman Catholic intellectuals with a solid position from which they could both defend themselves and counter the perceived socialist threat, but it also limited their political appeal. While officially nonconfessional, the People's Party was manifestly committed to Catholic principles. As a result, the party stood no chance of gaining support from Protestants, as we shall see, and to many less pious Catholics appeared closed and even backward-looking in a period of generalized socialist enthusiasm. A relatively more open stance may have aided the movement in gaining support, especially from the pool of supporters of the recently banned parties, thereby strengthening moderate politics in Czechoslovakia.

These criticisms notwithstanding, however, there is much positive to say about the positions adopted by Roman Catholic intellectuals. In contrast to their democratic socialist colleagues, they were fully aware of Marxist theory's potential dangers and consistently warned of the political danger of totalitarianism. Their concrete description of the features of a socialist Czechoslovak state were not only ultimately correct, but stood in sharp contrast to the vague notions of socialism expressed by democratic socialist intellectuals (or even those contained in the Communists' "Czechoslovak road" or the Czechoslovak Church's "Kingdom of God"). While rejecting capitalism, their resolute defense of private property and the private sector is unique, and their even more powerful rejection of materialism created space for their vision of a future Czech society based on policies of social amelioration rather than on the power of the idea of socialism. All in all, during a marked leftward swing in Czech political and cultural life, Roman Catholic intellectuals served their nation well. Their moderate plans for social justice—while perhaps neither grand nor appealing enough for those outside the Church—and defense of freedom and democracy without socialist adjectives are to be commended. Finally, their conceptions of proper political and social development mirrored their defense of Czech traditions and a Western orientation, providing Czech political Catholicism with admirable consistency.

12

Socialism and Protestant Intellectuals: The "Kingdom of God on Earth"?

To differing degrees, both the Evangelical Church of the Czech Brethren and the Czechoslovak Church embraced the political, social, and economic changes that followed the war. The larger and more important of these, the Czechoslovak Church, was far more radical in its support for the socialist transformation of the state, however. The Czech Brethren, and particularly that sect's towering figure, J. L. Hromádka, stood behind the new regime but showed more restraint and exhibited elements of the conceptual matrix visible in the ideas of democratic socialists, although Hromádka himself stood among the more radical Evangelicals. Nonetheless, the stances both groups adopted on the question of socialism provided largely unexpected support for the furthering of the radical socialist reorganization of Czech society. In this respect they can be seen politically as the left-wing religious analog to the Roman Catholic Church's moderate social reformism and support of the People's Party.

SOCIALISM AND CZECHOSLOVAK CHURCH INTELLECTUALS: THE "KINGDOM OF GOD ON EARTH"

The largely working-class Czechoslovak Church found itself in a fortuitous position after liberation. Despite charges of collaboration, it experienced rapid growth in membership as an institution, and its leading figures as individuals provided strong support for the cause of a radical socialism they saw politically embodied in the Communist Party. Church leaders, bolstered by the sense that their church stood at the forefront of the forces for change and by the increasing power its swelling membership brought, did not hesitate to urge their flock to participate in political life. The communist ideologist Arnošt Kolman's complaint that "religion is the opium of the masses . . . [because] it corrodes the believer's conscience and his will to consistently struggle for the decisive betterment of real life on this earth," could not be leveled at the spiritual positions of the Czechoslovak Church. Rather, the leadership actively worked to ensure that the day would soon come, as the leading theologian František Hník put it, when "religion will cease to be an opium . . . [but] will begin anew to represent an energizing force for making social organization pliant."[1] The instrumentality of this statement is symbolic of a problem that recurs throughout the writings of church leaders. The church's political commitment often gave rise to ambiguity about whether social change was desired in order to serve religious ends, or whether the church's religious views were crafted with social change and political impact in mind. In either case, Czechoslovak Church members were urged to take part in the socialist recasting of Czechoslovak society. Church leaders actively campaigned against what they termed "quietism" and "indifference," because "meek, weak-willed, and submissive people easily become just the apolitical mass that reaction and fascism most easily and successfully turn to the advantage of their goals." At his investment as the church's new patriarch, František Kovář proclaimed that "all church indifference to the historic movement of society . . . [is] a resignation of faith that the life of human society can be remade in the image of the Kingdom of God." Further, in a comment that mimics communist literature's heroic optimism, Kovář pointedly noted that "Jesus did not know such resignation."[2]

While some democratic socialist and Roman Catholic intellectual leaders argued for the adoption of a position above politics—or at least a separation of political and intellectual activities—the Czechoslovak Church and its leadership saw no such division between their worldly and spiritual responsibilities. One lay member urged the clergy in this direction, boldly proclaiming, "We are not afraid of words about socialism from our pulpits."[3] For the church's most vocal adherents, energetic participation in political life was a priority that drew them into strange formulations of Christian doctrine:

> There must be an end to the suicidal opinion that the church must be apolitical. On the contrary, for religious and free Christian reasons the church must always clearly support the strivings of those who are trying to make our national society more human, fuller and more beautiful. Here Jesus' words hold true: Who is not with us is against us.[4]

Despite their general support for Edvard Beneš, in practice they ignored the warning he gave an assembly of church leaders: "Beware that the church does not involve itself directly in politics." The only note of concern expressed within the church's intellectual leadership over the enthusiasm with which political activity was pursued appeared in an editorial on the eve of the communist assumption of power. In early 1948, a professor of theology, Zdeněk Trtík, cautioned, "We have in the church too many exponents of politics and worldly currents, but in political parties and public life many fewer exponents of Christianity and the calling of the church."[5] By that time, church theologians and lay intellectuals had traveled so far down the road toward creating what could be called "Christianity with a socialist face" that it was too late to attempt to create "socialism with a Christian face."

The church's zeal for political engagement in the cause of radical socialism was echoed in its theological demands for a new Christianity, which was to be achieved by means of a revolution in the faith. These demands reached their peak in the statements of professor of theology Otto Rutrle and those of František Linhart, the founder of the Association of Religious Socialists.[6] For these men especially, the war had marked a watershed in both theological and sociopolitical terms. As we have seen, the concept of crisis played a role in the interpretive structure of postwar Czechoslovakia, and played a particularly large one in the thought of the Czechoslovak Church. For Linhart, the world was

> in a deep crisis and needs a new orientation. . . . Today's world needs a new unity, and not only political and social unity, but above all spiritual unity. Historical, ecclesiastical Christianity can no longer provide this unity, since it is founded on outdated idealistic and dualistic thought. Today's world can only be given this unity by a new form of Christianity.[7]

Rutrle also believed that the emerging postwar world did "not only need a unifying world view, but also a unifying life principle. . . . The world needs—and in my judgment we are called to create—a new, real Christianity."[8]

Pronouncements desiring unity were rife in all spheres of public life in the wake of the war, as youth, labor, and professional organizations all struggled to reconstruct in a stronger and more resilient form a civil society disrupted by war. What sets apart the Czechoslovak Church's call for a new Christianity to fulfill the unifying function is its explicitly *revolutionary* aspect. For them, Christianity was a historically and theologically revolutionary faith, and they interpreted its history in much the same way as had Zdeněk Nejedlý. They recognized that many people saw Christianity as inherently opposed to revolutionary acts, "when old orders were hastened out violently with guns and bloodshed." Nonetheless, they held that this view sprang "from an incorrect conception of religion and Christianity and from an incorrect view of revolution."[9] For Linhart particularly, Christianity had from its very roots been revolutionary and, in fact, "Jesus' fundamental thought [was] the thought of world revolution." Although this revolutionary current had been oppressed and forced underground, he argued, it had always remained alive and waiting to resurface.[10] The era of capitalism had been only the latest in a string of oppressive forces, but its injustices had strengthened the revolutionary element of Christianity. Under capitalism, Jesus' ethos could live "only as an ethos of revolution, as a morally inexorable demand for the radical transformation of society." This view was by no means an extreme one within the church, as these last words appeared in the church's official and unanimously approved Pronouncement of the Second General Assembly.[11]

Not only was revolution supported as an intrinsic element of the church's reading of the Christian message, but also because church leaders believed a "new Christianity" was necessary for what can be called social and institutional reasons. Traditional Christianity, in the form of the Roman Catholic Church, for example, had lost much of its sway over the masses, and the growth of the Czechoslovak Church in the immediate postwar period gave its leadership some indication that it was delivering a welcome message. For those like Linhart, Christianity stood at a crossroads, forced to choose between maintaining outdated traditions and experiencing a radical religious revolution:

> Either it will choose to maintain its place in the new world and fulfill its calling in the history of humankind—and then it will have to accept the fundamental principles of the new thinking and undergo the most radical changes, it will have to go through a complete revolution, a revolution far more radical than the Reformation—or it will lose its meaning in the new world and live on in vain [*stane se solí zmařenou*]. There are no other paths open to it.[12] . . . Revolution . . . is necessary, if Christianity is to have a positive function in today's world. . . . It is felt increasingly clearly that the world political, social, and economic revolution, if its results are to be lasting, must be completed by a spiritual and religious revolution. This world revolution is in reality the fruit of the spirit of Jesus.[13]

Given his position as founder of the Association of Religious Socialists, there can be little doubt of the contours of the "new thinking" to which Linhart referred. He returned to this theme almost obsessively, and the influence of his views can be seen in the lengths to which many of his colleagues went in integrating them.

For Rutrle and Linhart, Christianity could only fulfill its true calling by expressing itself "in the conceptual categories and terms of the contemporary development of humanity."[14] This meant abandoning much of the language of the "spirit" Catholic intellectuals were striving so hard to defend, "since between traditional conceptions and the spirit of the new era there is a deep contradiction." In the new era, one that expressed itself in the "empirical, realistic, and progressive" truths the church found in the thinking of scientific socialism, religion must be "just as empirical as science."[15] There was much debate within the church over the implications of this, notably at its Fourth Theological Conference, held in August 1946, but little in the way of practical, programmatic results. Nonetheless, one aspect was certain:

This new form of Christianity will incorporate as its fundamental elements socialism and communism, which is in reality the fruit of the spirit of Christianity.
The task of Christians who understand the sign of the times and grasp their calling in it, is to work toward this goal, toward a new conception of Christianity
and toward its synthesis with socialism and communism.[16]

Two interesting points arise from the formulation of this sentiment. First, the
use of the singular "is" with socialism and communism reveals that Linhart,
at least, did not distinguish between the two. While Catholics did the same
in a negative sense, Linhart and other Czechoslovak Church leaders did so in
a positive one. Further, whereas Catholic leaders overwhelmingly rejected
the notion of any sort of synthesis between Christianity and communism, the
Czechoslovak Church actively supported the endeavor. Even Pavel Tigrid
(the only Catholic to admit even the possibility of some kind of synthesis between Catholicism and communism) argued that Christianity had to remain
firm and wait for communism to move toward it. Linhart reversed this, arguing that Christianity should reformulate itself so that it would be in more
agreement with communist principles. This sentiment was also implied in
the statement of František Hník, then serving as dean of the Theological Faculty, who argued, "The future of humanity is dependent on whether there
will be success in showing the compatibility of Christian spiritual values with
the positive results of the social revolution."[17] Again, it was the values of the
Christian faith that must be shown to be compatible with socialism, rather
than the converse.

This idea of synthesis, which permeated democratic socialist thought
along the conceptual axes East/West and socialism/democracy, found particular resonance among Czechoslovak Church thinkers searching for the
content of their new Christianity. The church's postwar theological conference was almost entirely devoted to the theme of "harmonizing Christianity
with scientific socialism (Trtík)," both in theological and practical terms. In
contrast to Catholicism, the Czechoslovak Church establishment found that
spirit and matter were in no way opposed and that there was "no reason why
materialism and metaphysics should not mutually respect one another
(Hník)." Cooperation between socialism and Christianity was not only "possible, [but] even necessary (Spisar)."[18] This line of thinking reached its peak
in Linhart's writing, when in early 1947 he made it a divinely ordained responsibility: "This synthesis is . . . a demand that God has imposed on our
era. The time is right for it. Let us not disappoint in the fulfilling of this task,
which God Himself has given us today!"[19]

The energies expended by the Czechoslovak Church leadership in the
search for a synthesis of socialism and Christianity were matched by those
devoted to an unrelenting criticism of capitalism. This was founded on phenomena tied tightly to the immediate postwar period, since Czechoslovak
Church intellectuals believed that the war had signaled "the total destruction

and ruination of the world built on the selfish morality, liberalism, and capitalism of the last century."[20] Further, even before Andrei Zhdanov had enunciated the "two camps" theory, church leaders like František Roháč had reached the conclusion that the war had brought about a division of "the world into two halves—capitalist and socialist." For them, the war had led "the majority of the lands in Europe" in the correct direction: "from profiteering society to socializing and socialist society."[21] Their final source of condemnation was drawn from the adoption of the Marxist argument that fascism and war were the logical results of capitalist development. The most important single document the church released in the period, the Pronouncement of the Second General Assembly, made this crystal clear by declaring:

> As Christians, we therefore consider it extremely necessary that the liberated peoples be aware that world fascism was a camouflaging maneuver of imperialist capitalism, that the existence of fascism and its growth into a social force has its origin in the historical development of class society, in its necessary internal socioeconomic and politicocultural contradictions, and that there will not be true peace and security in the world until the transition from a profiteering society to a socialist social order is complete.[22]

Surprisingly, given their radical tone, church intellectuals expressed a feeling of laggardliness in turning the church to full-fledged support of radical socialism. Although historically progressive, the church felt it necessary to indulge in an episode of self-criticism for not having earlier stood in the front ranks of the opponents of the capitalist order. Rutrle condemned the "sins of the church" in sanctioning the previously existing order and failing to renounce "one of the most powerful opponents of God—selfish capital."[23] According to the usually restrained Hník, the Christian churches had failed both themselves and society by maintaining "their alliance with the capitalist and imperialist vampires." They failed themselves because they failed to "diagnose the *essence* and *character* of the dark power" of capitalism. As a result, "the correct analysis—profiteering society, its development and maturity to the stage of world imperialism—came from elsewhere," i.e., from the camp of scientific socialism.[24] This interpretation fit well with the sudden upsurge in church membership after the war. Church leaders believed that by failing to accept the Marxist-Leninist interpretation of history and therefore often "standing against the true needs of the working class," the church's access to that class had been limited and the message of socialism became associated with anti- or areligious actors. They saw this as the case despite the fact that industrial workers had constituted the largest single group on the membership rolls already before the war. With its adoption of a more radical political orientation after the war, however, the church had grown rapidly, especially among the working class. Church leaders drew the lesson from this, distancing their present political incarnation from the "historical error" that had led them to appear as "open enemies of the working people," and repeatedly reiterating their condemnation of capitalism.[25]

The church's abhorrence of capitalism was trumped only by its overzealous praise of "scientific socialism" and its Marxist bearers. While this may very well have been tinged by a perceived need to compensate for their failure to diagnose the evils of capitalism early enough, it is unquestionable from the number and variety of speakers and the intemperance of their statements that the sentiment was genuine. The church's intellectual leadership expressed its position by support for the theory and representatives of "scientific socialism." Linhart, the most radical exponent of the line, maintained that a "new philosophical king had arrived in Karl Marx." For him, Marxist theory and Czech experience had made one fact clear: "We must today, *today* place ourselves on the side of socialism and communism." According to the minutes of the theological conference, "[Linhart] pronounced dialectical materialism, understood by him as dialectical realism, to be the only correct philosophy."[26] While he may have been the most radical, his judgments were reflected in the meditations of other members of the church's theological leadership. For František Roháč, it was not an overstatement to observe that Marx's "life and work constitutes one of the most heroic discoveries in modern history." While never heaping praise on communist theory, Hník similarly demanded that the church never "use its spiritual potential to come out conceptually or politically in opposition to dialectical materialism," promising in early 1946 that the church would be among the first "to attempt to forge a new theory of radical social change."[27] The church's patriarch, František Kovář, took advantage of the platform of the Communist Party pamphlet *My Relationship to the Communist Party of Czechoslovakia* to express his support for "scientific socialism," and one church member revealed elsewhere that plans for postwar political cooperation between the party and the church had already been agreed upon during the occupation.[28]

Perhaps even more important than political support was the legitimacy the Czechoslovak Church gave "scientific socialism" through the use of its theological authority. Many linked Christian ideals and socialism generally, with Hník's comments among the least outrageous. He found that Marx's "scientific socialism" maintained much of "the moral heritage of the New Testament message" and that socialism "indisputably . . . conforms to the moral orientation of Jesus' Gospel" far more than capitalism.[29] The church not only found that Marxian socialism was "compatible with Christian norms," but that in the cases of the nationalizations and socialist reforms in the sphere of property relations "the Christian, as a disciple of Jesus, can and must agree with socialism."[30] More egregious were Linhart's argument that communism represented "the fruit of [Jesus'] spirit" and Roháč's loaded claim that "*the ethos of Jesus' Gospel is the ethos of the classless society.*"[31] This latter statement was absorbed into the church assembly's

Pronouncement, with the added injunction "It is . . . a moral and religious duty to work so that the development of our society hastens toward the overcoming of class distinctions as consciously and quickly as possible."[32]

The blending of theological pronouncement and political agitation reached its height in the church's employment of the concept of the Kingdom of God, the realm in which the will of God is fulfilled. The laity was admonished to base its "political participation and labors" on "the ideas and demands of the Kingdom of God in the spirit of Jesus."[33] The link between the Kingdom of God, radical socialist politics, and the church's commitment to that politics was made by intellectual leaders both within and outside its hierarchy. As the newly inaugurated Bishop of Prague—and hence the church's second most important figure—Miroslav Novák, argued: "We move with the socialist strivings not because we need to swim with the current of the times, but because we see in the instituting of a socialist society the first and necessary precondition for Jesus' message of the Kingdom of God on Earth, a message of the Kingdom of brotherhood, love, and freedom finally becoming a reality."[34] That socialism was only a precondition for the Kingdom of God and required a spiritual component for its fulfillment was mentioned solely by Hník. Similarly, none denied that the Kingdom need not be delayed until after death or until the resurrection of Jesus. As Alois Spisar repeatedly stressed, the Kingdom of God was not "life after death, but also temporal life, life in this world, here on Earth, . . . the better order that . . . we want to build after two world wars." The radical socialist order for which the church strove was not only a morally perfect one, as one might expect to hear from a religious institution, but "a paradise *on Earth—a paradise*" that would bring "the bliss and joy that gushes forth from *material* wealth in the highest conceivable measure."[35] In addition to the problematic nature of the theology in these statements, the church's stress on the worldly benefits of the future socialist order provides an interesting contrast to the Catholic intellectual position that held that by stress on production and material betterment, communism was no more than the successor to the failed idolatrous values of capitalism. It is true that the church never directly proclaimed the Communist Party the political institution that would bring about the Kingdom of God on Earth. The roles played by scientific socialism, dialectical materialism, and the classless society in their theology and public pronouncements, however, leave little doubt with which party its sympathies lay.

The church's exceptional relationship with the Soviet Union only reinforces this conclusion. While criticism of the Soviet Union was taboo, many democratic socialists, and Roman Catholics in particular, restricted their praise of the Soviet Union to specific issues, primarily gratitude to the Red Army for its struggle in liberating Czechoslovakia. Not so the Czechoslovak Church. In contrast to warnings from Catholics concerning the persecution of religious believers in the USSR, Hník opened his ruminations on the topic with a citation from Stalin, and concluded "The Kremlin has adopted a position of benign tolerance toward religion; today in Russia all clergymen have full freedom of confession."[36] While it is true that there was a substantial relaxation of control over religion in the Soviet Union during the war years, it considerably overstates the case to maintain there was "full freedom" for clergymen. In the church's attempt to place itself politically behind the Soviet Union, religious issues were often left to the side. In one such instance, Bishop Novák stressed the similarities between his church and the Russian Orthodox Church. Further, a representative of the Soviet Union was present at the church's Fourth Theological Conference.[37] The only remark potentially critical of communism came from Hník, who suggested in one article that scientific socialism should revise its generally negative view of religion, although just a few months previously he had counseled his coreligionists that, in fact, they should be more tolerant of communism's atheism in order "to make cooperation with Marxism in the striving for the revival of human dignity possible."[38]

Given this almost literally messianic view of the potentials of socialist development it comes as little surprise that the church actively supported a regime dominated by the alliance of the Communist Party and left-wing Social Democrats. The conceptions of People's Democracy and the National Front government, central to the Communist Party's notion of a "Czechoslovak road," were considered by church spokespeople as bulwarks of the new order. Patriarch Kovář continually reminded the public of the church's "full political and moral solidarity" with the regime, and Bishop Novák stated proudly that "our religious communities are one of the most morally reliable forces of [socialist] construction" after the Communist Party victory in the 1946 parliamentary elections.[39] This support was also manifested in commentary on directly political issues, a step from which other religious institutions—notably the Roman Catholic Church—shied away for fear of mixing politics and religion too deeply. Such concern was only expressed on one occasion, and even on that occasion it was immediately dismissed. Patriarch Kovář wrote to the Prime Minister in late 1945 to declare his pleasure at the outcome of the negotiations over the first wave of nationalizations:

> In the name of all the members of the church, I express the conviction that this great work—which guarantees true freedom and equality and creates the preconditions for the material and spiritual advancement of the Czech and Slovak people—will be led successfully to its goal. . . . It could be considered as somewhat uncommon that church spokespeople have an interest in a decision concerning economic matters. However, in the free Christianity to which our church belongs, it was clear already before the war that the moral health and spiritual maturity of nations—just like their civilizational progress and cultural growth—can only be guaranteed when it steps away from the vicious circle of crises and ruinations that profiteering society carries within itself.[40]

Beyond the nationalizations, the most significant facets of the church's commentary on directly political issues concerned the Two-Year Plan and the limit on the number of permitted political parties implemented during the war. The approval given the plan, the success of which was a key ingredient of the Communist Party's "Czechoslovak road" strategy, was notable for its rhetorical vehemence. More revealing, however, were the way the Czechoslovak Church characterized its support and the role the church offered to play in ensuring its success. Hník, in a view typical for the church, stressed that the plan was more than a means for rebuilding the land in the wake of the war. He saw it as a "great socio-ethical experiment," much as Patriarch Kovář saw it as an essentially "moral question." Although the plan would have wide-ranging effects on the economic and labor freedoms of the Czechoslovak public, Hník argued that "for the good of the plan it is necessary to call for people to submit to limitations on their freedom in a disciplined fashion." In the communist-sponsored drive for what Kovář called "conscious social discipline," the patriarch similarly pledged the church's support in raising the nation's "devotion to labor and voluntary discipline."[41] This institutional support was also pledged retroactively in the case of the banning of the prewar right-wing parties, a move that had significantly strengthened the Communist Party's role in the government. Patriarch Kovář cited his predecessor's support for restrictions on the number of parties during the interwar period and somewhat contortedly called for "the reduction in the number of political parties to be carried out, in order to allow for a more complete and effective development of the principles of democracy."[42]

These examples of church support for specific policy instruments of the developing People's Democracy reveal that it was committed to the practical implementation of the radical social change it espoused. By engaging directly in debate over specific political issues, rather than discussing general political ideas and goals, however, the church became even more intertwined with political developments and left itself open to political abuse by its radical socialist allies. More importantly, the church's spokesmen showed what can only be regarded as careless negligence of the potential consequences of their actions. In an atmosphere of enthusiasm for socialism, the continuous effort of portraying themselves as among the most committed to revolutionary change revealed a lack of concern for basic freedoms. This was witnessed in the claim that limitations on entering professions or on the free movement of labor should be supported by calls for "conscious social discipline," and that the amputation of a large measure of the political spectrum would aid in perfecting democracy. These are not only questionable on their face, but in the atmosphere of postwar Czechoslovakia represented dangerous ground for religious authorities to tread.

This flexibility in views of democracy and freedom and the willingness to place the church at the service of the radical re-engineering of society led the church brain trust to further statements that can be looked back upon only with amazement. Democracy, as normally conceived of and as was practiced in prewar Czechoslovakia, was disparaged, and on one occasion it was noted that "even Hitler came to power with the help of the elections he won."[43] For the Czechoslovak Church, true democracy lay in radicalizing the socialist call for democracy in all spheres of life. Similarly, true freedom could only lead in one direction. As František Hník put it, it was an "act directed against God [*protibožský čin*]" to limit freedom and make people into "powerless tools":

> In this sense the Christian worldview is in dialectical opposition to the spirit of capitalism, to the spirit of fascism, and to every rapacious power of imperialism. Opposed to this, we meet with the true source of genuinely human society and we find the deepest justification for the communism of love [*zdůvodnění komunismu lásky*].[44]

On the road to realizing these radically reconfigured conceptions of freedom and democracy, the church pledged itself, as had democratic socialist intellectuals, to "educate the new man" and create a "new humanism" that would "certainly be different from the enlightenment humanism of the past epoch of liberalism."[45] It was comments like these that caused the Roman Catholic editorialist Pavel Tigrid to note, in regard to communist and democratic socialist use of the same rhetoric, that "they call their enslavement of man a 'new humanism' . . . Moral slovenliness, the mockery of idealism, insensitivity to iniquity, cowardice in conviction, and audacity in beastliness: these are the inevitable milestones on the road to this 'better tomorrow.'"[46]

Tigrid's comment is symptomatic of the relationship between the Roman Catholic and Czechoslovak churches, although more commonly and more virulently such expressions came from the side of the Czechoslovak Church. As one would expect from a sect that had grown out of the "Los von Rom" movement, held radical socialist beliefs, and was striving toward a "new Christianity," the Czechoslovak Church viewed the Roman Catholic Church as the incarnation of religious and political reaction. The church's leading weekly called Catholicism a "fascist form of Christianity," whose leaders were aware that "the man of the future, living in a society of social justice and lasting peace, will look for other forms of piety and devotion than those that the Vatican can offer."[47] In contrast to the Czechoslovak Church's engagement in the cause of a revolution in Christianity, it was argued that the Vatican could only muster strength for a "tight defense of orthodox formulations of faith."[48]

As was the case for the communists, the political positions of Roman Catholicism were more important to the Czechoslovak Church leaders than the existing theological differences. Rather than embracing the new order in the people's democracies, the Catholics' "anti-Soviet crusade" had shown that "in the fateful conflicts of humankind they truly do not want to place themselves on the side of . . . the uninterrupted progress of life." Referring to Roman Catholicism, the

Czechoslovak Church assigned itself the responsibility to "do everything in its power to help expose and beat back all nefarious intentions aiming to prevent the arrival of a new organization for our life even at the price of a new war." For Prague Bishop Miroslav Novák, the Vatican's "mask ha[d] lost its impenetrability" by late 1946 and revealed the Catholic Church to be a dangerous opponent of socialism.[49] Even those within the Czechoslovak Church's intellectual leadership who refused to insult the Catholic Church as a religious institution criticized its political positions. At the church's theological conference, one participant emphasized the importance of "distinguishing between the religious values and political tendencies of Catholicism." Another argued that, although the search for elements in the Catholic Church receptive to the new Christianity should continue, the Czechoslovak Church nonetheless had a "duty to expose all Vatican cooperation with politically and religiously reactionary forces."[50]

The animosity expressed toward the Roman Catholic Church was not mirrored in the Czechoslovak Church's views of the Protestant churches. In its relationship to them, there was a mixture of goading and encouragement toward radicalism, as well as a concern that the Czechoslovak Church maintain its position as the most progressive of churches. Like the Evangelical Church of the Czech Brethren and the Communist Party, the Czechoslovak Church claimed that in the spirit of "the Hussite traditions above all, we again [stand] in the front ranks of progressive humanity."[51] Czechoslovak Church leaders considered the Evangelicals theologically and politically closest, and rhetorically pushed and pulled members of that church toward the political left. J. L. Hromádka was hailed as a man whose "conception of religion can be socially very radical" and a man who had "stood in the front ranks of the so-called political and cultural left." Nonetheless, while "he himself stands on the side of the positive forces of history . . . organized followers of his way of thinking already stand on the opposing side."[52] In this vein, the Evangelical Church and other Protestant churches were called upon to "unfetter themselves from their bonds with the spirit of the capitalist system," while Bishop Novák promised to help "liberal-minded groups and exceptional individuals . . . to convince their own churches that it is not their task to hold back the rise of the new world."[53] The Czechoslovak Church, despite its meetings with other Christian groups, swore to maintain its political position in order not to "lag behind Christian churches in the East and the West." František Roháč summed up the Czechoslovak Church's relationship with all other Christian sects: "I think that it matters less whether and how much the other historic churches consider [the Czechoslovak Church] still Christian or not Christian enough, and it matters more that all the progressive and creative forces of humanity can consider it their comrade in arms."[54]

Given all of the preceding, it should come as no surprise that the intellectual leadership of the Czechoslovak Church praised the outcome of the February 1948 crisis. In the immediate aftermath of the communist assumption of power, church leaders manifested the same traits that had made them the most radical religious force in the nation. Again, a mixture of socialist and religious rhetoric came to the fore, with František Hník writing that the nation had "needed a purifying storm," and that with the rise of the Communist Party to total power, "We are truly grasping the spiritually transforming essence of Jesus' Gospel. We are seizing upon the prophetic core of the entire content of the Bible."[55] While the Kingdom of God had not been realized with the change in government, the way was now clear. According to Patriarch Kovář, speaking on the fourth of March in the name of the church's leadership council, the "historic days" the nation had just passed through had placed it "on a more secure and rapid road to the realization of social equality and progress . . . [toward] a society without class hatred and contradictions. Such a society is a precondition for the realization of the Kingdom of God on Earth."[56] In keeping with their earlier denigration of democracy, the days of "liberal democracy . . . the mechanical aggregation of voices" were seen to have come to an end, and the church claimed partial credit for the victory.[57] Despite the elation church leaders felt in the wake of the February events, they had outpaced their membership. Zdeněk Trtík seemed to be aware of this, but rather than counseling restraint, he argued the clergy should continue even further: "The relationship of our church public would be much more positive to socialism than it is now if all the clergy, on whom this depends, were to show how a Christian's positive relationship to the practical goals of socialism grows from *his own Christian foundation of faith*."[58]

There is little to add to the statements of the church's intellectual and ecclesiastical leadership. Their theological radicalism found a perfect partner in a communist ideology that had largely muted its atheist rhetoric, and the church strove to meet radical socialism more than halfway. Perhaps the most significant facet of this short examination is the political conclusion that can be drawn from it. The church's radical theological, social, and political adventurism not only did not cause disaffection among the laity, but resulted in a 20 percent increase in adherents before 1948, so that the church comprised roughly one-eighth of the Czech population. This can only be viewed as a measure of the popularity of radical views in the Czech population. It seems that the revolutionary enthusiasm of the Czech public witnessed by the phenomenal growth of the Communist Party had a theological analogue in the growth of the Czechoslovak Church, revealing a weakness in Czech culture that contributed to the nation's slide into dictatorship.

SOCIALISM AND EVANGELICAL INTELLECTUALS: THE "SOCIAL AND POLITICAL TENDENCY OF THE FUTURE"

Although many of the concepts key to the Czechoslovak Church's radicalism do not appear in the Evangelical message, in the essentials there was a great deal of consensus between the two largest non-Catholic religious denominations. Like the Czechoslovak Church, the Evangelical movement encouraged political activity on the part of their church's adherents, although still maintaining that it "would lose trust if [it] were to recommend wholeheartedly a definite party. Above all, it must concern a clear orientation."[59] The orientation this church settled on was clearly inclined toward socialism, as we shall see, but unlike its Czechoslovak Church analogs, it consistently stressed that while it was a "liberalistic error that religion was a private matter," the individual must "ensure for himself *before* entry into *whichever* party . . . *full freedom* for his *religious conviction.*"[60]

The Evangelicals' leader on the public stage, J. L. Hromádka, exhibited some unease at the political role that he came to play. On the one hand, he asked his public to "excuse [him] for becoming involved in politics," and proclaimed that he did "not want to agitate" and was even "afraid of agitation." On the other hand, his fear was evident neither in his espousal of his particular brand of socialism nor in his encouragement of the public to take part in the socialist transformation. In the same speech in which he proclaimed his aversion to agitation, he urged his listeners to play an active role in political life, arguing that church adherents could not "shrink from politics," because "the great church of our national neighbor to the north and west, the Germans, arrived on the brink of catastrophe because it supposed that with a lack of interest in political responsibility it would better carry out its religious calling."[61] The message was clear: German Protestants (even if the Nazi Party had found disproportionate electoral support among them) had not been active enough in political affairs and had been punished with the reactionary Nazi regime. In such a conceptual field, the Evangelicals' monthly journal, *Křest'anská revue,* could proclaim: "Today apoliticism is rejected and condemned on all sides as a poisonous mycelium in which fascism thrives. There is not allowed to be an apolitical person or apolitical culture, not even apolitical religion!"[62]

While this spur to political activity had a religious analog in the Czechoslovak Church with its call for a "new Christianity," the Evangelicals showed no such inclination. In fact, rather than encouraging religious and socialist revolution the church placed itself closer to the democratic socialist elements in the center of the political spectrum. While it recognized, in the words of the theologian František Bednář, that Czechs were "in a social revolution that is seizing the whole world and concerns more than industry," it also urged caution.[63] Church leaders had been reassured that the revolution had not adopted an anti-religious attitude, and this treatment must have influenced their positions.[64] Even Hromádka, who saw the contemporary events as "the greatest international revolution yet" and argued that his flock should "become accustomed to it," restrained himself from pushing for an expansion of the revolution. He argued that, although the revolutionary transformation of Czechoslovak society was not yet completed, the nation needed a period of calm. In his view, the course of future action should ensure "that we truly defend and morally and spiritually strengthen the gains won by the present revolution."[65] This argument echoes those of democratic socialist intellectuals who had welcomed the initial reforms but argued that the revolution was over and calm development necessary.

Although Evangelical intellectual leaders proved more reluctant revolutionaries, they rivaled their Czechoslovak Church colleagues in their praise of and pledges of active support for socialism. The theologian Josef Souček extolled the "joy" that he felt because the Czechs had "decided clearly, solidly, seriously and fearlessly to build our new life on new foundations . . . [with] the construction of socialism."[66] Hromádka, who often seemed almost obsessed with the historic meaning of Munich and the Second World War, judged that there was no need for discussion: all of Europe was on the road to socialism; it was a "historical fact." In Hromádka's view only insidious reaction opposed socialism, attempting "either out of fear or selfishness to obstruct the current of history."[67] The bourgeoisie, through its behavior at the time of Munich, had "unconsciously dug its own grave."[68] In such a situation he judged that there was no room for fence-straddlers. In a long speech given before a large audience in December 1947, with international and domestic tensions rising, he urged his audience to choose sides. One who wanted to "serve the Lord" and be among the "co-constructors of tomorrow, must already decide now where he wants to stand. He cannot wait for 'relations' to develop in such a way that he is comfortable with them." By this time, the argument for the calm consolidation of the revolution's gains had lost its importance for Hromádka, and he implied that there was no room for his followers to be both progressive and opposed to the communists.[69] Much of this stemmed from Hromádka's estimation of the international situation. In the printed version of this speech, two telling chapter titles, "The Danger from the Right" and "The Responsibility of the Left," clearly indicate his appraisal. At that time, only three months before the Communist assumption of total power, he was "convinced that the danger that today threatens humanity . . . threatens more from the right than from the left."[70] Consequently, he argued that the responsibility of Evangelical leaders lay in minimizing the danger from the right. He therefore urged a more activist path, particularly in winning over the youth:

> It is necessary to convince namely the young people, students, workers, farmers, apprentices, and small businessmen. They must understand what moral and spiritual properties the new society we want to build contains . . . How is it today that so many young and sincere people remain not only indifferent to the socialist future, but are either unfriendly toward it or view it with cynicism?[71]

That Hromádka could maintain such a stance so late in the postwar developments was only possible because of the positions he and other church leaders had consistently maintained since the war's end, positions that endorsed the People's Democratic system and stressed the changed nature of Czechoslovak communism. For Evangelical leaders, the People's Democracy represented "the best guarantee of freedom," and they were determined to support it.[72] While they condemned capitalism, saying that "Nothing was so far from the Christian spirit," their attitude toward the foundation of the new regime was wholly positive. Not only was "talk of a just social transformation . . . understandable and gratifying," but it spurred them to argue that already in 1945, "Evangelicals [were] only a step away from socialism."[73] Nonetheless, the church leaders' message to the nation characteristically declared, "it is not possible to build anything without Christian moral foundations."[74]

Their support was most evident in the attitude they adopted toward the Two-Year Plan. Church leaders praised the work that previously had been accomplished in rebuilding the republic, but proclaimed themselves still "far from satisfied."[75] For this reason, the success of the Two-Year Plan was considered absolutely necessary. There were, however, significant additional reasons for the emphasis Evangelicals placed on the plan. The enthusiasm with which the Czechoslovak Church endorsed the plan played a role in the Evangelical response. Evangelical leaders were cognizant of the rapid growth of the Czechoslovak Church and did not want to appear to be lagging behind that denomination. International prestige also accounted in some measure for the increased attention given the plan. In addition to the rebuilding aspect of the plan, Evangelicals stressed that "abroad they are watching us and anxiously waiting for us to flounder, wanting to demonstrate through us that the road upon which we have embarked leads nowhere and that it is better to maintain the old, capitalist practices."[76] Here the prestige was national, but it mirrors the prestige Communists attached to the plan for political reasons. The credence given the "Czechoslovak road" strategy by this statement is notable, as is the support given socialism generally. While stopping short of considering the fulfillment of the plan to be a divine mission, as had the Czechoslovak Church, Evangelicals nonetheless saw their church's participation as a "joyous duty," an "opportunity . . . to bear witness through increased fervor."[77]

Although devoting less attention to Marxist theory than either the Czechoslovak or Roman Catholic churches, the Evangelicals recognized the power of communist ideas and the need to formulate a position toward it. In the view of Břetislav Hladký, editor of *Kostnické jiskry*, communism, bolstered by its successes, had sounded a clarion call to all other movements, "above all Christianity, to overcome it or be overcome by it."[78] At an Evangelical conference in the late summer of 1946, the influence of J. L. Hromádka led to the adoption of a resolution that acknowledged that communism was "a most striking and radical sociopolitical and cultural movement, which to a large extent gives this era its character." In response to the power of communism, the Evangelical Church leadership maintained that it could "have no *religious* objections" to communism, but stressed that religious conviction had to take precedence over political belief. Nonetheless, they did take a small step toward condoning communism by pointing out that "our faith and morality often reflect our material interests rather than our obedience to the living God."[79]

In a reaction that bears witness to the success of the Communist Party's reinvention of itself, church leaders stressed the changed character of the party, particularly its view of religion. Hromádka observed that many people interpreted the Communists' tolerant attitude toward religion as a mere smoke screen while they waited for a "suitable time" for attack. He, however, believed that the Communist Party had truly changed and contrasted it favorably to the Roman Catholic, but nominally nonconfessional, People's Party.[80] The Communist Party's behavior after liberation testified to, in the view of the church, "the deep changes in the party."[81] *Kostnické jiskry*'s editor considered the new, tolerant face of the Communist Party toward religion to be

> a sincere expression—undeformed by tactics—of today's communist think-
> ing. . . . [I]t is a markedly different voice than that to which we have become ac-
> customed from the prewar ranks of the proletarian unbelievers. This new rela-
> tionship coincides with the new position on the church that official Russia has
> recently adopted.[82]

This impression was only reinforced by the Zdeněk Nejedlý's pronounce-ment that he stood against the separation of church and state. This was wel-come, if surprising, news for a community that had "prepared for [separation] and had come to terms with it."[83]

Evangelical intellectuals manifested a further weakness that was common in the democratic socialist camp: the belief that Czech communists were Czechs first and communists only second. One author held that "our com-munists are not always attentive students of Moscow," and that "our com-munists are more cosmopolitan than most." The success of the Communist Party's moderation is witnessed in the Evangelical statement, "[It] wants to be a mass and national party. Class struggle is admittedly a reality, but it is not a stressed program." The reputation of the Evangelical Church would only suffer if "it continue[d] in the old [antipathetic] conceptions, which today cor-respond to almost nothing." The author concluded with a responsible pre-election analysis: "It would be good if the [Communist] Party comes out of the elections strong enough to bear this responsibility [of governing] but not strong enough that it gains a taste for dictatorially excluding the others from cooperation."[84] Hromádka took this electoral hope for Communist electoral success even further by arguing that without "a powerful and disciplined Communist Party the danger of social and political reaction cannot be warded off." While falling short of endorsing the Party, Hromádka had no difficulty in proclaiming communism a better society.[85] Similarly, in one of the most outrageous statements of the era, František Bednář (a professor of church law no less) urged students and professors at the School of Theology to "above all, look at *the goals* of the various systems and in no way at their perhaps revolutionary and transitional methods of action" in deciding whom to support politically.[86] Similarly, Hromádka dismissed the threat of dictatorship from the Communist Party. He argued that dictatorship had been historically necessary in Russia, and placed his trust in the "Communist philosophers and officials [who] stress the temporary and transitional character of the socialist dictatorship of the proletariat." He implied—in keeping with the "Czechoslovak road"—that the Czech variant of communism would not need the dictatorship of the proletariat because different conditions obtained in Czechoslovakia than had held in Russia. For him, "the reality remains that communism, regardless of its idea or practice of dictatorship, is fundamentally not absolutist or totalitarian."[87]

Given the stress Hromádka placed on the international context, the Communists' "Czechoslovak road" also gained in credibility from the Evangelical leader's views of the USSR. In contrast to both Catholic intellectuals' warnings and the close relationship of the Czechoslovak Church to the USSR, Hromádka maintained two independent viewpoints, both of which strengthened the "Czechoslovak road." In one major article he stressed that Czechs had "no right to doubt" the freedom of the clergy in the USSR and praised the culture of the Soviet Union. He considered the morality of the Soviet youth as especially exemplary, providing an interesting contrast to the suspicions he harbored of young Czechs. Simultaneously, he maintained in the same article and elsewhere that communism should not be equated with the conditions obtaining in the USSR.[88] By the former he aided the communists only generally, but the latter had a more pernicious effect, by strengthening the notion that there could be a "Czechoslovak" variant of not only the road to socialism but of the end product as well. The employment of these two arguments together also implies that there was public suspicion of the USSR and of communist society: if the Soviet Union was worthy of Hromádka's high praise, why then stress that Czechoslovak communism could be different? Of the elements of the "Czechoslovak road to socialism" pointed out earlier, only two received critical commentary within the church. The mass membership drives the Communists Party sponsored and its call for gaining 51 percent of the vote were obliquely criticized. Evangelicals expressed some concern that these could lead to the doling out of privileges to party members and "lower [the Party's] moral quality" through dilution across a wider membership.[89]

Because the Evangelicals were not on the road to a "new Christianity," they were, on the whole, less committed to achieving a synthesis between communism and Christianity. This does not mean that they did not see an affinity. In fact, Hromádka saw communism as having "the character of a religious movement" and as the inheritor of many of Christianity's most important elements. He recognized the difficulty of reconciling this with Marxist atheism at a 1946 Evangelical conference: "It ranks among the most

intriguing paradoxes of our history that so much of the Christian heritage became the slogan of socialist representatives marching under an anti-religious
and anti-church banner."[90] This argument was supported by *Kostnické jiskry*
in an article that compared the early Christian church and communism and
concluded that "as long as we are faithful to Christ, we will in the end also
be socialists and in the most pure sense communists."[91] Although Hromádka
noted the historical irony, he did not go any further in examining the potential implications, believing instead that the atheism often expressed by communist ideologues was unimportant. Since for him "the classical theory of
communism is (as has often been shown) secularized Christian theology,"
the movement's atheism should be seen as "a practical reaction to the forces
of pre-socialist society rather than a positive, philosophically more important
position."[92] For another writer in the church, communism could not be accused of amorality, for it was bringing with it the "*new morality*" of the work
brigades. Even in the classless society of the future, the "*fundamental moral
questions*" would remain, he argued, for decisions regarding how to treat
"the selfish, the envious, [and] the oppressors" would endure.[93] Here the pro-
jected function of morality in a socialist society became coterminal with decisions on the appropriate meting out of socialist justice.

Although the Evangelical Church did not imply that the Communist Party
was the vanguard of the Kingdom of God, as did the Czechoslovak Church,
the concept did play some role in church rhetoric. Stanislav Čapek argued that

> It is possible to realize the Kingdom of God only through a change of character,
> spirit, and heart, not by a change in the social order. Paradise on Earth will not
> grow immediately after the removal of a few hundred capitalists . . . . Socializa-
> tion, étatization, and nationalization are not a magic formula.[94]

This was the standard argument in the circle around *Kostnické jiskry*. As
Amadeo Molnár argued, "The Kingdom of God, yes, and a Kingdom of God
on Earth, but a kingdom that relies above all on God, on His government. It
is not primarily about the transformation of society and its order."[95]
Hromádka was the lone radical in these terms, seeing the Kingdom of God
in a similar way to the Czechoslovak Church. For him, communism was also
a stepping-stone toward it, although the transformation must continue even
beyond it: "our history will not stop even with communism."[96]

Evangelical intellectuals criticized their colleagues in both the Roman
Catholic and Czechoslovak churches. Evangelicals were quick to point out
that Czech Catholics had served their nation well in the war and had proven
themselves more resistant to the allure of fascism than their co-religionists in
other lands. Nonetheless, the memory of Catholicism's association with the
Austro-Hungarian Empire remained with Evangelical intellectuals. Because
they perceived that "Communism and Catholicism are two powers that are
mutually exclusive," the Evangelical Church considered any cooperation
with the People's Party impossible.[97] This was in part because Evangelicals

"had no small objection to the idea of defending Christianity through the help of a definite political party," and believed that their place was "close to those who are moving pioneeringly forward."[98] More important, however, was the confessional issue. Doubts were legitimately cast on the non-confessional nature of the People's Party, and an analysis of the electoral situation revealed that Evangelical small businessmen and farmers would not vote for the party for confessional reasons. In short, it was clear "that for reasons of conscience we cannot vote for the People's Party. . . . In essence, there are historical and spiritual reasons that prevent a Czech Evangelical from having a positive position toward this party."[99] Further inhibiting Evangelical-Catholic cooperation was the distrust Evangelical intellectuals had of the wider Catholic world. While *Kostnické jiskry* only went so far as to question why the Catholic press, so critical of communist politics, was not as critical of the Vatican's, Hromádka was more venomous. He saw communism and "international Catholicism" as two forces that could end up in a "catastrophic conflict." Even in this, his major concern was that Western Protestants would not understand the true nature of the conflict and would erroneously support "the anti-Soviet Catholic front."[100]

Evangelicals were on only slightly better terms with the Czechoslovak Church. Squabbles occasionally broke out over issues as small as the wording of Czechoslovak Church documents.[101] It seems that the Evangelicals' patronizing attitude toward their Czechoslovak Church brethren was related to the latter's postwar growth and radicalism as much as to the Evangelicals' consideration of the denomination as composed of theologically unsound newcomers. In a blistering, two-part article from late 1947, Hladký expressed indignation at his church being considered "orthodox" and traditional by the Czechoslovak Church. He accused his attackers of still being infected with Catholicism, of having "the remains of a Catholic lack of understanding and Catholic rationalist moralism" in a dangerous mix with "a progressivist and modernist ideology." He condemned the Czechoslovak Church as having "a grab-bag of ideas" that made it difficult for Evangelical intellectuals "to take this church theologically seriously." Finally, perhaps out of envy at the Czechoslovak Church's ability to gain converts, he stabbed at the Czechoslovak Church's recent foundation, writing, "We look at it with indulgence, as at a younger sister, who must go through her childhood years before one can talk to her seriously."[102]

On issues of freedom and democracy, the stance the church adopted was, as on other issues, one having evolutionary socialist conceptions and a base in Christian belief. In this sense the church held that freedom had to be tempered by self-discipline and that "true democracy grows from the principles of Christian morality."[103] More radical views also existed within the church, with Hromádka's again among the most extreme. He maintained that the West only played "the game of democratic methods" and became "peevish or angry when other nations decided on a different type of political behavior." It was this variety of "democratic formalism" that had been present in the interwar Czechoslovak Republic, had become "a tool of privilege and capital interest," and had been unwilling or unable to defend the state.[104] This view was echoed in *Kostnické jiskry*, where Czechoslovakia's shift from a "liberal" to "a people's or socialist" democracy was sketched, and the conclusion drawn that "a Reformation church cannot be anything but positive to this change."[105] Hromádka, not one for understatement, indirectly accused democratic socialist intellectuals of acting as a Trojan horse for evil capitalists:

> Doesn't one smell, behind all these ringing slogans about "free democracy," behind all these endeavors to "defend personal freedom" and "free enterprise" . . . the material, economic interest of big industry and financial concerns?

For a man often portrayed in a positive light for his role in the 1968 attempt to create "socialism with a human face," Hromádka's statements betrayed a dangerous lack of concern for the fate of his countrymen. In perhaps the most outrageous of these, he maintained the position that the country should depend more heavily on the organization of socialist construction, and less on "individual or press freedom. Discipline, service, responsibility, self-control and self-sacrifice are in certain circumstances more important than human rights."[106]

Despite Hromádka's dangerous misjudgments of the international situation and of the development potential of Czech communism, there was one point on which he saw the situation clearly and critically: the relative practical and conceptual strengths of the communist and noncommunist forces. He weighed the ideas and practices of the two camps and emerged convinced of the political superiority of left-wing forces in the nation. Not only did he believe that the left "represents by its program, level of organization and certainty . . . the social and political tendency of the future," but that the "communists and radical (or left-) socialists have a program. They know how the social order should look, they are conceptually certain and solid." The Communist Party appeared to him the leading force in the nation, because it "has the clearest program . . . is the most disciplined and . . . knows where it is going." In contrast to this, he correctly identified one source of the democratic socialists' weakness, that they were "dismally dispersed." Nonetheless, even here he became carried away by his own insight, attributing the democratic socialists' lack of unity and conceptual clarity to being "united only by a mood of dissatisfaction, anti-communist indignation, and fear."[107] This final comment differs only in rhetorical degree from Václav Kopecký's ranting that in opposition to communism there stood no strong conceptual system, but only "reaction, decadence, pessimism, nihilism, existentialism, marasmus, putrefaction, finality, and death," a fitting note on which to end the examination of Protestant views.[108]

This analysis of the Czechoslovak Church and the Evangelical Church of the Czech Brethren shows that the view common since the 1950s, that the Protestant churches were a focus of dissent and resistance, is only partly true. While it is certainly the case for the Roman Catholic Church in the first post-war years, it is certainly not for the two most prominent non-Catholic denominations. Although far smaller than their Catholic counterpart, they still represented a sizable portion of the Czechoslovak population. Their willingness to enlist in the cause of radical social change and to use their spiritual and theological authority to foster enthusiasm on the part of their flocks betrays either a failure or lack of will to see the potential dangers to their land.

The primary differences between the two churches are matters of rhetorical heat and willingness to partake in directly political discussion. The Czechoslovak Church gave itself over wholeheartedly to political radicalism (which was rewarded in February 1948) and theological radicalism (which was not, as their new Christianity was never found and the Kingdom of God never came). The Evangelical Church was more restrained and remained theologically more traditional, but nonetheless placed itself largely at the service of a radical socialist political program. Nevertheless, it is relatively easier to find sympathy for the Evangelicals, who seem at least to have been attempting to ride the currents of history and to infuse the radical socialist movement with Christian principles. Unfortunately, its by far most visible leader, Hromádka, was also among its most radical. His responsibility continues beyond the communist assumption of power, as a result of his continuing support for the regime even at its harshest. The behavior of the intellectual, theological, and ecclesiastical leaders of the million-member Czechoslovak Church, on the other hand, was irresponsible and dangerous in the extreme. By outpacing even the Communist Party, they only fanned the flames of political radicalism, leading their flocks toward the gates of a spiritual and material paradise they called the Kingdom of God, which, in reality, became gates more resembling those of a concentration camp. Although Czechoslovak Church adherents apparently began to suspect this, they did not shrink back from their leaders until months after February 1948. By then, the church's bill for its adventurism had come due.

Conclusion

The End of Czechoslovak Democracy and the Rise of Communism in Eastern Europe

> The world does not evolve according to textbooks, but according to people. If the communists continue to be more agile, more energetic, and more intrepid than others, then in the end they will win, and they would deserve victory.
>
> —Ferdinand Peroutka, "Hlavní úkol naší politiky"

> Our, the democrats', fault was not so much political as rather moral. Together with the Communists, we deceived our own nation, here consciously, there unconsciously, and sometimes we did not dare to speak the truth.
>
> —Pavel Tigrid

In February of 1948 the Communist Party, and its allies in the other parties, gained total power in Czechoslovakia. The events of those days have been much discussed, and there is no need for their extensive recapitulation here. In the following, we will return to the questions posed in the introduction concerning the ease with which the communists acceded to this power. A fundamental reason for the weakness of the democratic forces, I will contend, lay in the culture communists and noncommunists alike, with the general exception of Roman Catholics, together created in the period between May 1945 and those February days. In many ways, February represented only the culmination of a break in the continuity of modern Czech history, not the break itself. Munich and the Second World War caused the true break in the continuity of Czech political, social, and cultural development, one that only became visible in 1945. The experiences of 1938–1945 triggered a set of radical changes that manifested themselves after liberation, changes that considerably eased the Communists' road to total power. The war did not constitute a break only in Czech continuities, however. It reshuffled the social, political, and economic deck across Eastern Europe, as the first chapter of this study showed. The Czech example was in some ways unique—for example, the Poles had no Munich, but rather Soviet invasion and the atrocities of the Katyń forest—but in other ways the Czech case sheds light on the shifting attitudes and perspectives caused by the war. With the Cold War now over, and the eastern half of the Continent on its "return to Europe," the time is ripe for a reassessment of how communism came to power in the region, one distanced from our knowledge that the story ended in the horrors of Stalinism.

THE END OF CZECHOSLOVAK DEMOCRACY

When the representatives of the National Socialist, People's, and Slovak Democratic parties handed in their resignations on February 20, 1948, over the matter of Communist Party abuse of the police force, they were not aware that they had signed their political death warrants. Above all, they believed that President Beneš would not accept their resignations, and that either the Communists would have to retreat on the police issue or that new elections would be called. They also felt they had an issue whose importance would be clear to the public and that the public would support them. Finally, they anticipated that the government crisis would be solved in a parliamentary-democratic way, through negotiations among the party leaderships, parliament, and the president. None of this was the case.

In resigning, these noncommunist ministers made several errors of a tactical nature. Crucially, they failed to secure the resignations of a majority of ministers, neither gaining the support of right-wing Social Democrats nor, as a bare minimum, that of the non-party foreign minister, Jan Masaryk. This left the status of the government in doubt, since the resignation of a majority of ministers was constitutionally necessary for the government to fall and new elections to be required. Equally importantly, they had not prepared for any other solution to the crisis they had initiated, such as the one with which the Communists presented them by mobilizing the public on the streets. In a sense, the Communist Party received precisely what it desired: its opponents had deserted the government and taken only one step (consulting the president) in preparation for the final confrontation. As Klement Gottwald put it six weeks later: "At first, I couldn't believe it would be so easy. But then it turned out that this is just what happened— they handed in their resignations. . . . I prayed that this stupidity over the resignations would continue and that they would not change their minds."[1]

The response the Communist Party mustered to the resignations was impressive. Within days, hundreds of thousands of protesters were flooding the streets of Czech cities and towns, filling the squares to hear Gottwald's speeches to the nation. The Communist Party's leader called for action committees to be formed in all institutions of public life, the mission of which was to remove the party's opponents from positions of influence. These committees were rapidly and enthusiastically formed across the country, including—odd though it may sound—in the Union of Friends of the United States (*Svaz přátel* USA). Huge daily marches were held in support of the party, and a one-hour general strike was held on February 24th, gaining the participation of millions of workers.[2] The following day, a crowd of 250,000 pro-communist demonstrators in Prague, and hundreds of thousands elsewhere across the nation, waited for Beneš to declare whether he would accept the Communist Party's solution to the crisis. Their proposal was for the president to accept the ministers' tendered resignations and to allow the Communists to fashion a government composed of their party's representatives and selected members, i.e., fellow travelers, from the other parties. In support of the opposing camp, which hoped for Beneš to accept the resignations, declare the government fallen, and call for elections, a few thousand students marched past the Prague Castle, demonstrating no more than their support for the president. Likewise, the President's Chancellery received 5,327 resolutions supporting the Communists' solution, and only 150 opposing. The last hope for popular support for the noncommunist forces, the peasantry, failed to provide opposition to the Communist Party: "only those [farmers] influenced by the Communists spoke out."[3] In the face of all this, Beneš conceded defeat and accepted Gottwald's cabinet. The communist victory was complete. Just as in 1945, when the society was radically reconstructed in distinction to its prewar incarnation, "this break in continuity evoked no widespread public protest."[4] In fact, Vilém Prečan has observed that "With a certain, but not great, amount of exaggeration it is possible to say that broad segments of the Czech nation welcomed the power monopoly of the [Communist Party], if not with flying banners then at least without general, visible, or marked opposition."[5]

Why were the noncommunists so ill-prepared for the final showdown? Why could they not call out supporting masses to counter those protesting for the Communist Party? Their weakness lay both in tactics and in the overall political mood of the postwar Czech nation. Tactically, since they had not foreseen the crisis leaving the government's meeting rooms and becoming a public event on the streets of the country, they failed adequately to inform their local representatives about the planned resignations and to prepare their supporters for the possible consequences. Their party structures and affiliated organizations neither knew precisely what was happening nor what their response should be. Pavel Tigrid has criticized this, pointing out that all the most important activity took place in Prague:

> To average Czechoslovak people, namely, those who lived outside of Prague, the victory of [the Communist Party] in February 1948 must have seemed like a lightning-quick knockout blow, delivered to an unguarded opponent unexpect-

edly in the third or fourth round of a fight that everybody expected with certainty would go the distance and carefully according to the rules. But the knockout came, and few knew how it really happened that overnight the Communists were in power. For that matter they do not know even today what really happened, how the democratic defender so quickly surrendered his title. It was almost exclusively a Prague affair. The nation behaved at that time as has almost become a tradition in periods of crisis, when (also almost traditionally) a clear order on what to do does not arrive.[6]

In this respect, the Roman Catholic People's Party, based in Moravia and with less than 15 percent support in and around Prague, became largely an onlooker to the Prague-centered public events. This was only reinforced by the fact that the journals on the religious wing of Czech postwar political Catholicism were also based in Moravia, while those on its political wing, *Obzory* and *Vývoj*, were among the first to be shut down.[7] Furthermore, the supporters of political Catholicism were not given to public displays to the same degree as were those of other groups. For different reasons, the Social Democrats also played a minor role. They lay paralyzed, "dreading a Communist defeat just as much as a Communist victory," and calling for the maintenance of a National Front government that had ceased to exist. This is hardly surprising, as the continuation of the National Front was "the only basis for preventing the fragmentation of the party."[8] All of these factors contributed to making this final showdown one between two socialist opponents—National Socialists and Communists—with the largely Moravian Roman Catholics and debilitated Social Democrats consigned, in large measure, to the sidelines.

The perilous state of noncommunist affairs had roots in the National Socialist political leadership's intellectual inability to foresee any possible solution to the crisis other than the parliamentary-democratic one upon which they counted. Even after the waves of demonstrations had commenced, they urged their supporters to remain calm, rather than to counterprotest. Not only did they not encourage their supporters, they agreed, according to Prokop Drtina, that "as long as it was not urgently necessary, we did not want to proceed to appealing to the support of the public."[9] The same holds true for National Socialist intellectuals, who committed what Peter Hruby has called "moral and national hara-kiri." As illustration, he recalls the following episode from February 24:

> I went to Professor František Kovárna. . . . I hoped to find him in the middle of preparations for countering the *coup* and wanted to offer help. . . . He said that our nation would not follow such a demagogue as Gottwald, that President Beneš was holding everything in his hands, and that surprisingly I, who always seemed to be so calm, was exaggerating, becoming hysterical for no good reason, should go home and calm down, that nothing would happen, and that there was no need to take any action.[10]

These and other procedural and tactical deficiencies in the noncommunist camp have been noted before, but a perhaps even more fundamental weakness lies in the less visible sphere of cultural and political attitudes. With the partial exception of Roman Catholics, who remained largely outside the course of the February events, the public discourse carried on by the democratic socialist intellectuals dangerously weakened the national political self-understanding. The Czech noncommunist public either largely could not see the implications of the events transpiring around them, or saw them as nothing radically new. This larger conceptual crisis in Czech democracy has only rarely been brought to light. Vladimir Kusin has observed, "The rallying cry of 'defense of democracy' and 'resistance to a police State' did not have the expected effect on the population."[10] Likewise, Otto Friedman has argued that organizing resistance

> was particularly difficult for Czech democrats, who had persisted in minimizing the difference between Western democracy and Soviet "democracy" and had thereby failed to prepare their followers for the danger of a Communist *putsch*. . . . No wonder that at this hour of peril the democratic leaders did not know how loyal their closest democratic collaborators were and whether they were willing to risk their lives to defend one kind of "democracy" against another. . . . Instead of stigmatizing the Czech Communists' subservience to Stalin and their deceptive idealization of the Soviet dictatorship, some democratic leaders lent support to Communist propaganda by their own publicity. In this manner, they demoralized their own adherents.[12]

For this state of affairs, democratic writers, political thinkers, journalists, and social critics—the broadly construed noncommunist intellectual leadership—bear a heavy share of blame. These intellectuals mirrored a weakness of their society, one which

> allowed itself to be carried away on a wave of utopian faith characteristic of a politically immature nation: that now it would be able—all at once and in the near future—to solve the problems not only of its own external security, but also to ensure freedom, social justice, and affluence.[13]

Democratic socialist intellectuals particularly served as conceptual shepherds, guiding their nation to an end whose features were unclear, but which they promised would be a socialist (even if necessarily not communist) paradise. Once Czech society was refashioned and the socialist citizen properly educated, socialist culture would be ethically advanced, socialist organization would bring material benefits, and the socialist individual would be a higher being. In this way, by "forecasting the victory of socialism over capitalism in Czechoslovakia they were in the enviable position of prophets who assist in the fulfillment of their own prophecies."[14]

They were indeed in such a position. The broadly construed intellectual caste in Czech society had the historically developed legitimacy to speak for the nation. It enjoyed authority and sympathy among the lower and middle classes and a history of Slavism and political activism that suited the postwar environment admirably. Its function in the twentieth century, as the Czech sociologist Arnošt Bláha defined it, was to perform a "spiritualizing function," understood as "the creation of spiritual values, [and] the organization and unifying of society in their name."[15] In postwar Czech society social reform was on the public agenda, as can be seen in the popularity of the nationalization decrees and the fact that in 1946 over three-quarters of the Czech public, in an "undisputed and spontaneous" display of enthusiasm, cast their votes to expressly socialist parties.[16] Democratic socialist intellectuals sought to "spiritualize" socialism and "organize and unify" the society for a socialism that, even to the group's leaders, remained little more than a self-reflexive conceptual matrix. Their responsibility for this task was not only self-assumed, however. They had been called by their nation to provide moral and political leadership, and they had welcomed the task.

The experiences of Munich and the Second World War had made possible the rethinking of the meaning of the nation, its organization and orientation. By calling into question prewar certainties, these experiences decidedly created the conditions for the Czech nation "to become the victim of some 'adventure,' some derailing from prior cultural and historical ties."[17] How the cultural and historical ties would be reconfigured was fought out in the battles examined in part 2 of this study. Communist intellectuals strove to recreate the idea of the Czech nation and to align it with their vision of the proper socialist society, one whose at least general model was the USSR. Their "revision of the national character" reinterpreted the entire national history to accent both its socialist and Slavic features. In this task they had support from both of the prominent Protestant churches active in the period, the million-member Czechoslovak Church and the smaller and more politically moderate Evangelical Church. Democratic socialist intellectuals either adopted compromise positions on the issues discussed, or argued in favor of a synthesis that would purportedly lead to a higher form of "Czechness" and potentially avert the onrushing Cold War. Roman Catholics alone largely resisted this wholesale rethinking of the Czech nation's meaning.

Through their participation in this reinterpretation, noncommunist intellectuals contributed to an atmosphere that weakened Czechs' democratic defenses. Again, the experiences of World War II provided the springboard. Czech intellectuals denigrated the West for its participation in the Munich tragedy and praised the USSR for the physical and, more importantly, moral strength it had shown in defeating the Axis forces. This strength was understood as proof that the Soviet Union's social order was more just and efficient. In a larger sense, Soviet culture was also seen as superior, because the socialist qualities it imbued in the state's citizens were seen as having made possible the wartime victory. Czech intellectuals denigrated their own interwar republic and either placed the Communist-led postwar republic on a pedestal or saw it as a beneficial "correction" of its interwar antecedent. This break with the prewar era can also be witnessed in the scorn heaped on "liberal democracy" and "liberal freedom," and the concomitant raising of Tomáš G. Masaryk's socialist pedigree. The most powerful evidence of the shift in mentality was revealed symbolically, in the differing meanings attached to the holidays of October 28th and May 5th. Not only was the latter seen as overcoming or completing the former, but its identification with a young and politically active generation testifies to the allure of radicalism in postwar Czech society.

The politically loaded reinterpretations of the national past, present, and future culminated in a large-scale swing in Czech cultural self-consciousness away from historic ties to the West and toward the Slavic and socialist East. The Czech intellectual caste presided over this, the most fundamental shift in self-representation the nation has ever undergone. All political currents, with the partial exception of the Roman Catholic, trumpeted the glories of an ill-defined "Slavic solidarity" and stood behind President Beneš's plans for a "new Slavic politics." Democratic socialists' efforts to salvage a portion of the Czech nation's Western self-understanding gave rise to a messianic vision of saving all of humanity by uniting the socialism of the East with Western cultural and political freedoms. The Czech nation was held to be uniquely capable of carrying out a synergetic synthesis whose contours remained unclear and whose practical possibility was never rigorously examined.

As a result, Czechs' traditional understandings of themselves and their nation lost their moorings, revealing evident political dangers. Above all, this ongoing reorientation affected traditional notions of freedom, democracy, and socialism, as well as conceptions of political behavior as a whole. If the interwar republic, praised a mere decade before, was imperfect to a high degree, then the fundamental political philosophy on which it rested must also be suspect. Further, the reinterpretations favored the left wing of an already truncated political spectrum. This wing was dominated by the Communist Party, whose Marxism offered a coherent and comprehensive cultural and political philosophy that provided consistent answers to the questions raised by the war. Communist ideology's considerable explanatory power was magnified by the support of Protestant religious leaders and presented a sharp contrast to democratic socialists' synthetic and compromise positions, positions which both lacked Marxism's solid theoretical foundation and differed considerably from one another. Roman Catholicism proved more immune to this, since it rested on a centuries-old conceptual framework. Moreover, the faith of Roman Catholic believers better insulated them against the collapse of values brought about by Munich and the war.

When the debate over the meaning of socialism intensified, the communists reaped the political rewards of their success in the "revision of the national character." In the battle over socialism, the Communist Party's moderation played distinctly to its advantage, and in many ways the Communist cultural offensive was more radical than its political offensive. The party's leading politicians and intellectuals were able to capitalize on the popularity of the postwar reorganization of the state to claim many features of postwar Czechoslovak government policy as their own. Further, the party was able to claim the title of socialist party *par excellence* and thus avoid discussing precisely where their "Czechoslovak road" would lead the state. The strategy of maintaining a commitment to the major elements of the people's democratic system—particularly the National Front, the Two-Year Plan, and parliamentary democracy (through the politics of gaining a majority of the vote)— brought them rhetorically closer to their democratic socialist opponents. Throughout this debate they could rely on the wholehearted support of often irresponsible Czechoslovak Church leaders and on that of the more circumspect leadership of the Evangelical Church. In the struggle over the meaning of socialism, just as in the struggle over the nation's history and orientation, the Communist Party essentially outmaneuvered its opponents, proving itself the "more agile, more energetic, and more intrepid" political force, precisely as Peroutka had feared.

The effects of the shift in national self-understanding on the events of February cannot be precisely measured, but the intellectual complicity of Protestant and democratic socialist leaders in Czechoslovakia's fate must be recognized. The latter group's enthusiasm for socialism both led, and to some extent was led by, the nation into a venture whose outcome it never clearly formulated. President Beneš's admitted that he had no "clear and precise" notion of the end state of Czechoslovakia's "socializing democracy," and Hubert Ripka later conceded that the democratic socialist endeavor was a "political experiment, which was not without audacity."[18] Democratic socialists' recognition that they were experimenting with the future of their nation neither dampened their enthusiasm by nourishing caution, nor encouraged an intellectually rigorous debate over the implications of socialism in their land. Moreover, it led to no critical public examination of developments in the fraternal "people's democracies," one that might have revealed the hazards of their experiment.

The Communists could rely on both the theoretical foundation of Marxism and the practical elements—the fulfilling of the Two-Year Plan and the winning of a majority—contained in the "Czechoslovak road." In opposition to this, democratic socialists could muster only vague notions of a "new democracy," a "socializing democracy," a "socialist humanism," and a messianic vision of uniting Eastern socialism with Western freedom. As in the debates over the nation's history and meaning, democratic socialists found themselves internally disunited, theoretically bereft and, after the elections of 1946, increasingly on the defensive. The costs of this became evident in February, when their supporters, if they were to act at all, were to stand up and defend freedom and democracy in Czechoslovakia. The former of these issues had led to the initially sharpest conflict between communist and democratic socialists, in the clash between the Kulturní obec and the Kulturní svaz. However, democratic socialists sacrificed the opportunity to launch an analysis of the internal conditions of the state thus presented on the altar of socialist solidarity. Instead, they professed their hope for some vague socialist-communist convergence on the road to a classless society.

In February 1948 the issues must have seemed unclear to the Czech public. Were true democrats to stand up for liberal democracy, socialist democracy, the people's democracy, or socializing democracy? Were they to counter the communists on the streets and in the action committees for liberal freedom, socialist freedom, or a higher freedom to be achieved by synergetic synthesis? Was opposition to the Communist Party an act inimical to the ideals of the "new Slavic politics?" Were Czechs to risk bloodshed, or at least the loss of their careers, to support the democratic socialist "struggle for the new man" instead of the communists' same struggle? Even granting that democratic socialists were both democratic (as they understood democracy), and socialist (as they understood socialism), one has to ask if they presented their ideas and ideals clearly, coherently, and consistently enough for the public to be able to clearly distinguish between what "we," the true democrats, stood for, and what "they," the incipient totalitarians, stood for. The road to the Communist Party's domination of Czechoslovakia was paved with democratic socialists' good intentions, but also by their failure to explain clearly their vision of the Czechoslovak future and to differentiate it from that of a Communist Party that commanded an enormous membership, was well organized, and had internally coherent views not only of the recent past, but also of the steps to be taken in the present. In this sense, the democratic socialists' loss was tragic in the truest sense of the word.

In many ways, however, democratic socialists were shackled by the times in which they acted. The experiences of Munich, occupation, and war had not made moderation a virtue, and the allure of Marxism and the Soviet Union reached a crest across Europe as a whole after the defeat of Nazi Germany. The argument can be made that if Czechoslovakia and France, whose nexus of intellectual and political action mirrors the Czechs', were to have traded locations and sizes, the French would have ended up in much the same predicament as the Czechs, although without the recalcitrant Slovaks to drag along behind them. Nonetheless, Czech democratic socialists had been co-creators already during the war of the institutional, political, and cultural contexts in which they would be operating after liberation. In this sense, the flaws of Czechoslovak democracy can be found in the wartime past, in Czech intellectuals' plans for the future in both the underground resistance and the London exile. As Vilém Hejl has argued:

> The February tragedy was already prepared in London. . . . The majority of the exile government blindly trusted Beneš and without objection accepted and peddled the vague terms "revolutionary politics," and "new democracy," "Slavism" and "socialization," without even thinking about who would carry out this "revolution," against whom and by what means, how much democracy would survive in the "new democracy," how "socialization" would appear in practice, and what the meaning of "Slavism" in the international position of the republic would be.[19]

THE COMING OF COMMUNISM TO EASTERN EUROPE

What lessons does the collapse of postwar Czech democracy hold for the historian of twentieth-century Eastern Europe? Above all, it shows that the war had proved a spur to social radicalism, putting a definitive end to the prewar regimes. Czechoslovakia, because of the length of time that elapsed between the end of the war and the Communist Party's achievement of total power, gives us a more visible window into the public mood of the region. The almost three years of ideological and political struggle in that country meant that the public forum of the press remained relatively unhindered and that we have a much better possibility of recreating the discussions of the period there than elsewhere. As I have shown, those discussions were indicative of a public mood favorable to radical social reform, and particularly to communism broadly construed.

It would be beyond the scope and intent of this study to attempt to delineate the sources and levels of support for communist politics across the Eastern European region. However, a few observations are in order before concluding with ideas on unexplored paths of research on various social groupings likely to have provided the communists with support. Above all, there were only three states in which the Communist Party undeniably had widespread authority: Yugoslavia, Bulgaria, and Czechoslovakia. While it is impossible to gauge the true level of support Tito's party had, it is very likely that, had the 1945 elections taken place freely and fairly, the communists would have received a majority of the ballots cast, perhaps even as many as two-thirds.[20] Given the Bulgarian Communist Party's intimidation and outright terror, combined with the high level of Soviet support, it is impossible to assess the true popularity of that party. However, the Fatherland Front officially received almost three-quarters of the Bulgarian vote in October 1946, with the Communists alone taking a majority of all ballots cast. It is reasonable to conclude that the party could count on the support of between one-quarter and one-third of the population.[21] Finally, as we have seen, the communists received 38 percent of the Czechoslovak vote in the free elections of 1946, clear evidence of their political authority.

In the other states of the region, the communists and their allies in "national front" coalitions surely had less support. Nonetheless, it is crucial to note that they had a not inconsiderable level of popularity, in comparison with the miniscule support they would likely have gathered before the war. In the Hungarian elections of 1946, the Communist Party received 17 percent of the vote. While the party's leaders were clearly dissatisfied with the results, this figure still means that, for whatever reason, over one in six Hungarian voters gave the party their vote.[22] In Poland, often seen as the country most inhospitable to communist politics, the results of the elections of January 1947 were so fraudulent as to invalidate drawing any conclusions. However, recent work on the 1946 referendum under the direction of Andrzej Paczkowski provides us with a window into Polish public opinion.[23] His team found in a reconstruction of that vote that perhaps 27 percent of Polish voters voted with the Polish Workers' Party to abolish the interwar senate. This indicates that almost one-quarter of the population was willing to support the communists on an issue that was of little consequence in itself, but which the opposition intended to use to chasten the Polish Communists.

In the remaining two Eastern European states, Romania and Albania, reasonable figures are very difficult to ascertain. In the former, after massive irregularities and intimidation, the communist-led National Democratic Bloc won some 70 percent of the vote and 347 of the 383 parliamentary seats. Given the erosion of Romania's traditional parties, the communists would likely have done very well in any case.[24] Whether they would have received, either through real belief, opportunism, or resignation, a majority of the ballot must at this time remain an open question. Still, a reasonable assessment would place Romanian support for the Communists at between one-quarter and one-third.[25] Albania remains the most inscrutable, since the elections of December 1945 resulted in an overwhelming victory for the Democratic Front, and no other data that have become available have shed any light on the true sensibilities of the Albanian population in the immediate aftermath of the war.

The preceding paragraphs have been intended to demonstrate that, unlike in the Cold War version of the immediate postwar period with which I and many others grew up, communism did not come to Eastern Europe solely on the backs of Red Army tanks. There was at least substantial support for the Communist parties of the region in each country, and quite significant support in several. This should come as no surprise, given the events these populations experienced during the war or even since 1918. As the first chapter of this study described, Eastern Europeans lived through a maelstrom in the first half of the twentieth century. They experienced right-wing national dictatorships, economic collapse, and then a war almost incomprehensible in its brutality. Those that survived, and particularly the youth among them, were

truly ripe for revolution. The fact that perhaps one-quarter of them were willing to support their national Communist parties fits with the observation
made in the initial chapter that those parties' Western European counterparts
received over 10 percent of the vote in eight countries, reaching 28 percent
in France. This indicates that, while the wartime experiences on the two
halves of the continent are comparable, there is likely a link between the
heightened levels of death, destruction, and brutality on its eastern half and
a similarly high level of political radicalization in the wake of the war.

One conclusion that should be drawn from this is that a rethinking of the
dominant periodization needs to occur. Driven by the dominating presence
of the Cold War and the allure of communism as a subject, Eastern European
history has traditionally been taught and written about with the war's conclusion as a starting point. This makes sense: the war ended and a new era
began. However, thinking about Eastern Europe in this way conceals the
massive impact the war had on the region. In order to understand what happened in the region after 1945, it is absolutely necessary to understand what
happened there between 1938 and 1945. Undoubtedly, knowledge of the
character and developments of the interwar years also adds much to understanding what happened after the war. However, it is clear that one cannot
talk about communist Eastern Europe without discussing World War II, the
event that made the rise of communist dictatorships possible.

Among these populations, who then supported the Communists' aims, in
all or in part? There were a number of social groups that stood to benefit
from the Communists' policies, and future research aiming to present a more
nuanced view of how the communists came to total power in the region
should look first at them. Perhaps foremost among them should come the
working class, the group in whose name the Communist Party claimed to
speak. Much of the Communists' attention was devoted to this stratum, and
just how effective their message was is poorly understood. The growth of
this class during the war gave it new strength, and the necessities of reconstruction made it politically important. Certainly some sections of the Eastern
European proletariat had stood behind left-wing politics before the war, and
it seems reasonable to assume that this faction would grow in its aftermath.
This is not to represent the working class as anything resembling a monolithic bloc. As Padraic Kenney's work has shown, there were significant differences along sectoral, regional, and gender lines in the way in which sub-
sections of the working class approached, and were approached by, the
Communist Party.[26] Between this study and Jon Bloomfield's work, we have
some notion of the proletariat's reaction to communism, but much work, especially in the Balkans, still needs to be done.[27]

Considering the percentage of the Eastern European population involved
in agriculture, the peasantry has also been woefully under-researched, and
not just for the immediate postwar period. The Communist parties sorely

needed at least the passivity of the rural population, if not its outright support. In the first years after the end of the war, there were a number of reasons for the peasantry, especially the small-holders among them, to support the party. The Communists stood squarely behind land reform and, by actually carrying it out, presented a stark contrast to the interwar capitalist regime's failed promises. Those who benefited from the reform would likely be more apt to support Communist initiatives in other areas, although even those landholders who did not directly gain from the reforms may well have supported them. Further, and despite the Soviet example, collectivization was not discussed publicly, although there can be little doubt that the peasants were suspicious. Much as Kenney showed with the working class, the coming of communism to the countryside seems to have been a process in which the peasantry had considerable agency, which they used to secure their interests against those of the Communist Party. This can perhaps best be seen in Melissa Bokovoy's work on Yugoslavia, although similar processes likely occurred across the region.[28]

There are also smaller but still significant groups whose views should be heard. Elements of the bureaucratic class may have been quite receptive to the Communists' plans, since the powers and social status of this caste would have appreciated markedly in the first postwar years, given the expanding powers of the state. Although positions in the civil service had already been coveted before the war, the expansion of the bureaucracy and the range of activities in which one could make one's mark decidedly raised the attractiveness of working for the state. It also opened the gates to higher income and social status for many outside the social groups from which this caste was traditionally recruited. Similarly, the populations being resettled into areas from which German, Hungarian, or other populations had been expelled should be looked at in more detail. I anticipate many new works on these groups coming out in the next decade, works that likely will bear out the hypothesis that resettled populations had a greater reliance on the state, owed their new possessions to it, were more atomized, and were therefore more likely to support the Communists. Less significant numerically, but important for dispelling a common Eastern European stereotype, are the Jews. It seems reasonable to conclude, as Charles Gati did, that Jews gave rather more support to the Communist Party than their non-Jewish fellow citizens, although not a significant amount more.[29]

Finally, I would hope that this study encourages others to look at the Eastern European intelligentsia. Intellectuals had a perhaps unique public authority across the region, largely derived from the role they played in the nineteenth-century struggles for their nations' independence, an authority that continued deep into the twentieth century. When not silenced by dictatorial governments of the left or right—and, in the case of dissidents under communism, often even when they are—they have a powerful impact on how their societies think and, ultimately, how they behave. They gave voice to the revolutions that swept away the region's Communist dictatorships in the late 1980s and, I would argue, played a significant role in the coming of those dictatorships in the 1940s. Intellectuals certainly seem to outpace their societies in their activism for social change, they certainly also seem to reflect and guide public desires. While social radicalism in the 1940s was clearly most powerful among intellectuals in Czechoslovakia and Yugoslavia, it stands to reason that it was evident to varying degrees elsewhere as well.

It is clear from this short overview that further research will be necessary before we can claim to have a complete picture of the rise of communism in Eastern Europe. Certainly, as noted in chapter 1, the Soviet Union and the Red Army played a role in the process, but aspects of public sympathy, participation, and, some would call it, collaboration, have been unjustly overlooked for much of the last half-century. Only when we have more evidence of the mentality of the region's peoples can we reach consensus on how the Communist Party came to dominate political, cultural, and social life. There are encouraging signs that just such a rethinking is beginning to occur, as a new generation of historians, freed from the burden of the Cold War and able to utilize materials previously kept away from scholars by the regimes of the Soviet bloc, looks at the second half of the twentieth century anew.

Appendix

DOCUMENT 1: ANNOUNCEMENT OF
THE ESTABLISHMENT OF *KULTURNÍ OBEC*

Českým kulturním pracovníkům

Zakládáme Kulturní obec, organizaci, která soustředí a sdruží kulturní pracovníky všech oborů k práci na široké a pevné ideové základně. Varování prožitky hrůzného období fašismu, spojujeme osud světové kultury s osudem pracujícího člověka, osud národní kultury s osudem českého lidu k výstavbě nové společnosti, spravedlivější a svobodnější.

Dějinné sociální a politické změny naší státní a národní základny, k nimž došlo roku 1945, probouzejí mírové budovatelské úsilí českého a slovenského lidu a žadají si souběžného kulturního programu, který by vyrůstal jak z pokrokové národní tradice, tak i z nového vývoje světového.

Potřeba takového programu je dána jednak současným vnitřním existenčním problémem české kultury, jednak jejím dějinným národním posláním. Naš lid za druhé světové války a v jejím vítězném zakončení jednou provždy překonal svou závislost na zhoubných předmnichovských poměrech, mezinárodních i vnitrních. Vstupuje však do nové kostelace dějinných sil, v níž by neobstál, kdyby svou existenci nezdůvodnil pokrokovým rozvinutím svého národního charkteru do svébytné národní kultury.

Proto dnes dáváme popud k vzniku Kulturní obec, spojující pracovníky vědecké, umělecké, lidovýchovné, osvětové a všechny ostatní dělniky ducha ze všech městských a venkovských kulturních středisek k takovým programovým úkol ů m, jejichž ideje by nejen zhojily mravní následky druhé světové války, překonaly ceský 'strach z malosti' a lhostejnost k veřejným otázkám, ale také probudily sebevědomí demokratického národa, žijící z vlastní práce.

Vyzýváme všechny, kdož ať ve městech nebo na venkově pracují a chtějí pracovat v tomto duchu bojovného a činorodého humanismu a vědeckého socialismu, aby vstoupili do naší Kulturní obce![1]

To All Czech Cultural Workers

We are founding Kulturní obec, an organization that will bring together and concentrate cultural workers from all fields to work on a wide and solid ideological foundation. Warned by the experience of the horrible era of fascism, we link the fate of world culture with the fate of the working man, the fate of the national culture with the fortunes of the Czech people in the construction of a more just and free society.

The historic social and political changes in the foundations of our state and nation that came in the year 1945 have awakened the peaceful constructive efforts of the Czech and Slovak people and call for a parallel cultural program that grows from our progressive national traditions as well as from recent world developments.

The need for such a program is given partly by Czech culture's contemporary internal subsistence problems and partly by its historical national calling. Our people during the Second World War and in its victorious conclusion once and for all overcame its dependence on its pernicious pre-Munich relationships, both international and domestic. However, it is entering into a new constellation of historical forces, in which it will not get by if it does not justify its existence through the progressive development of its national character into a distinctive national culture.

That is why today we are taking the initiative in originating Kulturní obec, uniting scientific, artistic and educational workers and all other workers of the spirit from all urban and rural cultural centers for these programmatic tasks, whose ideas will not only heal the moral consequences of the Second World War, and overcome the Czech "fear of smallness" and indifference to public affairs, but also awaken the self-consciousness of a democratic nation, living from its own labor.

We call to all of those, whether working in the city or in the countryside, who want to work in this spirit of active and fighting humanism and scientific socialism to join our Kulturní obec.

E. F. Burian, Václav Dobiáš, Franktišek Halas, Vl. Haškovec, Bohuslav Havránek, Ferd. Herčík, Ant. Hobza, A. Hoffmeister, Jindřich Honzl, Václav Husa, Otakar Chlup, Josef Kittrich, A. Kolman, V. Kopecký, Ladislav Koubek, Miroslav Kouřil,Vincenc Kramář, Jiří Kroha, Lubomír Linhart, M. Majerová, Vincenc Makovský, B. Mathesius, J. Mukařovský, Zdeněk Nejedlý, S. K. Neumann, V. Nezval, Ivan Olbracht, Vl. Procházka, M. Půjmanová, Božena Půlpánová, Jaroslav Průcha, Václav Rabas, Václav Řezáč, Ludvík Svoboda, L. Štoll, Jan Škoda, Fr. Trávníček, Otakar Vávra, Boleslav Vomáčka, Václav Vaněček, Bedrich Vaníček.

DOCUMENT 2: ANNOUNCEMENT OF THE ESTABLISHMENT OF *KULTURNÍ SVAZ*

Kulturním pracovníkům!

Největším kladným výsledkem fysického a mravního rozvratu, do něhož fašismus lidstvo uvedl, zůstává nepochybně už *vítězství tvořivé individuální i sociální práce* v celém vzdělaném světě i ve státě našem. Sama dnešní vláda československá je představitelkou tohoto vítězství a budovatelkou nového sociálního a hospodářského řádu, naší národní společnosti *ve smyslu vývoje politické demokracie v demokracii hospodárskou a sociální.*

V tomto duchu také kulturní činitelé osvobozené vlasti s radostí přijímají svůj podíl na budovatelských úkolech. Zároveň však tvrdí, že kultura je "vrcholným strážcem především neporušitelnosti lidských práv" a že je úkolem demokratického státu "hájit vývoj co možno bez všeho násilí duchovního i fyzického ve smyslu striktního plnění práva a spravedlnosti stejné pro všechny občany v duchu režimu demokracie stanoveného a demokraticky prováděného" a že tedy kultura "*musí zůstat ve svém sociálním prostředí především svobodná,* t.j. automní". (Z projevu dr. Edvarda Beneše na sjezdu českých spisovatelů.)

Kultura nemusí být politická, *politika však musí býti kulturní.* V politickém dění splní kultura své sjednocující poslání jen tehdy, zůstane-li pro politiku svéprávnou autoritu, i když není pochyby, že distribuce kulturních statků musí býti včleněna do státního plánu. Tím ostražitěji musíme bdíti nad tím, aby zůstala nedotčena *tvůrčí svoboda práce duchovní, vědní i umělecké, a svoboda života náboženského,* jakož i institucí, které jsou jejich orgánem.

Voláme proto kulturní pracovníky, aby se s námi sdružili v KULTURNÍ SVAZ, v němž by se pěstovala a chránila svoboda o osobitost duchovní tvorby proti jakýmkoliv zásahům a pokusům podrobit ji vlivům mocenským a stranickým, a jenž by byl ohniskem iniciativní myšlenky, usilující o uskutečnění rovnováhy svobodné osobnosti ve společnosti socialisticky spravedlivé.[2]

To All Cultural Workers!

The greatest positive consequence of the physical and moral breakdown, to which fascism led humanity, undoubtedly remains *the victory of creative individual and social work* across the entire civilized world and in our state.

Today's Czechoslovak government itself is a representative of this victory and the constructor of a new social and economic order, of our national society *in the sense of the development of our political democracy into an economic and social democracy.*

In this spirit the cultural actors of our liberated homeland also accept with joy their share of the tasks in this construction work. At the same time, however, they maintain that culture is "above all the supreme sentry guarding the inviolability of human rights" and that it is the task of a democratic state "to defend developments whenever possible without any spiritual or physical violence in the sense of the strict fulfilling of the law and justice similarly for all citizens in the spirit of a regime established for democracy, democratically exercised" and that consequently culture *"must remain in its social environment above all free,* i.e., autonomous." (From the speech of Dr. Edvard Beneš at the Congress of Czech Writers.)

Culture must not be political, *politics however must be cultural.* In political activity culture will fulfill its unifying calling only if it remains for politics a self-ruling authority, even if there is no doubt that the distribution of cultural property must be incorporated into a state plan. Because of this we must more diligently ensure that *the creative freedom of spiritual, scholarly and artistic work, and the freedom of religious life* and the institutions that are its organs remain untouched.

Therefore we call cultural workers to join with us in KULTURNÍ SVAZ, in which the freedom of the individuality of spiritual creation will be cared for and defended against any kind of interference or attempts to subordinate it to power and party political influences, and which will serve as the focus of stimulating ideas, striving for the realization of the balancing of the free individual in a socialistically just society.

Sixty-six signatories follow, including Kamil Bednář, Jan Bělehrádek, Vojta Beneš, Boh. Bouček, Vratislav Bušek, Václav Černý, Pavel Eisner, Emil Filla, J. B. Foerster, Václav Chalupecký, Jaromír John, Josef Kopta, Fr. Kovárna, J. B. Kozák, Josef Král, Karel Krejčí, Jaroslav Kvapil, Josef Lada, Vitězslav Novák, Otakar Odložilik, Josef Palivec, Ferdinand Peroutka, Karel Pokorný, Karel Polák, Jaroslav Seifert, Karel Stloukal, Karel Scheinpflug, Olga Scheinpflugová, Frana Šrámek, V. V. Štech and Jan Zrzavý.

DOCUMENT 3: ANNOUNCEMENT OF PRELIMINARY AGREEMENT BETWEEN THE REPRESENTATIVES OF *KULTURNÍ OBEC* AND *KULTURNÍ SVAZ*

Kulturní verejnosti

Naší základnou je *činorodný humanismus*, ve smyslu socialistického vývoje, to jest úsilí o lidskost v cíli i prostředcích. Humanismus, který—jak řekl

Masaryk—není filantropickou kostí, hozenou ukřivděným, nýbrž usiluje o kolektivní spravedlnost a při tom dbá každého mravně hodnotného jednotlivce. Za hlavní nástroj tohoto humanismu považujeme *socialismus*. Prijímajíce jako jeho hospodářský předpoklad socialisaci a boj proti vykořisťování člověka, vidíme hlavní smysl své práce ve vytvoření jeho obsahu duchového a mravního.

Vyznáváme *svobodu* ukázněnou, odpovědnou celku i vlastnímu svědomí, svobodu lidí věcných usilujících o pravdu, vzájemně se respektujících.

Toto vše pokládáme za postupné splňování nejlepších tradic a úkolů našich dějin a za cestu k *demokracii* stále lidovější a dokonalejší.

V tomto duchu budeme hájit svobodu bádání, tvorby, projevu i odpovědné kritiky, a zavazujeme se, že těmto cílům chceme svorně zasvětit všechno své úsilí.

Sloužíce takto svému národu, sloužíme i světu, jehož plodné duchovní podněty budeme vždy radostně přijímat.

Máme za to, že tato ideová základna dává možnost, aby se spojily kulturní síly národa k úkolům, které čekají.[3]

To the cultural public

Our basis is *active humanism*, in the sense of socialist development, that is, the striving for humanity in ends and in means. Humanism, as Masaryk said, is not a philanthropic bone thrown to those who have been wronged, but strives for collective justice and thereby cares for each morally valuable individual.

We consider *socialism* to be the primary tool of this humanism. Accepting socialization and the struggle against human exploitation as its economic precondition, we see the main meaning of our work in the creation of its spiritual and moral content.

We will profess a *freedom* that is disciplined, responsible to the whole and to our own conscience, a freedom of people eternally striving for truth and respecting one another.

We consider this all to be the gradual fulfillment of the best traditions and missions of our history, and to be the path to a *democracy* ever more perfect and of the people.

In this spirit we will defend the freedom of research, creation and responsible criticism, and we pledge unanimously to devote ourselves with all of our efforts to these goals.

Serving our nation in this way we also serve the world, whose fruitful spiritual impulses we will always joyfully accept.

We believe that this conceptual basis allows the possibility of uniting the cultural forces of the nation for the tasks that await.

K. J. Beneš, Václav Běhounek, Jan Bělehrádek, E. F. Burian, Václav Černý, Václav Dobiáš, Jan Drda, Ladislav Fikar, František Halas, Jan Kopecký, Josef

Kopta, J.B. Kozák, Bohuslav Kratochvíl, Ivan Olbracht, Ferdinand Peroutka, Václav Řezáč, Jaroslav Seifert, Ladislav Štoll, Otakar Wünsch.

DOCUMENT 4: RESOLUTION OF THE FOUNDING GENERAL ASSEMBLY OF *KULTURNÍ JEDNOTA*

Plni dobré vůle, plni víry v socialistickou budoucnost své země a jednotni v zásadách, jež jsme si stanovili z pocitu odpovědnosti za kulturní růst národa v nové, lidové demokracii, sešli jsme se, abychom soustředili tvořivé lidi a vykročili k práci.

Kulturní jednota chce být ohniskem jednotné kulturní iniciativy, aniž se její členové zřikají své názorové a tvůrčí osobitosti, se stálou snahou podřizovat se zájmům celku a pravdy. Při tom soudíme, že pohled s mnoha stran, zaměřený k jednomu cíli, přispěje k poznání podstaty. Věříme, že tato kulturní synthesa poroste ze součinnosti se všemi kulturními a politickými orgány lidu a státu, jimž chceme sloužit, pomáhat a radit, učíce se od lidu, a jsme přesvědčeni, že naše práce se uplatní tou měrou, jak budeme schopni řešit velké ideové problémy společenské proměny. Tvůrčí kritikou, ověřující nosnost myšlenek, chceme podnítit v životě národa a v jeho kultuře plodný ideový kvas, třídění duchů a činy hodné současna. Chceme, aby naše kultura byla vskutku morální zbrojnicí našeho lidu a spolutvůrcem nového, pevného národního chrakteru.

Naléhavost úkolů, které čekají, je podtržena skutečností, že lidstvo je na historickém rozmezí svého vývoje. Naplněni hrdostí, že náš národ, prošlý kalvarií, je součástí přední vlny onoho proudu, jímž se dnes vlévá do dějin pokrok pod slovanským sluncem svobody, mírotvorné práce, spravedlnosti a lidství, manifestujeme v předvečer výročí osvobození, ve dnech, naplněných doma budováním a ve světě vulí k míru, svou snahu obnažit a vypálit zbylá ložiska fašismu a křivd a podpořit nadějné klíčení a růst nových, vyšších tvarů demokracie a kultury. K tomu vás všechny zveme, bratrsky se obracejíce k slovenským kulturním pracovníkům, připraveni s nimi podat ruku všem demokratickým silám světové kultury při práci na velkém díle.[4]

Full of goodwill, full of faith in the socialist future of our land and united on the principles that we have laid down for ourselves from a feeling of responsibility for the cultural growth of the nation into a new, people's democracy, we have met to concentrate creative people and move forward to work.

Kulturní jednota wants to be the focal point of a united cultural initiative, without its members renouncing their individuality of ideas and creativity, with the continuing desire to subordinate itself to the interests of the whole and those of truth. For this we judge that the view from many sides, aimed at one goal, will contribute to the understanding of its essence. We believe that this cultural synthesis will grow from cooperation with all cultural and political organs of the people and the state—which we want to serve, help and advise, learning from the people—and we are convinced that our work will make its presence felt to the same extent that we are able to solve the great intellectual questions of the social transformation. By creative criticism, attesting to the power of thought, we want to instigate the fruitful fermentation of ideas in the life of the nation and in its culture by the assortment of great minds and by actions worthy of our times. We want our culture to truly be the moral armory of our people and the co-creator of a new, robust national character.

The urgency of the tasks that await is emphasized by the fact that humanity is at a historical turning point in its development. Filled with pride that our nation, having passed through its Calvary, is part of the leading wave of this current through which progress is today flowing into history under the Slavic sun of freedom, peacemaking activity, justice and humanity, we demonstrate—on the eve of the anniversary of our liberation, in days filled with building at home and with the will for peace in the world—our desire to expose and expunge the remaining centers of fascism and injustice and to support the hopeful buds and growths of new, higher forms of democracy and culture. To this we call you all, also turning fraternally to Slovak cultural workers, to be prepared to extend your hand to all the democratic forces of world culture laboring on this great work.

Notes

Note: Where abbreviations (e.g., lowercase initials) are used in place of authors' names, articles were published under these abbreviations. In some cases (those not followed by a name in brackets), the author signified could not be determined with certainty.

INTRODUCTION

1. Here and throughout this study the capitalized "Communist" will refer to the Communist Party, its viewpoints, and its members. The uncapitalized variant will be used to refer to those, for example on the left wing of the Social Democratic Party, who were sympathetic to the communist movement, but not members of the Communist Party.

2. Norman Naimark, "Revolution and Counterrevolution in Eastern Europe," in *The Crisis of Socialism in Europe*, ed. Christiane Lemke and Gary Marks (Durham and London: Duke University Press, 1992), 63.

3. The Edvard Beneš Society has reprinted many of the former president's writings from the interwar period.

4. See, for example, the English version of Ripka's memoirs, which begins by stating that "Czechoslovak democracy was left to defend itself alone against an enemy infinitely more powerful than itself," and that its postwar history was the story "of the vain struggle of a little democracy against the active force of totalitarian Communism." Hubert Ripka, *Czechoslovakia Enslaved* (London: Victor Gollancz, 1950), 7, 12.

5. The question of the constitutionality of the Communist Party's assumption of power in 1948 has been the source of debate since that year. In any case, the word "coup," so often associated with the event, is misleading, unless democratic political actors can be seen as starting a Communist coup. As M. R. Myant has argued, the debate over constitutionality "can lead to evasion of the central issues on both sides. The *general* constitutionality of the solution to the crisis can be used as a cover for the real essence of the change, which was the complete transformation of the political power structure. Alternatively, unconstitutional acts can be presented as the explanation for the defeat of the resigning ministers, thereby diverting attention from their political weaknesses without which the Communists' victory could not have been so simple." M. R. Myant, *Socialism*

and Democracy in Czechoslovakia 1945–1948 (Cambridge: Cambridge University Press, 1981), 208. Here and throughout, unless otherwise noted, any emphasis appears in the original.

6. The best of these is his *Nekrvavá revoluce* (Prague: Mladá fronta, 1993), the first part of which is essentially his well-known *The Short March* (London: C. Hurst, 1987). See also, for example, his textbook *Československo v letech 1945–53*, 2 vols. (Prague: SPN, 1990), his *Pravda o Československu 1945–48* (Prague: Panorama, 1990), or his *Pět kapitol o únoru* (Brno: Doplněk, 1997). The first of these concentrates on social and economic developments, the second is devoted almost exclusively to national problems, and the final concentrates on politics and the February crisis itself.

7. Kaplan, *Nekrvavá revoluce*, 11. Unless otherwise noted, all translations throughout this study have been made by the author.

8. This would include his *Stát a církev v Československu 1948–1953* (Brno: Doplněk, 1993), *Nebezpečná bezpečnost. Státní bezpečnost 1948–1956* (Brno: Doplněk, 1999), and his collaborative effort with Vladimír Pacl, *Tajný prostor Jáchymov* (České Budějovice: ACTYS, 1993), among others.

9. Alexej Kusák, *Kultura a politika v Československu 1945–1956* (Prague: Torst, 1998) and P. Prokš, "Československo. Politická moc a sovětizace (1945–1948)," in *Sovětizace východní Evropy*, ed. Miroslav Tejchman (Prague: Historický ústav, 1995), 39–77.

10. The best of these are Jaroslav Opat, *O novou demokracii* (Prague: Academia, 1966), Jaroslav Kladiva, *Kultura a politika 1945–1948* (Prague: Svoboda, 1968), and the volume edited by Kladiva and V. Lacina, *Československá revoluce 1944–1948* (Prague: Academia, 1966).

CHAPTER 1

1. Norman Naimark, "Revolution and Counterrevolution in Eastern Europe," in *The Crisis of Socialism in Europe*, ed. Christiane Lemke and Gary Marks (Durham: Duke University Press, 1992), 63.

2. Here, as indicated in this chapter's title, I owe a great debt to Hugh Seton-Watson, whose landmark *The East European Revolution* (New York: Praeger, 1951) has made a lasting impression on me. I also fully acknowledge my intellectual debt to my graduate school advisor, Norman Naimark, in particular for the article cited above. Finally, many of my ideas were deeply influenced by Jan Gross's "The Social Consequences of War: Preliminaries for the Study of the Imposition of Communist Regimes in East Central Europe," *East European Politics and Societies* 3 (1989): 198–214. In the following, I have relied on standard reference works for facts and figures and have avoided unnecessary citation.

3. On the Red Army's activities in Poland, see John Micgiel, "'Bandits and Reactionaries': The Suppression of the Opposition in Poland, 1944–1946," in *The Establishment of Communist Regimes in Eastern Europe, 1944–1949*, ed. Norman Naimark and Leonid Gabianskii (Boulder, CO: Westview, 1997), 93–110.

4. Though these courts seem to have been used politically by the Communists in all the other countries of the region, they were generally aboveboard in Czechoslovakia. See Benjamin Frommer, "Retribution against Nazi Collaborators in Postwar Czechoslovakia" (Ph. D. diss., Harvard University, 1999).

5. Gross, 206.

6. It should be pointed out that these figures, while consensus ones, probably do not reflect the true state of affairs. The Communists coerced people into joining, signed up entire villages without villagers' consent, and enrolled entire factories' workforces without their knowledge. Still, the growth of the Communist parties of the region was phenomenal.

7. See, for example, Arthur Marwick, *War and Social Change in the Twentieth Century. A Comparative Study of Britain, France, Germany, Russia and the United States* (London: Macmillan, 1974); Michael Scriven and Peter Wagstaff, eds., *War and Society in 20th Century France* (New York: Berg, 1991); Harold L. Smith, ed., *War and Social Change. British Society in the Second World War* (Manchester: Manchester UP, 1986); Alan Milward, *War, Economy*

and Society, 1939–1945 (Berkeley: University of California Press, 1977); Gordon Wright, *The Ordeal of Total War, 1939–1945* (New York: Harper, 1968); Richard Polenberg, *War and Society. The United States, 1941–1945* (New York: Lippincott, 1972); and Pitirim A. Sorotkin, *Man and Society in Clamity. The Effects of War, Revolution, Famine, Pestilence on Human Mind, Behavior, Social Organization and Cultural Life* (New York: E. P. Dutton, 1942). One of the few to discuss the experience of war in the smaller European lands is Wacław Długoborski, ed., *Zweiter Weltkrieg und sozialer Wandel. Achsenmächte und besetzte Länder,* Kritische Studien zur Geschichtswissenschaft 47 (Göttingen: Vandenhoeck & Ruprecht, 1981).

8. Marwick, 11–13.

9. These figures should be treated as estimates only. Differing sources give different figures, depending on the mode of aggregation, territories included, and so on.

10. Ulrich Herbert, *Hitler's Foreign Workers. Enforced Foreign Labor in Germany under the Third Reich,* trans. William Templer (Cambridge: Cambridge University Press, 1997), 462. These figures do not include the few thousands from other Eastern European countries.

11. The figures in this paragraph are taken from E. A. Radice, "Territorial Changes, Population Movements and Labour Supplies," in *Interwar Policy, the War and Reconstruction,* vol. 2 of *The Economic History of Eastern Europe 1919–1975,* ed. M. C. Kaser and E. A. Radice (Oxford: Clarendon Press, 1986), 324–25.

12. The breakdown is as follows: flight before military fronts—5,650,000, forced deportations to the Soviet Union—488,000, repatriation to the Soviet Union—5,000,000, organized postwar transfers—9,937,000, unorganized postwar resettlement—1,760,000, and internal postwar resettlement—8,300,000. All figures in this paragraph are from Paul Robert Magocsi, *Historical Atlas of East Central Europe,* A History of East Central Europe, vol. 1 (Seattle: University of Washington Press, 1993), 164–66.

13. The figures in this and the following paragraphs were gleaned from Kaser and Radice, Derek H. Aldcroft and Stephen Morewood, *Economic Change in Eastern Europe since 1918* (Aldershot: Edward Elgar, 1995); John R. Lampe, *The Bulgarian Economy in the Twentieth Century* (London: Croom Helm, 1986); Zbigniew Landau and Jerzy Tomaszewski, *The Polish Economy in the Twentieth Century,* trans. Wojciech Roszkowski (London: Croom Helm, 1985); Fred Singleton and Bernard Carter, *The Economy of Yugoslavia* (London: Croom Helm and New York: St. Martin's Press, 1982); and Ivan T. Berend and György Ránki, *The Hungarian Economy in the Twentieth Century* (New York: St. Martin's Press, 1985).

14. These figures are taken from Aldcroft and Morewood, 93.

15. These figures are drawn from Ezra Mendelsohn, *The Jews of East Central Europe between the World Wars* (Bloomington: Indiana University Press, 1983).

16. I hasten to add that not just the Nazis viewed the intelligentsia as a threat. The Red Army's massacre of Polish army officers at the Katyn forest and elsewhere, the deportations to Siberia from the Soviet-occupied zone of Poland, and the persecution of noncommunist intellectuals by the NKVD after the war all fit this pattern as well.

17. Even the states could not muster the necessary supplies for the first, harsh postwar months. The UN Relief and Rehabilitation Administration provided large-scale support, contributing $1,159,200,000 in aid (at gold parity of $35/oz., meaning roughly 10 billion dollars at today's prices), 40 percent of which was food aid, to Poland, Hungary, Czechoslovakia, and Yugoslavia alone. This information is drawn from R. Notel, "International Finance and Monetary Reforms," in Kaser and Radice, 522.

18. The information in this and the following paragraph is taken from Aldcroft and Morewood, 77–78.

19. On this, see E. A. Radice, "Changes in Property Relationships and Financial Arrangements," in Kaser and Radice, 332–33 and 337–46.

20. See Władysław Brus, "Postwar Reconstruction and Socio-Economic Transformation," in Kaser and Radice, 564–641.

21. See, on Czechoslovkia, *Za svobodu* (Prague: Nova svoboda, 1945), Václav Kural, *Vlastenci proti okupaci. Ústřední vedení odboje domácího 1940–1943* (Prague: Univerzita Karlova,

Ústav mezinarodních vztahu, 1997), and Detlef Brandes, *Die Tschechen unter deutschem Protektorat*, 2 vols. (Munich: R. Oldenbourg, 1969, 1975); on Poland, *Wizje Polski. Programy polityczne lat wojny i okupacji 1939–1944*, ed. Kazimierz Przybysz (Warsaw: Elipsa, 1992), Janusz W. Gołębiowski, "Sprawa nacjonalizacji przemysłu i odbudowy gospodarki narodowej w programach ważnieszych stronnictw politycznych podezas II wojny światowej," and Władysław Góra, "Reformy agrarne w programach partii I stronnictw politycznych w latach okupacji hitlerowskiej," in *Wojna i okupacja na ziemiach Polskich 1939–1945*, ed. Władysław Góra (Warsaw: Książka i wiedza, 1984), 527–84; on Hungary, see István Pintér, *Hungarian Anti-Fascism and Resistance, 1941–1945* (Budapest: Akadémiai Kaidó, 1986); and on Romania, see Stephen Fischer-Galați, "Prelude to Communist Totalitarianism, August 1944–March 1945," in *Romania: A Historic Perspective*, ed. Dinu C. Giurescu and Stephen Fischer-Galați (Boulder, CO: East European Monographs, 1998), 391–407, esp. 397–98.

22. See Karel Kaplan and Jiří Sláma, *Die Parlamentswahlen in der Tschechoslowakei 1935–1946–1948. Eine Statistische Analyse*, Veröffentlichung des Collegium Carolinum 53 (Munich: R. Oldenbourg, 1986), 58–59 and 118–19.

23. See Béla K. Király and Nándor F. Dreiziger, eds., *East Central European Society in World War I* (Boulder: Social Science Monographs; New York: Distributed by Columbia University Press, 1985), and Ivo Banac, ed., *The Effects of World War I: The Class War after the Great War*, (New York: Columbia University Press, 1983).

24. François Furet, *The Passing of an Illusion: The Idea of Communism in the Twentieth Century* (Chicago: University of Chicago Press, 1999), 352, 356.

25. These figures are taken from Alice Teichova, *The Czechoslovak Economy 1918–1980* (London: Routledge, 1988), 28. On the vagaries of the Czech land reform, and especially its relationship to the national question, see Eagle Glassheim, "Crafting a Post-Imperial Identity: Nobles and Nationality Politics in Czechoslovakia, 1918–1948" (Ph. D. diss., Columbia University, 2000).

26. The most successful project was Yugoslavia's, which expropriated virtually all the landed estates of 50–300 hectares, a step that "totally destroyed the large estates and established the role of peasant farms all over the country." Ivan T. Berend, "Agriculture," in *Economic Structure and Performance between the Two Wars*, vol. 1 of *The Economic History of Eastern Europe 1919–1875*, ed. M. C. Kaser and E. A. Radice (Oxford: Clarendon, 1975), 155. The majority of figures in this paragraph are drawn from this essay.

27. Of course, much of this good will was squandered as a result of the Soviet military's reprehensible behavior toward the people they had liberated.

28. Marwick, 12–13.

29. For this and the following two paragraphs, see the works cited in note 13, as well as Vojtech Mastny, *The Czechs under Nazi Rule* (New York: Columbia University Press, 1971), 82, and Ivan T. Berend, "The Composition and Position of the Working Class During the War," in György Lengyel, ed., *Hungarian Economy and Society During World War II*, trans. Judit Pokoly (Boulder, CO: Social Science Monographs, 1993), 151–68.

30. On the character of Czech workers in the immediate postwar years, see Jon Bloomfield, *Passive Revolution: Politics and the Czechoslovak Working Class, 1945–1948* (New York: St. Martin's, 1979). On the Polish working class, see Padraic Kenney, *Rebuilding Poland: Workers and Communists, 1945–1950* (Ithaca: Cornell University Press, 1997).

31. The phrase, as well as much of the data reported in this and the following paragraphs, is from Dudley Kirk, *Europe's Population in the Interwar Years* (Geneva: League of Nations, 1946). Other data is taken from Milan Hauner, "Human Resources," in Kaser and Radice, eds., *Economic Structure*, 74–82.

32. All statistics in this paragraph are taken from Statistical Office of the United Nations, *Demographic Yearbook*, vols. 1, 4, 8, 9 and 11 (New York: United Nations, 1948, 1952, 1956, 1957, 1959).

33. On the Yugoslav youth, see Petar Kačavenda, "The Youth of Yugoslavia in War and Revolution," in *War and Revolution in Yugoslavia, 1941–1945*, ed. Branko Prnjat, trans. Margot and Boško Milosavljević (Belgrade: STP, 1985), 186–99. On Bulgaria, see K. Vassilev, ed., *A Short History of the Bulgarian Communist Party* (Sofia: Sofia Press, 1977), 222.

34. Of course, Germans were scattered across the region, so one can argue that other states, such as Romania and Yugoslavia (with the Hungarian minority in the Vojvodina) faced the same danger. Nonetheless, Czechoslovakia was surely unique in the scale of its minority problem, and the interest taken by the revisionist powers in the fate of their co-nationals in the state.

35. I realize the problematic nature of the normative use of the "West," and that social conditions varied widely across the western half of the continent. Here it is used as a shorthand, in order to point out the similarities that existed between the Czech lands and the more developed economies, more fully elaborated civil societies, and democratic polities that were a general feature of Western Europe, and the differences that existed between them and the less industrialized and less politically experienced lands to the south and east, whose civil societies were also less well articulated.

CHAPTER 2

1. Fiona Björling, "Who Is the We of the Intelligentsia in Central and Eastern Europe?" in *Intelligentsia in the Interim. Recent Experiences from Central and Eastern Europe*, ed. Fiona Björling (Lund, Sweden: Lund University, 1995), 7.

2. Even such a resolutely non-intellectual political figure as Ronald Reagan could not be omitted in a discussion of the development of the American *Zeitgeist* of the 1980s. In some ways, the intellectuals included here, because of the public nature of their discussions, could be labeled the "chattering classes," although this is equally ambiguous.

3. What, for example, would one do with Václav Havel in the 1970s? In the 1990s? Much the same can be said for a host of Eastern European former dissidents who acquired political positions after the fall of Communism: Jiří Dienstbier, Petr Pithart, Adam Michnik, Tadeusz Mazowiecki, and Emil Constantinescu, among many others, come to mind.

4. Jan Hajda, "The Role of the Intelligentsia in the Development of Czechoslovak Society," in *The Czechoslovak Contribution to World Culture*, ed. Miroslav Rechcegl (The Hague: Mouton, 1964), 308–10.

5. On the national revival, and particularly the role of eighteenth-century intellectuals in it, see Hugh LeCaine Agnew, *Origins of the Czech National Renascence* (Pittsburgh: University of Pittsburgh Press, 1993).

6. Antonín Liehm, "[Interview]," in *The Politics of Culture*, ed. Antonín Liehm, trans. Peter Kussi (New York: Grove, 1973), 41–42.

7. Robert Auty, "Changing Views on the Role of Dobrovský in the Czech National Revival," in *The Czech Renascence of the Nineteenth Century*, ed. Peter Brock and H. Gordon Skilling, eds. (Toronto: University of Toronto Press, 1970), 18.

8. "The Age of Dobrovský" is the title of the first chapter of Tomáš G. Masaryk's *Česká otázka* (Prague: Svoboda, 1990).

9. Stanley B. Kimball, "The Matice Česká, 1831–1861: The First Thirty Years of a Literary Foundation," in Brock and Skilling, 53–73.

10. Miroslav Hroch, *Die Vorkämpfer der nationalen Bewegung bei den kleinen Völkern Europas* (Prag: Karlova Univerzita, 1968), 54, 61. Antonín Robek's studies, *Městské lidové zdroje národního obrození* (Prague: Univerzita Karlova, 1977) and *Lidové zdroje národního obrození* (Prague: Univerzita Karlova, 1974), deal respectively with the importance of small towns and villages in the early period of the national revival.

11. Jan Hajda, "The Development of the Intelligentsia between the Wars," in *The Intelligentsia and the Intellectuals*, ed. Aleksander Gella (Beverly Hills, CA: SAGE, 1976), 216. For a similar view, see David W. Paul, *The Cultural Limits of Revolutionary Politics. Change and Continuity in Socialist Czechoslovakia* (Boulder, CO: East European Monographs, 1979), 151ff.

12. Gary Cohen, *The Politics of Ethnic Survival: Germans in Prague, 1861–1914* (Princeton: Princeton University Press, 1981), 29.

13. Stanley Z. Pech, *The Czech Revolution of 1848* (Chapel Hill: University of North Carolina Press, 1969), 310, 333–35.

14. Pech, 123–38; the citations appear on pages 131 and 135.

15. Alexej Kusák, "Nationalbewußtsein und Nationalpädagogik als Aspekte der tschechischen und slowakischen Literatur 1945–1948," in *Die Tschechoslowakei 1945–1970*, ed. Nikolaus Lobkowicz und Friedrich Prinz (Munich: R. Oldenbourg, 1978), 239–40.

16. Czech universities offered 891 courses to the general public in the years 1898–1908, achieving a total attendance of some 200,000. Simultaneously, the activities of the Workers' Academy (Dělnická akademie, 1896), Central Workers' School (Ústřední škola dělnická, 1896), and the Union for Adult Education (Osvětový svaz, 1905), among others, commenced. Friedrich Prinz, "Das kulturelle Leben 1867–1939: Vom österreichisch-ungarischen Ausgleich bis zum Ende der ersten tschechoslowakischen Republik," in *Handbuch der Geschichte der böhmischen Länder*, vol. 4, ed. Karel Bosl (Stuttgart: Anton Hiersmann, 1970), 191.

17. I have relied here on Stanley B. Kimball, *Czech Nationalism. A Study of the National Theatre Movement* (Urbana: University of Illinois, 1964), 79 and 91. This excellent study reveals much about the ties between Czech culture and political nationalism in the nineteenth century and is still one of the most valuable sources on Czech nationalism available in the English language.

18. Jaroslav Opat, *Filozof a politik T. G. Masaryk 1882–1893* (Prague: Melantrich, 1990), 218–27.

19. Kramář was also motivated to take up the cause of Slavism at this time by the falling fortunes of his Young Czech Party, hoping to find in it political regeneration. The Tsar's reforms removed a major stumbling block for Social Democrats, who were sympathetic to the Slav idea, but not one that looked toward an absolutist, reactionary Russia.

20. Paul Vyšný, *Neo-Slavism and the Czechs, 1898–1914* (Cambridge: Cambridge University Press, 1977), 45, 49–50. On the Congress, see pp. 91–124.

21. Věra Olivová, *The Doomed Democracy. Czechoslovakia in a Disrupted Europe. 1914–1938* (Montreal: McGill-Queen's University Press, 1972), 111. Martin Bachstein has determined that 75 percent of the Castle group were civil servants, journalists, educators, or priests and that 60 percent had advanced degrees. In keeping with the social origins of the Czech intelligentsia, 49 percent of the group came from towns having under 5000 inhabitants. See Martin Bachstein, "Die sociologische Struktur der 'Burg'—Versuch einer Strukturanalyse," in *Die "Burg." Einflußreiche politische Kräfte um Masaryk und Beneš*, vol. 1, ed. Karl Bosl (Munich: R. Oldenbourg, 1973), 66–67.

22. Julius Firt, "Die 'Burg' aus der Sicht eines Zeitgenossen," in Bosl, 106–7. On the group's activities in creating the image of Czechoslovakia as a perfect democracy, see Andrea Orzoff, "Battle for the Castle: The Friday Men and the Czechoslovak Republic, 1918–1938" (Ph. D. diss., Stanford University, 2000).

23. Vojtech Mastny, *The Czechs under Nazi Rule: The Failure of National Resistance. 1939–1942* (New York: Columbia University Press, 1971), 82–83.

24. Václav Černý, *Křik koruny české. Paměti 1938–1945. Náš kulturní odboj za války* (Brno: Atlantis, 1992), 159. Černý maintains that "during the war the working class behaved generally tamely, and compliantly worked for the occupying power for the meager enough privileges of special fat and tobacco rations." Václav Černý, *Paměti IV* (Toronto: 68 Publishers, 1983), 136.

25. Mastny, 127. Five pages later Mastny notes that Nazi racial scientists determined that Czechs possessed even better racial characteristics than Sudeten Germans.

26. Mastny, 223.

27. As Detlef Brandes has written, "people and groups living illegally in the Protectorate undertook acts of sabotage, defended themselves against attacks and now and again raided small German offices. Still, these phenomena cannot be compared with the partisan warfare in the Soviet Union, Yugoslavia, or France." Detlef Brandes, *Die Tschechen unter deutschem Protektorat*, vol. II (Munich: R. Oldenbourg, 1975), 106.

28. Demonstrations in the early years of the war were generally small and non-violent, with Czech opposition limited largely to the wearing of armbands in the national colors and turning their lapel pins, which read "NS" for the only legal party in the Protectorate (*Národní souručenství*), upside down so that they read "SN," taken to mean "Death to the Germans" (*Smrt Němcům*).

29. Eventually, the closure was made permanent. Mastny, 110–18, here 117. See also Detlef Brandes. *Die Tschechen unter deutschem Protektorat*, vol. 1 (Munich: R. Oldenbourg, 1969), 84–95.

30. M. R. Myant, *Socialism and Democracy in Czechoslovakia 1945–1948* (Cambridge: Cambridge University Press, 1981), 26.

31. These phrases are attributed to Karl Hermann Frank, State Secretary in the Protectorate, in Brandes, vol. 1, 130, 133. Here we can see evidence for the Czech case of the attack on the bourgeoisie and the intelligentsia.

32. Vilém Prečan, "Heydrichuv stín nad Prahou," in Vílém Prečan, *V kradeném čase. Výběr z studií, článků a úvah z let 1973–1993* (Brno: Doplněk, 1994), 36.

33. Cited in Brandes, vol. 1, 213, 236.

34. Brandes, vol. 2, 23–24, and Černý, *Křik*, 281.

35. Brandes, vol. 1, 266.

36. Černý, Křik, 144–45. Again, unless otherwise noted, all emphasis appears in the original.

37. Černý, *Křik*, 396–97.

38. See, for example, the comments of Minister of Post František Hála in "Silná lidová strana, pevná hráz demokracie," *Lidová demokracie*, 19 May 1946, 2, the anonymously authored "Co má inteligence na srdci I," *Svobodné noviny*, 18 September 1945, 1, or Václav Běhounek, "Inteligence neví kudy kam?" *Práce*, 8 October 1945, 1.

39. This argument was made by such leaders as Ferdinand Peroutka and Václav Černý. The citation is from Julien Benda, *The Treason of the Intellectuals* (New York: Norton, 1969), 46. A translation of Benda's book appeared in Czechoslovakia under the title *Zrada intelektuálů* (Prague: S.V.U. Mánes, 1929).

40. Bohuslav Kratochvíl, *Veřejný život a intelligence* (Prague: Dělnické, 1946), 5–6.

41. Vladimír Ruml, "Inteligence a pracující třída," *Lidová kultura* 1, no. 13 (1945):1, and Lumír Čivrný, "Osobnost a kolektiv," in *Účtování a výhledy. Sborník prvního sjezdu českých spisovatelů*, ed. Jan Kopecký (Prague: Syndikát českých spisovatelu, 1948), 61. See also the Russian S. Kovaljov's contribution to the debate in the left-wing social democratic weekly, "Inteligence v socialistickém státě," *Cíl* 2 (1946): 287, 294. Many translations from Russian were offered to the public, primarily but not exclusively by communist-dominated journals.

42. po., "Místo inteligence je po boku lidu," *Tvorba* 14 (1945): 49. Kratochvíl mirrors this, writing that "It is not possible to stand by the side. . . . There is a necessity to express oneself, to choose." Kratochvíl, 10.

43. Oldřich Kerhart, "O výchovu pravé inteligence," *Život* 20 (1946/7): 15.

44. Miroslav Hořina, *Poslání inteligence v národě a ve státě* (Prague: ČAT-Universum, 1947), 15.

45. Kratochvíl, 6–7, and Lumír Čivrný, "Kultura proti nástupu reakce," *Tvorba* 15 (1946): 180.

46. Jan Drda, "Radostná tvář socialismu," *Rudé právo*, 13 June 1945, 3.

47. Čivrný, "Kultura," 180, and Milada Divišová, "Inteligence bez rozpaků," *Tvorba* 14 (1945): 142.

48. Čivrný, "Kultura," 181, and Josef Zika, "Problem intelligence," *Mladá fronta*, 1 November 1945, 1.

49. Ivan Olbracht, "Moje odpověď'," *Tvorba* 15 (1946): 177.

50. Václav Běhounek, "Inteligence neví kudy kam?," *Práce*, 8 October 1945, 1 and Zika, 1.

51. Běhounek, 1.

52. Gustav Bareš, "Cesta naší politiky," *Tvorba* 15 (1946): 674.

53. Ruml, 1.

54. Karel Severa, "Cesta ke kultuře," *Obzory* 3 (1947): 229. See also František Kafka, "Jediný celek," *Svobodné noviny,* 27 April 1947, 1. Despite this, Roman Catholics also strove "to gain for its ideals the intelligentsia above all," to which it accorded *"the leading role in the spiritual, economic and social life of the nation."* Antonín Pimper, *Křesťanský solidarismus* (Prague: ČAT-Universum, 1946), 104–5.

55. Pavel Tigrid, "Výzva k velikosti," *Lidová demokracie,* 3 November 1946, 2.

56. Ferdinand Peroutka, "Člověk je víc než politik," *Dnešek* 1 (1946/7): 427.

57. See, for example, po., 49 and Klement Gottwald, cited in "Klement Gottwald o kultuře," *Růst* 2 (1948): 73.

58. Ruml, 1. Cf. po., 49 and Josef Hejduk, "Lid a intelligence," *Tvorba* 14 (1945): 62–63.

59. Čivrný, "Kultura," 180.

60. See, for example, the comments of Josef Rybák, "Naše kulturni úkoly," *Rude právo,* 25 December 1947, 5, and Ivan Olbracht and Lumír Čivrný in Kopecký, 39 and 74, respectively.

61. Jan Čep, "Mezinárodní hnutí katolické intelligence," *Vyšehrad* 2 (1947): 310.

62. Jaroslav Nečas, "Spisovatel a dnešek," *Kolo* 11 (1946/7): 191, and Kafka, 1.

63. Edvard Beneš in Kopecký, 19 and 22.

64. Vladimír Vévoda, "Povinnost vzdělancu v dobách zmatku," *Lidová demokracie,* 1 November 1947, 5.

65. Alfred French, *Czech Writers and Politics 1945–1969* (Boulder, CO: East European Monographs, 1982), 30.

CHAPTER 3

1. Zdenek Suda, *Zealots and Rebels. A History of the Communist Party of Czechoslovakia* (Stanford, CA: Hoover Institution, 1980), 79. No less a figure than Stalin was named Comintern reporter on a subcommittee appointed to sort out the problems inside the party. The party had 132,000 members at its inception, but only 21,000 by the time of its fifth congress in February 1929.

2. Suda, 165.

3. Of respondants 6.4 percent responded, "Disagree, but recognize its good points," and only 1.9 percent responded, "Disagree entirely." Čeněk Adamec, Bohuš Pospíšil, and Milan Tesař, *What's Your Opinion? A Year's Survey of Public Opinion in Czechoslovakia* (Prague: Orbis, 1947), 14.

4. These were, in the Czech lands, the Communist Party of Czechoslovakia, the National Socialist Party, the Social Democratic Party, and the People's Party. In Slovakia, only the Communist Party of Slovakia and the Democratic Party were allowed. This asymmetric alignment accorded the Communist Party the ability to receive mandates from both parts of the republic, the only party with such a possibility.

5. The consequences of this were grave, and the democratic pedigree of the decision to limit the number of parties is also open to criticism, since the decision was made by exiled political representatives, without any consultation with the nation. Interestingly, President Beneš himself pushed for the limitation on parties, first suggesting a reduction to three parties. See Václav Pavlíček, *Politické strany po únoru. Příspěvek k problematice Národní fronty,* vol. 1 (Prague: Svobodné slovo, 1966), 72. The move was, however, popular. In March 1946, 57.5 percent of those surveyed considered four parties "sufficient" while, perhaps more shockingly, 34.2 percent held that four was "too many." Adamec et al., 13.

6. It should be pointed out that Communist Party of Czechoslovakia could not derive the same sort of advantages gained by its sister parties in the region from the prolonged presence of the armed forces of the USSR, for all Allied forces were withdrawn from the soil of Czechoslovakia by the end of 1945.

7. Vilém Prečan, "Politika a taktika KSČ 1945–1948," in Vilém Prečan, *V kradeném čase. Výběr ze studií, článků a úvah z let 1973–1993* (Prague: ÚSD, 1994), 117.

8. Zdeněk Mlynář, *Nightfrost in Prague*, trans. Paul Wilson (New York: Karz, 1980), 2.

9. Antonín Liehm, ["Interview"], in *The Politics of Culture*, ed. Antonín Liehm, trans. Peter Kussi (New York: Grove, 1973), 47–48, 50.

10. This figure is taken from Jan Kašpar, "Členská základna komunistické strany Československa v letech 1945–1949," *Československý časopis historický* 19 (1971): 1–25. Many of the statistics in this are reprinted in G. Wightman and A. H. Brown, "Changes in the Levels of Membership and Social Composition of the Communist Party of Czechoslovakia, 1945–1973," *Soviet Studies* 27 (1975): 396–417. A careful comparison of these reveals that at some times figures for the Czech lands alone are given, and at others the figures from both the Czech lands and Slovakia are given. Because of this, unless otherwise noted, the figures given are for both parts of the country. Partial data on Slovak membership shows that from 197,365 members at the end of 1945, the party actually shrank to a membership of 127,638 by the end of 1947. Therefore, we can safely assume that the growth discussed in the text can be ascribed to Czechs' entry into the party.

11. Marie Švermová, "Jsme milionovou stranou národa," *Rudé právo*, 31 March 1946, 5.

12. In January 1948, the National Socialists could claim 602,056 members. This figure becomes less impressive when one recognizes that one-third of these were not dues-paying members. Pavlíček, 102.

13. Paul Zinner, *Communist Strategy and Tactics in Czechoslovakia, 1918–1948* (London: Pall Mall, 1963), 125.

14. Pavlíček, 99. Also important is that while only 9.2 percent of the party fell under the label of "Intelligentsia," 22.3 percent of the Central Committee fell into this category. See Daniel Kubát, "Über die Frage der tschechoslowakischen kommunistischen Intelligenz seit dem Zweiten Weltkrieg," *Zeitschrift für Ostforschung* 11 (1962): 691.

15. Hubert Ripka, *Únorová tragedie* (Brno: Atlantis, 1995), 58. The longer quotation is from Prokop Drtina, *Československo můj osud*, vol. 2 (Prague: Melantrich, 1992), 172–73. Ambassador Steinhardt of the U. S. also vouched for the freedom of the elections. See Walter Ullmann, *The United States in Prague, 1945–1948* (Boulder, CO: East European Quarterly, 1978), 54.

16. Jiří Sláma and Karel Kaplan, *Die Parlamentswahlen in der Tschechoslowakei 1935–1946–1948* (Munich: R, Oldenbourg, 1986), 41–42, 59–67 passim.

17. Pavel Tigrid, *Kapesní průvodce inteligentní ženy po vlastním osudu* (Prague: Odeon, 1992), 221.

18. Ladislav Štoll, "Po velkém rozhodnutí," *Tvorba* 15 (1946): 337.

19. Ladislav Karel Feierabend, *Politické vzpomínky*, vol. 3 (Brno: Atlantis, 1996), 315.

20. Zinner, 113.

21. On the history of the party, see especially Karel Kaplan, *Das verhängnisvolle Bundnis. Unterwanderung, Gleichschaltung und Vernichtung der tschechoslowakischen Sozialdemokratie 1944–1954* (Wuppertal: POL, 1984).

22. This had been replaced in June of 1943 with the slogan "Death to the German Occupiers!" (Smrt německým okupantům!). After the war, no slogan appeared.

23. Jaroslav Kladiva, *Kultura a politika* (Prague: Svoboda, 1968), 228. All other circulation figures are taken from K. F. Zieris, *Nové základy českého periodického tisku* (Prague: Orbis, 1947), 24–25.

24. The membership figure is from April of 1946. Jon Bloomfield, *Passive Revolution: Politics and the Czech Working Class, 1945–1948* (New York: St. Martin's, 1979), 124. This is to date the best Western history of the union movement in this period.

25. This label, while reinforcing the fact that even the primary noncommunist intellectual opposition maintained a socialist standpoint, is not meant to imply that they followed the Social Democratic Party's political lead. Again, that party and particularly its intellectual supporters traveled with the Communist Party throughout most of the immediate postwar period. Although some intellectuals on the right wing of that party are included in this group, the majority will appear among the communists.

26. Statistical analysis has revealed that, while the party was supported from all sectors of the economy, "among civil servants [it] led with around two-thirds of the vote." Sláma and Kaplan, 66.

27. Karel Kaplan, *Nekrvavá revoluce* (Prague: Mladá fronta, 1993), 54, 403.

28. M. R. Myant, *Socialism and Democracy in Czechoslovakia, 1945–1948* (Cambridge: Cambridge University Press, 1981), 114.

29. Myant, 114, 116, 120.

30. As the young George Kennan noted already in March of 1939: "The Czechs take to political parties like ducks to water, and the smaller the party, the greater their loyalty to its cause and the fiercer their jealousy of all the others. For many years the Czech political parties have sat around the board and split any and all political spoils with the exactitude of small boys dividing a stolen melon. Their preoccupation with the relative size of their share, rather than with the extent of what there was to divide, has been one of the contributing factors in the catastrophe which has overcome the nation." George F. Kennan, *From Prague after Munich: Diplomatic Papers, 1938–1940* (Princeton: Princeton University Press, 1968), 99.

31. Ullmann, 98.

32. This became more apparent after the 1946 parliamentary elections, in which the National Socialists—traditionally rather a Bohemian phenomenon—gained over 30 percent of the vote in only 8 of the 110 Bohemian districts, while surpassing that barrier in 22 of the 46 Moravian constituencies. The People's Party was rooted in Moravia, and the increased tensions can be partly attributed to the overlap in strength. Sláma and Kaplan, 116–18.

33. Ullmann, 95.

34. Zinner, 116.

35. The only complete biography of Beneš in English is Zbyněk Zeman and Antonín Klimek's *The Life of Edvard Beneš, 1884–1948* (Oxford: Clarendon, 1997). See also the recent critical biography by Toman Brod, *Osudný omyl Edvarda Beneše 1939–1948* (Prague: Academia, 2002).

36. Jan Křen, *Bílá místa v našich dějinách?* (Prague: Lidové noviny, 1990), 70.

37. Václav Černý, *Paměti IV* (Toronto: 68 Publishers, 1983), 205.

38. Milan Otáhal, *Ferdinand Peroutka. Muž přítomnosti*, Slovo k historii 33 (Prague: Melantrich, 1992), 9.

39. He was offered release on two occasions, contingent upon his agreement to restart Přítomnost with a Nazi bias. He refused both times. On the return trip to Buchenwald after the first of these offers, in 1943, he was convinced he was to be "disposed of [zneškodit]." In the event the train was bombed, his papers burned, and he escaped execution. See Lev Braun, "Peroutka v otázkách a odpovědích," in *Muž přítomnosti*, ed. Jaroslav Strnad (Zürich: Konfrontace, 1985), 60. On Peroutka's life during and after World War II, see Pavel Kosatík, *Ferdinand Peroutka. Pozdější život (1938–1978)* (Prague-Litomyšl: Paseka, 2000).

40. See Peroutka's diary entry from 26 February 1948, in which he maintains that Bohumil Mathesius had promised the Communist Party to gain Peroutka's support for them already in 1945. Strnad, 147. The Temporary National Assembly was designed to serve until the 1946 parliamentary elections, and its members were divided largely among "clubs" corresponding to the permitted parties. Peroutka was a member of the National Socialist club.

41. Many of these are contained in the collections *Budeme pokračovat* (Toronto: 68 Publishers, 1980) and *Úděl svobody. Výběr z rozhlasových projevů 1951–1977* (Prague: Academia, 1995).

42. The high regard in which he is held can also be seen in the amount of his writings that have been reprinted. Among the most important are his *O věcech obecných*, 2 vols. (Prague: SPN, 1991), *Budování státu*, 5 vols. (Prague: Lidové noviny, 1991), *Sluší-li se být realistou* (Prague: Mláda fronta, 1993), *Deníky, dopisy, vzpomínky* (Prague: Lidové noviny, 1995), and *Byl Edvard Beneš vinen?* (Prague: H&H, 1993).

43. As early as 1931, his editor at *Lidové noviny*, Zdeněk Bořek-Dohalský, noted, "For the left Peroutka is difficult for he continually criticizes it. For the right he is dangerous, for he scorns it in everything." Otáhal, 1.

44. The citation is from a *Přítomnost* article of 1937, cited in Myant, 23. Already in 1925 the journal had run an article series entitled "Why Am I Not a Communist?" in which Peroutka suggested that the communist slogan should not be "Proletarians of All Lands, Unite!" but rather "Poisonous and Confused Literati of All Lands, Unite!" Reprinted in *Proč nejsem komunistou?* ed. Jaromír Hořec (Prague: Lidové noviny, 1991), 81.

45. Petr Fidelius, "Byl Peroutka liberál?" *Kritický sborník* 11 (1991): 30. Fidelius concludes that Peroutka contributed nothing new to Czech liberalism.

46. Eva Hartmannová, "Místo doslovu (Zamyšlení nad výběrem publicistiky F. Peroutky)," *Tvar* 1992, no. 4, 4–5.

47. Josef Čermák, "Hrst vzpomínek na profesora Václava Černého," in *Václav Černý. Sborník z konference konané 4.11.1993 na Dobříši,* ed. Marie Langerová (Prague: Obec spisovatelů, 1994), 94.

48. He tellingly notes that "I had even less taste for signing on with the National Socialists than the Communists." Černý, *Paměti IV,* 25–26.

49. See Dobrava Moldanová, "Poznámka k Černého polemice s historickým materialismem jako metodou literární kritiky," in Langerová, 64–65.

50. Although criticized as occasionally incorrect factually (in a more blatant example, he places Khrushchev's denunciation of Stalin in 1957), they remain an important source if it is borne in mind that "The author of the *Memoirs* is . . . a moralist and an intellectual who wants to share with the reader not only his memories and evidence, but also his reflections and understanding." Jan Vladislav, "(Další) poznámky k Pamětem Václava Černého," in Langerová, 27.

51. A partial list of these includes the following: *Paměti,* 3 vols. (Brno: Atlantis, 1992–94), *Tvorba a osobnost,* 2 vols. (Prague: Odeon, 1992–93), *Eseje o české a slovenské próze* (Prague: Torst, 1994), *O povaze naší kultury* (Brno: Atlantis, 1991), *První a druhý sešit o existencialismu* (Prague: Mladá fronta 1992), *Vývoj a zločiny panslavismu* (Prague: Institut pro středoevropskou kulturu a politiku, n.d. [1994]), *V zúženém prostoru* (Prague: Mladá fronta, 1994), and *Skutečnost svoboda* (Prague: Český spisovatel, 1995).

52. On Černý's anti-Semitism (based on comments in his memoirs), see both page 9 of Jaroslav Dresler, "Václava Černého účtování se Stalinismem" and page 24 of Josef Kalvoda, "Paměti Václava Černého," both in *Paměti Václava Černého v kritickém zrcadle exilu a disentu,* Edice TVARy, Series A, Number 6 (Prague: Tvar, 1995).

53. All periodicals had to be sponsored by organizations in the postwar era, as private periodical publishing was banned. The Association of Cultural Organizations (*Sdružení kulturních organisací*) was an umbrella group composed of some 63 organizations. Václav Černý served as vice-chairman. For more information, see "Sdružení kulturních organisací," *Svobodné noviny,* 10 November 1946, 2. The Association was often criticized in the Communist and left-wing Social Democratic press as being secretive and directed against socialism. See, for example, "Kdo je Sdružení kulturních organisací?" *Cíl* 2 (1946): 340–42.

54. All circulation data, except where noted, is from Zieris, 25, 27.

55. William Diamond, *Czechoslovakia Between East and West* (London: Stevens and Sons, 1947), 220, and Kladiva, 58.

56. It was considered National Socialist because it succeeded the prewar *Lidové noviny* (*The People's News*) and was financed largely by the family of the prominent party member Jaroslav Stránský. These charges were often denied, albeit implausibly. See, for example, Jan Bělohrádek, "Co chtějí *Svobodné noviny?*" *Svobodné noviny,* 30 November 1947, 2.

57. Eva Hartmannová, "'My' a 'oni': hledání české národní identity na stránkách Dneška z roku 1946," in *Strankami soudobých dějin. Sborník statí k pětašedátinám historika Karla Kaplana,* ed. Karel Jech (Prague: ÚSD, 1993), 94, 105.

58. The long series of reports on the situation in the frontier regions was written by Michal Mareš. *Dnešek* was also accused of being too German-friendly for defending Czech women who had married German men and were being expelled with their husbands. vd., "Je Dnešek volnou tribunou Němců?," *Tvorba* 16 (1947): 76–77.

59. The circulation figures are from Moldanová, 63.

60. *Masarykův lid* claimed to be a non-party weekly aimed at the youth but was undoubtedly part of the CNSP machinery. See "Masarykuv lid vychází znovu," *Masarykův lid* 15 (1945/6) n.p. *Svobodný zítřek* and *Dnešek* were often linked in the minds of their communist opponents. In the most witty example of this, the following equation was established: "'Today' + 'Tomorrow' (A Free) = Yesterday! (Dnešek + Zítřek (Svobodný) = Včerejšek!)" "Hádanka," *Cíl* 2 (1946): 223.

61. Martin Conway, introduction to *Political Catholicism in Europe 1918–1965*, ed. Martin Conway and T. Buchanan (Oxford: Clarendon Press, 1996), 2.

62. Miloš Trapl, *Politika českého katolicismu na Moravě 1918–1938* (Prague: SPN, 1968).

63. Rudolf Urban, *Die slavisch-nationalkirchlichen Bestrebung in der Tschechoslowakei mit besonderer Übersichtigung der tschechoslowakischen und der orthodoxen Kirche*, Slavisch-Baltische Quellen und Forschungen 9 (Leipzig: Markert & Petters, 1938), 86–7. Urban also notes here that "In the Prague suburbs populated mainly by workers it looked even worse for the Catholic Church." It is also important to note that the Church's losses were negligible among the German and Slovak portions of the population.

64. See the analysis of the results of the 1935 elections in Sláma and Kaplan, 25.

65. Trapl, 43–46.

66. On this incident, see Kurt Huber, "Die 'Burg' und die Kirchen," in *Die "Burg". Einflußreiche politische Kräfte um Masaryk und Beneš*, vol. 2, ed. Karel Bosl (Munich, R. Oldenbourg, 1975), 181–96, passim.

67. The Vatican also recognized the valuable contribution of the party in this episode, and its head, Monsignor Šrámek, was decorated by Pope Pius XI.

68. Trapl, 79.

69. They predicated their stance on the need to guarantee Czech industrial-sector employment through increased exports and to solidify alliances after the reentry of Germany into European politics.

70. Václav Vaško, *Neumlčená. Kronika katolické církve v Československu po druhé světové válce*, vol. 1 (Prague: Zvon, 1990). Vaško cites figures showing that of the 159 Czech clergymen imprisoned in Dachau, 143 were Roman Catholic (pp. 22–23). See also Karel Kaplan, *Stát a Církev v Československu 1948–1953* (Prague: ÚSD, 1993), 12.

71. Further, only 63.8 percent of all Czechs claimed to believe in the existence of God and only 32.8 percent that Jesus was the incarnation of God. Františekek Müller, "Výzkum veřeného mínění o náboženství v životě českého člověka," *Katolík* 9, no. 22 (1946):2.

72. Vaško, 41.

73. František Hála, "Silná lidová strana, pevná hraz democracie," *Lidová demokracie*, 19 May 1946, 1.

74. Karel Kaplan, *The Short March* (London: C. Hurst, 1987), 48, 54.

75. The party constantly, and correctly, stressed that it was the government whose political direction had changed, not the party's own. Though the efficacy of this strategy can certainly be debated, it was followed up to the level of Minister of Health Adolf Procházka. See Adolf Procházka, "Čsl. strana lidová ve vládě Národní fronty," *Lidová demokracie*, 3 April 1946, 3.

76. Müller, 2.

77. See the photograph accompanying "Naším cílem je svobodná, kulturní, lidová republika," *Lidová demokracie*, 20 May 1945, 1.

78. K. N., "Diktatura proletariátu," *Lidová demokracie*, 26 May 1946, 1.

79. Karel Kaplan states that in the summer of 1946, when the pre-election struggle for the former Agrarian supporters reached its peak, the People's Party counted 200,000 peasants among its ranks, the Communists 129,000, the National Socialists 89,500, and the Social Democrats 77,600. See Kaplan, *Short March*, 56.

80. True to tradition, the party received 27.5 percent of the Moravian vote, but only 16.2 percent of the Bohemian. Similarly, they gained 30 percent of the total Catholic vote, while almost none of the non-Catholic. See Sláma and Kaplan, 66.

81. Adolf Kajpr, "Demokracie vždy a všude," *Katolík* 9, no. 13 (1946):2, and Adolf Kajpr, "Tak je po volbách," *Katolík* 9, no. 11 (1946):1.

82. The way in which the expulsion of Koželuhová was handled drew criticism from *Katolík*, among others. Adolf Kajpr pointed out the failure to meet the standards of true democracy, as there was first silence on the issue and then a suspicious unanimity. See Kajpr, "Demokracie," 2.

83. Between October of 1947 and February of 1948, only 680 of the new members of the Communist Party came from the ranks of the People's Party, while 2657 came from the National Socialists and 3,343 from the Social Democrats. Kaplan. *Short March*, 108 and 115.

84. Fr. Günzl, "List redakci 'Obzorů,'" *Obzory* 1 (1945) 213, and Redakce, "Svoboda psání aneb svoboda lhání," *Tvorba* 16 (1947): 7. Other attacks can be found, for example, in Acer, "Stránský, Firt, Ducháček, Tigrid—mluví dnes v jménu katolicismu," *Tvorba* 16 (1947): 36, F. J. Kolár, "'Obzory' proti dvouletému plánu ve vlastní straně," *Tvorba* 15 (1946): 479, and František Pexa, "Nadhodnota z Obzorů na vybájeném ostrově," *Tvorba* 15 (1946): 717.

85. More serious, however, were attacks that attempted to link the journal with the Germans, a tactic even more potentially damaging than the charge of being reactionary. Tvorba accused *Obzory* of being defeatist, and condemned its editorials as recalling the pre-Munich "capitulatory propaganda of the Agrarian-united fifth column." Redakce, 7.

86. Jiří Taufer, "Temný obzor 'Obzorů,'" *Tvorba* 14 (1945): 282–83.

87. The journal, which was "more outspokenly anti-communist than other journals," even drew fire from Moscow. In the publication of the All-Slav Committee, *Slavjane*, *Obzory* was pilloried as "working against the Soviet Union and against friendly relations between Czechoslovakia and the Soviet Union." Its contributors were described as "ill-disposed reactionaries [who] do not represent the Czechoslovak nation," and *Slavjane* concluded with the ominous warning that "One cannot continue to harm the interests of the Czechoslovak government . . . without punishment." This episode is described in Zinner, 177.

88. Myant, 124.

89. Redakce, 7. On the end of *Obzory* and *Vývoj* see Zinner, 212.

90. Vaško, 49.

91. On the career of Braito, who also served ten years in Communist prisons, see Karel Mácha, *Glaube und Vernunft. Die böhmische Philosopie in geschichtlicher Übersicht*, vol. 3 (Munich: K. G. Saur, 1989), 169, and Zdeněk Rotrekl, *Skrytá tvář české literatury* (Brno: Blok, 1993), 28–31. Rotrekl also makes several strong points for Moravian specificity in "Poválečný literární život v Brně 1945–1948," in his *Barokní fenomén v současnosti* (Prague: Torst, 1995), 186–221.

92. Vaško, 208.

93. *Církev československá v životě národa. Memorandum presidentu republiky, ústavodárnému národnímu shromáždění, vládě republiky a veřejným činitelům* (Prague: Informační a tisková rada církve čsl., 1946), 11.

94. Rudolf Urban, *Die Tschechoslowakische Hussitische Kirche* (Marburg/Lahn: J. G. Herder Institute, 1973), 157.

95. The reform movement had presented a list of demands to Pope Benedict XV, but his willingness to compromise on the language issue proved both too little and too late. On the reform movement, see Rudolf Urban, *Die slavisch-nationalkirchlichen Bestrebungen*, 13–19. On the organizing of the church, see the critical work by the Catholic Ludvik Nemec, *The Czechoslovak Heresy and Schism. The Emergence of a National Czechoslovak Church*, Transactions of the American Philosophical Society, new series, vol. 65, part 1 (Philadelphia: The American Philosophical Society, 1975), 17–22. On Church doctrine, see both of the above-cited works, although a concise formulation can be found in Patriarch Adolf Procházka's article "Die Tschechoslowakische Nationalkirche," in *Die Kirchen der Tschechoslowakei*, ed. Friedrich Siegmund-Schultze (Leipzig: Leopold Klotz, 1937), 176–80.

96. The Czechoslovak Church was thwarted in its aim for two reasons. On the one hand, the leaders of the new state, President Masaryk and Foreign Minister Beneš, wished to maintain good relations with the Vatican. On the other hand, the example of the Habsburg Empire had convinced Masaryk and Beneš that weaker ties between church and state lessened the danger of abuse.

97. Nemec, 33.

98. Nemec, 31, 60–61.

99. Procházka, "Die Tschechoslowakische Nationalkirche," 177.

100. The words are those of the nationalist poet Viktor Dyk, cited in Nemec, 68.

101. On this complicated episode, see Urban, *Die slavisch-nationalkirchlichen Bestrebungen*, 89–114 and 125–41.

102. *Církev československá*, 20.

103. At that time, "the party-political ties of the Czechoslovak Church went so far that it was many times accused of being a mere church appendage of the National Socialist Party." Urban, *Die slavisch-nationalkirchlichen Bestrebungen*, 294.

104. Nemec, 11.

105. This figure and those that follow are drawn from Urban, *Die slavisch-nationalkirchlichen Bestrebungen*, 202–3 and *Církev československá*, 13–17.

106. Urban, *Die slavisch-nationalkirchlichen Bestrebungen*, 245. The breakdown was 13.8 percent in Bohemia and 8.3 percent in Moravia.

107. *Církev československá*, 17.

108. Urban, *Die slavisch-nationalkirchlichen Bestrebungen*, 88–89.

109. Urban, *Die slavisch-nationalkirchlichen Bestrebungen*, 249–51, and *Die Tschechoslowakische Hussitische Kirche*, 215. Similar figures were reported by Anežka Ebertová. She found that in the 1930s 45.8 percent of the membership came from the working class, with 72.9 percent of these workers coming from industry and manufacturing. See her "Církev v proměnách," in *Padesát let československé církve*, ed. Miloslav Kaňák (Prague: Husova československá bohoslovecká fakulta, 1970), 118.

110. *Církev československá*, 15–16.

111. Urban, *Die Tschechoslowakische Hussitische Kirche*, 151–52 and *Církev československá*, 9.

112. Urban, *Die Tschechoslowakische Hussitische Kirche*, 148.

113. Urban, *Die Tschechoslowakische Hussitische Kirche*, 148–52.

114. Miloslav Kaňák, "Stručný nárys dějin čs. církve vzhledem k jejímu vzniku a pulstoletnému vývoji," in Kaňák, 27.

115. *Církev československá*, 21.

116. Much the same kinds of demands were made, and partially fulfilled, with respect to Roman Catholic holdings after the communist assumption of power in 1948.

117. Urban, *Die Tschechoslowakische Hussitische Kirche*, 158.

118. Kaplan, *Stát a církev*, 124. Kaplan names two members of the church's central council (Miroslav Kouřil and Bishop Novák) as well as the secretary of the church's national committee František Hub, and the leading journalists Václav Lorenc and František Roháč.

119. *Církev československá*, 10, 19.

120. Kaplan, *Stát a církev*, 124–25.

121. Many of the early pastors in the Czech evangelical churches were drawn from Slovakia. See Ferdinand Hrejsa, "Kirchengeschichte Böhmens," in Siegmund-Schultze, 82–85.

122. The ongoing but unsuccessful discussions were also damaged by confessional sectarianism fueled from the Augsberg confession's celebrations of Luther in 1880 and 1883 and the Reformed (Helvetian) church's celebration of the anniversary of the Helvetian confession in 1866. On the complicated history of the confessions in the nineteenth century, see Rudolf Říčan, *Das Reich Gottes in den böhmischen Ländern. Geschichte des tschechischen Protestantismus*, trans. Bohumír Popelář (Stuttgart: Evangelisches Verlagswerk, 1957), 149–82, here 167–68.

123. There were 260,000 Augsbergers and 120,000 Helvetians in the Austrian half of the Dual Monarchy as a whole. See Říčan, 175.

124. On the history of the movement in the late nineteenth century, see Paul Mai, "Die tschechische Nation und die Los-von-Rom Bewegung," in *Festschrift für Bernhard Stasiewski. Beiträge zur Ostdeutschen und Osteuropaischen Kirchengeschichte*, ed. Gabriel Adriáni und Joseph Gottschalk (Cologne: Böhlau, 1974), 171–85.

310 Notes to Chapter 3

125. The importance of Constance arises from the Council of Constance, which condemned Hus as a heretic and ordered his execution.

126. The vast majority of the remaining evangelicals were ethnic Germans belonging to the Lutheran church. These statistics are drawn from Řičan, 190ff, Urban, *Die slavisch-nationalkirchlichen Bestrebungen*, 203–4, and Vratislav Busek, "Church and State," in *Czechoslovakia*, ed. Vratislav Busek and Nicholas Spulber (New York: Praeger, 1957), 141.

127. František Bednář reports that some 109,740 new members in the years 1919–1930 had formerly been members of the Roman Catholic Church, with 55,769 joining in the years 1921 and 1922. See Fr. Bednář, "Die Tschechisch-Brüderische Evangelische Kirche," in Siegmund-Schultze, 130.

128. These figures are drawn from Bohdan Chudoba, "Czech Protestants and Communism," *America: National Catholic Weekly Review* 82 (1949): 149 and Bohumil Jiří Frei, *Staat und Kirche in der Tschechoslowakei vom Februarumsturz zum Prager Frühling 1968*, vol. IV (Munich: Robert Lerche, 1973), 458–59.

129. Chudoba, 150.

130. Sláma and Kaplan, 66–7. It is notable that the Communist Party of Slovakia outdistanced its Democratic Party rival among Slovak Protestants in the 1946 parliamentary elections as well.

131. There has been much work on Hromádka both within Czechoslovakia and abroad. An important source is Hromádka's autobiography *Proč žiji*, much of which is reprinted in *J. L. Hromádka. Pravda a život* (Prague: Ekumenický institut, 1969). It is also available in German, as *Mein Leben zwischen Ost und West* (Zürich: Theologischer Verlag, 1971). Among the most important domestic secondary works are Josef Smolík, *J. L. Hromádka. život a dílo* (Prague: Ekumenická rada, 1989), Martin Salajka, *Naše doba. Z ekumenického odkazu J. L. Hromádky* (Prague: Ekumenická sekce Husovy fakulty, 1978), and Aleš Havlíček, ed. *Nepřeslechnutelná výzva* (Prague: Oikoymenh, 1990). The best Western works on Hromádka are Dorothea Neumärker, *Josef L. Hromádka. Theologie und Politik im Kontext des Zeitgeschehens* (Munich: Kaiser, 1974), Charles C. West, *Communism and the Theologians. Study of an Encounter* (London: SCM, 1958), Paul Mojzes, *Christian-Marxist Dialogue in Eastern Europe* (Minneapolis: Augsburg, 1981), and Hans Ruh, *Geschichte und Theologie: Grundlinien der Theologie Hromádkás* (Zürich: EVZ, 1963). For a Marxist view, see Milan Machovec, *Marxismus und dialektische Theologie: Barth, Bonhoeffer und Hromádka in atheistischkommunistischer Sicht*, trans. Dorothea Neumärker (Zürich: EVZ, 1962).

132. Smolík, 65 and Mojzes, 111.

133. Josef Smolík, 52–53 and 72–80, passim. Hromádka's view of Catholicism changed after February 1948, when he and his *Křesťanská revue* supported the attacks of the Communist regime on the Catholic Church. See Kaplan, *Stát a církev*, 123.

134. J. L. Hromádka, "Církevní a náboženské situace v SSSR," *Křesťanská revue* (1931/2): 99–105. As Dorothea Neumärker notes, "Hromádka's image of the Soviet Union, which he had not yet visited at that time, was painted in rapturous romantic colors (schwärmerisch-romantisch Züge trug)." After he visited the land for the first time, in 1947, he recorded that his impression was "very strong. . . . One perceives no social barriers among the masses." Neumärker, 101, 108.

135. J. L. Hromádka, "Na hřbitově starého světa," in J. L. Hromádka and Otakar Odložilík, *S druhého břehu* (Prague: F.Borový, 1946), 122.

136. Various articles by J. L. Hromádka, cited in West, 51–55.

137. West, *Communism and the Theologians*, 55, 68, 77. See also Neumärker's comment that in Hromádka "history and the reign of God were placed in a very close connection, even equated." Neumärker, 96.

138. For this and other comments favorable to the regime written immediately after the takeover, see J. L. Hromádka, "Po únorové krisi," *Křesťanská revue* 15 (1948): 68–72 and "Mezi včerejškem a zítřkem," *Náboženská revue* 19 (1948): 321–27 among many others.

139. J. L. Hromádka, *Proč žiji*, in *Pravda a život*, 110.

140. Smolík, 106.

141. Dorothea Neumärker on Hromádka's continued alliance with the state through the harshest period of Stalinism. Neumärker, 134.

142. West, 63–64.

143. Cited in Neumärker, 130.

144. Mojzes, 114. He was also awarded honorary doctorates from the University of Warsaw (1961) and Humboldt University (1959), and the highest non-military Soviet award—the Lenin Prize for International Friendship and Peace—was bestowed upon him in 1958.

CHAPTER 4

1. Jan Čep, "Křesťan před budoucností," *Vyšehrad* 3 (1947/8): 91.

2. Ludvík Forman, "Na křizovatce," *Obzory* 2 (1946): 614–15, J. L. Hromádka, "Na prahu nové éry," *Svobodný zítřek* 1, no. 1 (1945): 1–2, Bohuslav Kratochvíl, "Mezník v kulturním rozvoji národa," *Cíl* 2 (1946): 209–16. It is interesting to note, given Hromádka's later career, that he recycled this title in 1949, after the Communist Party's assumption of power.

3. Alois Spisar, "Proč mravní chaos dneška?," *Náboženská revue* 17 (1946): 86–91, Miloš Dvořák, "Ke kořenum kulturní krise," *Akord* 13 (1946/7): 121–26, Jan Babor, "Krise kulturního života?," *Svobodný zítřek* 3, no. 45 (1947): 5.

4. Ferdinand Peroutka, "Druhá výstavba," *Svobodné noviny*, 28 September 1946, 1.

5. Edvard Beneš, *Demokracie dnes a zítra* (Prague: Fr. Borový, 1946), see especially pp. 64–87 and 169–96. For a contemporary discussion of his conception of the depth of democracy's crisis, see the article by his biographer František Hník, "Česká humanitní tradice a Edvard Beneš," *Náboženská revue* 18 (1947): 129–49, esp. 147ff. Beneš' speech appeared in all the major dailies. See, e.g., *Lidová demokracie*, 25 December 1946, 1–2.

6. F. Jiřík, "Křesťanský paradox," *Obzory* 3 (1947): 505. A very similar argument, although also placing part of the blame for the Church's decreasing role in public affairs on the Church itself, is made by Jan Čep in "Křesťan a svět," *Vyšehrad* 2 (1947): 1–3.

7. Pavel Tigrid, "Krise lidskosti," *Lidová demokracie*, 25 August 1946, 1–2. He was supported in this argument by many religious leaders, but also the professor of biology Zdeněk Frankenberger. See his "Československá kultura mezi Západem a Východem," *Lidová demokracie*, 4 January 1948, 12.

8. Čep, 91.

9. J. B. Kozák, "T. G. Masaryk a osobní odpovědnost," *Svobodný zítřek* 3, no. 37 (1947): 2.

10. Jan Patočka, "Masaryk včera a dnes," *Naše doba* 52 (1945/6): 305, 310.

11. Pavel Tigrid, "O tom pocitu nesvobody," *Lidová demokracie*, 3 October 1945, 1.

12. Kamil Bednář, "Kamil Bednář o umění," *Vývoj* 2 (1947): 303. For reference, as there are two pages numbered 303 due to faulty pagination, this appears in number 27 of the volume, dated 2 July.

13. J. L. Hromádka, "Naše orientační postava," *Svobodný zítřek* 1, no. 8 (1945): 2.

14. Spisar, 88–89.

15. Alois Spisar, "Mravnost a jednotný světový názor," *Český zápas* 29 (1946): 250.

16. Zdeněk Nejedlý, "Za lidovou a národní kulturu," reprinted in his *O kulturu národní a lidovou* (Prague: Melantrich, 1948), 37. The speech was delivered on 25 May 1945.

17. Jiří Hájek, "Umění v novém národním životě," *Tvorba* 14 (1945): 33.

18. Václav Kopecký, "Dělničtí delegáti ze závodů se sešli, aby se zabývali kulturou," *Lidová kultura* 1, no. 7 (1945): 2, and Ladislav Štoll, "Úvodem," *Nová mysl* 1, no. 1 (1947): 1.

19. Gustav Bareš, "O kulturu nového národního obrození," in his *Listy o kultuře* (Prague: Svoboda, 1947), 13, 15.

20. This is from Kopecký's speech to a conference of party intellectual workers (*Konference ideových pracovníků KSČ*) delivered 9 January 1948 and reprinted as his *Zápas o nové vlastenectví* (Prague: ÚV KSČ, 1948), here page 3.

21. Václav Kopecký, "Výsledky kulturního budování republiky," in _Můj poměr ke KSČ_ (Prague: KSČ, 1946), 9. The style corresponds to the man. Kopecký, from his experience in the USSR, was shrewd enough to adapt the Soviet writers' definition of socialist realism—"realist in form, socialist in content"—and define the new Czechoslovak culture as "national in form and progressive in content," stressing the national component. Note also that, in keeping with the moderate political strategy of the Communist Party, he used "progressive" in place of even "socialist."

22. Nejedlý, 29.

23. Jaromír Lang, "Naše ideové úkoly," _Lidová kultura_ 1, no. 24 (1945): 1.

24. Václav Kopecký, "O národní a státní ideologii nového Československa," _Rudé právo_, 31 March 1946, 3.

25. Nejedlý, 28.

26. Jan Štern, "O vlastenectví a internacionalismu," _Tvorba_ 16 (1947): 1002–3.

27. Kopecký, _Zápas_, 26.

28. Rudolf Slánský, "Komunistická strana v boji za svobodu národa," _Rudé právo_, 29 March 1946, 5 and Nejedlý, 29. All parties and organizations devoted much energy to honoring their war dead, perhaps a sign of the Czech "martyr complex" described by Robert Pynsent in his _Questions of Identity. Czech and Slovak Ideas of Nationality and Personality_ (London: Central European University Press, 1994), 147ff.

29. See, for example, Klement Gottwald, "Republice více práce—to je naše agitace!" and "Hlavním obsahem politiky naší strany je práce," in his _Spisy_, vol. 12 (Prague: SNPL, 1955), 265–68 and 321–23.

30. Zdeněk Nejedlý, _Komunisté—dědici velikých tradic českého národa_ (Prague: Sekretariát ÚV KSČ, 1947), 39–41. On the Communist Party's views of the trial of the Protectorate government's leadership and that of the leader of the wartime Slovak state, see Brad Abrams, "The Politics of Retribution: The Trial of Josef Tiso," _East European Politics and Societies_ 10 (1996): 255–92.

31. Ferdinand Peroutka, "Tři místo jednoho—a co z toho," _Dnešek_ 1 (1946/7): 30.

32. For example, in a speech to the United States Congress in 1947, Foreign Minister Jan Masaryk refuted the idea that the Communists wished to expel other parties from government and said "I have known Gottwald many years. He is an excellent [_výtečný_] person and a great Czech patriot." _Národní osvobození_, 25 January 1947, 1. Masaryk's doctor later claimed that Masaryk had made these statements in order to obtain increased American engagement in Czechoslovakia. See Toman Brod, _Cesta československých komunistů k moci v letech 1945–1948_, vol. 1 (Prague: Magnet, 1990), 83. His view may have changed a half-year later, after the Soviets had vetoed Czechoslovak participation in the Marshall Plan. At that time he uttered the now famous line that "I went to Moscow as the Foreign Minister of an independent sovereign state; I returned as a lackey of the Soviet Government." Robert Bruce Lockhart, _Jan Masaryk: A Personal Memoir_ (London: Putnam, 1956), 66. On the embarrassing prostration of the Czechoslovak delegation that ordered the withdrawal from the Marshall Plan, see Bradley F. Abrams, "The Marshall Plan and Czechoslovak Democracy: Elements of Interdependancy," in _The Marshall Plan: Fifty Years After_, ed. Martin A. Schain (New York: Palgrave, 2001), 93–116. This and other claims of Soviet "interference" in the sovereign affairs of Czechoslovakia made particularly in the memoirs of exiled anti-communist politicians lose much of their luster when they constantly refer to their self-initiated "consultations" with Moscow or the Soviet Ambassador in Prague over internal Czechoslovak affairs. If one constantly seeks "advice" from the USSR and always follows it, can one then complain about Soviet "interference"?

33. Robert Bruce Lockhart, _My Europe_ (London: Putnam, 1952), 635 and 643.

34. Hugh Seton-Watson, _Nationalism and Communism. Essays, 1946–1963_ (London: Methuen, 1964), 121, and Josef Korbel, _The Communist Subversion of Czechoslovakia 1938–1948_ (Princeton: Princeton University Press, 1959), 142.

35. This was the view of the Brno leadership of the National Socialist Party, who ascribed their party's electoral loss in 1946 to its failure "to shake the patriotism of the Communist Party and displace it from the position of the most national party." From an internal party memorandum cited in Václav Pavlíček, *Politické strany po únoru. Příspěvek k problematice Národní fronty*, vol.1 (Prague: Svobodné slovo, 1966), 87.

36. Gustav Bareš, "Cesta naší kultury," *Tvorba* 15 (1946): 673. See also the comment that "historicism plays in the Czech nation a role only rarely seen in other places." Václav Husa, "Po sjezdu," *Kulturní politika* 3, no. 5 (1947/8): 1.

37. Zdeněk Nejedlý, "Historie a její význam pro nás," *Nová mysl* 1, no. 1 (1947): 12. The placement of this article, in the first issue of the Communist Party's new theoretical organ, underscores the importance of history.

38. František Marek, "Východ a Západ," *Vyšehrad* 3 (1947/8): 176. Emphasis added. The congress to which he refers is the Second Congress of Czechoslovak Historians, which took place in October of 1947. Its primary importance lies in the facts that 750 people took part (almost entirely Czechs), that historical materialism played a prominent role in the discussions, and that the conference attracted front-page coverage in the daily press. Can one imagine a conference of proportional size, or with similar coverage, taking place in any Western European country?

39. Jiří Síla, "Český socialismus," *Práce*, 23 December 1945, 1–2.

40. Nejedlý, *Komunisté*, 17–18.

41. Zdeněk Nejedlý, *Komunisté—dědici velikých tradic českého národa* (Prague: Práce, 1978), 38. The reason for the use of this reprint is that several pages are missing from the only extant first edition in the National Library in Prague.

42. Zdeněk Nejedlý, *Odkaz našich národních dějin* (Prague: ÚV KSČ, 1948), 4.

43. Of those who gave a response, 24% placed "The Hussite wars" first, 22% "The reign of King Charles IV," and 21% "The present time." The question was "Which period of Czech history do you consider to be the most glorious?" When much the same question was put in October of 1968 (therefore after the Warsaw Pact's crushing of the Prague Spring), the "age of Hus" came in a close second (36%) to the interwar republic (39%). Charles IV dropped to third (31%), and the 1945–48 period to sixth, with only 9%. The figures were higher in the latter case as respondents were allowed to name two periods. The second question read "Which personalities in our history do you esteem most?" See Archie Brown and Gordon Wightman, "Czechoslovakia: Revival and Retreat," in *Political Culture and Political Change in Communist States*, ed. Archie Brown and Jack Gray (London: Macmillan, 1977), 164–65, 179–80.

44. The author has here relied on Howard Kaminsky's *A History of the Hussite Revolution* (Berkeley: University of California Press, 1967).

45. Nejedlý, *Komunisté* (1978), 42.

46. Ladislav Štoll, "Husitská tradice a naše budoucnost," *Rudé právo*, 6 July 1945, 1.

47. Fr. Jungmann, "Strana velkých tvurcu naší kultury," *Lidová kultura* 2, no. 13 (1946): 1.

48. J. Dubský, "Táborská demokracie vzorem," *Rudé právo*, 5 July 1946.

49. Zdeněk Nejedlý, "Husuv den," *Rudé právo*, 5 July 1946, 1.

50. Zdeněk Nejedlý, "Hus a naše doba," *Rudé právo*, 5 July 1947, 3 and Síla, 1.

51. Arnošt Kolman, *Co je smyslem života?* (Prague: Orbis, 1947), 45.

52. Nejedlý, *Komunisté* (1978), 45.

53. Zdeněk Nejedlý, "K revisi národního charakteru," *Tvorba* 16 (1947): 571.

54. Nejedlý, *Komunisté* (1978), 45.

55. Nejedlý, *Komunisté* (1978), 43.

56. Václav Lorenc, "V duchu Husitské revoluce," *Český zápas* 29 (1946): 149.

57. František Roháč, *Jednota v našich národních tradicích* (Prague: Akademický klub Tábor, 1947), 17.

58. Lorenc, 149–50.

59. T. G. Masaryk, *Jan Hus. Naše obrození a naše reformace* (Prague: Jan Kanzelsberger, 1990), 105, 166.

60. Jan Kozák, "Proč tedy nejste komunistou," *Svobodný zítřek* 2, no. 17 (1946): 1.

61. Václav Žižka, "S východem a západem," *Masarykův lid* 14–15 (1945/6): 12.

62. A. Novotný, "Stále živý program," *Svobodný zítřek* 1, no. 11 (1945): 2.

63. František Loubal, "Dědici národních tradic?," *Svobodný zítřek* 3, no. 24 (1947): 5, 12.

64. Arnošt Klíma and Petr Zenkl, "Debata o vědeckém socialismu," *Dnešek* 1 (1946/7): 78.

CHAPTER 5

1. The literature on this shameful episode in European diplomatic history is vast. The only treatment of the crisis and the ensuing conference dealing in depth with Czech activities is Igor Lukes' excellent *Czechoslovakia between Stalin and Hitler: The Diplomacy of Edvard Beneš in the 1930s* (Oxford: Oxford University Press, 1996).

2. Vilém Hejl, *Rozvrat. Mnichov a náš osud* (Toronto: 68 Publishers, 1989), 30.

3. BVL [Bohuslav Václav Lohniský], "Podzim 1938 a dnešek," *Český zápas* 39 (1946): 213.

4. A survey taken in 1946 revealed that of those Czechs whose opinion of the Western powers had changed only since the end of that year's Paris Peace Conference, 79% looked on them "less favorably." Čeněk Adamec, Bohuš Pospíšil, and Milan Tesář, *What's Your Opinion? A Year's Survey of Public Opinion in Czechoslovakia* (Prague: Orbis, 1947), 18.

5. Antonín Trýb, "My, staří," *Věda a život* 11 (1945): 419.

6. Adolf Kajpr, "Sisyfova práce?," *Katolík* 9, no. 17 (1946): 2.

7. Zdeněk Trtík, "Výstraha Mnichova," *Český zápas* 30 (1947): 223.

8. Pavel Tigrid, "Je Západ reakcionářský?," *Lidová demokracie*, 4 August 1946, 1.

9. "Manifest Národní fronty Čechů a Slováků k 28. říjnu 1945," *Lidová demokracie*, 28 October 1945, 1.

10. Václav Lorenc, "15. březen varuje," *Český zápas* 29 (1946): 43–44.

11. The interwar Czechoslovak Republic had signed mutual defense treaties with both the USSR and France. The provisions calling for the military assistance of the USSR, however, were contingent upon a French declaration of war and the assistance of that state's troops. (Interestingly, the Czechoslovak side placed this condition in the treaty.) As the French were co-signers of the Munich Accords and hence would not be coming to Czechoslovakia's aid, the USSR was relieved of its obligation.

12. Václav Lorenc, "Přízraky Mnichova," *Český zápas* 29 (1946): 213.

13. Lorenc, "15. březen," 44.

14. Cited in František Hník, "Česká humanitní tradice a Edvard Beneš," *Náboženská revue* 18 (1947): 147.

15. Jaroslav Stránský, "Sedmý listopad a my," *Svobodný zítřek* 1, no. 7 (1945): 1.

16. Prokop Drtina,"Žádné Mnichovanství staré ani nové," *Svobodný zítřek* 3, no. 47 (1947): 3. He was raked over the coals by Miroslav Galuška, who accused him of "glorifying" the "greatest historical fault of the Czech bourgeois ruling class" and accused Drtina's National Socialist Party of "preserving 'Munich-ism.'" Miroslav Galuška, "Nové Mnichovanství," *Rudé právo*, 8 November 1947, 2.

17. Drtina, 3. The claim that the USSR was willing to come to Czechoslovakia's aid even beyond its treaty obligations, long doubted by most scholars, has been definitively rebutted. See Lukes, 209–63, passim.

18. Tigrid, 1–2.

19. Adolf Kajpr, "I u nás je duch Mnichova," *Katolík* 11, no. 6 (1948): 1.

20. Karel Dvořák, "Mnichov a dnešek," *Vývoj* 2 (1947): 899.

21. Hubert Masařík, cited in Telford Taylor, *Munich: The Price of Peace* (London: Hodder and Staughton, 1979), 49.

22. Kajpr, 1.

23. Interestingly, the article was issued in book form in 1937 (just before Munich) and reissued in 1947, just as the reevaluation of the national character was taking place. Tomáš G. Masaryk, *Problém malého národa* (Prague: Neutralita, 1990).

24. Cato, "Evropská jednota a my," *Dnešek* 2 (1947/8): 302.

25. Lorenc, "Přízraky," 213.

26. Jiří Hájek, "Umění v novém národním životě," *Tvorba* 14 (1945): 33.

27. Gustav Bareš, "Ke sjezdu spisovatelů," *Tvorba* 15 (1946): 370.

28. Hájek, 34.

29. Zdeněk Nejedlý, "K revisi národního charakteru," *Tvorba* 16 (1947): 571.

30. Jan Stránský, *East Wind over Prague* (London: Hollis and Carter, 1950).

31. Although Red Army abuses in Czechoslovakia were undoubtedly less widespread than in the defeated powers of Eastern Europe, they have yet to be systematically researched. Still, hearsay testimony indicates significant maltreatment of the civilian population. For example, Jan Stránský reports (again only after his flight) an orgy of rape in Brno, claiming that as a result 2000 women asked for admission to local hospitals and thereby indicating the number was far higher. Thievery was apparently also rampant, especially that of watches. Stránský reports that Red Army soldiers would merely point their guns at civilians and demand their watches, saying "*davay chasi,*" and that this even happened to Minister of Finance Vavro Šrobár. He also reported that "whenever the documentary film of the Yalta conference was shown in the cinemas, and whenever the scene was thrown on the screen of Roosevelt sitting next to Stalin and looking at his watch, the public always yelled with great gusto the well-known Russian words: '*Davay chasi!*' I have seen it happening several times myself, and I also know that the Communist Minister of Information finally ordered the 'Roosevelt wrist-watch scene' to be cut out of the film." See Stránský, 29 and 32–55.

32. Gustav Bareš, "Diskuse," *Kritický měsíčník* 2 (1946): 16.

33. Quoted in Alt [J. Albrecht], "Zdeněk Nejedlý o úkolech české filosofie," *Vyšehrad* 1, no. 16 (1945/6): 17–18.

34. Vitězslav Nezval's speech at the Congress of Czech writers, in *Účtování a výhledy. Sborník prvního sjezdu českých spisovatelů* ed. Jan Kopecký (Prague: Syndikát českých spisovatelů 1948), 104.

35. Kajpr, "Sisyfova," 2.

36. Vladimír Hellmuth-Brauner, "Svět, který jsme zdědili a který tvoříme," *Vyšehrad* 1, no. 6 (1945/6): 3.

37. Prokop Drtina, "Vítězná revoluce a naše vítězství," *Svobodný zítřek* 1, no. 7 (1945): 1.

38. The most prominent Protestant leader of the time, J. L. Hromádka, did not fault the Soviet Union for signing the pact, writing that "from the first we were certain that it was a tactically unavoidable and brilliant step. . . . We knew [after Munich] that the European reactionary forces wanted to take advantage of the disintegration of the peace system and liquidate—if necessary with Hitler's and Mussolini's help—'the Bolshevik danger.' . . . Then came the 22nd of June, 1941! After a few weeks it was obvious that the socialist government was the master of the situation in its land." See J. L. Hromádka, "Mezi válkou a mírem," *Kostnické jiskry* 30 (1945): 56.

39. Marie Voříšková, "Být Evropanem," *Vyšehrad* 1 (1945/6): 2. A similar view from the Roman Catholic camp can be found in J., "Krise umění," *Vývoj* 2 (1947): 44.

40. J. L. Hromádka, "Na prahu nové éry," *Svobodný zítřek* 1, no. 1 (1945): 1.

41. See, for example, J. Pecháček, "Zákon všech revolucí," *Lidová demokracie*, 18 July 1945, 1.

42. František Hník, "Svoboda a řád," *Svobodný zítřek* 1, no. 6 (1945): 2.

43. Ironically, a report written by Walter König-Beyer of the Race and Settlement Head Office concluded, "A rough estimate of the racial structure of the Sudetenland . . . shows that from a purely numerical point of view the racial picture of the Czech people is considerably more favorable today than that of the Sudeten German population." He estimated that 45% of Czechs were "nordic, dinaric or westic," 40% "unbalanced' racial mixtures," and 15% "racially alien."

The figures for Sudeten Germans were 25%, 55%, and 20%, respectively. This was in harmony with Reichsprotektor Konstantin von Neurath's observation that among the Czechs generally there was a "high number of fair-haired people, who would not stand out unfavorably even in central and southern Germany." See Vojtech Mastny, *The Czechs under Nazi Rule: The Failure of National Resistance, 1939–1942* (New York: Columbia University Press, 1971), 127, 132.

44. V. V. Štech, "Umění v národě a státě," *Dílo* 34 (1945/6): 10.

45. Arnošt Kolman, *Diskuse s univ. prof. dr. Arnoštem Kolmanem* (Prague: Orbis, 1946), 23. Note again the communist stress on strength.

46. Jiří Hájek, "Jsme nositele nové doby," *Mladá fronta*, 9 May 1945, 2.

47. Albina Dratvová-Kozák, "Jednota filosofická k oslavě TGM," *Svobodné noviny*, 12 March 1946, 5.

48. Ferdinand Peroutka, "Co se stalo," *Dnešek* 1 (1946/7): 145.

49. Pavel Tigrid, "Mravní profil voleb," *Lidová demokracie*, 1 June 1946, 1.

50. Bohuslav Brouk, "O znehodnocení hodnot," *Svobodný zítřek* 3, no. 2 (1947): 3. Cf. František Kovárna, "Proti zosobňování institucí," *Svobodný zítřek* 2, no. 43 (1946): 5.

51. Bohuslav Brouk, "Kdo vystoupil, je vyloučen," *Dnešek* 1 (1946/7): 725. Brouk wrote the article after resigning from the Communist Party. He emigrated to Paris after the Communist assumption of power and eventually settled in London.

52. Stránský, 47. Later he relates the following conversation during a campaign visit with a farmer, who argued that "I am a Communist. . . . If democracy wins, nobody will punish me, nobody will chase me out of my farm, nobody will put me in prison. The worst that might happen is that a few people will say 'Look at old Novotny, he was in the Communist party, the silly old fool!' . . . But if on the other hand it is the Communists who win and I am no longer a member— well, Mister, there would be hell to pay." Stránský, 131.

53. Pavel Tigrid, "Mravní profil," 1.

54. František Hála, "Co potřebuje naše kultura?," *Lidová demokracie*, 25 December 1946, 1.

55. Ferdinand Peroutka, "Druhá výstavba," *Svobodné noviny*, 28 September 1946, 1.

56. Mastny, 157.

57. Edvard Beneš, "K připravnému výboru Československé protifašistické společnosti," in *EB národu. Z projevů presidenta republiky v letech 1946–1947*, ed. František Škarvan (Prague: Zemská rada osvětová, 1946), 26.

58. Pavel Tigrid, "O evropský ethos," *Lidová demokracie*, 13 July 1946, 1 and Zdeněk Nejedlý, "Kulturní politika třetí republiky," *Věda a život* 11 (1945): 277. At that time Nejedlý was serving as minister of education and culture. See also the similar comments of the novelist Jan Drda in "Radostná tvář socialismu," *Rudé právo*, 13 June 1945, 3 and those of the communist Minister of Information Václav Kopecký in Karel Teige, "Entartete Kunst," *Kvart* 4 (1945/6): 42.

59. Václav Lorenc, "Naše místo není u brzda," *Český zápas* 29 (1946): 105.

60. Václav Molkop, "Poselství sněmu k církvi a národu," *Český zápas* 29 (1946): 7.

61. The democratic socialist view of fascism was, however, marked by the widespread contemporary notions that fascism sprang from the "mystical German" deification of the state or "the Prussian spirit of the mechanization of life." See Kovárna, 5, or Jaroslav Nebesář, "Žijeme zase v demokratickém státě," *Panorama* 21 (1945/6): 10.

62. The press restrictions forbade, among others, criticism of the National Front government or the foreign policy of the state (i.e., alliance with the Soviet Union and in some cases even the Soviet Union itself). As tensions heightened, so did restrictions, as Karel Kaplan has described: "Already in the summer of 1947, the [Communist-controlled] Ministry of the Interior published guidelines on the prosecution of 'anti-state statements' . . . . Many district [State Security] commanders understood the general message to mean that criticism of Marxism, the Union of Youth, the trade unions, or the Communist Party was a punishable act. The non-Communist ministers protested unsuccessfully . . . . Gottwald and Kopecký not only defended this type of action, but they praised the security forces for conscientiously carrying out their tasks." See Karel Kaplan, *The Short March* (London: C. Hurst, 1987), 141.

63. Edvard Beneš, "[In Response to a Letter from *United Nations World*]," *Svobodný zítřek* 3, no. 10 (1947): 2.

64. Hník, 2.

65. From František Halas's speech, reprinted in Kopecký, 14.

CHAPTER 6

1. Joseph Rothschild, *East Central Europe between the Two World Wars* (Seattle: University of Washington Press, 1974), 134.

2. Hugh Seton-Watson, *Eastern Europe between the Wars, 1918–1941* (Boulder, CO: Westview, 1982), 185.

3. Jan Strakoš, "Masarykův odkaz politický," *Obzory* 3 (1947): 542.

4. Karel Kreibich, "Marxismus, bolševismus a násilí," *Tvorba* 15 (1946): 164–65. Kreibich went on to become the Czechoslovak ambassador in Moscow, 1950–52.

5. Jiří Hájek, "Kroky k Mnichovu, které udělala první republika," *Cíl* 2 (1946): 597.

6. Gustav Bareš, "Cesta naší kultury," *Tvorba* 15 (1946): 673. J. L. Hromádka sympathized with this viewpoint, as with so many other communist commentaries, writing that particularly "the Agrarian Party ideologically and practically tilted toward the side of European reaction and in its way supported fascist or at least semi-fascist ideas. By this it crippled the strength and solidity of the Czechoslovak state. . . . [This] was the most fateful and most dismal mistake of the First Republic." J. L. Hromádka, "Pohled na první republiku," *Křesťanská revue* 13 (1946): 177.

7. Jiří Hájek, "Generace 28. října a generace 5. května," *Generace* 1 (1946/7): 4.

8. Jarmila Jelínková-Papírníková, "Dopis čtenáře, který se F. Peroutkovi nehodil," *Tvorba* 15 (1946): 426–27. The letter had originally been sent to Peroutka's *Dnešek*, which did not print it.

9. Gustav Bareš, "[Untitled]," *Tvorba* 15 (1946): 180.

10. Jiří Hendrych, "Morálka naší doby," *Tvorba* 15 (1946): 793–95. Heda Kovály noted, "Our conditioning for the revolution had begun in the concentration camps. Perhaps we had been most impressed by the example of our fellow prisoners, Communists who often behaved like beings of a higher order. Their idealism and Party discipline gave them strength." Heda Kovály, *Under a Cruel Star: A Life in Prague, 1941–1968* (New York: Penguin, 1986), 59.

11. František Weyr, "Co to má znamenat?," *Svobodné noviny*, 16 November 1946, 1.

12. Jaroslav Blažek, "Znalost historie první republiky," *Dnešek* 2 (1947/8): 36–37.

13. Ferdinand Peroutka, "Není navratu," *Svobodné noviny*, 25 November 1945, 1.

14. See, for example, Kamil Novotný, "Umění a lid," *Česká osvěta* 39 (1946): 11.

15. Josef Macek, "Jak si to uděláme, tak to budeme mít," *Naše doba* 52 (1945/6): 1–4. The title of this piece, "As We Sow, So Shall We Reap," consciously recalled not only the Bible, but also the words Stalin used in guaranteeing the Soviet Union's non-interference in Czechoslovakia's internal affairs. In the same journal, F. M. Dobiáš also criticized the number of parties sharing in power in the prewar republic and the atomization of that society as a whole. See F. M. Dobiáš, "Obrožené Československo," *Naše doba* 53 (1946/7): 52–57.

16. Josef Macek, "Vláda i oposice věrná lidu," *Naše doba* 53 (1946/7): 145–49.

17. Karel Hrbas, "Demokracie hledá sebe," *Národní osvobození*, 12 August 1945, 1.

18. Edvard Beneš, *Demokracie dnes a zítra* (Prague: Čin, 1947), 64–72.

19. Beneš, 216–17.

20. Beneš, 81.

21. Ferdinand Peroutka, "Dík minulosti," *Svobodné noviny*, 28 October 1945, 1.

22. Jaroslav Pavela, "Za první republiky," *Lidová demokracie*, 5 February 1946, 1.

23. Bohdan Chudoba, "Křesťanská orientace," *Obzory* 1 (1945): 260–1.

24. Bohdan Chudoba, "Lid či třídy?," *Obzory* 2 (1946): 21–2.

25. J. L. Hromádka, "Naše orientační postava," *Svobodný zítřek* 1, no. 8 (1945): 1.

26. J. B. Kozák, "T. G. Masaryk a osobní odpovědnost," *Svobodný zítřek* 3, no. 37 (1947): 2. The article is also reprinted in J. B. Kozák *O lidu a lidech* (Prague: Vl. Žikeš, 1948), 161–67.

27. Jaroslav Pokorný, "Zásadní poznámka," *Lidová kultura* 2, no. 10 (1946): 1.

28. Adolf Novotný, "T. G. Masaryk časově naléhavý," *Svobodný zítřek*. 3, no 10 (1947): 1.

29. Jiří Hájek, "TGM k dnešku," *Tvorba* 16 (1947): 190. The noncommunist former Masaryk collaborator, Lev Sychrava, also expressed the concern that official celebrations were sinking to the level of "formal cults" that "tempt superficiality." See Lev Sychrava, "Masaryk hovoří k dnešku," *Národní osvobození*, 7 March 1947, 1.

30. Edvard Beneš, "List Dr Edvarda Beneše k ústavujícímu valnému shromáždění Masarykovy společnosti 7. března 1946," *Česká mysl* 40 (1946–8): 120.

31. Kozák's comments are reported by Albína Dratvová in "T. G. M. a dnešek," *Svobodné noviny*, 27 December 1945, 5.

32. Jiří Zhor, "Její tvář," *Dnešek* 2 (1947/8): 355.

33. Václav Kopecký, "T. G. Masaryk a nová republika," *Rudé právo*, 7 March 1946, 2.

34. Hájek, 190. Lumír Čivrný, "Kultura proti nástupu reakce," *Tvorba* 15 (1946): 180–81.

35. JR, "Veliká bojová tradice března," *Rudé právo*, 7 March 1948, 1.

36. Václav Kopecký, "Do boje za vítězství nového československého vlastenectví," *Rudé právo*, 10 January 1948, 1.

37. Kopecký, "T. G. Masaryk," 2.

38. Josef Rybák, "Nad Masarykovým odkazem," *Rudé právo*, 7 March 1948, 1.

39. Vladimír Procházka, "Masarykova osobnost," *Rudé právo*, 14 September 1947, 2, and František Götz, "V čem je Masaryk předchůdcem dnešního socialistického humanismu," *Tvorba*. 15 (1946): 331. See also M. Kárný, "T. G. M.," *Rudé právo*, 14 September 1945, 1.

40. Vladimír Procházka, "Masarykova osobnost," *Tvorba* 16 (1947) 735 and Ludmila Koutníková, "Masaryk a dnešek," *Lidová Kultura* 2, no. 10 (1946): 2.

41. Quoted in Václav Cháb, "Zd. Nejedlý: Úkol české současné filosofie," *Národní osvobození*, 5 February 1946, 4.

42. lš [Ladislav Štoll], "T. G. Masaryk," *Tvorba* 14 (1945): 113–14.

43. Procházka, "Masarykova osobnost," *Tvorba*. 735–36.

44. Procházka, "Masarykova osobnost," *Rudé právo*. 2.

45. Rybák, 1.

46. E. F. Burian, "Odkaz TGM," *Kulturní politika* 3, no. 1 (1947): 7.

47. Koutníková, 2.

48. Pokorný, 1.

49. Kárný, 1. See also Josef Rybák's statement that even if Masaryk was not a socialist, he "fought with all his being for the world." Rybák, 1. The retroactive proclamation of the socialist status of historical individuals was an integral part of the Communist reinterpretation of the Czech past.

50. Jan Hostáň, "My a TGM," *Lidová kultura* 2, no. 10 (1946): 2. See also Vladimír Procházka's comment that Masaryk "went with and stood by the side of the workers." Procházka, "Masarykova osobnost," *Rudé právo*, 2.

51. See, for example, Štoll, 113–14 or Kárný, 1.

52. Kopecký, "T. G. Masaryk," 31.

53. Procházka, "Masarykova osobnost," *Tvorba*, 736.

54. Burian, 7.

55. Robert Konečný, "Masarykův odkaz," in his *Živá slova* (Brno: Zář, 1946), 35.

56. Ferdinand Peroutka, "Dědictví," *Svobodné noviny*, 14 September 1945, 1. Notably, the phrase "I never twiddled my thumbs" ("jsem nikdy nesloužil ruce v klín") has the secondary meaning "I never gave up."

57. From an interview in *Masarykův lid* reprinted in *EB národu. Z projevů presidenta republiky v letech 1945–1946*, ed. František Škarvan (Prague: Zemská rada osvětová, 1946), 35–36.

58. Edvard Beneš, "Žádné násilí a teror, ani duchovní ani fysický," *Lidová demokracie*, 14 September 1947, 1.

59. Jan Slávik, "Jeho věčný hlas," *Svobodný zítřek* 2, no. 10 (1946): 5. The citation is from Tomáš G. Masaryk, *Otázka sociální* (Prague: Čin, 1946), 698.

60. Jan Patočka, "Masaryk a naše dnešní doba," *Křesťanská revue* 13 (1946): 35.

61. Kozák, 1. The debate of the non-partisan *Filosofická jednota* (Philosophical Unity) club is reported in Albína Dratvová, "T. G. M. a dnešek," *Svobodné noviny*, 22 December 1945, 5.

62. Beneš, "Žádné násilí" 1. See also Jan Patočka's comment that Masaryk's conception of "humanist democracy" is "never identical with the state in the conception of classical liberalism, with its social atomism and the unscrupulousness of the individual." Patočka, 37.

63. Beneš, "List Dr Edvarda Beneše," 122–23.

64. Josef Král, "Masaryk a dnešek," *Svobodný zítřek* 2, no. 10 (1946): 1–2. See also his further comments from a lecture given at *Filosofická jednota* in Albína Dratvová, "Jednota filosofická k oslavě TGM," *Svobodné noviny*, 12 March 1946, 5.

65. As Toman Brod has correctly pointed out, "the Czechs were the only national society in the world that . . . voluntarily decided in its majority for a *socialist* future. Despite the fact that almost half of this may have had in mind a socialism *different* from the Moscow type . . . the leftist tendencies in postwar Czechoslovakia were spontaneous and undisputed." Toman Brod, *Cesta československých komunistů k moci*, vol. 1 (Prague: Magnet, 1990), 37–38.

66. Lev Sychrava, "Je třeba ještě revoluce?," *Národní osvobození*, 16 February 1946, 1.

67. Kozák. 1–2.

68. Ladislav Rieger, "O základy humanismu," *Česká mysl* 40 (1946–8): 235.

69. Edvard Beneš, "Žádné násilí," 1 and "List Dr Edvarda Beneše," 122.

70. Masaryk saw revolution as a moral duty against violent, oppressive regimes and in cases in which the physical or spiritual life of a nation was endangered. Král, 2.

71. Vladimír Úlehla, "Slovanský filosof," *Svobodné noviny*, 7 March 1947, 1.

72. Peroutka, "Dědictví," 1.

73. See, for example, Dratvová, "Jednota filosofická," 5 or Král, 1.

74. He lists Spencer and Hume as the most important of the Anglo-Saxons Masaryk brought to Czech thought. Dr. js [Jan Strakoš], "Živoucnost T. G. Masaryka," *Lidová demokracie*, 14 September 1945, 1.

75. Jan Strakoš, "Tomáš G. Masaryk mezi námi," *Lidová demokracie*, 7 March 1946, 1.

76. The First Republic was criticized in *Tvorba* precisely for placing too much emphasis on Jesus (spiritual power) and not turning quickly enough in the 1930s to the worldly power of Caesar, seen as embodied in the Soviet Union. See M. Černý, "S kým je dnes Masaryk?," *Tvorba* 15, no. 10 (1946).

77. Jan Strakoš, "Tomáš G. Masaryk," 1–2, and "Živoucnost," 2. The latter of these claims is drawn from the writer Karel Čapek's interview with Masaryk, in which Masaryk gives as the strongest argument for democracy "faith in man, in his spirit and immortal soul; that is true, metaphysical equality. Ethically, democracy is based on the political realization of love of one's neighbor. The eternal to the eternal cannot be indifferent, the eternal cannot misuse the eternal, it cannot exploit and violate it." See Tomáš G. Masaryk, *Masaryk on Thought and Life: Conversations with Karel Čapek*, trans. M. and R. Weatherall (New York: Macmillan, 1938), 190.

78. Jan Strakoš, "T. G. Masaryk stále živý," *Lidová demokracie*, 7 March 1947, 1–2. See also his "Tomáš G. Masaryk," 2.

79. "K svobodě člověka," *Vývoj* 2 (1947): 3.

80. František Škarvan, "Nad Masarykovou Otázkou sociální," *Křesťanská revue* 14 (1947): 40–41.

81. Miloslav Trapl, "Masarykuv poměr k socialismu," *Křesťanská revue* 14 (1947): 210–11.

82. František Hník, "V čem následoval T. G. Masaryka," *Český zápas* 30 (1947): 209.

83. F.R., "Masaryk a socialismus," *Český zápas* 29 (1946): 41. This argumentation is strikingly reminiscent of the common folk belief in Imperial Russia that the Tsar was a good, honest father to his people, who was either unaware of the problems of his people or was deceived by his advisors.

84. František Linhart, "Masaryk a náš náboženský úkol," *Český zápas* 29 (1946): 69, 75, 81.

CHAPTER 7

1. That the capital was "liberated" by Russian troops was one of the legitimizing foundation myths of the communist regime in Czechoslovakia. In fact, however, the Prague Uprising had already succeeded in negotiating a cease-fire and the withdrawal of German units from the city, such that the Russian units that sped 200 kilometers through the night to "liberate" the city "arrived to a Prague already liberated by its own force and diplomacy and almost completely empty of Germans." Václav Cerny, *Křik koruny ceské. Paměti 1938–1945* (Prague: Atlantis, 1992), 392. On the withdrawal of the Germans and arrival of the Russians, see also Detlef Brandes' encyclopedic history of the occupation *Die Tschechen unter den deutschen Protektorat*, vol. 2, (Munich: R. Oldenbourg, 1975), 113–47, and Rudolf Ströbinger, *Poker um Prag. Die frühen Folgen von Jalta* (Zürich: Edition Interfrom, 1985), 80–87.

2. The perusal of these weeks in any of the immediate postwar years will show this to be true, but the most egregious examples can be found in *Mladá fronta* from 1946. The issue of May fifth devoted five and one-half of its eight pages to the uprising (with the week following containing reminiscences every day), and the issue of May ninth contained no less than four poems extolling the virtues of the Soviet Army. Tellingly, the Social Democratic Party daily *Právo lidu* maintained much the same line in 1946—before the party's poor electoral showing and during its period of maximum cooperation with the Communist Party—but in 1947 turned to a more moderate approach, stressing the importance of the first of the month and remaining restrained on the ninth.

3. The expulsion, or "transfer" (*odsun*) as it was termed throughout the period of communist rule, was a further legitimizing myth of the party-state. The Communist Party was the most rhetorically strident on the "German question" in the immediate postwar period and, after the party's assumption of power in 1948, could point to the Soviet Union as the guarantor of Czechoslovakia's borders against "revanchism" from West Germany. In an intense and fascinating emigré and *samizdat* debate beginning in the late 1970s, many Czech intellectuals argued that the expulsion was not only morally wrong, but had damaging effects on the political, economic, and moral development of the nation, contributing to the Communist Party's rise to total power and the ferocity of the early 1950s. On this debate, see Bradley F. Abrams, "Morality, Wisdom and Revision: The Czech Opposition of the 1970s and the Expulsion of the Sudeten Germans," *East European Politics and Societies* 9 (1995): 234–55.

4. Klement Gottwald, "Jednota lidu—jednota v budování—jednota ve věrnosti SSSR a slovanské politiky," *Rudé právo*, 28 October 1947, 1. The term "construction" (adj. *budovatelský*, n. *budování*) here and below should be understood as meaning "the building of socialism." Cf. also B. Kvasnička, "Historické 28. říjny," *Rudé právo*, 28 October 1947, 3.

5. Ladislav Rieger, "28. října—svátek národního budování," *Lidová kultura* 2, no. 37 (1946): 1.

6. Josef Smrkovský, "Splnit ideje, za které lidé umírali," *Rudé právo*, 27 October 1946, 2. Smrkovský can be seen as paradigmatic for the experience of his generation. His life story shows an early enthusiasm for communism, the onset of disillusion after the show trials of the 1950s, radical reformism in the Prague Spring of 1968, and finally exclusion from the party after the Warsaw Pact invasion.

7. See, for example, the coverage given to October 28th in *Svobodné noviny*.

8. The statement was reprinted in all the major dailies. See, for example, "Manifest Národní fronty Čechů a Slováků k 28. říjnu 1945," *Svobodné noviny*, 28 October 1945, 1.

9. Gustav Bareš, "28.X.1918 a ruská revoluce," *Rudé právo*, 28 October 1947, 3.

10. Josef Kubát, "Říjen pokračuje květnem," *Právo lidu*, 27 October 1946, 2.

11. Ladislav Štoll, "Zdroje československé samostatnosti," *Rudé právo*, 28 October 1945, 1. See also the argument that the decision to base the new parliament on election results from 1911, "which had long ago ceased to correspond to the will of the people," had the result of "paralyzing revolutionary feelings." Vladimír Koucký, "Naše demokracie," *Rudé právo*, 21 October 1945, 1.

12. Eduard Bass, "28. říjen," *Svobodné noviny*, 28 October 1945, 1.

13. Ferdinand Peroutka, "Čím je nám 28. říjen," *Svobodné noviny*, 27 October 1946, 1.

14. Vladimír Sís, "Příkaz 28. říjen," *Lidová demokracie*, 28 October 1947, 3. Another Roman Catholic observer tried to shore up October 28th's position by stressing that the illegal celebration of the day under Nazi rule in 1939 was the first act of resistance to the occupation, perhaps trying to counter the Communist stress on the fifth of May as a "fighting" holiday. See d, "28. říjen a 17. listopad,1939," *Lidová demokracie*, 28 October 1945, 2.

15. Petr Zenkl, "28. říjen programem," *Svobodné slovo*, 27 October 1946, 1.

16. Jan Vaněk, "Duch 28. října," *Právo lidu*, 28 October 1947, 1.

17. Zenkl, 1.

18. "Manifest Národní fronty," 1 and Bass, 1.

19. Otakar Machotka, "28. říjen a 5. květen," *Svobodné slovo*, 27 October 1946, 3.

20. J. Závodský, "Smysl 28. října," *Kostnické jiskry* 30 (1945): 171 and Bedřich Bobek, "V tento den sváteční," *Lidová demokracie*, 28 October 1947. The massive Slovak National Uprising commenced on 29 August 1944.

21. "Manifest Národní fronty," 1.

22. Petr Zenkl, "Vule k životu i spolupráce," *Svobodné slovo*, 5 May 1946, 1.

23. More ominously to our eyes today, he also noted that they also shared the quality of having two defining personalities, one Czech and one foreign. October twenty-eighth was defined by Tomáš G. Masaryk and Woodrow Wilson, while the fifth of May was seen in the light of Edvard Beneš and Josef Stalin. Jaroslav Werstadt, "Dvacátý osmý říjen po 28 letech," *Svobodný zítřek* 2, no. 43 (1946): 1–2.

24. Albert Pražák, "Podstata 5. května," *Rudé právo*, 5 May 1946, 1 and "Dva velké dny," *Svobodné slovo*, 28 October 1945, 1.

25. Vilém Nový, "Nový duch 28. října," *Rudé právo*, 27 October 1946, 1.

26. Peroutka, 1.

27. Machotka, 3.

28. Otakar Machotka, "Patý květen 1945," *Svobodný zítřek* 2, no. 18 (1946): 3.

29. Vitězslav Nezval, "5. května—živá krev našich dějin," *Kulturní politika* 2, no. 29 (1946/7): 3.

30. Machotka, "Patý květen," 3.

31. Jiří Zhor, "Proměny," *Dnešek* 1 (1946/7): 65–66.

32. František Halas, "Hlásíme se," 26 June 1945, 1.

33. Helena Koželuhová, "Co je vlastně revoluce?," *Lidová demokracie*, 3 March 1946, 1.

34. Karel Severa, "Dvě revoluce," *Výroj* 2 (1947): 395–96.

35. Jan Strakoš, "Symbol národní a státní svébytnosti," *Lidová demokracie*, 27 October 1946. See also d, "Nesmíme zapomenout," *Lidová demokracie*, 5 May 1946, 1.

36. See, for example, the issues of *Lidová demokracie* surrounding 5 May 1947. Other organs of the noncommunist press, such as *Svobodné noviny*, followed a similar pattern.

37. Karel Štainer-Veselý, "Uskutečnit mravní ideály revoluce," *Práce*, 4 May 1947.

38. Albert Pražák, "Stavíme nový barikády," *Dnešek* 1 (1946/7): 418.

39. František Günzl, "List redakci 'Obzoru,'" *Obzory* 1 (1945): 213.

40. Josef Smrkovský, "Povstání českého lidu," *Rudé právo*, 5 May 1946, 1–2. See also the preelection Social Democratic Party's *Právo lidu*, which condemned the "slanders of the doommongers, fence-sitters, and compromisers [*pomluvy svěků, opatrníků a kompromisníků*]" who had argued that an uprising with the war already essentially won was unnecessary. Josef Mecer, "S holýma rukama," *Právo lidu*, 5 May 1946, 2.

41. Hořec and Miroslav Sigl collected memoirs of the group of young intellectuals surrounding *Mladá fronta* in a volume with the notable title *Generace 1945* (Prague: Rio-press, 1997).

42. Jaromír Hořec, "Nový 28. říjen," *Mladá fronta*, 27 October 1946, 2.

43. Pražák, "Dva velké dni," 1 and E. F. Burian, "[Leader]" *Kulturní politika* 3, no. 7 (1947): 1–2.

44. Jiří Hájek, "Generace 28. říjen a generace 5. květen," *Generace* 1 (1946/7): 4.

45. Hájek, "Generace 28. říjen," 4, and "Tvář generace" in Hájek's *Generace na rozhraní* (Prague: Mladá fronta, 1946), 104.

46. Hájek, "Tvář generace," 104–8.

47. Hájek, "Tvář generace," 108–9.

48. Hájek, "Tvář generace," 112–14.

49. Hájek, "Generace 28. října," 5.

50. Jiří Hájek, "Jsme nositeli nové doby," *Mladá fronta*, 9 May 1946, 2.

51. Václav Černý praised the younger generation for taking part in the social changes of the era, rather than remaining in opposition as the literary avant-garde had during the First Republic. However, he was also the only voice critical of *Generace*, writing that "'Generace' does not suffice as a program. Only Jiří Hájek—to the detriment of real work—has made do with it for seven months already." See Václav Černý, "První číslo 'Generace,'" *Kritický měsíčník* 6 (1945): 245.

52. "Květen 1945—Náš květen," *Mladá fronta*, 5 May 1946, 1–2, and Václav Kutný, "Květnové povstání revolucí mladých," *Mladá fronta*, 5 May 1946, 1. On the role of the youth in the uprising see, for example, the series of articles running in this newspaper from the first to the sixteenth of May 1947.

53. Stanislav Maleček, "Odkaz květnové revoluce," *Mladá fronta*, 5 May 1946, 2 and Kutný, 1. Maleček was also a contributor to *Generace*.

54. Josef Träger, "Tvaří k východu. K diskusi naší kulturní orientace," *Tvorba* 15 (1946): 102. The democratic socialist art critic František Kovárna also noted that the "moral pressure of foreign occupation" and the isolation it had brought formed young intellectuals into a true generation, unlike the generation that had experienced the First World War. See František Kovárna, "Dvojí výtvarná tvář za války," *Kritický měsíčník* 6 (1945): 212–13.

55. Antonín Pimper-Klaušovský, "Staří a mladí," *Lidová demokracie*, 30 December 1945, 1.

56. Pavel Tigrid, "Mravní profil voleb," *Lidová demokracie*, 1 June 1946, 1.

57. Ferdinand Peroutka, "Druhá vystavba," in his *Tak nebo Tak* (Prague: Fr. Borový, 1947), 195.

58. Josef Grňa, "Problematika fašismu. Světová revoluce," *Dnešek* 1 (1946/7): 327.

59. Vratislav Bušek, "Proč jsem národním socialistou II," *Masarykův lid* 15 (1945/6): 54.

60. Bohumil Černý, "Mravní hodnoty revoluce," *Masarykův lid* 15 (1945/6): 526–7. See also the right-wing Social Democrat Josef Hudec's article "Na prahu socialismu," *Dnešek* 1 (1946/7): 389–90.

61. Jaroslav Stránský, "O revoluci a právu," *Svobodný zítřek* 2, no. 5 (1946): 1–2. It should be pointed out that Communist Party intellectual and cultural leaders only used the term "revolution" in the phrase "national and democratic revolution," as it fit poorly into the conceptual cluster surrounding the moderate course the party consistently advocated. It is also interesting to note that Stránský felt compelled to argue using terms appealing to both the right ("insane revolution") and the left ("counterrevolution.")

62. Ferdinand Peroutka, "Duch v revoluci," *Svobodné noviny*, 6 February 1946, 1.

63. Ferdinand Peroutka, "Chvála roku 1946," *Dnešek* 1 (1946/7): 641.

64. Koželuhová, 1–2.

65. Severa, 396.

66. KBH, "Křesťanství v zrcadle naší národní povahy," *Katolík* 10, no. 21 (1947): 2.

67. Dominic Pecka, "Cesta do sociální obnovy," *Vyšehrad* 3 (1947/8): 96.

68. František Bednář, "Křesťanství a dnešní světová revoluce," *Svobodný zítřek* 2, no. 8 (1946): 1.

69. "Tábor je náš program," *Český zápas* 30 (1947): 120.

CHAPTER 8

1. Pavel Tigrid, "Věčná otázka našich dějin," *Lidová demokracie*, 14 July 1946, 1–2. This idea was expressed most often in the form employed by J. B. Čapek, that the question of national

orientation constituted the "problem of our entire history." J. B. Čapek, "K dnešním úkolum národní kultury," *Naše doba* 53 (1946/7): 156.

2. Jindřich Chalupecký "Konec moderní doby" in his *Obhajoba umění 1934–1948* (Prague: Orientace, 1991), 158. The article originally appeared in the journal he edited, *Listy* 1 (1946): 1–23.

3. Dominik Pecka, quoted in "Československá kultura mezi západem a východem," *Lidová demokracie*, 1 January 1948, 5. This massive survey of 78 leading noncommunist intellectuals was published in two issues of the Roman Catholic People's Party newspaper, the first appearing on 1 January 1948 (hereafter LD1) and the second three days later (hereafter LD2).

4. František Vrba, "K socialistické kritice dneška," *Generace* 1, no. 3 (1946/7): 6.

5. Klement Gottwald, "Masaryk k dnešku," *Tvorba* 16 (1947): 729.

6. Dr. Václav Wagner, chairman of the State Memorials Office, LD2, 15.

7. Vojta Beneš, "Mezi západem a východem," *Český život* 1 (1947): 146–47.

8. Evžen Klinger, "Stíny Mnichova," *Mladá fronta*, 28 September 1947, 2.

9. Jiří Zhoř, "Její tvář," *Dnešek* 2 (1947/8): 354.

10. Václav Molkop, "Poselství sněmu k cirkvi a národu," *Český západ* 29 (1946): 7. See also J. L. Fischer, LD1, 1.

11. František Stehlý "K výročí říjnové revoluce," *Lidová demokracie*, 7 November 1946, 1, and Josef Macurek, *Slovanská idea a dnešní skutečnost* (Brno: Zemská osvětová rada, 1947), 25.

12. Jaromír Uhlíř, "Česká otázka," *Masarykův lid* 14–5 (1945/6): 7.

13. Edvard Beneš, *EB národu. Z projevů presidenta republiky v letech 1945–1946*, ed. František Škarvan (Prague: Zemská rada osvětová, 1946), 56, and Macurek, 22–23. See also Beneš' comments at the end of his *Úvahy o slovanství* (Prague: Čin, 1947), 304.

14. Ludvík Kuba, LD1, 4.

15. František Bednář, "Nedostatky a kazy našeho života," *Svobodný zítřek* 2, no. 49 (1946): 1.

16. Josef Rybák, "Naše kulturní úkoly," *Rudé právo*, 25 December 1945, 5.

17. Edvard Beneš, *Úvahy*, 260.

18. Ladislav Štoll, "Východ a západ," *Rudé právo*, 19 August 1945, 1.

19. Diary entry from 17 April 1945, reproduced in Ferdinand Peroutka, *Muž přítomnosti* (Zürich: Konfrontace, 1985), 126.

20. See, for example, Pavel Reiman, "Dvě cesty literárního vývoje," *Tvorba* 14 (1945): 261.

21. Čapek, 157, and Josef Macurek, cited in Josef Brambora, "Na sjezdu historiku," *Práce*, 9 October 1947, 4.

22. Lumír Čivrný, "Poznámky k diskusi o sjezdu spisovatelu," *Tvorba* 15 (1946): 507.

23. Václav Řezáč, "O novou kulturní orientaci," *Práce*, 26 August 1945, 3.

24. Lev Sychrava, "'Spravná' ideologie," *Národní osvobození*, 19 October 1947, 1. For a similar view see Miloš Dvořák, LD1, 3.

25. Antonín Klatovský, "Svoboda a socialismus," *Dnešek* 2 (1947/8): 168.

26. Klatovský, 183.

27. Václav Černý, "Ještě jednou: Mezi východem a západem. (K problematice socialistické kultury u nás, 1.)," *Kritický měsíčník* 6 (1945): 143. See also Vojta Beneš's comment that "The soviets did not drop from the heavens. . . . they are the work of centuries and are not so terribly far from Western European development." Vojta Beneš, 147.

28. Otakar Machotka, "Západ či východ?," *Svobodný zítřek* 1, no. 5 (1945): 5, 10.

29. See, for example, the comments of the literary critic and former member of the Prague Linguistic Circle Jan Mukařovský in "K otázce tak zvané orientace," *Tvorba* 15 (1946): 148–49.

30. J. L. Hromádka, "Poslání Československa v dnešní Evropě" in his *O nové Československo* (Prague: Henclova tiskárna, 1946), 25.

31. Mil. Kaňak, "Víra v dějinný pokrok prolegomenon historického bádání," *Náboženská revue* 17 (1946): 35 and "Úvaha o zpusobu a metodě historického bádání v ČCS," *Náboženská revue* 17 (1946): 286.

32. Karel Polák, "Rozhovor o kultuře," *Vývoj* 2 (1947): 676.

33. Jaroslav Stránský, "Sedmý listopad a my," *Svobodný zítřek* 1, no. 7 (1945): 2.

34. Černý, 144.

35. Prokop Maxa, "Význam Slovanského sjezdu v Bělehradě," in *Slovanský sjezd v Bělehrad r. 1946*, ed. Václav Burian, A. Frinta and B. Havránek (Prague: Orbis, 1947), 8, and Emanuel Poche, LD2, 13.

36. Macůrek, 5–6.

37. Lev Sychrava, "Slovanské zrádcování," *Národní Osvobození*, 11 December 1947, 1.

38. V. V. Štech, "Umění v národě a státě," *Dílo* 34 (1945/6): 10.

39. Zdeněk Nejedlý, cited in Václav Cháb, "Říjnová revoluce a Slovanstvo," *Národní osvobození*, 9 October 1947, 5. See also Josef Macůrek's comment that in order to fulfill their "special mission," Slavs should strive "to make it impossible that the Slavic world appears as a reactionary or retarding element." Macůrek, 36.

40. Beneš wrote another, shorter book on the matter, which contributed nothing new to his ideas and seems intended to popularize the topic. See Edvard Beneš. *Nová slovanská politika* (Prague: Čin, 1946). Milan Hauner has addressed Beneš's revival of Slavism in his "Von der Verteidigung der 'kleinen Völker' zum neuen Slawismus. Edvard Beneš und der Slawismus," in *Geschichtliche Mythen in den Literaturen und Kulturen Ostmittel- und Südosteuropas*, ed. Eva Behring, Ludwig Richter, and Wolfgang F. Schwarz (Stuttgart: Franz Steiner, 1999), 293–309.

41. Edvard Beneš, *Úvahy*, 253–54.

42. Edvard Beneš, *Úvahy*, 254, 256.

43. Edvard Beneš, *Úvahy*, 282.

44. Edvard Beneš, *Úvahy*, 281, 291. It is interesting and more than a little ominous that Beneš used the less common term *souručenství*, as the only legal political party under the Nazi occupation was named *Národní souručenství* (National Solidarity).

45. Edvard Beneš, *Úvahy*, 268.

46. Edvard Beneš, *Úvahy*, 269, 265.

47. Edvard Beneš, *Úvahy*, 265, 196.

48. Molkop, 7.

49. an, "Církve a jednota Slovanstva," *Český zápas* 30 (1947): 64. The stress on uniting religion and science is reminiscent of the church's solution to the crisis it saw Czech society experiencing. It is also interesting to note that it is almost exclusively communists and representatives of the Czechoslovak Church who use the word "Slovanstvo," which is tied to the Russian, in place of the more common Czech word "Slovanství."

50. Jaroslav Pravda "Všeslovanská vzájemnost a solidarita politická," "Všeslovanská vzájemnost a solidarita kulturní," and "Jeden za všechny a všichni za jednoho heslem všeslovanským," *Masarykův lid* 15 (1945/6): 88–89, 133–34, 498–99. The quoted material appears in the first of these articles, but is representative of the tone taken throughout.

51. Adolph Procházka, "Bilance osvobozovací zahraniční práce a nárys ústavního života republiky," *Lidová demokracie*, 20 May 1945, 2.

52. Jan Strakoš, "Tomáš G. Masaryk mezi námi," *Lidová demokracie*, 7 March 1946, 1, and "Karel Havlíček Borovský a dněek," *Lidová demokracie*, 28 July 1946, 1–2.

53. Vladimír Sís, "Po slovanském sjezdu," *Lidová demokracie*, 29 December 1946, 1.

54. Pavel Tigrid, "Odpověď Barešovi, aneb: co chceme," *Obzory* 3 (1947): 400. See Beneš's comments in *Úvahy*, 279.

55. Václav Černý, "Mezi východem a západem," *Kritický měsíčník* 6 (1945): 70.

56. Černý, "Mezi východem a západem," 71.

57. Černý, "Mezi východem a západem," 72. As an example of how tenacious the struggle over the nation's orientation was, in 1947 Černý published a scholarly work on Czech courtly poetry, in which he demonstrated its roots in the songs of French and Italian troubadours of the fourteenth century. The study came under intense fire from communist intellectuals, who accused it of being merely a way of encouraging the Western orientation. Václav Černý, *Staročeská milostná lyrika* (Prague: Družstevní práce, 1947).

58. Černý, "Mezi východem a západem," 73.

59. Černý, "Ještě jednou," 142.

60. Černý, "Mezi východem a západem," 71.

61. Černý, "Ještě jednou," 143–44.

62. Černý, "Mezi východem a západem," 73.

63. Černý, "Ještě jednou," 144.

64. Černý, "O naší moderní socialistické tradici a co s ní souvisí. (K problematice socialistické kultury u nás, 5.)," *Kritický měsíčník* 7 (1946): 179.

65. Černý, "Ještě jednou," 141.

66. Černý, "O naší moderní socialistické tradici." 179.

67. J. B. Čapek, "K dnešním úkolům národní kultury," *Naše doba* 53 (1946/7): 157.

68. On the Roman Catholic view, see Adolph Procházka, "Naše národní individualita," *Lidová demokracie*, 6 October 1945, 1 or Al. Birnbaumová, LD2, 11, and for the communists, among many others, "Východ či západ?" *Kulturní politika* 1, no. 1 (1945/6): 1.

69. See, for example, Klement Gottwald, "Masaryk k dnešku," *Tvorba* 16 (1947): 729, and Pavel Reiman, "Dvě cesty literárního vývoje," *Tvorba* 14 (1945): 261–62.

70. Tigrid, "Věčná otázka," 1.

71. Karel Falta, "My a západ," *Masarykův lid* 14–5 (1945/6): 120, and Jaroslav Nečas, "Naše kulturní situace," *Masarykův lid* 14–5 (1945/6): 478. Analogous comments appear, for example, in Miroslav Rutte, LD2, 14, Jaroslav Šimsa, "Lednový traktát," *Naše doba* 52 (1945/6): 56–57, and Vojta Beneš, 147.

72. The citation is from Sychrava, 1. See also František Hála, LD1, 4, J. L. Hromádka, "Naše problematika," *Svobodný zítřek* 1, no. 3 (1945): 2, or Václav Běhounek, "Na východ či na západ?," *Práce*, 15 July 1945, 8, among many others.

73. Albert Pražák, "Změna doby v našem písemnictví," *Naše doba* 52 (1945/6): 11, Vl. Hellmuth-Brauner, "Svět, který jsme zdědili a který tvoříme," *Vyšehrad* 1, no. 6 (1945/6): 3 and J. L. Fischer, LD1, 4.

74. Redakce, "O co usilujeme a co odmítáme," *Obzory* 1 (1945): 214. Among other examples, see Fr. Marek, "K dni zrození demokracie," *Katolík* 10, no. 29 (1947): 3 or Sychrava, 1.

75. Zdeněk Kalista, LD1, 4.

76. See, for example, Klatovský, 182, A. Novotný, "Stále živý program," *Svobodný zítřek* 1, no. 11 (1945): 2 or František Hník, "Národní revoluce a svoboda," *Český život* 29 (1946): 92.

77. Chalupecký, 159–60. See also the historian J. L. Fischer's comment that the bridge concept came from the Czech "taste for compromise." J. L. Fischer, "Západ či Východ?," *Svobodné noviny*, 18 October 1946, 1.

78. Čivrný, 507.

79. From a speech given 14 July 1946 in Kroměříž, which was reprinted in Edvard Beneš, *EB národu*, 50.

80. For the former, see the leading National Socialist Petr Zenkl's comments in Jindřich Chalupecký, "O naší kulturní politiky," *Lidová kultura* 3, no. 10 (1947): 1, and for the latter see Tigrid, "Věčná otázka," 1, among many others.

81. Bohumil Laušman, LD1, 5. See also Karel Polák's comment in LD1, 5, and Václav Žižka, "S východem a západem," *Masarykův lid* 15 (1945/6): 13.

82. nb, "Západ, východ a my uprostřed," *Svobodný zítřek* 2, no. 46 (1946): 2.

83. Redakce, 214.

84. Havel-Hrbas, "Demokracie hledá sebe," *Národní osvobození*, 12 August 1945, 1. See also Vojta Beneš, 147.

85. Sychrava, 1.

86. Jan Slavík, "Tvář státu v zrcadle voleb," *Svobodný zítřek* 1, no. 23 (1946): 2.

87. Jaromír Hořec, "Dějinný generační úkol," *Mladá fronta*, 21 October 1945, 1.

88. Karel Polák, "Rozhovor o kultuře," *Vývoj* 2 (1947): 676. See also Professor Zdeněk Frankenberger, LD2, 12.

89. Hála, 4. See also Nečas, 478.

90. Žižka, 13. Among many analogous comments, see especially those of Sychrava, 1, and Jaroslav Seifert, "O umění" *Vývoj* 2 (1947): 867.

91. Jan Dokulil, LD1, 3 and Nečas, 478.

CHAPTER 9

1. To the author's knowledge this view was only held by one contemporary observer. In late 1947, Karel Kosík called the people's democracy a "revolutionary process, when the national, democratic revolution grows into a socialist revolution." Karel Kosík, "O nové cestě k socialismu," *Lidová kultura* 3, no. 42 (1947): 8. It is interesting to note that the journal's editorial board published this article, which came out immediately after the announcement of the "Czechoslovak road," with the disclaimer that they disagreed with some statements in it. They were likely aware that the freedom of action that the "Czechoslovak road" implied might be curtailed by Moscow and wished to protect themselves against an erroneous interpretation of the policy. The argument on the growth of the revolution into a truly socialist one can be found in Jaroslav Cesar and Zdeněk Snítil, *Československá revoluce 1944–1948* (Prague: Svoboda, 1979) and, more subtly made, in Jon Bloomfield, *Passive Revolution: Politics and the Czechoslovak Working Class, 1945–1948* (New York: St. Martin's, 1979).

2. Hubert Ripka, *Czechoslovakia Enslaved. The Story of the Communist Coup d'Etat* (London: Gollancz, 1950), 12 and 27. This has recently appeared in Czech translation (*Únorová tragedie. Svědectví přímého účastníka* [Prague: Atlantis, 1995]), but appeared first in French with the telling title *Le Coup de Prague: Une Révolution Préfabriquée* (Paris: Plon, 1949). This position was also adopted by Paul Zinner, who wrote,"The question is frequently asked whether the Communists in Czechoslovakia and elsewhere in Eastern Europe proceeded according to a plan conceived and elaborated in advance. The answer in the Czech case is certainly affirmative." Paul Zinner, *Communist Strategy and Tactics in Czechoslovakia. 1918–1948.* (London: Pall Mall, 1963), 117.

3. A variation on this argument posits that the party had a public program designed to assure it public support and a "secret" one for seizing power. This argument is made, for example, by Toman Brod in his *Cesta československých komunistů k moci v letech 1945–1948*, vol. 1 (Prague: Magnet, 1990), 39 and 84. As will become apparent, the discussions even in the closed confines of the Central Committee render this argument invalid. If leading communist political actors could not even privately discuss such a "secret program," there can be little doubt that no such program existed.

4. Václav Pavlíček, *Politické strany po únoru. Příspěvek k problematice Národní fronty*, vol.1(Prague: Svobodné slovo, 1966), 61–62. See also Karel Bartošek's opening speech at the landmark 1966 historical conference devoted to the early postwar period. He concludes, "It would be naive to think that the revolutionary development in Czechoslovakia was carried out in the years 1945–1948 'according to plan' and more precisely to conceptions created beforehand." Karel Bartošek, "Československá společnost a revoluce," in *Československá revoluce v letech 1944–1948. Sborník příspěvků z konference historiků k 20. výročí osvobození ČSR*, ed. J. Kladiva and V. Lacina (Prague: Academia, 1966), 43. The entire "Prague Spring" was fruitful for reflection on the 1945–1948 period and particularly for ruminations on the "Czechoslovak road," as reform communist historians strove to create space for a "socialism with a human face." They argued that the "Czechoslovak road" and the entire development of the state had been aiming toward a democratic socialist order until thrown off its natural course into Soviet-style totalitarianism by Stalin and the "cult of personality."

5. Brod, 63.

6. Josef Beld, "Československá cesta k socialismu," *Příspěvky k dějinám KSČ* 7 (1967): 18.

7. J. Kolár, "Socialisační snahy v roce 1918," *Tvorba* 14 (1945): 275.

8. Brod, 62–63.

9. This is from a speech made to party functionaries in Prague on 5 July 1945. "O politice Komunistické strany Československa v dnešní situaci," in his *Spisy*, vol.12 (Prague: SNPL, 1955), 80–81, 83. This reiterated Gottwald's sentiments as expressed in Slovakia three months earlier: "Does this mean that already today it is time for us to place as our immediate goal a soviet republic, a socialist state? No! On the contrary, it would be a great strategic mistake if the party were to have such immediate prospects. In spite of the favorable situation the nearest goal is not soviets and socialization, but the truly consistent carrying through of the democratic, national revolution." See "Projev na konferenci funkcionářů Komunistické strany Slovenska," in *Spisy*, vol. 12, 15.

10. Gustav Bareš, *Naše cesta k socialismu* (Prague: ÚV KSČ, 1948), 14.

11. Karel Kaplan and Pavel Reiman, "Vývoj názorů na revoluci v Československu," in *Sborník historických prací o naší cestě k socialismu*, Digest 2, Supplement 2 (Prague, 1966). Cited in Martin Schultze Wessel, "Vom Tabu zum Mythos? Der 'spezifische Weg zum Sozialismus' in der Tschechoslowakei," in *Kommunismus in Osteuropa. Konzepte. Perspektiven und Interpretationen im Wandel*, ed. Eva Schmidt-Hartmann (Munich: R. Oldenbourg, 1994), 246.

12. Jaroslav Kladiva, *Kultura a politika 1945–1948* (Prague: Svoboda, 1968), 221. The latter of these claims is attributed to Jiří Veltruský, *Byrokracie, demokracie a dělnická třída* (Prague: Sociální demokracie, 1945), 19. The author could not verify this, but in the second edition Veltruský does accuse the Communist Party of bureaucratism and absurdly states that the party's politics had isolated it on the *right* of the political spectrum. Jiří Veltruský, *Byrokracie, demokracie a dělnická třída*, (Prague: Propagační oddělení ČSSD, 1946), 7–8, 19.

13. Bloomfield, 74–79.

14. Belda, 14–15. While Belda argues that this was due to fear of isolation on the left, it is at least equally plausible that, as all political forces in the nation were united behind the communist-inspired Košice program, there was no need to go further at that time.

15. See, for example, "Klid a neklid mezi námi," *Svobodný zítřek* 2, no. 7 (1946): 1 or Stanislav Budín, "Jakou politiku?," *Kulturní politika* 3, no. 13 (1947/8): 1. At that time the party could have taken advantage of the rabid anti-Germanism and revolutionary feeling of the Czechs as well as the aid the Red Army could have provided, and which it in fact did provide to other Eastern European Communist parties. Budín saw this as evidence that the party had no such thoughts even at the late date of his writing.

16. Marie Švermová, "Jsme milionovou stranou národa," *Rudé právo*, 31 March 1946, 5.

17. Rudolf Slánský, "Sněm budovatelů," *Rudé právo*, 31 March 1946, 1.

18. Václav Kopecký, "O národní a státní ideologie nového Československa," *Rudé právo*, 31 March 1946, 4.

19. Rudolf Slánský, Václav Nosek and Klement Gottwald, "Pozdrav soudruhu J. Stalinovi," *Rudé právo*, 29 March 1946, 1.

20. Klement Gottwald, "Komunistická strana při budování nové republiky," *Rudé právo*, 30 March 1946, 3–5. This speech is reprinted in his *Spisy*, vol. 12, 351–73.

21. Jaroslav Opat, "K metodě studia a výkladu některých problémů v období 1945–1948," *Příspěvky k dějinám KSČ* 5 (1965): 75. See also Michal Reiman's comment that "[t]he program of the Gottwald government itself shows that the construction of socialism in Czechoslovakia appeared differently to the party after the Eighth Congress than later interpretations relate. The truth is that this program in essence grew from the given structure . . . It counted on more serious changes only in agriculture." Michal Reiman, "Koncepce KSČ 'O specifické cestě k socialismu' v naší revoluci," in Kladiva and Lacina, 170.

22. Klement Gottwald, "O naší československé cestě k socialismu," in his *Spisy*, vol. 12, 230. This is taken from a speech made to party functionaries from the factories in October of 1946.

23. The main point of Stalin's words was related in the *Daily Herald* by one of the participants, an M. Phillips: "There are two roads to socialism: one Russian and one British. It is clear that each conceives of achieving the socialist goal in its own way. The Russian road is shorter, but less easy

and brings bloodshed with it. Nonetheless, it is necessary to bear in mind that Marx's and Lenin's adherents do not consider this road as the only one leading to socialism. The parliamentary road does not bring bloodshed with it, but is a longer march." Cited in Karel Kaplan and Michal Reiman, "Naše revoluce a myšlenky o socialismu," *Plamen* 7, no. 12 (1965): 114.

24. The fact that the Communist party of Czechoslovakia's sister party, the Communist Party of Slovakia, could muster only 31% against only one serious contender—the Democratic Party— was merely a slight hindrance. The Communists soon found the "bourgeois" parties willing allies in curtailing the power of the Democratic Party and the autonomy of Slovakia in general. On this, and the lack of unity between Czech and Slovak noncommunist political parties in general, see the author's "The Politics of Retribution: The Trial of Jozef Tiso," *East European Politics and Societies* 10 (1996): 255–92.

25. Cited in Kaplan and Reiman, 114.

26. Klement Gottwald, *Deset let*, ed. Gustav Bareš (Prague: Orbis, 1948). The history of this book mirrors the history of the "Czechoslovak road to socialism." First published in 1947, it went through several editions through 1949, with all editions of Gottwald's many speeches and references to the "Czechoslovak road" (although notably remaining blank for the period of the Nazi-Soviet Pact). It was even recommended that all read it in order to understand the theory. (See Gustav Bareš, "Pramen živé vody. Co nám řekl Stalin," *Tvorba* 16 [1947]: 356.) Thereafter, these portions were excised. Similarly, when the definitive collection of Gottwald's works was issued in the 1950s, almost all mentions of the "Czechoslovak road" had been removed.

27. Fr. Lužický, "O ruzných cestách k socialismu," *Tvorba* 15 (1946): 796–97.

28. Gustav Bareš, "Socialismus je v životném zájmu národa a republiky," *Rudé právo*, 11 January 1948, 4.

29. These appeared in different forms in the works of different authors, but remained constant into 1948. See, for example, František Nečasek, "Klement Gottwald o naší cestě k socialismu," *Tvorba* 15 (1946): 705–6 near the beginning of the period, and as an example from just before the party's achievement of total power see Bareš, *Naše cesta*, 9–12. Note also that Václav Kopecký's conception of the "new Czechoslovakia" in early 1948 rests on these same ideas. Václav Kopecký, *Zápas o nové vlastenectví* (Prague: ÚV KSČ, 1948).

30. See K. R., "Lidová lidovláda?," *Tvorba* 14 (1945): 189–90.

31. Nečasek, 705.

32. Kopecký, *Zápas*, 37–38. Kopecký based his view on Zhdanov's writings. See also the comment that "it is necessary to emphasize the conception of the People's Democracy as our specific national transitional form from capitalism to socialism." K. Lukeš and V. Ruml, "Gottwald: politik, státník, budovatel," *Tvorba* 16 (1947): 93.

33. Bareš, *Naše cesta*, 28.

34. Bareš, *Naše cesta*, 34.

35. On the history of the idea of planning, see Zdeněk Snítil, "O dvouletce a jejím místě v politice KSČ v roce 1946," *Příspěvky k dějinám KSČ* 7 (1967): 669–98.

36. Čeněk Adamec, Bohuš Pospíšil, and Milan Tesař, *What's Your Opinion? A Year's Survey of Public Opinion in Czechoslovakia* (Prague: Orbis, 1947), 15. To the question "Do you know the contents of the Two-Year Plan thoroughly, or only in its main outline, or not at all?" posed in September 1946 16% answered "Thoroughly," 57% "Main Outline" and 27% "Not at all." To the November 1946 question "Do you believe that the Two-Year Plan will succeed entirely, or partly, or not at all?" 41% responded "Entirely successful," 36% "Partly successful," 4% "Fail," and 19% "Don't know."

37. See ojn, "Nepřátele dvouletky půjdou do žaláře," *Práce*, 30 January 1947. While the popularity of such measures is impossible to gauge, 70% approved of fining those who were late to work (including 87% of those over the age of 50, i.e., those who would best remember the interwar republic), while only 17% disapproved. See Adamec et al., 29.

38. Jaromír Hořec, "Přemyšlení o reakci," *Mladá fronta*, 1 December 1946, 2.

39. Klement Gottwald, "Zasedání Ústředního výboru KSČ 22.–23. ledna 1947," *Spisy*, vol. 13 (Prague: SNPL, 1957), 292.

40. Gottwald, "O naší Československé cestě," 231.

41. Arnošt Kolman, *Co je smyslem života?* (Prague: Orbis, 1947), 23.

42. See, for example, Lumír Čivrný, "Poznámky k diskusi o sjezdu spisovatelů," *Tvorba* 15 (1946): 507.

43. Cited in Brod, 52.

44. Gottwald, "O naší Československé cestě," 231.

45. Nečasek, 706 and Jiří Hendrych, "Od 40 Procent k většině národa," *Tvorba* 16 (1947): 374.

46. See, for examples outside of the Communist Party press, the cartoon and poem set "Na startu," *Kulturní politika* 2, no. 6 (1946/7): 1, or the poem by the apolitical poet Kamil Bednář, "Dvouletý plan." *Lidová kultura* 3, no. 11 (1947): 1. The fairy tale is called "Pohádka o dvouletce" and appears in the early issues of 1947. Despite this ludicrous example, the journal solemnly set itself the task of "convinc[ing] all doubters of the high cultural values of the Two-Year Plan." František Jungmann, "Dvouletka a kultura," *Lidová kultura* 2, no. 36 (1946): 2.

47. Gustav Bareš, "Cesta naší kultury," *Tvorba* 15 (1946): 673–74.

48. Čivrný, 508.

49. On the history of the idea, see Reiman, 400–12.

50. Nečasek, 706.

51. Bareš, *Naše cesta*, 34.

52. On the situation inside the party at this time, see M. R. Myant, *Socialism and Democracy in Czechoslovakia, 1945–1948* (Cambridge: Cambridge University Press, 1981), 140–41.

53. The maintenance of the National Front was made public from the outset. See Hendrych, 706. It was also reiterated inside the secrecy of the Central Committee at least as late as June of 1947 by Rudolf Slánský. See Pavlíček, 89.

54. Gottwald apparently believed that a certain correlation existed between the number of party members and its vote. Since one million members had brought 40% of the vote, he called for a rise in the party rolls to 1.5 million, thereby calculating a majority. Most of the new members gained in this drive already voted Communist and the desired inroads into the middle classes were not successfully made.

55. Discussion of the majority covers three pages in Klement Gottwald, "Osnova referátu na zasedání Ústředního Výboru KSČ 27. listopadu 1947," in his *Spisy*, vol. 14 (Prague: SNPL, 1958), 190–93, here 193. Gottwald made these optimistic statements although, according to the Social Democratic leader Bohumil Laušman, roughly a month later he apparently thought the KSČ percentage of the vote would only remain stable and "no longer spoke of the 51 percent." Bohumil Laušman, *Kdo byl vinen?* (Vienna: n.p., 1953), 181. The press release on this meeting stressed "The National Front—One Hundred Percent Yes!" and closed with the same words expressing confidence in the party's ability to gain a majority. See Klement Gottwald, "Referát na zasedání Ústředního Výboru KSČ 27. listopadu 1947" in his *Spisy*, vol. 14 (Prague, SNPL, 1958), 203 and 206. For similar sentiments expressed publicly in January 1948, see Reiman and Kaplan, 116.

56. Eduard Táborský, *Prezident Beneš mezi Západem a Východem* (Prague: Mladá fronta, 1993), 253 (available in English as *President E. Beneš between West and East, 1938–1948* [Stanford: Hoover, 1981]). Táborský believed that the Communists would get "perhaps 25% of the votes." Hubert Ripka similarly believed that the party would lose eight to ten of its forty percent. Ripka, 182.

57. Ripka, 47.

58. Myant, 131.

59. Karel Kaplan, *Nekrvavá revoluce* (Prague: Mladá fronta, 1993), 134. Cf. Kaplan's statement that these findings were "exaggeratedly favourable" in his *Short March*, 149.

60. Dana A. Schmidt, *Anatomy of a Satellite* (Boston: Little, Brown, 1953), 327. See also John Brown [pseud.], *Who's Next? The Lesson of Czechoslovakia* (London: Hutchinson, 1951).

61. mch [Pavel Machonin?], "Nedokončený pruzkum," *Dějiny a současnost* (1968) 7:44.

62. That the Communist Party would likely remain the largest was recognized even by Ripka: "Even if the Communists remained relatively the strongest party—which was to be expected. . ." Ripka, 185. If Laušman is right (see note 55), this is the result Gottwald also anticipated.

63. Karel Kaplan, *Das verhängnisvolle Bundnis. Unterwanderung, Gleichschaltung und Vernichtung der tschechoslowakischen Sozialdemokratie 1944–54* (Wuppertal: POL, 1984) 62–66.

64. Cited in Jaroslav Kladiva. *Kultura a politika*, 237.

65. Jaroslav Kladiva, "Význam 'Československá cesta k socialismu' v politických a ideových zápasech let 1946–1947," *Nová mysl* 20, no. 17 (1966): 8.

66. Vratislav Bušek, "Dvě cesty socialismu," *Svobodné slovo*, 1 October 1946, 1.

67. Cited in Kladiva, *Kultura a politika*, 229.

68. Kladiva, "Význam," 9.

69. Radical socialist intellectuals looked primarily in the National Socialists' ranks for the "reaction" that they held threatened the country. They also made much of an open letter from an interwar National Socialist senator, who bemoaned the "bad situation created by today's leadership of the National Socialist Party, composed to a general extent of new people for whom the original ideology of the party is entirely foreign. . . . It is necessary for the true National Socialists to be able to remind the leadership of our party that our party must be socialist as it was, if it is not to harm its future development and expansion." Ferdinand Šťastný, "Pro socialistický blok," *Práce*, 18 September 1947, 1.

70. Jaroslav Kladiva cites negative reactions from Zlín, Olomouc, Mladá boleslav and Prague 8. Kladiva, *Kultura a politika*, 221. The August demand is cited in Jaroslav Opat, *O novou demokracii. Příspěvek k dějinám národně demokratické revoluce v Československu v letech 1945–1948* (Prague: Academia, 1966), 223.

71. Meeting of the Central Committee, 25–26 September 1946. Cited in Reiman, 405.

72. Nečasek, 705–6.

73. Opat, "K metodě," 70–71.

74. "Dvouletka—nejblížší etapou na cestě k socialismu," *Rudé právo*, 5 October 1946, Lenin's *Letters from Afar* and Stalin's *Fundamentals of Leninism*, for example, are cited in respectively Nečasek, 705, and Bareš "Pramen," 356.

75. František Pexa, "Lenin mluví k dnešku," *Tvorba* 16 (1947): 64–65.

76. Lukeš and Ruml, 93. See also the comment that Gottwald's ideas were "a brilliant example of creative Marxist analysis" in Nečasek, 705.

77. Kopecký, *Zápas*, 41–43.

78. Kolman, 29.

79. Luděk Forman, "Včera a dnes," *Obzory* 2 (1946): 809.

80. For example, 140,000 copies of the *History of the Communist Party of the Soviet Union (Bolshevik)* and almost 100,000 of Stalin's *On the Great Patriotic War of the Soviet Union* had been sold by the end of 1947, and Klement Gottwald's *Deset let* had gone through six editions totaling 70,000 copies. This at a time when few books were bought due to the postwar austerity. Jaroslav Kladiva, "Boj o duši národa v předvečer února 1948," *Československý časopis historický* 15 (1967): 69–70. The citation is from page 70.

81. Václav Běhounek, "'Překonavatelé' marxismu," *Kulturní politika* 1, no. 34 (1945/6): 1, 4.

82. Josef Kubat, "Mravnost socialismu," *Práce*, 19 January 1947, 1. The final comment may have been directed at the National Socialist Party's Otakar Machotka, whose *Socialism českého člověka* had been published the year before. The view that Marxism's opponents were caricaturing the materialism of socialist theory was also the view of left-wing Social Democrats like Radim Foustka, who wrote that "Materialism and Marx's historical materialism are currents of thought that have nothing in common. . . . Marxism does not deny the powerful influence that ideas and great people have on history, it does not deny the influence of cultural and other actors." Radim Foustka, *O pevnou půdu pod nohama* (Prague: Ústřední akční výbor čs. sociální demokracie, 1945). Cf. also his *Dialektický materialismus jako způsob myšlení* (Prague: Práce, 1946).

83. See, for example, Kolman, 7, and, for a similar social democratic view Foustka, 5.

84. Běhounek, 1.

85. Ladislav Štoll, "O naší národní ideologii," *Rudé právo*, 10 March 1946, 2.

86. For just one example, see Heda Kovály's comments that "The Communists at that time kept stressing the scientific basis of their ideology. . . . The result [of the war] was a sudden loss of personal and national identity. . . . The democratic government of Thomas Masaryk had instilled in us the certainty that some things could no longer happen. . . . When it happened in our time and in a form far worse than we could imagine, it felt like the end of the world. . . . we came to believe that communism was the very opposite of Nazism, a movement that would restore all the values that Nazism had destroyed." Heda Margulius Kovály, *Under a Cruel Star: A Life in Prague, 1941–1968* (New York: Penguin, 1986), 58 and 64–65.

87. Kopecký, *Zápas*, 51 and 53. The effect of socialism's "scientific" basis on Czech consciousness can of course not be proven, but the testimonials of many former communists ensure its plausibility. See, among many others, Mlynář's rueful comment that "the ideology contained in this [communist] literature gives someone who in reality knows very little or nothing at all the self-assurance of someone who has mastered the very laws that govern the development of mankind and the world." Zdeněk Mlynář, *Nightfrost in Prague*, trans. Paul Wilson (New York: Karz, 1980), 2–3.

88. K. Moškovič explored a different route, arguing that "The dictatorship of the proletariat and its entire development does not have to be the same in our country as in the USSR." Felix Oliva posed the question, and P. Reiman provided the consensus view. All cited in Kaplan and Reiman, 113.

89. Arnošt Kolman, "Otevřený dopis univ. prof. Dr J. B.Kozákovi," *Tvorba* 15 (1946): 305–6.

90. Hendrych, 373.

91. Gustav Bareš, *Naše cesta*, 33–34.

92. Jaroslav Opat, *O novou demokracii*, 225.

93. Gustav Bareš, "Odpověď lidem, kteří ničemu nenaučili," *Rudé právo*, 6 March 1946, 1. In this case, Bareš was characterizing Ferdinand Peroutka as straying dangerously close to such opinions.

94. Kopecký, *Zápas*, 43.

95. Walter Ullmann, *The United States in Prague, 1945–1948* (Boulder, CO: East European Quarterly, 1978), 108–9.

96. These are the final words of Bareš's *Naše cesta k socialismu*, 35.

97. "Svoboda včera a dnes," *Rudé právo*, 28 January 1948, 2, and Václav Kopecký, "O národní a státní ideologii nového Československa," *Rudé právo*, 31 March 1946, 4.

98. Kopecký, *Zápas*, 21–22, 45.

99. Opat, *O novou demokracii*, 227.

100. See, for example, Belda, 7, or Bloomfield, 120.

101. Vilém Prečan, "Politika a taktika KSČ 1945–1948," in his *V kradeném čase. Výběr z studií, článků a úvah z let 1973–1993* (Prague: ÚSD, 1994), 124.

102. Karel Kaplan, *Znárodnění a socialismus*, (Prague: Academia, 1968), 183.

103. Zhdanov's penultimate preparatory memorandum placed the French, Italians, and Czechoslovaks on the dock of parties to be harshly dealt with. It was only in his final reading that the Communist Party of Czechoslovakia was removed. Grant Adibekov, "How the First Conference of the Cominform Came About," 5. Although the Czechoslovaks received little criticism, the Communist Party of the Soviet Union was clearly disturbed by the failure of the party to show considerable progress. A Soviet party Foreign Political Department memorandum drawn up before the Cominform meeting indicted Gottwald's team for missing the opportunity to seize power while the Red Army was still on Czechoslovak soil, for not taking the nationalizations far enough, and for failing to resolve the national question (which had led to the growth of "reaction" in Slovakia). Anna Di Biagio, "The Establishment of the Cominform," 19–20. Both of these appear in *The Cominform. Minutes of the Three Conferences 1947/1948/1949*, ed. Giuliano Procacci (Milan: Fondazione Giangiacomo Feltrinelli, 1994).

104. Prečan, 122 and 124, and Korbel, 142.

105. Bareš, "Pramen živé vody," 356.
106. Pavlíček, 59 and 62.
107. Brod, 65.
108. Korbel, 142.
109. Kovály, 63. She also argues on page 100 that in 1950 "For some time it had been rumored that Gottwald drank, and that he had taken to drinking out of desperation over the Soviet failure to keep their word to let us run our country our own way." While this does not meet any standards of historical evidence, she equally has no reason to deceive.
110. Brod, 66. Even Prečan is willing to cede a bit on this point, noting that "If we have before our eyes the later fates of the great part of this pre-February leadership and many other functionaries of the Communist Party, the question arises of whether these people suspected what awaited them when they became absolute rulers: that they would feel themselves in a far less meaningful role than they had played to that time, that they would be only place-holders, Stalin's marionettes even, delivered to the tender mercies of his compassions and quirks." Prečan, 128.
111. I agree with the assessments of the works that have argued that the "Czechoslovak road" was not abandoned until late in the summer of 1948, after the Yugoslav Communist Party was expelled from the Cominform. This line pervades the Czech analyses of the immediate postwar period from the 1960s, and has been adopted by M. R. Myant as well. Two brief introductions to the fate of the "Czechoslovak road" after February 1948 can be found in Robert K. Evanson, "The Czechoslovak Road to Socialism in 1948," *East European Quarterly* 19 (1985): 469–92, and Karel Kaplan, *The Rise of a Monopoly of Power in the Hands of the Communist Party of Czechoslovakia, 1948–1949*, 2 vols., "The Experiences of Prague Spring, 1968" Research Project, Study 2, n.p.: self-published, 1979.

CHAPTER 10

1. This term, although confusing in English, is necessary. The Czech *socializující demokracie* implies, by the employment of the gerundial form as a present active participle, that Czech society was moving toward but had not yet achieved the status of socialist. An even greater ambiguity concerning the final shape Czechoslovak society would take than that noted in the "Czechoslovak road to socialism" is evident here.
2. Ferdinand Peroutka, "Není návratu," *Svobodné noviny*, 25 November 1945, 1.
3. Ferdinand Peroutka, "Když spáč procitne . . . ," *Dnešek* 1 (1946/7): 1. President Beneš concurred: "I think we all agree: we agree with the just given analysis of liberal society, with its criticism, with its condemnation . . . and we are also agreed that we cannot return to it. . . . We accept the idea that liberal society is theoretically and in practice overcome." Speech upon receiving an honorary Doctor of Law degree, 15 December 1945, in Edvard Beneš, *EB národu. Z projevu presidenta republiky v letech 1945–1946*, ed. František Škarvan (Prague: Zemská rada osvetová, 1946), 39.
4. Ferdinand Peroutka, "Odpověď pravici," *Svobodné noviny*, 19 February 1946, 1 and "Volby—a co po nich?" *Svobodné noviny*, 26 March 1946, 1.
5. Peroutka. "Odpověď," 1.
6. Antonín Klatovský, "Svoboda a demokracie," *Dnešek* 1 (1946/7): 562.
7. V. G., "Socialistický realismus," *Dnešek* 2 (1947/8): 67. This idea was expressed in harsher terms by communists like Miloš Kopecký: "The future of the nation cannot be defended by people who . . . still live in the spiritual world of the bourgeoisie . . . their influence must be mercilessly banished from schools, from books of quotations, from thought and from the general, smaller daily morality of the people." Miloš Kopecký, "Ještě komunistova odpověď," *Dnešek* 1 (1945/6): 123.

8. Nikolaus Lobkowicz, *Marxismus-Leninismus in der CSR. Die tschechische Philosophie seit 1945* (Dordrect, Holland: D. Reidel, 1961), 27.

9. Josef Král, "Cesty české filosofie," *Česká mysl* 40 (1946–8): 12.

10. Otakar Machotka, *Socialism českého člověka* (Prague: CSNS, 1946), 4, and František Dědek, "Pokrok, reakce a sklon k frázím," *Svobodný zítřek* 3, no. 33 (1947): 3. Despite this praise, the only comments critical of Marx himself came in the work of the leading National Socialist Party ideologue Otakar Machotka, in a book whose nationalist fervor and anti-Semitic overtones he must later have regretted. In a crude attempt to win votes and stress his party's nationalism, Machotka characterized Marx as "foreign" to the Czech mentality. Marx's teachings, particularly his views on revolution, were characterized as an expression of his "psychological features," which were a combination of "German hardness and ruthlessness" with an "oriental fantasy and radicalism . . . of Jewish origin." Marx's Jewish heritage was also seen as the cause for his internationalism: "Certainly Marx's internationalism is connected with the fact that the author of *Capital* belonged to a nation that for millennia had no home and was dispersed among all the nations of the earth. The natural basis for national feeling was lacking in him." Machotka, 11 and 14–16.

11. Václav Černý in *Můj poměr ke KSČ. Projevy z řad pracující inteligence* (Prague: KSČ, 1946), 24.

12. E. A. Saudek, "Od manifestu k tvorbe," *Tvorba* 15 (1946): 407 and Gustav Bareš, "Diskuse," *Kritický měsíčník* 7 (1946): 14.

13. František Vrba, "K socialistické kritice dneška," *Generace* 1, no. 3 (1946/7): 10, and "Složitý dr Václav Černý," *Generace* 1, no. 3 (1946/7): 22.

14. Otakar Machotka, "Politické strany a mravnost," *Svobodný zítřek* 2, no. 35 (1946): 1. Cf. his "Mravní hodnoty a politika," *Svobodný zítřek* 2, no. 32 (1946): 3.

15. Inocenc Arnošt Bláha, *Kultura a politika* (Brno: Zemská osvetová rada, 1946), 9.

16. Václav Černý, "Pár slov o kulturním ethosu. (K prob. soc. kultury u nás, 4.)," *Kritický měsíčník* 7 (1946): 65.

17. "Debaty okolo marxismu," *Generace* 1, nos. 4–5 (1946/7): 37.

18. Edvard Beneš, in *Účtování a výhledy*, ed. Jan Kopecký (Prague: Syndikát českých spisovatelu 1948) 26.

19. Jaroslav P. Blažek, "Rozhovory s komunisty," *Dněšek* 2 (1947/8): 705. See also JUC. L. V., "[Letter to the Editor]" *Dněšek* 1 (1946/7): 126, and the philosopher Jan Patočka's comment that there was "undoubtedly . . . something of pantheism" in Marxist socialism. Jan Patočka, "Masaryk vcera a dnes," *Naše doba* 52 (1945/6): 306.

20. Ferdinand Peroutka, "Komunistova odpověď," *Dněšek* 1 (1946/7): 48.

21. Václav Černý, "Hrst poznámek o polemice věcné a nevěcné," *Kritický měsíčník* 7 (1946): 70. He was forced to confirm his socialism again in an article entitled "Attacks on Me, or Trojan Horses without Greeks" after two subsequent articles by Jaroslav Pokorný in a communist-dominated trade union weekly, "Dr. V. Cerného převrat leninismu" and "Dr. V. Černý na pokračování," *Lidová kultura* 2, nos. 6 and 7 (1946): both page 2. See Václav Černý, "Útoky na mně aneb Trojští koně bez Řeku," *Kritický měsíčník* 7 (1946): 156–59.

22. Jan M. Michal, "Postwar Economic Development," in *A History of the Czechoslovak Republic 1918–1948*, ed. Victor S. Mamatey and Radomír Luža (Princeton: Princeton University Press, 1973), 439.

23. Ferdinand Peroutka, "Nesrozumitelný dnešek," *Svobodné noviny*, 27 January 1946, 1.

24. "Do voleb a po nich," *Svobodný zítřek* 2, no. 6 (1946): 1.

25. Jan Kozák, "Proč tedy nejste komunistou?" *Svobodný zítřek* 2, no. 18 (1946): 1.

26. Jan Patočka, "Ideologie a živote v ideji," *Kritický měsíčník* 7 (1946): 12, and Jan Bělehrádek, "Proč jsem sociálním demokratem," *Dněšek* 1 (1946/7): 101.

27. J. S. and Josef Macek, "Co je socialismus?" *Dněšek* 1 (1946/7): 174.

28. Černý, "Pár slov," 66–67, and "Diskuse," *Kritický měsíčník* 7 (1946): 24.

29. Ferdinand Peroutka, "Co jest reakce?" *Dněšek* 1 (1946/7): 289–90, and "Rozjímání," in his *Tak nebo tak* (Prague: F. Borový, 1947) 170–71, 173.

30. Peroutka, "Když spáč procitne. . . ," 2.

31. Václav Černý, "Pár slov," 63. Later Černý glossed over the ambiguities of socialist humanism by making the two components identical: "Once more: socialism is humanism, and because it is humanism it is never against man. Its hatred is for institutions, bourgeois society, fascism." Václav Černý, "Hrst poznámek k socialistickému realismu," *Kritický měsíčník* 8 (1947): 352.

32. František Kovárna, *O kulturu v socialismu* (Prague: Melantrich, 1946), 23.

33. Peroutka, "Není návratu," 1.

34. Beneš, in Kopecký, 19.

35. From a speech delivered in Ostrava, 17 July 1946. Reprinted in Beneš, *EB národu*, 40.

36. Arnošt Bláha, "Socialismem k lepší lidství," *Lidová kultura 3*, no. 6 (1947): 9.

37. Machotka, *Socialismus*, 17, 20.

38. Beneš is cited in čt. "Boj o nového člověka trvá," *Svobodné noviny*, 15 December 1946, 1. See also, for example, Robert Konecný, *Demokracie* (Prague: Československý obec sokolský,1947), 16, or F. M. Dobiáš, "Obrozené Ceskoslovensko," *Naše doba* 53 (1946/7): 54.

39. J. B. Čapek, "O nový humanismus," *Naše doba* 52 (1945/6): 354, and Machotka, *Socialismus*, 18.

40. Václav Černý, "Básníkova trnitá cesta do socialistické společnosti," *Kritický měsíčník* 6 (1945): 241. Beneš also admitted that he had no precise idea of where he was leading the nation: "A new world and a new life are being created. We do not have a precise and entirely clear conception of these new things, but we are searching for them, we are creating them, we are struggling for them." Cited in čt, 1.

41. Edvard Beneš, cited in čt, 1.

42. "Resoluce sjezdu ceských spisovatelu," in *Účtování a výhledy*, ed. Jan Kopecký (Prague: Syndikát českých spisovatelů, 1948), 265.

43. Bohuslav Brouk, "O nový životní styl," *Dnešek* 1 (1946/7): 330, and František Kovárna, "Národní kultura a socialismus," *Svobodný zítřek 2*, no. 38 (1946): 5.

44. Václav Černý, "Diskuse," 24. Slightly later he went further, stating that "I am a socialist . . . I fear for the fate of socialist culture in their [i.e., the Communists'] hands." Václav Černý, "Hrst poznámek o polemice," 70.

45. Václav Černý, "Ještě jednou: Mezi východem a západem," *Kritický měsíčník* 6 (1945): 144.

46. Hubert Ripka, "Jakou demokracii, a jaký socialismus," *Svobodný zítřek* 2, no. 19 (1946): 4, and Václav Žižka, "S východu a západu," *Masarykův lid* 15 (1945/6): 13. Ripka went on to point out that "the Soviet regime is in harmony with Russian national traditions and with the needs of the Soviet national environment."

47. Hubert Ripka, "Diktatorská totalita nebo demokracie?" *Svobodný zítřek* 2, no. 21 (1946): 1, 4.

48. Eva Hartmannová, "'My' a 'oni': hledání české národní identity na stránkách *Dneška* z roku 1946," in *Strankami soudobých dějin. Sborník statí k pětašedesátinám historika Karla Kaplana*, ed. Karel Jech (Prague: ÚSD, 1993), 99.

49. See Ferdinand Peroutka, "Před Havlíčkovým jubileem," *Dnešek* 1 (1946/7): 177–78, and Čestmír Adam, "Českoslovenští marxisté v krisi III," *Masarykův lid* 15 (1945/6): 269.

50. Peroutka, "Volby," 1. This statement was criticized as defeatist by some members of Peroutka's National Socialist readership. See Ferdinand Peroutka, "Komunisté mezi námi," in Peroutka, *Tak nebo tak*, 86.

51. See, for example, K., "Po volbách do Ústavodárného Národního shromáždění," *Naše doba* 52 (1945/6): 355.

52. Ferdinand Peroutka, "Co se stalo," *Dnešek* 1 (1946/7): 146.

53. Josef Hudec, "Povoleblní meditace," *Dnešek* 1 (1946/7): 161.

54. Cited in Walter Ullmann, *The United States in Prague, 1945–1948* (Boulder, CO: East European Quarterly, 1978), 54.

55. Peroutka, "Komunisté," 87.

56. Peroutka, "Komunisté," 84–85. The mythologizing of a heroic and infallible Czech "people," in both this period and others, has been bitingly criticized in Vilém Hejl, *Rozvrat. Mnichov a náš osud* (Toronto: 68 Publishers, 1989), 192–94.

57. [Anon.], "Co jest reakce?," *Dnešek* 1 (1946/7): 334.

58. J. S. and Macek, 172–4.

59. Antonín Klatovský, "Svoboda a socialismus," *Dnešek* 2 (1947/8): 167, and Vratislav Bušek, "Dvě cesty socialismu," *Svobodné slovo*, 1 October 1946, 1. See also the comment that the Communist Party had merely adopted the prewar program of the Social Democrats. Emanuel Kučera, "Dopis starého komunisty," *Dnešek* 1 (1946/7): 127.

60. Hubert Ripka, "Stalin oživuje naděje," *Svobodný zítřek* 2, no. 40 (1946):1, 3, and František Kovárna, "Kulturní autonomie nebo kulturní konfekce," *Naše doba* 53 (1946/7): 203.

61. [Anon.], "Svoboda a kazeň," *Dnešek* 1 (1946/7): 801.

62. Lev Sychrava, "Vulgární materialismus," *Národní osvobození*, 14 January 1947, 1.

63. Edvard Beneš, in Škarvan, 38.

64. K., "Lidová demokracie," *Naše doba* 52 (1945/6): 27.

65. Bláha, *Kultura a politika*, 8–9.

66. Pavel Tigrid, *Kapesní průvodce inteligentní ženy po vlastním osudu* (Prague: Odeon, 1992), 205.

67. Peroutka, "Co jest reakce?" 290.

68. Ferdinand Peroutka, "Budování a synthesa," *Svobodné noviny*, 14 July 1946, 1 and Klement Gottwald, "Zasedání Ústředního výboru KSC 22.-23. ledna 1947," in his *Spisy*, vol. 13 (Prague: SNPL, 1957), 292.

69. Robert Konečný, "Do druhého roku svobody," in his *Živá slova* (Brno: Zář, 1946), 81.

70. K. J. Beneš, "Kulturní plánování," *Cíl* 2 (1946) 349. Beneš wrote four articles on the topic of cultural planning, and *Cíl* devoted an entire issue (number 14 of 1946) to much the same issue.

71. Josef Macek, "Socialismus a svoboda," *Naše doba* 54 (1947/8): 52.

72. Ferdinand Peroutka, "Tři místo jednoho—a co z toho," *Dnešek* 1 (1946/7): 31.

73. Ripka, "Jakou demokracii," 4.

74. Fr. Turek, "Jak se na to dívají čtenáři Svobodných novin," *Dnešek* 2 (1947/8): 731.

75. Kozák, "Proč tedy nejste komunistou," 2.

76. Ferdinand Peroutka, "Hlavní úkol naší politiky," *Dnešek* 1 (1946/7): 49.

77. As noted already in 1950, it "was particularly difficult for Czech democrats, who had persisted in minimizing the difference between Western democracy and Soviet 'democracy' and had thereby failed to prepare their followers for the dangers of a Communist *putsch*. The Communist *coup d'état* in Hungary might have taught them a valuable lesson, had they paid attention to it. But they did not." Otto Friedman, *The Break-Up of Czech Democracy* (London: Gollancz, 1950), 91. Vilém Hejl also makes this point, more provocatively asking "did it not occur to anyone to look outside the Czechoslovak backyard, to trace the fates of the democratic parties of Bulgaria, Romania, Hungary, and Poland?" Vilém Hejl, *Rozvrat*, 146.

78. Prokop Toman, "Císařovy nové šaty, kritika kritiky," *Svobodný zítřek* 2, no. 12 (1946): 5.

79. Jan B. Kozák, "Odpověď p. kolegovi A. Kolmanovi," *Svobodný zítřek* 2, no. 21 (1946): 2, and Peroutka, "Co se stalo," 145.

80. Václav Černý, "F. X. Č.', aneb ještě jedna ofensivka, již se věru bát nemusím," *Kritický měsíčník* 8 (1947): 238–9. The reference to F. X. Šalda draws on the communist argument that Černý was trying to dominate the cultural discourse as Šalda had before the war. Note that Černý implicitly excluded his communist opponents from his idea of the national whole in this statement, maintaining that they were a foreign element and not part of "our culture and our socialism."

81. Ferdinand Peroutka, "Co jest reakce?" 289–90.

82. [Anon.], "Co jest reakce?" 334 and Dědek, 3. Dědek argued that "There are two possibilities: progress or reaction. Already by not giving ourselves to one or to the other, we help reaction. Reactionary politics is unscientific, therefore a politics based on metaphysics belongs here. . . . A progressive politics is based on science. There is only one science of human society as the foundation of politics: real, empirical sociology. . . . It is not a politics based on any kind of ideology."

83. Jan Slavík, "Reakce pozvedává hlavu," *Svobodný zítřek* 3, no. 4 (1947): 13.

84. Ferdinand Peroutka, "Vysvětlení budoucího času," *Svobodné noviny*, 12 October 1947, 1.

85. Edvard Beneš, "[In Response to a Letter from United Nations World]," *Svobodný zítřek* 3, no. 10 (1947): 2, Ripka, "Diktatorská totalita," 1, and Slavík, "Reakce, 3.

86. Peroutka, "Hlavní úkol," 19, and Klatovský. "Jsou všichni," 223.

87. Ferdinand Peroutka, "Chvála roku 1946," *Dnešek* 1 (1946/7): 641.

88. Václav Černý, *Pameti*, vol. 4 (Toronto: 68 Publishers, 1983), 25.

89. Ladislav Görlich, "Co je a co není socialismus," *Český život* 2 (1948): 6.

90. Klatovský, "Svoboda a socialismus," 167, and Konečný. *Demokracie.* 11.

91. Edvard Beneš, in Škarvan, 38, Konečný, *Demokracie*, 17, and Ferdinand Peroutka, "V předvečer," *Svobodné noviny*, 23 September 1945, 1. As the ideas in Beneš' *Demokracie dnes a zítra* have received attention in other studies, I shall discuss primarily other democratic socialist intellectual notables' propagation of the same ideas. On Beneš, see particularly the body of work by his secretary, Eduard Táborský, and the critical view taken throughout Vilém Hejl's *Rozvrat*, esp. 96–100.

92. Vladimír Hellmuth-Brauner, "Idea minulé a dnešní demokracie," *Svobodné noviny*, 25 July 1945, 1, and Robert Konečný, "Svoboda v řadu," in his *Živá slova*, 25.

93. Klatovský, "Svoboda a socialismus," 168.

94. Václav Černý, "Pozdrav mrtvým . . . ," *Kritický měsíčník* 6 (1945): 13. Černý was commended for this statement by the communist sympathizer Bohuslav Kratochvíl in his "Dnešní místo a úkol intelligence," *Česká osveta* 39 (1946): 198.

95. Hellmuth-Brauner, 1, and Konečný, "Do druhého roku," 79. Not surprisingly, spiritual democracy escaped even an attempt at definition.

96. Josef Macek, "Většina a menšina v demokracii," *Naše doba* 54 (1947/8): 97.

97. Jaroslav Nebesář "Žijeme zase v demokratickém statě," *Panorama* 21 (1945/6): 11.

98. Klatovský, "Svoboda a socialismus," 183.

99. Oldrich Procházka, "Naše národní individualita," *Svobodné noviny*, 15 June 1947, 1.

100. [Anon.], "Svoboda," 801.

101. Peroutka, "Komunistova odpověd'," 48, and "Budování," 1. He repeated this sentiment a third time, in his "Před Havlíčkovým jubileem," 178.

102. Hubert Ripka, "Co je československá sociální demokracie?" *Svobodný zítřek* 2, no. 20 (1946): 1–2. In this he closely follows the ideas of President Beneš.

103. Vratislav Bušek, "Národ se bránil: 1348–1648–1848–1948," *Svobodný zítřek* 3, no. 52 (1947): 3.

104. Klatovský, "Svoboda a socialismus," 166.

105. "Ceským kulturním pracovníkům," *Rudé právo*, 6 October 1946, 1. See Document 1 of the Appendix for the complete text.

106. This episode is a fascinating one in the intellectual history of postwar Czech history that, for reasons of space, cannot be addressed here. Suffice it to say that democratic socialists responded timidly, and that the following assessment by Toman Brod is essentially correct: "The Czechoslovak echo was . . . commensurate to the typical atmosphere ruling the land, which made it impossible for the *Leningrad* scandal to finally become a subject for the analysis of Soviet conditions in general. Even the most courageous commentators limited themselves mainly to the demand and hope that a similar thing could never come about in Czechoslovakia." Brod, 99. Václav Černý reviewed the most important responses and criticized the affair most comprehensively in his "Sovetská čistka, česká kocovina a leccos jiného," *Kritický měsíčník* 7 (1946): 385–92.

107. Jaroslav Kladiva, "Kulturní jednota," *Impuls* 1 (1966): 571–72.

108. "Kulturním pracovníkům," *Svobodné slovo*, 13 October 1946, 1. See Document 2 of the Appendix for the complete text.

109. See, for example, the democratic socialist vk, "O svobodu kultury," *Masarykův lid* 15 (1945/6): 498, the Social Democrat kšk [Karel Šourek], "Abychom si rozuměli alespoň v kultuře, čili Kulturní obec a Kulturní svaz," *Cíl* 2 (1946): 642, and the communist Jiří Hájek, "Rozkol nebo vyjasňování v české kultuře," *Tvorba* 15 (1946): 693.

110. See, for example, Václav Běhounek, "Není to mnoho?"*Práce*, 15 October 1946, 2, František Götz, "Rozdvojení na ceské kulturní frontě." *Národní osvobození*, 16 October 1946, 5, or Bohuslav Březovský, "Rozdvojení nebo vyjasnění?" *Národní osvobození*, 19 October 1946, 5.

111. For example, the differences were played down by commentators as diverse as Ferdinand Peroutka, "Rozkol v české kultuře?," *Dnešek* 1 (1946/7): 481, and F. F. Burian, "[Leader]," *Kulturní politika* 2, no. 5 (1946/7): 1, among many others, although theirs contained the implicit suggestion that the opposing organization was unnecessary.

112. Peroutka, "Rozkol," 481–82.

113. K. J. Beneš, 2. See also Karel Polák, "Potřebujeme jednotné kulturní organisace," *Právo lidu*, 20 October 1946, 1.

114. F. F. Burian, "[Leader]," *Kulturní politika* 2, no. 6 (1946/7): 1–2. This point was also made by Jiří Hájek, who accused Kulturní svaz's membership of having a strong admixture of "decidedly fascist and definitely reactionary elements." Hájek, 693.

115. On the potential formation of an anti-communist front, see Ladislav Štoll, "O svobodu. K rozkolu v české kultuře," *Tvorba* 15 (1946): 715, and Václav Běhounek, "Obec přes palubu?" *Práce*, 5 November 1946, 2. For Stránský's comments, see "Poslání kulturních organisací," *Národní osvobození*, 3 November 1946, 1.

116. The Kulturní svaz decision not to publish further names is in *Svobodné noviny*, 27 October 1946, 2. Lists of additional signatories to the two organizations' manifestos can be found in *Rudé právo*, 20 and 27 October 1946 and *Svobodné slovo*, 15–17 October 1946.

117. "Českým kulturním pracovníkum," *Rudé právo*, 20 October 1946, 1.

118. "Kultura má sjenocovat národa," *Mladá fronta*, 20 October 1946, 1.

119. "Kulturní obci a Kulturnímu svazu," *Svobodné noviny*, 27 October 1946, 2.

120. The first public announcement of these meetings came in the October 26 edition of *Právo lidu*.

121. Published simultaneously in many organs, the complete text appears as Document 3 of the Appendix.

122. This was perhaps as a result of Lumír Čivrný's definition of the complete term as "the law of the path from understanding to action ties the *new* humanism to the fruitful idea of scientific socialism." Lumír Čivrný, "Od myšlenky k činum, (K ustavení Kulturní obce)," *Tvorba* 15 (1946): 641.

123. Jan Kozák noted this concern in *Kulturní jednota a její program. Projevy pronesené na ustavující valné hromadě "Kulturní jednoty" v Dome umelců dne 27. dubna 1947*, ed. J. B. Kozák (Prague: Orbis, 1947), 14.

124. Pavel Eisner, "Jednota akční," *Kulturní politika* 2, no. 9 (1946/7): 1.

125. Ferdinand Peroutka, "Aby nebylo třeba psát satiru," *Dnešek* 1 (1946/7): 626.

126. Nineteen meetings were held during the five-month period between the publication of the proclamation announcing agreement and the actual inaugural meeting of Kulturní jednota. They were chaired by Bohumil Kratochvíl, until he was named ambassador to Great Britain in December of 1946, and thereafter by J. B. Kozák. The participants included all of those who signed the unifying proclamation and Arnošt Bláha, Alois Cervinka, and J. L. Fischer, among others, and took place largely in the offices of *Kulturní politika*. The minister of information and the minister of culture and education were kept informed on the progress of the meetings, and Kozák briefed President Beneš personally. See Kozák, *Kulturní jednota*, 14, 18.

127. The entire text of the resolution appears as Document 4 of the Appendix.

128. Václav Běhounek, "Kulturní jednota skutkem," *Kulturní politika* 3, no. 33 (1947): 3.

129. That Kozák went over to the communist side in February of 1948 has been described as extremely painful to President Beneš (as related by his brother). See Peter Hruby, *Fools and Heroes. The Changing Role of Communist Intellectuals in Czechoslovakia* (Oxford: Pergamon, 1980) 6.

130. Kozák, *Kulturní jednota*, 8, 10, 13.

131. Kozák, *Kulturní jednota*, 18–19.

132. Kozák, *Kulturní jednota*, 23–24.

133. Kozák, *Kulturní jednota*, 24, 27–29.

134. Kozák, *Kulturní jednota*, 31–33.

135. Kozák, *Kulturní jednota*, 33, 35–36.

136. Štoll, 714.

137. Kozák, *Kulturní jednota*, 46.
138. Kozák, *Kulturní jednota*, 47.
139. Brod, 91.
140. Hejl, 158.
141. Friedman, 102–3.
142. Lumír Čivrný in *The Politics of Czech Culture*, ed. Antonín J. Liehm, trans. Peter Kussi (New York: Grove, 1973), 316.

CHAPTER 11

1. The election results were as follows:
   In Bohemia:　　　People's Party 16.27%, Communist Party 43.25%.
   In Moravia:　　　People's Party 27.56%, Communist Party 34.46%.
   In Slovakia:　　　Democratic Party 61.43%, Communist Party 30.48%.
2. John H. Whyte, *Catholics in Western Democracies. A Study in Political Behavior* (Dublin: Gill and Macmillan, 1981).
3. In Belgium, the new non-sectarian party, the *Union démocrate belge*, soon collapsed, but the Belgian Catholic Party was reconstructed as the Christian Social Party. As with the Czech People's Party, it was formally nonconfessional. Only the Netherlands, where the Catholic People's Party was the only one in Europe to retain the word "Catholic" in its title, and in Italy, where the Christian Democrats were closer to the Church than the prewar Popular Party, were exceptions.
4. Whyte, 88.
5. Whyte, 90.
6. Whyte, 91, 93.
7. For information on this, one should merely flip through Václav Vaško, *Neumlčená. Kronika katolické církve v Československu po druhé světové války*, vol. 1 (Prague: Zvon, 1990), esp. 201–28.
8. Karel Kaplan, *Stát a církev v Československu v letech 1948–1953* (Prague: ÚSD, 1993) 11. On the question of Church schools, see Vaško, 177–84.
9. "Osudový zápas" is the title of the first chapter of Ghelfand's *Dialektický materialismus* (Prague: Universum, 1947), 5, 8.
10. R. M. Dacík, "Nevědecké přednášky o 'vědecké filosofii'," *Na hlubinu* 21 (1947): 383. The only Catholic author who considered the possibility of synthesis was Pavel Tigrid, who argued that one could be achieved only if the communists changed entirely and Christians held firm until they did. See Pavel Tigrid, "Rozdíly," *Lidová demokracie*, 17 November 1946, 1.
11. Ivo Ducháček, "Proč jsem lidovcem," *Dnešek* 1 (1946/7): 102.
12. Bedřich Bobek, "Poslání lidové strany," *Lidová demokracie*, 3 April 1946, 1.
13. The sudden change in Communist tactics toward Catholicism can be partially ascribed to the party's large-scale electoral defeat in Slovakia, the most intensively Catholic region of the country, and to the upcoming trial of the leader of the wartime Slovak Republic, the Catholic priest Dr. Jozef Tiso.
14. Kaplan, 19.
15. Vaško, 44.
16. Zdeněk Nejedlý, "Slovo o náboženství," in his *Slovo o náboženství* (Prague: Melantrich, 1948), 21–22 and 25–26.
17. Nejedlý, 12, 24, and 31.
18. f. r., "Husitská tradice a komunisté," *Tvorba* 15 (1946): 434.
19. Adolf Kajpr, "Komunismus a království Boží," *Katolík* 9, no. 10 (1946): 2 and "Ještě o sociální otázce," *Katolík* 10, no. 6 (1947): 3.
20. Jindřich Středa, "Katolík a revoluce," *Katolík* 10, no. 44 (1947): 3.
21. Rudolf Beck, "Katolický hlas proti marxismu," *Nová mysl* 2 (1948): 97.

22. The Jesuit S. S. Ghelfand made this point twice in the space of one month at the time of the 1946 elections, in the Catholic camp's most widely circulated periodical, the People's Party daily *Lidová demokracie*. See "Materialismus—věda nebo víra?" *Lidová demokracie*, 21 May 1946, 5, and "Kritika jediné kritiky," *Lidová demokracie*, 15 June 1946, 2.

23. Dominik Pecka, "Kredo moderního člověka," *Vyšehrad* 2 (1947): 69. The passing comparison of Marxism and fascism is a Catholic device more often used by writers on the more "political" wing of Catholic thought.

24. Pavel Tigrid, "Aby nebylo omylu," *Obzory* 2 (1946): 40.

25. fm [František Marek], "Ideologie v pohybu," *Katolík* 9, no. 27 (1946): 2. From the other wing, see, for example, Miloš Šolle, "K filosofii dialektického materialismu," *Obzory* 2 (1946): 217–18.

26. rs, "Proč nejsme socialisty," *Lidová demokracie*, 9 April 1946, 1 and Ghelfand, *Dialektický materialismus*, 87–88.

27. Dominik Pecka, "Kredo," 69–70 and "Společnost a společenství," *Vyšehrad* 1, no. 8 (1945/6): 1. S. S. Ghelfand also noted that "evil is not in manners of production, evil is in us." "Marxismus a křesťanství," *Lidová demokracie*, 27 February 1946, 2.

28. Pavel Tigrid, "Vánoční rozjímání," *Lidová demokracie*, 23 December 1945, 1.

29. S. S. Ghelfand, *Marxismus a křesťanský sociální reformismus. K výročí papežských okružních listů "Rerum novarum" a "Quadragesimo anno"* (Prague: n.p., 1946).

30. Aloys Skoumal, in *Účtování a výhledy. Sborník prvního sjezdu českých spisovatelů*, ed. Jan Kopecký (Prague: Syndikát Českých Spisovatelu, 1948), 48. On page 86, Ludvík Svoboda took issue with Skoumal, saying that the Communists wished for "the recreation of the spirit and society to be carried out in parallel." On the Catholic view of the place of revolution in the European tradition, see Marie Voříšková, "Být Evropanem," *Vyšehrad* 1, no. 1 (1945/6): 4.

31. Adolf Procházka, "Čsl. strana lidová ve vládě národní fronty," *Lidová demokracie*, 3 April 1946, 4.

32. Jaroslav Richter, *Socialismus a křesťanství* (Prague: ČAT-Universum, 1947), 42–43.

33. Antonín Pimper, *Křesťanský solidarismus* (Prague: ČAT-Universum, 1946), 70–71. See also Bohdan Chudoba's comment that the idea of the dictatorship of the proletariat merely recreates the conditions of capitalism, with one class oppressing another. Bohdan Chudoba, "Lid či třídy?" *Obzory* 2 (1946): 22.

34. K. N., "Diktatura proletariátu," *Lidová demokracie*, 26 May 1946, 1.

35. "K svobodě člověka," *Vývoj* 1 (1946): 3.

36. This speculation is based on information in Vaško, 237.

37. Beck, 97.

38. Ghelfand, *Marxismus*, 15, and *Dialektický materialismus*, 13.

39. Ghelfand, *Marxismus*, 28–30, and *Dialektický materialismus*, 77–80. This argument is repeated by him in "A přece překonaná doktrina!," *Obzory* 3 (1947): 432–33. Furthermore, it was taken up in the anonymous "Lidově demokratický nebo socialistický řád?" *Lidová demokracie*, 31 March 1946, 6, and by Bohdan Chudoba in his *Co je to křesťanská politika* (Prague: Universum, 1947), 68.

40. Ghelfand, *Dialektický materialismus*, 78.

41. Rudolf Beck, 102, see also Radim Foustka's admission that Ghelfand's argument is an "effective trick." Radim Foustka, "Jesuitská polemika s marxismem," *Cíl* 3 (1947): 455.

42. Foustka, 455, and Beck, 103.

43. Šolle, 217.

44. Chudoba, "Lid či třídy?" 22.

45. "Lidově demokratický nebo socialistický řád?" *Lidová demokracie*, 31 March 1946, 1.

46. Helena Koželuhová, "Volby poučejí," *Lidová demokracie*, 2 December 1945, 1.

47. Adam Hrubě, "Ústavní názory našich komunistu," *Obzory* 4 (1948): 23.

48. F. Jiřík, "Mezi dvěma frontami," *Obzory* 4 (1948): 104. See also "Abychom opravdu věrni zustali," *Obzory* 2 (1946): 322.

49. Marius [pseud.], "Československá demokracie v krisi?" *Obzory* 2 (1946): 441, and Luděk Forman, "Včera a dnes," *Obzory* 2 (1946): 809.

50. K. S., "O příští směr," *Lidová demokracie*, 15 June 1946, 1.

51. Tigrid, "Aby nebylo omylů," 38.

52. K. N., 1.

53. Vojtěch Šťastný, "Idea politické demokracie," *Obzory* 2 (1946): 745. *Obzory* believed that the political successes involved with the instantiation of the Two-Year Plan had led to a surge of Communist Party optimism witnessed in the call for 51% of the vote, but argued that by mid-1947 even the communists themselves had realized that the goal could not be reached. Jan Kolár, "Oč jde," *Obzory* 3 (1947): 375.

54. Pavel Tigrid, "Odpověď Barešovi, aneb co chceme," *Obzory* 3 (1947): 400.

55. J. Bilý, "O svobodu," *Vývoj* 2 (1947): 1043.

56. S. S. Ghelfand, "Co je socialismus?" *Vývoj* 1 (1946): 52. See also his *Dialekticky materialismus*, 87.

57. Pavel Tigrid, "V domě oběšencově . . . ," *Obzory* 3 (1947): 85, and his "Mravní profil voleb," *Lidová demokracie*, 1 June 1946, 2.

58. Pavel Tigrid, "Kde je reakce?" *Lidová demokracie*, 1 February 1947, 1.

59. Rather than from one of the many offended Communists, the quotation is taken from a left-wing Social Democrat. See Foustka, 455.

60. Redakce, "O co usilujeme a co odmítáme," *Obzory* 1 (1945): 214, and Ducháček, 102.

61. Ghelfand, *Dialektický materialismus*, 87. From the political wing, see the comments of Pavel Tigrid, who noted that totalitarianism can come from either side of the political spectrum in his "Aby nebylo omylů," 38. This point was also made by Dominik Pecka, in "Pokroková republika nebo autoritivní stát?" *Katolík* 10, no. 6 (1947): 2.

62. Jan Kolár, "Krise našeho věku," *Obzory* 3 (1947): 544.

63. Richter, 29–31.

64. Chudoba, *Co je to*, 42. See also Ghelfand, *Dialektický materialismus*, 54–57, and his "Marxismus a fašismus," *Obzory* 2 (1946): 425–27.

65. Kajpr, "Komunismus," 2, and Pimper, 81.

66. Chudoba, *Co je to*, 13 and 58.

67. Richter, 21–22.

68. Ghelfand, *Dialektický materialismus*, 84, *Marxismus*, 41, Chudoba, *Co je to*, 76–77, and Pimper, 138–40.

69. Dominik Pecka, "Křesťanství a aktivita," *Na hlubinu* 22 (1948): 10.

70. Richter, 17, 19, and 33.

71. Miloslav Skácel, "Co je to socialismus?" *Obzory* 3 (1947): 72–73.

72. [Anon,], "Konec komunismu bestialismus," *Na hlubinu* 21 (1947): 381, and Chudoba, *Co je to*, 15.

73. Šolle, 218.

74. Kajpr, "Komunismus," 2, and František Marek, "Poslední revoluce měšťáka?" *Katolík* 10, no. 18 (1947): 3.

75. Dominik Pecka, "Osoba a osobnost," *Vyšehrad* 2 (1947): 249, and Miloš Dvořák, "Co říká F. X. Šalda dnešku," *Akord* 13 (1946/7): 284.

76. Bohdan Chudoba, "V politice nejde jen o stát," *Obzory* 3 (1947): 156. Pecka similarly stressed that what he called "modern collectivism" was "nothing more than state capitalism," and Ghelfand argued that communists "yearn for liberation from the tyranny of private capitalism and want to introduce a much more severe and ruthless capitalism—state capitalism." Pecka, "Osoba," 249, and Ghelfand, "Marxismus," 427.

77. Bohdan Chudoba, "Doprava? Doleva?" *Obzory* 2 (1946): 231, and *Co je to*, 56–57. See also his *Majetek, práce a sociální úkoly* (Prague: ČAT-Universum, 1946), 7.

78. Ghelfand, *Marxismus*, 25.

79. Pecka, "Osoba," 249.

80. Kajpr, "Komunismus a království Boží," 2.

81. Marek, 3.

82. F. Jiřík, "Mezi dvěma frontami," 104. This is one of the rare instances in which Catholic doctrine was expressly labeled a form of "socialism."

83. Adolf Kajpr, "Drama atheistického humanismu," *Katolík* 9, no. 1 (1946): 3.

84. Silvestr Braito, "Křesťanství a sociální otázky," *Na blubinu* 21 (1947): 66.

85. Artur Pavelka, "Soudruh Ježíš Kristus," *Katolík* 11, no. 3 (1948): 3.

86. These are taken from the chapter headings of Michael Fogarty, *Christian Democracy in Western Europe, 1820–1953* (Notre Dame: University of Notre Dame Press, 1957), v–vi.

87. Šolle, 218.

88. Adolf Kajpr, "V čem se vlastně rocházíme?," *Katolík* 9, no. 4 (1946): 1, and Dominik Pecka, "Křesťanský realismus," *Vyšebrad* 2 (1947): 17–18.

89. Václav Chytil, "Socialismus a sociální reformismus," *Obzory* 3 (1947): 624, 640.

90. Ghelfand, "Co je socialismus?" 51, and Richter, 49.

91. Pecka, "Křesťanství a aktivita," 8.

92. Jaromír John in Kopecký, 76, and Richter, 21.

93. Tigrid, "Vánoční rozjímání," 2, and "Abychom opravdu věrní zůstali," 322.

94. Pimper, 80 and 85. See also Ghelfand, *Marxismus*, 45.

95. Richter, 17. See also Chudoba, *Co je to*, 76, and Ghelfand, *Marxismus*, 33.

96. Richter, 35, Chudoba, *Co je to*, 73, and Josef Zvěřina, "Katolicismus a komunismus," *Svobodné noviny*, 19 October 1946, 1.

97. Tigrid, "V domě oběšencově . . .." 85 and Zvěřina, 1.

98. Jon Bloomfield, *Passive Revolution. Politics and the Czechoslovak Working Class 1945–1948*, (New York: St. Martin's, 1979), 71.

99. Bohdan Chudoba, "Křesťanská orientace," *Obzory* 1 (1945): 260–61, rs, 1 and Ghelfand, *Marxismus*, 32–34.

100. Jan Kolár, "O svobodě," *Obzory* 3 (1947): 369.

101. Pavel Tigrid, "Smysl Mnichova," *Obzory* 3 (1947): 557, and Kolár, 375.

102. Richter, 37.

103. In this respect, the even more conservative, clericalist position of the People's Party's Slovak analogue, the Democratic Party, certainly contributed to the failure to develop political cooperation among non-Communist parties across the state.

CHAPTER 12

1. Arnošt Kolman, *Co je smyslem života?* (Prague: Orbis, 1947), 52, and František Hník, "Duchovní základy nového humanismu," *Náboženská revue* 17 (1946): 331.

2. Jarmila Glazerová, "Česká kultura církvi československé," *Český zápas* 29 (1946): 11, and František Kovář, "Projev patriarchy PhDr Františka Kováře při uvedení v úřad," in *Církev československá v službách pokroku*. (Prague: Informační a tisková rada církve čsl., 1946), 8.

3. V. Štrunc, "Církev československá a ekumenický ideal," *Český zápas* 30 (1947): 39.

4. Václav Molkop, "Církev a politika," *Český zápas* 29 (1946): 3–4.

5. Beneš' words are reported in Josef Souček, "Političnost a nepolitičnost křesťanství," *Křesťanská revue* 14 (1947): 293. An example of the church's views of Beneš can be seen in František Hník's review of the president's *Demokracie dnes a a zítra* in *Náboženská revue* 17 (1946): 166–69. Trtík's comments are from his "Proč království Boží není snem," *Český zápas* 31 (1948): 4. Notably, this concern did not stop Trtík from participating in the Church's orgy of enthusiasm, as the title of the article, "Why the Kingdom of God Is Not a Dream," indicates.

6. It is important to reiterate that Linhart, who had served as an Evangelical pastor in the interwar period, has been placed with the Czechoslovak Church because his views correspond with those of the church and he published them almost exclusively in its press and through its publishing institutions.

7. František Linhart, *Dialektický materialismus a křesťanství* (Prague: Tábor, 1947), 46–47.

8. Otto Rutrle, "K současnému poslání křesťanské církve," *Náboženská revue* 17 (1946): 15, and "Jeden jest vůdce váš, Kristus," *Český zápas* 29 (1946): 191.

9. "Tábor je náš program," *Český zápas* 30 (1947): 120.

10. Linhart, 37–38.

11. "Poselství II. řádného sněmu církve československé," *Náboženská revue* 17 (1946): 60. The assembly took place in January of 1946, and was attended by delegates from 273 religious communities. Even the National Socialist *Masarykův lid* reprinted the document, commenting that it was worthy of particular attention because the Czechoslovak Church had grown so rapidly in a period in which Czechs were not much concerned with religion. Arnošt Polavský, "Otázky doby v svobodně křesťanském pojetí," *Masarykův id* 15 (1945/6): 135–36.

12. Linhart, 31.

13. František Linhart, "Křesťanství na rozcestí," *Náboženská revue* 17 (1946): 293.

14. Otto Rutrle, "Jeden jest," 191.

15. Linhart, "Křesťanství," 77.

16. Linhart, *Dialektický materialismus*, 47.

17. Hník, 330.

18. The citations are from the minutes of the conference taken by Zdeněk Trtík and reprinted in "Čtvrtá theologická konference duchovenstva čs. církve v Broumově-Olivětíně 1.-8. srpna 1946," *Náboženská revue* 17 (1946): 148–64.

19. František Linhart. "K situaci náboženského socialismu v Československu," *Český zápas* 30 (1947): 28.

20. Rutrle, "K současnému poslání," 14.

21. František Roháč, "Otázky doby a naše křesťanství," *Náboženská revue* 17 (1946): 25.

22. "Poselství," 60.

23. Rutrle, "K současnému poslání," 16.

24. On this, see František Hník, "Křesťanova orientace ve dnešním světě," *Náboženská revue* 17 (1946): 68.

25. Roháč, "Otázky doby," 24–25.

26. Linhart, "K situaci," 28 and Zdeněk Trtík, cited in Trtík, "Čtvrtá theologická konference," 151.

27. František Roháč, cited in Trtík, "Čtvrtá theologická konference," 162, and František Hník, "Křesťanova orientace" and "Poměr církve k veřejnému životu," *Náboženská revue* 17 (1946): 11.

28. František Kovář in *Můj poměr ke KSČ. Projevy z řad pracující inteligence* (Prague: KSČ, 1946), 48, and Václav Vyšohlíd, "Hledá se společný jmenovatel," *Český zápas* 29 (1946): 142.

29. Hník, "Duchovní základy," 324, and "Poměr církve," 11.

30. Václav Molkop, "Poselství sněmu k církvi a národu," *Český zápas* 29 (1946): 8, and Alois Spisar, "Spolupráce křesťanství s komunismem," *Český zápas* 29 (1946): 185.

31. Linhart, *Dialektický materialismus*, 34 and Roháč, "Otázky doby," 26.

32. "Poselství," 60.

33. Alois Spisar, "Křesťan a politika," *Český zápas* 29 (1946): 133.

34. Miroslav Novák, "Projev biskupa Dr Mir. Nováka při uvedení v úřad," in *Církev Československá*, 18–19. The only argument offered for the necessity of socialism was offered by Zdeněk Trtík, who maintained that justice in interpersonal relations was a condition for entry into the Kingdom of God, that a condition for justice in interpersonal relations was a "just economic and social order," and that the hallmark of an unjust social order was class struggle. See Zdeněk Trtík, "Spravedlnost podmínkou království Božího," *Český zápas* 29 (1946): 220.

35. Alois Spisar, "Proč mravní chaos dneška?" *Náboženská revue* 17 (1946): 86, and "Církev a království Boží," *Český zápas* 29 (1946): 48.

36. Hník, "Křesťanova orientace," 65.

37. Novák, "Projev biskupa," 19, and Trtík, "Čtvrtá theologická konference," 150.

38. Hník, "Duchovní základy," 327, and "Poměr církve," 4.

39. Kovář, "Projev patriarchy," 9, and Novák, "Projev biskupa," 20. See also Kovář's statement that the "entire public has already many times had the possibility to be convinced of the positive position of the Czechoslovak Church to the people's democratic regime." František Kovář, "Církev československá dvouletce," *Český zápas* 29 (1946): 249.

40. Kovář, "Projev patriarchy," 12.

41. Hník, "Duchovní základy," 328, and František Kovář. "Velké dny církve československé," *Český zápas* 29 (1946): 226. Interestingly, Hník published an article on the same topic in the National Socialist Party weekly *Svobodný zítřek* slightly later, in which he still termed the plan a "great socio-ethical experiment," but dampened his enthusiasm and dedication on other points. See František Hník, "O základy nového humanismu," *Svobodný zítřek* 3 (1947): 2.

42. Kovář, "Projev patriarchy," 11. The unwieldy number of political parties had been a topic of criticism before the war, though the idea of removing the consistently largest party, the Agrarians, was certainly not part of the discussion.

43. J. Světlý, "Problémy demokracie," *Český zápas* 30 (1947): 280.

44. Hník, "Mravní problém dneška a křesťanské principy," *Český zápas* 29 (1946): 194.

45. Hník, "Křesťanova orientace," 71, and Novák, "Projev biskupa," 18. In the same piece, Novák vowed to "help this new man . . . be born and find himself."

46. Pavel Tigrid, "Krise lidskosti," *Lidová demokracie*, 25 August 1946, 1.

47. Světlý, "Problémy demokracie," 280, and "Kdo jsou tihle Slované," *Český zápas* 30 (1947): 91.

48. Rutrle, "K současnému poslání," 18.

49. Václav Lorenc, "Přízraky Mnichova," *Český zápas* 29 (1946): 213, and Miroslav Novák, "Projev biskupa," 19.

50. Trtík, "Čtvrtá theologická conference," 149, and Václav Vyšohlid, "O *Český zápas*," *Český zápas* 30 (1947): 57.

51. "Poselství," 60.

52. Vyšohlid, "Hledá se," 142. See also Patriarch Kovář's positive review of a book co-authored by Hromádka, "J. L. Hromádka a Otakar Odložilík: S druhého břehu," *Náboženská revue* 17 (1946): 126–28.

53. Hník, "Duchovné základy," 326, and Novák, "Projev biskupa," 19.

54. Hník, "Poměr církve," 10, and Roháč, "Otázky doby," 26.

55. František Hník, "V duchu T. G. M. k očistě republiky," *Český zápas* 31 (1948): 51.

56. František Kovář, "Prohlášení k věřícím a veřejnosti," *Český zápas* 31 (1948): 51.

57. Otto Rutrle, "Boží slovo nad světem," *Český zápas* 31 (1948): 57.

58. Zdeněk Trtík, "Zkouška charakteru," *Český zápas* 31 (1948): 60.

59. Ladislav Blecha, "Úvaha politická," *Kostnické jiskry* 31 (1946): 131.

60. B. Hl. [Břetislav Hladký], "Proč marxismus?" *Kostnické jiskry* 32, no. 46 (1947): 3, and Jan A. Pellar, "Krok kupředu!," *Kostnické jiskry* 31 (1946): 217.

61. J. L. Hromádka, "Poslání Československa v dnešní Evropě," in his *O nové Československo* (Prague: Henclova tiskárna, 1946), 15, and "Jednota národa v pravdě," in his *Jednota národa v pravdě* (Prague: Evangelické dílo, 1946), 8–9, 24.

62. _or, "Nepolitičnost," *Křesťanská revue* 13 (1946): 102.

63. František Bednář, "Poslání theologických fakult v dnešní světové revoluci," in *Hledej pravdu. Sborník o sjezdu evangelických akademiků v listopadu 1945 v Praze* (Liptovský Sv. Mikuláš: Transocius, n.d.), 75.

64. Doc. Dr Ant. Boháč, "Naše poslání," *Kostnické jiskry* 31 (1946): 2. Boháč was the church's synodal curator.

65. J. L. Hromádka, "Naše odpovědnost v poválečném světě," in *J. L. Hromádka. Pravda a život* (Prague: Ekumenický institut, 1969), 62, and J. L. Hromádka, *Komunismus a křesťanství* (Rovnečný na Moravě: Evangelické dílo, 1946), 13–14.

66. Josef Souček, "Po roce," *Křesťanská revue* 13 (1946): 97.

67. J. L. Hromádka, "Poslání Československa v dnešní Evropě," 25, and *Komunismus a křesťanství*, 8.

68. J. L. Hromádka, "Na prahu třetí republiky," *Kostnické jiskry* 30 (1945): 85.

69. Hromádka, "Jednota národa," 20. He said "Is it not possible to build the new, postwar order on a decidedly socialist but yet noncommunist foundation? . . . the logic of relations will become the tool of reactionary forces if [parties] stand against the communists" (23–24).

70. Hromádka, "Jednota národa," 18–19 and 31.
71. Hromádka, "Jednota národa," 32–33.
72. B. Hladký, "Komunismus a náboženství," *Kostnické jiskry* 30 (1945): 160.
73. Boháč, "Naše poslání," 1, and Jan Sláma, "Poměr evangelistického křesťana k veřejnosti," *Kostnické jiskry* 30 (1945): 109.
74. "Poselství k církvi a národu," *Kostnické jiskry* 32, no. 4 (1947): 1.
75. Stanislav Čapek, "Solidní stavba," *Kostnické jiskry* 31 (1946): 253.
76. Vladimír Harych, "K dvouletnímu programu," *Kostnické jiskry* 31 (1946): 268.
77. Jaroslav Nečas, "Evangelíci a dvouletka," *Kostnické jiskry* 31 (1946): 273.
78. B. Hl. [Břetislav Hladký], "Komunismus a křesťanství," *Kostnické jiskry* 32, no. 13 (1947): 2.
79. Pellar, 217.
80. Hromádka, "Poslání Československa," 21. See also his comment that while "We are not naive children, who imagine the Soviet government will turn to Christianity and that the Soviet youth will now be educated in Sunday schools," the Czechoslovak public must recognize that there had been "deep changes" in the Soviet Union's attitude toward religion. J. L. Hromádka, "Mezi válkou a mírem," *Kostnické jiskry* 31 (1946): 56.
81. Blecha, 132.
82. B. Hladký, "Komunismus a náboženství," *Kostnické jiskry* 30 (1945): 160.
83. Josef Závodský, "Odluka církve a státu?" *Kostnické jiskry* 31 (1946): 58.
84. Blecha, 132.
85. Hromádka, *Komunismus a Křesťanství*, 14–15 and 34–35.
86. Bednář, "Poslání theologických fakult," 81.
87. Hromádka, "Naše odpovědnost," 68.
88. Hromádka, "Naše odpovědnost," 69 and 71. See also his "Naše problematika," *Svobodný zítřek* 1, no. 3 (1945): 2. For his more extensive comments on the Soviet Union, see "Hovoříme se profesorem Hromádkou," *Kostnické jiskry* 32 (1947), no. 49:1 and no. 50:2.
89. Although some of this criticism was directed at all the parties, the Communist Party was obviously the intended target, given that it was the only party with a reasonable chance of gaining a majority. Stanislav Čapek, *Úvod do sociální otázky* (Prague: Kostnická jednota, 1947), 43.
90. Hromádka, *Komunismus a křesťanství*, 41 and 43.
91. Amadeo Molnár, "*křesťanství* a komunismus," *Kostnické jiskry* 31 (1946): 77.
92. Hromádka, "Naše odpovědnost," 67.
93. Jan Pellar, "Mravnost a dialektický materialismus," *Křesťanská revue* 15 (1948): 48 and 51.
94. Čapek, *Úvod*, 29. See also his comment that the Kingdom of God should not be "'of this Earth,' sinful and blemished, but a Kingdom of God on this Earth." Čapek, "Solidní stavba," 253.
95. Molnár, 76.
96. Hromádka, *Komunismus a křesťanství*, 37.
97. B. Hladký, "Komunismus a křesťanství," *Kostnické jiskry* 32, no. 13 (1947): 2
98. J. B. Souček, "Jak politicky uplatňovat naše křesťanství?" *Kostnické jiskry* 30 (1945): 86.
99. B. Hladký, "Evangelíci a lidová strana," *Kostnické jiskry* 30 (1945): 103, and Blecha, 132.
100. Blecha, 132, and Hromádka, *Komunismus a křesťanství*, 19–20.
101. See, for example, -ž [Luděk Brož], "Československá církev a světová rada církví," *Kostnické jiskry* 32, no. 31 (1947): 3, and the response of the Czechoslovak Church's F. M. Bartoš, "O svobodné křesťanství," *Kostnické jiskry* 32, no. 33 (1947): 3.
102. B. Hl. [Břetislav Hladký], "Náš poměr k československé církvi," *Kostnické jiskry* 32 (1947), no. 47:4 and no. 48:3.
103. See, for example, Boháč, "Naše poslání," 1 and B. Hl. [Břetislav Hladký], "Komunismus a křesťanství," *Kostnické jiskry* 32, no. 13 (1947): 2.
104. Hromádka, "Naše odpovědnost," 66.
105. Boháč, 1.
106. Hromádka, "Naše odpovědnost," 63 and 65. His view that the democrats were abusing the term freedom was supported by Břetislav Hladý, who argued that those "who today speak of the

Church and Christian cultural values, about religious freedom and Christian democracy or humanism, have in mind capitalism and their social privileges." Hladý, "Komunismus a křest'anství," 2.

107. Hromádka "Jednota národa v pravdě," 31–32, and "Poslání Československa," 12.

108. Václav Kopecký, *Zápas o nové vlastenectví* (Prague: ÚV KSČ, 1948), 53.

CONCLUSION

1. Cited in Karel Kaplan, *The Short March: The Communist Takeover of Czechoslovakia, 1945–1948* (London: C. Hurst, 1987), 179.

2. In Prague 200,300 workers took part, while there were only 98 strike breakers. M. R. Myant, *Socialism and Democracy in Czechoslovakia* (Cambridge: Cambridge University Press, 1981), 203. This was in conjunction with voting on a resolution of the Congress of Factory Councils, which supported demands made by the Communist Party and which passed overwhelmingly. In another tactical mistake, the anti-communist leaders handed in their resignations two days before this Congress met in Prague, assembling 8,030 mostly communist delegates in the capital.

3. Kaplan, 182 and 185.

4. Eva Schmidt-Hartmann, "Das Konzept der 'politischen Kultur' in der Tschechoslowakei," in *Sowjetisches Modell und nationale Prägung. Kontinuität und Wandel in Ostmitteleuropa nach dem zweiten Weltkrieg*, ed. Hans Lemberg (Marburg/Lahn: J. G. Herder Institut, 1991), 195.

5. Prečan, "Politika a taktika KSČ 1945–1948," in his *V kradeném čase. Výběr ze studií, článků a úvah z let 1973–1993* (Prague: ÚSD, 1994), 116. Milan Kundera perceived February in much the same way: "And so it happened in February of 1948 the Communists took power not in bloodshed and violence, but to the cheers of about half the population. And please note: the half that cheered was the more dynamic, the more intelligent, the better half." Milan Kundera, *The Book of Laughter and Forgetting*, trans. Michael Henry Heim (New York: Penguin, 1981), 8.

6. Pavel Tigrid, *Marx na Hradčanech* (New York: Edice Svědectví, 1960), 10. For a Communist evaluation of the mood in Prague immediately preceding and during the crisis, see Miroslav Bouček, *Praha v únoru 1948* (Prague: NPL, 1963).

7. Václav Kopecký's words of six weeks earlier must still have been ringing in communists' ears: "agents of foreign enemies, of a foreign imperialism. . . . measures must be taken against *Obzory* and *Vývoj*, which, as journals of the People's Party, fully evidence that they are agents of foreign reaction." Václav Kopecký, *Zápas o nové vlastenectví* (Prague: ÚV KSČ, 1948), 24. There were rumors that Pavel Tigrid had fled the country, further weakening the Catholic cause. Myant, 214.

8. Myant, 215.

9. Prokop Drtina, *Československo můj osud. Kniha života českého demokrata 20. století*, vol. 2 (Prague: Melantrich, 1992), 515. Eva Schmidt-Hartmann has taken this as a departure point for a perhaps exceedingly harsh judgment of the National Socialist leadership's democratic sensibilities. She writes that by their reliance on "cabinet politics. . . . their 'democratic consciousness' must fundamentally be called into question. A politician, who shows so little respect for the role of the public—as is throughout the case in the memoirs examined here—cannot be termed a democrat or even a defender of democracy without further evidence." Eva Schmidt-Hartmann, "Demokraten in der Sackgasse. Das Bild der kommunistischen Machtübernahme in den Memoiren besiegter tschechischer Politiker," *Kommunismus und Osteuropa. Konzepte, Perspektiven und Interpretationen im Wandel*, ed. Eva Schmidt-Hartmann (Munich: R. Oldenbourg, 1994), 211.

10. Peter Hruby, *Fools and Heroes: The Changing Role of Communist Intellectuals in Czechoslovakia* (Oxford: Pergamon, 1980), 5

11. Vladimir V. Kusin, "Czechoslovakia," in *Communist Power in Europe. 1944–1949*, ed. Martin McCauley (London: MacMillan, 1977), 83.

12. Otto Friedman, *The Break-Up of Czech Democracy* (London: Victor Gollancz, 1950), 91 and 98.

13. Prečan, 117.

14. Alfred French, *Czech Writers and Politics, 1945–1969* (Boulder, CO: East European Monographs, 1982), 47.

15. Arnošt Bláha, *Sociologie intelligence* (Prague: Orbis, 1937), 59.

16. Toman Brod, *Cesta československých komunistů k moci*, vol. 1 (Prague: Magnet, 1990), 38.

17. Prečan, 116.

18. Edvard Beneš, cited in čt, "Boj o nového člověka trvá," *Svobodné noviny*, 15 December 1946, 1 and Hubert Ripka, *Czechoslovakia Enslaved* (London: Victor Gollancz, 1950), 312.

19. Vilém Hejl, *Rozvrat. Mnichov a náš osud* (Toronto: 68 Publishers, 1989), 115.

20. See Alexsa Djilas, *The Contested Country: Yugoslav Unity and Communist Revolution, 1919–1953* (Cambridge: Harvard University Press, 1991), 159.

21. This estimate relies on two assumptions. It takes at face value the Agrarian Nikola Petkov's assertion that had the elections been free, fair, and accurately counted the opposition Agrarians would have won 60% of the vote, leaving some forty percent for the Fatherland Front. Further, it assumes that the Communist Party's share of the Front vote remained constant at 75%.

22. Charles Gati has pointed out that "The war years and the destruction of the country made economic change of a radical type quite appealing. . . . [T]here was considerable appeal, among the population at large, in radical, perhaps socialist or social-democratic, transformation. . . . Hungary was in a radical mood." Cited in Michael Charlton, *The Eagle and the Small Birds* (London: British Broadcasting Corporation, 1984), 59. Gati elaborates on the possibilities for this in "The Domestic Context," chapter 2 of his *Hungary and the Soviet Bloc* (Durham, NC: Duke University Press, 1986), 44–72. See also William O. McCagg, Jr., "Communism and Hungary, 1944–1956" (Ph. D. diss., Columbia University, 1965).

23. The referendum was on three issues: the abolition of the interwar senate, the distribution of agricultural land to the peasantry and the nationalization program for industry, and the ratification of Poland's new borders. The leader of the largest opposition party, the Peasant Party's Stanisław Mikołajczyk, took this opportunity to make a show of opposition strength by asking his supporters to vote against the first of these. See Andrzej Paczkowski, *Referendum z 30 czerwca 1946 r.* (Warszawa: ISP PAN, 1993), 159.

24. Here I am following the evaluations of both Keith Hitchens and Stephen Fischer-Galați. See Keith Hitchens, *Rumania 1866–1947* (Oxford: Oxford University Press, 1994), 533 and Stephen Fischer-Galați, *Twentieth Century Rumania* (New York: Columbia University Press, 1970), 104.

25. Hitchens reports on the above-cited page that "independent sources suggest that the National Peasants were on their way to a landslide victory with about 70 per cent of the vote." Even allowing for this, most of the remainder would fall to the Communists.

26. Padraic Kenney, *Rebuilding Poland: Workers and Communists, 1945–1950* (Ithaca: Cornell University Press, 1997).

27. Jon Bloomfield, *Passive Revolution: Politics and the Czech Working Class, 1945–1948* (New York: St. Martin's, 1979).

28. Melissa K. Bokovoy, *Peasants and Communists: Politics and Ideology in the Yugoslav Countryside, 1941–1953* (Pittsburgh: University of Pittsburgh Press, 1998).

29. See "A Note on Communists and the Jewish Question" in Gati, *Hungary*, 100–7, esp. 105–7.

APPENDIX

1. *Rudé právo*, 6 October 1946, 1.
2. *Svobodné slovo*, 13 October 1946, 1.
3. *Rudé právo*, 7 November 1946, 4.
4. J. B. Kozák, ed., *Kulturní jednota a její program* (Praha: Orbis, 1947)

Bibliography

Abrams, Bradley. "Morality, Wisdom and Revision: The Czech Opposition of the 1970s and the Expulsion of the Sudeten Germans." *East European Politics and Societies* 9 (1995): 234–55.

———. "The Marshall Plan and Czechoslovak Democracy: Elements of Interdependancy." In *The Marshall Plan: Fifty Years After*, edited by Martin A. Schain, 93–116. New York: Palgrave, 2001.

———. "The Politics of Retribution: The Trial of Josef Tiso." *East European Politics and Societies* 10 (1996): 255–92.

———. "The Second World War and the East European Revelation." *East European Politics and Societies* 16 (2002): 623–64.

Adamec, Čeněk, Bohuš Pospíšil and Milan Tesař. *What's Your Opinion. A Year's Survey of Public Opinion in Czechoslovakia*. Prague: Orbis, 1947.

Agnew, Hugh LeCaine. *Origins of the Czech National Renascence*. Pittsburgh: University of Pittsburgh Press, 1993.

Aldcroft, Derek H. and Steven Morewood. *Economic Change in Eastern Europe Since 1918*. Aldershot: Edward Elgar, 1995.

Banac, Ivo, ed. *The Effects of World War I: The Class War after the Great War*. New York: Columbia University Press, 1983.

Bareš, Gustav. *Listy o kultuře*. Prague: Svoboda, 1947.

———. *Naše cesta k socialismu*. Prague: ÚV KSČ, 1948.

Belda, Josef. "Československá cesta k socialismu." *Příspěvky k dějinám* KSČ 7 (1967).

Benda, Julien. *The Treason of the Intellectuals*. New York: Norton, 1969.

———. *Zrada intelektuálů*. Prague: S.V.U. Mánes, 1929.

Beneš, Edvard. *Demokracie dnes a zítra*. Prague: Čin, 1947.

———. *Nová slovanská politika*. Prague: Čin, 1946.

———. *Úvahy o slovanství*. Prague: Čin, 1947.

Berend, Iván T. and György Ránki. *Economic Development in East-Central Europe in the 19th and 20th Centuries*. New York: Columbia University Press, 1974.

Berend, Ivan. "The Composition and Position of the Working Class During the War." In *Hungarian Economy and Society During World War II*, edited by György Lengyel. Translated by Judit Pokoly, 151–68. Boulder, CO: Social Science Monographs, 1993.

Björling, Fiona. "Who Is the We of the Intelligentsia in Central and Eastern Europe?" In *Intelligentsia in the Interim. Recent Experiences from Central and Eastern Europe*, edited by Fiona

Björling. Lund, Sweden: Lund University, 1995.

Bláha, Inocenc Arnošt. *Kultura a politika*. Brno: Zemská osvětová rada, 1946.

————. *Sociologie Inteligence*. Prague: Orbis, 1937.

Bloomfield, Jon. *Passive Revolution. Politics and the Czech Working Class 1945–1948*. New York: St. Martin's, 1979.

Bokovoy, Melissa K. *Peasants and Communists. Politics and Ideology in the Yugoslav Countryside. 1941–1953*. Pittsburgh: University of Pittsburgh Press, 1998.

Bosl, Karl and Ferdinand Seibt, eds. *Kultur und Gesellschaft in der ersten tschechoslowakischen Republik*. Munich: R. Oldenbourg, 1982.

Bosl, Karl, ed. *Die "Burg." Einflußreiche politische Kräfte um Masaryk und Beneš*. 2 vols. Munich: R. Oldenbourg, 1973, 1975.

Bouček, Miroslav. *Praha v únoru 1948*. Prague: NPL, 1963.

Bradley, John F. N. *Czech Nationalism in the Nineteenth Century*. Boulder, CO: East European Monographs, 1984.

————. *Politics in Czechoslovakia, 1945–1990*. Boulder, CO: East European Monographs, 1992.

Brandes, Detlef. *Die Tschechen unter deutschem Protektorat*. 2 vols. Munich: R. Oldenbourg, 1969, 1975.

Brock, Peter and Gordon Skilling. *The Czech Renascence of the Nineteenth Century*. Toronto: University of Toronto Press, 1970.

Brod, Toman. *Cesta československých komunistů k moci v letech 1945–1948*. 2 vols. Prague: Magnet, 1990.

————. *Osudný omyl Edvarda Beneše, 1939–1948*. Prague: Academia, 2002.

Brouček, Miloslav. *Československá tragedie*. New York[?]: M. Brouček, 1956.

Brown, Archie and Gordon Wightman. "Czechoslovakia: Revival and Retreat." In *Political Culture and Political Change in Communist States*, edited by Archie Brown and Jack Gray, 159–96. London: Macmillan, 1977.

Brown, John (pseud.) *Who's Next? The Lesson of Czechoslovakia*. London: Hutchinson, 1951.

Burian, Václav, A. Frinta and B. Havránek, eds. *Slovanský sjezd v Bělehrad r. 1946*. Prague: Orbis, 1947.

Busek, Vratislav. "Church and State." In *Czechoslovakia*, edited by Vratislav Busek and Nicholas Spulber, 130–53. New York: Praeger, 1957.

Chalupa, Vlastislav. *Communism in a Free Society: Czechoslovakia 1945–1948*. Chicago: Czechoslovak Foreign Institute in Exile, 1958.

Chalupecký, Jindřich. *Obhajoba umění 1934–1948*. Prague: Orientace, 1991.

Charlton, Michael. *The Eagle and the Small Birds*. London: British Broadcasting Corporation, 1984.

Chudoba, Bohdan. "Czech Protestants and Communism." *America: National Catholic Weekly Review* 82 (1949).

————. *Co je to křest'anská politika*. Prague: ČAT-Universum, 1947.

————. *Majetek, práce a sociální úkoly*. Prague: ČAT-Universum, 1946.

Církev československá v službách pokroku. Prague: Informační a tisková rada církve čsl., 1946.

Církev československá v životě národa. Memorandum presidentu republiky, ústavodárnému národnímu shromáždění, vládě republiky a veřejným činitelům. Prague: Informační a tisková rada církve čsl., 1946.

Cohen, Gary. *The Politics of Ethnic Survival: Germans in Prague, 1861–1914*. Princeton: Princeton University Press, 1981.

Conway, Martin. Introduction to *Political Catholicism in Europe, 1918–1965*, edited by Tom Buchanan and Martin Conway, 1–33. Oxford: Clarendon Press, 1996.

Čapek, Stanislav. *Úvod do sociální otázky*. Prague: Kostnická jednota, 1947.

Černý, Václav. *Eseje o české a slovenské próze*. Prague: Torst, 1994.

————. *Křik koruny české. Paměti 1938–1945. Náš kulturní odboj za války*. Brno: Atlantis, 1992.

————. *O povaze naší kultury*. Brno: Atlantis, 1991.

———. *Paměti IV*. Toronto: 68 Publishers, 1983.

———. *Paměti*. 3 vols. Brno: Atlantis, 1992–94.

———. *První a druhý sešit o existencialismu*. Prague: Mladá fronta. 1992.

———. *Skutečnost svoboda*. Prague: Český spisovatel, 1995.

———. *Staročeská milostná lyrika*. Prague: Družstevní práce. 1948.

———. *Tvorba a osobnost*. 2 vols. Prague: Odeon, 1992–93.

———. *V zúženém prostoru*. Prague: Mladá fronta, 1994.

———. *Vývoj a zločiny panslavismu*. Knihovna střední evropy 1. Prague: Institut pro středo-evropskou kulturu a politiku, n.d. [1994].

Červinka, František. *Zdeněk Nejedlý*. Prague: Melantrich, 1969.

Československý biografický slovník. Prague: Academia, 1992.

Diamond, William. *Czechoslovakia Between East and West*. London: Stevens and Sons, 1947.

Djilas, Alexsa. *The Contested Country. Yugoslav Unity and Communist Revolution 1919–1953*. Cambridge: Harvard University Press, 1991.

Długoborski, Wacław, ed. *Zweiter Weltkrieg und sozialer Wandel. Achsenmächte und besetzte Länder*. Göttingen: Vandenhoeck & Ruprecht, 1981.

Dresler, Jaroslav. "Václava Černého účtování se Stalinism." In *Paměti Václava Černého v kritickém zrcadle exilu a disentu*. Edice TVARy. Series A, Number 6. Prague: Tvar, 1995.

Drtina, Pavel. *Československo můj osud*. 2 vols. Prague: Melantrich, 1992.

Ebertová, Anežka. "Církev v proměnách." In *Padesát let Československé církve*, edited by Miloslav Kaňák. Prague: Husova československá bohoslovecká fakulta, 1970.

Eubank, Keith. *Munich*. Norman: Oklahoma University Press, 1963.

Feierabend, Ladislav Karel. *Politické vzpomínky*. Vol. 3. Brno: Atlantis, 1996.

Fidelius, Petr. "Byl Peroutka liberál?" *Kritický sborník* 11 (1991).

Fischer-Galaţi, Stephen. "Prelude to Communist Totalitarianism, August 1944–March 1945." In *Romania: A Historic Perspective*, edited by Dinu C. Giurescu and Stephen Fischer-Galaţi, 391–407. Boulder, CO: East European Monographs, 1998.

Fischer-Galaţi, Stephen. *Twentieth Century Rumania*. New York: Columbia University Press, 1970.

Fogarty, Michael. *Christian Democracy in Western Europe 1820–1953*. Notre Dame: University of Notre Dame Press, 1957.

Foustka, Radim. *Dialektický materialismus jako způsob myšlení*. Prague: Práce, 1946.

———. *O pevnou půdu pod nohama*. Prague: Ústřední akční výbor čs. sociální demokracie. 1945.

Frei, Bohumil Jiří. *Staat und Kirche in der Tschechoslowakei vom Februarumsturz zum Prager Frühling 1968*. Vol. 4, Dokumente und Tabellen. Munich: Robert Lerche, 1973.

French, Alfred. *Czech Writers and Politics 1945–1969*. Boulder, CO: East European Monographs, 1982.

Friedman, Otto. *The Break-Up of Czech Democracy*. London: Victor Gollancz, 1950.

Furet, François. *The Passing of an Illusion. The Idea of Communism in the Twentieth Century*. Chicago: University of Chicago Press, 1999.

Gati, Charles. *Hungary and the Soviet Bloc*. Durham, NC: Duke University Press, 1986.

Gella, Aleksander, ed. *The Intelligentsia and the Intellectuals*. Beverly Hills, CA: SAGE, 1976.

Ghelfand, S. S. *Dialektický materialismus*. Prague: Universum, 1947.

Ghelfand, S. S. *Marxismus a křesťanský sociální reformismus. K výročí papežských okružních listů "Rerum novarum" a "Quadragesimo anno."* Prague: n.p., 1946.

Glassheim, Eagle. "Crafting a Post-Imperial Identity: Nobles and Nationality Politics in Czechoslovakia, 1918–1948." Ph.D. diss., Columbia University, 2000.

Góra, Władysław, ed. *Wojna i okupacja na ziemiach Polskich 1939–1945*. Warszawa: Książka i wiedza, 1984.

Gottwald, Klement. *Deset let*. Edited by Gustav Bareš. Prague: Orbis, 1948.

———. *O kultuře a úkolech inteligence*. Prague: Min. informací a osvěty, 1949.

———. "Projev na konferenci funkcionářů Komunistické strany Slovenska v Košicích 8. Dubna 1945." In *Spisy*, vol. 12. Prague: SNPL, 1955.

———. *Spisy*. Vols 12–14. Prague: SNPL, 1955–58.

Gross, Jan. "The Social Consequences of War: Preliminaries for the Study of the Imposition of Communist Regimes in East Central Europe." *East European Politics and Societies* 3 (1989): 198–214.

Hajda, Jan. "The Role of the Intelligentsia in the Development of Czechoslovak Society." In *The Czechoslovak Contribution to World Culture*, edited by Miroslav Rechcigl, 307–12. The Hague: Mouton, 1964.

Hájek, Jiří. *Generace na rozhrání*. Prague: Mláda fronta, 1946.

Hartmannová, Eva. "Místo doslovu (Zamyšlení nad výběrem publicistiky F. Peroutky)." *Tvar*, no. 4 (1992): 4–5.

———. "'My' a 'oni': hledání české národní identity na stránkách *Dneška* z roku 1946." In *Strankami soudobých dějin. Sborník statí k pětašedesatnám historika Karla Kaplana*, edited by Karel Jech, 93–109. Prague: ÚSD, 1993.

Hauner, Milan. "Von der Verteidigung der 'kleinen Völker' zum neuen Slawismus. Edvard Beneš und der Slawismus." In *Geschichtliche Mythen in den Literaturen und Kulturen Ostmittel- und Südosteuropas*, edited by Eva Behring, Ludwig Richter and Wolfgang F. Schwarz, 293–309. Stuttgart: Franz Steiner, 1999.

Havlíček, Aleš. *Nepřeslechnutelná výzva*. Prague: Oikoymenh, 1990.

Hazareesingh, Sudhir. *Intellectuals and the French Communist Party*. Oxford: Clarendon Press, 1991.

Hejl, Vilém. *Rozvrat. Mnichov a náš osud*. Toronto: 68 Publishers, 1989.

Herbert, Ulrich. *Hitler's Foreign Workers. Enforced Foreign Labor in Germany under the Third Reich*. Translated by William Templer. Cambridge: Cambridge University Press, 1997.

Hertz, Alexander. "The Case of an Eastern European Intelligentsia." *Journal of Central European Affairs* 11 (1951).

Hitchens, Keith. *Rumania 1866–1947*. Oxford: Oxford University Press, 1994.

Hledej pravdu. Sborník o sjezdu evangelických akademiků v listopadu 1945 v Praze. Liptovský Sv. Mikuláš: Transocius, n.d.

Hoensch, Jörg. "Die Ausschaltung der nichtsozialistischen Parteien in Ostmitteleuropa." In *Sowjetisches Modell und nationale Prägung. Kontinuität und Wandel in Ostmitteleuropa nach dem zweiten Weltkrieg*, edited by Hans Lemberg, 71–96. Marburg/Lahn: J.-G. Herder Institute, 1991.

Hora, Josef. *Srdce a vřava světa*. Prague: Boravy, 1929.

———. *Svědectví o puči*. 2 vols. Prague: Melantrich, 1992.

———. "Západ a Východ." In *Srdce a vřava světa*. Praha: Borovy, 1929: 34–35.

Hořec, Jaromír. *Doba ortelů. Dokumenty—vzpomínky—iluze a skutečnosti*. Brno: Scholaris, 1992.

Hořec, Jaromír, ed. *Proč nejsem komunistou?* Prague: Lidové noviny, 1991.

Hořec, Jaromír and Miroslav Sígl. *Generace 45*. Prague: Rio-press, 1997.

Hořina, Miroslav. *Poslání inteligence v národě a ve státě*. Prague: C.A.T-Universum, 1947.

Hroch, Miroslav. *Die Vorkämpfer der nationalen Bewegung bei den kleinen Völkern Europas*. Praha: Karlova Univerzita, 1968.

Hromádka, J. L. and Otakar Odložilík. *S druhého břehu*. Prague: F. Borový, 1946.

———. *Jednota národa v pravdě*. Prague: Evangelické dílo, 1948.

———. *Komunismus a křesťanství*. Rovnečný na Moravě: Evangelické dílo, 1946.

———. *Mein Leben zwischen Ost und West*. Zürich: Theologischer Verlag, 1971.

———. *O nové Československo*. Prague: Henclova tiskárna, 1946.

Hruby, Peter. *Daydreams and Nightmares: Czech Communist and Ex-Communist Literature, 1917–1987*. Boulder CO, East European Monographs, 1990.

———. *Fools and Heroes*. Oxford: Pergamon, 1980.

J. L. Hromádka. *Pravda a život.* Prague: Ekumenický institut, 1969.

Judt, Tony. *Past Imperfect: French Intellectuals. 1944–1956.* Berkeley: University of California Press, 1992.

Kačavenda, Petar. "The Youth of Yugoslavia in War and Revolution." In *War and Revolution in Yugoslavia 1941–1945,* edited by Branko Prnjat. Translated by Margot and Boško Milosavljevič, 186–99. Belgrade: STP, 1985.

Kalvoda, Josef. "Paměti Václava Černého." In *Paměti Václava Černého v kritickém zrcadle exilu a disentu.* Edice TVARy. Series A, Number 6. Prague: Tvar, 1995: 20–5.

Kaminsky, Howard. *A History of the Hussite Revolution.* Berkeley: University of California Press, 1967.

Kaplan, Karel. *Československo v letech 1945–53.* 2 vols. Prague: SPN, 1990.

———. *Das verhängnisvolle Bundnis. Unterwanderung, Gleichschaltung und Vernichtung der tschechoslowakischen Sozialdemokratie 1944–1954.* Wuppertal: POL, 1984.

———. *Nebezpečná bezpečnost. Státní bezpečnost 1948–1956.* Brno: Doplněk, 1999.

———. *Nekrvavá revoluce.* Prague: Mladá fronta, 1993.

———. *Pět kapitol o únoru.* Brno: Doplněk, 1997.

———. *Pravda o Československu 1945–8.* Prague: Panorama, 1990.

———. *The Rise of a Monopoly of Power in the Hands of the Communist Party of Czechoslovakia, 1948–1949.* 2 vols. "The Experiences of Prague Spring, 1968" Research Project, Study 2. Unknown Location: Self-Published, 1979.

———. *Stát a církev v Československu 1948–1953.* Prague: ÚSD, 1993.

———. *The Short March. The Communist Takeover in Czechoslovakia 1945–1948.* London: C. Hurst, 1987.

Kaplan, Karel and Vladimír Pacl. *Tajný prostor Jáchymov.* České Budějovice: ACTYS, 1993.

Kaser, M. C. and E. A. Radice, eds. *The Economic History of Eastern Europe 1919–1975.* 3 vols. Oxford: Clarendon Press, 1985–86.

Kašpar, Jan. "Členská základna komunistické strany Československa v letech 1945–1949." *Československý časopis historický* 19 (1971): 1–25.

Kennan, George F. *From Prague after Munich. Diplomatic Papers, 1938–1940.* Princeton: Princeton University Press, 1968.

Kenney, Padraic. *Rebuilding Poland: Workers and Communists, 1945–1950.* Ithaca: Cornell University Press, 1997.

Kimball, Stanley B. *Czech Nationalism: A Study of the National Theatre Movement.* Urbana, IL.: University of Illinois Press, 1964.

Király, Béla and Nándor F. Dreiziger, eds. *East Central European Society in World War I.* Boulder, CO: Social Science Monographs, 1985.

Kirk, Dudley. *Europe's Population in the Interwar Years.* Geneva: League of Nations, 1946.

Kladiva, Jaroslav and V. Lacina, eds. *Československá revoluce v letech 1944–1948. Sborník příspěvků z konference historiků k 20. výročí osvobození ČSR.* Prague: Academia, 1966.

Kladiva, Jaroslav. "Boj o duši národa v předvečer února 1948." *Československý časopis historický* 15 (1967): 51–70.

———. *Kultura a politika 1945–1948.* Prague: Svoboda, 1968.

———. "Kulturní jednota." *Impuls* 1 (1966).

———. "Význam 'Československá cesta k socialismu' v politických a ideových zápasech let 1946–1947." *Nová mysl* 20 (1966) no. 17, pp. 6–10; no. 18, pp. 6–10.

Kolakowski, Leszek. *Der Mensch ohne Alternative. Von der Möglichkeit und Unmöglichkeit, Marxist zu sein.* Munich: Piper, 1960.

Kolman, Arnošt. *Co je smyslem života?* Prague: Orbis, 1947.

Konečný, Robert. *Demokracie.* Prague: Československý obec sokolský, 1947.

———. *Živá slova.* Brno: Zář, 1946.

Kopecký, Jan, ed. *Účtování a výhledy. Sborník prvního sjezdu českých spisovatelů.* Prague: Syndikát českých spisovatelů, 1948.

Kopecký, Václav. *Zápas o nové vlastenectví*. Prague: ÚV KSČ, 1948.

Korbel, Josef. *The Communist Subversion of Czechoslovkia, 1938–1948*. Princeton, NJ: Princeton University Press, 1959.

Kosatík, Pavel. *Ferdinand Peroutka. Pozdější život (1938–1978)*. Prague/Litomyšl: Paseka, 2000.

Kovály, Heda Margulius. *Under a Cruel Star: A Life in Prague, 1941–1968*. New York: Penguin, 1986.

Kovárna, František. *O kulturu v socialismu*. Prague: Melantrich, 1946.

Kozák, J. B., ed. *Kulturní jednota a její program. Projevy pronesené na ustavující valné hromadě "Kulturní jednoty" v Domě umělců dne 27. dubna 1947*. Prague: Orbis, 1947.

Král, Václav, ed. *Das Abkommen von Munich 1938. Dokumente*. Prague: Academia, 1968.

Kratochvíl, Bohuslav. *Veřejný život a inteligence*. Prague: Dělnické, 1946.

Křen, Jan. *Bílá místa v našich dějinách?* Prague: Lidové noviny, 1990.

Kubát, Daniel. "Über die Frage der tschechoslowakischen kommunistischen Intelligenz seit dem Zweiten Weltkrieg." *Zeitschrift für Ostforschung* 11 (1962).

Kundera, Milan. *The Book of Laughter and Forgetting*. Translated by Michael Henry Heim. New York: Penguin, 1981.

Kural, Václav. *Vlastenci proti okupaci. Ústřední vedení odboje domacího 1940–1943*. Prague: Univerzita Karlova, Ústav mezinarodních vztahů, 1997.

Kusák, Alexej. *Kultura a politika v Československu 1945–1953*. Prague: Torst, 1996

———. "Nationalbewuβtsein und Nationalpädagogik als Aspekte der tschechischen und slowakischen Literatur 1945–1948." In *Die Tschechoslowakei 1945–1970*, edited by Nikolaus Lobkowicz and Friedrich Prinz, 237–58. Munich: R. Oldenbourg, 1978.

Kusin, Vladimir. "Czechoslovakia." In *Communist Power in Europe 1944–1949*, edited by Martin McCauley, 73–94. London: MacMillan, 1977.

———. *The Intellectual Origins of the Prague Spring*. Cambridge: Cambridge University Press, 1971.

Langerová, Marie, ed. *Václav Černý. Sborník z konference konané 4.11.1993 na Dobříši*. Prague: Obec spisovatelu, 1994.

Laušman, Bohumil. *Kdo byl vinen?* Vienna: n.p., 1953.

Liehm, Antonín, ed. *The Politics of Culture*. Translated by Peter Kussi. New York: Grove, 1973.

Linhart, František. *Dialektický materialismus a křesťanství*. Prague: Tábor, 1947.

Lobkowicz, Nikolaus. *Marxismus-Leninismus in der ČSR. Die tschechoslowakische Philosophie seit 1945*. Dordrect, Holland: D. Reidel, 1961.

Lockhart, Robert Bruce. *Jan Masaryk. A Personal Memoir*. London: Putnam, 1956.

———. *My Europe*. London: Putnam, 1952.

Lukes, Igor. *Czechoslovakia between Stalin and Hitler. The Diplomacy of Edvard Beneš in the 1930s*. Oxford: Oxford University Press, 1996.

Mácha, Karel. *Glaube und Vernunft. Die Böhmische Philosopie in geschichtlicher Übersicht*. Part III: 1900–1945. Munich: K. G. Saur, 1989.

Machotka, Otakar. *Socialism českého člověka*. Prague: ČSNS, 1946.

Machovec, Milan. *Marxismus und dialektische Theologie: Barth, Bonhoeffer und Hromádka in atheistischkommunistischer Sicht*. Translated by Dorothea Neumärker. Zürich: EVZ, 1962.

Macků, Jan. "On the Problem of the Intelligentsia in the Process of Social Change." In *Sborník prací filsofické fakulty Brněnské university*, edited by Dušan Jeřábek, 113–22. Řada sociálněvědná (G) ročník 14.

Macůrek, Josef. *Slovanská idea a dnešní skutečnost*. Brno: Zemská osvětová rada, 1947.

Magocsi, Paul Robert. *Historical Atlas of East Central Europe*. Seattle: University of Washington Press, 1993.

Mai, Paul. "Die tschechische Nation und die Los-von-Rom Bewegung." In *Festschrift für Bernhard Stasiewski. Beiträge zur Ostdeutschen und Osteuropaischen Kirchengeschichte*, edited by Gabriel Adriáni und Joseph Gottschalk, 171–85. Cologne: Böhlau, 1974.

Mamatey, Victor S. and Radomír Luža, eds. *A History of the Czechoslovak Republic, 1918–1948.* Princeton: Princeton University Press, 1973.

Mannheim, Karl. *Ideology and Utopia.* London: Routledge, 1976.

———. *Man and Society in an Age of Reconstruction.* New York: Harcourt, Brace, 1940.

Marwick, Arthur. *War and Social Change in the Twentieth Century. A Comparative Study of Britain, France, Germany, Russia and the United States.* London: Macmillan, 1974.

Masaryk, Tomáš G. *Jan Hus. Naše obrození a naše reformace.* Prague: Jan Kanzelsberger, 1990.

———. *Česká otázka.* Prague: Svoboda, 1990.

———. *Masaryk on Thought and Life. Conversations with Karel Čapek.* Translated by M. and R. Weatherall. New York: Macmillan, 1938.

———. *Problém malého národa.* Prague: Neutralita, 1990.

Mastny, Vojtech. *The Czechs under Nazi Rule: The Failure of National Resistance, 1939–1942.* New York: Columbia University Press, 1971.

McCagg, William O. "Communism and Hungary, 1944–1956." Ph. D. diss., Columbia University, 1965.

mch. [Pavel Machonin?] "Nedokončený pruzkum." *Dějiny a současnost* (1968) no. 7, p. 44.

Mendelsohn, Ezra. *The Jews of East Central Europe between the World Wars.* Bloomington: Indiana University Press, 1983.

Micgiel, John. "'Bandits and Reactionaries': The Suppression of the Opposition in Poland, 1944–1946." In *The Establishment of Communist Regimes in Eastern Europe, 1944–1949,* edited by Norman Naimark and Leonid Gabianskii, 93–100. Boulder, CO: Westview, 1997.

Milward, Alan. *War, Economy and Society, 1939–1945.* Berkeley: University of California Press, 1977.

Mlynář, Zdeněk. *Nightfrost in Prague.* Translated by Paul Wilson. New York: Karz, 1980.

Mojzes, Paul. *Christian-Marxist Dialogue in Eastern Europe.* Minneapolis: Augsburg, 1981.

Možný, Ivo. *Proč tak snadno? Některé rodinné důvody sametové revoluce.* Prague: SLON, 1991.

Můj poměr ke KSČ. Projevy z řad pracující inteligence. Prague: KSČ, 1946.

Myant, M. R. *Socialism and Democracy in Czechoslovakia, 1945–1948.* Cambridge: Cambridge University Press, 1981.

Naimark, Norman. "Revolution and Counterrevolution in Eastern Europe." In *The Crisis of Socialism in Europe,* edited by Christiane Lemke and Gary Marks, 62–83. Durham, NC: Duke University Press, 1992.

Nejedlý, Zdeněk. *Komunisté—dědici velikých tradic českého národa.* Prague: Práce, 1978.

———. *Komunisté—dědici velikých tradic českého národa.* Prague: Sekretariát ÚV KSČ, 1947.

———. *O kulturu národní a lidovou.* Prague: Melantrich, 1948.

———. *Odkaz našich národních dějin.* Prague: ÚV KSČ, 1948.

———. *Slovo o náboženství.* Prague: Melantrich, 1948.

Nemec, Ludvik. *The Czechoslovak Heresy and Schism: The Emergence of a National Czechoslovak Church.* Transactions of the American Philosophical Society, New Series, Volume 65, Part 1. Philadelphia: The American Philosophical Society, 1975.

Neumärker, Dorothea. *Josef L. Hromádka. Theologie und Politik im Kontext des Zeitgeschehens.* Munich: Kaiser, 1974.

Olivova, Vera. *The Doomed Democracy: Czechoslovakia in a Disrupted Europe, 1914–38.* London: Sidgewick and Jackson, 1972.

Opat, Jaroslav. "K metodě studia a výkladu některých problémů v období 1945–1948." *Příspěvky k dějinám KSČ* 5 (1965): 65–85.

———. *Filozof a politik T. G. Masaryk 1882–1893.* Prague: Melantrich, 1990.

———. *O novou demokracii. Příspěvek k dějinám národně demokratické revoluce v Československu v letech 1945–1948.* Prague: Academia, 1966.

Orzoff, Andrea. "Battle for the Castle: The Friday Men and the Czechoslovak Republic, 1918–1938." Ph. D. diss, Stanford University, 2000.

Otáhal, Milan. *Ferdinand Peroutka. Muž přítomnosti.* Slovo k historii 33. Prague: Melantrich, 1992.

Paczkowski, Andrzej. *Referendum z 30 czerwca 1946 r.* Warsaw: ISP PAN, 1993.

Pasák, Tomáš. "K problematice české kolaborace a fašismu za druhé světové války." In *Príspevky k dejinám fašizmu v Československu a Maďarsku,* edited by Ľudovít Halotík, 129–62. Bratislava: SAV, 1969.

Paul, David W. *The Cultural Limits of Revolutionary Politics. Change and Continuity in Socialist Czechoslovakia.* Boulder, CO: East European Monographs, 1979.

Pavlíček, Václav. *Politické strany po únoru. Příspěvek k problematice Národní fronty.* Vol. 1. Prague: Svobodné slovo, 1966.

Pech, Stanley Z. *The Czech Revolution of 1848.* Chapel Hill: University of North Carolina Press, 1969.

Peroutka, Ferdinand. *Budeme pokračovat.* Toronto: 68 Publishers, 1980.

———. *Budování státu.* 4 vols. Prague: Lidové noviny, 1991.

———. *Byl Edvard Beneš vinen?* Prague: H&H, 1993.

———. "Článek nikoliv lhostejný." *Svobodné noviny* 20 January 1946: 1.

———. "Co se stalo." *Dnešek* 1 (1946/7): 145.

———. *Deníky, dopisy, vzpomínky.* Prague: Lidové noviny, 1995.

———. "Hlavní úkol naší politiky." *Dnešek* 1 (1946/7): 49.

———. *Jací jsme.* Prague: Obelisk, 1924.

———. *O věcech obecných.* 2 vols. Prague: SPN, 1991.

———. *Sluší-li se být realistou.* Prague: Mláda fronta, 1993.

———. *Tak nebo tak.* Prague: F. Borový, 1947.

———. *Uděl svobody. Výběr z rozhlasových projevů 1951–1977.* Prague: Academia, 1995.

Pimper, Antonín. *Křesťanský solidarismus.* Prague: ČAT-Universum, 1946.

Polenberg, Richard. *War and Society: The United States, 1941–1945.* New York: Lippincott, 1972.

Prečan, Vilém. *V kradeném čase. Výběr z studií, článků a úvah z let 1973–1993.* Prague: ÚSD, 1994.

Prinz, Friedrich. "Das kulturelle Leben (1867–1939) vom österreichisch-ungarischen Ausgleich bis zum Ende der ersten tschechoslowakischen Republik." In *Handbuch der Geschichte der böhmischen Länder,* edited by Karel Bosl, vol. 4, 153–225. Stuttgart: Anton Hiersmann, 1970.

Prokš, P. "Československo. Politická moc a sovětizace (1945–1948)." In *Sovětizace východní Evropy,* edited by Miroslav Tejchman, 39–77. Prague: Historický ústav, 1995.

Przybysz, Kazimierz, ed. *Wizje Polski. Programy polityczne lat wojny i okupacji 1939–1944.* Warsaw: Elipsa, 1992.

Pynsent, Robert. *Questions of Identity: Czech and Slovak Ideas of Nationality and Personality.* London: Central European University Press, 1994.

Reiman, Michal. "O významu hesla 'Za většinu národa.'" *Příspěvky k dějinám KSČ* 4 (1964).

Richter, Jaroslav. *Socialismus a Křesťanství.* Prague: ČAT-Universum, 1947.

Ripka, Hubert. *Czechoslovakia Enslaved: The Story of the Communist Coup d'Etat.* London: Gollancz, 1950.

———. *Únorová tragedie.* Brno: Atlantis, 1995.

Robek, Antonín. *Lidové zdroje národního obrození.* Prague: Univerzita Karlova, 1974.

———. *Městské lidové zdroje národního obrození.* Prague: Univerzita Karlova, 1977.

Roháč, František. *Jednota v našich národních tradicích.* Prague: Akademický klub Tábor, 1947.

Rothschild, Joseph. *East Central Europe between the Two World Wars.* Seattle: University of Washington Press, 1974.

———. *Return to Diversity. A Political History of East Central Europe since World War II.* New York: Oxford, 1989.

Rotrekl, Zdeněk. *Barokní fenomén v současnosti.* Prague: Torst, 1995.

———. *Skrytá tvář české literatury.* Brno: Blok, 1993.

Ruh, Hans. *Geschichte und Theologie: Grundlinien der Theologie Hromádkas.* Zürich: EVZ, 1963.

Řičan, Rudolf. *Das Reich Gottes in den böhmischen Ländern. Geschichte des tschechischen Protestantismus.* Translated by Bohumír Popelář. Stuttgart: Evangelisches Verlagswerk, 1957.

Salajka, Martin. *Naše doba. Z ekumenického odkazu J. L. Hromádky.* Prague: Ekumenická sekce Husovy fakulty, 1978.

Schmidt, Dana Adams. *Anatomy of a Satellite.* Boston: Little, Brown, 1952.

Schmidt-Hartmann, Eva. "Das Konzept der 'politischen Kultur' in der Tschechoslowakei." In *Sowjetisches Modell und nationale Prägung. Kontinuität und Wandel in Ostmitteleuropa nach dem zweiten Weltkrieg,* edited by Hans Lemberg, 186–99. Marburg/Lahn: J. G. Herder Institut, 1991.

Schmidt-Hartmann, Eva, ed. *Kommunismus und Osteuropa. Konzepte, Perspektiven und Interpretationen im Wandel.* Munich: R. Oldenbourg, 1994.

Scriven, Michael and Peter Wagstaff, eds. *War and Society in 20th Century France.* New York: Berg, 1991.

Seton-Watson, Hugh. *Eastern Europe between the Wars, 1918–1941.* Cambridge: Cambridge University Press, 1946.

———. *Nationalism and Communism. Essays, 1946–1963.* London: Methuen, 1964.

———. *The East European Revolution.* New York: Praeger, 1951.

Siegmund-Schultze, Friedrich, ed. *Die Kirchen der Tschechoslowakei.* Ekklesia 5. Leipzig: Leopold Klotz, 1937.

Sláma, Jiří and Karel Kaplan. *Die Parlamentswahlen in der Tschechoslowakei 1935–1946–1948. Eine Statistische Analyse.* Munich: R. Oldenbourg, 1986.

Slapnicka, Helmut. "Die böhmische Länder und die Slowakei 1919–1945." In *Handbuch der Geschichte der böhmischen Länder,* edited by Karel Bosl, vol. 4, 1–98. Stuttgart: Anton Hiersemann, 1969.

Smith, Harold, ed. *War and Social Change: British Society in the Second World War.* Manchester: Manchester University Press, 1986.

Smolík, Josef. *J. L. Hromádka. Život a dílo.* Prague: Ekumenická rada, 1989.

Smutný, Jaromír. *Svědectví presidentova kancléře.* Prague: Mladá fronta, 1996.

Snítil, Zdeněk. "O dvouletce a jejím místě v politice KSČ v roce 1946." *Příspěvky k dějinám KSČ* 7 (1967).

Sorotkin, Pitirim. *Man and Society in Calamity: The Effects of War, Revolution, Famine, Pestilence on Human Mind. Behavior, Social Organization and Cultural Life.* New York: E. P. Dutton, 1942.

Statistical Office of the United Nations. *Demographic Yearbook.* Vols 1, 4, 8, 9, and 11. New York: United Nations, 1948, 1952, 1956, 1957, 1959.

Stransky, Jaroslav. *East Wind over Prague.* London: Hollis and Carter, 1950.

Strnad, Jaroslav, ed. *Muž přítomnosti.* Zürich: Konfrontace, 1985.

Ströbinger, Rudolf. *Poker um Prag. Die frühen Folgen von Jalta.* Zürich: Edition Interfrom, 1985.

Suda, Zdenek L. *Zealots and Rebels. A History of the Communist Party of Czechoslovakia.* Stanford, CA.: Hoover Institution, 1980.

Svoboda, Ludvík. *Marxismus a náboženství.* Prague: Život a práce, 1947.

Škarvan, František, ed. *EB národu. Z projevů presidenta republiky v letech 1945–1946.* Prague: Zemská rada osvětová, 1946.

Táborský, Eduard. *Prezident Beneš mezi Západem a Východem.* Prague: Mladá fronta, 1993.

Taylor, Telford. *Munich: The Price of Peace.* London: Hodder and Stoughton, 1979.

Teichova, Alice. *The Czechoslovak Economy, 1918–1980.* London: Routledge, 1988.

Tigrid, Pavel. *Kapesní průvodce inteligentní ženy po vlastním osudu.* Prague: Odeon, 1992.

———. *Marx na Hradčanech.* New York: Edice Svědectví, 1960.

Trapl, Miloš. *Politika českého katolicismu na Moravě 1918–1938.* Prague: SPN, 1968.

Ullmann, Walter. *The United States in Prague. 1945–1948.* Boulder, CO: East European Quarterly, 1978.

Urban, Rudolf. *Die slavisch-nationalkirchlichen Bestrebungen in der Tschechoslowakei mit besonderer Berücksichtigung der tschechoslowakischen und der orthodoxen Kirche.* Leipzig: Markert & Petters, 1938.

Urban, Rudolf. *Die Tschechoslowakische Hussitische Kirche.* Marburg/Lahn: J. G. Herder Intitut, 1973.

Vaško, Václav. *Neumlčená. Kronika katolické církve v Československu po druhé světové války.* 2 vols. Prague: Zvon, 1990.

Vassilev, K. ed. *A Short History of the Bulgarian Communist Party.* Sofia: Sofia Press, 1977.

Veltruský, Jiří. *Byrokracie, demokracie a dělnická třída.* Prague: Propagační oddělení ČSSD, 1946.

Viney, D. E. "Czech Culture and the 'New Spirit', 1948–1952." *Slavonic and East European Review* 31 (1952): 466–94.

Vyšný, Paul. *Neo-Slavism and the Czechs, 1898–1914.* Cambridge: Cambridge University Press, 1977.

West, Charles C. *Communism and the Theologians: Study of an Encounter.* London: SCM, 1958.

Whyte, John H. *Catholics in Western Democracies: A Study in Political Behavior.* Dublin: Gill and Macmillan, 1981.

Wightman, G. and A. H. Brown. "Changes in the Levels of Membership and Social Composition of the Communist Party of Czechoslovakia, 1945–1973." *Soviet Studies* 27 (1975): 396–417.

Wright, Gordon. *The Ordeal of Total War, 1939–1945.* New York: Harper, 1968.

Za svobodu. Prague: Nova svoboda, 1945.

Zieris, K. F. *Nové základy českého periodického tisku.* Prague: Orbis, 1947.

Zinner, Paul. *Communist Strategy and Tactics in Czechoslovakia, 1918–1948.* London: Pall Mall, 1963.

Index

Albania, 36; communists in, 10, 27, 35;
    interwar, 24, 25, 32; postwar
    elections in, 34, 285; World War II in,
    15, 16, 17, 23, 30
Allied Control Commissions (ACCs),
    11–12
Austro-Hungary, 83, 123; breakup of, 24,
    36, 83, 142; Catholic nature of, 40, 69,
    76, 84, 271; Czech life in, 37, 38, 40,
    45, 47, 98, 118, 120, 128; socialism
    under, 54, 229

Bareš, Gustav: and Czech character, 96,
    110, 111, 187; ideology of, 93, 120,
    121, 141; political assessments, 181,
    185, 186, 188, 195; press of, 59, 60
Battle of White Mountain (1620), 40, 98,
    229
Bednář, František, 84, 85, 154, 159, 266,
    269
Beneš, Edvard: background of, 44, 61;
    influence of, 64, 65, 72, 99, 111,
    182, 210, 219, 228, 229, 232, 279,
    284; nationalization program of, 21,
    120, 140, 204; political acts of, 105,
    276, 277; Slavicism and, 159,
    164–65, 166, 281; socialism and,
    172, 200, 203, 207, 213, 218, 283,

291, 292; speech to Congress of
    Czech Writers, 203, 207–8, 224, 228,
    292; views of, 51, 90, 96, 108, 115,
    116, 123–24, 126–27, 131–32, 133,
    158, 254
Björling, Fiona, 39
Bolshevism, 24, 28, 132, 136. See also
    Russian Revolution
Brod, Toman, 180, 181, 198, 231
Bulgaria, 164; communists in 12, 35,
    183, 223, 284; demographics in, 32,
    33, 34, 36; interwar, 25, 26, 27, 32,
    37; state ownership in, 19, 21, 22,
    37; USSR and, 10, 11, 12, 20, 28, 284;
    World War II in, 15, 16, 17, 23, 30,
    31, 34, 35, 38

Čapek, J. B., 170
Čapek, Karel, 44, 65
Čapek, Stanislav, 271
Černý, Václav, 67; influence of, 64;
    under Nazis, 45, 46, 47; press and,
    66, 68, 167; regarding socialism, 47,
    65, 169–70, 202, 203, 204, 206, 207,
    208, 216–17, 219, 292, 293; view of
    West, 162, 163, 167–71, 172, 202
Chudoba, Bohdan, 73, 74–75, 125, 237,
    243, 246, 248

collectivization, 27, 287; as ideology, 51, 229–31, 247, 293; religious groups and, 240, 245, 247–49, 251, 252

Congress of Czech Writers, 203, 207–8, 224, 228, 292

Czechoslovak Church, 76–78, 85, 107, 137, 252, 253–74; membership of, 5, 79, 175; other religions and, 85, 177, 238, 246, 251, 252; political stance of, 80–82, 92, 101, 107, 115–16, 136–38, 154, 162, 165–66, 174–75, 177, 182, 237, 246, 280, 282; Slavism and, 165–66, 174

Czechoslovak Republic, 7, 95, 122, 139, 154, 174, 223, 226; assessments of, 137, 148–49; communist views of, 118–20, 121, 125, 137, 144, 147; democratic socialist views of, 121, 122–24, 145, 175, 201, 213; formation of, 141; German crisis, 104–5, 108, 117; Masaryk, Thomas and, 125, 131–37; October 28th celebrations of, 141–43; People's Party view of, 124–25, 176; politics in, 190, 273; religion in, 69, 83

democratic socialists. *See* National Socialists, Social Democrats, *Kulturní svaz*

deportation: of anticommunists, 11; by Nazis, 15, 16, 18; of Germans, 16, 18, 19, 20, 21, 23, 55, 68, 78, 80, 84, 90, 94, 98, 131, 139, 140, 145, 158–59, 181, 185, 196, 209, 223, 288

Dnešek (*Today*) National Socialist press, 68, 114, 146, 152, 162, 211, 212, 215, 221

Dobrovský, Josef, 41

education, 40–41, 72, 118; during WWII, 45–46, 122, 152; growth of intelligentsia, 42, 43; socialist, 193, 201, 207, 232, 290

Evangelical Church of the Czech Brethren, 76, 77, 136, 138, 183; formation of, 82–83, 84; leadership of, 81, 85–87, 92, 102, 126, 159, 163; and other churches, 251, 264, 272; political stance of, 143, 175, 253, 266–74, 281, 282

February 1948 crisis: assessments of, 6, 8, 56, 88, 197, 275, 283; communist efforts during, 93, 127, 157, 179, 183, 186–88, 191, 195, 196, 215, 239; election speculation, 57, 188–89, 244; evangelicals during, 85; events of, 2, 3, 98, 103, 276–78; noncommunist intellectuals in, 90, 215, 216, 221; opposition groups during, 59, 61, 62, 67, 73, 75, 76, 82; public support during, 5, 56

Fierlinger, Zdeněk, 59, 75, 81

First Congress of Writers, 250

First Republic. *See* Czechoslovak Republic, Masaryk, Thomas

French Revolution, 160, 161, 168

Furet, François, 26

German evangelical churches, 80

Gottwald, Klement: and cultural crisis, 157, 170; in 1948 crisis, 5, 276–77; and elections, 57, 187–88, 191; leads Communist Party, 54, 55, 60, 182–83, 187, 212; nationalization by, 140, 182; perceptions of, 96, 191, 211–12, 278; and socialism, 52, 181, 186, 193, 213; and Stalin, 182, 183–84

Great Depression: capitalism debunked by, 22, 28, 29, 200–201; communism and, 54, 70; and demographics, 32–33, 118, 149; responses to, 19, 27, 37, 84, 122

Grňa, Josef, 152

Hájek, Jiří, 60; on cultural crisis, 93, 109, 110, 113; on Masaryk, 120, 127; on WWII effects, 148–49, 150

Hála, František (People's Party), 71, 73, 75, 115, 171

Halas, František (poet), 117, 146, 293

Havlíček, Karel, 42, 65, 168

Hitler, Adolf, 29, 46; East European allies, 23–24, 28, 35; interwar

influence, 37, 263; opposition to, 35, 70, 108, 153, 212, 218, 254; West's weakness regarding, 25, 104, 106–7, 109, 158, 160
Hník, František, 81, 117, 136–37, 254, 265
Hroch, Miroslav, 41
Hromádka, Josef Lukl: cultural crisis views of, 92, 112, 117, 125; as Evangelical Church leader, 84, 85–86, 264, 266–67, 272–73; socialism and, 86–87, 162, 253, 267–69, 270–71, 272, 273, 274
Hungary: communists in, 2, 10, 11–12, 35, 28, 216, 285; Czech leaders regarding, 87, 120; demographics in, 32, 33, 34, 36–37; interwar, 20, 24, 25, 26, 32, 37; population transfers in, 16, 32, 36, 181, 205, 287; WWII in, 10, 23, 28, 30, 31
Hussite Movement, 69, 83, 157; communist use of, 99–103, 127, 110, 174, 239, 266; and intelligentsia, 40, 76, 99; as nationalism, 97, 98–99; Taborites, 100, 102–3

Jews, 13, 18, 19, 20, 22, 128, 287
Jungmann, Josef, 41

Kaizl, Josef, 43
Kajpr, Adolf, 75, 76, 111, 237, 239, 246; on Munich, 107, 108, 109
Kaplan, Karel, 4, 80–81, 197, 238
Kolman, Arnošt, 59, 114, 186–87, 192, 194–95, 254, 290
Kopecký, Václav, 182, 196, 291; as communist leader, 59, 93, 95, 194, 273; "Czech road," and, 185, 191–92, 195; on Masaryk, 94, 127, 128, 30
Košice Program. *See* National Front
Koželuhová, Helena, 73, 74, 75, 147, 152, 243
Král, Josef, 132, 133, 292
Kramář, Karel, 43
Kratochvíl, Bohuslav, 48, 294
Kulturní obec: battle against *Kulturní svaz*, 200, 223, 225, 228, 230, 283;

founding as communist press, 222, 230, 289–91; unites with *Kulturní svaz* as *Kulturní jednota*, 226, 227
Kulturní svaz, 200; founded in opposition to *Kulturní obec*, 223–25, 283, 291–92; union with *Kulturní obec* as *Kulturní jednota*, 227–30, 292

land reform. *See* nationalization
Liehm, Antonín, 40, 41
Little Entente, 25
Lorenc, Václav, 101, 107, 109, 116

Machtka, Otakar, 143, 145, 203; and socialism, 64, 163, 207, 208, 214, 228, 229
Marwick, Arthur, 13, 14, 30, 34
Masaryk, Jan, 96, 276
Masaryk, Tomáš, 7, 43, 176; as intellectual, 41, 44, 109, 110, 123, 129, 161, 168, 190, 207, 211, 226; as politician, 65, 123, 157; and religion, 83, 102, 134–37; as symbol, 41, 68, 95, 98–99, 117, 119–20, 122, 124, 139, 147, 152, 174, 210, 244, 249, 281, 293
military tribunals, 11, 146
Munich Accords, 7, 24, 37, 45, 104–17, 275; communist response to, 54, 55, 56, 94, 95, 99, 119, 146, 174, 185; cultural crisis and, 48, 52, 86, 103, 155, 157–58, 165, 173, 280; Czech consequences of, 16, 22–23, 118, 276; People's Party and, 70, 72, 176, 236, 281; political effects of, 37, 123, 137, 149, 174, 175, 196, 228, 284; protestant churches and, 86, 267; psychological effects of, 146, 159, 163, 194;
Western abandonment, 25, 89, 120, 121, 160, 223, 290. *See also* "smallness," fear of

Naimark, Norman, vii, 2, 9
National Front (Košice Program) 48, 143, 56, 210, 226; communists and,

74, 96, 142, 179, 180, 181, 183,
185–86, 188, 189, 191, 218, 282;
democratic socialists and, 62, 72,
117, 200, 213, 204, 278; formation of,
55; Munich and, 107; in other
countries, 11, 285; religious groups
in, 80, 82, 236, 249, 262
nationalism:
anti-German, 11, 26, 40, 55, 90, 94, 100,
139, 159; communists and, 89, 95,
211, 181; interwar, 24, 36–37, 118.
See also pan-Slavism
National Socialists: accounts of 1948 by,
3–4, 189; and Catholics, 73, 193, 194;
and communists, 63, 179, 188, 191,
216, 223; constituency of, 57, 61–62,
73; cultural crisis and, 90, 102, 142,
143, 162–63, 172, 173; election
returns of 1946, *58*, 209–210;
February 1948 and, 276, 278;
ideological spectrum of, 59, 71, 77,
148, 152, 176, 190, 204, 211, 221,
278; leadership of, 64–67, 108; and
Masaryk, 119, 130; press and, 67–68,
75, 224–25; and Social Democrats,
189–90. *See also Kulturní svaz*,
individual leaders
National Theater, 43, 66
nationalization: commemoration of, 140,
145; communists and, 22, 27, 181,
182, 185, 186, 187, 287; cultural
aspects of, 50, 206; industry and,
19–20, 21, 22, 36, 120, 140, 185, 191,
204–5, 280; interwar, 24, 26, 119,
144; land reform as, 20–21, 120, 141;
Masaryk and, 130, 131, 211;
opposition to, 217, 250–51;
protestant views of, 259, 261–62,
271; social change and, 22, 205
Nejedlý, Zdenek, 59, 98, 102, 128, 223;
cultural crisis views, 93, 100, 101,
110, 164; ideology of, 111, 115, 129,
238, 255, 269, 291; nationalism and,
95, 96–97, 98
NKVD, 2, 11
Novák, Miroslav, Bishop of Prague, 80,
81, 260, 261, 264

Palacký, František, 41, 42, 159
pan-Slavism: communists and, 100, 115,
191, 280; conferences, 42, 43, 44 ;
and cultural orientation, 7, 107, 109,
110, 117, 156–74, 221; religious
groups and, 74, 77, 78; socialism
and, 7, 51, 100–103, 227, 228, 281,
283, 295; in WWII, 28, 29
People's Democracy: communists and,
93–94, 165, 175, 179, 185–86, 190,
192, 196, 228; democratic socialists
and, 102, 213, 217, 218, 232, 233;
intellegentsia role in, 48–50; Masaryk
legacy and, 128, 130–31, 138, 226;
religious groups in, 239, 243, 261,
262, 268; youth and, 139
People's Party: assessments of, 236–37;
communists and, 3, 72, 74, 115, 192,
216, 234, 244–45, 251, 269, 276;
election returns, *58*, 70, 252; history
of, 69–70, 77; liabilities of, 71–73;
political stance of, 135, 143, 147, 190,
204, 239, 241, 249, 278; press organs,
60, 68, 74–75, 124, 242; Protestants
and, 78, 271–72; as Roman Catholic
party, 63, 70, 252; Slavism and, 166.
See also Roman Catholics
Peroutka, Ferdinand, 1, 44, 51, 64,
65–66, 199; communism, views on,
65, 152, 202, 204, 205, 206, 209,
210, 214, 215, 216, 217, 218, 219,
232, 275, 282; cultural crisis views,
90, 96, 114, 115, 122–23, 124,
142–45, 151, 161; as Democratic
Socialist spokesman, 200–201, 213,
219, 221; and Masaryk, 130–31, 134;
press and, 67–68, 146, 224, 227,
292, 294
pětka, 25, 37
Poland: communists in, 10, 11, 12, 27,
28, 35, 183, 216, 285; demographics,
16, 32, 33, 34; interwar, 24, 25, 27,
28, 36; nationalization, 19, 20, 21, 22,
26; WWII destruction in, 10, 13, 15,
17–18, 23, 30, 31, 32–33, 36, 38, 45
Prague Spring (1968), 2, 67, 141, 189,
196, 273

Prague Uprising (May 5, 1944) 7, 46–47, 66, 89, 131, 139–55, 176, 281
Procházka, Adolf, 73, 80, 166, 170, 241
Procházka, Oldřich, 221
Procházka, Vladimir, 129, 130, 291
Protectorate of Bohemia, 23, 38, 46; conditions in, 30–31, 44–45, 107, 122, 149; Czechoslovak Church in, 79, 101; "protectorate mentality," 105, 110, 113, 115

Red Army, 16, 17, 75; historiography regarding, 2, 10, 36, 285, 288; liberation by, 34, 55, 100, 110–11, 112, 157, 159, 260; threat of, 10–11, 35, 123, 244
resistance movements, 13, 15, 21–22, 26, 33, 152; communist involvement in, 27–29, 34–35, 54–56, 117; Czech involvement in, 38, 45, 88, 94, 105, 114; intelligentsia in, 18, 45–47, 49, 61, 65, 66, 127, 284; Prague Uprising, 114, 148–50; religious groups in, 70, 72, 79, 85, 235, 236
Revolution of 1848, 41, 42, 43, 44, 82, 98
Ripka, Hubert, 3; anticommunism of, 208, 215, 218; and "Czech road," 208, 211; as National Socialist, 64, 221, 282;
Romania: communists in, 10, 11, 12, 27, 34, 35, 183, 285; demographics of, 18, 32, 34; interwar, 25, 27, 36–37; nationalization in, 19, 20, 21; World War II in, 15, 16, 17, 18, 23, 24, 28, 30, 31, 37
Roman Catholics, 40, 97, 101, 234–52, 260; antimaterialism of, 192, 193, 202, 203, 260; cultural views of, 51, 90–92, 166, 170–71, 174; generational effect on, 141, 142, 151; as intelligentsia, 53, 68–76, 87; and Masaryk, 119, 128, 130, 135–36, 137–38; Munich and, 106–7, 108; opposition to communism of, 3, 103, 105, 111–12, 116–17, 143, 166, 176–77, 182, 192, 193, 216, 219, 257,

263, 269, 270; and other churches, 99, 101, 158, 253, 256, 263–64, 271, 272, 274; political views of, 50, 112, 254, 261; Prague Uprising and, 146–47; views on revolution, 152, 154, 155. *See also* People's Party
Russian Orthodox Church, 76, 86, 135, 261
Russian Revolution: Czech views of, 141, 145, 161, 165, 172, 221; Eastern European fear of, 27, 142; of 1905, 44; Masaryk and, 133, 136; and Orthodox Church, 86. *See also* Bolshevism

Slovak Democratic Party, 276
Slovak National Uprising (1944), 17, 18, 23 , 38, 143
Slovak Republic, 104
Slovaks, 36, 37, 38, 55, 128, 130, 276, 284; communism and, 34, 35, 59, 94, 188, 233, 243; nationalism and, 25, 29, 104, 181; as Nazi ally, 23, 38, 79, 89, 91, 104; religion and, 78, 82, 261; socialism and, 210, 220, 290, 295; WWII, effects on, 15, 16, 17, 18, 30, 31, 143
"smallness," fear of, 105, 109, 146, 159, 163, 223, 290. *See also* Munich Accords
Social Democrats, 20, 67, 78, 130; and communists, 48, 53, 58, 71, 75, 120, 140, 142–43, 176, 179, 182, 189, 190, 193, 200, 209, 261; cultural crisis and, 89, 90, 92, 93, 103, 172; interwar, 24, 27, 28; National Front and, 276, 278; National Socialists and, 61, 63, 190; People's Party and, 72, 250; postwar status of, 59; press, 60, 68, 142, 192; radicalism of, 10, 12. *See also Kulturnia svaz*, individual leaders
Spisar, Alois, 81, 92, 257
Stalin, Josef, 29, 72, 189; Czech views of, 56, 109, 110, 111, 127, 129, 136, 169, 173, 191, 193, 202, 261
Stalingrad, 23, 24, 29

stalinism: Czech communists and, 10, 60, 119, 182–84,196, 211, 279; historiography of, 1, 3, 4, 179, 183, 276
Strakoš, Jan, 135, 166
Sudetenland, 22, 37; German confrontation over, 16, 38, 45, 105; population transfers in, 68, 80, 120, 131, 140, 145, 223. *See also* deportation, nationalization

Temporary National Assembly, 66, 140, 148
Third Republic: (Czech), 123–25; (French), 23
Tigrid, Pavel, 76, 151, 213, 275, 277; as Catholic spokesman, 73, 74, 237, 250; on communism, 114, 115, 244, 245, 257, 263; cultural crisis views, 90, 92, 107, 157, 167, 170–71; on materialism, 240, 241, 251; Munich and, 108; press and, 74, 75
Tito, Josip Broz, 35, 284
trade unions: Catholic, 235, 236; communists and, 27, 182; consolidation of, 32, 34, 92, 224, 236; press organs of, 50, 97, 140, 187; state opposition to, 24, 28
Trapl, Miroslav, 136
Tvorba (*Creation*): attacks Catholic position 75, 239; as communist press, 48–49, 60, 181, 191; cultural crisis and, 93, 110; and First Republic, 119, 120, 126; nationalism and, 95, 100
Two-Year Plan, 23, 223; as Communist agenda, 185, 186–87, 190, 282; intelligentsia support for, 145, 179, 213; religious support for, 262, 268

Union of Czech Youth, 151; *Mladá fronta*, 60, 140, 148, 150, 224, 226, 228
USSR, 29, 32, 243; Catholic views of, 70, 74; Czech communists and, 63, 128, 196, 205, 280; Czech cultural crisis and, 100, 108; "Czech road" and, 94, 98, 196, 197, 222; intelligentsia views of, 132, 136, 207; interwar, 70, 119; Protestant views of, 261, 270; and WWII, 11–12, 36, 54, 55, 111, 112, 117, 183, 184–85, 209, 210, 240, 281

Whyte, Johyn, 235, 237
World War I, 61; effects of, 32–33, 170; failed reforms after, 21, 25–27, 29, 120; nationalism after, 24, 36, 83; perceptions of, 113, 118, 119
World War II: Catholic Church and, 70, 235; collaboration during, 288; communists and, 54, 58; communists use accusations against, 96, 113; Czechoslovak Church and, 80, 253; political bans of, 24, 36, 55, 62; property confiscated, 20, 21, 35, 81, 205; by regimes, 28, 105, 145–46; tribunals of, 11; Western states and, 25. *See also* resistance movements, deportations, "smallness," individual countries

youth, 30, 42, 156, 165; communists and, 56, 57, 60, 128, 151, 218; generational differences, 4, 7, 32, 33; press, 60, 150, 226; radicalism of, 10, 33, 34, 56, 60, 139, 281, 285–86; religion and, 80, 84, 85, 176, 236, 255, 267, 270; socialism and, 148, 202; WWII, effects on, 149, 150, 151, 223. *See also* Hájek, Jiří
Yugoslavia: communist strength in, 14, 28, 35, 284, 287, 288; demographics in, 32, 33 , 34; interwar, 25, 37; state role in, 19, 25, 36; World War II destruction in, 15–17, 23, 30, 31, 32, 33, 38, 44

About the Author

Bradley F. Abrams is an assistant professor of history at Columbia University. He teaches Eastern European history of the nineteenth and twentieth centuries and specializes in the twentieth-century history of East-Central Europe. He received his Ph.D. from Stanford University and is the author of several articles on various aspects of postwar Czech and Slovak developments. He resides in New York City, with his wife, Irene Krarup, and two children, Helena and Alexander.